REAL WORLD
ADOBE ILLUSTRATOR 10

Deke McClelland

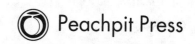
Peachpit Press

REAL WORLD ADOBE ILLUSTRATOR 10

Deke McClelland

Peachpit Press
1249 Eighth Street
Berkeley, CA 94710
510/524-2178
800/283-9444
510/524-2221 (fax)

Find us on the Web at www.peachpit.com.
To report errors, please send a note to errata@peachpit.com.

Peachpit Press is a division of Pearson Education.

Copyright © 2002 by Deke McClelland

Project Editor: Rebecca Gulick
Editors: Amy Thomas Buscaglia, Liza Weiman Hanks, and Wendy Katz
Contributing writers: Conrad Chavez, Wendy Katz, and Barbara Obermeier
Production coordinator: Kate Reber
Copyeditor: Brenda Benner
Compositor: Phyllis Beaty
Indexer: Karin Arrigoni
Cover design: Earl Gee, Gee + Chung Design
Cover and part opener art: Ron Chan
Interior design: Michele Cuneo, Mimi Heft, and Kate Reber

ISBN 0-201-77630-8

9 8 7 6 5 4 3 2

Printed and bound in the United States of America

ACKNOWLEDGMENTS

As all first-time authors discover to their great surprise, writing a book is not a solo activity. And that is true no matter how many titles you've chalked up. I've got a big "team" to thank in the creation of this book: all the staff at Peachpit Press, especially Rebecca Gulick and Kate Reber, my project editor and production coordinator; and Marjorie Baer, Peachpit's executive editor. Many thanks, too, to Amy Thomas Buscaglia, Liza Weiman Hanks, and Wendy Katz for keeping my prose in check, my numbers sequential, my figures up to date, and my train of thought more or less on track (everyone needs an editor!); to Brenda Benner for copyediting; and to Phyllis Beaty and Karin Arrigoni for compositing and indexing this manuscript through the wee hours of the night(s).

Thanks also go to Conrad Chavez and Barbara Obermeier for their valuable contributions of technical expertise, product knowledge, and many great suggestions. And to Mordy Golding of Adobe for answering so many questions about new features and for letting his humor show through the entire grueling review process, even when he was asked to have it done "yesterday" about five times a week.

I'd also like to thank Ron Chan for creating the art for the cover and part openers, and Stephen Dampier for pre-empting a last-minute artistic emergency.

CONTENTS AT A GLANCE

TABLE OF CONTENTS

PART ONE
WELCOME TO ILLUSTRATOR 1

Chapter 7
Modifying and Combining Paths 193

Chapter 8
Developing a Flair for the Schematic 223

Chapter 9
The Magic of Transformations and Distortions 269

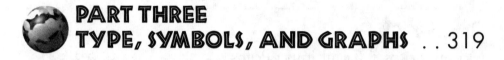

Chapter 20
Becoming Master of the Raster. 693

 PART FIVE
GOING PUBLIC 721

Chapter 21
Creating Web Graphics 723

Chapter 22
Animation and Data-Driven Graphics 777

INTRODUCTION

If you're reading this book, you probably have at least some idea of what Illustrator is and what it can do (although you may not know quite what you're getting into; most computer programs this charismatic can be addictive!). But I'll sum up: it's an incredibly powerful vector drawing program that helps you create just about any kind of image you can dream of, from basic drawings on up to complicated visual epics. It uses a lot of tools that mimic what you may have done (or wished you had done) using traditional tools such as pens, t-squares, and paints, and tools that can be found only in the digital world. It finds myriad ways to help you do your work faster and avoid duplication, yet it never squelches your creativity. Can you tell I like this thing?

You see Illustrator graphics every day in newspapers and magazines, in advertising, and on the Web. Artists use Illustrator to create diagrams, info-art, maps, logos, posters, photorealistic renderings, and all sorts of other illustrations that defy categorization. And so can you. You can draw high-contrast graphics with perfectly smooth edges. You can use tools and filters to alter a basic (or any) shape in ways you and your pencil hadn't imagined. You can edit the outline of any shape long after you create it. You can even integrate photographs that were corrected and enhanced in Adobe Photoshop or a similar application. In this new version of Illustrator, you can perform minor artistic miracles with gradients, blends, transparency, live effects, and Web-graphics capabilities that may knock your socks off.

Illustrator is as expansive, elaborate, and perplexing (to the outside eye) as any traditional, professional workshop on earth. Like any powerful collection of tools, Illustrator will demand your attention and reward your comprehension. That's why this book guides you through every feature of the program as if you've never seen a drawing application in your life. Every section not only explains how to perform a technique, but also provides enough background so you know why you'd want to. Though I hope they're pleasing to look at, the figures aren't meant to amaze, but educate. Soon enough, you'll be able to amaze yourself.

The Structure of This Book

Real World Adobe Illustrator 10 contains 25 chapters organized into five distinct parts. Each part explores a simple concept in exhaustive and engaging detail. My hope is that at the end of every part, you will feel confident enough with the material to see that the explanations are really just starting-out points for your own explorations. Once you understand the topics, you can invent techniques on your own without the slightest hesitation.

- **Part One, Starting:** The first part's four chapters introduce the fundamental aspects of Illustrator 10. I explain how Illustrator differs from other graphics programs and introduce you to Illustrator's network of tools and palettes. I'll tell you everything there is to know about the file formats supported by Illustrator 10. If you're familiar with previous editions of Illustrator, this part will get you up and running in no time at all. You may even get to skip ahead.

- **Part Two, Working with Shapes:** These five chapters tell you how to create basic graphic elements in Illustrator. I'll introduce you to the fundamental shape-creation tools—such as the polygon, line, star, and spiral—and explain how you can change shapes, combine them, make holes in them, smooth them out, and otherwise coax them into becoming whatever you want them to be. I make sense out of the all-powerful but oft-confusing pen tool and Bézier curves. This section also covers "management" features that will help you keep your shapes in line, literally and figuratively. I'll explore the tools and controls for measuring, aligning, and arranging elements, as well as those that will organize the elements of your document for easier retrieval, focused attention, or for use in other documents.

Part Three, Type, Symbols, and Graphs: Chapters 10 and 11 devote close attention to Illustrator's strong and easy-to-use text editing tools and to the larger topic of creating and editing text. But don't think that just because type is in a separate section from shapes and other images, it isn't as artistic an element in your illustrations as those graphics are. Chapter 12 introduces the symbolism tools, an exciting new way of working with repeating elements. I close this section with a look at one of Illustrator's most overlooked features, graphing.

Part Four, Color and Effects: I've devoted several pages to showing you how color works and how (and with what features) to use it. Even if you didn't happen to be using Illustrator, you'd find a lot in Chapter 14 to help you understand working with digital color. Chapter 18 looks at how the transparency options affect objects. However, coloring doesn't just mean color, so there are also chapters to cover blending colors and shapes, masks and opacity masks, and other effects. This section also includes extensive coverage of Illustrator's new live distortion effects, which are "smart art" personified: they maintain the integrity of the individual elements of your designs while allowing you to perform amazing feats of transformation on them.

Part Five, Going Public: Then, of course, you'll want to share your masterpieces with the world, and so I'll tell you all about how to get your graphics wherever they need to go: to the Web, to other programs, and of course to print. And seeing how you're always in such a big hurry to get all those things done (isn't it always that way?) I've included a modest chapter on how to get the most out of Illustrator's Actions—a great way to automate repetitive tasks.

I've written the chapters so you can read them from beginning to end without finding the information either repetitive or overwhelming. If you prefer to read just when you're stumped, you can look up a confusing topic in the index. Or you can simply browse through the pictures until you come to something that looks interesting. But no matter how you approach the text, I hope that it snags you and teaches you more than you bargained for. If you look up from the book at your watch and think, "Dang, I've got to get back to work!" then I've done my job.

The Margin Icons

If I've written a paragraph that contains very important information or an offhand comment, I've included an icon next to the paragraph to distinguish it from the surrounding text.

Here are the five icons that you can expect to jockey for your attention.

 This icon points out features that are new to Illustrator 10. Sometimes, the paragraph tells you everything you need to know about the new feature. Other times, the icon introduces further paragraphs expounding on the same topic. Either way, you'll know it's something you didn't have in Illustrator 9 or earlier. If you already know Illustrator, you can get up to speed in Illustrator 10 by just reading these paragraphs.

 The latest version of Illustrator packs in even more features specifically for generating optimized Web graphics. I bring the most significant and useful ones to your attention using this handy Web icon.

 It seems like every book offers a tip icon. I've tried to steer clear of the boring old tips that every Illustrator user hears a million times and concentrate on the juicy stuff that most folks don't know. But keep in mind, these are fast tips. For the more involved killer techniques, you may have to read some text, too. Tips, as well as warnings and notes, are in italics to make them really stand out.

 This icon explains an action to avoid or that maybe won't work the way you expected it to. Few operations are hazardous in Illustrator, but many are time wasters. When I tell you what not to do, I try to include a preferable alternative as well.

 Occasionally I feel compelled to share my thoughts on a variety of subjects. Sometimes it's a bit of history, sometimes a technical clarification, other times it's a thoughtful observation, and every once in a while it's just a complaint. Whatever it is, you can skip it if it gets on your nerves.

Platform Nuts and Bolts

Adobe Illustrator 10 is a drawing program for both Windows and Macintosh computers. The differences in the program between these two types of computers are few and are mostly related to unique platform behaviors, such as the look and function of a palette's Close box. The biggest of these differences is that for keystroke combinations Windows employs the Ctrl key and the Alt key, whereas on a Mac you'd use the Command (Cmd) key (sometimes called the Apple or even Splat key) and the Option key. In this book, when I point out helpful keyboard shortcuts, the Windows version will appear first, followed by the Macintosh keystroke combination(s) in parentheses. The Windows key combinations will be joined with plus symbols, while their Mac brethren will be connected with hyphens. So when I tell you the quick way to save a document, for example, it'll say "Choose File » Save or press Ctrl+S (Cmd-S on the Mac)."

The other platform-specific convention you'll see in this book is (with apologies to any lefties out there who've switched their controls) "right-click" (Control-click on the Mac). Typically, this brings up a context-specific menu that repeats choices from a standard menu. The contextual menu can be a lot more convenient (if you're a keyboard person) and, to me, represents a general "have it your way, have it delivered right to your door" trend in our society that has trickled into software.

PART ONE
WELCOME TO ILLUSTRATOR

MEET ILLUSTRATOR 10

Adobe Illustrator—what is it, and what's new with version 10? That's the stuff of Chapter 1. This chapter provides a general overview of Illustrator 10, along with a brief preview of the new features. If you've never used Illustrator before, I'll tell you what it is and why you've probably heard its name bandied about. I'll show you where it fits into the world of computer graphics. Along the way you'll find out about Illustrator's relationship to its more popular sibling, Photoshop—a graphics program with an entirely different purpose.

If you're a longtime Illustrator enthusiast, this chapter provides some amusing—if not terribly insightful—analyses along with a practical assessment of Illustrator 10's new capabilities. I even tell you which chapters to turn to for more information on Illustrator's new features.

Adobe: the "Microsoft of Graphics"

To truly understand Illustrator, you have to know a bit about the company behind it, Adobe Systems Inc. One of the five largest software companies in this quadrant of the galaxy, Adobe is widely considered to be the one software developer that Microsoft cannot destroy. Adobe knows electronic graphics and design, and Microsoft never will. It's that simple.

Case in point: Photoshop, Adobe's phenomenally successful image-editing program, is widely considered the most powerful personal computer application for mucking around with computerized photographs. Photoshop is equally revered by expert and novice, young and old, educated and self-taught, primate and bottom-feeding slime fish. Photoshop isn't altogether perfect, but it has a universal appeal.

Microsoft, meanwhile, has squat. No high-end image editor now, and none planned for the future.

Adobe also makes Premiere, the number one program for editing digital video sequences. But there's absolutely nothing like it for messing around with moving images and creating simple animated effects.

Microsoft is currently unaware of any need for a video-editing package among the populace at large.

Are you beginning to see the trend? Adobe is absolutely steeped in the world of professional artistry and business graphics, and Microsoft hasn't even begun to compete. And perhaps it never will.

In the mind of your everyday, average industry analyst, Adobe is the "Microsoft of graphics." Like Microsoft, Adobe is a dominant force that not only lords over an entire discipline of computing with an iron fist, but also manages to consistently churn out quality software. Lesser companies regard Adobe with a combination of envy, respect, and fear. For better or worse, Adobe is currently where the artwork is.

Where Illustrator Fits In

Illustrator is important because its creation set current events in motion. Prior to Illustrator—back in the mid-1980s, when *the world was learning to pronounce Mikhail Gorbachev and Scritti Politti*—Adobe was a small company that had invented the PostScript printing language. PostScript revolutionized the world of typesetting and jump-started the career of at least one computer book author, but it didn't exactly make *Adobe* a household word (except in New Mexico, where adobe houses are quite common).

The problem with PostScript was its inaccessibility. In theory, PostScript let you design incredibly ornate, twisty-curvy lines and fill them with any of several million color options. But unless you wanted to resort to PostScript programming—the equivalent of instructing a friend to draw an object by reciting numerical coordinates over the phone—your options were limited to text surrounded by a few straight lines and rectangles.

Illustrator single-handedly changed all this. Before Illustrator, computer graphics looked blocky and turgid; after Illustrator, most folks couldn't tell computer graphics from those drawn with pen and ink. The transition couldn't have been more abrupt or more welcome.

Close, But Not Kin: Illustrator Versus Photoshop

Now in its fifteenth year, Illustrator is often seen as a kind of support program for Photoshop, thanks to the latter's dramatic and overshadowing success. Mind you, Illustrator's growth has been consistent and commendable over the years, and to this day it remains the world's most popular PostScript drawing program. But Photoshop manages to sell roughly twice as well as Illustrator, despite being nearly three years younger.

Truth be told, Adobe has tried to piggyback Illustrator on Photoshop's success. Since Photoshop was first released, Illustrator's popularity has mushroomed and the two programs have become more closely related. In fact, beginning with Illustrator 7, Adobe took this marriage one step further. Illustrator now has the look and feel of Photoshop. It still functions as Illustrator should, but the physical layout and the interface is similar to that of modern-day Photoshop. Adobe is simply trying to make Illustrator more accessible to the numerous Photoshop users.

Illustrator Does Smooth Lines; Photoshop Does Pixels

The easiest way to help you understand how Illustrator works is to start off by explaining how it *does not* work—which is precisely how Photoshop *does* work. As its name implies, Photoshop's primary purpose is to edit photographs. When you scan a photograph into a computer, the software converts it to a collection of tiny colored blocks called *pixels*. Each pixel is perfectly square, and one is perfectly adjacent to the next with no wiggle room between them. The primary purpose of Photoshop's hundreds of features is to adjust the colors of these pixels.

In Illustrator, each line, shape, and character of text is altogether independent of its neighbors. These independent elements are known collectively as *objects*, which is why Illustrator art is sometimes called *object-oriented*. Illustrator keeps track of each object by assigning it a separate mathematical equation. (Don't worry, there is no math in this book. Well, none that's important, anyway.) Illustrator later prints the lines, shapes, and text by sending the equations to the printer and letting the printer figure it out. The result is uniformly smooth artwork with high-contrast edges and crisp detail.

Like a longtime couple, Illustrator and Photoshop have taken on more of each other's personalities with each passing year, while retaining their own identities. Photoshop now has tools that create Illustrator-like paths and shapes, and Illustrator can treat its own graphics with Photoshop-style effects and filters. But Photoshop is still a pixel editor at heart, and Illustrator's objects are still described by smooth lines.

The Right Tool for the Right Job

As you might imagine, this difference in approach leads to a difference in purpose. Pixels are great for representing continuous color transitions, in which one color gradually changes into another. Such color transitions are the norm in real life, which is why pixels are so well suited to photographs. (Experienced/pretentious computer artists have even been known to call photographs *continuous-tone images*, but for our purposes, just plain *image* will suffice.)

Likewise, Illustrator is perfect for high-contrast artwork, which can vary from schematic or cartoonish to just barely stylized. This kind of computer art is known as a *drawing* or *illustration*.

Take as examples the two graphics in **Figure 1.1**. Both depict a sea lion in an attitude of aquatic grace, to be sure. But whereas the first is a photograph (snapped by Marty Snyderman and available at www.martysnyderman.com), the second is a line drawing I created in Illustrator. For the image on the left, I converted the color image to grayscale, corrected the brightness and contrast, and sharpened the focus, all in Photoshop. To achieve the illustration on the right, I had to meticulously trace the photograph in Illustrator and fill each shape with a different shade of gray.

The first image looks like a photo. But although the second is a recognizable member of the wildlife community, it is obviously executed by human hands, not snapped with a camera. This is the most significant difference between Photoshop and Illustrator.

Figure 1.1: A photographic image enhanced in Photoshop (left) compared with a line drawing created in Illustrator (right).

Flexible Resizing

Another difference is in the details. Photoshop's details can be grainy, but Illustrator's are forever smooth.

As you increase the size of a Photoshop image, the square pixels likewise grow and become more obvious. On the left side of **Figure 1.2**, for example, I've enlarged the sea lion image to 200, 400, and 800 percent. At each level of magnification, your eye is better able to separate the pixels into individual colored squares. As a result, a photograph looks great when printed at high *resolutions*, that is, when a lot of pixels are packed into a small space. But it begins to look coarse, jagged, and out of focus when printed at low resolutions, with fewer pixels per inch.

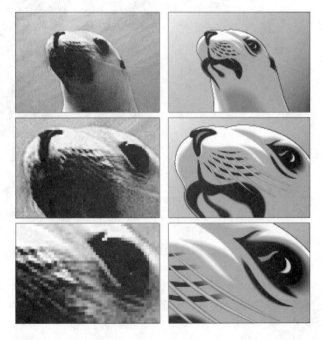

Figure 1.2: The results of magnifying the Photoshop image (left) and Illustrator drawing (right) to 200, 400, and 800 percent.

Illustrator art isn't like that at all. As shown on the right side of Figure 1.2, the drawing looks great no matter how much you enlarge it. Every line is mathematically accurate regardless of size. The downside, of course, is that it took me about 5 minutes to adjust the sea lion photo in Photoshop, but almost 3 hours to draw the sea lion in Illustrator. Apart from the photographic process itself, illustrations typically require a more sizable time investment than photographic images.

Objects and Pixels Together

The final difference between Photoshop and Illustrator is that with few exceptions Photoshop primarily handles pixels, while Illustrator primarily handles vectors. Don't get us wrong; Photoshop does have limited vector drawing capability, and Illustrator can work with images and rasterize vectors into bitmaps, but these capabilities are included as means to each program's own ends. In Photoshop, vectors are available as a more convenient way to create some kinds of pixel graphics, and in Illustrator, the pixel capability allows the creation of designs that can't be achieved through vectors alone. **Figure 1.3** shows the object-oriented sea lion layered in front of the original Photoshop image, so that the image serves as a background.

Figure 1.3: This inspiring creature is the product of Photoshop and Illustrator working together.

But to interpret Illustrator's acceptance of pixels as an advantage over Photoshop's relative ignorance of objects misses the point. Illustrator and Photoshop are designed to work together, now more than ever before. There may even be times when you prefer to convert an entire illustration to pixels inside

Photoshop, either to apply special effects that only Photoshop can handle or merely to simplify the printing process so the printer has to solve fewer equations. Illustrator and Photoshop are two halves of the artistic process, each taking up where the other one leaves off, each making up for the other one's weaknesses. It's the perfect marriage, and you're the lucky beneficiary.

The Lowdown on Illustrator 10

 If you're familiar with previous versions of Illustrator, then you probably already know the stuff I've told you so far (although it never hurts to revisit the basics every now and then). What you may not know is what the new Illustrator 10 has to offer that its predecessors did not. For you, I provide the following quick but riveting list, designed to get you up and running with little pain and lots of potential. Note that I also indicate which corresponding chapter spells out the new feature in detail, so you know where to turn when you need more information.

- **Live distortion (Chapters 9 and 19):** Using Illustrator's new warp effects and envelopes, you can quickly create a wide variety of live distortion effects. Because the effects are live, the content of the object can be altered even after the distortion has been applied. For example, you can resize a rectangle or edit text even while the distortion is applied. Warp effects let you arc, bulge, wave, and otherwise distort artwork and are useful for simulating nonflat surfaces and creating unusual perspective effects. With envelopes, any path created in Illustrator can be used as the basis for distorting an object. Envelopes are perfect for giving drawings three-dimensional perspective and can be especially fun when used with text, as **Figure 1.4** demonstrates. In the figure, I used the circle as an envelope to distort the text, creating a 3D effect.

Figure 1.4: Using a circle to distort text, editing the circle, then editing the text.

Liquify tools (Chapter 9): A new set of seven liquify tools—Warp, Twirl, Pucker, Bloat, Scallop, Crystalize, and Wrinkle—allow you to distort paths interactively by dragging over them. While live distortions affect entire objects, the liquify tools lets you distort parts of objects. These distortions can be minor adjustments or wild alterations. If you want to alter the path only slightly, one pass with a liquify tool will do. If you pass over the path repeatedly, the effect becomes more exaggerated and pronounced, as you can see in **Figure 1.5**. With the liquify tools you can apply everything from familiar pucker and bloat distortions to new crystallize and wrinkle effects.

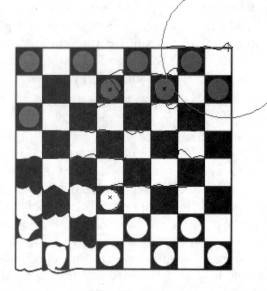

Figure 1.5: The Wrinkle liquify tool distorts the area you drag over.

Symbols palette and symbolism tools (Chapter 12): In the past, creating an illustration composed of many similar elements—like leaves on a tree, for example—was a time-consuming and labor-intensive process. Each object had to be copied, pasted, and then transformed into place. And if you wanted to change the basic object everywhere, you had to start all over from the beginning. But not anymore. Using the new Symbols palette, you can define any object as a symbol and then add instances of the symbol to your illustrations as many times as you want. In addition to being convenient, using symbols in an illustration reduces file size because all the instances of a symbol are linked to the original object stored in the Symbols palette. This can save quite a bit of precious memory in larger illustrations. This also means that if you need to change every instance of the symbol, you have to redefine the symbol only once—what a timesaver! But Illustrator goes beyond a basic implementation of symbols with the strange but wonderful idea of having a number of symbols behave as a single object. You can spray a number of symbols onto the artwork, then alter the sprayed instances of symbols using the new symbolism tools. You can see an example of this in **Figure 1.6**. You can shift, scrunch, resize, spin, tone, or style the symbols, and each symbol in the set will react independently and uniquely, and the changes remain applied even if you redefine the symbol.

 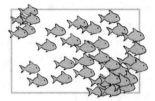 

Figure 1.6: A school of fish built up from a single fish symbol (left) with the symbol sprayer tool (center) and shaded with the toning tool (right).

- **Updated Pathfinder palette with new compound shape options (Chapter 7)**: Combining shapes is easier than ever before with Illustrator 10's new, more powerful Pathfinder palette. Offering more intuitive controls than in previous versions, the Pathfinder palette makes it easier to combine shapes and more accurately choose the appropriate compound option. Compound shapes are also now live objects and can still be transformed and edited once compounded.

- **Line, arc, grid, and polar grid tools (Chapter 5)**: Illustrator 10 adds several new drawing tools that users have been requesting for years. Now you can quickly draw lines and arcs without having to use the pen tool. Use the grid tool to create rectangular grids with up to 999 horizontal or vertical dividers. Useful primarily for map-type illustrations, the polar grid tool renders grids with concentric circles and as many dividers as you specify.

- **Select menu (Chapter 6)**: The selection commands that used to live under the Edit and Object menus have been promoted to a Select menu of their very own. That's quite a promotion!

● **Magic wand (Chapter 6)**: The magic wand tool has been an essential part of Photoshop for years, and now Illustrator has its own version of the tool. You can use the magic wand to select objects that have a similar fill, stroke, opacity, or blending mode. The Magic Wand palette lets you adjust the tolerance of the tool to specify how similar the objects' colors, strokes, or opacities must be in order to be included in the selection.

● **Object-based slices and manual slicing tools (Chapter 21)**: After a Web graphic is sliced into several smaller graphics files, it's often difficult to make changes to the image without reslicing it. With the introduction of object-based slices, Illustrator 10 tackles this problem head on by making it easier to edit sliced graphics. Instead of the traditional method of slicing an image into a series of rectangles before being displayed in the browser, object-based slices use each object's bounding box to guide the placement of slices. Since object-based slices are based on each object's bounding box, the position of the slices will update automatically when you modify the graphic. In other words, once you set it up, you don't have to worry about it again. If you want more control over slicing, use the new manual slicing tools, which let you locate slices wherever you like. Manual slices don't update automatically, but they also don't have to be tied to specific objects within the illustration.

● **Slicing options (Chapter 21)**: Illustrator 10 can optimize each slice of an illustration separately. This allows you to specify the optimal file format and setting for each individual slice. For example, a slice containing only text will download and render fastest if it's saved in straight HTML, while a photograph will most efficiently optimize in the JPEG format. Slices can even be saved in the Macromedia Shockwave (SWF) format. With this amount of control over the slicing and optimization process, you can produce Web images that both load quickly and look great.

● **Support for CSS layers (Chapter 21)**: Now slices also can be exported as Cascading Style Sheet (CSS) layers. With CSS layers, slices can overlap each other and take advantage of transparency. With a bit of scripting, you can make different layers display in different contexts. For example, you can have one set of layers display on weekdays and another on weekends. Or you can have a layer with English-language text and another with French to match the local browser settings.

Data-driven graphics for the Web (Chapter 22): This incredibly powerful feature allows you to automatically feed graphics from a database into Illustrator templates. Let's say you have to design a Web catalog with products, prices, and page headings that don't change. You can draw a template containing the basic design of the page, and designate areas that will contain the parts that change (products, information, etc.). You assign variables to the changeable parts and let a database and a script fill them in as needed. With this feature and a little scripting, you can use a template and a database to dynamically generate Web pages.

Improved animation support (Chapter 22): Illustrator 9 allowed you to export files in the SWF format, commonly associated with Flash animations. Illustrator 10 expands on this capability by giving you more control over the animations you export. Now you can select whether your animations play a fixed number of times or constantly loop, and you can automatically generate the HTML code that allows an SWF file to play in the Web browser. To ensure that animations are more compact, symbols and instances are automatically converted to Macromedia Flash style symbols and instances. If a symbol is used many times in a drawing, it is saved only once in the file, with all other instances being based on the original symbol.

Native support for Mac OS X: If you're using this radical update to the Mac OS, Illustrator will take advantage of its features, such as vastly improved memory management and Apple's Aqua user interface.

Improved SVG support (Chapter 22): Adobe continues to build its support for this open, XML-based vector graphics format for the Web. It's now possible to open and edit SVG files exported from Illustrator, because Illustrator can embed the original file in the SVG file. More excitingly, Illustrator has added a number of live SVG effects. The key thing about SVG effects is that they save network bandwidth by not being rendered until they reach the browser. The filters themselves are rather innovative because they are live (so you can edit the object while the effect is applied) and because they are effects not normally expected for vectors, such as blurs and drop shadows.

Flare tool (Chapter 5): The new flare tool can simulate lens flares and add lighting effects to illustrations. Using just the mouse, you can draw a flare and set the location and number of its rays. Double-click a flare to display the Flare Tool Options dialog box, where you can adjust the center, halo, ray, and ring settings.

As with any new version of Illustrator, there are several questions to be answered. What's the best new feature? Are there problems that will need fixing in the next version? How will Illustrator 10 affect your style of art? Will it improve your life? The only way to answer these questions is to forge ahead. There's a lot to learn, so let's get going.

CHAPTER 2

THE INTERFACE

Whenever folks speak about Illustrator, someone always seems to drop the word "elegant" into the conversation. And, truly, it fits. Despite its occasional flaws, Illustrator has always delivered a rare combination of a logical interface and extremely reliable performance. And what, I ask you, could be more elegant than that?

But even an elegant application can bewilder and vex the user it has sworn to serve. The biggest strike against Illustrator is that it doesn't always work like other programs. Illustrator provides three different arrow tools where most other programs manage to make do with one. Many commands are missing from the menus and are available only through floating palettes. You change the performance of many tools by clicking *with* them rather than double-clicking *on* them. The pen tool takes some getting used to with its Bézier control handles.

The end result is that the elegant Illustrator is hard to learn. But once you come to terms with it, which takes some concentrated and patient effort, you'll never go back to other illustration programs. This chapter introduces Illustrator to new users, reminds casual users how it works, and brings longtime users up to speed. Here's where I explain the interface, briefly describe the tools and palettes, and examine every single one of the preference settings in excruciating detail.

There is nothing that says you have to read this stuff sequentially. Feel free to skip around, read bits and pieces over the course of several weeks, or cut out the pages and paste them over your bathroom mirror. Follow whatever learning style makes you smart in the shortest amount of time.

Getting Illustrator Up and Running

Most folks are pretty clear on how to start up a program with the Mac OS or Windows system software, and Illustrator is no exception. For example, you can double-click the Adobe Illustrator icon, which looks as though someone gold-plated the statue of liberty. Or you can double-click an Illustrator file. Or you can drag some other file onto the Illustrator application icon. Some folks call this technique *launching* a program, others call it *running* a program—but whatever you call it, you have to do it before you can use Illustrator.

Setting Aside Memory

 For those of you using a Macintosh running Mac OS 9 or earlier, prior to starting up Illustrator, you may want to adjust the amount of memory (called RAM, like the sheep) that your Mac assigns to the application. To do this, first select the Adobe Illustrator application icon and choose File » Get Info » Memory. Change the Preferred Size value to assign more RAM to Illustrator. (Even though you can also change the Minimum Size value, don't do it! Lowering this value can wreak havoc on Illustrator's performance and may even prevent the program from running.) Mac OS 10.1 utilizes modern memory management and automatically allocates memory to applications as they need it.

The Splash Screen

After you launch Illustrator, the splash screen shows you that your computer is obeying your instructions. Little messages tell you that Illustrator is loading fonts or reading plug-ins. This is a perfect time to get a cup of coffee.

If you ever want to look at the splash screen again, choose About Illustrator from the Apple menu if you're on a Mac (it's in the Illustrator menu if you're running OS 10.1 on the Mac), or from the Help menu on Windows. There's no practical reason you'd ever want to do this, but there are a couple of silly features that you might find mildly amusing.

- Wait a while to see a list of credits. Whoopee.

- Press the Alt key (Option key on the Mac) to see the credits roll by quickly. Super whoopee. (Unfortunately, this does not work on Mac OS 10.1)

- Click or press any key to make the splash screen go away.

There you have it, a bunch of silly information that won't do you a lick of good, except to clog your mind when you're in your dotage.

The Illustrator Desktop

After the splash screen goes away, you will see the onscreen elements. Illustrator 10 does not automatically create a new illustration window. You have to choose the New command from the File menu and make a few decisions about the document. This may add a few seconds to your projects, so make sure you budget your time accordingly.

If you've been working on the Windows or Mac system for any amount of time, you're probably familiar with the basic desktop elements labeled in **Figures 2.1** (Windows) and **2.2** (Mac). If you're new to the world of computing or new to Illustrator, go ahead and read the descriptions. (Labeled items from the figures appear in italic type.)

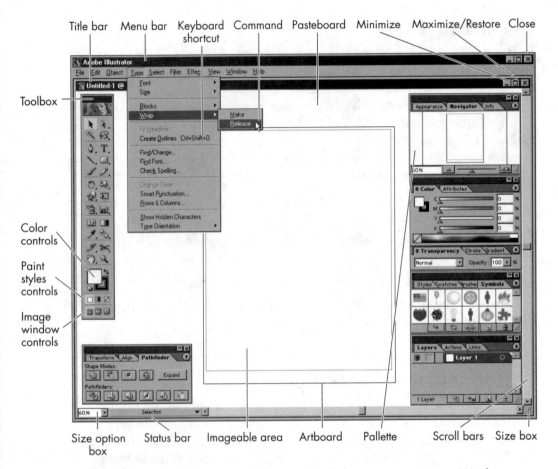

Title bar Menu bar Keyboard Command Pasteboard Minimize Maximize/Restore Close
                      shortcut

Toolbox

Color
controls

Paint
styles
controls

Image
window
controls

Size option   Status bar   Imageable area   Artboard   Pallette   Scroll bars   Size box
box

Figure 2.1: The fully annotated Illustrator 10 desktop, as it appears on Windows.

If a right-pointing arrowhead follows a command name, choosing the
command displays a submenu of additional commands. To choose
Type » Wrap » Release, for example, you would click the word Type
in the menu bar to open the Type menu. You would then move down
to the Wrap command, then over to the submenu, and then click the
Release command. This closes the menu and applies the command.

The *menu bar* provides access to Illustrator's ten menus. Click a menu
name to display a list of *commands* that perform various operations.
To choose a command, drag your cursor on top of it so it becomes
highlighted, then release. *Keyboard shortcuts* appear to the right of
commands. If a command is dimmed, it isn't applicable to the current
situation and you can't choose it.

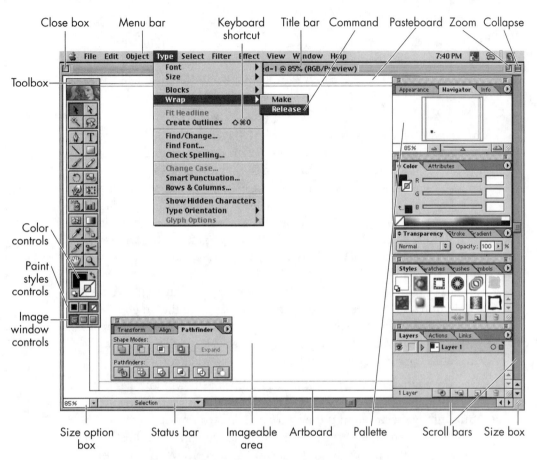

Figure 2.2: Here's the Illustrator 10 desktop as it appears on the Mac.

The *toolbox* includes 24 default tools and 52 alternate tools. To select a tool, click its icon. I'll briefly introduce all 76 tools in the "Using Tools" section later in this chapter. The bottom portion of the toolbox offers three sets of controls. The *color controls* let you change the colors of an object's stroke and fill as well as interchange colors. The *paint styles controls* let you select a solid color, a gradient, or none (that is, see-through) for your fill or stroke. And in the final row, the *image window controls* give you control over the display of the foreground window.

The toolbox is known generically as a *palette*. In addition to the toolbox, Illustrator provides a number of other palettes, all of which are detailed in the "Using Palettes" section of this chapter.

- The *illustration window* is the large window in the middle of the desktop. A window appears for every open illustration. The *title bar* lists the name of the document, the relative viewing size, the document color mode, and the type of preview currently chosen. If the illustration has not been given a name, the name appears as "Untitled," followed by a number.

- You can move the illustration window by dragging the title bar. Close the illustration by clicking in the *close box* in the upper-left corner on the Mac or in the upper-right corner in the Windows environment. Drag the *size box* in the bottom-right corner of the window to enlarge or reduce the size of the window manually. Macintosh users can click the *zoom box* on the right side of the title bar to expand the window to fill the entire screen. Click the zoom box again to reduce the window to its previous size. For Windows users, this corresponds to the *maximize/restore box* that sits just to the left of the close box. To the left of that, Windows provides the *minimize box*, which reduces Illustrator to a button on the Windows taskbar without quitting the program. (The Macintosh equivalent is the *collapse box,* which hides the entire window with just the title bar visible.) In Mac OS 10, all the options (maximize, minimize, and close) are in the upper-left corner.

- The page with the drop shadow in the middle of the window is the *artboard*. This represents the size of the drawing you want to create. Surrounding the artboard is the *pasteboard*. You can move objects out to the pasteboard, and these objects will be saved with your illustration but they will not print. Experienced artists typically use the pasteboard as a storage area for objects they can't quite bear to delete when they print directly from Illustrator. (Warning: Objects on the pasteboard of documents exported and placed into other programs, such as QuarkXPress or InDesign, will print.) The dotted line around the *imageable area* shows the portion of the artboard your printer can actually print. Most printers can't print to the extreme edges of a page.

- Together, the artboard and pasteboard are generically known as the *drawing area*.

- The *scroll bars* appear along the right and bottom edges of the illustration window, as they do in most Mac and Windows applications. They allow you to move your drawing with respect to the window to better see various portions of your illustration. Click one of the arrows at the end of a scroll bar to nudge the drawing a small distance; click in the gray area of a scroll bar to move the drawing a greater distance. Drag the tab in either scroll bar to move the drawing manually.

The *size option box* in the lower-left corner of the illustration window lets you change the view size of your artwork. Simply click the size option box, enter any permitted value, and hit Enter (Return on the Mac). You can reduce the view to as little as 3.13 percent of the actual size, allowing you to easily see the largest possible artboard size that Illustrator permits. Going to the other extreme, you can expand a square inch to a respectable 6 1/3 square feet by choosing 6400 percent.

The *status bar* just to the right of the size option box lists all kinds of moderately useful information about the program. Click the status bar to display a pop-up menu of status bar options, as shown in the top example of **Figure 2.3**. You can have the status bar list the active tool, the date and time, the amount of RAM going unused inside Illustrator, the number of available undos and redos, or the type of color profile assigned to the document.

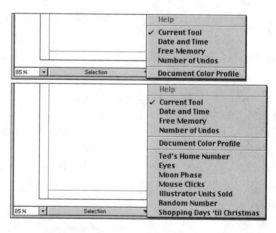

Figure 2.3: These are the pop-up menus that appear when you click (top) and Alt-click or Option-click (bottom) on the status bar.

Press the Alt key (or the Option key on the Mac) as you click the status bar to access the additional options shown in the bottom example of Figure 2.3. Most of these options are very silly—Random Number and Shopping Days 'til Christmas—but two are actually useful. If you use Illustrator on an older PowerBook, you might appreciate the Eyes option, which brings up a pair of eyes that follow your cursor around the screen. No more lost cursor! And if you can't get Illustrator to work correctly, then check out Ted's Home Number. You won't really get Ted, who used to be one of the Illustrator product managers—you'll get Adobe's technical support line.

Context Menus

Originally only Windows had context menus, sometimes called shortcut menus, but after they were introduced to the Mac platform, Adobe added context menus to Illustrator with great results. On the Mac platform, you open context menus by holding the Control key and clicking with the mouse. Under Windows, you click with the right mouse button.

 In Mac OS 10, you can access contextual menus by right-clicking with a two-button mouse.

There are several benefits to working with context menus. First, they appear anywhere on the screen—you don't have to move your mouse all the way up to the top of the screen to get the menu. Second, they display their items in the context of what is currently selected. So if you invoke the context menu while your cursor is over a ruler, for example, you get options for switching the units of measurement for the rulers. But if you right-click or Control-click a selected object on the artboard, you get a context menu with completely different options.

Online Resources

Click the Venus icon at the top of the toolbox to open the Adobe Online dialog box, shown in **Figure 2.4**. This screen gives you access to Adobe's Web site, where you can register Illustrator, download updates, look up support articles, read tips and tricks from other Illustrator users, and purchase other Adobe products. If you have a live Internet connection, click the Go Online button to get started. Or if you just want to download the latest product updates, click the Updates button instead. You can also click Preferences to tell Illustrator to check for updates automatically.

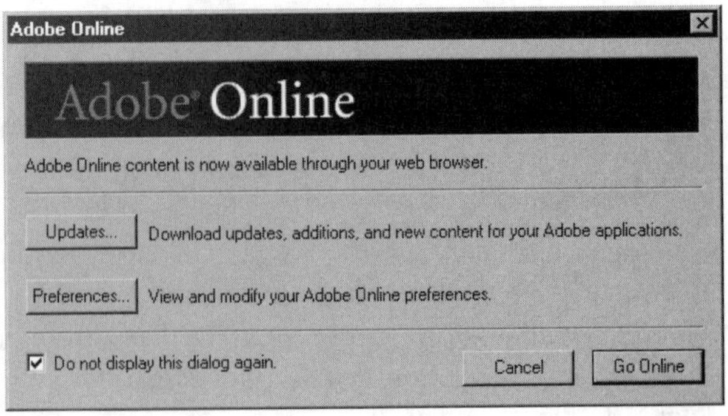

Figure 2.4: The Adobe Online dialog box gives quick access to Adobe's Web site.

Unless you want to bypass the Adobe Online dialog box in the future, be sure to turn off the Do Not Display This Dialog Again check box before you click Go Online. If you leave this option turned on, as it is by default, clicking the Venus icon or choosing Adobe Online from the Help menu will take you directly to Adobe's Web site forever after.

Using Tools

The toolbox, like any other palette, is entirely independent of all other desktop elements, so if you reduce the size of a drawing window, the toolbox remains unchanged, with 24 tools visible and easily accessible. The toolbox serves, and is positioned in front of, any and all open illustrations. You can move the toolbox by dragging its title bar and hide it by choosing the Window » Hide Tools command. To redisplay the toolbox, choose Window » Show Tools.

 You can hide the toolbox and all other palettes by pressing the Tab key. Press Tab again to bring all the palettes back. To get rid of all palettes except the toolbox, press Shift-Tab (that is, hold the Shift key and then tap the Tab key).

As with other graphics and publishing programs, you select a tool in Illustrator by clicking its icon in the toolbox. Illustrator highlights and colors the active tool so it stands out prominently. Even folks in the next cubicle can't help but know which tool you're using.

The toolbox contains 24 tool *slots*. In addition to the default tools occupying these slots, Illustrator offers 52 alternate tools that are initially hidden. For example, Illustrator hides the smooth tool and the erase tool under the pencil tool. To use one of these hidden tools, you have to click and hold the ellipse icon to display a pop-up menu of alternates, as demonstrated in **Figure 2.5**. Select the desired tool as you would a command—that is, by highlighting the tool and releasing the mouse button. Slots that offer alternate tools have tiny right-facing arrowheads in their lower-right corners.

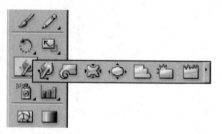

Figure 2.5: To select an alternate tool, click and hold a toolbox icon that features a small arrowhead.

Slots have an added benefit of letting you tear off the tools so they appear in their own little row. Just drag your cursor over to the *tearoff* icon (indicated by the small arrowhead) at the end of the slot. Release the mouse. That slot appears in its own little toolbar. (Despite the name, you don't actually tear the slot off the toolbox. You just choose it and it tears off by itself.) You can then position the toolbar anywhere on your window. You can even create multiple toolbars for the same tools.

All 76 default and alternate tools appear in the composite screen shot in **Figure 2.6**. These tools, aside from the new ones, work just as they did in Illustrator 9.

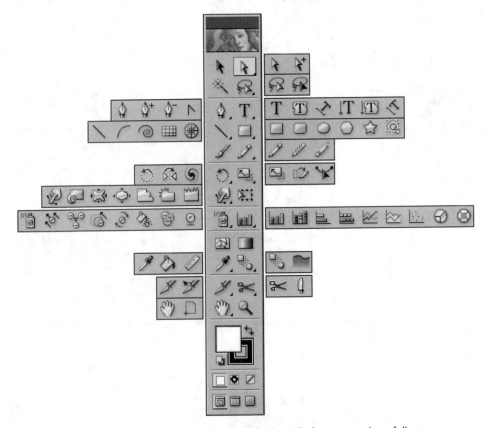

Figure 2.6: The toolbox with all the default and alternate tools in full view.

Illustrator allows you to switch to any of the tools, or access the controls in the toolbox, by pressing the appropriate key, as shown in **Figure 2.7**. Many of the default settings are the same shortcuts that Photoshop uses. They don't all make sense on first glance, but if you realize that the tool that makes rectangular areas is the *marquee (M)* tool in Photoshop, you'll understand why the rectangle tool uses the letter M in Illustrator. After all, the R key can't be assigned to the rectangle, rotate, and reflect tools simultaneously. Fortunately, Illustrator 10 lets you assign your own keys to any of the tools. So if you want to set R for *rectangle*, and A for rotate *around*, and M for reflect in a *mirror*, you can do so.

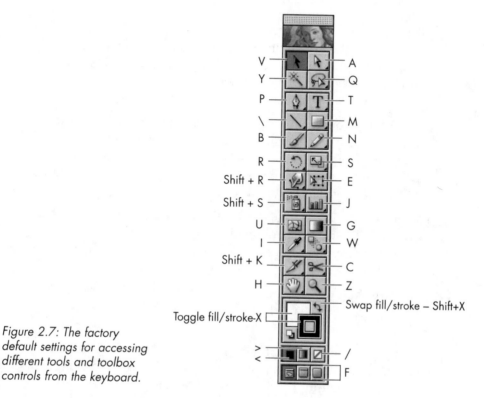

Figure 2.7: The factory
default settings for accessing
different tools and toolbox
controls from the keyboard.

   The following paragraphs explain how to use each of Illustrator's 76 tools in the illustration window. For example, if an item instructs you to *drag*, click the tool's icon to select it and then drag inside the drawing area; don't drag on the icon itself. These are intended as introductory descriptions only. If a tool name appears in italics, that indicates that the tool's description appears later in the list. Subsequent chapters contain more information, which is why I include chapter numbers in the descriptions. Double-clicking some tools brings up that tool's preferences. For example, double-clicking the magic wand tool brings the Magic Wand palette into view. Double-clicking the symbolism tools let you set individual preferences for that tool.

Selection (Chapter 6): The selection tool—which I usually called the "arrow tool" in deference to its appearance—is active when you first start Illustrator. Use this tool to select objects that you've created so you can manipulate them. Click an object to select the entire object. Drag an object to move it. You can also use the selection tool to select text blocks.

Direct selection (Chapter 6): Click with this hollow arrow to select individual anchor points and segments in a line or shape. This is also the perfect tool for editing the Bézier control handles that govern the curvature of segments. Press Alt (Option on the Mac) while this tool is active to access the *group selection* tool.

Group selection (Chapter 6): Click with this tool (or just Alt-click or Option-click with the direct selection tool) to select whole objects at a time. Though it frequently acts the same as the standard arrow tool, the group selection tool lets you select individual objects inside groups, whereas the arrow tool selects *all* objects in a group.

Magic wand (Chapter 6): Click with this tool to select objects that have a similar stroke, fill, or opacity. You can adjust the tolerance of the tool to determine how similar the objects have to be in order to be selected.

Lasso (Chapter 6): Drag with this tool to select entire objects within a non-rectangular area. When you release the mouse, any objects within the lasso area will be selected.

Direct-select lasso (Chapter 6): Drag with this tool to select the individual points within a non-rectangular area. When you release the mouse, any points or paths within the lasso area will be selected.

Pen (Chapter 6): This is Illustrator's most powerful drawing tool and the one that's most responsible for Illustrator's success. Use the pen tool to draw a line as a series of individual points. Click to add corners to a line, drag to add arcs. You can also Alt-drag (Option-drag on the Mac) on an arc to change it to a cusp. Illustrator automatically connects your points with straight or curved segments. Press Alt (Option on the Mac) while this tool is active to access the *convert anchor point* tool.

Add anchor point (Chapter 6): Click a segment with the add anchor point tool to insert a new point into a line. Press Alt (Option on the Mac) to access the *delete anchor point* tool.

Delete anchor point (Chapter 6): Click a point with this tool to remove the point while leaving the line intact. That's why I'd rather call this the "remove point" tool—"deleting" a point would create a hole. Press Alt (Option on the Mac) to access the add-anchor-point tool.

Convert anchor point (Chapter 6): Use this tool to change a corner in a line to an arc or vice versa. Click an arc to make it a corner; drag on a corner to make it an arc.

Type (Chapter 10): Click with this tool and then enter text from the keyboard to create a line of type in the standard left-to-right format. To create a text block with type that automatically wraps from one line down to the next, drag with the type tool and then start banging away at the keyboard. You can also use this tool (or one of the other five type tools) to highlight characters in a text block—allowing you to edit or format them. Press Shift while this tool is active to access the *vertical type* tool.

Area type (Chapter 11): Click a line or shape to create text that wraps inside an irregular boundary. Press Alt (Option on the Mac) to access the *path type* tool. Press Shift to access the *vertical area type* tool.

Path type (Chapter 11): Click a line or shape to create text that follows the contours of the object, better known as text on a curve. Press Alt (Option on the Mac) to access the area type tool. Press Shift to access the *vertical path type* tool.

Vertical type (Chapter 11): Very similar to the type tool, this tool arranges text vertically, the way Japanese script appears. Click with this tool and then enter text from the keyboard to create an ascending column of type. To create a text block with type that automatically wraps from one column to the next (from right to left), drag with the vertical type tool and then start them magic fingers fluttering. Press Alt (Option on the Mac) to access the *vertical path type* tool. Press Shift to access the type tool.

Vertical area type (Chapter 11): Click a line or shape to create text that fills an irregular boundary column. Press Alt (Option on the Mac) to access the *vertical path type* tool. Press Shift to access the area type tool.

Vertical path type (Chapter 11): Click a line or shape to create text that follows the contours of the object. As you probably guessed, one letter will stack upon the next to form a column that follows the curve. Press Alt (Option on the Mac) to access the vertical area type tool. Press Shift to access the path type tool.

Line segment (Chapter 5): Drag with this tool to draw a straight line. Shift-drag to create lines that are parallel to, perpendicular to, or at a 45-degree angle from the x and y axis. Click with this tool to define the angle and length of a straight segment in a dialog box.

Arc segment (Chapter 5): Drag with this tool to create concave or convex arcs. Shift-drag to draw a proportional arc. Press the C key while you drag to create a closed arc. Press the F key while you drag to flip the arc 180 degrees. Click with the arc tool to define the arc in a dialog box. Press the up and down arrow keys to change the radius of the arc.

Spiral (Chapter 5): Drag to draw a spiraling line, like a stylized pig's tail. To change the number of times the line twists inside itself, click with the tool in the drawing area.

Rectangular grid (Chapter 5): Drag with this tool to draw a rectangular grid. Shift-drag to create a perfectly square grid. Double-click the tool in the toolbox, or click with the tool in the illustration window, to specify the size of the grid and number of dividers it will contain. Press the up and down arrows to add or remove rows. Press the left and right arrows to add or remove columns. Press the Z, X, C and V keys to "skew" the rows and columns (this all applies to the *polar grid* tool as well).

Polar grid (Chapter 5): Drag to draw an elliptical grid consisting of concentric circles divided by lines that stretch from the center point of the ellipse to the outer edge, similar to a dart board or radar screen. Shift-drag to create a circular polar grid. As with the rectangular grid tool, you can click with the tool to specify the size of the grid and the number of dividers.

Rectangle (Chapter 5): Drag with this tool to draw a rectangle. You can also Shift-drag to draw a square or Alt-drag (Option-drag on the Mac) to create a rectangle from the center outward. Click with the tool to enter numerical dimensions for your rectangle.

Rounded rectangle (Chapter 5): If you want your rectangles to have rounded corners, use this tool. To adjust the roundness of the corners of future shapes, click with the tool in the drawing area. Shift-drag to draw a rounded square. As you may have guessed, you can Alt-drag (Option-drag on the Mac) to create a rounded rectangle from the center outward.

Ellipse (Chapter 5): This tool works just like the rectangle tool, except that it makes ellipses and circles. Shift-drag to draw a circle or Alt-drag (Option-drag on the Mac) to draw an ellipse from the center outward.

Polygon (Chapter 5): When you drag with this tool, you draw a regular polygon, such as a triangle or pentagon. Click with the tool to change the number of sides.

Star (Chapter 5): Drag with this tool to draw a star with symmetrical points. Alt-drag (Option-drag on the Mac) to constrain the star so opposite arms are perfectly aligned, as for a five-pointed American star or a Star of David. Click with the tool to change the number of points. You can also press the Spacebar to reposition the object while drawing it. This actually applies to all the drawing shape tools.

Flare (Chapter 5): The flare tool creates a lens flare effect similar to one you might find in a photograph. Click-and-drag once to create the center, the rays, and the halo. Release the mouse button, position the cursor, and click-and-drag to create the rings. To create a custom flare, click with the flare tool and specify your options in the Flare Option box.

Paintbrush (Chapter 5): This tool creates an open path that is automatically styled with one of the calligraphy, artistic, scatter, or pattern brushes. Double-click the icon to set the sensitivity of the paintbrush. Like the *pencil* tool, the paintbrush can also be used to modify a previously drawn brushstroke.

Pencil (Chapter 5): The pencil tool makes a free-form line when you drag with it, much as if you were drawing with a pencil. If you are not satisfied with the final result, simply drag over the part of your path you wish to correct and the offending snippet toes the line.

Smooth (Chapter 6): Use the smooth tool to reposition points and reshape paths quickly. After you drag with this tool, Illustrator will add or remove points (or even move points) in an attempt to streamline the path and smooth it out.

Erase (Chapter 6): With the erase tool, you drag over a segment of an entire path to remove it. This allows you to open closed paths and delete unnecessary paths easily.

Rotate (Chapter 6): This tool lets you rotate selected objects. Click with the tool to determine the center of the rotation, and then drag to rotate the objects around this center. Or just drag right off the bat to position the center of the rotation smack dab in the center of the selected objects. You can also Alt-click (Option-click on the Mac) with the tool or double-click the rotate tool icon in the toolbox to specify a rotation numerically.

Reflect (Chapter 9): Use this tool to flip objects across an axis. Usually it's easiest to just drag with this tool, or Alt-click (Option-click on the Mac) to flip horizontally or vertically.

Twist (Chapter 19): Formerly known as the twirl tool, this tool lets you twist selected objects around a fixed point with the rotation occurring more intensely in the center of the object rather than in its edges. (Why the name change? Because Illustrator 10 introduces a brand new *twirl* tool, which I discuss a few short paragraphs from now.) Click to set the center point and then drag to twist, or just start dragging to twist around the object's exact center. To twist numerically, Alt-click (Option-click on the Mac) with the twist tool or choose Filter » Distort » Twist. You can also use Effect » Distort & Transform » Twist to twist an object without permanently distorting its shape.

Scale (Chapter 9): This tool and the two other transformation tools, *reflect* and *shear*, work just like the rotate tool. The only difference is that the scale tool enlarges and reduces selected objects.

Shear (Chapter 9): Drag with the oddly named shear tool to slant or skew selected objects. The effects of Shift-dragging are generally easier to predict; when the Shift key is down, the shear tool slants objects horizontally or vertically.

Reshape (Chapter 6): Click-and-drag with this tool on an open path to deform the path in a free-form manner. The result of the deformation is entirely dependent on which points of the object were selected.

Warp (Chapter 9): Drag over an existing object with this tool to alter its path. The path will stretch in the direction that you drag. If you drag toward the center of the object, the path will curve toward the center. If you drag away from the center, the path will appear concave. Double-click the warp tool icon to modify the brush size and spacing used for warping.

Twirl (Chapter 9): Not to be confused with the twist tool described earlier, the twirl tool lets you create swirling distortions within an object. Drag over any portion of an object to twirl only that portion. Use short, circular drags to create a swirling effect.

Pucker (Chapter 9): Drag over a path with the pucker tool to deflate an object by moving control points toward the cursor.

Bloat (Chapter 9): Drag over a path with the bloat tool to inflate an object by moving surrounding points away from the cursor.

Scallop (Chapter 9): The scallop tool lets you rough up the path of an object. When you drag over an object, the scallop tool adds random arcs to the outline or the path of the object. You can adjust the complexity and detail of the scalloped edge by double-clicking the scallop tool icon in the toolbox.

Crystallize (Chapter 9): Drag over an object with this tool to create crystal-like, spiked distortions along the object's path. Double-click the crystallize tool icon to adjust the intensity of the effect.

Wrinkle (Chapter 9): Drag with the wrinkle tool to add wrinkles—both arcs and spikes—to the path of an object. Double-click the tool icon to adjust the intensity of the distortion.

Free transform (Chapter 9): The free transform tool allows you to scale, rotate, reflect, and shear as well as properly four-point distort selected paths, all right on screen. A lame version of this tool that uses a dialog box is found under Filter » Distort » Free Distort. This is the Free Distort filter that was removed when the free transform tool was introduced in Illustrator 8. However, a live version of the Free Distort filter is found under Effect » Distort & Transform » Free Distort. This allows you to transform an object without permanently changing its shape.

Symbol sprayer (Chapter 12): The symbol sprayer lets you place instances of a selected symbol from the Symbols palette on the artboard. You may select a symbol that Illustrator has provided, or create your own custom symbol. Click once to place a single symbol instance or drag to leave a trail of instances, better known as a set, behind your path. With all the symbolism tools, the Alt (Option) key reverses the effect. So for example with the symbol sprayer, pressing and dragging adds symbol instances to your set. Adding the Alt (Option) key while you drag removes symbol instances. For the *symbol scruncher*, adding Alt (Option) moves instances further apart.

Symbol shifter (Chapter 12): Drag with this tool over a series of selected symbol instances to shift their position. Double-click the tool icon to define how wide an area you want the symbol shifter to affect and the amount of space that symbol instances are shifted.

Symbol scruncher (Chapter 12): The symbol scruncher lets you move a series of selected symbols instances closer to each other. The more you drag over the instances, the closer they will get to each other—eventually overlapping. Double-click the tool icon in the toolbox to set the symbol scruncher options.

Symbol sizer (Chapter 12): The symbol sizer allows you to increase or decrease the size of the symbol instances. Click-and-drag to increase the size of the instances. Hold down the Alt key (Option key on a Mac) to decrease the size. Double-click the tool icon in the toolbox to set the tool's options.

Symbol spinner (Chapter 12): Use this tool to rotate a series of selected symbol instances. Just drag over the symbol instances in the direction that you want to rotate them.

Symbol stainer (Chapter 12): The symbol stainer lets you colorize symbol instances. Choose a fill color and click or drag over the instance(s). The hue of the instance changes to the fill color while retaining the original luminosity (shadows, midtones, and highlights). Hold down the Alt key (Option key on a Mac) to decrease the amount of colorization.

Symbol screener (Chapter 12): The symbol screener changes the transparency of symbol instances. Drag over instances to make them more transparent. Alt-drag (Option-drag on the Mac) to decrease the level of transparency.

Symbol styler (Chapter 12): Click or drag with this tool to apply the selected style in the Styles palette to symbol instances.

Column (Chapter 13): Drag with this tool to specify the rectangular boundaries of a standard column graph. Shift-dragging constrains the boundary to a square and Alt-dragging (Option-dragging on the Mac) forms rectangular boundaries from the center out. Illustrator then presents you with a spreadsheet in which you can enter your data. Double-click the graph tool icon in the toolbox to specify the options for the graph you want to create.

Stacked column (Chapter 13): This tool and the seven other graph tools that follow work like the column graph tool, except that dragging with this tool specifies the boundaries of a stacked column graph.

Bar (Chapter 13): Drag with this tool to specify the boundaries of a standard horizontal bar graph.

Stacked bar (Chapter 13): Drag with this tool to specify the boundaries of a stacked horizontal bar graph in which each graph entity appears farther to the right.

Line (Chapter 13): Drag with this tool to specify the boundaries of a line graph—you know, your basic dot-to-dot with a few labels to make it look official.

Area (Chapter 13): Drag with this tool to specify the boundaries of an area graph. It's the color-within-the-lines evolution of the line graph.

Scatter (Chapter 13): Drag with this tool to specify the boundaries of a scatter graph, one in which only the points are plotted.

Pie (Chapter 13): Drag with this tool to specify the boundaries of a pie graph. Enough said.

Radar (Chapter 13): Drag with this tool to specify the boundaries of a radar graph. This is the ideal graph for confusing anyone attending your presentation.

Mesh (Chapter 15): Click inside an object to convert the object to a mesh object and add a mesh point. Drag to move a mesh point. Click inside an existing mesh object to add additional mesh points. Alt-click (Option-click on the Mac) a mesh point to delete it.

Gradient (Chapter 15): Drag inside a selected object that's filled with a gradation to change the angle of the gradations, as well as the location of the first and last colors. Shift-drag to constrain your drag to 45-degree increments.

Eyedropper (Chapter 10) Click an object or text with the eyedropper to copy the appearance, color, and text attributes. These attributes can then be applied to other objects or text using the *paint bucket*. Set the eyedropper options by double-clicking the icon in the toolbox.

Paint bucket (Chapter 10): Click an object or text to apply the attributes sampled by the paint bucket. Set paint bucket options by double-clicking the tool icon in the toolbox.

Measure (Chapter 8): Drag with this tool to measure the distance between two points. Alternatively, you can click in one spot and then click in another. Illustrator displays the measurements in the Info palette.

Blend (Chapter 17): The blend tool allows you to create custom gradations. After selecting two or more objects with one of the arrow tools, use the blend tool to click a point in one object, then click a point in the others. Illustrator creates a collection of intermediate shapes between the two objects and fills these with intermediate colors. You can also create blends using the Object » Blend » Make command.

Auto trace (Chapter 5): Click or drag within 6 screen pixels of a raster image to trace a line around the image. This tool is easily Illustrator's worst; you're almost always better off tracing images with the pen or pencil.

Slice (Chapter 21): This tool lets you slice up an image into a series of smaller images. Drag to create rectangular slice areas, which you can optimize separately for the Web. Different Web effects can be associated with the slices.

Slice select (Chapter 21): The slice select tool allows you to select slices. Hold down the Shift key to select multiple slices.

Scissors (Chapter 7): Click a line to cut it into two. Illustrator inserts two points at the spot where you click, one for each line.

Knife (Chapter 7): Drag with the knife tool to cut shapes into new shapes, just as if you had dragged through them with a real knife. The knife tool is a little *too* sharp though; it cuts through any objects in its path, whether they're selected or not.

Hand (Chapter 3): Drag with the hand tool to scroll the drawing inside the illustration window. It is much more convenient than the scroll bars. You can also double-click the hand tool icon in the tool-box to fit the entire artboard into the illustration window.

Page (Chapter 3): Drag with the page tool to move the imageable area within the artboard. Unless the artboard is larger than the printed page size, you don't have to worry about this tool. Double-click the icon in the toolbox to automatically reposition the imageable area to the lower-left corner of the artboard.

Zoom (Chapter 3): Click with this tool to magnify the size of the illustration. (This doesn't affect the printed size of the drawing, just how it looks onscreen.) Alt-click (Option-click on the Mac) to zoom out. You can also draw with the tool to surround the exact portion of the illustration you want to magnify. Double-click the zoom tool icon to view your drawing at the very same size it will print.

Using Dialog Boxes

When you choose any command whose name includes an ellipsis (…)—such as
File » Save As… or Type » Find/Change…—Illustrator has to ask you some questions before it can complete the operation. It asks you these questions by displaying a dialog box.

A *dialog box* is a window that comes up onscreen and demands your immedi-
ate attention. You can sometimes switch to a different application while a dialog
box is onscreen, but you can't do any more work in Illustrator until you address
it, either by filling out a few *options* and clicking the OK button, or by clicking
the Cancel button.

Options naturally vary from one dialog box to the next, but there are eight
basic kinds of options in all. **Figure 2.8** shows examples of these option types as
they appear in two of Illustrator's dialog boxes. Also labeled is the title bar, which
tops just about every dialog box these days. If the dialog box is blocking some
important portion of your illustration, just drag the title bar to move it to a more
satisfactory location.

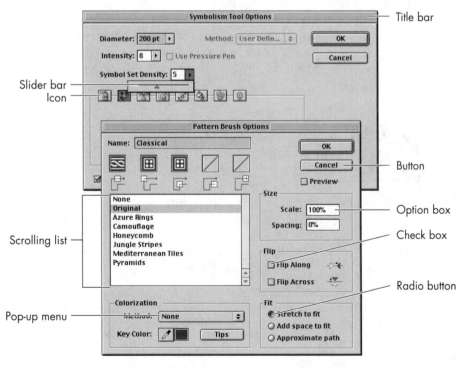

Figure 2.8: Two dialog boxes with major elements labeled.

Here's a quick rundown of the different kinds of dialog box options:

- **Radio buttons:** When you can select only one option from a group of options, a round radio button precedes each option name. To select a radio button, click either the button itself or the name of the option following the button. This deselects all other radio buttons in the group. A radio button filled with a black dot is selected; a hollow radio button is not.

- **Check boxes:** When you can select several options in a group, square check boxes come before the option names. To turn a check box on or off, click either the box itself or the option name. An *x* indicates a selected check box; a deselected check box is empty.

- **Pop-up menus:** A pop-up menu looks like a word in a box. Click the word or the triangle next to it to display a menu of options and select the desired option from the menu just as you would a command from a menu.

- **Option boxes:** If a dialog box were a test, radio buttons, check boxes, and pop-up menus would be multiple-choice questions; whereas option boxes (also called *numerical fields* by the nerd faction) are fill-in-the-blank questions. Option boxes are typically reserved for numbers, such as dimensions or color percentages. To select the current value in an option box, double-click it. Enter a new value from the keyboard.

If a dialog box contains lots of option boxes, you can advance from one to the next by pressing the Tab key. To go in the other direction, press Shift-Tab.

- **Scrolling lists:** When Illustrator really wants to pack in a lot of options, it presents them inside a scrolling list. Use the scroll bar on the right side of the list to check out more options. Then click the option you want to use. When a scrolling list is in a dialog box, you can select only one option from the list. Palettes, however, display their own form of scrolling lists. These scrolling lists let you select multiple options by Shift-clicking to select contiguous listings or Ctrl-clicking (Cmd-clicking on the Mac) to select noncontiguous listings.

 *In most cases, you can select a specific option from a scrolling list by typing the first few letters of its name. For example, pressing the P key selects the first option whose name begins with a P. You may want to first make sure the list is active by clicking it. If an option box is active, typing replaces the value instead.*

 **Icons:** In a few rare cases, Illustrator just doesn't feel like being locked into all the other options it has at its disposal, so it resorts to small graphic icons. These icons are like radio buttons in that you can select just one icon from a group. Illustrator either highlights or underlines the selected icon.

 **Slider bars:** If you come across a horizontal line or colored bar with one or more triangles underneath it, you've encountered a slider bar. Drag the slider triangle back and forth to lower or raise the value, which is usually displayed in an option box. (You can also enter a different option box value if you prefer.)

 **Buttons:** Not to be confused with radio buttons, standard dialog box buttons look like words inside rectangles or rounded rectangles. Click a button to make something happen. Two of the most common buttons are OK, which closes the dialog box and applies your settings, and Cancel, which closes the dialog box and cancels the command. Some dialog boxes offer Copy buttons, which apply settings to a copy of a selected object.

 *Instead of clicking on the OK button, you can press the Enter key (Return key on the Mac). Press Escape or Ctrl+period (Cmd-period on the Mac) to cancel the operation.*

A dialog box that conveys information rather than requests it is called an *alert* box. As its name implies, the purpose of an alert box is to call your attention to an important bit of news. Some alert boxes warn you about the consequences of an action so you can abort it and avert a hideous outcome. Others are just Illustrator's way of whining at you. "I can't do that," "You're using me wrong," and "Don't you think I have feelings, too?" are common alert box messages. (OK, that's an exaggeration, but it's not far from the truth.) The Disable Warnings setting in the General Preferences dialog box, which I discuss shortly, can help reduce Illustrator's complaints.

Using Palettes

A palette is nothing more than a dialog box that can remain open while you fiddle about inside the software. You can show or hide any of Illustrator's numerous palettes (including the toolbox) by choosing the appropriate command.

 Illustrator 10 consolidates all of the palette commands on the Window menu. Choose the name of a palette to toggle its visibility onscreen. A checkmark next to the palette name indicates that the palette is currently displayed. No checkmark means it is hidden.

 To hide all palettes, including the toolbox, press Tab. To redisplay them, press Tab again. Illustrator displays only those palettes that were onscreen before you pressed Tab the first time. If you press Shift-Tab, you hide all the palettes except the toolbox.

Figure 2.9 shows a couple of typical palettes from Illustrator. As you can see, palettes offer many of the same kinds of options that you find inside dialog boxes, including option boxes, sliders, and the like. A bar tops off each palette. Drag the bar to move the palette on screen. Illustrator's palettes snap into alignment with other palettes; they also snap into alignment with the edges of the screen.

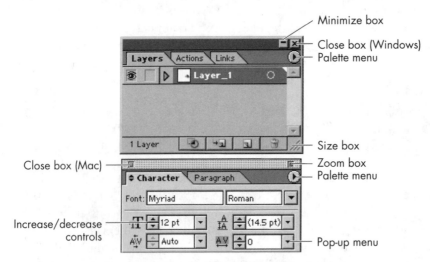

Figure 2.9: Two palettes with common options labeled.

Options vary more widely in palettes than they do in dialog boxes. Some are so specific to the function of the palette, there's no point in explaining them here. So for now, I'll just cover the ones that you see quite a bit in Illustrator and other applications (including Photoshop).

- **Close box:** Mac users click in the close box in the left corner of the title bar to close the palette. Windows users will find their close boxes in the right corner.

- **Zoom box:** Palettes offer zoom boxes, known as minimize buttons under Windows, on the right sides of their title bars. When you click in the zoom box, Illustrator changes the size of the palette, either making it larger to show the options or reducing its size to show just the panel tab. In the case of the Tabs palette, clicking in the zoom box aligns the palette with the active text block.

- **Palette menu:** Click the right-pointing arrowhead located at the top right of any palette to display the palette menu, then drag to choose the desired command. Palette menus are context-sensitive. In other words, the commands are relevant to the purpose of the palette.

- **Size box:** Drag the size box to change the size of particular palettes.

- **Increase/decrease controls:** Some of the option boxes in palettes have controls that let you increase or decrease the values in the box. Click the up arrow to increase the value; click the down arrow to decrease it.

- **Pop-up menu:** If you see a little down-pointing arrowhead in a box, this indicates a pop-up menu. Drag from the arrowhead to display the menu and select your favorite option.

 After you enter a value into a palette's option box, you can press Enter (Return on the Mac) to make the value take effect and to return control to the drawing area. To make a value take effect and keep the palette in focus (that is, not return control to the drawing area), press Shift-Enter (Shift-Return on the Mac).

 When the drawing area is in focus, press Ctrl+tilde (~) (Cmd-tilde on the Mac) to return focus to the last-used palette. Illustrator will try to activate the last option you used in that palette. Because not all options remain active once you've selected them (such as the Gradient Type pop-up menu or the Caps and Joins buttons in the Stroke palette), it may highlight one of the palette's nearby option boxes instead.

Customizing a Palette's Appearance

Palettes allow you to change the attributes of your artwork on the fly, but they can also clutter up the screen and considerably limit your view. If you have tons of money to spend, you can always get a second monitor to display just your palettes while you work on your main monitor. Or you can change the look and construction of palettes so they take up less room on your screen.

The default arrangement of the palettes groups certain palettes together, as *panels* within a single palette. To change a panel's group, click-and-drag on the panel's tab and move the panel to its new location, as shown in **Figure 2.10**. One of three things happens. First, if you end your drag on an area free of palettes, you separate the panel from its original group. Second, if you move the tab onto another panel in a different palette, the panel you move will join the new group as the newest and rightmost member of that group. When you drag a panel onto a new palette, Illustrator will indicate that it is ready to let the panel join the destination palette's little family by ringing the palette with a strip of black. So if you really need to free up some screen real estate, you can group all your palettes into one humongous group.

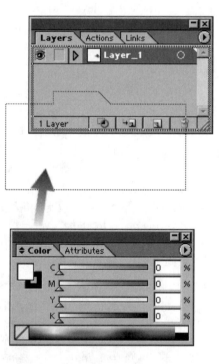

Figure 2.10: Here, the Color palette is being dragged into the Layers palette group.

The third result of dragging a panel is that you will *dock* the panel below a palette. Docking a palette results in a *meta-palette*. Once you have formed a meta-palette, you have the option of adding palettes to either group, as described above, or even of making an *ultra-meta-palette* by dragging another palette onto the bottom of the meta-palette.

Most palettes have more than one display size. For example, there are three display sizes for the Color palette: full options, basic options, and tab only. Full options shows all the color controls as well as the color ramp. Basic options contains just the color ramp. Tab only shows just the panel tab. If a palette has different display sizes, you will see two little arrows in the panel tab. Click the up or down arrows to cycle through the different sizes for the palette. **Figure 2.11** shows the three sizes for the Color palette.

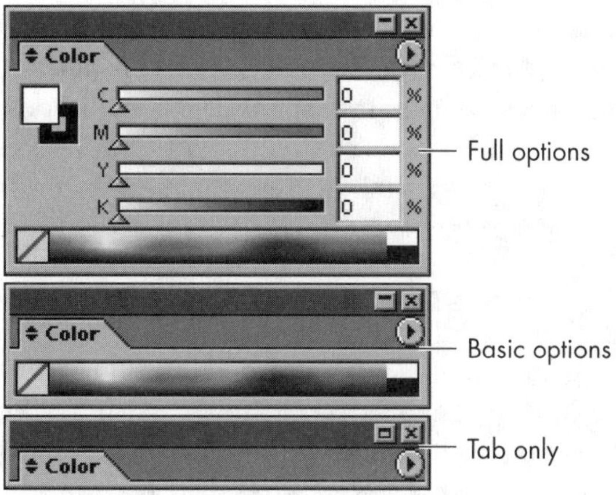

Figure 2.11: The three display options for the Color palette.

Full options

Basic options

Tab only

Even if you don't see the arrows in the panel tab, double-click any panel's tab to reduce the palette and cycle through its different sizes. You will eventually shrink the palette to its smallest size, just as though you had clicked on the palette's zoom box. This is an especially useful function when you have meta-palettes, as described earlier in this section.

So what does all this mean? It means that you have considerably more freedom in designing your workspace. If you find that, for the most part, you use only the Color, Stroke, and Layers palettes, then combine them into a single palette, a meta-palette, or even an ultra-meta-palette and close all the other palettes. With your single palette, controlled by a single zoom box, you'll have considerably more unobstructed space to create your artwork.

Accommodating Your Personal Style

No two folks draw alike. It's a cliché, but it happens to be true (except in the case of very close twins). For those who draw to a different drummer—in other words, all of us—Illustrator provides the Edit » Preferences submenu (or the Illustrator » Preferences submenu in Mac OS X), which provides nine commands that allow you to edit a variety of attributes controlling Illustrator's performance. All of these commands affect Illustrator's *global* preferences—that is, preferences that affect every single illustration you create or edit in the future. (In the next chapter, I discuss Document Setup and other commands that affect one illustration at a time.)

Choosing any of the commands in the Preferences submenu displays the corresponding dialog box; all of these dialog boxes share a few identical elements. A pop-up menu appears at the top, and four buttons line the right side of each Preferences dialog box. The pop-up menu allows you to switch quickly to any of the other Preferences dialog boxes. The four buttons include both the standard OK and Cancel, which implement or ignore your changes while also closing the dialog box, and Previous and Next. As you have probably surmised, clicking on Previous takes you to the previous Preferences dialog box, and clicking on Next advances you to the next one.

General Preferences

Choosing Edit » Preferences » General (or Illustrator » Preferences » General in Mac OS X) or pressing Ctrl+K (Cmd-K on the Mac) displays the General Preferences dialog box, shown in **Figure 2.12**. Here you can control the way some tools behave, whether dialog boxes display warnings, plus much, much more.

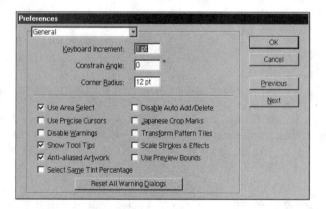

Figure 2.12: Here's where you make Illustrator conform to many of your whims.

The following list describes each option available in this dialog box. Of course, you may feel that you don't have the background to understand many of these options. But have no fear, most options are covered in context in one or more chapters, as the descriptions indicate. For now, content yourself with the certain knowledge that these pages contain an invaluable resource you can refer to over and over throughout your happy and productive illustrating years.

Here are the options, in their order of appearance in the General Preferences dialog box:

- **Keyboard Increment (Chapter 8):** Illustrator allows you to move selected objects from the keyboard by pressing one of the four arrow keys. Each keystroke moves the selection the distance you enter into this option box. The default value is 1 point, equivalent to one screen pixel at the 100 percent view size. That's a subtle nudge.

- **Constrain Angle (Chapters, 5, 9, and others):** If you press the Shift key while dragging an object, you constrain the direction of its movement to a multiple of 45 degrees; that is, straight up, straight down, left, right, or one of the four diagonal directions. These eight angles make up an invisible, er, thingamabob called the *constraint axes*. You can rotate the entire set of constraint axes by entering a value—measured in degrees—in the Constrain Angle option box. This value affects the creation of rectangles, ellipses, and text blocks, as well as the performance of transformation tools.

- **Corner Radius (Chapter 5):** This option sets the default roundness for the rounded rectangle tool. A value of 0 creates perpendicular corners; larger values make for progressively more rounded rectangles. However, this is just the default setting. You can change the amount as you are working using the Rounded Rectangle dialog box. You never need to come back here to change the setting.

- **Use Area Select (Chapter 6):** This option controls how you go about selecting filled objects in the preview mode. When it's checked, you can click anywhere inside an object to select the object, so long as the object is filled. When the option is off, you can select an object only by clicking its points and segments. Experienced users can turn this option off so they can select objects behind other objects easily without the fills getting in the way.

- **Use Precise Cursors:** When this option is checked, Illustrator displays crosshair cursors in place of the standard cursors for all drawing and editing tools. These special cursors let you better see what you're doing, but they're not so fun to look at.

 In truth, there's no reason to select this check box. Just press the Caps Lock key to access the precise cursors when the check box is off. If the check box has been mysteriously turned on, pressing Caps Lock displays the standard cursor.

Disable Warnings: Turning on this check box commands Illustrator to resist its temptation to tell you incessantly that you don't know what you are doing. For instance, when this option is off, as it is by default, clicking even slightly off an object's point with the convert anchor point tool will result in Illustrator's scolding you. Disabling this warning won't correct the problem—you will still have to repeat the operation from the beginning—but you won't have to close the warning box first. Leave this on if you're just starting out so you have some idea of *why* Illustrator is yelling at you. Turn it off when you're fed up with the complaints.

Show Tool Tips: This option is responsible for those little yellow rectangles that pop up displaying the name of the tool or palette option when you hold your cursor over it. In the beginning, it's probably a good idea to leave this option selected. It helps novices become accustomed to Illustrator's different features. Even experienced users can profit from it, because Illustrator now shows icons instead of names in palettes such as Pathfinder and Character. If the tips make you crazy, though, turn this off.

Anti-aliased Artwork (Chapter 20): With this option on, your document will have a smoother onscreen appearance. This gives you a better idea of what your vector artwork will look like when printed on a PostScript printer, because your final hardcopy will not have all the jagged imperfections that show up onscreen. This option doesn't affect placed graphics, but it does impact the appearance of artwork you rasterize inside of Illustrator.

Select Same Tint Percentage (Chapter 14): In Illustrator 8 and earlier, there was a problem using the selection commands on tints of spot colors. If you had two objects filled with Pantone 185 and another filled with a 50% tint of Pantone 185, the Select » Same » Fill Color command would select all three objects as one. Introduced in version 9, this option fixes that problem. Tints of colors need to have the same percentages before they are chosen by the selection commands.

Disable Auto Add/Delete (Chapter 6): By default, the pen tool will automatically change to the add anchor point tool or delete anchor point tool as the situation demands. For example, if you position the pen tool over a point of a selected path, the pen tool will temporarily transform into the delete anchor point tool, ready to out the damn spot. If you prefer the pen tool to limit its personalities to only one identity, check this box.

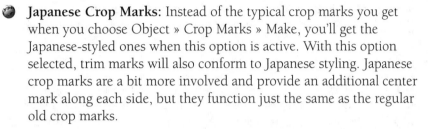

Japanese Crop Marks: Instead of the typical crop marks you get when you choose Object » Crop Marks » Make, you'll get the Japanese-styled ones when this option is active. With this option selected, trim marks will also conform to Japanese styling. Japanese crop marks are a bit more involved and provide an additional center mark along each side, but they function just the same as the regular old crop marks.

Transform Pattern Tiles (Chapter 15): When an object is filled or stroked with a tile pattern, you can specify whether the pattern moves, grows, shrinks, or rotates as you move, scale, or rotate the object. Fortunately, you can turn this option on or off in the dialog boxes for the transformation tools. This setting affects only transformations created manually.

Scale Strokes & Effects (Chapter 16): When you scale an object proportionally—so that both height and width grow or shrink the same amount—Illustrator can likewise change the thickness of the stroke or effects, such as feathering, that are assigned to the object. If you are working on a project where all strokes must be half a point, you want to turn this option off. Like the Transform Pattern Tiles option, you can turn this setting on and off in the dialog boxes for the transformation tools.

Use Preview Bounds (Chapter 8): By default, both the Transform and Info palettes display a selected path's physical attributes without considering the path's stroke weight. For example, the Info palette would normally list a 40-point by 20-point rectangle with a 10-point stroke as having a width of 40 points and a height of 20 points. With the Use Preview Bounds option on, the Info palette would list this same rectangle with a height of 50 points and a width of 30 points. The 10-point stroke would add 5 points to each side. In addition to stroke weight, the preview bounds can also apply to drop shadows, glows, and other effects that extend far beyond the boundaries of the original object.

Reset All Warning Dialogs: As you work in Illustrator, you will encounter various dialog boxes that Adobe thinks are giving you important information that will make you a happier and smarter Illustrator person. After a few dozen times reading the same dialog box, you may find yourself cursing at the screen. Sometimes, however, there is a little check box that says "Don't show again." If you turn on that check box, you will never see the specific dialog box again, unless you click the Reset All Warning Dialogs button—then you get to reread all those informational messages you had forgotten.

Type & Auto Tracing

The next Preferences command, Edit » Preferences » Type & Auto Tracing (or Illustrator » Preferences » Type & Auto Tracing in Mac OS X), displays the lovely and functional dialog box shown in **Figure 2.13**. Here you will find options related to text manipulation. If you're familiar with this dialog box from Illustrator 9, you can just skip to the next section. None of the options have changed in Illustrator 10.

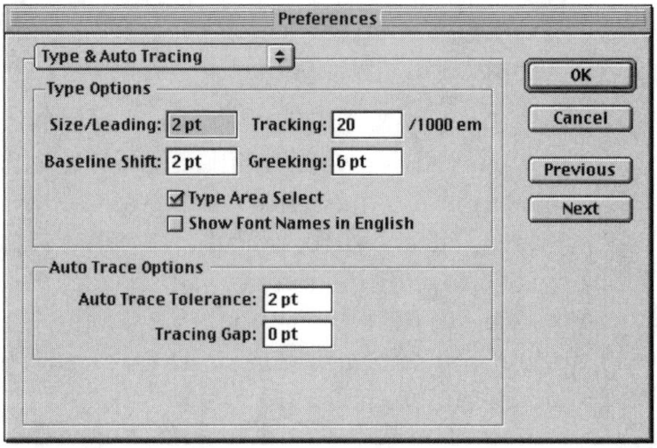

Figure 2.13: Use this dialog box to set a handful of text preferences.

- **Size/Leading (Chapter 10):** Just as you can nudge objects from the keyboard, you can likewise adjust the size and leading of selected text with keystrokes. To define the increment of each keystroke, enter a value in this option box.

- **Baseline Shift (Chapter 10):** Baseline shift raises and lowers characters relative to the baseline, ideal for creating superscript and subscript type. To define the increment for raising and lowering selected type, type a new value into this option box.

- **Tracking (Chapter 10):** To keep large text looking good, you may want to adjust the amount of space between neighboring characters, called *kerning* or *tracking*. You can modify the kerning from the keyboard by the increment you enter in this option box. This value is always measured in 0.001 em space. (An em space is as wide as the current type size is tall.)

- **Greeking:** If text gets smaller than this value, Illustrator shows the text blocks as gray bars, an operation called *greeking*. Both type size and view size figure into the equation, so that 6-point type greeks at 100-percent view size and 12-point type greeks at 50 percent. Greeking speeds the screen display because gray bars are easier to draw than individual characters.

Type Area Select (Chapter 10): Just as the Use Area Select option of General Preferences gives you control over how you go about selecting filled paths, the Type Area Select option lets you choose just how careful you have to be when you're trying to select text and text blocks. When this option is deactivated, you have to click the path in which the type resides. With this option checked, you have a bit more freedom, since you need to click only within the bounding box that surrounds the type.

Show Font Names in English: If you have fonts loaded on your system that use alphabets other than the Latin alphabet, check this option to force Illustrator to show the font in its English equivalent. This assumes that the font contains this information in its code; Illustrator cannot translate the fonts' names on its own.

Auto Trace Tolerance (Chapter 5): This complex little option controls the sensitivity of *both* the pencil and the auto trace tools. Any value between 0 and 10 is permitted, and it is measured in points. Low values make the tools very sensitive, so that a pencil path closely matches your cursor movements or an auto trace path closely matches the form of the imported template. Higher values give Illustrator license to ignore small jags and other imperfections when creating the path.

Tracing Gap (Chapter 5): Tracing templates frequently contain loose pixels and rough edges. Using the Tracing Gap option, you can instruct Illustrator to trace over these gaps. A value of 0 turns the option off, so that the auto trace tool traces rough edges as they appear in the template. A value of 1 allows paths to skip over single-pixel gaps; a value of 2 (the highest value allowed) allows paths to hurdle two-pixel gaps.

Units & Undo

The Edit » Preferences » Units & Undo (or Illustrator » Preferences » Units & Undo in Mac OS X) command focuses on the units that Illustrator uses in different dialog boxes, as well as the number of undos that are at your disposal. Please take a moment to revel in the glory that is **Figure 2.14**.

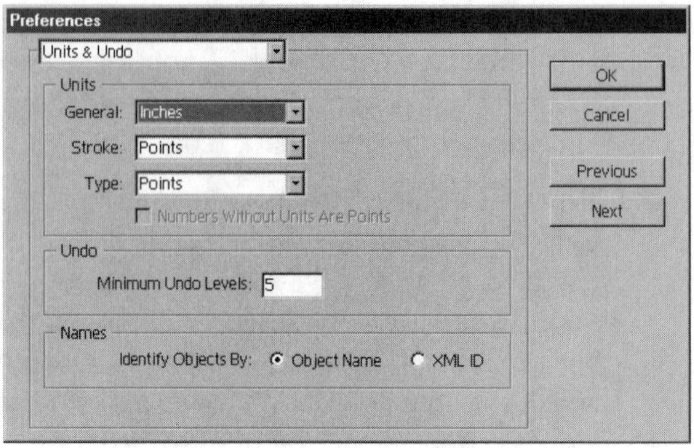

Figure 2.14: Select any measuring system your heart desires in the Units & Undo Preferences dialog box.

- **General (Chapter 8):** Select Points, Picas, Inches, Centimeters, Millimeters, or Pixels from this pop-up menu to specify the system of measurement to use throughout all dialog boxes (including this one) as well as in the horizontal and vertical rulers. Unlike the similar option in the Document Setup dialog box—which affects just the one drawing you're working on—this option applies to *all* future illustrations in addition to the one you're working on.

- **Stroke (Chapter 16):** Let's say you're one of those people who thinks in inches. Most likely you will want to set the general measurement to inches. But do you *really* want to specify stroke weights in inches? Not unless you enjoy thinking in hundredths of an inch. This setting gives you the luxury of defining strokes as points in an inches world.

- **Type (Chapter 10):** You *could* select an option from this pop-up menu to specify the measurement system used specifically for type. But no one in his right mind *would* do this, since points are the standard for measuring type in nearly every corner of the globe. The only exception to this rule is that a unit called Q (equal to 0.25 millimeters or roughly 1.4 points) has a strong foothold in Japan. Honestly, leave this option set to Points, the default. (Incidentally, this option controls the units used by three options in the General Preferences dialog box—Size/Leading, Baseline Shift, and Greeking.)

- **Numbers Without Units Are Points (Chapter 10):** Though this may sound like a nonsensical mantra, it's meant to explain that, provided you've chosen Picas as your general units, you have more freedom with the way you enter numbers into dialog boxes. With this box checked, Illustrator will assume that any number you enter into an option box without specifying a unit, such as 72 instead of 72 *pt*, should be in points and not picas. Otherwise, Illustrator will convert unitless numbers to picas—72 becomes 60 (6 picas and no points).

Minimum Undo Levels (Chapter 5): Here you enter the minimum number of undos and redos that Illustrator can perform in a row. Notice the word *minimum,* though. Most of the time Illustrator will give you far more than the minimum number of undos. However, if your graphics are very complex, Illustrator will lower the number of undos. This setting simply sets the absolute minimum number of undos you can have.

Identify Objects By (Chapter 22): This option lets you select a naming convention for dynamic objects. Since dynamic objects are often exported to other Adobe products as SVG templates, certain naming conventions must be followed. Specifically, if you wish to use XML (Extensible Markup Language) for scripting dynamic object interaction, select the option to identify objects by XML ID versus Object Name.

Guides & Grid

Descending the list, you'll find the Edit » Preferences » Guides & Grid command. This dialog box, shown in **Figure 2.15**, allows you to choose the color and style of both guides and grids. You can also set the size and spacing of a grid. To see the actual guides and grid, you must choose the corresponding Show command in the View menu.

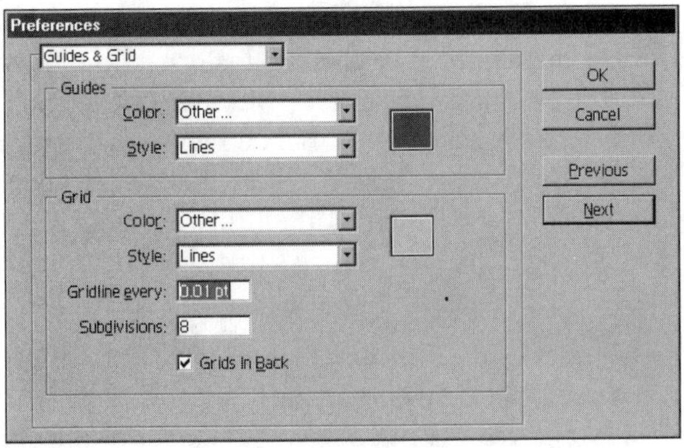

Figure 2.15: Choose the color and style of your grids and guides here.

Color (Chapter 8): From these pop-up menus, choose from nine predefined colors for your guides and grids. If you prefer to define your own color, then either choose Other from the pop-up menu or double-click the color box just to the right of the menu. The Color dialog box will display, where you construct your own color by clicking on the spectrum in the upper-right portion of the dialog box. Also, if you become quite smitten with your creation, you can save it by clicking the Add to Custom Colors button.

- **Style (Chapter 8):** From these pop-up menus, you decide whether your guides and grid will appear as dashed or solid lines. If you select the Dots option, you will see only the major gridlines and not all the additional subdivisions.

- **Gridline every (Chapter 8):** Enter the size that you want your square grids to be. You can specify the units of this number or simply enter a number and have Illustrator use whatever units you set in the Units & Undo Preferences dialog box.

- **Subdivisions (Chapter 8):** Here you state the number of times you want to divide your grid both horizontally and vertically.

- **Grids In Back (Chapter 8):** When you're using a grid, you have the choice of having the grid overlaid on the pasteboard, partially obscuring parts of your artwork, or having it appear in the background, giving your work the appearance of lying on top of graph paper. Simply select this option to place the grid in the background, where it's less intrusive.

Smart Guides & Slices

Provided you have selected the View » Smart Guides command (Ctrl+U or Cmd-U), additional information and path outlines appear and disappear as you move your cursor over the different elements of your artwork. Smart guides are meant to help you align paths as you transform and move them by showing you when your transformation coincides with different intersection points within your artwork. Many people feel overloaded with information when they turn on the smart guides. The Smart Guides & Slices Preferences dialog box (shown in **Figure 2.16**) lets you control what type of information is displayed when you turn on the smart guides, as well as set the angles that the guides work along. This preferences dialog box also controls the display and color of slice numbers and lines.

- **Text Label Hints (Chapter 8):** With this option selected, several different labels (including path, anchor, align, intersect, and page) may pop into view as you move your cursor or drag paths around the screen. They indicate that your cursor is over a special point of interest, helping you determine whether you have found the right spot. I suggest that you turn off this option. Artwork consisting of many paths is complex enough without the additional muddling these labels can add.

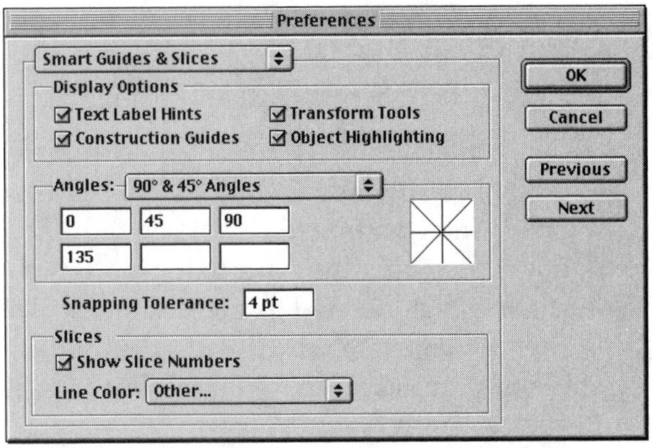

Preferences

Smart Guides & Slices

Display Options
☑ Text Label Hints   ☑ Transform Tools
☑ Construction Guides   ☑ Object Highlighting

Angles: 90° & 45° Angles

| 0 | 45 | 90 |
| 135 | | |

Snapping Tolerance: 4 pt

Slices
☑ Show Slice Numbers
Line Color: Other...

OK
Cancel
Previous
Next

Figure 2.16: The Smart Guides & Slices Preferences dialog box lets you turn off or modify the feedback information given when smart guides is turned on.

Construction Guides (Chapter 8): One of the main functions of smart guides is the alignment guides that pop up as you move or transform paths. True to intuition, these guides spring forth to tell you when the present location is in alignment with your starting point. You use the Angles option (discussed below) to decide where to position these guides. If you want Illustrator to display even more alignment information, select the Construction Guides option. In addition to showing you when your present location is aligned with respect to your starting point, Illustrator also alerts you when you are in alignment with respect to various aspects of the other paths in your artwork. This allows you to position paths relative to two separate points.

Transform Tools (Chapter 8): Illustrator's alignment guides appear when you are manipulating a path with one of the arrow tools, or transforming a path with one of the four traditional transformation tools. If you want the alignment guides to appear only when you're using one of the arrow tools and not when you're using one of the transformation tools, simply deactivate this option.

Object Highlighting (Chapter 8): When this option is on, Illustrator highlights the outline of a path, making it appear to be selected as long as you position an arrow or transformation tool over the path. This is helpful when you're dealing with a number of overlapping paths, some of which are very small or just barely exposed. Otherwise, this option is better left off.

Angles (Chapter 8): With these six option boxes, you decide at what angles Illustrator will inform you whether your present onscreen position aligns with either your initial position or one of the points of some other path in your artwork—that is, provided Construction

Guides is selected. You can choose from one of seven predefined sets of angles or enter the angular values that best suit your needs. Package designers and others creating 3D perspectives may want to set their own angles here.

- **Snapping Tolerance (Chapter 8):** Here you decide within how many points (ranging from 0 to 10) you must position your cursor (that is, how close you must come to the various points of interest) before the alignment guides and text labels appear. The default value is 4 points. Higher numbers make the smart guides appear more readily; lower numbers mean you have to get closer to objects before the smart guides appear.

- **Show Slice Numbers (Chapter 21):** When slicing objects for the Web, the slices will appear on the artboard. Check this option to enable your slice numbers to show.

- **Line Color (Chapter 21):** You can specify the color of the lines separating your slices by choosing a color from the Line Color pop-up menu. Choosing Other will take you to various color model wheels where you can select a custom color. Slices add many additional lines to your screen, so you may want to make them as unobtrusive as possible.

Hyphenation Options

Moving right along, you can choose Edit » Preferences » Hyphenation (or Illustrator » Preferences » Hyphenation in Mac OS X) to exclude words from Illustrator's automatic hyphenating capabilities (covered in Chapter 10). Although most Illustrator users go their entire careers without ever giving a second thought to automatic hyphenation, you may feel compelled to rule out the occasional proper noun, so that Johnson never appears as John-son. Here's how:

1. Choose Edit » Preferences » Hyphenation to display the dialog box captured for time immemorial in **Figure 2.17**.

2. Select a language from the Default Language pop-up menu to determine which set of rules Illustrator uses to hyphenate your words. For example, you wouldn't want Hungarian hyphenation if you were writing in Finnish.

3. Enter the word you want to protect from hyphenation harm into the New Entry option box.

If you enter the word without any hyphens, it will never be hyphenated. If you place hyphens in the word, it will be hyphenated only at those places. So for example, if you enter the word therapist as therapist, it will be hyphenated that way only.

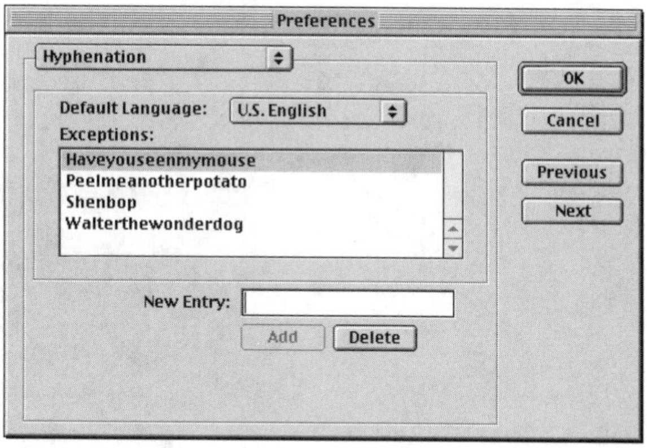

Figure 2.17: Choose how Illustrator hyphenates some words and prevent some words from ever being hyphenated using the Hyphenation Preferences dialog box.

Preferences

Hyphenation

Default Language: U.S. English
Exceptions:

Haveyouseenmymouse
Peelmeanotherpotato
Shenbop
Walterthewonderdog

New Entry:

Add   Delete

OK
Cancel
Previous
Next

4. Click the Add button. The word appears in the scrolling list of Exceptions.

5. If you decide you've added a word in error, select it from the scrolling list and click the Delete button.

6. Click the OK button to exit the dialog box.

Your hyphenation information is saved with the application that created the file. If you transfer the file to a different computer, the text may hyphenate differently. If you share files with others, it's a good idea to make sure everyone sets the same hyphenation exceptions.

Plug-ins & Scratch Disks

These preferences are more maintenance issues that cover how Illustrator interacts with the rest of your computer. The Edit » Preferences » Plug-ins & Scratch Disks (or Illustrator 10 » Preferences » Plug-ins & Scratch Disks in Mac OS X) command lets you direct Illustrator to the folder that contains the plug-ins you want to use. By default, all Illustrator plug-ins are installed in the Plug-ins folder inside the same folder that contains the Illustrator application. But because plug-ins consume a large amount of RAM, you may want to organize your plug-ins into a series of separate folders. This may make Illustrator perform faster or get it to work better on Macs with little memory. Then you can use the Edit » Preferences » Plug-ins & Scratch Disks (or Illustrator 10 » Preferences » Plug-ins

& Scratch Disks in Mac OS X) command to tell Illustrator which set of filters you want to use the next time you start the program.

1. Choose Edit » Preferences » Plug-ins & Scratch Disks. The dialog box shown in **Figure 2.18** will appear.

2. Click the Choose button and locate the folder that contains the set of plug-ins you want to use next.

3. Click the OK button.

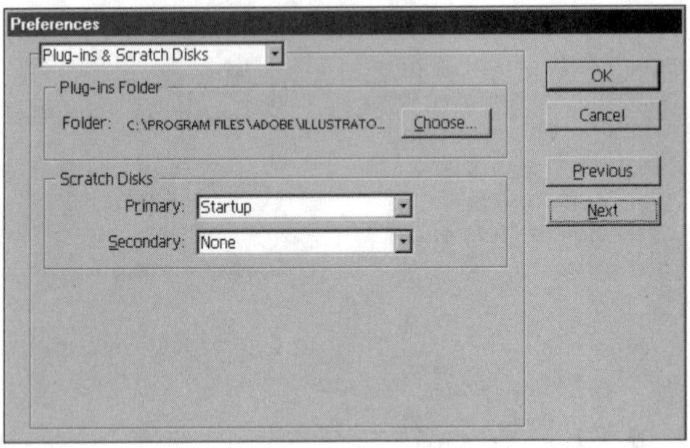

Figure 2.18: The Plug-ins &
Scratch Disks Preferences
dialog box lets you determine
how Illustrator allocates hard
disk space to use as extra
memory.

4. Quit Illustrator by pressing Ctrl+Q (Cmd-Q on the Mac).

5. Launch Illustrator again to load the program as well as the new set of plug-ins.

You also have the option of specifying the location of a primary and secondary *scratch disk*—the virtual memory that Illustrator uses when your RAM is full. Because virtual memory resides on your hard drive, reading and writing to virtual memory will slow Illustrator considerably. Choose the location of the first place that you want Illustrator to use for virtual memory from the Primary pop-up menu shown in Figure 2.18. From the Secondary pop-up menu, you select the location of the scratch disk that supplements Illustrator's memory when the first scratch disk is full. If you have a second hard drive or another form of storage media, you can use this as your secondary scratch disk.

When an application writes to the scratch disk, it likes to write in a contiguous area. (Hey, you wouldn't like it if you had to run all over your house just to write a letter to your folks.) Your scratch disks will be more contiguous if you regularly run utility programs to defragment your scratch disks (like organizing all your notepaper in one box). If you feel Illustrator is acting sluggishly, make sure your scratch disks are defragmented.

Files & Clipboard

The next entry in the Edit » Preferences (Illustrator 10 » Preferences in Mac OS X) submenu is the Files & Clipboard command. This command opens the Files & Clipboard dialog box (shown in **Figure 2.19**), which controls how files are named, how links are updated, and the format for items copied to the Clipboard.

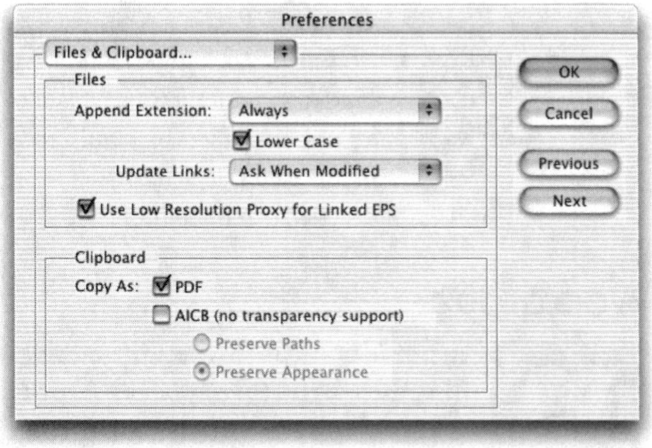

Figure 2.19: The Files & Clipboard Preferences dialog box controls aspects of saving files, linking files, and how images copied to the Clipboard are handled.

- **Append Extension (Chapter 4):** This setting appears only in the Macintosh version of Illustrator. It allows you to automatically add the three-letter file extension to the names of saved and exported files. Windows users don't have this preference because all files automatically get the file extension added to the name of the file—that's one of the basic tenets of the Windows operating system. But the Macintosh does not use file extensions. If you routinely send files from the Macintosh to Windows, you probably should set this option to Always.

- **Update Links (Chapter 4):** When you place images from other programs in Illustrator, they keep a link to the original file. If you modify the original file, the linked image needs to be updated in Illustrator. This option controls how the updates happen: automatically, manually, or with a dialog box that asks if you want to update the modified links.

- **Use Low Resolution Proxy for Linked EPS (Chapter 4):** By default, linked EPS files are displayed at low resolution. If you uncheck this option, your files will be displayed at high resolution, but that degrades your system's performance, so turn the option back on if you want to speed things up.

Clipboard (Chapter 7): These options control how much information gets sent to the Clipboard. This doesn't do anything if you copy from one Illustrator document to another. But if you copy from Illustrator and then paste into other programs, you may need to set these options. For instance, older programs may not be able to handle PDF information or transparency. Changing your options here can help you copy and paste.

PDF is the default setting. If you want to paste into Photoshop and get the "paste as pixels, paths or shape layers?" dialog box, you'll need to choose an AICB format. It is possible to select BOTH options simultaneously, but you'll take a minor performance hit.

Workgroup

 Last but not least is the Edit » Preferences » Workgroup (or Illustrator 10 » Preferences » Workgroup in Mac OS X) command, which helps you manage workflow in a data-driven, networked environment (**Figure 2.20**). The purpose of workgroup management is to prevent two people from trying to update a file at the same time. As you may well know, nothing is more frustrating than having someone else save over your hard work. The options in this dialog box help you avoid such mishaps and otherwise control how Illustrator functions in a workgroup setting.

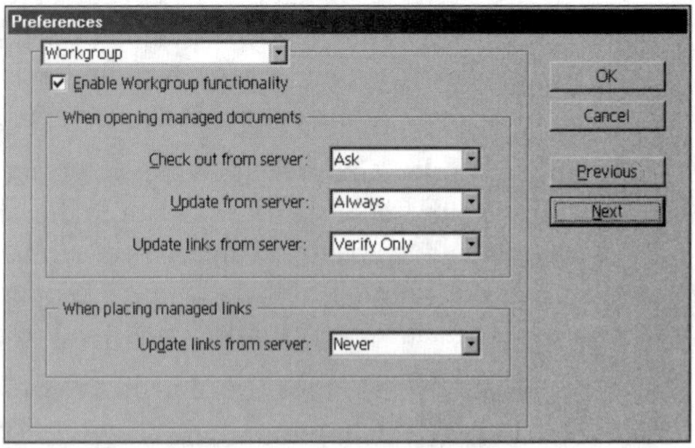

Figure 2.20: The Workgroup Preferences dialog box helps you manage your Illustrator workflow in a networked environment, where multiple people need to access the same files.

 Enable Workgroup functionality: This option determines whether Illustrator uses the workgroup management tools at all. Turn it off and Illustrator will completely ignore these features. If you leave the option on, the management features are enabled.

Check out from server: If you set this option to Ask, a dialog box will appear when you attempt to open a file that has not been checked out from the server. The dialog box will ask if you want to check out the file. If you elect to do so, other users will be able to open the file and edit it locally, but they won't be able to save a new copy to the server. When this option is set to Never, you won't be given the option to check out a file when you open it. Instead, Illustrator will automatically open a local copy. Finally, when this option is set to Always, files will automatically be checked out from the server when you open them.

Update from server: If a file has been updated on the server and this option is set to Ask, a dialog box will appear asking if you'd like to download the latest version of the file from the server. If set to Never, a local copy of the file will be displayed. If you want the updated version, you need to manually retrieve it from the server. If you have this option set to Always, the latest version of the file will be downloaded from the server automatically.

Update links from server: You may often work with files that contain dynamic links to other files. If one of these linked files is updated, the file containing the link might need to be updated as well. If you select Ask from this pop-up menu, every time you open a file that contains links, Illustrator will present a dialog box that gives you the option to update the links. If you set this pop-up to Never, a local copy of the illustration will be opened without updating the links. Selecting Always tells Illustrator to automatically update links within every file you open. If you just want Illustrator to find any broken links and flag them with an icon in the Links palette, choose Verify Only.

When placing managed links: This option lets you choose how to manage links within files you place (File » Place) into Illustrator documents. Choosing Always will always update the links within the file being placed; Ask will display a dialog box asking if you wish to update the links; and Never will place a local copy of the file without updating the links.

The Prefs File

All global preference settings are saved on a Macintosh to a file called Adobe Illustrator 10.0 Prefs, located in the Adobe Illustrator 10 folder in the Preferences folder inside the System folder. On Windows, they are saved to the AIPrefs file in the folder where you installed Illustrator. Illustrator also saves a list of open palettes, as well as the physical location of the palettes onscreen, in the preferences file. These settings affect every file that you create or modify from this moment on (until you next change your preferences).

On Mac OS X, the prefs file is located at users/<username>/library/preferences/Adobe Illustrator 10/.

 To reset all preferences and related dialog boxes to their original settings, quit Illustrator and drag the Adobe Illustrator 10.0 Prefs file into the Trash or rename the AIPrefs file. Then relaunch Illustrator; a spanking-clean, new preferences file will be created. This can be a particularly good thing to do when Illustrator starts flaking out on you. If you've customized the program exactly the way you want, you probably don't want to lose those preferences. Make a backup copy of the preferences file and save it on a backup disk. Then the next time the program starts acting flaky, most likely your preferences file has gotten corrupted. Whip out your backup copy of the preferences file and swap your nice, clean preferences file for the dirty, old corrupted one.

Illustrator updates the Adobe Illustrator 10.0 Prefs file *every* time you quit the program, and *only* when you quit the program. If you crash or force-quit Illustrator by pressing Ctrl+Alt+Delete (Cmd-Option-Escape on the Mac), Illustrator leaves the preferences file untouched. Therefore, if you want to force Illustrator to save your preferences, quit the program by pressing Ctrl+Q (Cmd-Q on the Mac).

 If you're the adventurous type, you may want to try your hand at editing the Adobe Illustrator 10.0 Prefs file (or the AIPrefs file) in a word processor, such as Apple's SimpleText or Windows Notepad. After quitting Illustrator, open the Adobe Illustrator 10.0 Prefs or the AIPrefs file. You'll see a list of items in code. There's an item to turn off the splash screen (/showSplashScreen); you can even change the default typeface and size (/faceName and /faceSize). Limit your changes to numerical values and items within parentheses. In most cases, 0 means off and 1 means on. (If you totally muck things up, you can always throw away the Prefs file and let Illustrator create a fresh one.)

The Startup File

The other method for changing Illustrator's global preferences is to edit the startup files contained in the Plug-ins folder. You can change the custom colors, gradients, tile patterns, and path patterns available to every illustration. Perhaps more alluring, you can change the illustration window size, the view size, and the position of the artboard inside the window. You can also edit the default style that controls the fill and stroke attributes that are applied to objects when you press the letter D. These are minor adjustments, of course, but even minor adjustments can go a long way toward creating a more comfortable environment.

1. Open the Adobe Illustrator Startup_CMYK or _RGB file.

2. The file contains all kinds of styles, patterns, gradients, and colors. Read Chapters 14 through 16 for information about editing these or creating your own. Placement is not important; just fill a shape with whatever color, pattern, or gradation you want to add.

3. Size the illustration window as desired by dragging the size box.

4. Magnify the window to the desired view size using the zoom tool, as explained in Chapter 3.

5. Use the hand tool to scroll the artboard to the desired position (also described in the next chapter).

6. Use File » Document Setup and click the Print Setup button (Page Setup button on the Mac) to make any desired changes to the size and shape of the artboard and imageable area (Chapter 3).

7. Choose View » Show Rulers or press Ctrl+R (Cmd-R on the Mac) if you want the rulers to come up every time you start Illustrator.

8. Close the file (Ctrl+W or Cmd-W on the Mac) and press Enter (Return on the Mac) to save it to disk.

From now on, every new illustration you create will subscribe to these adjusted settings.

CHAPTER 3

THE ARTBOARD

Decisions, decisions! When you first open Illustrator 10, you've got all your tools ready, but no document to start working on. Right away you need to make some decisions about your artwork. Some of these decisions are easy; others may confuse you. This chapter shows you how to tackle them all.

Because every illustration begins as a new document—even existing drawings were new once—I explain the first option in this chapter. You'll also learn everything you need to know about modifying the artboard, specifying the size of pages for print, magnifying your drawing, and changing the way your illustration looks on screen. For the lowdown on opening existing files and several other exciting topics, I enthusiastically refer you to Chapter 4.

Preparing a New Illustration

Preparing a new illustration is not that different from most other things in life. Good planning often leads to success. The following sections explain the options available to you for setting up your illustration, so you can plan accordingly.

Creating a New Document

When you choose File » New or press Ctrl+N (Cmd-N on the Mac) you are confronted by the New Document dialog box, shown in **Figure 3.1**, which requires you to make some basic decisions about your illustration. But don't worry, any choices you make here can be changed easily later on. Besides, the following few subsections provide a blow-by-blow account of how to deal with the various options in the New Document dialog box.

 Press Ctrl+Alt+N (Cmd-Option-N on the Mac) to bypass the New Document dialog box and create a new document based on the last used settings.

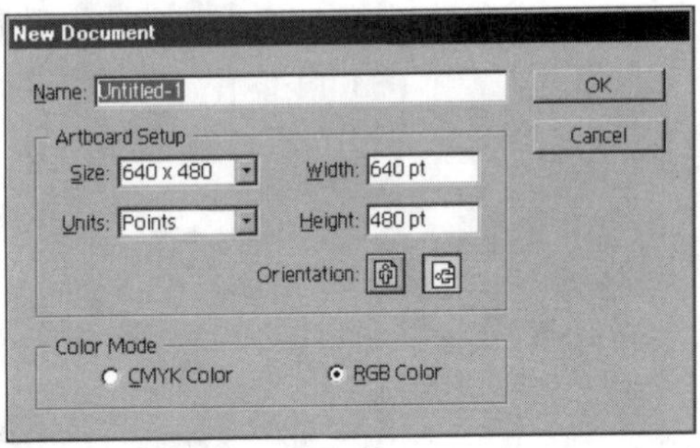

Figure 3.1: Here's where you tell Illustrator how to set up your new document.

The first option is easy; what name would you like the document to have? Because the default—"Untitled" followed by a number—is a rather bland name for a document, you should think of something snappy. If you tend to work in multiple Illustrator documents at the same time, use something descriptive such as "Business Card" or "Lunch Menu," so you can quickly pick out the correct document from the names listed at the bottom of the Window menu.

 Don't let entering a name for the file fool you: Your file is not actually saved or written to disk when you give it a name here. The only thing that entering the name does is put the name up in the title bar of the document. You still have to execute the File » Save command to actually make a permanent copy of the document on a disk.

Basic Artboard Setup

Sometimes you may care about the size of the artboard; sometimes you may not. It depends on what kind of document you want to create.

If you're creating a drawing, logo, or other graphic that you intend to place into a layout program—such as InDesign, PageMaker, or QuarkXPress—or export to the Web, then you aren't interested in how big the artboard is in Illustrator. When you import an Illustrator drawing into a page-layout program or export to a Web format, all blank portions of the artboard are cropped away, leaving just the graphic itself. Heck, you can create the entire graphic in the pasteboard if you like. Therefore, the size of the graphic is all that matters.

But issues such as page size, orientation, and placement are important anytime you are going to print directly from Illustrator or make a PDF file. The Artboard Setup section of the New Document dialog box has several options. It becomes critical when building a small document. Although touted as an illustration program, Illustrator is well suited to producing full-page fliers, double-sided mailers, posters, and even full Web pages.

 New to Illustrator 10, the Artboard Setup section of the New Document dialog box lets you plan ahead for such occasions. Here's how the options work.

- 🌑 **Size:** This pop-up menu offers ten preset artboard sizes plus a Custom setting. The last seven options let you quickly access some common document sizes, including Letter, Legal, A4, and others, which are useful for illustrations you plan to print directly from Illustrator or export to PDF. The Custom option is selected automatically if you deviate from any of the preset sizes offered in the list.

- 🌑 The 640 x 480 and 800 x 600 options correspond to common monitor resolutions, making them good choices for Web page layouts and full-screen Web graphics. But keep in mind that a viewer's browser window will take up some of the available screen space. So if your illustration fills an entire 640 x 480 artboard, it probably won't quite fit within a standard-size browser window. Choose the 468 x 60 option to set the artboard to the size of a standard Web advertising banner.

- **Units:** From the Units pop-up menu, you can choose which measurement system you prefer. Points and picas are common measurements used in print design. (Font size is commonly measured in points.) If you're more comfortable working in inches, millimeters, or centimeters, those units are available as well. You'll want to choose Pixels if you're producing Web illustrations since that's the unit of measure on the Web.

 Illustrator will automatically convert unit values in the Width and Height boxes. For example, if your chosen units is points and you want to enter values in inches, just type the value, followed by in. Illustrator automatically converts the measurement to points. You can also enter values in millimeters (mm) or picas (p). For example, 55p6 stands for 55 picas plus 6 points, which is 666 points or 9.25 inches. This automatic conversion works in any Illustrator palette or dialog box that accepts numeric values.

- **Width and Height:** The Width and Height option boxes let you customize the size of your artboard. If you're going to be printing to a nonstandard paper size or are gearing your illustration toward a specific screen size for the Web, enter the appropriate dimensions here.

- **Orientation:** Here's where you specify the orientation of your artboard. If your illustration is taller than it is wide, click the Portrait button on the left. If your document is wider than it is tall, choose the Landscape option on the right.

Selecting a Color Mode

Don't panic. You don't have to take a course in color management to select the proper Color Mode setting. Even if you guess, there are only two choices, so you've got a 50-50 chance of being right. First, you need to decide whether Illustrator will limit your colors to either CMYK colors, which are usually used for print jobs, or RGB colors, which are used for Web graphics. So if your job is going to be separated by a commercial printing process, you should select CMYK. If it's going to the Web, select RGB. Wait, did I hear someone ask, "What if the job is going to be printed *and* published on the Web?" In that case, you should choose CMYK—the needs of the commercial print job come first. It's not such a big deal if you have CMYK colors in a Web graphic, but RGB colors in a print job can cause problems when the illustration is separated.

Unlike what happens in Photoshop, in Illustrator choosing RBG doesn't make your file any smaller. There are no extra channels in Illustrator that make a CMYK file bigger than an RGB one.

Once you've made your selections in the New Document dialog box, click OK, and your document window appears. But before you hunker down and get to work, there are a few additional page setup features you may find worthy of your attention. The following sections explain all.

The Artboard Versus the Printed Page

In Illustrator, you specify the size and orientation of the artboard in one step and the size and orientation of the printed page in another. This may seem flat-out bizarre—aren't the artboard and the printed page the same thing?—but it makes sense given Illustrator's flexible approach to pages. See, in Illustrator, you can create humongous pages, just shy of 19 by 19 feet—larger than many bedrooms. Because very few printers can handle this extreme page size, Illustrator lets you divide your artwork onto several printed pages if you so desire.

Now, you probably aren't looking to print 19-by-19-foot artwork, but you still might find a use for an artboard that's larger than the printed page.

Say that you want to create a 17-by-22-inch poster in Illustrator. Although this size is rather small for a poster—most are twice that large—it's awfully large for a printer. Office printers, for example, top out at 11 by 17 inches. This means you'll probably have to print your poster onto several pages and paste the pages together by hand (at least in the proofing stage).

Since you specify the size of the artboard when you first create your document, your next order of business is to set the size of the printed page. You can then go back and adjust the size of the artboard, if necessary, using the Document Setup dialog box. In fact, you can keep adjusting the page and artboard sizes until the dogs come home. The sections that follow show you how.

Setting Up the Printed Page

To specify the size of the pages Illustrator prints, you first need to make sure you have the proper printer selected. Mac people using System 9.1 need to select the Chooser command from the Apple menu. On the left side of the Chooser dialog box you'll see a scrolling list of icons. These icons are *printer drivers*. Select the proper driver for your printer:

- If you're using a PostScript-compatible printer, select the PS Printer icon. If PS Printer is not available, select LaserWriter 8. (The two are virtually identical. PS Printer comes from Adobe and is therefore probably more recent; LaserWriter 8 comes from Apple.)

● If you own a non-PostScript printer, select the icon named after your printer. It may even look like your printer.

After you select the proper driver, click the close box or press Cmd-W to close the Chooser dialog box.

Mac folks using System 10.1 have it even easier. If you are connected to a USB printer, OS 10.1 selects if for you automatically. If you are using network printers, use Print Center to select your desired printer from the Printer list.

Windows folks can change printers by clicking the Start button on the Windows taskbar and then choosing the Settings » Printers shortcut. Double-click the Add Printer icon and follow the instructions in the Add Printer Wizard. You will have the opportunity to select a printer driver from a slew of drivers that come with Windows or to add one that comes from your printer's manufacturer on a separate disk. After choosing a printer and finishing with the Add Printer Wizard, return to Illustrator.

Next, choose File » Print Setup (Ctrl+Shift+P) on Windows to display the Print Setup dialog box shown in **Figure 3.2**. On the Mac, choose File » Page Setup (Cmd-Shift-P) to bring up the Page Setup dialog box, which looks a bit different from its Windows equivalent but offers the same essential options. Different printer drivers change the dialog box, but for the time being, only two options in this dialog box matter: Size (Scale on the Mac) and Orientation. (For descriptions of the others, read Chapter 24.)

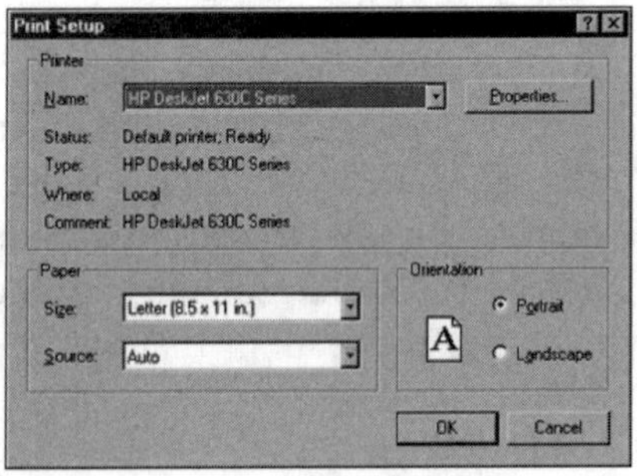

Figure 3.2: Called Print Setup on Windows and Page Setup on the Mac, here's where you change the size and the orientation of the page when it is printed.

● **Paper Size:** From this pop-up menu—which goes by different names depending on which platform and operating system you're using— select the paper size you want to print on. As you might imagine, it's important to make sure your printer can handle the paper size you select. Don't select Tabloid (11 by 17 inches), for example, if your printer maxes out at Legal (8.5 by 14 inches). A4, B5, and others are European page sizes.

Orientation: You can create an upright page (Portrait) or turn it over on its side (Landscape), depending on whether you want a page that's taller than it is wide (the default) or one that's wider than it is tall.

After you respond to these two options, click the OK button or press Enter (Return on the Mac). Illustrator automatically redraws the dotted outlines inside the artboard. One outline represents the border of the printed page, and the other represents the size of the imageable, or printable, area.

 If the size of the printed page is the same size as the artboard, you won't see the outside border of the printed page. You need to make the artboard bigger to see the border of the printed page.

 Naturally, when you prepare illustrations for the Web, paper size and printer choice are irrelevant. Since the imageable area refers only to printed output, it's also of no consequence for Web graphics. So you can simply ignore the dotted outline that represents the imageable area on the artboard. Or if you find the outline annoying, you can hide it by choosing View » Hide Page Tiling

Modifying the Artboard

Not happy with the artboard size you specified when you created your document? Not a problem. Choose File » Document Setup or press Ctrl+Alt+P (Cmd-Option-P on the Mac) to bring up the Document Setup dialog box shown in **Figure 3.3**. Then make sure the Artboard option is selected from the pop-up menu in the upper-left corner. (I'll discuss the other two options—Printing & Export and Transparency in Chapters 24 and 18, respectively.) Most of the settings in the Artboard section of this dialog box simply duplicate the Artboard Setup options in the New Document dialog box. But a few additional settings control the relationship between the artboard and the printed page. Whatever their purpose, here's how the Artboard Document Setup options work.

 If you're paying close attention, you can see there's a Print Setup or Page Setup button in the Document Setup dialog box. It's a back door to the Print Setup area in case you realize you need to make some changes in that dialog box without leaving the Document Setup.

Figure 3.3: Use the Document
Setup options to change the
size and orientation of the
artboard at any time you like.

Size: This pop-up menu offers the same predefined artboard sizes found in the New Document dialog box.

Units: Select an option from this pop-up menu to change the measurement system for the current drawing.

Use Print Setup: Select this check box (called Use Page Setup on the Mac) if you want to match the artboard to the printed page size.

Width and Height: Use these option boxes to enter a custom artboard size.

Orientation: Click the left or right button to change the orientation of the artboard to portrait or landscape, respectively.

Show Images In Outline: When this setting is turned off, a placed image does not display properly in the outline mode. Instead, it appears as a rectangle, bisected by two diagonal lines. When the check box is selected, Illustrator shows a monochrome version of the image in the outline mode. Placed images of all varieties *always* show up in the preview mode—and of course they always print—regardless of the status of the Show Images In Outline check box.

Single Full Page: The three radio buttons next to the Show Images In Outline check box determine how Illustrator prints oversized artboards. Single Full Page is the default setting. It instructs Illustrator to display just one set of dotted lines and print just one page, regardless of the size of the artboard. Some artists like to use this option with a slightly oversized artboard so they can adjust the way the illustration fits on the page using the page tool.

Tile Full Pages: Select this option to display as many whole pages as will fit in the drawing area. No partial pages are allowed.

This is the option to select when creating a multipage document such as a newsletter. Illustrator numbers the page boundaries inside the artboard so you know the order in which the pages will print.

 Tile Imageable Areas: By selecting the Tile Imageable Areas radio button, you tell Illustrator to chop up the artboard into as many imageable areas as will fit, thus ensuring no gap between an object printed half on one page and half on another.

 *Select the Tile Imageable Areas option when subdividing poster-sized artwork onto many printed pages.*

Once you exit the Document Setup dialog box (by pressing Enter or Return, naturally), you'll see the altered page boundaries against the altered artboard. To adjust the position of the page boundaries, read on.

Positioning the Pages on the Artboard

You can't move the artboard. (That is, you can scroll around so that it looks like it moves inside the illustration window, but you can't actually change its location.) The artboard is always positioned smack-dab in the center of the pasteboard. However, you can move the page boundaries with respect to the artboard using the page tool. (If you can't raise the bridge, lower the water.)

The page tool is the first alternate tool in the hand tool slot. Select this tool and then click or drag inside the artboard to set the location of the lower-left corner of the imageable area of a printed page. If you selected the Tile Imageable Areas or Tile Full Pages option in the Document Setup dialog box, a network of page boundaries emanates from the point at which you release the mouse button. If just one page boundary appears even though you selected the Tile Full Pages radio button, it's because this is the only whole page that fits at this location. Drag again with the page tool or increase the size of the artboard to see more pages.

 To automatically line up the page boundaries with the lower-left corner of the artboard, double-click the page tool in the toolbox.

 Always use the page tool to change the placement of an illustration on a page. It's easier and faster than trying to move a huge squad of graphic objects and text blocks with the arrow tool. If you need more wiggle room, increase the size of the artboard one or more inches all around.

Hiding the Page Boundaries and Artboard

If the dotted page boundaries get in your face, choose View » Hide Page Tiling to make them go away. This is, of course, merely a temporary measure. You can make the page boundaries reappear at any time by choosing View » Show Page Tiling. As I mentioned before, if you're creating artwork that will be exported to a layout program, you don't need to be concerned with the artboard. Choose View » Hide Artboard. If the idea of working without an artboard frightens you, choose View » Show Artboard to get it back.

Getting Around in Illustrator

Illustrator works a lot like other graphics programs. You can zoom in to take a closer look at a detail and out to view your illustration in its entirety. You also can scroll the illustration to bring different bits and pieces into view. And if you own an older, slower machine, you can view objects in a special wireframe mode that speeds screen display.

The next few sections explain how to get around quickly and expertly. If you don't know them already, pay special attention to the keyboard shortcuts. Using navigational shortcuts rather than selecting tools and commands expedites the artistic process more than any other single factor.

Fit-in-Window and Actual Sizes

Illustrator provides 23 preset *view sizes*, which are the magnification levels that Illustrator uses to display your drawing in the illustration window. Illustrator also allows you to specify any view size between 3.13 and 6,400 percent by entering the value into the size option box or dragging with the zoom tool. Magnified view sizes show great detail but permit you to see only small portions of the illustration at a time. Reduced view sizes show you a larger portion of the drawing area but may provide insufficient detail for creating and manipulating objects.

Assuming that you haven't altered the Adobe Illustrator Startup file, Illustrator displays every new illustration at a *fit-in-window size*, which reduces the artboard so it fits inside the illustration window. The specific magnification level required to produce the fit-in-window size depends on the size of your monitor and the size of the artboard. In **Figure 3.4**, for example, the artboard fits in the window at 64 percent magnification.

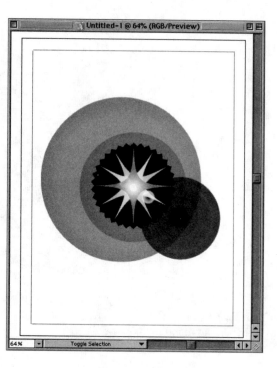

Figure 3.4: A typical
illustration viewed from far
away at fit-in-window size.

 You can return to fit-in-window size at any time by choosing View » Fit In Window or pressing Ctrl+0 (Cmd-0 on the Mac). If this key equivalent doesn't necessarily remind you of anything, just double-click the hand tool icon in the toolbox. (To help you remember this shortcut, think of using that hand tool to push back the illustration.)

Another useful view size is *actual size*—or 100 percent view—which shows the visible details of your illustration on screen more or less as they will print. **Figure 3.5** shows an example.

 Actual size is not an exact representation of your illustration, and even approximate accuracy assumes your monitor displays 72 pixels per inch. Many monitors can pack in more pixels, causing an illustration viewed at actual size to appear quite a bit smaller than it prints. If you want to get a truly accurate feel for how your illustration will print, then print it (as described in Chapter 24).

 You can switch to actual size by choosing the View » Actual Size command or pressing Ctrl+1 (Cmd-1 on the Mac). (The number 1 stands for 100 percent.) But if you can't remember the keystrokes, double-click the zoom tool icon in the toolbox (the one that looks like a magnifying glass).

Figure 3.5: Switch to actual size to see your illustration at the size it will print.

Magnifying as the Mood Hits You

You can access each of Illustrator's 23 preset view sizes using the zoom tool. Select the zoom tool and click in the illustration window to magnify your drawing to the next-higher view size. For example, when you're viewing an illustration at actual size, clicking with the zoom tool takes you to 150 percent. Clicking again takes you to 200 percent. Each view affords greater detail but shows a smaller portion of your artwork.

Drag with the zoom tool to surround the portion of the illustration that you want to magnify with a dotted rectangle called a *marquee*. Illustrator zooms in until the surrounded area fills the entire screen, as demonstrated in **Figure 3.6**. Whereas clicking with the zoom tool lets you step through the 23 preset view sizes, the marquee takes you to the view size that most closely reflects the exact area you drag on. Notice that in the right portion of Figure 3.6, which shows the result of dragging with the zoom tool, the size box indicates a view size of 129.52 percent. If you were to click with the zoom tool or click the Zoom In button inside the Navigator palette, the view size would step up to the next size, 300 percent.

Once you get a feel for marqueeing, try out the following techniques in mid-drag to make your zooms more precise.

Press the spacebar in the middle of a drag to move the marquee. To change the shape of the marquee again, just release the spacebar.

 If you decide in mid-drag that you don't want to magnify the illustration after all, drag back to the spot where you started so the dotted marquee disappears, and then release. Illustrator knows you chickened out and leaves the view size unchanged.

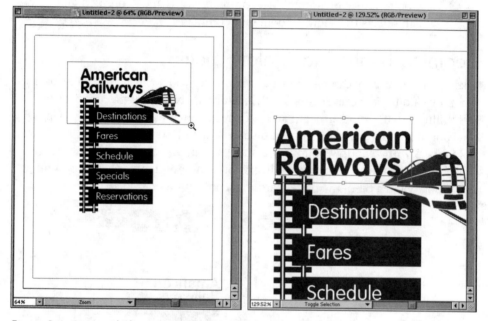

Figure 3.6: Drag with the zoom tool to surround an area with a marquee (left). Illustrator then magnifies that area to fill the window (right).

When you press the Alt key (Option key on the Mac), the cursor displays an inset minus sign, showing you that it's all set to zoom out. Alt-clicking (Option-clicking on the Mac) with the zoom tool reduces the view size to the next lower view size. You can see more of your artwork but less detail.

The zoom tool cursor is empty when your current view size is at either the maximum (6,400 percent) or minimum (3.13 percent) level of magnification. At that point, you can zoom in or out no further.

You can also zoom in and out using a whole mess of keyboard shortcuts.

 To access the zoom tool temporarily when some other tool is selected, press and hold the Ctrl and spacebar keys (Cmd and spacebar on the Mac)—the same shortcut as found in InDesign, PageMaker,

Photoshop, and FreeHand. Releasing the keys returns the cursor to its previous appearance.

 You can zoom in one level by pressing Ctrl++ (plus sign) (Cmd-+ on the Mac), the shortcut for View » Zoom In.

 Press Ctrl+Alt+spacebar (Cmd-Option-spacebar on the Mac) to get the zoom-out cursor. Again, all the best applications use this shortcut.

 Or zoom out by pressing Ctrl+– (minus sign) (Cmd-– on the Mac), which selects the View » Zoom Out command.

Zooming by the Navigator Palette

Like other Adobe applications, Illustrator also gives you a Navigator palette to help you move around in your document. By default, the Navigator palette displays the active illustration's entire artboard and a red rectangular *window boundary*. This window boundary represents the current display of the illustration window. As shown in **Figure 3.7**, the window boundary is smaller than the artboard that it overlaps. This means that the corresponding illustration window shows only this portion of the artboard and a bit of the pasteboard that flanks it on one side.

Figure 3.7: The Navigator palette lets you easily switch to any view size, including the preset values. The palette also allows you to scroll quickly to any location on the pasteboard.

The Navigator provides three ways to change the illustration window's view size.

 Click the zoom-in button to magnify to the next larger preset view size. Click the zoom-out button to reduce the view to the next smaller preset size.

 Click along the zoom slider to change the view size. Click all the way to the left to zoom out all the way to the smallest view size, which is 3.13 percent. Click all the way to the right to zoom in to the maximum level of magnification, 6,400 percent. You can also drag the slider triangle to zoom in or out dynamically.

 Click the zoom option box and enter any value between 3.13 and 6,400 to change the view size to that percent.

The Navigator palette offers a few other useful features.

 Click in the palette's window to reposition the boundary window such that it's centered on your click. Drag in the palette's window to move around the window boundary. As you drag, Illustrator will automatically update the illustration window to reflect your movements.

 Press the Ctrl key (Cmd key on the Mac) while the cursor is over the Navigator palette's window, and it changes to a magnifying lens. Ctrl+drag (Cmd-drag on the Mac) to change the size of the window boundary. This is similar to dragging with the zoom tool in the illustration window, except that the window boundary will always remain proportional to the dimensions of the illustration window.

 By default, the Navigator palette displays only those paths that appear on the artboard. If any paths straddle the edge of the artboard, this option will truncate their appearance in the Navigator palette's window. To see all the paths that will fit into the window at the current view size, including those that reside on the pasteboard outside the boundaries of the artboard, deselect View Artboard Only from the Navigator palette's pop-up menu.

 Select Palette Options from the palette's pop-up menu to change the color of the window boundary. You can choose from a list of predefined colors or create your own by double-clicking the color box.

  *The Navigator can be enlarged so you can see more details in the artwork, so it can act as a second window displaying your illustration. This way you can zoom in on one area while keeping an eye out on the overall big picture.*

Those of us who grew up on early versions of Illustrator used to create multiple views in a single illustration by choosing Window » New Window. Illustrator doesn't create a copy of the artwork, but rather makes a second illustration window that lets you track changes. There's no difference between this and creating a larger Navigator palette as mentioned in the previous tip.

Dragging the Drawing

Because most screens aren't as large as a full page, you probably won't be able to see your entire illustration at actual size or larger. Therefore, Illustrator lets you move the artboard inside the illustration window, a technique known as *scrolling*. It's like looking through a pair of binoculars, in a way. You can see the action more clearly, but you can see only part of the action at a time. To look at something else, you have to move the binoculars (and your head) to adjust your view. This is what happens when you scroll in Illustrator.

One method for scrolling the drawing area is to use the two scroll bars, located at the bottom and right side of the window. But only saps use the scroll bars, because Illustrator provides a better tool: the hand tool. Located at the bottom-left of the toolbox, the hand tool allows you to drag the drawing area inside the window. As you drag, the hand cursor changes to a fist to show you that you have the illustration in your viselike grip.

 To access the hand tool when some other tool is selected, press and hold the spacebar. Then drag as desired. Release the spacebar to return the cursor to its previous appearance.

 When a text block is active, pressing the spacebar results in a bunch of spaces. You can get around this by pressing the Ctrl key (Cmd key on the Mac), then pressing the spacebar, and then releasing the Ctrl or Cmd key. As long as you keep the spacebar down, the hand tool is yours and the text block remains active.

Changing the Display Mode

Another way to control what you see on screen is to change the *display mode*—that is, how you see individual objects on screen. There are two basic modes.

 In the *preview mode*, you see objects and text in full color, more or less as they will print. (Again, Illustrator does its best with this what-you-see-is-what-you-get stuff. It's only software, after all.) Illustrator displays your drawing in the preview mode by default, and you can return to it at anytime by choosing View » Preview or pressing Ctrl+Y (Cmd-Y on the Mac).

If you own a slow computer, you can speed up Illustrator's screen redraw by choosing View » Outline or press Ctrl+Y (Cmd-Y) again. Illustrator's *outline mode* is what other programs call a *wireframe* or *key-line* mode: Text appears in black, graphic objects have thin outlines and transparent interiors, and there's not a color in sight. **Figure 3.8** shows how outline and preview modes compare.

Figure 3.8: A relatively complex illustration displayed in outline view (top) and in preview mode (bottom).

 The outline mode used to be called the artwork mode in Illustrator 8 and earlier. Someone at Adobe must have felt the term artwork was confusing. I agree; outline is a much better way to describe the display.

The outline mode is very fast because Illustrator doesn't have to display complicated visual effects such as blends and gradients. However, it takes some time to get used to. You basically have to imagine how the colors, strokes, gradations, and other effects are going to look. That's why most experienced artists switch back and forth between the outline and preview modes by pressing Ctrl+Y (Cmd-Y).

Fortunately, Illustrator lets you choose different preview options for different layers (see Chapter 8), so you can set the active layer to preview mode while other layers with gradients and blends are in the outline mode.

Creating a View You Can Come Back To

Do you find yourself switching back and forth between the same views over and over? First you zoom in on an individual leaf in a tree, then you scroll down and zoom out a little to examine the trunk, and next you zoom out two or three increments to take in the whole tree. Then you magnify the leaf again and start the process over. This kind of zooming and scrolling back and forth between key locations in your illustration can eat up all kinds of valuable drawing time.

Luckily, Illustrator has a solution. You can save specific views of your illustration and then return to them at the press of a key. When you choose View » New View, Illustrator asks you to name the current view of your illustration. Enter a name and press Enter (Return on the Mac). Illustrator saves the view size, the relative location of the page in the illustration window, and even the display mode.

Illustrator appends the view name to the bottom of the View menu. From now on, you can return to this exact view size, page position, and display mode just by choosing the view name.

 You can create 25 views. All views are saved with the illustration and change from one illustration to the next. That is, the views saved with one drawing will not necessarily be the views that are saved with any other drawing.

To change the name of a view, or to delete one or more views, choose View » Edit Views. Then select a view from the scrolling list in the Edit Views dialog box and enter a new name, or press the Delete button to get rid of it. If you want to delete many views at a time, you can Shift-click a view name to select consecutive views or Ctrl+click (Cmd-click on the Mac) to select nonconsecutive views.

CHAPTER 4

FILES AND FORMATS

One of the strengths of Illustrator is its ability to work with many different file formats. Whether you are sharing files between the Mac and PC, saving illustrations to place in a layout program, or exporting graphics to the Web, you will find that Illustrator supports file formats suited to your needs. In the end, the hardest thing about having all these file formats available is deciding which ones to use.

In this chapter, I'll make sure you're familiar with the basic but critically important steps of opening and saving your files correctly, including how to get around your computer's file structure to find things. I'll also discuss the different file formats and the ways each is used, and how to take artwork from other sources and make it part of your illustration. Finally—you'll be able to stop wondering what's the difference between an EPS and a PDF!

Opening Files

Fortunately, not every Illustrator session begins with creating a new document from scratch. To open an existing illustration saved to disk, choose File » Open or press Ctrl+O—that's the letter O (Cmd-O on the Mac). Alternatively, you can open a recently used illustration by choosing File » Open Recent Files and selecting a name from the drop-down menu.

You can open four kinds of files in Illustrator.

- Drawings previously created in Illustrator (and saved in any of the Illustrator native formats).

- Drawings created in FreeHand or some other drawing program and saved in either the Illustrator file format or the format native to the other drawing program.

- Documents created in InDesign, QuarkXPress, Photoshop, or FreeHand and exported in EPS format (or other programs that can export in EPS format), or documents converted to PDF.

- Images saved as TIFF, JPEG, or some other compatible format.

If you open an illustration (a line drawing saved in any of a number of different formats, including both the Illustrator and the FreeHand native formats), it pops up on screen in a new illustration window. You can edit any line, shape, or word of text as explained in the chapters that follow. Similarly, you can open and edit the lines, shapes, or text from vector EPS documents. (You can't do much, if any, editing of this nature in a raster image you open in Illustrator, though you can still apply filters and other effects to it. For more on this, see Chapter 20.) You can also edit the shapes and text inside opened PDF files, although it is possible that you may lose some objects in the PDF conversion.

When you open a TIFF file or another image, Illustrator displays the image in a new illustration window. You can move or transform (scale, rotate, flip, or skew) images, as well as apply Photoshop filters and effects (as described in Chapter 20). But it's just not possible to edit them in the same way that you edit object-oriented illustrations.

I'll discuss individual file formats and the special ways to deal with them later on in the section "Why All These Formats?" But first, let's briefly go over the basics of opening a file from disk. If you already know all about opening files, feel free to skip this section.

Using the Open Dialog Box

When you choose File » Open, Illustrator displays the Open dialog box, shown in its Windows and Mac incarnations in **Figures 4.1** and **4.2**, respectively. Your only job here is to locate and select the drawing with which you want to work. The dialog box lets you search through the folders on all available hard drives, CD-ROMs, and floppy disks. Sometimes you can even preview what the file looks like before you open it.

Figure 4.1: The Open dialog box is your tool for locating files stored on disk. This is the Windows version.

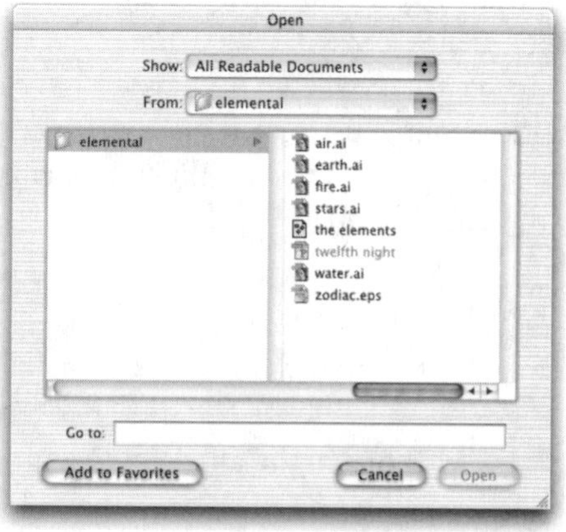

Figure 4.2: The Open dialog box as it appears on a Mac running OS 10.1. As you probably know if you're using this system, when you click once on a file name, you'll see a preview (if there is one) in the right-hand pane.

The Folder Bar and Scrolling List

When you're in the Open dialog box, you and your mouse can get to any location on your computer or network to select any existing file. At the top of the box you'll see a *folder bar*, showing your current folder name—your location within the file hierarchy. Click on that bar to see the nested folders, and drag to switch to a *parent folder*; that is, one of the folders that contains the current folder.

In this way, you can navigate to anywhere on the drive or to other connected computers (not that I recommend opening files over a network, mind you).

Below the folder bar is a scrolling list that contains the names of all the files and folders inside the current folder. Since you're seeing this through the Open dialog box, the files you'll see will be based on the option you've selected in the Files of type option box (Show option box on the Mac), covered in the "Showing Fields" section further down. Once you've found the file, select it in the scrolling field and click the Open button, or just double-click on the filename.

Using the Preview

The Open dialog box includes a thumbnail preview of the selected illustration or image. The beauty of the preview is that you don't have to open the graphic to remember what it looks like. The preview feature is constantly on in Windows (though if your file hasn't been saved with previews or does not support previews, you will just see a gray box) and in Mac OS 10.1; in Mac OS versions earlier than 10 you can turn it on or off with the Show/Hide Preview button in the Open dialog box.

To see the preview you have to have saved a thumbnail along with the file inside either Illustrator 6 or later (previous versions didn't support previews) or Photoshop 2.5.1 or later. Illustrator can also display the PICT previews included with some EPS files.

Showing Files

The Open dialog box has a Files of type pop-up menu (called Show on the Mac) where you can choose what types of files you want to see. The choices are:

- **All Formats:** Called All Documents on the Mac, this option lets you see all of the files in whatever location you're looking, whether Illustrator can open them or not.

- **All Readable Formats:** Called All Readable Documents on the Mac, this option lets you see all of the files that Illustrator knows it can open. This option is the default and helps you focus on the files you want to work with, and not waste time with the others.

- **File Types:** You can also choose to display only a specific type of file that Illustrator knows it can open. For instance, you may want to open only CorelDraw files. You can choose that file type to list only those files. This list also helps you understand which file types Illustrator does recognize.

Placing and Linking

 If you import a lot of fancy pictures, you may be very pleased to know you can now control the resolution of your screen preview of linked EPS graphics. By default, Illustrator is set up to display placed EPS files at low resolution. If you want to see a crisper, more gratifying image, go to the Files & Clipboard Preferences dialog box and uncheck the Use Low Resolution Proxy for Linked EPS option. That'll improve your picture, but decay your performance, so turn the option back on if you want to speed things up again.

If you want to add an illustration or image to the illustration you're working on, choose File » Place. Rather than create a separate illustration window, Illustrator places the graphic in the foreground window. The graphic appears selected so you can begin working on it immediately. You can move or transform a placed graphic, but you can't edit it, even if the graphic was created using Illustrator. You can also apply Photoshop filters to placed images (unless the placed image is an Illustrator EPS, as this chapter explains later).

The Place Dialog Box

The Place dialog box looks and works like the Open dialog box, except it offers three additional check-box options.

- **Link:** When this check box is selected, Illustrator tags the physical location of the image or illustration without integrating it into the current working file, so the file's size therefore does not increase. Graphics so placed are considered *linked*. If you turn off this check box, Illustrator will save the placed item as part of your artwork, resulting in a larger file. These "added" images are then called *embedded images*.

- **Template**: If you select this check box, Illustrator automatically creates a new template layer (directly below the current layer) expressly for this image. A template layer is automatically set as visible, locked, and nonprinting. By default, the image will be dimmed by 50 percent. (For more information on layers, see Chapter 8.) Images acting as templates in this manner are ideal for tracing. (For more information on tracing and the auto trace tool, see Chapter 5.)

- **Replace:** Instead of simply placing an image or illustration, you can replace a previously placed graphic with a new one. First select the graphic that you want to replace in your artwork. Then choose File » Place, select the new graphic from the scrolling list, turn on the Replace check box, and press Enter (Return on the Mac).

The Links Palette

Illustrator offers a palette devoted to the organization and keeping of all your placed graphics, both linked and embedded. For each graphic you place in a document, Illustrator creates a *link* in the Links palette, which you can display by choosing Window » Links. The link includes the graphic's name and a thumbnail preview of the graphic, as shown in **Figure 4.3**.

The link may also include one of three small informational icons, labeled in Figure 4.3.

Embedded: This icon means all the information about the graphic is incorporated in the Illustrator file. You can create an embedded graphic by deselecting the Link check box when you place the file, by choosing Embed Image from the Links palette menu, or by applying any of the commands that rasterize an image within the file (see Chapter 20).

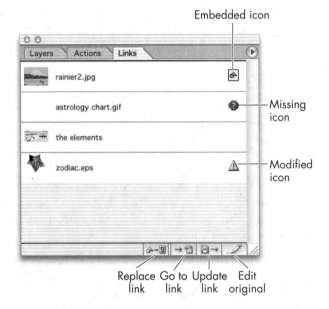

Figure 4.3: Within the confines of the Links palette, you can organize, find, and change the embedded status of all placed graphics in your document.

Missing: This icon never shows up when you first place an image. It appears when you open a file that contains a linked image that Illustrator can no longer locate. Perhaps you've moved the file to a new location or—shudder!—you've thrown the file away. Whatever the case, this icon alerts you that the original is no longer available. You can either relink the image or replace it with another image.

Modified icon: If you change a linked image outside of Illustrator, Illustrator displays the modified icon. This is a gentle reminder that you need to update the linked image.

No icon whatsoever: This lack of an icon tells you that you have a linked image in proper working order.

The Links palette's pop-up menu contains options that let you view and modify the images associated with the different links. The first five options require that either an image is selected in your document or that a link is selected in the Links palette. The full list of options are as follows:

Go to Link: With a link selected, choose this option (or click the second icon from the left along the bottom of the palette) and Illustrator will select the image associated with the link and center it in the document window.

Update Link: If you've modified the original file of a linked image currently open in Illustrator, this command lets you update the image. Select the image's link and choose this option (or click the second icon from the right along the bottom of the palette).

Edit Original: Choose this option to open the original image in the application in which it was created. If the original image wasn't created on your computer, the image will open in the most appropriate application (as dictated by your operating system and the image's format). This option affects only linked images because embedded images, as integrated parts of your document, no longer have originals.

Replace: If you decide that an image is wrong for your document, select its link from the Links palette and choose this option. The standard Place dialog box will display. Select the image that you'd prefer in the place of the original. As was the case when you placed the original image, you'll have the option of linking or embedding the new image via the Link check box.

NEW 10 **Placement Options:** Choose this option to display the Placement Options dialog box (**Figure 4.4**), which contains five Preserve modes. If you select Transforms from the Preserve pop-up menu, the linked file will be stretched to fit the bounding box. Choose Proportions (Fit) to fit the entire linked graphic into the bounding box while preserving its original proportions. If you choose Proportions (Fill), the entire bounding box will be filled, but parts of the linked graphic may be cut off to allow the original proportions to be preserved. The File Dimensions option retains the original dimensions of the linked file, regardless of how the bounding box is sized. The Bounds mode acts much like Transforms in that the linked graphic will be the same size as the bounding box. But in the Bounds mode, if that linked graphic is replaced, the new graphic will not be stretched to fit the bounding box.

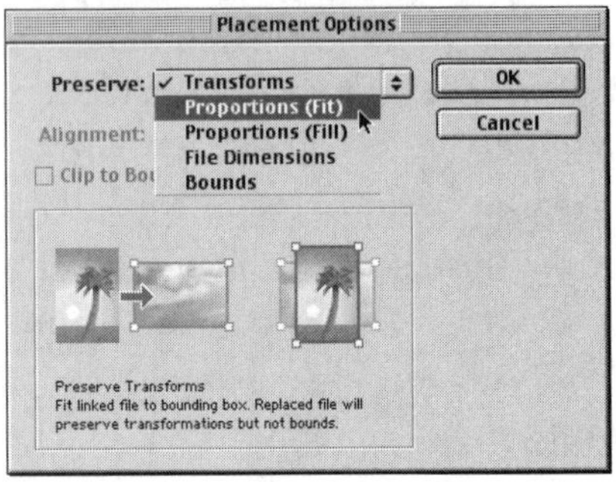

Figure 4.4: The Placement Options dialog box of the Links palette.

The Alignment icon lets you choose a point from which to align the image. The Clip to Bounding Box option prevents the image from overlapping the bounding box. As you experiment with these options, you'll see that this one works with only some of the methods.

 Verify Workgroup Link: If you're working in a networked environment and your linked graphic is shared among several systems, you don't have complete control over the location of the original image. Someone else may move it or delete it without your knowledge. This option lets you verify the link over a workgroup to determine if the unthinkable has happened.

 Save Workgroup Link: Similarly, if a link is established over a network, this option allows you to save the link.

Embed Image: Choose this option to encode a linked image's information into your document. This embeds the image, just as though you had deactivated the Place dialog box's Link check box when first placing the image.

Information: With a link selected, choose this option (or double-click the link) to display the Link Information dialog box. Here you'll find information about the image, including its name, location on disk, size in bytes, kind (that is, its file format), creation and modification dates, and any changes that you made to its scaling or angular orientation.

 Show: You can opt to show all links in the Links palette or just those in which you are interested.

 Sort: Choose the appropriate option to sort the links by name, kind, or status. Sorting links by status groups the links into those that are missing, modified, or up-to-date.

 Palette Options: Choose this option to display the Palette Options dialog box, where you can select the size of the thumbnail images representing each of the linked files. You can also select whether or not to show transparency interactions among linked files. Sometimes transparent elements within linked files don't play nicely together.

Saving Your Work to Disk

Whenever the topic of saving files comes up, I am tempted to jump on a soapbox and recite shopworn slogans:

 Save your illustration early and often!

 The only safe illustration is a saved illustration!

 An untitled illustration is a recipe for disaster!

 If you're about to switch applications, hit Ctrl+S (Cmd-S on the Mac)! If you hear thunder, hit Ctrl+S! If a child enters your room, hit Ctrl+S!

I guess I'm trying to say it's really important to save. I ought to know—I've lost immeasurable amounts of work, and of course a lot of hours, by not saving in time. So do it!

Four Saves and an Export

And if you think I'm being a fanatic about saving, just look at Illustrator's File menu. There are four—count 'em, *four*—different commands with a Save in them: Save, Save As, Save A Copy, and Save For Web. And if that isn't enough, there's an Export command to boot. So when should you use what?

Save: This is the command that writes the current information about the named file on the disk. If there is no file on the disk, then Illustrator treats the Save command as a Save As. The shortcut for this most-basic-of-all-commands is Ctrl+S (Cmd-S on the Mac).

Save As…: Notice the ellipsis? Anytime you see an ellipsis after a command name, you know there's a dialog box that follows. The command can't be completed until you do something with the dialog box. The Save As command is where you can name the file, make decisions about its format, and then write the file to disk. You can also use the Save As command to make different versions of your document. When you Save, Save As, or Save A Copy, you are creating a file that is in the Illustrator family: an Illustrator file, an EPS file, a PDF file, an SVG file, or an SVG Compressed file. All these file types can be opened and modified by Illustrator; not so with the Save For Web and Export commands. The keyboard shortcut for Save As is Ctrl+Shift+S (Cmd-Shift-S on the Mac).

 If you're saving to PDF or SVG and have even the remotest intention of editing your file in the future, be sure to keep the Preserve Illustrator Editing Capabilities option checked.

 Remember, even if you named the file when you first created the document, you must perform a Save As command to actually name the file on disk.

Save A Copy…: You may be wondering, why would anyone want to save a *copy*? Doesn't Save As do that? Well, yes, but when you choose Save As, you're usually planning to change the name of the file you're working on, and when you've done so, you'll be in the newly named version of the file. But when you choose Save A Copy, you send a copy of the newly named file off to sit on disk, and you're still working on the original file. Imagine you're about to do something really strange to your document. Before you make that drastic move, use Save A Copy to make a copy of your work at that point under a name like "Before I messed up the art." Then you can do whatever you want to the file. Days later, when the client sees the bizarre version and is backing toward the door, you know you still have the safer version saved as a copy. The keyboard shortcut for Save A Copy is Ctrl+Alt+S (Cmd-Option-S on the Mac).

Save For Web…: This command really isn't a save but an export. However, unlike the actual Export command, Save For Web (see Chapter 21) opens up a large dialog box—actually a mini-program inside Illustrator—where you can play around with different Web formats, sizes, and optimization settings for Web files. People used to pay big money to get programs like Save For Web, and here it is, free with Illustrator. The keyboard shortcut for Save For Web is the finger-twisting Ctrl+Shift+Alt+S (Cmd-Shift-Option-S on the Mac).

Export: The Export command gives you a list of different file formats into which Illustrator can convert your file. Most of these convert your elegant line drawings into pixelated facsimiles.

Using the Save Dialog Box

If the foreground window is untitled, as it is when you work on a new illustration, choosing File » Save or pressing Ctrl+S (Cmd-S on the Mac) displays the Save As dialog box shown in **Figure 4.5**. This is Illustrator's way of encouraging you to name the illustration, specify its location on disk, and select a file format. After you save the illustration once, choosing the Save command updates the file on disk without bringing up the Save As dialog box.

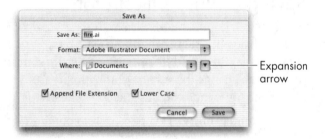

Figure 4.5: The Save As
dialog box lets you name
your file.

——Expansion
arrow

 If you think the dialog box shown in Figure 4.5 above looks a little skimpy, it's because it's the "lite" version of the amazing expanding and contracting dialog box in Mac OS X. The big arrow next to the Where field lets you show the file and folder panes of the window as well as the New Folder and Add to Favorites buttons.

Choose File » Save As or press Ctrl+Shift+S Cmd-Shift-S on the Mac) to change the name, location, or format of the illustration. Choosing the Save As command always brings up the Save dialog box. If you didn't give your document a name when you first created it, here's another chance. Use the navigation buttons to find the area where you want to save your file.

Mac users can choose to add a file extension to the name and to have that extension in lowercase. This is extremely helpful if you routinely send your files to your Windows friends or if you need to post your files on Unix servers that like lowercase extensions. (Windows users, you don't have to care about this because your files always get the file extension added automatically.)

Selecting a File Format

The most complex option in the Save dialog box is the Save as type pop-up menu on Windows or the Format pop-up menu on the Mac, which lets you specify the file format you want to use to preserve your illustration. Your choices are Illustrator, Illustrator EPS, Adobe PDF, SVG, or SVG Compressed. I explain why and when you'd want to use each of these formats in the "Why All These Formats?" section later in this chapter. But first, let's take a look at the only two formats that save every shred of information in your illustration, making them the formats you're likely to use most: the native Illustrator format and Illustrator EPS.

 If you save an illustration in any format other than Illustrator 10 or Illustrator 10 EPS, make sure you have created a backup version of the illustration first in the Illustrator 10 format! Otherwise, you are needlessly and deliberately throwing away some amount of your hard work.

Saving a Native Illustrator File

If you choose the Illustrator format in the Save dialog box, you are faced with another dialog box (shown in **Figure 4.6**) where you need to set which version of Illustrator you would like to make your file compatible with. The only time you need to change the version compatibility is if you need to send your file to some poor soul who hasn't upgraded to Illustrator 10.

- **Compatibility:** This pop-up list contains all the previous versions of Illustrator back to 3.0. If you don't care about previous versions of Illustrator, leave the most recent version selected so you don't lose anything.

- **Create PDF Compatible File** (available only if you're saving in Illustrator 10 format): This option includes PDF data within your file to make the file compatible with other Adobe products. That means if you don't check this option, you can't place (or open) this file in, say, Photoshop, InDesign, or Acrobat. Unless you're truly a stand-alone Illustrator user, it's probably best to just leave this option checked and forget about it. It'll add a few bytes to your file size, but consider it the cost of doing business with Adobe.

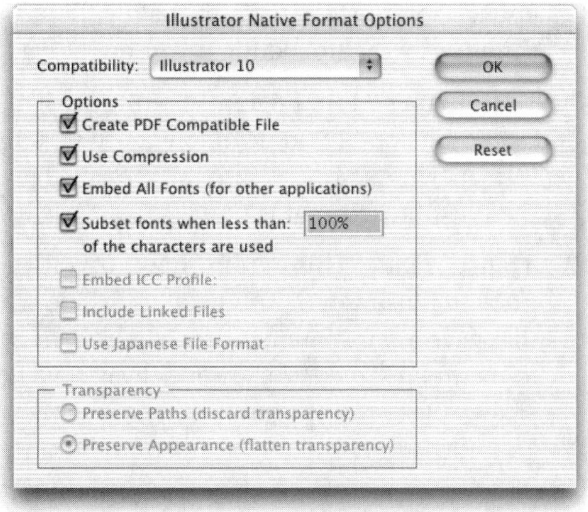

Figure 4.6: The Illustrator Native Format Options dialog box lets you choose which version of Illustrator should be able to open and play with your file.

Use Compression (also available only if you're saving in Illustrator 10 format): This option automatically compresses the data as it saves the file. Test it sometime: It makes a big difference!

Embed All Fonts: Don't get excited—this check box doesn't do quite what you might think it does, or maybe what you secretly want it to do. If you select this option, Illustrator will include the fonts used with the file. But that doesn't mean that you can send the file to someone to work on who doesn't own those fonts and they'd be able to use them. It means only that the fonts are included with the file if you place it into a layout program such as InDesign.

Subset Fonts: Once you've decided to embed all fonts, you then have another question: How much of the font do you want to embed? For instance, if you have used a font for only one single character, do you really want to embed all characters in the font? This option lets you choose to embed only those characters used. However, if you want to make sure the entire character set is included, set this to 100 percent.

Embed ICC Profile: Select this if you want to keep the color management information attached to the file. Deselect this if you would like another application to handle the color management.

Include Linked Files: The name of this option tells it pretty much like it is: It embeds the files that are linked. Having selected this option, if you place the saved file into a layout program, there will be enough information to print the file. But this doesn't mean you can throw away the linked file if you might want to work on it again.

🌑 **Use Japanese File Format:** If you save in a version of Illustrator before version 6, you need to choose this if you want the Japanese file format. This is not the case for present-day Illustrator, because now the Illustrator format is universal.

🌑 **Transparency:** This option shows up only if you save in a version prior to Illustrator 9. You need to decide what to do with any objects that have a transparency, drop shadow, or other special effect assigned to them. Preserve Paths throws away the effect but keeps the path shapes. Preserve Appearance rasterizes the image. (Check out Chapter 18 for an in-depth look at Illustrator's transparency features.)

Saving an EPS Illustration

To use an illustration in InDesign or QuarkXPress, select Illustrator EPS from the Save as type (Format on the Mac) pop-up menu in the Save dialog box. After you click the Save button or press Enter (Return on the Mac), Illustrator displays the EPS Format Options dialog box depicted in stunning detail in **Figure 4.7**. You can probably figure out the majority of these options on your own, but we may as well run through them, if only to eliminate all possible confusion.

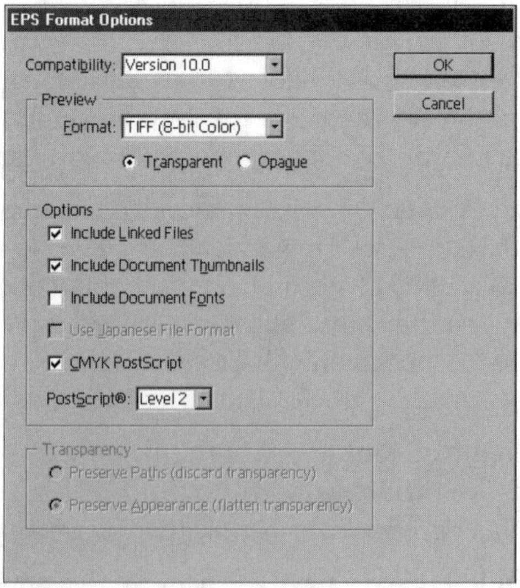

Figure 4.7: Illustrator presents you with a world of options when saving an EPS file.

Compatibility: This pop-up menu is the same as the one for the native Illustrator format.

 Preview: These options control the screen preview that Illustrator attaches to an EPS file. If you're sending the file to a Windows machine, choose TIFF (8-bit Color). Choose Tiff (Black & White) only if the program you're sending the file to doesn't support color. You can also set the preview to transparent or opaque if you choose a TIFF preview. On the Mac, you can also choose Macintosh (8-bit Color) to generate a PICT preview, but you should avoid this option if you'll be sharing the file with Windows colleagues. Only choose Macintosh (Black & White) if you're going out to an application that does not support color.

 *If you are going to send your work to QuarkXPress on the Macintosh, you can choose the TIFF preview. QuarkXPress can handle the TIFF preview information.*

 *Remember, the preview doesn't change the actual information in the file. However, some non-PostScript printers do use the information in the preview to print the file.*

 Include Linked Files: This is the same as the one for the native Illustrator format. Check this option if you would like to send just one EPS file.

Don't throw away the original linked files if you choose this option. You still need to have the original linked images if you want to edit your file.

 Include Document Thumbnails: Always select this check box. It creates a thumbnail of the illustration so you can preview it from the Open dialog box inside Illustrator, Photoshop, and an increasing number of other programs.

 Include Document Fonts: If you use a font in your illustration that you're not sure is as popular with your audience as it is with you, select this option. The file will be a bit larger (depending on the size of the font file), but you ensure that your document will appear with the font you intended. Just remember, someone who doesn't own the fonts still won't be able to edit the file.

Use Japanese File Format: Same story as in the Illustrator Native Format Options dialog box that discussed a few pages ago.

 CMYK PostScript: With this option selected, Illustrator will automatically convert RGB colors to their CMYK equivalents as needed.

 PostScript Level: When you send your artwork to a PostScript printer, there are different levels of PostScript that are used to print the file. Level 3 is the most sophisticated and can handle any effect or feature in Illustrator. Level 2 is less complex. Some features, such as the gradient mesh, are converted into raster images if the printer uses Level 2. Level 1 is the most primitive. If you know your printer can handle Level 3 information, choose it. If not, use Level 2. Don't pick Level 1 unless you've been specifically told to do so by someone important, like your service bureau.

 Transparency: These, too, are the same as the options in the Illustrator Native Format Options dialog box.

Illustrator is pretty clever. In most cases you can just press Enter (Return on the Mac) to quickly get you out of the EPS Format Options dialog box. The default settings ensure there's no loss of information even if you weren't paying a lick of attention to what you were doing. That's the kind of service any decent program is all too happy to perform.

Saving as an SVG

SVG stands for Scalable Vector Graphic. I'll discuss the SVG format at length in Chapter 22 and will fully discuss file-saving options there, when you have more SVG information under your belt. For right now, it's enough to say that SVG is a new Web graphics format that supports animation and dynamic scaling. Although not yet widely supported by browsers, and (perhaps because of that) not wildly embraced by Web designers, SVG files have the potential to be an important player in the Web graphics game.

Why All These Formats?

File formats are different forms and methods in which files can be written, saved, or exported to disk. Just as VHS and 8mm are different videotape formats, TIFF and PCX (for example) are different image formats. By supporting a wider variety of formats, Illustrator can accept graphics from all kinds of Macintosh and Windows applications.

The following sections describe most of the formats that Illustrator 10 supports. I'll tell you how each format works and what good it is, and I'll offer additional instructions as needed.

Native Illustrator

The native Illustrator format—the one Illustrator likes best—is a type of PostScript file. If you know how to program in PostScript, you can even open the file (as a text file) in a word processor and edit it line by line. There are nine variations on the basic Illustrator format, each corresponding to a different version of the software.

Illustrator 10 can open Illustrator files from all past versions. But, of course, the older the versions get, the less exciting stuff they did. Following is a quick list of what's *not* supported as you traverse back through the versions—sort of like an archaeological snapshot of the evolution of the program's features. This list is not an exhaustive description of what each one will support.

- **Illustrator 10.0:** This format saves every little thing you can do in Illustrator 10.

- **Illustrator 9.0:** This format does not support symbols and instances, variables, and other information related to data-driven graphics and SVG interactivity.

- **Illustrator 8.0:** This format does not support appearances, transparency, live object effects, and live raster effects.

- **Illustrator 7.0:** This format does not support the extended blend capabilities, gradient meshes, and specialized brushstrokes.

- **Illustrator 6.0:** This format does not support grids, the expanded template capabilities, and some file formats.

- **Illustrator 5.0/5.5:** The Illustrator 5 format does not support imported image files or thumbnail previews.

- **Illustrator 4.0 (for Windows):** This Windows-only version of the Illustrator format is almost identical to the Illustrator 3 format. (Illustrator 4 also supported grids and TIFF templates—neither of which was possible on the Mac side until Illustrator 7—but this hardly matters, in terms of format.)

- **Illustrator 3.0/3.2:** This format doesn't support gradients, layers, large artboard sizes, tabs, and columns or rows. It converts gradient fills to blends and combines all objects onto a single layer. Objects in the pasteboard may be lost.

- **Illustrator 88:** This format does not support compound paths, area and path text, text blocks with more than 256 characters, custom guides, and charts. All paths remain intact, but they may not serve their original function. Text blocks are divided into pieces; area and path text may be broken up into individual letters.

- **Illustrator 1.0/1.1:** This format supports only paths and small text blocks. What it doesn't support could fill a book (such as this book): tile patterns, masks, placed EPS images, and colors (that's right, colors).

-  *Although Illustrator 10.0 can open both 88 and 1.0/1.1 files, it cannot save back to those formats. If there is some obscure reason you need files in those formats, use Macromedia FreeHand, which does support saving files in those formats.*

Formats for Printing and Mobility: Adobe PDF and EPS

Illustrator might like the native Illustrator format best, but, of course, there are a lot of other "hosts" out there waiting to receive and use your artwork. In this section we'll look at the two most popular formats for getting your files seen and understood by the most universal audience possible. An EPS file is a top choice for placing into layout programs for high-end output. A PDF file is an excellent choice to be printed on its own, retaining the look and colors of your original no matter where it goes, but its utility goes way further than that, extending into the prepress and online realms as well.

Portable Document Format (PDF)

PDF files are becoming increasingly commonplace because you can view and print them from any machine that has the Adobe Acrobat Reader software, which is a free download from Adobe. You can trade PDF files with other Mac and Windows users, regardless of which program you used to create the original file or which fonts you used to format the text. PDF ensures that fonts, colors, and other elements look the same on any computer. Illustrator also allows you to edit text and graphic objects within the Acrobat document itself.

Further, PDF is becoming a strong player in prepress, or maybe I should say pre-prepress: It gives you the convenience of making it very easy to package files for remote printing. I'll cover PDF and its relation to prepress in detail in Chapter 24.

PDF has also become a popular choice for Help files and for Web documents that need to appear identically (and readily accessible) on all machines. PDF files on the Web can now also be indexed by search engines such as Yahoo.

Encapsulated PostScript (EPS)

The EPS format combines a pure PostScript description of an illustration with a preview so you can see what the image looks like on screen. Years ago EPS files were the only way to get Illustrator artwork into page-layout programs, and it still remains the best format for doing so. You can also store images in the EPS format. Although it's not the most efficient format for images in terms of file size, EPS images print faster and with less chance of problems, which is why the format is a favorite of high-end service bureaus.

Web Image Formats: GIF, JPEG, and PNG

Don't worry, I wouldn't forget to cover Web formats, without which, of course, no self-respecting twenty-first-century program would be able to hold up its head. While they all share the description of "popular, Web-friendly, raster format with some form of compression," each of the following has its own strengths and is best suited for a particular type of graphic.

Some of these formats may be available as a direct export option, but they are all available in the Save for Web dialog box, where you've got a lot more control over them anyway (as explained in Chapter 21).

Graphics Interchange Format (GIF89a)

Originally designed for transferring compressed graphics with a modem, GIF is the most extensively used graphics format on the Web. It supports up to 256 colors and LZW compression, as does TIFF (mentioned later). Although you can use the Export command to create GIF images (provided you actually take the time to install the plug-in, which has become optional), you'll get more bang for your buck by using the Save For Web command.

JPEG

Named after the folks who designed it—the Joint Photographic Experts Group—JPEG is the other widely used Web graphics format and is best used for compressing photographs and other *continuous-tone* images, in which the distinction between immediately neighboring pixels is slight. Any image that includes gradual color transitions qualifies for JPEG compression. JPEG is not well suited to screen shots, line drawings, and other high-contrast images. Like GIF images, you have much more control using the Save For Web command to create JPEG files.

Portable Network Graphics (PNG)

Designed to outperform and eventually replace GIF, PNG compression doesn't sacrifice quality and supports both 24-bit and 48-bit images. Thus, PNG files are larger than GIF, JPEG, or TIFF files (unless you are exporting a grayscale image), and are generally best suited for smaller images. Once again, although you can use the Export command to create PNG files, you have more control using the Save For Web dialog box. Although older browsers don't support PNG, the latest versions do.

Web Vector Formats: Shockwave Flash and SVG

With the Web formats already mentioned you have to worry, one way or another, about size and pixelation and loss, which is an inelegant way of leading up to saying, I am so happy that vector formats are finally gaining ground in the online scene. The small size and eminent scalability and fidelity of these formats will appeal both to your artistic side and your Webmaster side.

Shockwave Flash (SWF)

Shockwave Flash files can be both very intricate and very compact, and are creating a buzz in the Web graphics world. SWF animations are commonly called Flash files, but Flash (FLA) files are actually the native file format created by Macromedia Flash.

Time was, it was hard to get anyone from Adobe to even *use* the term SWF— Macromedia's proprietary format for Web animations. Now there are *two* Adobe products—Illustrator and LiveMotion—that create SWF animations.

I think it's a good business decision to conclude that if you can't beat 'em, join 'em. See Chapter 22 for more detailed information about SWF.

 Although Illustrator can create SWF animations, it doesn't let you create the buttons, actions, or scenes, nor add sounds that many finished SWF animations have. For that you'll need to use either Macromedia Flash or Adobe LiveMotion.

Scalable Vector Graphics (SVG) and Scalable Vector Graphics Compressed (SVGZ)

Welcome to the world of the future. SVG is a vector file format, designed for Web graphics creation, that can be coded directly into XML documents. SVG files offer many benefits over other formats: They are smaller than GIF or JPEG files, can be scaled up or down, can be made part of searches, and can handle animation. So why aren't there loads of SVG files posted on the Web? Because as of the publication of this book, most people don't have the browsers necessary to view SVG files, and I'm not sure when support for SVG will be incorporated into the main browsers. Meanwhile, Adobe's SVG plug-in is already available, so it's not too soon to play around with this format.

By the way, SVGZ is nothing more than the compressed version of SVG; but you can't edit SVGZ files using a text editor as you can with regular SVG files. See Chapter 22 for more on SVG.

TIFF and the Rest

Illustrator recognizes a dizzying number of graphics formats. Granted, some of these are starting to fade away, but there are probably a few Amiga users out there (and you know who you are) who will be happy to know that they're still supported, somehow, somewhere.

The remainder of this section describes formats you'll find in the Files of type (Show on the Mac) menu in the Open dialog box. If they've already been covered above, I won't repeat them. And since TIFF is by far the most common, I'll start with that, and then resort to alphabetical order so as not to play favorites. Many of these formats are found in both the Open and Export dialog boxes.

Tag Image File Format (TIFF)

Developed by Aldus (which is now part of Adobe) to standardize electronic images so you could easily import them into PageMaker, TIFF is one of the most widely supported formats across both the Macintosh and Windows platforms. Unlike PICT (discussed shortly), it can't handle object-oriented artwork, but it is otherwise unrestricted, supporting 16 million colors and virtually infinite resolutions.

Photoshop lets you apply LZW compression to a TIFF image, which substitutes frequently used strings of code with shorter equivalents. This makes the files smaller on disk without altering so much as a single pixel. Imaging professionals call this kind of compression *lossless*, because it preserves the integrity of each and every scanned color. Illustrator likewise supports LZW compression. It also opens both the Mac and Windows varieties of TIFF, so you never have to worry that your Photoshop images won't be compatible with Illustrator.

Amiga Interchange File Format (IFF)

The Amiga was an experiment in desktop computers pioneered by Commodore in the 1980s. Illustrator lets you open and save IFF files. IFF is the Amiga's all-around graphic format, serving much the same function as PICT on the Mac.

AutoCAD Drawing (DWG) and AutoCAD Interchange (DXF)

AutoCAD is a program used by engineers and architects. DWG is the standard file format created by AutoCAD. DXF is the tagged data format of those files.

BMP (Bitmap)

BMP is the native format for the cheesy little Paint utility that ships with Windows. Like PCX, BMP supports 16 million colors and high resolutions. If there is any way that you can avoid working with BMP files, do so. However, if you get a BMP image, rest assured that you can place it into your illustration.

Computer Graphics Metafile (CGM)

CGM is a vector-based file format that is used by a wide variety of programs. Think of CGM as the common language among different vector programs.

CorelDraw 5, 6, 7, 8, 9, 10 (CDR)

Although it can't export in the CorelDraw format, Illustrator does let you open files created in CorelDraw versions 5, 6, 7, 8, 9, and 10. Of course, not all effects and attributes will translate correctly when opened in Illustrator.

FilmStrip (FLM)

FilmStrip is the format used by Adobe Premiere and Adobe Photoshop. FilmStrip organizes frames into a long vertical strip. A gray bar separates each frame. Although Photoshop is a far more useful program for editing FilmStrip files, you can open and add to these files in Illustrator.

FreeHand 4, 5, 6, 7, 8, 9 (FH4, FH5, FH6, FH7, FH8, FH9)

Why would Adobe let you open FreeHand files in Illustrator? After all, isn't Macromedia FreeHand Illustrator's number one competitor? Well, yes, but that doesn't mean you shouldn't be able to translate FreeHand files into your own Illustrator artwork. Of course, don't expect all the FreeHand attributes to make it across the border. But it does help greatly when you're working desperately Sunday night and need to add the client's FreeHand logo into your Illustrator page.

Kodak Photo CD

Photo CD is the affordable photographic scanning technology that leaves some flatbed scanners in the dust. You can take a roll of undeveloped film, color negatives, or slides in to your local Photo CD dealer and have the photos scanned onto a CD-ROM at 2,048 by 3,072 pixels for about $2 per photo. Each CD holds 100 images, allowing you to acquire a library of images without taking up a lot of room in your home or office. Better yet, Photo CDs are designed to resist the ravages of time and last well into the twenty-second century (longer than any of the people using them now).

Metafiles (WMF, EMF)

Metafiles are actually the broad description of any files that contain commands that are used to draw graphics. Strictly speaking, Illustrator files are a type of metafile. WMF stands for *Windows Metafile,* the 16-bit files used by the Windows operating system to display pictures. EMF stands for *Enhanced Metafile,* a more advanced form of the Windows metafile, which contains 32-bit information.

PC Paintbrush (PCX)

PCX is the extension that PC Paintbrush assigns to images saved in its native file format. PCX used to be a very popular image file format, largely because PC Paintbrush has been around for so long. PCX images can include up to 16 million colors.

Photoshop 6 (PSD)

Illustrator can open and place images stored in Photoshop's native format. This means you do not have to save a copy of a Photoshop file as a TIFF or EPS to add it to Illustrator documents. Even better, you can open Photoshop files and any Photoshop layers can be converted into distinct images in Illustrator—complete with transparency and with masks applied.

PICT (PIC, PCT)

The PICT (*Macintosh Picture*) format is a graphics exchange format Apple designed more than ten years ago and has updated irregularly over time. You can save both object-oriented illustrations and photographic images in the PICT format, but the format isn't ideally suited to either. Frankly, TIFF is better for images, and EPS is better for illustrations. But that doesn't mean PICT doesn't have its uses; it's perfectly good for slide output and screen presentations.

Pixar (PXR)

When it wasn't busy creating award-winning blockbusters such as *Toy Story* original and sequel, *A Bug's Life,* and *Monsters Inc.,* Pixar created a few 3D graphics applications for the Mac, including MacRenderMan, ShowPlace, and Typestry. The company works its own 3D magic using mondo-expensive Pixar workstations. Illustrator can open a still image created on a Pixar machine.

Targa

TrueVision's Targa and NuVista video boards let you overlay computer graphics and animation onto live video. The effect is called *chroma keying* because typically a key color is set aside to let the live video show through. TrueVision designed the Targa format to support 32-bit images that include so-called *alpha channels* capable of displaying the live video. Illustrator doesn't know a video from a rodeo, but it can place a still Targa image.

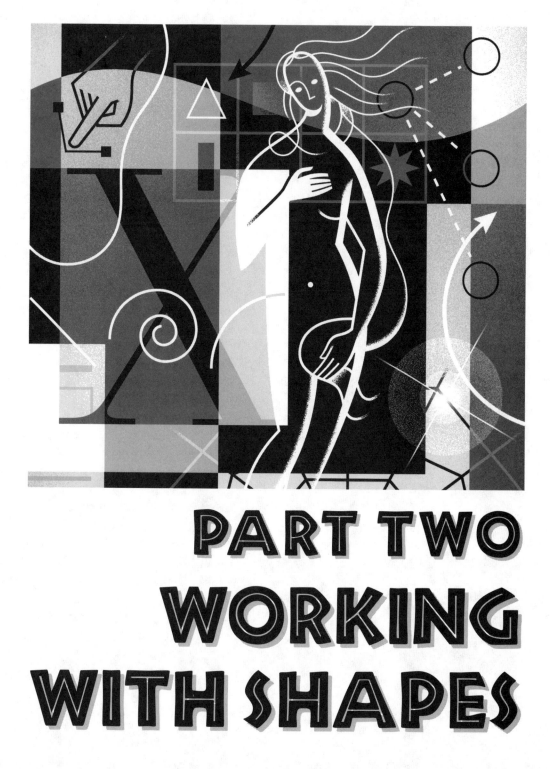

PART TWO
WORKING
WITH SHAPES

CREATING LINES AND SHAPES

Heaven help the experienced artist who encounters Illustrator for the first time. If you've drawn with pencil and paper, or sketched inside a painting program such as Photoshop, but you've never used Illustrator before, now is a good time to open your skull, remove your brain, and replace it upside down. Drawing with an illustration program is a very different adventure, and though it pains me to say it, your previous experience is as likely to impede your progress as to expedite it.

Drawing in Illustrator is actually a three-part process: You draw lines and shapes, you manipulate these objects and apply special effects, and you stack the objects one in front of another like pieces of paper in a collage.

This means the lines and shapes are forever flexible. You can select any object and edit, duplicate, or delete it, regardless of its age or location in the illustration. Pencil and paper do not give you this degree of control.

But Illustrator's flexibility comes at a price. It takes a lot of time and a fair amount of object-oriented savvy to create even basic compositions. There are no two ways about it—Illustrator is harder to learn and more cumbersome to use than conventional artists' tools.

In this chapter, I'll explain how to use Illustrator's most straightforward drawing tools. If you're feeling a little timid—particularly after this pessimistic introduction—have no fear. With this chapter in front of you, you'll be up and running within the hour. If you're the type who prefers to dive right in and investigate basic functions on your own, you can discover how these tools work, largely without my help. For you, this chapter explains options, suggests keyboard tricks, and points out small performance details that many novice and intermediate users overlook.

But before we start, let's look at how lines and shapes work inside Illustrator. You'll better understand how drawing tools work if you first understand what you're drawing.

Everything You Need to Know About Paths

Any line or shape you create in Illustrator is called a *path*. (Now that I've introduced that word I'll stop saying "lines or shapes" all the time; the one word comprises both.) Conceptually, a path is the same as a line drawn with a pencil. A path may start at one location and end at another, as in the case of an open line. Or it may meet back up with itself to form a closed shape. (A piece of string is an open path; a rubber band is a closed one.) Paths can range in length and complexity from tiny scratch marks to elaborate curlicues that loop around and intersect like tracks on a roller coaster.

The cartoon face in **Figure 5.1** contains 12 paths. Of the paths, ten are open (lines) and two are closed (shapes). So that you can clearly distinguish open from closed, I've given the lines thick outlines and the shapes thin ones. The closed paths surround the face, with the white shape mostly covering the gray one. The open paths represent the face's features.

Figure 5.1: A simple cartoon composed of open paths (thick outlines) and closed ones (thin).

All paths—whether open or closed—are made up of basic building blocks called *anchor points* (or just plain *points*). The simplest line is a connection between two anchor points—one at each end. (Anyone familiar with a little geometry will recognize this principle: A minimum of two points are needed to define a line.) But Illustrator can just as easily accommodate paths with hundreds of points, one connected to another like dots in a connect-the-dots puzzle.

Points and Segments

Figure 5.2 shows the points required to create the cartoon face. I've applied thinner outlines to the lines and made the shapes transparent so you can better see the square points. The most complicated path contains 11 points; the least complicated contains two.

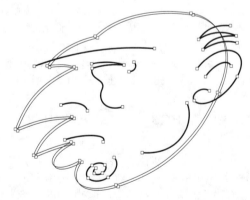

Figure 5.2: The small white squares represent the points needed to create the cartoon in Illustrator.

The bits of line between points are called *segments*. A segment can be straight, as if it were drawn against the edge of a ruler. A straight segment flows directly from one point to another in any direction. A segment may also curve, like the outline of an ellipse. Curved segments connect two points in an indirect manner, bending inward or outward along the way.

Strokes and Fills

Although a line drawn with a dull pencil is heavier than a line drawn with a sharpened one, the thickness of any line fluctuates depending on how hard you press the pencil tip to the page. In Illustrator, the thickness (or *weight*) of an out-line is absolutely consistent throughout the course of a path. In other words, different paths can have different weights, but the weight of each path is constant (as Figure 5.1 shows).

The thickness of an outline is called the *stroke*. In addition to changing the weight of the stroke, you can change its color. Strokes can be black, white, gray, or any of several million colorful variations.

 Just because the weight of each path is constant doesn't mean that the appearance of the path has to remain constant. Illustrator's brushes (discussed in Chapter 16) allow you to create strokes that have the appearance of different weights—even though the stroke weight remains constant.

You can also color the interior of a path by assigning it a *fill*. Like a stroke, a fill may be black, white, or any color. In Figure 5.1, the shapes that encircle the face are filled with white and gray. You can even assign a transparent fill, as in the case of the shapes in Figure 5.2.

Doing and Undoing

I said we were going to jump into the topic of drawing, but again, a detour, this time to offer a few words of assurance. *Don't worry about making mistakes,* because in Illustrator you can almost always fix them. Illustrator provides you with the ability to nullify the results of previous operations. In fact, Illustrator lets you retract several operations in a row. So when drawing anxiety sets in, remember this simple credo: *Undo, redo, relaxum.* That's Latin for "Chill, it's just a computer."

Undoing Consecutive Operations

Edit » Undo—or its universal shortcut, Ctrl+Z (Cmd-Z on the Mac)—lets you negate the last action performed. For example, if you move a point and decide you don't like how it looks, choose Edit » Undo Move and the new point disappears. More to the point (ha ha), Illustrator returns you to the exact moment before you moved the point. Better yet, you can *always* undo the last action, even if you have since clicked somewhere on the screen or performed some minor action that the command does not recognize.

You can even undo an operation performed prior to the most recent Save operation (although you cannot undo the Save command itself). For example, you can delete an element, save the illustration, then choose Edit » Undo Clear to make the element reappear. It's a real lifesaver.

Illustrator lets you undo up to 200 consecutive operations. This powerful feature takes a great deal of the worry out of using this awe-inspiring application. You can reverse even major blunders one step at a time.

To change the number of possible consecutive undos, choose the Edit » Preferences » Units & Undos command (Illustrator » Preferences » Units & Undos in Mac OS 10.1) to display the Units & Undo Preferences dialog box, and then enter a new value in the Minimum Undo Levels option box. The word *Minimum* appears in the option name because Illustrator permits you to undo as many operations as it can store in its undo buffer, regardless of the option value. The value merely sets aside space in your computer's memory so Illustrator can undo at least that many operations. As a result, you may be able to undo 200 path operations even if the Minimum Undo Levels value is set to 5.

 To monitor how many undo levels are available at any given time, select the Number of Undos option from the status bar pop-up menu in the lower-left corner of the illustration window.

After you exhaust the maximum number of undos, the Undo command appears dimmed in the Edit menu. Pressing Ctrl+Z (Cmd-Z on the Mac) will produce no effect until you perform a new operation. And remember, Illustrator can undo operations performed in the current session only. You can't undo something you did back before the most recent time you started Illustrator.

 Let's say you need to make a quick 156 undos. Are you going to press Ctrl+Z (Cmd-Z) once for each of the offending steps? Not even! Instead, you're going to press and hold these keys for a couple of seconds. This will let you start jumping back through the history of your drawing in units of five undos at a time. It's like watching a movie of your work coming undone.

Redoing Undo Operations

Just as you can undo as many as 200 consecutive actions, you can redo up to 200 consecutive undos by choosing Edit » Redo or pressing Ctrl+Shift+Z (Cmd-Shift-Z on the Mac). You can choose Redo only if the Undo command was the most recent operation performed; otherwise, Redo is dimmed. Also, if you undo a series of actions, perform a new series of actions, and then undo the new series of actions to the point where you had stopped undoing previously, you can't go back and redo the first series of undos. Instead, you can either continue to undo from where you left off or redo the later set of actions.

 What if you want to make a bunch of quick redos? Same as the preceding tip, except that now you can see your artwork come together in fast motion by holding Ctrl+Shift+Z. This is especially fun to do right after you've done 200 undos.

Reverting to the Last Saved File

If your modifications to an illustration are a total botch, you can revert to the last saved version of the file by choosing File » Revert or pressing F12. It's like closing a file, electing not to save changes, and reopening the file in one step. You probably won't need this command very often, but keep in mind that it's there when things go terribly wrong.

If you haven't done anything to an illustration since you last saved it, or if you've never saved the drawing, the File » Revert command is dimmed.

And now, without further ado—I really mean it this time—let's start drawing.

Creating Simple Shapes

Illustrator offers six tools for creating rectangles, ellipses, and other basic, closed shapes. The default tool you see in the toolbox is the rectangle (fourth row from the top, on the right); the others are all alternatives in the same slot. You select them by clicking and holding on the rectangle tool slot, as shown in **Figure 5.3**. Now simply drag to the right until your tool of choice is highlighted.

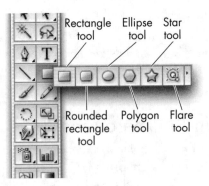

Figure 5.3: Illustrator offers five different shape tools.

 Holding the Alt key (Option key on the Mac) as you click the tool in the toolbox will toggle you through the tools in that slot.

Drawing a Rectangle

To draw a rectangle, select the rectangle tool and then click and drag inside the drawing area. The point at which you start dragging sets one corner of the rectangle; the point at which you release sets the opposite corner, as shown in **Figure 5.4**. The two remaining corners line up vertically or horizontally with their neighbors. (Illustrator creates a fifth point called the *center point* in the center of the shape. If you move the rectangle or change its size, Illustrator repositions the center point so it remains in the center of the shape.)

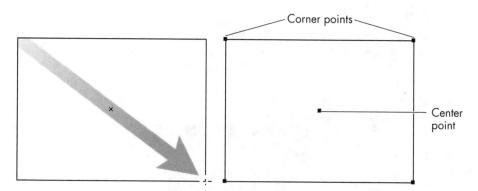

Figure 5.4: Drag from one corner to the opposite corner to draw a rectangle.

You can also use the rectangle tool as follows:

- If you press the Alt (Option on the Mac) key while drawing with the rectangle tool, the start point of your drag marks the center of the rectangle. As before, the release point becomes a corner point.

 You can press and release Alt or Option in mid-drag to switch between dragging from corner to corner and center to center. Give it a try.

- Shift-drag with the rectangle tool to draw a perfect square. You can press and release the Shift key in mid-drag to switch between drawing a rectangle or a square. Isn't it great how Illustrator lets you change your mind?

- Shift+Alt-drag (Shift-Option-drag on the Mac) with the rectangle tool to create a square from center to corner.

- Press the tilde (~) key while dragging with the rectangle tool to create a series of rectangles, all of which border on a common point. Press Alt+~ (Option-~ on the Mac) while you drag to create a series of concentric rectangles.

- Press the spacebar while dragging to move the rectangle rather than change its size. When you get it positioned properly, release the spacebar and continue dragging or release.

Drawing by the Numbers

You can also enter the dimensions of a rectangle numerically. Click with the rectangle tool—that's right, just click inside the drawing area—to display the dialog box shown in **Figure 5.5**. Here you can enter values for the Width and Height options. After you press Enter (Return on the Mac) or click OK, Illustrator creates a rectangle to your exact specifications.

Figure 5.5: Click with the rectangle tool to enter the exact width and height of your rectangle.

Want to create a square? You could enter the same value in both option boxes, but frankly that's too much effort. Just enter the desired size into the Width option box, and then click the word Height to duplicate the value. Or vice versa.

Because the Rectangle dialog box doesn't give any placement options, the point at which you clicked with the tool serves as the upper-left corner point of the shape. If you want the click point to be the center of the shape, Alt-click (Option-click on the Mac).

You'll see this information scattered elsewhere, but it may help you to know that every shape tool has a dialog box that functions similarly. Of course, the options are different based on the shape itself, but in terms of how it works, where and when it draws a shape, and how it saves the settings, they all work the same, and the point on the page where you click to pop up the dialog box will be the starting point for your shape.

Notice that both option boxes in Figure 5.5 include the letters *pt*, an abbreviation for points (1/72 inch). Font size is commonly measured in points. This refers to the unit of measure you set using the General Units option in the Units & Undo Preferences dialog box. The unit of measure can alternatively be inches (in), millimeters (mm) or centimeters (cm), or pixels (px). You can enter spaces between the number and the measurement abbreviation, but you don't have to. If you enter a value without an abbreviation, Illustrator assumes the active unit of measurement—by default, points.

The exception to this is when you have selected Picas for the General Units option and then elected to activate the Numbers Without Units Are Points check box—also found within the Units & Undo Preferences dialog box. Illustrator will then assume that any numbers you enter into the Rectangle dialog box (or any other dialog box for that matter) should be interpreted as points and not as picas.

 To make life a little easier for you, all of the numeric fields in Illustrator allow for automatic unit conversion. For example, if the default units in your document are set to points but your client barks, "Quick, make a box 4 centimeters square," you can just enter 4 cm and Illustrator will automatically convert it to equivalent points.

You use the Rectangle dialog box only to create new shapes, not to modify existing ones. If you want to change the size of a rectangle you've already drawn, you can use any of the transformation options covered in Chapter 9. However, the easiest option is to use Illustrator's Transform palette (**Figure 5.6**). Make sure the rectangle is selected so that its points are visible. (Use the arrow tool to click the shape if it is not selected.) Then, if the Transform palette is hidden, choose Window » Transform or press Shift-F8. Next, enter new values in the W and H option boxes. Illustrator resizes the rectangle automatically.

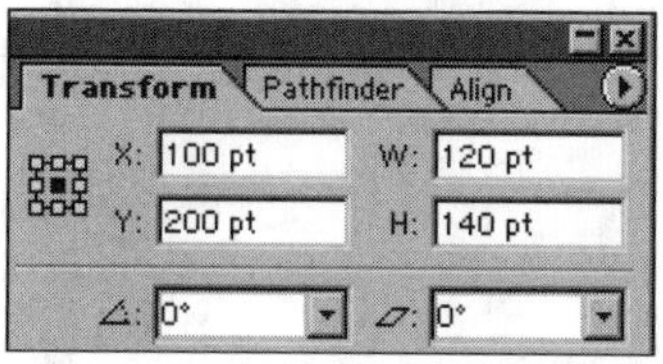

Figure 5.6: The Transform palette offers the easiest way to change the dimensions of an existing rectangle—by modifying the W and H values.

The reference points on the left side of the Transform palette let you choose the point around which the transformation should take place. The default position for the reference point is the center of the object. If you click the reference point icon, you can change that position to top or bottom, left or right, or side center.

Rounding off a Rectangle's Corners

To draw a rectangle with rounded corners, select the rounded rectangle tool from the shape tools slot and drag away. Illustrator creates a shape with eight points—two along each side with a curved segment around each corner, as in **Figure 5.7**.

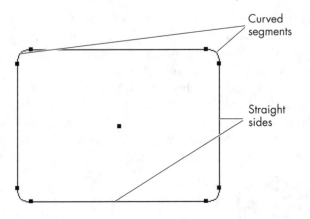

Curved
segments

Straight
sides

*Figure 5.7: Illustrator uses
curved segments to join
straight sides in a rounded
rectangle.*

You control the roundness of the corners by changing the Corner Radius value in the General Preferences dialog box. You can also click with the rounded rectangle tool and enter a value for the Corner Radius option in the Rounded Rectangle dialog box. The option in these two places functions identically, but of course it's more efficient to use the Rounded Rectangle dialog box.

Just how does the Corner Radius value work? As you may recall from your school days, radius is the distance from the center of a circle to any point on its outline. You can think of a rounded corner as being one quarter of a circle, as shown in the first example of **Figure 5.8**.

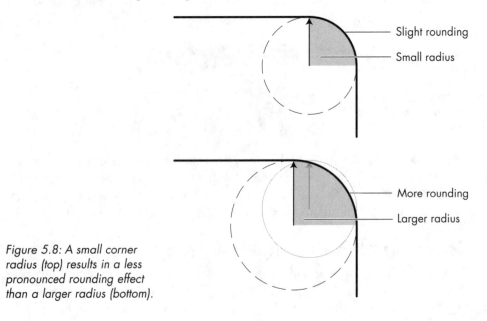

Slight rounding

Small radius

More rounding

Larger radius

*Figure 5.8: A small corner
radius (top) results in a less
pronounced rounding effect
than a larger radius (bottom).*

A less scientific way of changing the roundness of the corners is to "eyeball" it while you're actually drawing the rectangle. As you're dragging the shape with the rounded rectangle tool, use your arrow keys to modify the radius. The up and down arrow keys will alter the value incrementally; the left and right arrow keys will take the radius to its minimum and maximum, respectively.

There's no easy command to change a corner radius once your rectangle's complete, but don't worry—should you desire to achieve this lofty goal, there's a live effect that can help you change the roundness of existing corners. You'll find out all about it in Chapter 19.

Drawing an Ellipse

When it comes to drawing ellipses and circles, the trusty ellipse tool is all you need. Simply click-and-drag along a diagonal line to form graceful and sublime rings of spherical excellence. Your ellipse fills the imaginary rectangle you create as you drag.

If you're an old-time Illustrator user, you may remember that many years ago (before version 8) Illustrator drew ellipses from arc to arc with the imaginary rectangle inside the ellipse—not outside as it does now. But because the folks at Adobe know that old habits die hard, Illustrator still lets you draw the old way. Start your ellipse as you would normally—by dragging with the tool. Once you're into the drag, press the Ctrl key (Cmd key on the Mac). The ellipse will resize accordingly. Be sure to hold the Ctrl or Cmd key through the completion of the drag.

In most other respects, the ellipse tool works much like the rectangle tool.

- Alt-drag (Option-drag on the Mac) with the ellipse tool to create an ellipse outward from the center. As always, the release point becomes the middle of an arc, determining the size and shape of the ellipse.

- Shift-drag to draw a perfect circle. Alt+Shift-drag (Option-Shift-drag on the Mac) to draw a circle from the center point outward.

- Press the tilde (~) key while dragging with the ellipse tool to create a series of ellipses. Press Alt+~ (Option-~ on the Mac) while you drag to create a series of concentric ellipses.

- Press the spacebar while dragging to move the ellipse rather than change its size. When you get it positioned properly, release the spacebar and continue dragging or release.

Click in the drawing area to bring up the Ellipse dialog box. It contains Width and Height options for specifying the width and height of the shape. The shape aligns to your click point by the middle of the upper-left arc. If you Alt-click (Option-click on the Mac) with the ellipse tool, the ellipse aligns by its center.

 Use the W and H values in the Transform palette to change the width and height of an ellipse that you've already drawn.

Simple Shapes at an Angle

When drawing a shape with the rectangle, rounded rectangle, or ellipse tool, you may find that your path rotates at an odd angle, as demonstrated in **Figure 5.9**. Don't worry—you aren't misusing the tool, Illustrator isn't broken, and you don't need an eye exam. Someone has gone and changed the Constrain Angle value in the General Preferences dialog box.

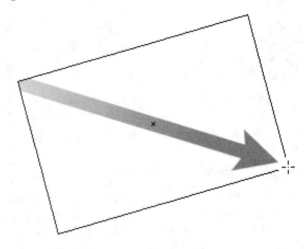

Figure 5.9: The result of drawing a rectangle after rotating the constraint axes by 15 degrees.

The *constraint axes* control the angles at which you move and transform objects when pressing the Shift key. But they also control the creation of rectangles, ellipses, and text blocks. If the Constrain Angle value is set to anything besides 0, Illustrator rotates a rectangle or an ellipse to that angle as you draw. The Constrain Angle value has no impact on the creation of stars, polygons, or spirals whatsoever—even if you hold down the Shift key while drawing one of these shapes, they will still align to the horizontal axis despite the option box's value.

If someone has indeed reset your Constrain Angle, choose Edit » Preferences » General or press Ctrl+K (Cmd-K on the Mac, or choose Illustrator » Preferences »

General in Mac OS 10.1). Enter 0 into the Constrain Angle option box and press Enter (Return on the Mac). Someone ought to put a password on that thing!

Drawing a Regular Polygon

A regular polygon is a shape with multiple straight sides—each side is identical in length and meets its neighbors at the same angle. An equilateral triangle is a regular polygon, as is a square. Other examples include pentagons, hexagons, octagons, and just about any other shape with a *gon* in its name. **Figure 5.10** shows a few regular polygons for your visual edification.

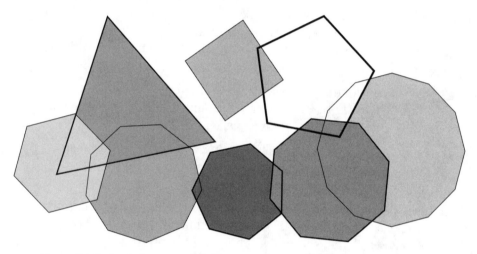

Figure 5.10: A whole mess of regular polygons, ranging from 3 to 12 sides.

To draw a polygon, select the polygon tool and drag in the drawing area. You always draw a polygon from the middle outward, whether you press the Alt key (Option key on the Mac) or not. The direction of your drag determines the orientation of the shape.

 By default, Illustrator draws hexagons (six-sided shapes) with the polygon tool. You can change the number of sides while dragging with the polygon tool by pressing the up and down arrow keys. The up arrow key adds a side; the down arrow key deletes one.

Another way to change the number of sides (I've already hinted about this earlier in the chapter) is to click with the polygon tool in the drawing area. Illustrator displays the Polygon dialog box, which lets you specify a Radius value and a number of sides.

The **Radius** value is the distance from the center of the shape to any corner point in the shape. Therefore, a regular polygon with a radius of 100 points would fit entirely inside a circle with a radius of 100 points.

 The **Sides** value can be anything from 3 to 1000. Shapes with more than 20 sides look like circles with bumps.

As always, the values you enter into the Polygon dialog box affect all future polygons you create. You cannot make changes to an existing polygon using the Polygon dialog box. If you want to change the size of a polygon, use the scale tool, as discussed in Chapter 9. To change the orientation of a polygon, use the rotate tool, also covered in Chapter 9. But if you want to change the number of sides, you have to delete the polygon and redraw it.

Following are a few more (marginally useful) things you can do with the polygon tool:

 Shift-drag with the tool to constrain a polygon's orientation so the bottom side is horizontal. (This is the same way Illustrator draws a shape when you click with the polygon tool.)

 Press the spacebar while dragging to move the shape rather than change its size. When you get the polygon positioned properly, release the spacebar and continue dragging or release.

 Press the tilde (~) key while dragging to create a series of concentric polygons. This is a singularly bizarre technique. It's great for getting oohs and ahs from your friends, but it's rarely practical.

Drawing a Star

Illustrator lets you draw regular stars, in which each spike looks just like its neighbors. To draw a star, drag with the star tool, which is the fifth tool in the rectangle tool slot. Illustrator draws the shape from the center outward.

You can modify the performance of the star tool by pressing Ctrl+Alt (Cmd-Option on the Mac) as you drag. But to explain adequately what you're doing, we need a small geometry lesson. A star is made up of two sets of points, one at the points where the spikes meet and one at the tips of the spikes. These points revolve around one of two imaginary circles, which form the inner and outer radiuses of the star, as pictured in **Figure 5.11**.

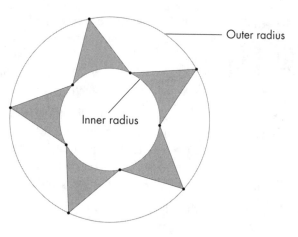

Outer radius

Inner radius

Figure 5.11: The inner and outer points in a star revolve around two imaginary circles.

When you drag with the star tool, Illustrator scales the two radiuses proportionately, so that the inner radius is exactly half the outer radius (as in Figure 5.11). If you don't like this particular arrangement, you can gain more control in the following ways:

- Press Ctrl (Cmd on the Mac) while dragging to scale the outer radius independently of the inner radius. So long as the Ctrl (or Cmd) key is down, the inner radius remains fixed. You can even drag the outer radius inside the inner radius to make the outer radius the inner radius. Then you can adjust the inner radius while the outer one is fixed. To resize both radiuses proportionally again, release Ctrl (or Cmd) and keep dragging.

- Alt-drag (Option-drag on the Mac) to snap the inner radius into precise alignment so that opposite spikes align with each other. The top sides of the left and right sides of a five-sided star, for example, form a straight line.

- Because Ctrl and Alt (Cmd and Option on the Mac) have mutually exclusive effects on a star, they cannot be in effect at the same time. If you do hold down both of these command keys, Alt (Option on the Mac) takes precedence.

 Let's say you used the Ctrl key (Cmd key on the Mac) in conjunction with the star tool and went way too far with the outer radius, so that you could draw only stars consisting of a number of spindly arms emerging from the center. You would probably have a heck of a time correcting this problem with just the Ctrl (or Cmd) key. Here's the solution: Click and drag with the star tool. While dragging, press Ctrl+Alt (Cmd-Option on the Mac) simultaneously. The star will return to a more regular shape.

As with the polygon tool, you can add or delete spikes from a star by pressing the up or down arrow key in mid-drag. You can also move a star in progress by pressing the spacebar or orient the star upright by pressing Shift. And—not to overlook the least important tip of all—you can press the tilde (~) key to create concentric stars.

Probably the funkiest of all the hidden tool tips is that in addition to creating a regular star, the star tool lets you draw a double star. That's the type of star where the lines are visible across each other—not that there's a huge demand for such a shape, but it is an interesting variation on the traditional star.

To draw a double star, here's what you need to do:

1. Drag with the star tool and hold down the mouse button throughout these steps.

2. Press the down arrow key until you have a three-sided star, the fewest number of sides permitted.

3. Tap both the Ctrl and Alt keys (Cmd and Option keys on the Mac).

4. Press the up arrow key until you've reached the desired number of sides. Once you're at four sides, you'll see the double star configuration.

5. Adjust the double star's size, placement, and orientation as you would a regular star's—with the Ctrl (or Cmd) key, Shift key, and spacebar, respectively.

To take full advantage of its duality, be sure to press the Ctrl key (Cmd key on the Mac) while you're drawing a double star. This allows you to vary the size of one star independently of the other.

 If you tire of the double-star configuration and want to return to drawing more traditional stars, you simply need to tap both the Ctrl and Alt keys (Cmd and Option keys on the Mac) once again. The star tool will then draw stars as usual.

Click in the drawing area with the star tool to bring up the Star dialog box. As shown in **Figure 5.12**, this dialog box permits two Radius values, one for the outer radius and one for the inner. You can also specify the number of spikes. (Illustrator calls these "points," so don]t confuse them with the points between segments. There are twice as many points as spikes—for example, a path with five spikes has ten points.)

Figure 5.12: You'll get a dialog box to specify the precise inner and outer radius values by clicking with the star tool.

The Flare Tool

 The flare tool, a new member of the drawing tools, definitely stands heads above its more mundane neighbors. This fascinating tool lets you create effects such as lens flares, shown in **Figure 5.13**, by making a flare object consisting of a center, a halo and rays and rings. The great thing about the flare is that it is photo realistic, yet totally vector based in its structure. Because the flare is live, it can also be edited and adjusted to your heart's content. The flare tool comes equipped with lots of options that can be manipulated to produce numerous variations.

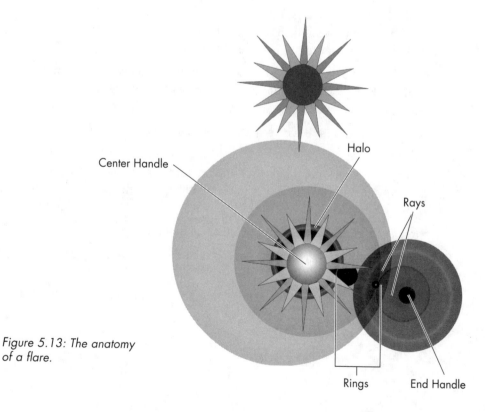

Figure 5.13: The anatomy of a flare.

Creating Flares

To create a quick flare using the default settings, simply select the flare tool, press Alt (Opt on a Mac) and click where you want to the flare to appear. No fuss, no muss. It's amazing something so complex looking can be so easy to create.

 Although it isn't mandatory, you may want to create your flares over an object. That way it appears there's a reason for the flare and it's not just an orphan effect floating around looking for a place to shine.

To create a flare with different settings, select the flare tool and click where you want your flare. Make your setting adjustments in the Flare Options dialog box that appears and click OK. If after making your adjustments you decide you would rather stick with the default settings, double-click the flare tool, and in the Flare Options dialog box, press Alt (Opt on a Mac) and click on the Reset button.

If you're more of a control freak, you'll probably want to create your very own flare. Let's walk through those steps.

1. Position the flare tool where you want the center handle to be located.

2. Press and drag to establish the size of the center, the size of the halo, and the length and rotation angle of the rays.

   If you press the Shift key while you are dragging, you can constrain the angle of the rays. Press the up or down arrows to add or subtract rays. And press the Ctrl (Cmd on a Mac) to hold the flare's center in place.

3. Release your mouse once you've reached the desired size of your halo and rays.

4. Unlike the other drawing tools, the Flare tool is a two-step tool. Press and drag again from the center (although it doesn't necessarily have to be the center) to create the rings.

   Press the tilde (~) key to redraw the rings in a random format.

5. Release your mouse wherever you want to the end handle to be located.

   Put on your sunglasses and admire your bright and shiny new flare.

Editing Flares

If you aren't satisfied with your flare, you can easily edit it by selecting the flare object and double-clicking the flare tool. In the Flare Options dialog box, change your settings and then click OK. You can also drag the center or end handles with the flare tool to change the length or angle of the flare.

If you need to do some serious editing, expand the flare by choosing Object >> Flare, which will convert all the flare components into editable chunks.

Most of the options in the Flare Options dialog box, shown in **Figure 5.14**, are self-explanatory, but here's a little information on those that aren't.

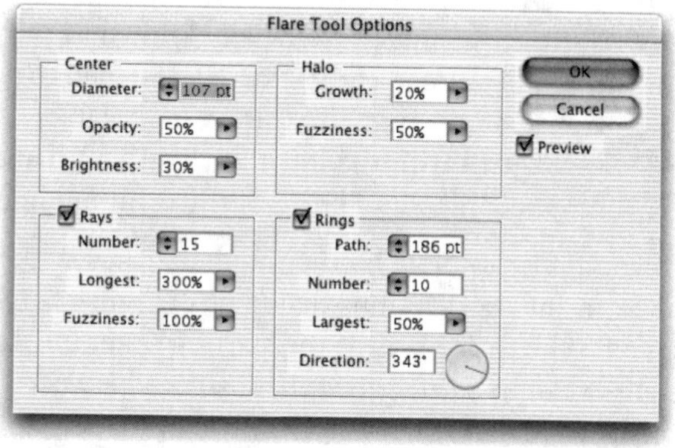

Figure 5.14: The Flare Options dialog box offers settings to customize your flare.

- Fuzziness refers to the feathering effect of the halo and rays. A value of 0 will give sharper edges, while a value of 100 will give a wispier, fuzzier look.

- The % growth of the halo is in reference to the overall size of the flare.

- The path of the rings refers to the distance of the path between the center handle and the end handle.

Lines, Arcs, Spirals, and Grids

If you've been using Illustrator in previous incarnations, you'll have found ways of drawing whatever shapes you need (and it's amazing how many shapes you find you actually do need). Illustrator 10 has added a few new utensils that many users will appreciate for their ease of use—the line segment tool, the arc tool, the rectangular grid tool, and the polar grid tool. Now these join company with the spiral tool (as shown in **Figure 5.15**) to help you make short work of many of your drawing tasks.

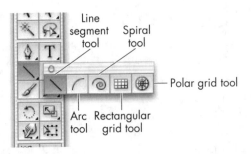

Figure 5.15: Drawing just got easier again.

Drawing a Line

The line tool (officially known as the line segment tool) is a new feature in Illustrator 10 designed to make quick work of drawing simple lines. To draw a line segment, simply drag in the drawing area with the line tool. The length and direction of your drag determines the length and angle of the resulting line.

If you prefer to draw by the numbers, click with the line tool to bring up the Line Segment Tool Options dialog box (**Figure 5.16**). The point at which you click with the tool serves as the starting point for the line. Enter a value in the Length option box to specify the distance between the starting and ending point. You can be very precise—up to 1/100 of a point. Enter an Angle value from 0 to 360 degrees to determine the direction the line segment will travel from the starting point. Click the Fill Line check box if you want lines to be assigned the current fill color (otherwise, they will have no fill color). I can't imagine why you might want your line to have a fill, but you never know.

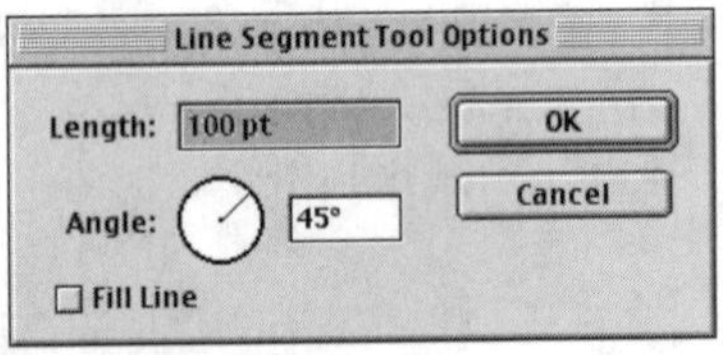

Figure 5.16: The Line Segment Tool Options dialog box lets you specify the length and angle of your line.

The line tool, like the shape tools, offers several additional options.

- Alt-drag (Option-drag on the Mac) with the tool to draw a line from the center outward in both directions.

- To move the line as you draw it, press the spacebar.

- Press the tilde key (~) to create a series of line segments as you drag with the tool.

Shift-drag to constrain a line so that it's perpendicular to, parallel to, or at a 45-degree angle from the horizontal and vertical axes. Such lines are sometimes called *orthogonal*.

Drawing an Arc

    An arc is simply a curved line segment—you can think of it as one quarter of an ellipse. In the old days, the only way to draw and arc was to pick up the somewhat laborious pencil tool (discussed later in this chapter) or the even more laborious pen tool (covered in Chapter 6). But Illustrator 10 changes all that with the introduction of the new arc tool, which provides an easier and more convenient way to tackle your basic arc drawing tasks.

To draw an arc, select the arc tool—it's the second tool in the line tool slot—click at the point where you want the arc to begin, and drag in the drawing area. The length and direction of your drag determines the length and direction of the arc segment.

To draw an arc with specific properties, click with the arc tool to display the dialog box pictured in **Figure 5.17**. Here's how the various options work.

    To see a dynamic preview of the slope of an arc, double-click on the arc tool in the toolbox.

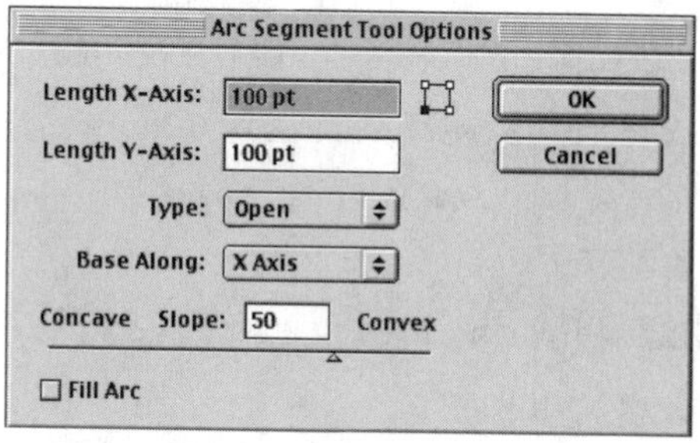

Figure 5-17: Click once with the arc tool in the drawing area to bring up this dialog box, where you can fine-tune your arc settings.

Arc Segment Tool Options

Length X-Axis:	100 pt
Length Y-Axis:	100 pt
Type:	Open
Base Along:	X Axis
Concave Slope:	50 Convex
☐ Fill Arc	

OK

Cancel

    Length: Type the width and height of the arc in the Length X-Axis and Length Y-Axis option boxes, respectively. The box with four points to the right of the Length X-Axis option determines the origin point of the arc.

    Type: This option lets you select whether you would like the arc to be drawn as an open or closed path. If you choose Closed, the arc will appear similar to a piece of pie.

- **Base Along:** Use this pop-up menu to specify the direction of the arc segment. Choose X Axis or Y Axis to draw the base along the X (horizontal) or Y (vertical) axis, respectively.

- **Slope:** This option lets you determine whether your arc curves inward (concave) or outward (convex) and to what degree. Drag the slider at the bottom of the box or enter a value between –100 for concave to 100 for convex (0, of course, being a straight line). This is shown in **Figure 5.18**.

- **Fill Arc:** When checked, this option fills the internal area of the arc with the current fill pattern. When unchecked, the arc has only a stroke.

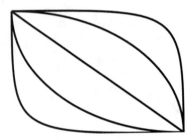

Figure 5.18: Arcs of the same length, drawn from the same point, with slopes of (from left to right) –100, –50, 0 (for reference), 50, and 100. These arcs are all drawn with their base along the X axis.

Like the other line and shape tools, the arc tool responds to several keyboard modifiers.

- Alt-drag (Option-drag on the Mac) with the arc tool to draw an arc that extends from both sides of the point clicked.

- If you want to move the arc as you draw it, hold the spacebar.

- Press and hold the tilde key (~) as you drag to create multiple arc segments.

- To switch between drawing a concave and convex arc press the X key.

- Shift-drag with the arc tool to constrain the proportions of the arc so it is even on both sides of the origin point.

Creating a Spiral

Spirals don't exactly lend themselves to a wide range of drawing situations, but I must admit, I've found they sometimes come in very handy. (In fact, the spiral tool made the lovely chin dimple in Figure 5.1.)

But wouldn't you know it, spirals are one of the most difficult things to create in Illustrator. Oh sure, you can draw them easily enough; just drag with the spiral tool and the spiral grows outward from its center. But controlling the number of times the spiral wraps around itself requires a fair amount of dexterity and reasoning.

Let's start with the Spiral dialog box (**Figure 5.19**). To access this dialog box, click with the spiral tool—the third tool in the line tool slot—inside the drawing area. The Spiral dialog box contains the following options:

- **Radius:** Enter a Radius value to specify the size of the spiral. This represents the distance from the center of the shape to the last point on the spiral.

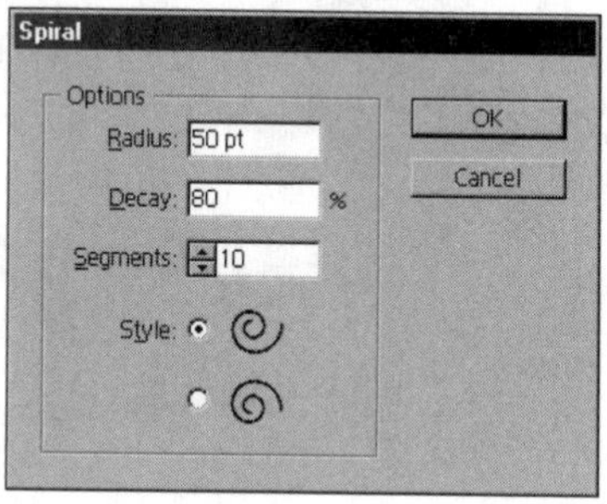

Figure 5.19: The Spiral dialog box allows you to specify the Radius and Decay of the spiral.

- **Decay:** The Decay value determines how quickly the spiral loops in on itself. **Figure 5.20** demonstrates the effects of several decays. As you can see, small values result in short loops. Larger values—up to 99.99 percent—result in more tightly packed spirals.

- *Here's where things get weird. If you enter a value of 100 into the Decay option box, the spiral coils on top of itself, creating a circle. Values above 100 (up to 150 percent) turn the spiral inside out, looping it in the opposite direction and outside the radius, as in the bottom two examples of Figure 5.18.*

- **Segments:** Enter the number of curved segments between points into the Segments option box. Each segment represents a quarter coil in the spiral.

- **Style:** Select a radio button to coil the spiral counterclockwise or clockwise. (This assumes a Decay value of less than 100 percent. If the Decay is higher than 100, the spiral coils in the opposite direction.)

By itself, an increased Segments value may not result in more coils. Strange, but true. You have to raise both the Decay and Segments values to wind the coils more tightly. This is because Illustrator drops segments when Decay is too low to accommodate them.

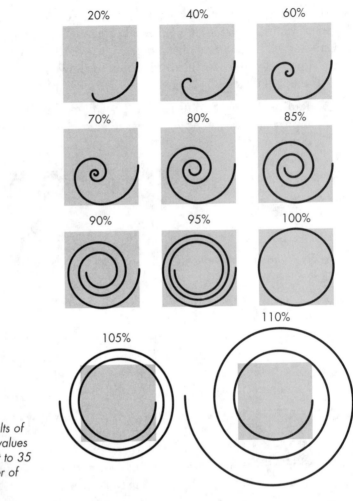

Figure 5.20: The results of changing the Decay values while the radius is set to 35 points and the number of segments is set to 10.

That's a lot of talk about making spirals, but we're not quite done. I wouldn't be giving you the whole story if I didn't let you know that you can modify your coils without resorting to the Spiral dialog box. It takes a little getting used to, but it works. Here's how.

- When you drag with the spiral tool, you're changing the radius and rotating the spiral around. You'll want to get that straight before you go any further.

- Press the Ctrl key (Cmd key on the Mac) while dragging to modify the decay. Drag outward to lower the decay; drag inward to raise it. If you drag inward past one of the coils, the spiral flips on itself, indicating a decay of more than 100 percent.

Don't press the Ctrl or (Cmd key) the moment you start dragging or you'll pop the Decay value to some ridiculously low number such as 7 percent. Start dragging and then press Ctrl (or Cmd) in mid-drag. Release the key to modify the radius again.

 Press the up or down arrow keys while dragging with the spiral tool to raise or lower the number of segments in a spiral.

 You can also change the number of segments by pressing the Alt or Option key. Alt-drag (Option-drag on the Mac) toward the center of the spiral to delete segments and reduce the radius. Drag outward to both add segments and increase the radius, thus better accommodating the new coils.

 If you press both Ctrl and Alt (Cmd and Option on the Mac) simultaneously, Ctrl (or Cmd) takes precedence (unlike with the star tool, where Alt or Option is dominant).

 You can also press the spacebar while dragging with the spiral tool to reposition the path. Shift-drag to constrain the spiral to some 45-degree angle.

 As if it's not goofy enough to be able to create concentric polygons and stars, you can create a series of spirals by pressing the tilde (~) key as you drag. Just the thing to embellish the next annual report!

Getting on the Grid

Until now, grids in Illustrator were a behind-the-scenes element for helping control where things go on your pages. With these new shape tools, they've graduated to design elements. Whenever you have to create charts, maps, or other serious grown-up things like that, the rectangular and polar grid tools will make it a lot easier. And since by now you're an old pro at using the other shape tools, the controls for these will be practically second nature. But we'll run through them anyway.

Drawing a Rectangular Grid

Simplest first: To draw a rectangular grid, select the rectangular grid tool—the fourth option in the line tool slot in the toolbox—and click and drag diagonally.

To draw a rectangular grid with specific properties, just click in the drawing area with the rectangular grid tool to display the dialog box pictured in **Figure 5.21**. Here's what the various options do.

 The point where you click in the drawing area to activate the dialog box also sets the origin point for the shape you're about to create; this works with the grid tool and all of the other drawing tools as well.

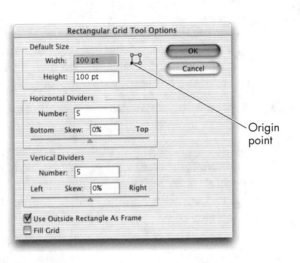

Figure 5.21: Welcome to the Rectangular Grid Tool Options dialog box. The location where you click the mouse determines the starting point for your object, but the Origin Point proxy establishes which way it goes from there.

- **Default Size** determines width and height of the entire grid.

- **Horizontal Dividers** sets the number of rules you want to have *between* the top and bottom of the grid.

- **Vertical Dividers** sets the number of rules you want to have *between* the side edges of the grid.

- **Skew** bunches up the dividers toward one side or the other of the grid.

- **Use Outside Rectangle As Frame** creates a separate rectangle to be the outside edge (and fill, if specified) of the grid.

- **Fill Grid** applies the current fill color to the grid; if this option is not checked, no fill is applied.

Now it's time to tell you what extra controls you can use via keyboard commands while you're dragging to draw a grid.

- Alt (Option on the Mac) extends the grid outward from all sides of the origin point.

- Shift-drag constrains the grid to a square.

- Shift+Alt (Shift-Option on the Mac) constrains the grid to a square as it extends from the origin point.

- The spacebar temporarily suspends the act of drawing and allows you to move the whole grid.

- The tilde (~) key creates multiple concentric grids as you draw.

Finally, as with the spiral tool, there are even more things you can do to change the composition and appearance of your grid as you create it.

- To add or remove horizontal lines, use the up or down arrow keys.

- To add or remove vertical lines, use the right or left arrow keys.

- To increase or decrease the skew value of the horizontal dividers by 10%, press the V key or F key, respectively.

- To increase or decrease the skew value of the vertical dividers by 10%, press the C key or X key, respectively.

Drawing polar grids

Bull's-eye! When's the last time you had to draw concentric circles with radial dissecting lines? It's so much easier to let Illustrator do it than go the painstaking manual route—even with the new line tool.

To draw a polar grid, select the polar grid shape tool (finally, we come to the last tool in this slot!) and click-and-drag diagonally.

To set up your polar grid with specific properties, you guessed it, just click on your page with the polar grid tool selected to bring up the Polar Grid Tool Options dialog box. Here are the options available in the dialog box, as shown in **Figure 5.22**.

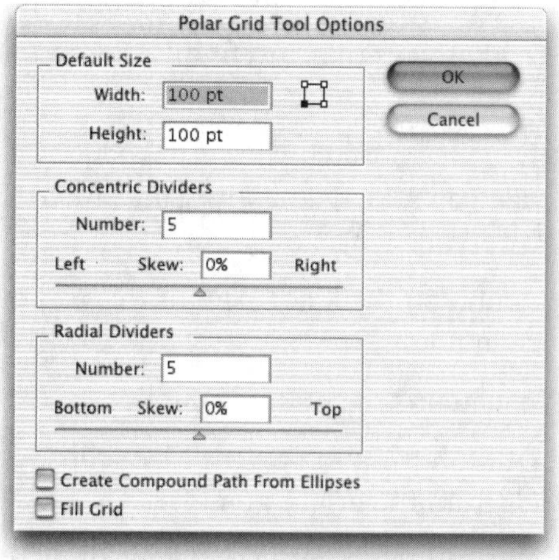

Figure 5.22: The Polar Grid Options dialog box.

- **Default Size** allows you to set the width and height values for the entire grid.

- The **Origin Point** icon sets the direction, or maybe better to call it the trajectory, in which the grid is drawn.

- **Concentric Dividers** is the number of circular divisions you want in the grid (not counting the outside edge).

- **Left/Right Skew** is how much the radial dividers bunch in their spacing around the circle, like the hands on a clock. (Be forewarned: yes, this Skew setting belongs with the Radial Dividers option, not the Concentric one—living proof that even really good programs have bugs. These features work fine; the skews are just reversed from where they should be, at least in the debut version of Illustrator 10.) Zero is, of course, for even spacing.

- **Radial Dividers** is the number of radial dividers or "rays" you want between the center and the circumference of the grid.

- **Bottom/Top Skew** is how much the concentric circles get bunched up toward the inner or outer edges, respectively, of the grid. (Once again, this feature should go with Concentric dividers; the documentation correctly describes how these functions work together. Just remember to reverse the skew settings!)

- **Create Compound Path From Ellipses** converts the concentric circles into a separate compound path and fills every other circle. The look will remind you of that old tractor-fed computer paper with alternating green and white stripes.

- **Fill Grid** applies the current fill color to the grid; if unchecked, no fill is applied.

And, finally, you can watch your grid change before your very eyes, live and in person, while you're dragging, by using any of the following keyboard commands—everyone sing along now:

- Alt (Option on the Mac) extends the grid outward from all sides of the origin point.

- Shift constrains the grid to a circle.

- Shift+Alt (Shift-option on the Mac) constrains the grid to a circle as it extends from the origin point.

- The spacebar temporarily suspends drawing activity to allow you to move the object.

- The tilde (~) key allows you to create multiple polar grids.

- The up and down arrow keys add or remove concentric circles, respectively.

- The right and left arrow keys add or remove radial lines, respectively.

- The X and C keys weight the concentric dividers toward the inside or outside by 10%, respectively.

- The V and F keys weight the radial dividers clockwise or counter-clockwise by 10%, respectively.

Drawing Free-Form Paths

The tools we've discussed so far are all well and good. But Illustrator's true drawing power lies in its ability to define free-form lines and shapes. Such paths may be simple shapes such as zigzags or crescents, or they may be intricate polygons and naturalistic forms. It all depends on how well you can draw.

The pencil tool (fifth down on the right side of the toolbox) works much like a real pencil and lets you draw anything you want. Heck, the pencil cursor even looks like a pencil.

When you first select the pencil tool, the pencil cursor displays with a small (almost microscopic) x in the lower-right corner. This indicates you are drawing a new, independent path. As you drag with the tool, Illustrator tracks the cursor's motion with a dotted line. After you release the mouse button, Illustrator automatically assigns and positions the points and segments needed to create your path. The path you created adopts the traditional fill and stroke characteristics as dictated by the values set in the various palettes (including the Color and Stroke palettes). For more information on fill and stroke, read the way-fab and truly meaty Chapters 15 and 16.

Adjusting the Tolerances

Alas, automation is rarely perfect. (If it were, what need would these machines have for us?) Try as it might, Illustrator doesn't always do such a hot job of drawing pencil paths. When the program finishes its calculations, a path may appear riddled with far too many points, or equipped with too few.

Fortunately, you can adjust the performance of the pencil tool to accommodate your personal drawing style using the Fidelity and Smoothness Tolerances options found in the Pencil Tool Preferences dialog box. To change how the pencil tool works, double-click the pencil tool icon in the toolbox. This opens the Pencil Tool Preferences dialog box (**Figure 5.23**).

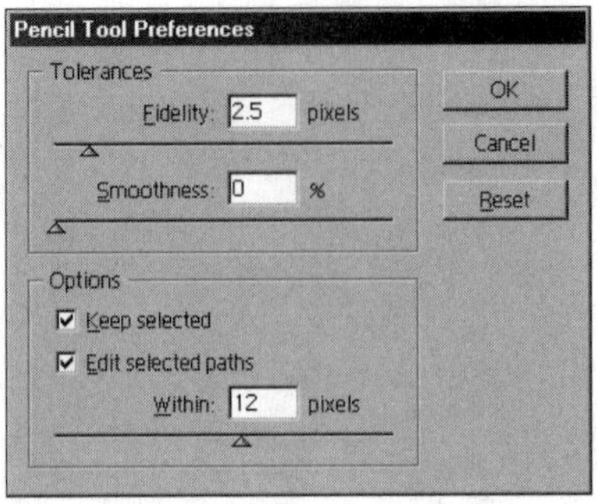

Pencil Tool Preferences

Tolerances

Fidelity: 2.5   pixels

Smoothness: 0   %

OK

Cancel

Reset

Options

☑ Keep selected

☑ Edit selected paths

Within: 12   pixels

Figure 5.23: Use this dialog box to specify exactly how Illustrator will mimic your mouse movements when you're dragging with the pencil tool.

In the Fidelity option box, enter any value between 0.5 and 20, or if you prefer, use the slider bar to select a value within the same range. Illustrator measures the Fidelity value in screen pixels. Fidelity determines how far from the path the individual point may stray. A value of 2.5, for example, instructs the program to ignore any jags in your cursor movements that do not exceed 2.5 pixels in length or width. Setting the value to 0.5 makes the pencil tool extremely sensitive; setting the value to 20 smoothes the roughest of gestures.

A Fidelity value of 2 or 3 is generally adequate for most folks, but you should experiment to determine the best setting. Keep in mind that Illustrator saves the Fidelity value, and it remains in force until you enter a new value into the Pencil Tool Preferences dialog box.

Smoothness is the other tolerance value that affects the pencil tool's behavior. It dictates how many points are needed to complete the path. Smoothness values can range from 0 to 100 percent, and you can enter that value into the Smoothness option box or set it via the slider bar. The higher the value, the smoother the pencil path.

You can't alter either the Fidelity or the Smoothness value for a path after you've drawn it, because Illustrator calculates the points for a path only once, after you release the mouse button.

The other features of this dialog box are also worth mentioning. The first is the Keep selected check box. When you select this option, a path remains selected just after creation, allowing you to extend or close it.

The second option is Edit selected paths. When this is selected, you can specify how close the pencil tool has to come before it can modify selected paths. (Rather than clutter up the rest of this chapter with how to modify paths, it's covered in great detail in Chapter 7.)

If you trust the Adobe engineers more than your own preferences, click the Reset button, which sets all the options back to their factory defaults.

Extending and Closing a Path

Normally, when you drag with the pencil tool, the result is an open path. This is true even if the starting point of your draw coincides perfectly with the final point. In this case, Illustrator will create two points so that the initial point overlaps the final point. This is not the limit of its capabilities, however: You can also use the pencil tool to create closed paths or extend any open path, lengthening it or even closing it.

To create a closed path from scratch, press Alt (Option on the Mac) while dragging with the pencil tool and hold it through the completion of the drag. As you do this, the pencil cursor changes slightly. It still looks like a pencil, but now the eraser end is filled and a small *o* replaces the *x* that usually appears to the right, as shown in **Figure 5.24**. Upon your drag's completion, Illustrator automatically adds a segment that connects the first and last points. The right side of Figure 5.22 shows how Illustrator adds this segment. If the two endpoints coincide, holding the Alt (Option on the Mac) key creates a single point that marks both the beginning and the end of the closed path.

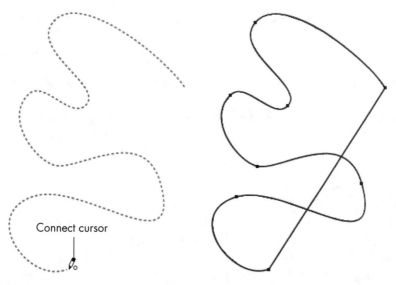

Connect cursor

Figure 5.24: Hold down the Alt key (Option key on the Mac) while you drag with the pencil tool (left), and Illustrator automatically closes your path regardless of where you start and end your drag (right).

On the other hand, if you want to extend an existing open path, select the path and position the pencil cursor over either end of the line. You'll know you're ready to go when you get the connect cursor (the standard pencil cursor without the x, as seen in **Figure 5.25**). Drag away—Illustrator treats your cursor movements as an extension of the existing path.

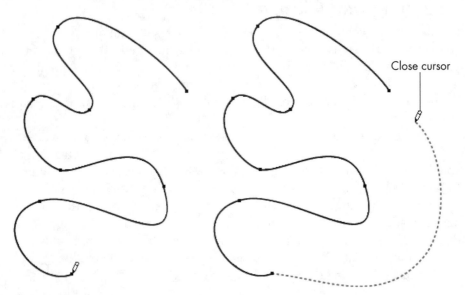

Close cursor

Figure 5.25: Drag from an endpoint to extend a path (left). Drag back to the other endpoint to close it (right).

Finally, to close a selected open path with the pencil tool, you might think you need to hold the Alt (or Option key) as in the case of creating a closed path from scratch. Amazingly, this is not so. In this case Illustrator understands that if you extend a path, you probably want to close it. So all you need to do is bring the pencil tool onto the open point and the path will close with a single point.

Painting Paths

The paintbrush tool (fifth tool down on the left side of the toolbox) is the other free-form path creation tool. Like the pencil, the paintbrush follows your mouse movements. When you release the mouse, Illustrator automatically assigns and positions points and segments to the path. So what's the difference between the two tools?

The big difference between the tools is that the paintbrush automatically assigns special types of strokes—called brushes—to the paths it draws. These brushes allow you to create the look of pen and ink, calligraphy, natural media, and even supernatural strokes. **Figure 5.26** shows how applying brushes to a simple path can dramatically change the path's appearance.

The brushes the paintbrush applies to a path are located in the Brushes palette (which you can see by pressing F5). The Brushes palette is covered in full detail in Chapter 16, but for now, just select a brush from the palette list and drag with the paintbrush to draw an open path. To draw a closed path, press and hold the Alt key (Option key on the Mac) after starting the drag.

Figure 5.26: The plain illustration on the left was changed by applying different brushes to the path. Nothing was moved, altered, or in any way changed except by applying the brushes.

As with the pencil tool, you can adjust the fidelity, smoothness, and edit distance of the paintbrush by double-clicking the tool icon in the toolbox. The Paintbrush Tool Preferences dialog box (**Figure 5.27**) appears. Most of the options are identical in form and function to the pencil tool preference settings shown back in Figure 5.21.

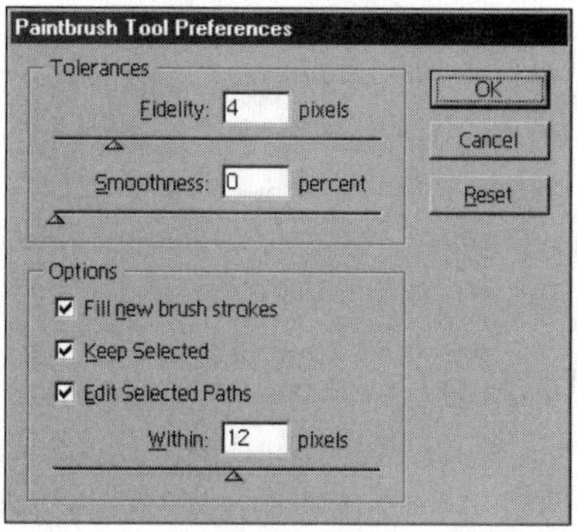

Figure 5.27: Here's where you specify the behavior of the paintbrush tool.

Most of the time, you'll want to turn off the Fill new brush strokes option. The result is a more natural-looking brushstroke.

But there's one additional option that requires some explanation: Fill New Brush Strokes. When this check box is turned on (as it is by default) the paintbrush applies the active fill color to any paths you draw. It then applies a stroke from the Brushes palette using the active stroke color. When the option is off, the paintbrush behaves in a more sophisticated manner. First, it determines whether there is a stroke color. If there is, the paintbrush discards any fill and keeps the stroke color applied to the color of the brush. If there is no active stroke color, the paintbrush swipes the current fill color and uses it for the stroke. It then deletes the fill color. In other words, with the option turned off, you will never have a filled brushstroke.

Tracing Templates

Any time you place a file into Illustrator or open a raster image, you have the option to make the image a template. Templates are images on special layers that make it (slightly) easier to trace illustrations. The image used as a template can be black and white, grayscale, or color.

When the template image comes into Illustrator, it comes in on a new layer that is given special template status. A template layer is positioned under the current layer and set to not print. Any images on the template layer are ghosted (dimmed) to 50% of their regular shades, and the layer is locked so you can't inadvertently move the image. You can set all these options yourself by creating a new layer, placing the image, and setting all the layer options, but it's much easier to just place the image as a template. If you are the do-it-yourself type, see Chapter 8, where all the options for layers are fully covered.

Unfortunately, you still can't scan images directly into Illustrator. Ideally, you ought to be able to scan in some line art and make it into an illustration in minutes without opening other programs.

Using the Auto Trace Tool

After placing a template in your illustration (as described in the "Placing and Linking" section of Chapter 4), you can trace the edges manually using any of Illustrator's drawing tools. But if you want Illustrator to do the work for you, your only choice is the auto trace tool. Despite its faults, there are certainly times when you may find it useful, so here's how you use it. First, select the auto trace tool (the alternative tool in the blend tool slot). **Figure 5.28** shows just that, with a tracing template all ready to go.

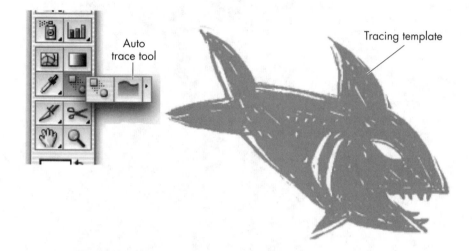

Auto trace tool

Tracing template

Figure 5.28: With the template in place, choose the auto trace tool.

 If you're really serious about tracing and like to scan your own handiwork, you'll want to check out Adobe Streamline. Not only can this dedicated tracing program trace multiple paths at once, it can also give you much more control over the tracing paths, and it can be set to trace an entire folder of images.

You can use the auto trace tool in one of two ways.

 Click within six pixels of an edge in the tracing template. Illustrator automatically encircles that area with a closed path.

Drag from within six pixels of an edge to within six pixels of some other portion of that same edge. Illustrator traces an open path between the point at which you click and the point at which you release.

For example, to trace around the outside of the fish, I clicked at the top of the fin, as in the top example in **Figure 5.29**. (Illustrator always creates a point at the spot on the template nearest your click, so it's best to click near a corner.) To trace the eye, I clicked just to the right of its edge, as shown in the lower example.

Click point 1

Click point 2

Figure 5.29: I clicked above the fin to trace the outside of the fish (top). Then I clicked beside the eye to trace inside its edge (bottom).

Dragging is a less common way to trace shapes, but it can be useful if you want to trace one portion of the template automatically and the rest manually. After you complete your drag, Illustrator traces clockwise around exterior edges, as demonstrated in **Figure 5.30**, and counterclockwise around interior edges. This is true even if it's tracing the longer of the two distances between where you started your drag and where you released.

You can temporarily hide a template layer to get a better view of your artwork. Click that layer's Visibility button in the Layers palette—it's the little circle, triangle, and square icon where the eyeball is for regular layers. The template disappears. To bring the template back into view, click again where the icon was.

Figure 5.30: When you drag from one side of an exterior surface to another (top), Illustrator traces between the two points in a clockwise direction (bottom).

Adjusting Auto Tracing Sensitivity

If you are dissatisfied with Illustrator's tracing accuracy, you can adjust the auto trace tool's sensitivity by changing the Auto Trace Tolerance value in the Type & Auto Tracing Preferences dialog box. An Auto Trace Tolerance value of 0 instructs Illustrator to trace every single pixel of a bitmapped template. If you raise the value to 10, the software ignores large jags in the outline of a template and smoothes out all kinds of details.

Generally speaking, it's better to have too many points than too few. After all, you can always delete points later. So for the most reliable auto tracing, set the Auto Trace Tolerance value no higher than 2.

Tracing Across Gaps

The auto trace tool is most effective in tracing the borders between the black and white areas in a template. But it can also trace gray areas and areas with broken or inconsistent outlines. To accommodate such rough spots, Illustrator provides a Tracing Gap option in the Type & Auto Tracing Preferences dialog box.

You can set this value to any value from 0 to 2. The default value of 0 instructs Illustrator to never pass over the gap. A value of 1 permits Illustrator to jump one-pixel gaps. If you raise the value to 2, Illustrator can jump a two-pixel gap. This is a useful setting when you're tracing photographs and other images with loose pixels.

Yet One Tool Beats Them All

Before I close this chapter, I want to leave you with a parting bit of wisdom. We've tackled all but one of Illustrator's drawing tools, and that remaining tool—the pen tool—is far and away the best of all. It is infinitely more flexible than the rectangle, ellipse, and other shape tools, and more precise than the pencil, paint-brush, and auto trace tools. (The pen tool is also mightier than the sword tool, but that's another story.) It is, in fact, the only tool you really need. There was a time when the pen, rectangle, and ellipse tools were all Illustrator offered—yet there wasn't a thing you couldn't draw. And if you use either Adobe Photoshop or InDesign, you know that they, too, use the same pen tool. So mastering the Illustrator pen can help you when working in other applications.

That's why the next chapter is so important. It shows you how to edit the paths you create with the tools in this chapter, and how to create more exacting shapes with the pen. These features require more work, but they'll reward your effort several times over.

EXACT POINTS AND PRECISION CURVES

Much as Illustrator tries, at a price range of $149 to $399, it just can't live up to the 25¢ pencil when it comes to smooth, real-time drawing. Whether you use Illustrator's pencil, paintbrush, or auto trace tool, you still get the same thing— paths divided by anchor points. A drawing tablet and stylus help, but only to communicate smoother lines to Illustrator; they don't help Illustrator better interpret your beautiful work.

Each version of Illustrator does a better job of interpreting pencil paths. Look how far we've come since Illustrator 88 (the first version to offer the tool). So one might expect Illustrator 2010 to perform even better and Illustrator 2525 to be right on the money. In the meantime, we can either suffer with clunky paths, or we can fix them.

That said, it would be a sin if fixing paths weren't what this chapter is all about. I'll explore a whole mess of path-editing theories—you'll see how to move anchor points and bend segments to get lines as smooth as water droplets and as organic as flower petals. I'll also cover the pen tool—the only tool in all of Illustrator that lets you draw paths correctly the first time out. And just when you think Illustrator couldn't be any dreamier, I'll throw in some pointers for adding, deleting, and converting points.

If Illustrator is nothing else, it's the most excellent path creation and manipulation tool the world has ever enjoyed. This chapter tells why.

Selecting Like a House on Fire

The job of sprucing up paths rests on the shoulders of five very sturdy tools. These are the selection tools, available from the top two-and-a-half slots in the toolbox (**Figure 6.1**). Clicking or dragging on a point or segment with one of these selects all or part of a path. The tools differ only in the extent of the selection they make.

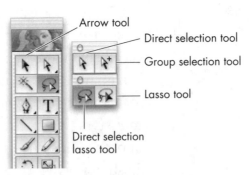

Figure 6.1: The three selection tools are all you need to move anchor points, bend segments, and whip paths into shape. The lasso tools select but don't move points and paths.

Arrow tool
Direct selection tool
Group selection tool
Lasso tool
Direct selection lasso tool

Arrows or Lassos?

Choosing your "weapon" for selection all depends on what you want to do with that selection once you've, um, captured it. The arrows (also known as the selection, direct selection, and group selection tools) are the most powerful of selection tools. Not only can they select objects and points, but if you drag with them, they move things around.

Lassos (also known as the lasso and direct select lasso tools) aren't as powerful as the arrow tools. They can only select things; if you want to move the selection around, you have to switch to an arrow.

 Ordinarily you would see a bounding box around objects that are selected using the selection tool. This bounding box can be used to scale or rotate selected objects. However, I think the bounding box gets in the way of working with selection basics, so I've hidden it from these illustrations. To hide (or show) the bounding box, choose View » Hide (or Show) Bounding Box. Or take the time to memorize the vital keystroke Ctrl+Shift+B (Cmd-Shift-B on the Mac).

The Plain Black Arrow Tool

The selection tool—which I call the arrow tool to distinguish it from its selection pals—is the most straightforward of the bunch. When the arrow tool is active, you can click anywhere along the outline of a path to select the path in its entirety. If the Use Area Select check box is turned on inside the General Preferences dialog box, you can also click inside the path to select it, provided the path has a fill (as discussed in Chapter 15). All points become visible as filled squares, as **Figure 6.2** demonstrates.

Figure 6.2: Click any part of a path with the arrow tool (left) to select the entire path (right).

After selecting a path with the arrow tool, you can move it, apply a transformation, or perform any other manipulation that affects the path *as a whole*. You cannot move points or bend segments. If the path has been grouped with other paths (as explained in Chapter 7), the arrow tool selects the entire group, prohibiting you from altering one grouped path independently of another.

Here are a few other ways to select paths with the arrow tool.

- When you click a path, you not only select the path you click, you also deselect any previously selected path. To select multiple paths, click the first path and then hold the Shift key as you click each additional path you want to select (this is called a *Shift-click*). The Shift key prevents Illustrator from deselecting paths as you click new ones.

Another way to select multiple paths is to *marquee* them. Drag from an empty portion of your drawing area to create a dotted rectangular outline, called a marquee. You select all paths that fall even slightly inside this outline when you release the mouse button. In **Figure 6.3**, for example, I dragged into the apple at least far enough to capture a piece of the leaf as well.

 You can combine marqueeing with Shift-clicking to select multiple paths. You can also drag a marquee while pressing Shift, which adds the surrounded objects to the present selection.

If you Shift-click an object that is already selected, Illustrator deselects it, as discussed in the upcoming section "Deselecting Stuff That You Want to Leave As Is."

To access the arrow tool temporarily when some other tool is active, press and hold the Ctrl key (Cmd key on the Mac). Release the key to return to the last tool you used. If pressing Ctrl (Cmd) gets you one of the hollow selection cursors instead, press Ctrl+Tab (Cmd-Tab on the Mac) and then press Ctrl (Cmd) again. To switch to the arrow tool without having to hold modifiers, press the V key.

Mac users, take note: If the preceding tip doesn't work, it's because the Mac OS has taken over the use of Cmd-Tab for switching between open applications. Fortunately, Adobe recognized the situation and added Control-Tab as another way to switch between the arrow tool and the hollow arrow tools.

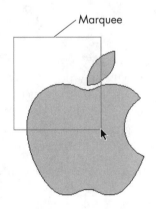

Marquee

Figure 6.3: By marqueeing partially inside both elements of the apple image (left), I selected them both (right).

The Hollow Direct Selection Tool

The direct selection tool is the hollow (white) arrow in the upper-right corner of the toolbox. Click with the direct selection tool to select an individual point or segment in a path. If you click a point, you select the point; if you click a segment, you select the segment. This works even if the path that contains the point or segment is part of a group.

 As you work with the selection arrows, you will notice little squares appear next to the cursor. These boxes indicate what type of object the arrow is over. When the cursor is over any point, a small white square appears, as shown in the left two examples of **Figure 6.4**. *Move it over a segment of a path and a black square joins the cursor, as you can see in the top-right example of Figure 6.4. Move it over a filled area (when Use Area Select is turned on) and it also displays the black square. These cursors inform you that if you click with the mouse, you will select the intended element.*

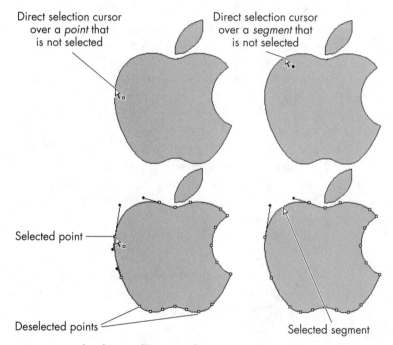

Figure 6.4: Position the direct selection tool over a point (top left) and the cursor gains a small hollow square. When it's over a segment (top right), the direct selection cursor gains a small black square. Select a single anchor point (bottom left) or segment (bottom right) by clicking with the direct selection tool.

Now that you know how the direct selection tool appears when you are selecting path elements, you might as well know how those path elements appear when you select them with the direct selection tool. Different elements have different ways of showing that they are selected. For example, when you select a point, it appears as a small filled square, as shown in the bottom-left example of Figure 6.4. If the point borders a curved segment, you can also see a Bézier control handle connected to the point by a thin lever.

 For those of you reading aloud to loved ones, Bézier is pronounced bay-zee-ay. Named after Pierre Bézier—the French fellow who designed this particular drawing model to expedite the manufacture of car bodies, of all things—Bézier curve theory lies at the heart of both Illustrator and the PostScript printing language. Sadly, Monsieur Bézier passed away on November 25,1999, at the age of 89. Fortunately, his name will forever be linked with the control handles and curves in vector drawing programs. Now, if only it were easy to remember which "e" to put the accent over.

When you select a path, Illustrator shows you both selected and deselected points. The deselected points appear as hollow squares, showing that they are part of a partially selected path, but are not themselves selected.

When you click a segment with the direct selection tool, Illustrator shows you the Bézier control handles for that segment—if there are any—as in the lower-right example of Figure 6.4. Unless some point in the path is also selected, all points appear hollow. Because Illustrator shows you only the control handles, you may find it a little confusing when selecting straight segments, which lack handles. You just have to click the segment and have faith that it's selected. (I wish Illustrator thickened the segment to provide some sort of visual feedback.)

You can also drag with the direct selection tool to marquee elements. All points and segments that lie inside the marquee become selected, even if they belong to different paths, as **Figure 6.5** shows.

The following list summarizes these and other ways to select elements with the direct selection tool:

- If the Use Area Select check box in the General Preferences dialog box is turned on (as it is by default), you can click inside a filled shape to select the entire path. This assumes that the shape has a fill, as addressed in Chapter 15.

- Shift-click a point or segment to add it to the current selection. You can also Shift-marquee around elements. (If you Shift-click a point or segment that's already selected, it becomes deselected. The same goes for Shift-marqueeing.)

Alt-click (Option-click on the Mac) a point or segment to select an entire path. This is a great way to select paths inside groups.

Alt-marquee or **Alt+Shift-click** (Option-marquee or Option-Shift-click on the Mac) paths to select multiple paths at a time.

To switch back and forth between the arrow tool and the direct selection tool, press Ctrl+Tab (Cmd-Tab on the Mac). If you last used the direct selection tool (as opposed to the arrow tool), you can access it while any other tool is active by pressing Ctrl or Cmd. If you last used the arrow tool, press Ctrl+Tab (Cmd-Tab on the Mac) and then press Ctrl (Cmd). To switch to the direct selection tool, press the A key.

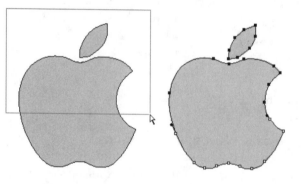

Figure 6.5: When dragging a marquee with the direct selection tool (left), all points and segments inside the marquee are selected (right).

The Sad Little Group Selection Tool

Adobe added the group selection tool to Illustrator so folks who were afraid to press the Alt or Option key could select paths inside groups. In other words, you can either Alt-click (Option-click on the Mac) a path to select it with the direct selection tool (temporarily accessing the group selection tool), or click the path with the group selection tool. If you're not afraid of the occasional extra keystroke, feel free to ignore the group selection tool. I never touch it. Honestly, it's useless.

If you don't believe me, and you'd prefer to know everything about everything, you can select the group selection tool by dragging from the upper-right slot in the toolbox. Then do any of the following:

Click a point or segment to select a whole path in a group. You can also select groups within groups by clicking multiple times on a path, but you can do this with the direct selection tool as well so long as you hold down the Alt (Option on the Mac) key. (All this grouping stuff is covered in Chapter 8.)

- Marquee paths with the group selection tool to select the paths, whether they fall entirely or partially inside the marquee.

- Shift-click a path to add it to the selection. You can also Shift-marquee if you get the urge.

- Alt-click (Option-click on the Mac) a point or segment to select it independently of its path. The Alt or Option key temporarily converts the group selection to direct selection.

See, what did I tell you? Dumb tool. Steer clear of it.

Lassoing Selections

You may have noticed that the marquees created by the arrow tools are always rectangular. But unless you're hopelessly, well, square, you are bound to want to select a non-rectangular area some day. The lasso tools let you round up selections in any shape you desire. And just like the selection tools, the lassos are divided into two selection modes.

The Black Lasso

The black lasso (officially known as the *lasso tool*) selects entire objects—even if you snare only parts of them within the lasso marquee (just like the selection arrow selects entire objects within its marquee). Simply drag the lasso around the objects you want to select. A line indicates the area that is being selected. When you release the mouse, all the objects that were within the lasso marquee will be selected as shown in **Figure 6.6**.

Figure 6.6: When the lasso is dragged around parts of the objects (left), a line indicates the area that is being selected. When the mouse is released, the two objects are entirely selected (right).

The White Lasso

The white lasso (officially known as the *direct select lasso tool*) selects parts of objects. Drag around the points or segments you want to select. When you release the mouse, only those points or segments that were within the lasso marquee will be selected. As shown in **Figure 6.7**, the direct select lasso allows you to select points that would require many different passes dragging with the arrow tools.

Figure 6.7: This selection around the "inner passage" of the apple was created with the direct selection lasso tool (left), and selects only the interior points of the illustration that were included in the lasso's reach (right).

Adding More Lasso Selections

The lasso tools work slightly differently than the other selection tools. If you hold the Shift key, you will see a small plus sign next to the lasso cursor. This indicates that the next loop of the lasso will add to the selection. But the lassos do not deselect selected items when you use the Shift key. They only add to the selection. To deselect as you lasso, you have to press and hold down the Alt key (Option key on the Mac).

Selecting Everything

If you want to select all paths in your drawing, choose Select » All or press Ctrl+A (Cmd-A on the Mac). Illustrator selects every last point, segment, and other element throughout the illustration, even if it's on the pasteboard. (An exception is if you've either locked an object so it can't be selected or selected a letter inside a text block, in which case Select All highlights all text in the story.)

Inversing the Selection

To select everything that's not selected and deselect what is selected, choose Select » Inverse.

Both the Select All and Select Inverse commands make it easier to select most of the objects in a complicated drawing. You can choose Select All and then Shift-click the objects you don't want to select. Or start off by clicking and Shift-clicking the stuff you don't want to select, and then choose Select » Inverse. Either way works fine; it's entirely a matter of personal preference.

Another way to select and manage objects is by using the Layers palette (covered in Chapter 8).

Hiding the Points and Handles

All those points, handles, and colored outlines that Illustrator uses to show that an object is selected can occasionally get in your way. If you're aware of your selection but you want to see the selected objects unadorned, choose View » Hide Edges or press Ctrl+H (Cmd-H on the Mac).

From that point on, no selection outline appears onscreen, even if you select a different object. To see the selection outlines again, you have to choose View » Show Edges or press Ctrl+H (Cmd-)H again.

The Select Menu

 If you've been using Illustrator 9, you'd be justified in going to the Edit menu for your selection needs. But it appears that selection has gotten to be such a hot item that, like other brash young stars, it got top billing—the Select menu, as shown in **Figure 6.8**.

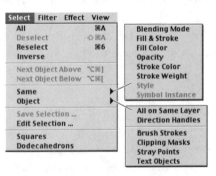

Figure 6.8: The Select menu and all of its submenu glory. If you don't have certain kinds of attributes or elements on the page, the choices are grayed out.

The choices on the Same and Object submenus of the Select menu are fairly self-descriptive, but since some of these concepts may be foreign to you, I'm going to perform a public service and list them here with references to the chapters where the terms and features are discussed in more detail.

Each of the options listed below is the only one that needs to match among objects being selected; that is, if you choose to match fill color, then the stroke color as well as the weight and all other attributes may vary.

- *Same » Blending Mode (Chapter 17)*
- *Same » Fill & Stroke (Chapters 15 and 16)*
- *Same » Fill Color (Chapter 15)*
- *Same » Opacity (Chapter 18)*

Same » Stroke Color (Chapter 16)

 Same » Stroke Weight (Chapter 16)

 Same » Style (Chapter 19)

 Same » Symbol Instance (Chapter 12)

 Object » All on Same (Chapter 8)

 Object » Direction Handles (Chapters 6 and 7)

 Object » Brush Strokes (Chapter 16)

 Object » Clipping Masks (Chapter 17)

 Object » Stray Points: (Chapter 6)

 Object » Text Objects (Chapters 10 and 11)

Once you have chosen one of these selection commands, that command is stored in Illustrator's memory. You can then choose Select » Reselect or Ctrl+6 (Cmd-6 on the Mac) to reapply whatever selection criterion was previously chosen. The benefit of this is if you've just selected and modified all red-filled objects, you can select one green object, choose Select Again, and then modify the green-filled ones.

 Another way to come back to a selection is to save it (Select » Save Selection). Once you've saved and named a selection, it will appear in the Select menu for easy loading (there are a couple of saved choices on my Select menu back in Figure 6.8). Obviously, this can be a big help if you think you're going to be making frequent visits.

There's one other choice—well, it's a set of two—on the Select menu that can help you navigate the objects on the page. You can move among objects by using the Next Object Above and Next Object Below commands, or Ctrl+Alt+] and Ctrl+Alt+[(Cmd-Option-] and Cmd-Option-[on the Mac). "Above" and "below" refer to the stacking order of objects on the page; by default, this is the order in which they were drawn.

The Edit Selection command is the bureaucrat of the family; it just allows you to delete or rename a selection.

Using the Magic Wand Tool

 Got Photoshop? Then your fingers (sometimes attached to your wishful brain) have probably been trying to use the magic wand tool in Illustrator before it even arrived. Now it's here, so now you can.

The magic wand is a little bit of magic, I think; what else would you call a tool that can act on your wishes with just a few clicks of information to go by? Oh, wait—that describes about a million other tools in Illustrator, too. Anyway, the magic wand tool is a welcome addition to the Selection family in that it allows you to make selections based on attributes—fill color, stroke color, stroke weight, opacity, and blending mode—in a very automated way. (In fact, for the most part, it does everything that the Select commands do, but a little bit more conveniently, in my opinion). You can limit it to working on the same layer or on all layers. (You can toggle this option in the palette's pop-up menu.)

When you click any object with the magic wand tool, it will then select any other existing objects that match the criteria you've specified in the palette, which is shown in **Figure 6.9**.

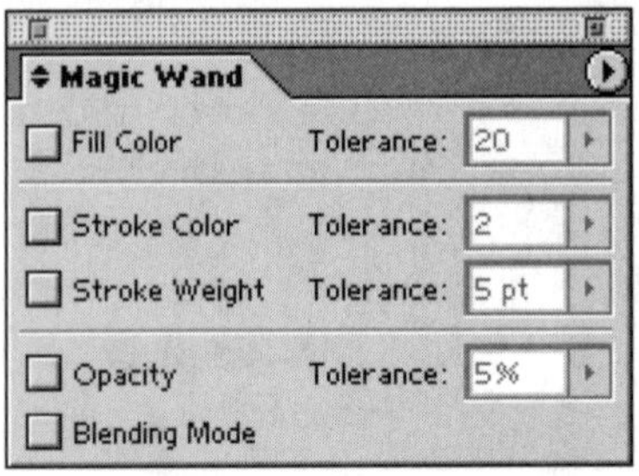

Figure 6.9: Here, the Magic Wand palette is opened to its full extent, but you can hide the stroke or transparency options if you don't use those frequently.

The Tolerance feature is helpful since it means you can specify a range of values for any of the options. The Blending Mode option selects any objects that have any blending mode applied. For more information about blending modes, see Chapter 17.

Deselecting Stuff That You Want to Leave As Is

Selecting is your way of telling Illustrator, "This thing is messed up, and now I'm going to fix it." If you don't want to do something to an object, you need to deselect it.

It's also OK if you say "unselect," or even "antiselect" or "get it out of the selection loop," but I've always found the unremarkable "deselect" easiest.

To deselect all objects, press Ctrl+Shift+A (Cmd-Shift-A on the Mac) or choose Select » Deselect (this works for all or however many items you have selected). Or, you can just click with one of the selection tools on an empty portion of the drawing area to deselect everything.

You can make more discrete deselections using the Shift key.

- To deselect an entire path or group, Shift-click the object with the arrow tool.

- To deselect a single point or segment, Shift-click it with the direct selection tool.

- To deselect a single path inside a group, Alt+Shift-click it (Option-Shift-click on the Mac) with the direct selection tool.

- You can also deselect elements and objects by Shift-marqueeing around them. Selected elements become deselected, and deselected elements become selected.

Dragging Stuff Around

Once you've selected a point or segment, you can move it around, changing its location and stretching its path. In fact, dragging with the direct selection tool is the single most common method for reshaping a path inside Illustrator. You can move selected points independently of deselected points. And you can stretch segments or move Bézier control handles to alter the curvature of a path. The next few pages explain all aspects of dragging.

Dragging Points

To move one or more points in a path:

1. Select the points you want to move with the direct selection tool.

2. Drag any one of them.

3. Squeal with delight.

When you drag a selected point, all other selected points move the same distance and direction. When you move a point while a neighboring point remains stationary, the segment between the two points shrinks or stretches in length to accommodate the change in distance, as demonstrated in **Figure 6.10**.

Figure 6.10: When you
drag a selected point
bordered by deselected
points (left), Illustrator
stretches the segments
between the points (right).

When you move a point, any accompanying control handles will move with it. As a result, the curved segments on either side of the point must not only shrink or stretch, but also bend to accommodate the movement. Meanwhile, segments located between two deselected points or two selected points remain unchanged during a move, as demonstrated in **Figure 6.11**. Illustrator lets you move multiple points within a single path (also shown in Figure 6.11), or in separate paths, as in **Figure 6.12**. This means you can reshape multiple paths at the same time.

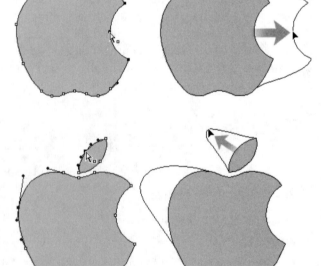

Figure 6.11: When you drag
more than one selected point
at a time (left), the segments
between the selected points
remain unchanged (right).

Figure 6.12: You can move
multiple points even when
selected points reside in
different paths.

While you move a point, Illustrator displays both previous and current locations of the point and its surrounding segments. This useful feature permits you to gauge the full effect of a move as it progresses. Also worth noting: When you drag a single selected point, Illustrator displays the point, any Bézier control handles associated with the two neighboring segments, and the neighboring deselected points, as shown back in Figure 6.10. When dragging multiple points, Illustrator hides the points and handles, as in Figures 6.11 and 6.12. I'd like to be able to see the points and handles, but Adobe thinks all that screen clutter might prove confusing.

Keeping Your Movements in Line

You can constrain your cursor movements horizontally, vertically, or diagonally by pressing the Shift key. For example, if you want to move a point horizontally without moving it so much as a smidgen up or down, press the Shift key while dragging the point with the direct selection tool.

You have to press Shift after you begin dragging—if you press Shift before you drag, you deselect the selected point that you click, which causes Illustrator to ignore your drag. Then you hold down the Shift key until after you release the mouse button. Always release the mouse button first, and then whatever modifier key you have pressed. If you release Shift first, you'll lose the constraint.

You can adjust the effects of pressing Shift by changing the Constrain Angle value in the General Preferences dialog box. This rotates the constraint axes. So a horizontal (0-degree) move becomes a 15-degree move, a 45-degree move becomes a 60-degree move, and so on.

Why would you ever want to do this? You may want to move a point along an angled object without letting the point and the object drift apart. For example, the top segment along the tent object in **Figure 6.13** is oriented at a 15-degree angle. To move the ball forward along the segment, I first rotated the constraint axes to 15 degrees and then dragged the object while pressing Shift.

Rather than change the Constrain Angle, you can also set the Smart Guides (glorified in Chapter 8) to a specific angle and then move objects.

Remember, the constraint axes also affect the creation of rectangles, ellipses, and text blocks. So you'll generally want to reset them to 0 degrees when you finish making your moves.

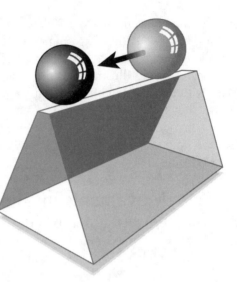

Figure 6.13: Rotating the constraint axes to 15 degrees allows the ball to be moved precisely along a 15-degree segment.

Snapping Point to Point

When dragging a point, you may find that it has a tendency to move sharply toward another point in your illustration. This effect is called *snapping,* and it's Illustrator's way of ensuring that points that belong together are flush against each other to form a perfect fit.

When you drag a point within two screen pixels of a second point on your drawing area, your cursor snaps to the stationary point, so that both point and cursor occupy the very same spot on the page. At the moment the snap occurs, your cursor changes from a filled arrowhead to a hollow arrowhead, as shown in **Figure 6.14**. (This is particularly useful after a long day in front of the screen, when your snap-perception capabilities have all but vanished.)

For example, you might drag the corner point of one rectangle until it snaps to the corner point of another. In this way, both rectangles sit exactly point to point.

Snap cursor

Figure 6.14: Your cursor changes to a hollow arrow-head when snapping a point to a stationary point.

Your cursor snaps to stationary points as well as to the previous locations of points currently being moved. (This last item is more useful than it sounds. You'll see—one day it'll come in handy.) Your cursor also snaps to text blocks and to guides (covered in Chapters 10 and 8, respectively).

You can turn Illustrator's snapping feature on and off by choosing the View » Snap to Point command or by pressing Ctrl+Alt+" (Cmd-Opt-" on the Mac). That's the double-quote character on your keyboard.

Dragging Segments

You can also reshape a path by dragging its segments. When you drag a straight segment, its neighboring segments stretch or shrink to accommodate the change in distance, as shown in the first example in **Figure 6.15**. However, when you drag a curved segment, you stretch only that segment. The effect is rather like pulling on a rubber band extended between two nails, as the second example illustrates.

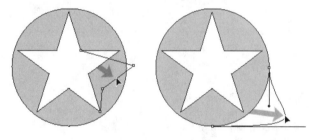

Figure 6.15: The difference between dragging a straight segment (left) and a curved segment (right).

Figure 6.16 examines in detail what happens when you drag on a curved segment. The longer the drag, the more the segment has to bend. More important is how the segment bends. Notice the two Bézier control handles on either side of the segment. The handles automatically extend and retract as you drag. Each handle moves along an imaginary line consistent with the handle's original inclination. The angle of a control handle does not change one whit when you drag a segment, thus guaranteeing that the curved segment moves in alignment with neighboring stationary segments.

 When dragging a segment, drag on the middle of the segment, about equidistant from both of its points, as you saw in Figure 6.15. This provides the best leverage and keeps you from losing control over the segment. (These things can spring away from you if you're not careful.)

If you want to move a control handle in a different direction, you have to drag the handle itself, as I describe in the "Dragging Control Handles" section later in this chapter.

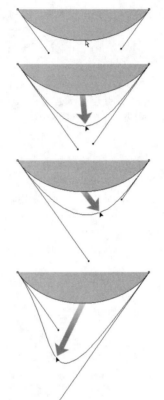

Figure 6.16: When you drag a curved segment, each Bézier control handle moves back and forth along a constant axis.

Nudging Points and Segments

Another way to move a selected element is to press one of the four arrow keys at the bottom of your keyboard (up, down, left, right). Not surprisingly, each of these keys nudges a selection in the direction of the arrow.

You can change the distance that a single keystroke moves a selected element by adjusting the Keyboard increment value in the General Preferences dialog box. For example, setting the value to 1 point is equivalent to one screen pixel when you view the illustration at actual size. However, you can set the value anywhere from 0.01 to 1296 points—that's a whopping 18 inches.

You can use arrow keys to move points as well as straight and curved segments. (Sadly, you can't move a single control handle with an arrow key; to do this, you must drag the handle with the direct selection tool.) This is very handy for stretching two segments exactly the same distance. Just click one segment, Shift-click the other, and whack away at the arrow keys as if you were getting paid by the keystroke.

The arrow keys move a selection with respect to the constraint axes. For example, if you change the constrain angle to 15 degrees, pressing the right arrow key moves the selection slightly upward, and pressing the up arrow moves it slightly to the left.

If pressing an arrow key doesn't seem to produce any noticeable result, a palette might be active. For example, if you just got through changing the size of a font in the Character palette, Illustrator may be forwarding the arrow key signal to the palette, even if no option appears to be active. To remedy this situation, press Enter (Return on the Mac) to deactivate the palette. Then press the arrow keys to nudge without hindrance.

Dragging Control Handles

The only element that I've so far neglected to move is the Bézier control handle. I've saved it for last because it's the most difficult and the most powerful element you can manipulate.

After referencing control handles several times in this chapter, it's high time I defined our terminology. The *Bézier control handle* (*control handle* or *handle* or *those funky little line things* for short) is the element that defines the arc of a segment as it exits or enters an anchor point. It tugs at a segment like an invisible thread. You increase the curvature of a segment when you drag the handle away from its point and decrease the curvature when you drag a handle toward its point.

To display a control handle, you can either select the point to which the handle belongs or select the segment it controls. You then drag the handle with the direct selection tool, just as you drag a point.

Figure 6.17 shows three paths composed of five points each. I drew the first path—the one that looks like a 2—with the pencil tool and assigned it a thick gray stroke. The second and third paths are based on the first; the only differences are the positions of the control handles and the curvatures of the segments. The points remain unmoved from one path to the next, and yet the results are unique.

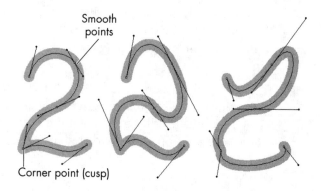

Figure 6.17: These three paths comprise five points apiece. The points remain stationary—only the control handles move.

Smooth points

Corner point (cusp)

The 2 comprises two smooth points around its loop and a special kind of corner point called a *cusp* where the loop and base meet. A cusp forms a corner between two curved segments. (It doesn't really matter what kinds of points the endpoints are, because no segments follow them.)

The other two paths contain the same points in the same order. So not only has no point been moved, no point has been converted to a different kind of point. As a result, the bottom-left point in each path remains a corner, permitting me to move the two control handles on either side of the point independently of each other. This is the very nature of a corner point.

Likewise, the points in the middle and upper-right portions of the path remain smooth points. When I move one control handle, the other moves in the opposite direction, making for a sort of fulcrum effect. This ensures a continuous arc through each point. Not only is there no corner at either location, but there's no hint of even the slightest crease. The path continues through the points as smoothly as a bend in the road.

 Dragging a control handle can turn ugly when you're working inside a very complex illustration. If the handle rests near a point or segment from a different path, Illustrator may think you're trying to drag the point or segment rather than the handle. To bring the handle out of the fray so you can get to it more easily, drag the curved segment that the handle controls (stretching the segment lengthens the handle). Then you can drag the handle without busybody points and segments horning in.

Bézier Rules

Figure 6.17 is proof of the old Bézier adage that just because you *can* drag control handles all over the place doesn't mean you *should*. Manipulating handles is not so much a question of what is possible as of what is proper. Several handle-handling rules have developed over the years, but the best are the *All-or-Nothing rule* and the *33-Percent rule*.

 The All-or-Nothing rule states that every segment in your path should be associated with either two control handles or none at all. In other words, no segment should rely on only one control handle to determine its curvature.

 The 33-Percent rule declares that the distance from any control handle to its point should equal approximately one-third the length of the segment. So one handle covers one-third of the segment, the other handle covers the opposite third, and the middle third is handle-free.

The left path in **Figure 6.18** violates the All-or-Nothing rule. Only one handle apiece controls each of its two curved segments, resulting in weak, shallow arcs. Such puny curves are sure to inspire snorts and guffaws from discriminating viewers.

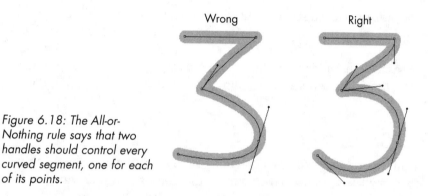

Figure 6.18: The All-or-Nothing rule says that two handles should control every curved segment, one for each of its points.

The right example in Figure 6.18 obeys the All-or-Nothing rule. As the rule dictates, the straight segment has no handles and the two curved segments have two handles apiece. The result is a full-figured, properly rendered path that is a credit to any illustration.

The first path in **Figure 6.19** violates the 33-Percent rule. The handles are either much too short or much too long to fit their segments. The result is an ugly, misshapen mess. In the second example, each handle is about one-third of the length of its segment. The top segment is shorter than the other two, so its handles are shorter as well. This path is smooth and consistent in curvature, giving it a more natural appearance.

 What happens if you violate either of these rules? Will the Bézier police come to arrest you? No. Will your jobs print? Yes. The real reason these rules exist is to help you create elegant curves that are easy to work with.

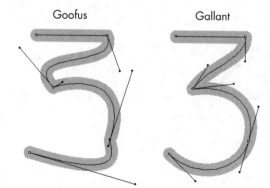

Figure 6.19: According to the 33-Percent rule, every control handle should extend about one-third the length of its segment.

The Great and Powerful Pen Tool

Now that you've had a taste of Bézier theory, it's time for full immersion. The pen tool is the absolute Bézier champ, capable of creating anything from schematic newspaper charts to detailed scenes of heightened reality. For nearly a decade, Illustrator's pen tool was the reigning virtuoso, and no other program offered anything that came close. Now Adobe has taken Illustrator's pen tool and, with a few microscopic exceptions, added it to InDesign. You can also find a more primitive version of the pen tool in Adobe Photoshop. It's a testament to the elegance of the original.

Pen Tool Basics

When drawing with the pen tool, you build a path by creating individual points. Illustrator automatically connects the points with *segments*. The following list summarizes how you can use the pen tool to build paths in Illustrator. These methods are described in more detail later in this chapter.

- **Path building:** To build a path, create one point after another inside the drawing area until the path is the desired length and shape. You create and position a point by either clicking or dragging with the pen tool. (Clicking creates a corner, dragging creates a smooth point.) Illustrator draws a segment between each new point and its predecessor.

- **Adjusting a point:** Midway into creating a path, you can reposition points or change the curvature of segments that you've already drawn. To move a point while you are still creating it, press and hold the spacebar. You can then reposition the point on the fly. Release the spacebar and continue creating points. If you've already created a point but want to modify it before moving on to the next point, just press the Ctrl key (Cmd key on the Mac) to access the direct selection tool, and drag the points, segments, and control handles as desired. When you've finished, release the Ctrl (Cmd) key and continue adding points.

- *If the arrow tool comes up instead of the direct selection tool while you're trying to modify a point, press Ctrl+Tab (Cmd-Tab on the Mac, or Control-Tab if Cmd-Tab gets taken over by the Mac OS and jumps you between your open applications).*

Be sure not to Ctrl-click (Cmd-click on the Mac) in an empty portion of the drawing area or on a different path. That will deactivate the active path, which means you can't add any more points to it without first reactivating the path (as described in the "Extending an open path" item, coming right up).

Closing the path: To create a closed shape, click or drag on the first point in the path. Every point will then have one segment coming into it and another segment exiting it.

Leaving the path open: To leave a path open (so it will have a specific beginning and ending), deactivate the path by pressing Ctrl+Shift+A (Cmd-Shift-A on the Mac) or choose Select » Deselect. Or you can press Ctrl (Cmd on the Mac) to get the arrow or direct selection tool and click an empty portion of the drawing area. Any of these will deactivate the path so you can move on and create a new one.

Extending an open path: To reactivate an open path, click or drag one of its endpoints. Illustrator is then ready to draw a segment between the endpoint and the next point you create.

Joining two open paths: To join one open path with another open path, click or drag an endpoint in the first path, then click or drag an endpoint in the second. Illustrator draws a segment between the two, bringing them together in everlasting peace and brotherhood.

That's basically all there is to using the pen tool. A click here, a drag there, and you've got yourself a path. But to achieve decent results, you need to know exactly what clicking and dragging will do and how to use these techniques to your best advantage. If the devil is in the details, the pen tool is Illustrator's most fiendish tool. I'll probe the pits of the pen, one level at a time, in the following sections.

Defining Points and Segments

Points in a Bézier path act as little road signs. Each point steers the path by specifying how a segment enters it and how another segment exits it. You specify the identity of each little road sign by clicking or dragging, sometimes with the help of the Alt key (Option key on the Mac).

The following items explain the specific kinds of points and segments you can create in Illustrator, with **Figure 6.20** providing examples.

Corner point: Click with the pen tool to create a corner point, which represents the corner between two segments in a path (or defines the end points of a single straight segment).

- **Straight segment:** Click at two different locations to create a straight segment between two corner points, like the first example shown in Figure 6.20.

After positioning one corner point, you can Shift-click to create a perfectly horizontal, vertical, or 45-degree segment between that point and the new one.

- **Smooth point:** Drag with the pen tool to create a smooth point with two symmetrical Bézier control handles. A smooth point ensures that one segment fuses into another to form a continuous arc.

- **Curved segment:** Drag at two different locations to create a curved segment between two smooth points, as the second example in Figure 6.20 illustrates.

- **Straight segment followed by curved:** After drawing a straight segment, drag from the corner point you just created to add a control handle. Then drag again at a different location to append a curved segment to the end of the straight segment, as the third example in Figure 6.20 illustrates.

- **Curved segment followed by straight:** After drawing a curved segment, click the smooth point you just created to delete the forward control handle. This converts the smooth point to a corner point with one handle. Then click again at a different location to append a straight segment to the end of the curved segment. This is shown in the fourth example in Figure 6.20.

- **Cusp point:** Here's how to convert a smooth point to a corner point with two independent handles (sometimes known as a *cusp point*). First, after drawing a curved segment, don't release the mouse button. Add the Alt key (Option key on the Mac) and pivot to change the direction of the forward control handle. Then drag again at a new location to append another curved segment (this could go in either direction). This creates a cusp as shown in the last example in Figure 6.20.

Old-timers may recall a different technique for converting a smooth point to a cusp. First you draw the curve segment and release the mouse button. Then you hold the Alt key (Option on the Mac) and position the cursor over the point you just created and drag the control handle out from the point. Finally, you draw a new curved segment. The only problem with that technique is that it is too easy to create a new point when you want to pull out the handle.

However, if your fingers are totally adapted to the old technique, don't try to retrain them.

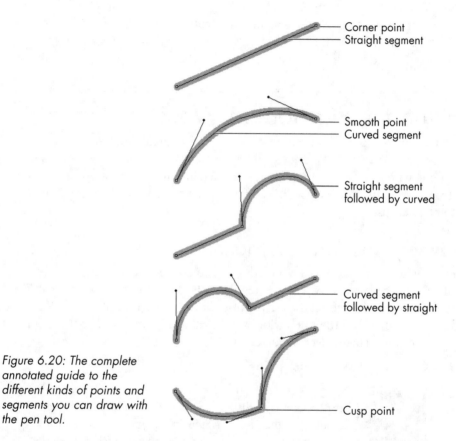

Corner point
Straight segment

Smooth point
Curved segment

Straight segment
followed by curved

Curved segment
followed by straight

Cusp point

Figure 6.20: The complete annotated guide to the different kinds of points and segments you can draw with the pen tool.

Modifying the Closing Point

When you close a shape, you click, drag, and Alt-drag (Option-drag on the Mac), just as you do when creating other points. But because you modify and close in one gesture, it seems a good idea to revisit these techniques within this slightly different context.

 Click the first point in a path to clip off any control handle that may have been threatening to affect the closing segment and you'll close the path with a corner point.

 If the first point in the path is a smooth point, drag it to make sure it remains smooth, thus closing the path with an arc.

If the first point is a corner point, drag to add a control handle that curves the closing segment, which creates a cusp point.

 To convert a smooth point to a cusp on closing, Alt-drag (Option-drag on the Mac) the first point in the path. In this case, you must press the Alt (Option) key before you start the drag—pressing it after you're into the drag has no effect.

Putting the Pen Tool to Work

That was a whole lot of information crammed into a small amount of type—perhaps too much. To make things a little clearer for those of you who are still struggling with this amazing tool, here's your chance to try out the pen tool in the next three sections, in which we'll work on corner points, then smooth points, and finally cusps.

Drawing Free-Form Polygons

Clicking with the pen tool is a wonderful way to create straight-sided polygons. Unlike the shapes you draw with the regular polygon tool, pen tool polygons may be any shape or size. These are pistol-packin' polygons of the Wild West, with no laws to govern their behavior or physical form. I'm talking outlaw polygons, so be sure to take cover as you click.

1. **Click to create a corner point.**

     Select the pen tool and click in the drawing area to create a corner point. The little x next to the pen cursor disappears to show you that a path is now in progress. The new corner point appears as a filled square to show that it's selected. It is also open-ended, meaning that it doesn't have both a segment coming into it and a segment going out from it. In fact, this new corner point—point A—is not associated with any segment whatsoever.

    If you were to stop working on this path right now, this stray point would remain on the page. If you deselect the point, it would be very hard to find. This is the type of point that the Select » Object » Stray Points command will find and let you delete.

2. **Click to add another corner point.**

    Click at a new location in the illustration to create a new corner point—let's call it point B. Illustrator automatically draws a straight segment from point A to point B, as demonstrated in **Figure 6.21**.

Notice that point A now appears hollow rather than filled, showing that point A is a member of a selected path, but is itself deselected. Point B is selected and open-ended. Illustrator automatically selects a point immediately after you create it and deselects all other points.

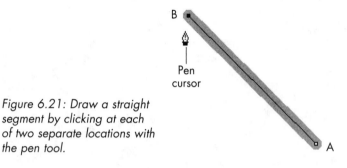

Figure 6.21: Draw a straight segment by clicking at each of two separate locations with the pen tool.

3. **Click to add yet another corner point.**

Click a third time with the pen tool to create a third corner point—point C. Since a point may be associated with no more than two segments, point B is no longer open-ended, as **Figure 6.22** verifies. Such a point is called an interior point.

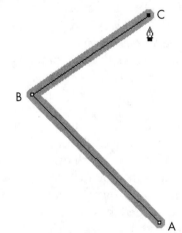

Figure 6.22: Point B is now an interior point, incapable of receiving additional segments.

4. **Click the first point in the path.**

You can keep adding points to a path one at a time for as long as you like. When you're finished, you can close the path by again clicking on point A, as demonstrated in **Figure 6.23**. Illustrator displays the close cursor to show you that it's ready to draw the last segment. If you don't see the close cursor (the pen cursor augmented with a little *o* in the bottom right), you don't have it positioned properly. Since point A is open-ended, it willingly accepts the segment drawn between it and the previous point in the path.

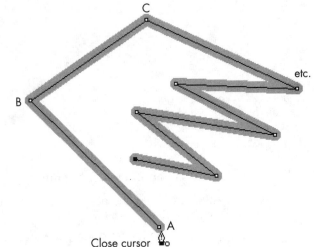

Figure 6.23: Clicking on the first point in a path closes the path and deactivates it. The next point you create will begin a new path.

 If you have the Text Label Hints option from the Smart Guides & Slices Preferences dialog box active (and Smart Guides enabled in the first place, of course), Illustrator displays the word anchor, *providing you with another visual clue that you're in a position to close the path.*

5.   Click to start a new path.

All points in a closed path are interior points. Therefore, the path you just drew is no longer active. Illustrator displays the new path cursor, as in **Figure 6.24**, to show it will draw no segment between the next point you create and any point in the closed path. To verify this, click again with the pen tool. You create a new independent point, which is selected and open-ended in two directions, just like point A. Meanwhile, the closed path becomes deselected, and the path-creation process is begun anew.

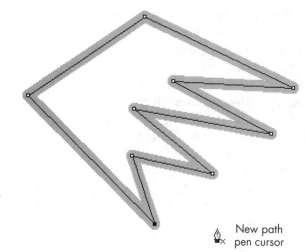

Figure 6.24: After you close
a path, Illustrator adds a little
x to the pen tool cursor to
show that the next point you
create starts a new path.

New path
pen cursor

Drawing Supple Curves

Free-form polygons are great, but you can create them in any drawing program,
even something old and remedial like MacDraw. The real advantage to the pen
tool is that it lets you draw very precise curves.

When you drag with the pen tool to create a smooth point, you specify the location of two control handles. Each of these handles appears as a tiny circle perched
at the end of a thin line that connects the handle to its point (**Figure 6.25**). These
handles act as levers, bending segments relative to the smooth point itself.

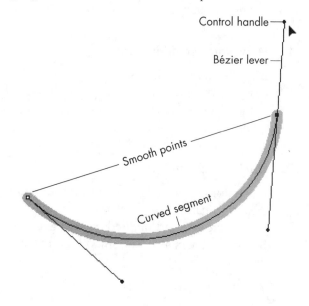

Control handle

Bézier lever

Smooth points

Curved segment

Figure 6.25: Drag with the
pen tool to create a smooth
point flanked by two Bézier
control handles.

The point at which you begin dragging with the pen tool determines the location of the smooth point; the point at which you release becomes a control handle that affects the *next* segment you create. A second handle appears symmetrically from the first handle, on the opposite side of the smooth point. This handle determines the curvature of the most recent segment, as demonstrated in Figure 6.25. You might think of a smooth point as if it were the center of a small seesaw, with the control handles acting as opposite ends. If you push down on one handle, the opposite handle goes up, and vice versa.

Smooth points act no differently than corner points when it comes to building paths. You can easily combine smooth and corner points in the same path by alternately clicking and dragging. However, if the first point in a path is a smooth point, you should drag rather than click the point when closing the path. Otherwise, you run the risk of changing the point to a cusp, as discussed in the next section.

Creating Corners between Curves

A smooth point must *always* have two Bézier control handles, each positioned in an imaginary straight line with the point itself. A corner point, however, is much more versatile. It can have zero, one, or two handles. To create a corner point that has one or two control handles (sometimes called a cusp), you must manipulate an existing corner or smooth point while in the process of creating a path. I'll demonstrate three examples of how this technique can work.

Deleting Handles from Smooth Points

The following steps explain how to add a flat edge to a path composed of smooth points.

1. Draw some smooth points.

Begin by drawing the path shown in **Figure 6.26**. You do this by dragging three times with the pen tool: First drag downward from point A, then drag leftward from point B, and finally drag up from point C (which is selected in the figure). The result is an active path composed of three smooth points.

2. Click the last point created.

Illustrator lets you alter the most recent point while in the process of creating a path. Suppose that you want to flatten off the top of the path to create a sort of tilted bowl, like the one in **Figure 6.27**. Because you can associate smooth points only with curved segments, you must convert the top two smooth points to corner points.

To convert the most recent point—the one on the left—position the pen tool over point C so the pen changes to the cusp cursor (the normal pen cursor with an additional little caret in the lower-right corner, as in Figure 6.26). Then click to amputate the forward handle, which does not yet control a segment.

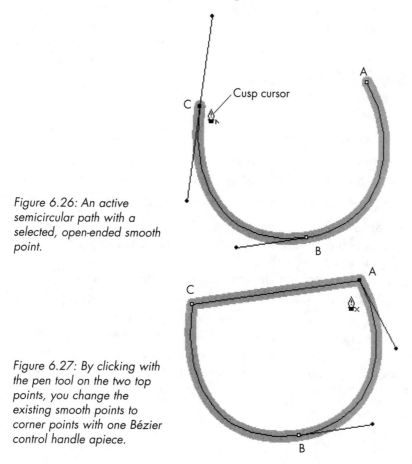

Figure 6.26: An active semicircular path with a selected, open-ended smooth point.

Figure 6.27: By clicking with the pen tool on the two top points, you change the existing smooth points to corner points with one Bézier control handle apiece.

3. **Click the first point in the path.**

You now have an open path composed of two smooth points (A and B) and a cusp (C). You still need to close the path and amputate a handle belonging to point A. A single operation—clicking on the first smooth point—accomplishes both maneuvers. It's that simple. With one click, you close the path and amputate the control handle that would otherwise have curved the closing segment. Hence, the new segment is straight, bordered on both sides by corner points with one handle each, as in Figure 6.27.

If you don't release the mouse button, you can delete the forward handle from point C by another method. You construct the path as explained in Step 1, except that you don't release the mouse button after dragging with the pen to form the forward control handle belonging to point C. Continue to hold down the mouse button, and press the Alt key (Option key on the Mac). You can now drag the forward handle independently of the backward handle. Drag the forward handle back into point C until it disappears. The advantage is you can modify the path as you drag. Just make sure the forward handle is completely gone.

Converting Smooth Points to Cusps

These steps show you how to close the path from Figure 6.26 with a concave top, resulting in a crescent shape.

1. Draw some smooth points.

Begin again by drawing the path shown in Figure 6.26 as described in the first step of the previous section.

2. Alt-drag (Option-drag on the Mac) down from the last point created.

The segments in a crescent are curved, but the upper and lower segments meet to form two cusps. You need to change the two top smooth points to cusps with two control handles apiece—one controlling the upper segment and one controlling the lower segment.

If you still have the mouse pressed as you create the smooth point, you can add the Alt (Option) key and pivot the control handle down. If you've already released the mouse, just hold Alt (Option) and position the cursor over the point, and then drag from point C. The existing handle disappears and a new handle emerges, as shown in **Figure 6.28**. This handle controls the next segment you create.

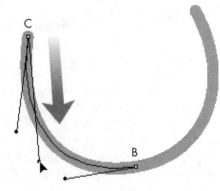

Figure 6.28: Press the Alt key (Option on the Mac) and drag from the selected smooth point to convert the point to a cusp.

3. **Alt-drag (Option-drag on the Mac) up from the first point in the path.**

You close the path in a similar manner, by Alt-dragging (Option-dragging on the Mac) upward from point A. Notice the location of the cursor as you drag, as **Figure 6.29** demonstrates. You drag in one direction, but the handle emerges in the opposite direction. This is because when dragging with the pen tool, you always drag in the direction of the forward segment—that is, the one that *exits* the current point. Illustrator positions the handle controlling the closing segment symmetrically to your drag, even if it is the only handle you're manipulating. It's kind of weird, but it's Illustrator's way.

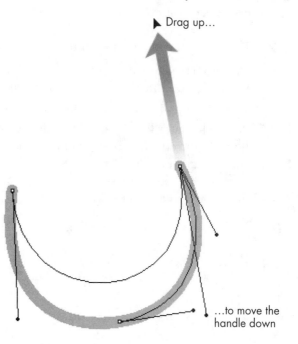

Figure 6.29: Close the path by Alt- or Option-dragging up from the first point in the path

Adding Handles to Corner Points

Last but not least, the next steps tell you how to add a curved segment to a path composed of straight ones.

1. **Draw some corner points.**

Begin by creating the straight-sided path shown in **Figure 6.30**. It doesn't matter how many points are in the path, so long as they're all corner points.

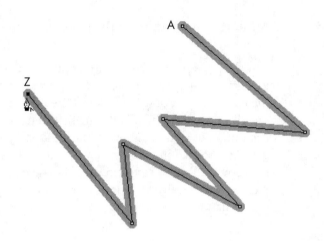

Figure 6.30: An active path
composed entirely of straight
segments with a selected,
open-ended corner point.

2.   Drag from the last corner point created.

Drag from the corner point you've created most recently (point Z in
the figure) to extract a single control handle, as shown in **Figure 6.31**.

You may think you need to hold the Alt (Option) key here, but you
don't. Illustrator knows that if you drag you want to create curves.
It won't convert the corner point to a smooth one, though. It simply
adds a Bézier handle to create a curve for the segment you're about
to create. (If you do press the Alt or Option key before you start the
drag, you'll still wind up with the same results.)

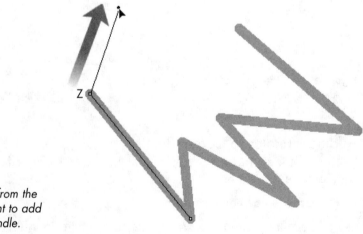

Figure 6.31: Drag from the
selected corner point to add
a Bézier control handle.

3. **Drag from the first point in the path.**

To close the path, drag from the first corner point in the path, as demonstrated in **Figure 6.32**. Once again, you drag in the direction opposite the emerging Bézier control handle. (Same as before, you don't need to hold the Alt or Option key.) Illustrator won't curve the first segment, only the one you're currently working on.

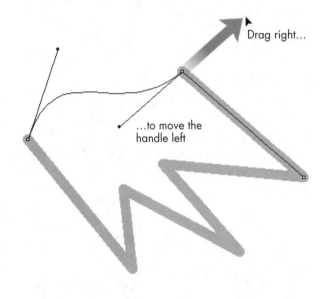

Drag right...

...to move the
handle left

Figure 6.32: Close the path
by dragging on the first
corner point in the path.

Smoothing, Erasing, Reshaping, and Simplifying (aka Fixing Things)

It happens—somewhere, sometime, somehow you're going to make a mistake. Perhaps you have created a pencil path that is too wobbly; perhaps you kept dragging with the pencil beyond where you should have; or maybe you just don't like one side of the shape anymore. Whatever the reason, the bottom line is that you're going to want to change it. Fortunately, Illustrator gives you several tools and a special command that can help reshape, smooth, and erase existing paths. These include the smooth tool, the erase tool, the pencil and paintbrush, the reshape tool, and the Simplify command. I'll start in with the aptly named smooth and erase tools, which can be found in the alternate slots for the pencil tool, as shown in **Figure 6.33**.

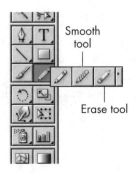

Smooth tool

Erase tool

Figure 6.33: The smooth and erase tools don't create new paths, but they help you modify existing ones.

Smoothing Things Out

The smooth tool works by modifying selected paths. As you drag across the path with the tool, the tool deletes points so that the modified path is closer to the path that you dragged. As **Figure 6.34** shows, the smooth tool works by deleting excess points as well as moving others. Multiple passes with the smooth tool will make a path progressively smoother.

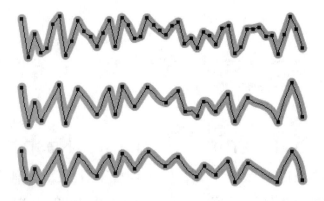

Figure 6.34: The smooth tool was dragged across the original path (top) at its highest setting. The middle example shows how the tool deleted many of the points. The bottom example shows how the smooth tool reshaped the path.

Double-click the smooth tool icon in the toolbox to open its preferences. There you can set the same Fidelity and Smoothness sliders found in the pencil tool preferences. The higher the Fidelity, the more the smooth tool will distort the selected path to the shape of the line that you draw with the smooth tool. The higher the Smoothness, the more the tool will move and delete points in the path.

Erasing Wayward Paths

Lady Macbeth would have loved the erase tool (out, damned path! out, I say!), which lets you delete any portion of a selected path. Simply select the erase tool (the third tool in the pencil tool slot), and drag along or across a selected path. The portion of the path over which you drag will be deleted. Unlike simply deleting a point, which deletes the segment until it reaches a new point, the erase tool adds points at the position where you start and end the drag. In other words, the erase tool can delete part of a path even if there are no anchor points, as **Figure 6.35** illustrates.

 Click with the erase tool on a selected closed path to delete the entire path. Poof! It's gone! If you try this on an open path, it behaves differently; it can delete or detach pieces of an open path, or remove chunks of the fill of an open path.

Figure 6.35: The erase tool was dragged across the original path (left). That portion of the path was deleted and two new anchor points were added as endpoints to the path.

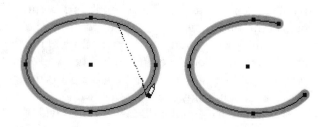

Reshaping with the Pencil and Paintbrush

Of course, the pencil and paintbrush tools can create paths, but they can also reshape them.

As you saw earlier, you can use the pencil tool to create or extend a path. You can also use it to reshape any selected path—even paths created with other tools. As shown in **Figure 6.36**, if you drag the pencil over a selected path, the path reshapes itself to follow the drag of the pencil.

Figure 6.36: The pencil tool was dragged in an arc over the straight line (top). This resulted in a reshaped path (bottom).

 The paintbrush can also reshape selected paths, but only those that have been styled with a brushstroke, as explained in Chapter 16. The pencil can reshape any selected path, including those styled with brushes. (That makes the pencil more powerful than the paintbrush.)

The Stretch Tool

Although Adobe put it in the same slot with the scale tool—for lack of a better location, I suppose—the reshape tool is not a true transformation tool, because you are not given an origin point. The tool does not act around any one point; instead, it stretches the selected portion of the path, anchoring it by the two points just outside that part.

Reshape is too generic a term, implying that the tool could ultimately square a circle. A better name for this would be the stretch tool. As you drag the selected points on a path with the reshape tool, that portion of the path stretches in or out, all the while remaining attached to the anchor points (the two points just outside the selected portion). Moderate use of the tool preserves the path's general shape. This tool comes in handy when you want to tweak the position of part of a path slightly while keeping the path's overall appearance. (Mapmakers love the tool for gently moving rivers without destroying their shape.)

Moving points (and their Bézier handles) with the direct selection tool gives you control over the exact position and shape of a curve, but it can also give rather stiff and labored results if you're not careful. The reshape tool gives you a quick and easy alternative to the labor-intensive selection tools. Unfortunately, the results of the reshape tool can be somewhat unpredictable and most likely won't give you a perfect fit.

To use the reshape tool, select some of the points in an open or closed path, or select an entire open path, with one of the arrow tools. When you use it on a fully selected open path, Illustrator assumes that the endpoints are the anchor points. Now simply drag with the reshape tool. You can start your drag on either a point or a segment of the path. If you start on a point, Illustrator stretches the path to fit your drag by changing the location of the selected points and the direction of their corresponding Bézier handles (though the handle sizes remain the same). On the other hand, if you start your drag on a segment, Illustrator adds a point to the path, and the Bézier handles of the surrounding points change size and shape accordingly.

In general, when you drag with the reshape tool, all the selected points move with respect to each other (and with respect to all the points not selected). You can also specify whether some of the selected points keep their original positioning with respect to one another. To do so, superselect them before you drag (the points will appear surrounded by a tiny square). Then, when you drag with the reshape tool, the superselected portion retains its original shape while moving with the rest of the selected portion, as shown in the lower portion of **Figure 6.37**. The three superselected points retain their original shapes.

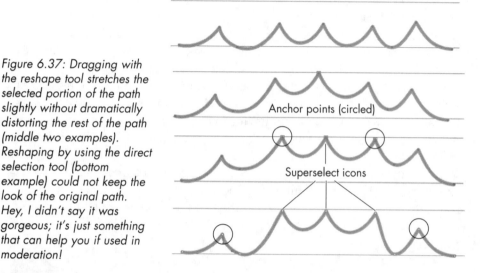

Figure 6.37: Dragging with the reshape tool stretches the selected portion of the path slightly without dramatically distorting the rest of the path (middle two examples). Reshaping by using the direct selection tool (bottom example) could not keep the look of the original path. Hey, I didn't say it was gorgeous; it's just something that can help you if used in moderation!

 To superselect points, Shift-click on selected points with the reshape tool, or marquee over the desired selected points to select multiples.

 Using the reshape tool on a wholly selected closed path is the same as moving the path with the arrow tool—Illustrator doesn't know where to anchor the path for the stretch.

Figure 6.37 gives you some examples of how the reshape tool works and how it compares to moving with the direct selection tool (I've included horizontal lines to help you compare the differences). The top example shows the original wavy line. I want to make the middle reach up higher, without losing its waves. The second one down shows what happens if you drag upward with the reshape tool on just the middle point—shown here with the superselection box. The path keeps its waves as it rises. The third example from the top shows what happens when you drag to superselect three of the points. They keep their shape as the rest of the path rises.

However, if you doubted that the reshape tool really did anything special, look at how the bottom example is all distorted. That's what you get when you just drag with the direct selection tool.

Simplifying Paths

If you draw your own shapes, you will most likely never need to simplify them. You will create only clean, simple, elegant paths. (That's why you are reading this book.) But many designers and artists receive files created from CAD (computer-aided design) programs, such as AutoCAD, which add hundreds of unnecessary points. Others use clip art, such as maps and cartoons that were created using programs such as Streamline and include many extraneous points. Still others inherit logos and other artwork designed by incompetent fools who added points willy-nilly.

So besides making selected paths look like the edge of an open zipper, why should you care if there are millions of points in your artwork? The primary reason is that it's easier to manipulate paths when they have fewer points. It's much easier to select one or two points if you don't have a huge pile of them in one microscopic section.

The other reason is that every single point takes up some part of the memory used to write the file. Excess points add to the file size; and the bigger the file, the more time it will take a print shop or a desktop printer to print the darn thing. And take it from me: you don't want to get a phone call at 2 a.m. from the manager of some service bureau who tells you, "Hey, dude, yer file won't print, man."

If you have a path in need of simplification as shown in **Figure 6.38**, you can apply the simplify command by choosing Object » Path » Simplify. The Simplify dialog box appears as shown in **Figure 6.39**. Adjust the settings as follows:

Figure 6.38: The outline of New York (top) has far too many points. After the Simplify command was applied (bottom) there are far fewer.

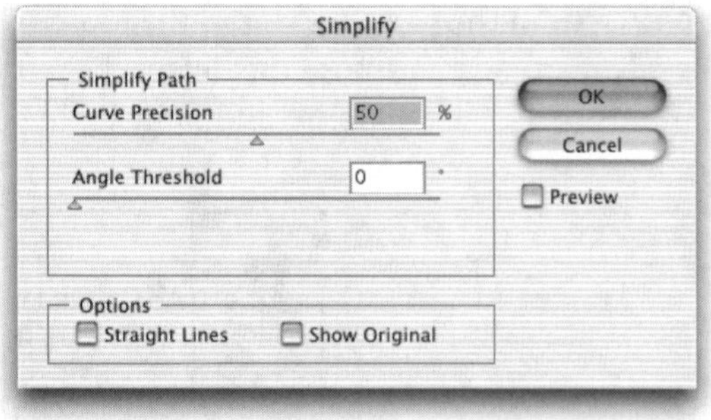

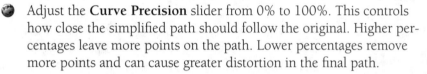

Figure 6.39: The Simplify dialog box is where you can throw out redundant points.

- Check **Preview** to add a display of the number of points in the original version of the object, as well as the number of points that will be in the object after you apply the command.

- Adjust the **Curve Precision** slider from 0% to 100%. This controls how close the simplified path should follow the original. Higher percentages leave more points on the path. Lower percentages remove more points and can cause greater distortion in the final path.

- Adjust the **Angle Threshold** slider from 0 to 180 degrees. This controls the smoothness of the corner points. The lower the Angle Threshold, the more likely sharp angles will be turned into smooth curves.

- Check **Straight Lines** to create straight lines between points.

- Check **Show Original** to add a red preview of the original path. This helps you see just how much your original artwork will be changed.

Operating on Points after the Path Is Done

With all of that under your belt, you may be feeling justifiably empowered and capable of taking on all the path-editing projects you can find. But there are still some unanswered questions. For example, how do you insert a point into a path? For that matter, how do you remove a point without breaking the path in half? And what do you do if you want to change a corner point in an existing path to a smooth point, or a smooth point to a corner? Aaaauuggghhh!

Illustrator provides three tools that let you *precisely* operate on existing points, whether drawn with the pen tool or any of the other tools. These are the add anchor point tool, the delete anchor point tool, and the convert anchor point tool. (All those anchors are weighing me down, so I'll just dump them overboard, leaving the shorter tool names listed in **Figure 6.40**.) To select one of these tools, you can drag from the pen tool slot in the toolbox and select the tool from the pop-up menu. You can also use the default keyboard shortcuts: plus (+) for add point, minus (-) for delete point, and Shift-C for convert point.

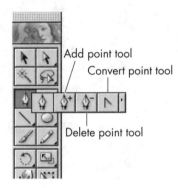

Add point tool
Convert point tool
Delete point tool

Figure 6.40: Drag from the pen icon to access three point-editing tools.

The smooth tool and the erase tool, discussed in the previous section, also let you modify existing paths, but because their behavior is somewhat arbitrary, the more precise add, delete, and convert point tools are preferred by most power users.

Adding Points to a Path

Like an imaginary creature, a path is constantly subject to revision and enhancement. Even if you created it years ago in a different version of Illustrator or even in a different program, it's not permanent. What I'm trying to say here is, if a path doesn't have enough points to get the job done, don't hesitate to add some.

- **Appending a point to the end of an open path:** If an existing path is open, you can add points to either end of it. First activate one of its endpoints by clicking or dragging it with the pen tool. When you position the pen tool over an inactive endpoint, you get the activate cursor, which looks like a pen with a little slash next to it. Drag from the point if you want to retain or add a control handle; click if you want to trim off a control handle or avoid adding one; and Alt-drag (Option-drag on the Mac) if you want to change the direction of a handle. Then click-and-drag to add more points to the path.

  You can also lengthen an open path by dragging from one of its endpoints with the pencil tool. In the unlikely event the path touches a portion of a tracing template, you can even use the auto trace tool.

- **Closing an open path:** Once the path is active, you can close it in any of the ways discussed in the "Putting the Pen Tool to Work" section earlier in this chapter. Just click, drag, or Alt-drag (Option-drag on the Mac) the opposite endpoint with the pen tool. You can also close a path with the pencil tool by dragging from one endpoint to the other. In either case, Illustrator adds a little *o* to the cursor to show a closing is in process.

 Insert a point into a segment: To insert a new interior point into a path, select the add point tool and click anywhere along a segment (except on an existing point). Illustrator inserts the point and divides the segment in two. Illustrator automatically inserts a corner or smooth point depending on its reading of your path. If the point does not exactly meet your needs, you can modify it with the convert point tool, as I'll explain a few paragraphs from now.

You don't have to actually switch to the add point tool. If you have the pen chosen, simply position the cursor over an empty spot on any segment. The regular pen cursor gains a little plus sign (so it looks just like the add point cursor). Click! If you don't see the plus sign, move the pen cursor closer to the path or make sure you haven't activated the Disable Auto Add/Delete check box inside the General Preferences dialog box.

The add point tool is great for filling out a path that just isn't making the grade. If a path isn't curving correctly, it may be that you're trying to make the existing points in the path do too much work. For example, the first path in **Figure 6.41** obeys both the All-or-Nothing and 33-Percent rules, but it still looks overly squarish. That's because it violates a lesser rule that says handles shouldn't point wildly away from each other. To smooth things out, I clicked on the path midway between the two points with the add point tool. In this case, Illustrator inserted a smooth point, because the segment is ultimately smooth at the point where I clicked. I then used the direct selection tool to adjust the control handles and get the more rounded curve shown in the second example.

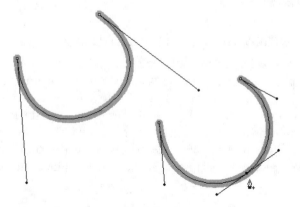

Figure 6.41: If a curve looks squarish no matter how much you monkey with the control handles (left), insert a point with the add point tool (right).

If you don't like the pen tool switching its function, go to the General Preferences dialog box and switch on the Disable Auto Add/Delete option. The pen tool will no longer let you add or delete points to existing segments.

*You don't have to change the preference settings to disable the add/delete option. If you press the Shift key you will temporarily disable the pen tool's capability to add or delete points to existing segments. This comes in handy when you're trying to position a new point over an existing segment of that same path, as shown in **Figure 6.42**. Once the drag is under way, release the Shift key or you will constrain the construction of the point's control handles.*

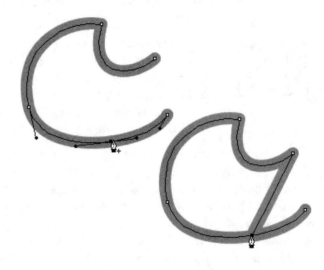

Figure 6.42: The left side shows what happens when you click an active path with the pen tool. You don't continue the path; you add a point. The right side shows what happens when the Shift key is pressed. A new point that extends the original path is created over the path. In both these examples, the Disable Auto Add/Delete check box is not selected.

Press the Alt key (Option key on the Mac) to access the add point tool temporarily when either the delete point or scissors tool is selected.

Removing Points from a Path

To delete an entire path, you just select it with the arrow tool and press the Backspace key (Delete on the Mac). If you love menus, you can choose Edit » Clear.

I said above that it's always OK to add points to a path if it needs some. Similarly, to borrow a page from that old Bézier adage, just because you can make millions of points in a path doesn't mean you should. (For more information about that subject, see the "Simplifying Paths" section earlier in this chapter.) To delete a point or segment, try out one of the following techniques:

Delete a point and break the path: To delete a point, select it with the direct selection tool and press the Backspace (Delete on the Mac) key. When you delete an interior point, you delete both segments associated with that point, resulting in a break in the path. If you delete an endpoint from an open path, you delete the single segment associated with the point.

Delete a segment: You can delete a single interior segment from a path without removing a point. To do so, click the segment you want to delete with the direct selection tool and press Backspace (Delete). Deleting a segment always creates a break in a path.

Delete the rest of the path: After you delete a point or segment, Illustrator selects the remainder of the path. If the path is broken into two parts, both parts will be selected. To delete the whole path, just press Backspace (Delete) a second time. This can be a handy technique if you don't want to switch to the arrow tool. Just click some portion of the path and press Backspace (Delete) twice in a row to delete the whole path.

 This is another place where you can inadvertently create stray points. If you delete the segment of a path that has only two points, those two points will still exist. You have to press Backspace (Delete on the Mac) again, or you'll leave those stray points on your page. If your illustration does have lots of lone points, choose Select » Object » Stray Points and delete them. For full-scale housecleaning, choose Object » Path » Clean Up; this lets you delete stray points, unpainted objects, and/or empty text boxes, all in one fell swoop.

Remove a point without breaking the path: If you want to get rid of a point but don't want to create a break in the path, select the delete point tool and click the point you want to disappear. Illustrator draws a new segment between the two points neighboring the deleted point.

 Just as the pen tool can add points to an active path, so can it delete points. Just move the pen tool over one of the points of an active path. When the tool is in place, the regular pen cursor gains a small minus sign in the lower-right corner, mimicking the appearance of the delete point tool. After you click, Illustrator redraws the path as demonstrated in the middle example of **Figure 6.43.**

Whereas the delete point tool allows you the freedom to delete a point from any path, selected or not, the pen tool's automated delete point feature works only on selected paths. If you don't like the pen tool deleting points, go to the General Preferences dialog box and switch on the Disable Add/Delete option.

Figure 6.43: The top example shows the original curve and the placement of the pen cursor. The second example is the result of clicking the middle point with the pen tool; the point is deleted. The third example shows what happens if you hold the Shift key as you click the segment; Illustrator constructs a new point in the same position as the existing point.

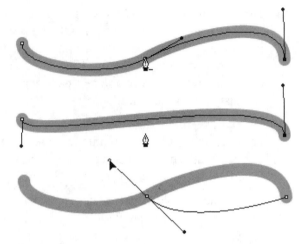

 As before, you can press the Shift key to disable temporarily the pen tool's capability to delete the points of a selected path. This comes in handy when you're trying to position a new point over an existing point of that same path, as shown in the bottom example of Figure 6.43.

 Press Alt (Option on the Mac) to access the delete point tool when the add point tool is active. Have you noticed that Alt (Option) is a toggle between the add and delete point tools? When one is active, Alt (Option) gets you the other.

Converting Points between Corner and Smooth

Of the tools discussed in this chapter, I would probably rank the direct selection tool as most important, the pen tool as number two, and this next tool—the convert point tool—as number three. The convert point tool lets you change a point in the middle of a path from corner to smooth or smooth to corner. When a path is shaped wrong, this tool is absolutely essential.

You can change the identity of an interior point in any of the following ways:

- **Smooth to corner:** Using the convert point tool, click a smooth point. This converts it to a corner point with no control handles.

- **Smooth to cusp:** Drag a control handle belonging to a smooth point to move it independently of the other control handle, thus converting the smooth point to a cusp.

- **Corner or cusp to smooth:** Drag from a corner point or cusp point to convert it to a smooth point with two symmetrical control handles.

Once you have the smooth point, you can use the convert point tool on either handle to change the point into a cusp.

Figure 6.44 shows a path created with the star tool. Like any star, it's made up entirely of corner points and straight segments. But with the help of the convert point tool, you can put some curve on that puppy, as the following steps show.

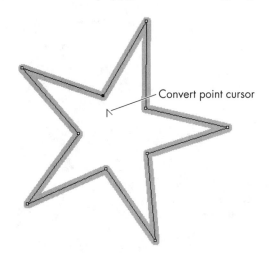

Figure 6.44: The convert point tool, poised to add some wiggle to the star.

1. **Drag from one of the points along the inner radius.**

   Select the convert point tool and drag from one of the inner radius points, as demonstrated in **Figure 6.45**. The corner point changes to a smooth point with symmetrical control handles, bending both neighboring segments.

Figure 6.45: Drag from a corner point to convert it to a smooth point.

2. **Drag the inside control handle outside the star.**

Drag the control handle that moved inside the star to a position outside the star, so that the two spikes form mirror images of each other, as demonstrated in **Figure 6.46**. This converts the smooth point to a cusp, permitting the control handles to move independently.

Figure 6.46: Drag the inside handle to a location outside the star, converting the smooth point to a cusp.

3. **Repeat Steps 1 and 2 on all the inner radius points.**

By dragging control handles from all the points and converting them to cusp points, you can create the flower shape shown in **Figure 6.47**. Yeah, I know, it violates the All-or-Nothing rule; each segment gets just one control handle. But after all, isn't that why we have rules—so we can occasionally ignore them and feel like we're getting away with something?

Figure 6.47: By dragging the control handles out of all the inner radius points, you get this lovely flower outline.

4. Continue to adjust the handles until they're just right.

With the convert point tool, click and drag on any handle that doesn't suit your fancy.

 If you're working with the pen tool, you can press Alt (Option on the Mac) to temporarily get the convert point tool.

 If all of this Bézier stuff is a little bit, ahem, hard to handle, remember this program is merciful and can help you undo your work. Go back to the section on "Doing and Undoing" in Chapter 5 for a refresher if you're feeling unsure.

MODIFYING AND
COMBINING PATHS

Now that you've had the opportunity to create
every kind of object available to Illustrator, it's
time to talk in earnest about messing up these
objects. This chapter specifically discusses how
to edit paths created with the drawing tools covered in Chapters 5 and 6. You can clone paths to
create copies, join paths together and hack them
apart, and carve holes in paths.

As the *pièce de résistance*, you can combine simple paths into highly intricate ones using an assortment of pathfinder commands. These commands allow you to use one path to change the shape of another. The pathfinder commands are for everyone who ever despaired that they can't draw.

With the exception of cloning, you can't apply the operations covered in this chapter to text unless you first convert the characters to paths using Type » Create Outlines or Ctrl+Shift+O (Cmd-Shift-O on the Mac). And you can edit elements inside graphs only if you first ungroup the graphs by pressing Ctrl+Shift+G (Cmd-Shift-G on the Mac) or by choosing Object » Ungroup.

In fact, you'll have to ungroup portions of the graph more than once to break apart the nested groups. To be sure, press Ctrl+Shift+G (Cmd-Shift-G on the Mac) four times to ungroup every single object in the graph. Or you can simply wait to see if Illustrator complains when you try to perform an operation; if it does, press Ctrl+Shift+G (Cmd-Shift-G on the Mac) and try again.

One Million Ways to Replicate

Adobe understands the benefits of duplicating paths, which is why it has blessed Illustrator with so many techniques for cloning and copying. Each of these is useful in different situations. If you aren't already familiar with these techniques, study these sections carefully and commit the techniques to memory. Those poor souls who don't understand duplication miss out on one of the key factors that gives Illustrator the edge over the common household pencil.

If you think you know pretty much everything about duplication already, at least skim the next few sections. I'm confident you'll pick up a handful of techniques that you never heard of, had forgotten, or hadn't considered in quite this context. I'm equally confident you'll find a way to put these new techniques to work in the very near future.

Plain Old Copying and Pasting

Most folks are familiar with the Clipboard, which is a portion of memory set aside to hold objects that you want to duplicate or transfer to another program. It's kind of like the Memory button on a calculator. You store something one minute and retrieve it the next. There are three commands that involve the Clipboard, and you're probably very familiar with them already: cut, copy, and paste.

- You can *cut* (delete) selected objects from the illustration while at the same time sending them to the Clipboard by pressing Ctrl+X (Cmd-X on the Mac) or by choosing Edit » Cut.

- You can *copy* selected objects to the Clipboard (without deleting them) by pressing Ctrl+C (Cmd-C on the Mac) or by choosing Edit » Copy.

- Press Ctrl+V (Cmd-V on the Mac) or Edit » Paste to retrieve the objects from the Clipboard. Illustrator *pastes* the objects in the center of the illustration window and leaves them selected so that you can immediately set about manipulating them.

- Before or after pasting, the objects remain in the Clipboard until the next time you cut or copy. Both commands shove out the old contents of the Clipboard and bring in the new.

- You can also use the Clipboard to hold objects that you want to transport to another program. For example, you can copy paths from Illustrator and place them inside an InDesign document using the standard Copy and Paste commands.

You might be thinking, "I understand C for Copy, but why X for Cut and V for Paste?" It's very simple, really, providing you know the secret code: the first few commands in the Edit menu are assigned the first few keys along the bottom row of the keyboard. Ctrl (or Cmd) in conjunction with Z, X, C, and V activate Undo, Cut, Copy, and Paste, respectively. This was built into the first Macintosh programs, long before Illustrator was created.

 Illustrator also adds neighboring keys D, F, and B to the duplication family—Ctrl+D (Cmd-D on the Mac) for Transform Again, Ctrl+F (Cmd-F on the Mac) for Paste In Front, and Ctrl+B (Cmd-B on the Mac) for Paste In Back, as shown in **Figure 7.1.**

Figure 7.1: Ever notice that all of Illustrator's duplication shortcut keys are clustered in one corner of the keyboard? Coincidence or alien intervention? You decide.

Creating Clones

The Clipboard isn't the only means for copying paths and segments in Illustrator. You can completely bypass the Clipboard—and leave the contents of the Clipboard intact—using a technique called *cloning*.

To clone a path, select it with the arrow or direct selection tool, begin to drag the path, press and hold the Alt key (Option key on the Mac) in mid-drag, release the mouse button, and release the keys. It's very important to press Alt

(Option) *after* you start to drag, because Alt-clicking (Option-clicking on the Mac) with the direct selection tool selects whole paths and groups. And you have to keep Alt (Option) pressed until after you release the mouse button to create the clone. So again: drag, press Alt (Option), release the mouse button, and release the keys. Illustrator positions the clone just in front of the original path.

You can also use the Alt (Option) key with the scale, rotate, reflect, and shear tools to clone a path while transforming it. Chapter 9 tells all there is to know on the subject.

Nudge and Clone

You might think that you could nudge and clone a path by pressing Alt (or Option) with an arrow key. And, provided you do not have any text or text block selected, this is exactly what you can do.

The arrow keys move the object by the amount specified by the keyboard increment value of General Preferences fame. Using the arrow keys with Alt (Option on the Mac) is a useful way to create clones that are evenly spaced from their originals.

Unfortunately, using Alt (Option) with the up or down arrow keys changes the leading for a text block. If you wish to nudge and clone the path of a text block without affecting the text, select the path by Alt-clicking (Option-clicking on the Mac) it with the direct selection tool and then press Alt+arrow key (Option-arrow key). Keep in mind that if the path you are cloning contains text within its borders, the new path is linked to the original path and will automatically fill with any text that does not fit inside the original.

To nudge and clone the path a considerably farther distance from the original, press Alt+Shift+arrow key (Option-Shift-arrow key on the Mac). This moves a path ten times the amount entered in the Keyboard Increment option box.

Cloning Partial Paths

If you Alt-drag or Alt+arrow key (Option-drag or Option-arrow key on the Mac) a path in which all points are selected, Illustrator clones the entire path. But you also can clone individual points and segments that you've selected with the direct selection tool. In fact, Illustrator was the first drawing program for the Mac that let you duplicate bits and pieces of a path. This precise control over partial paths is one of the primary ingredients that distinguishes a professional-level program such as Illustrator from the greater midrange morass.

Figure 7.2 shows what happens when you clone a single segment independent of the rest of the path. If you Alt-drag (Option-drag on the Mac) a straight segment (or press Alt+arrow key (Option-arrow key on the Mac) when the segment is selected), you clone the segment at a new location, as demonstrated in the two left-hand examples in the figure. If you clone a curved segment, you stretch the segment and leave its points at their original positions, as in the right-hand examples.

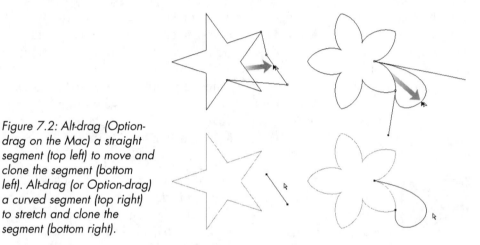

Figure 7.2: Alt-drag (Option-drag on the Mac) a straight segment (top left) to move and clone the segment (bottom left). Alt-drag (or Option-drag) a curved segment (top right) to stretch and clone the segment (bottom right).

When dragging or nudging one or more selected points, you clone the points as well as any segments connected to those points. Whether straight or curved, each segment between a selected point and a deselected point stretches to keep up with the drag, as **Figure 7.3** illustrates.

Figure 7.3: Alt-drag (Option-drag on the Mac) selected points (top examples) to clone all segments connected to those points (bottom).

Copying in Place

The problem with Alt-dragging (Option-dragging on the Mac) partial paths, therefore, is that doing so almost always results in distortions. This technique will drag a straight segment without changing it, but when you clone curved segments or selected points, they're going to stretch.

This is why so many experienced Illustrator artists duplicate partial paths using the Copy and Paste In Front commands. By simply pressing Ctrl+C (Cmd-C on the Mac) followed by Edit » Paste In Front or Ctrl+F (Cmd-F on the Mac), you can copy one or more selected points and segments to the Clipboard and then paste them directly in front of their originals. No stretching, no distortion; Illustrator pastes the paths just as they were copied.

Also worth noting, the Paste In Front command positions the pasted paths at the same spot where they were copied. (By contrast, Edit » Paste positions the paths in the middle of the illustration window, regardless of the placement of the originals.) Therefore, Ctrl+C, Ctrl+F (Cmd-C, Cmd-F on the Mac) creates a copy in place.

 Edit » Paste In Back or Ctrl+B (Cmd-B on the Mac) works just like the Paste In Front command, except that it pastes the copied paths in back of the selected elements. Unless you specifically want to change the stacking order of objects (as explained in Chapter 8), Paste In Front is usually preferable, because it permits you to easily select and edit paths after you paste them.

Cloning in Place

You can also create a quick duplicate directly on top of the original by pressing Alt+up arrow (Option-up arrow on the Mac) followed by the down arrow key. This creates a clone and then nudges it back into place.

What's the benefit? Why not just copy in place like we just did? Because that method replaces the contents of the Clipboard, whereas this one doesn't. And the more accustomed you become to working in this program, the more your brain will automatically know which is the appropriate method for your current task.

Creating a Series of Clones

After Alt (or Option)-dragging or Alt (or Option)+arrowing, you can repeat the distance and direction that a clone has moved by choosing Object » Transform » Transform Again or pressing Ctrl+D (Cmd-D on the Mac). This command creates a series of clones, as shown in **Figure 7.4**.

 You can also apply Object » Transform » Transform Again to a partially cloned path.

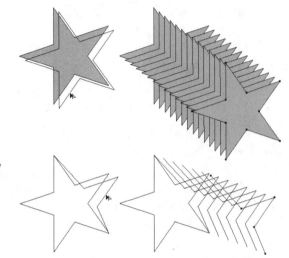

Figure 7.4: After cloning a path (top left), press Ctrl+D (Cmd-D on the Mac) to create a string of equally spaced clones (top right). If you create a series of partial clones (bottom), Illustrator applies the same movement to all points.

 The keystroke for Transform Again does not stand for Duplicate the object; it stands for Duplicate the action. For instance, if you drag an object 3 inches to the right, you can switch to another object and choose Transform Again. The second object will move the same distance as the first. But no duplicate will be created. The command duplicates only the move, not the object.

Expanding the Clone

A little-known command for cloning paths is Offset Path. This command clones a selected path and expands the outline of the clone an equal distance in all directions.

Select a path and choose Object » Path » Offset Path. The dialog box shown in **Figure 7.5** appears. Enter the numeric distance of the expansion into the Offset option box. If you want to create a slimmer, smaller path, enter a negative value. Then press Enter (Return on the Mac).

The Offset Path dialog box also offers the Joins and Miter Limit options, both of which affect how Illustrator draws the corners of the cloned paths. The default Joins setting (Miter) creates pointed corners, but you can also round off the corners (Round) or cut them short (Bevel). The Miter Limit value chops the corner short if the path threatens to grow too long. For more information on these basic stroking concepts, consult Chapter 16.

Figure 7.5: Enter a value into the Offset option box to specify how far Illustrator should expand a selected path. Positive values expand objects. Negative values shrink them.

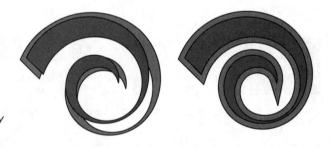

As shown in **Figure 7.6**, there are four things to notice about the clones created by the offset command.

- Offset Path is the one cloning operation that positions clones in back of their originals, so that all paths are plainly visible.

- You can enter negative values into the Offset option box. In that case, Illustrator places the diminutive clone in front of the original.

- Expanding a path using the offset command is not the same as scaling it. Object » Path » Offset Path adds an amount all around the path, as the light gray shape shows. By contrast, the scale tool enlarges interior areas so that they no longer align with the original.

Figure 7.6: The difference between scaling an object (left) and using the Offset command (right). Scale makes the object bigger, but it doesn't fit snugly around the original. The Offset command fits the clone snugly around the original.

The offset command treats closed paths as explained above. With open paths, the command creates a closed path that outlines the original path.

Dragging and Dropping

The one remaining method for duplicating objects allows you to drag an object from one illustration window and drop it into another. Naturally, you have to be able to see at the same time at least a little bit of the illustration window you're dragging from and the one that you're dragging into on your computer screen. Then, armed with the arrow tool or direct selection tool, simply drag one or more selected objects out of one window and into a background window, as illustrated in **Figure 7.7**. You can also use this technique to drag Illustrator objects onto InDesign pages.

There's no need to press the Alt key (Option key on the Mac) when dragging and dropping. Illustrator automatically clones the object, leaving the original in one window and adding a duplicate to the second. (As with other cloning techniques, the Clipboard contents remain unchanged.) After your drop, Illustrator brings the receiving window to the front, so that you can position the object and edit it if need be.

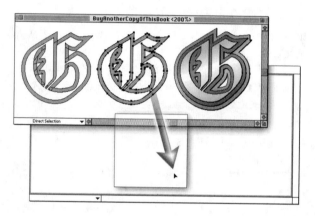

Figure 7.7: Drag selected objects from one window and drop them into another to clone objects between illustrations.

Dragging Scraps and Clips

You can create small files consisting of only the selected element by dragging objects from Illustrator and dropping them onto the Desktop. On a Windows system, these bits are called *scraps* (on the Mac, the word for them is *picture clippings*).

Picture clippings are little holding cells that keep objects until you need to use them later. On the Mac, when you drag and drop objects onto the Desktop, Illustrator works with the system software to create a picture clipping file, which looks like a frayed page with a bent corner. You can double-click the file icon at the Finder level to view its contents. (Illustrator doesn't have to be running for you to view the picture.)

The Windows scrap is created in the same manner (simply drag and drop selected items onto the desktop), but unfortunately, you cannot view its contents as you can on a Mac. Instead, double-clicking on a scrap launches Illustrator (if Illustrator is not already running) and opens the scrap as an independent window.

At any time in the future, you can add the objects from a picture clipping or a scrap into an illustration by dragging the scrap file or picture clipping and dropping it—into an Illustrator file or, similarly, into InDesign, Photoshop, or some other application that supports the Illustrator format.

If you've been using a Macintosh for any period of time, you probably know about the Scrapbook. After choosing the Scrapbook command from the Apple menu, you can paste items into the Scrapbook window to create a sort of Rolodex of Clipboard stuff. What nobody seems to know is that you don't have to copy objects from Illustrator to paste them into the Scrapbook. You can drag and drop Illustrator items to and from the Scrapbook without changing the contents of the Clipboard.

Staying within the Window

Instead of dragging an object outside the window, you might want to drag the object to a new position within the window. This is called *autoscrolling*. Because it is so easy to drag outside the window, you need a few tricks to make Illustrator automatically scroll the window as you drag an object.

First, you need to hover your cursor over a scroll bar or title bar. For example, after you grab an object, drag it onto the right scroll bar and hold it there; Illustrator scrolls to the right. If you drag the object onto the title bar, Illustrator scrolls upward.

But what if you want to scroll to the left, where no scroll or title bar appears? In this case, drag the object to the left edge of the window. Pause right over the thin edge of the window. It's tricky, but it works. When you've scrolled far enough, drag the object back into the window and drop it into place.

Joining Points and Paths

Enough duplicating already. It's time to do something different with all these paths we're making, starting with joining. Depending on the effect you're trying to achieve, a Pathfinder function, which I cover at the end of the chapter (see "Use a Path to Change a Path") may be a better alternative than the semimanual procedures discussed below. But, in the spirit of learning the hard way first, if only to appreciate the new and improved version, here we go.

Illustrator's Join command lets you join two open paths to create one longer open path. Or you can connect two endpoints in a single open path to form a closed path.

   Drag one endpoint onto another with the direct selection tool so that it snaps into alignment. Then select the two endpoints (by marqueeing around them with the direct selection tool) and choose Object » Path » Join, or press Ctrl+J (Cmd-J on the Mac). This fuses the two endpoints into a single interior point. Illustrator displays the Join dialog box, which lets you select whether you want to fuse the points into a corner point or a smooth point. Make your selection and press Enter (Return on the Mac).

If you don't see the Join dialog box as shown in **Figure 7.8** after pressing Ctrl+J (Cmd-J on the Mac), it's because your points aren't coincident—that is, one point isn't exactly, precisely snapped into alignment with the other. Press Ctrl+Z (Cmd-Z on the Mac) to undo the join, and then try again to drag one point into alignment with the other, or just press Ctrl+Alt+Shift+J (Cmd-Option-Shift-J on the Mac). The latter averages and fuses the points in one brilliant move.

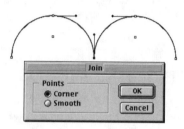

Figure 7.8: The Join dialog box appears only if two selected points are exactly aligned.

*If so much as 0.001 point stands between two selected points, Object » Path » Join connects the points with a straight segment. (That is roughly 0.3 micron, the size of one of your tinier bacteria—no joke—hence the insightful **Figure 7.9**.) So if you need a straight segment in a hurry, select two endpoints and press Ctrl+J (Cmd-J on the Mac).*

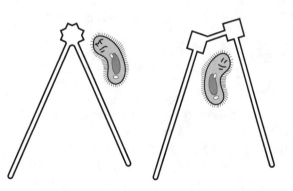

Figure 7.9: Choose Object » Path » Join to fuse two exactly aligned points into a single point (left). But if a bacterium can fit between the points (right), Illustrator connects the points with a straight segment.

If you aren't particularly concerned with the placement of your points, and you want to join the points into one, press Ctrl+Alt+Shift+J (Cmd-Option-Shift-J on the Mac). This brings the points together by averaging their locations and then joins them into a corner point. It's what's known as an Average/Join command.

- To undo the Average/Join, you must press Ctrl+Z (Cmd-Z on the Mac) twice in a row—once to undo the averaging and again to undo the join.

- To close an open path, you can select the entire path with the arrow tool and press Ctrl+J (Cmd-J on the Mac). If the endpoints are coincident, a dialog box comes up asking you how you want to fuse the points. Otherwise, Illustrator connects the points with a straight segment.

 Whatever you do, don't use the Average/Join command when an entire path is selected. Illustrator averages all points in the path into a single location, creating a very ugly effect. If you mess up and do what I told you not to do, press Ctrl+Z (Cmd-Z on the Mac) to make it better.

Splitting Paths into Pieces

The opposite of joining is splitting, and Illustrator provides five basic ways to split paths apart. We touched on two methods in Chapter 6: You can select a segment or an interior point with the direct selection tool and press the Backspace key (Delete key on the Mac). Or you can use the erase tool to dissolve sections of a path.

But what if you want to break apart a path without creating a rift? Or what if you want to break a path in the middle of a segment? The answer to either question is to use the scissors tool, knife tool, or the Slice command. The scissors tool creates a break at a specific point; the knife tool creates a free-form slice; and the Slice command uses a selected path to slice through all other paths that it comes in contact with. The only things lacking are a nail file and a toothpick.

Snipping with the Scissors

The scissors tool is one of Illustrator's earliest tools, predating just about every path-editing tool except the arrow tool. Its operation hasn't changed that much since the old days. You click anywhere along the outline of a path to snip the path at that point; the path need not even be selected. As **Figure 7.10** shows, you can click either a segment or a point.

Whenever you click with the scissors tool, Illustrator inserts two endpoints. As the bottom example in Figure 7.10 illustrates, you can drag one endpoint away from the other with the direct selection tool. The problem is, one endpoint is necessarily in front of the other. Why is that a problem? Every so often, you'll want to drag the point that's in back, and you won't be able to get to it because the front point is in the way.

Naturally, you can drag the front point out of the way, and then drag the rear point. But that means moving both points.

The solution is to select both points by drawing a marquee with the direct selection tool or direct select lasso tool. Then Shift-click the point to deselect the top point. Now just the bottom point is selected. Press an arrow key three or four times to nudge the bottom point so you can easily select it, and then drag it to the desired location.

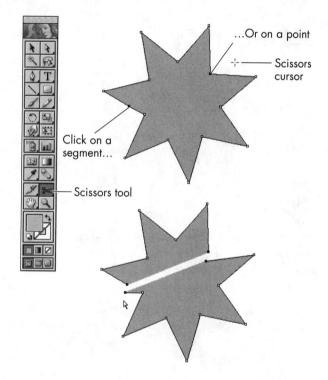

Figure 7.10: Snip a break in a path by clicking on the outline of the path with the scissors tool.

Wielding the Knife

The other path-splitting tool is the knife tool (the alternate tool in the scissors tool slot). It looks like a little Ginsu knife (you know, the one that cuts through tin cans and still slices and dices like a dream). The knife tool can cut through multiple paths at a time. The knife tool splits only paths and it doesn't affect text, unless the text is first converted to paths with the Create Outlines command.

 As long as one or more paths are selected, the knife tool will sever those paths but leave all unselected paths unchanged. On the other hand, if nothing in your document is selected, the knife happily chops any path that's in its, er, path.

Before you operate the knife tool, make sure that the objects you want to cut through are all assembled. Then just drag with the knife, much as you would with the pencil tool. As demonstrated in **Figure 7.11**, Illustrator's knife tool carves through all closed paths and all open filled paths that it comes into contact with.

 Although the knife tool has come a long way, it still has a couple of small quirks. The first is that it doesn't affect unfilled open paths. Second, it automatically closes filled open paths after it splits them into pieces.

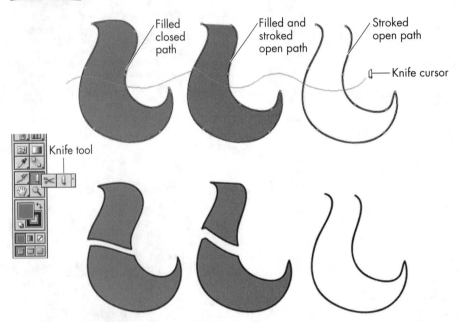

Figure 7.11: Drag with the knife tool (top) to cut through paths (bottom). Notice that the knife tool does not cut unfilled open paths. In addition, it closes the open filled path after it cuts it in two.

To make nice straight cuts, use the Alt key (Option key on the Mac) while you're dragging with the knife tool. Be sure to press Alt (Option) before you start your drag. If you press it after you're already into the drag, it will have no effect. Press and hold both Alt (Option) and the Shift key to constrain the slices to a multiple of 45 degrees (plus whatever value you've entered into the Constrain Angle option box in the General Preferences dialog box).

Cutting with a Path

The bad news about the knife tool is that it doesn't offer much control. You can't carefully position points and control handles to specify the exact directions of your incision, and you can't edit the cut after drawing it.

But the Divide Objects Below command gives you a lot more control (I think it's a lot more fun, too). This replacement for the Slice command (if you don't know how the word *slice* has been co-opted, you'll know after you've read Chapter 21) lets you use any path you've drawn in Illustrator to cut through filled objects that lie beneath it. Here's how to do it.

1. Assemble the filled objects that you want to hack to pieces.

2. Draw the path that you want to use to slice up the objects. You can use the pen tool, star tool, spiral tool, or any other drawing tool.

3. Position the path over the objects. Then choose Object » Path » Divide Object Below. Illustrator slices through all objects that the selected path overlaps and disconnects the pieces wherever the path dictates. But say goodbye to your original shapes, because they'll be gone.

In **Figure 7.12**, I used a spiral to divide a star. After cutting with the spiral, I drew a short straight line into the center of the shape with the pen tool (as noted in the figure) and repeated the command. This was so that I could fill different loops of the spiral with different colors. If you want that kind of luxury, you definitely have to divide twice; you can't Divide Objects Below with more than one cutting path at a time.

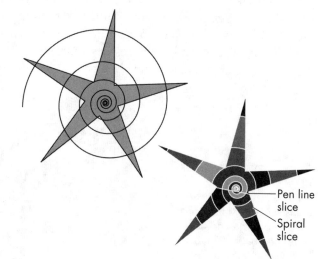

Figure 7.12: Using Object » Path » Divide Objects Below, I twice cut into a star, first with a spiral tool and then with a small straight line created with the pen tool.

Pen line slice

Spiral slice

Carving Holes in Paths

Illustrator lets you carve holes inside a path. You can see through these holes to objects and colors that lie behind the path. A path with holes in it is called a *compound path*, which is the subject of this section.

The most common kind of compound path is converted text. Consider the baroque character in **Figure 7.13**. This character is actually the combination of three paths—the serrated ruffles on the left side, the main body of the *B*, and the hole inside the *B* (filled with white in the figure). Illustrator automatically combined these three paths into a single compound path when I chose Type » Create Outlines.

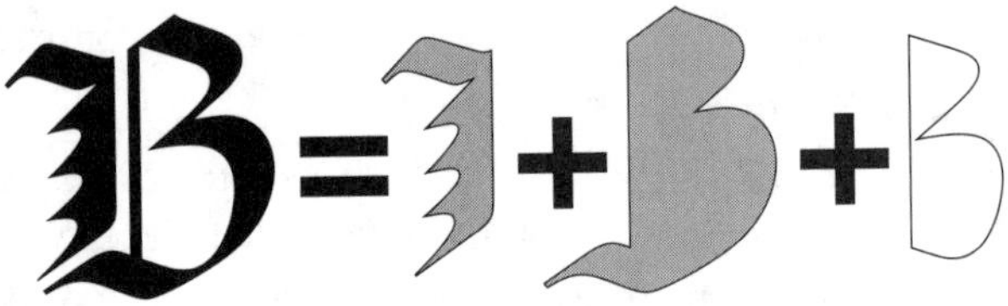

Figure 7.13: This character of type comprises three paths, all joined together into one compound path.

At this point you might be thinking, "Why do you need a path with a hole in it? Why not just stick the smaller path in front of the bigger path and fill the smaller path with the background color?" Here are two reasons why you might want authentic holes in your paths.

- First, the background may contain lots of different colors, as in **Figure 7.14**; it could even contain a photograph or a gradient. To create the first *B* in the figure, I filled to interior shape with light gray in an attempt to vaguely match the background, but it doesn't look right at all. The second B is a proper compound path, allowing us to see through the B to anything behind it.

Figure 7.14: Three filled paths set in front of a multi-colored background (left) compared with a compound path with a hole carved into it (right).

Second, working with opaque paths limits your flexibility. Even if you can get away with filling an interior path with a flat color, you'll have to change that color any time you change the background or move the objects against a new background. But with a compound path, you can move the object against any background without changing a thing. You can even add effects like drop shadows without modifying the compound path one iota. It's flexibility at its finest.

Creating a Compound Path

As I already mentioned, Illustrator automatically turns (converted) letters into compound paths. But you may want to create additional compound paths of your own. Doughnuts, ladders, eyeglasses, windows, ski masks, and slices of Swiss cheese are just a few of the many items that lend themselves to compound paths.

To make a compound path, do the following:

1. **Draw two shapes.**

    Make one smaller than the other. You can use any tool to draw either shape, and the paths can be open or closed. You'll probably want to stick with closed paths to ensure even curves and continuous strokes; with open paths, the fills get flattened off at the open edge.

2. **Select both shapes and choose Object » Compound Path » Make.**

    Or press the keyboard equivalent, Ctrl+8 (Cmd-8 on the Mac). Where the two shapes overlap, the compound path is transparent; where the shapes don't overlap, the path is filled.

     If you don't get any holes at all, you must have drawn the shapes in different directions. The solution is to select one of the shapes with the direct selection tool, click the Attributes palette, and click the Reverse Path Direction button that is not active. For a detailed explanation of this, read the "Reversing Subpath Direction" section a few short pages from now.

3. **Edit the individual shapes in the compound path with the direct selection tool.**

    After you combine two or more shapes into a compound path, select the entire path by clicking on it with the arrow tool. If you want to select a point or segment belonging to one of the subpaths—that's the official name for the shapes inside a compound path—press Ctrl+ Shift+A (Cmd-Shift-A on the Mac) to deselect the path and click an element with the direct selection tool. You can then manipulate points, segments, and control handles as usual. For example, **Figure 7.15** shows how the holes in the beautiful bouncing B have been moved and reshaped.

With the direct selection tool, Alt-click (Option-click on the Mac) a subpath twice to select the entire compound path. If you decide later to restore the compound path to its original independent parts, select the entire path and choose Object » Compound Path » Release, or press Ctrl+Alt+8 (Cmd-Option-8 on the Mac).

 If there's nothing behind your compound path, it may be hard to tell if you've actually created the compound. Turn on the page grid (Ctrl+" or Cmd-"). As long as the grid is in back, you'll see it through the compound path. For more information on grids, see Chapter 8, "Developing a Flair for the Schematic."

Figure 7.15: Use the direct selection tool to move and reshape the subpaths of a compound path.

Working with Compound Paths

Compound paths are very special and wonderful things that you can screw up very easily. If you know what you're doing, you can juggle tens or hundreds of subpaths and even add holes to existing compound paths. But by the same token, you can accidentally add a hole when you don't mean to, or you may encounter a perplexing error message when editing a subpath in a manner that Illustrator doesn't allow.

The following tidbits of information are designed to help eliminate as much confusion as possible:

- You can't connect a subpath from one compound path with a subpath from a different compound path or a different group, whether with the Join command or the pen or pencil tool. This may sound like something you'll never want to do, but I promise one day, you'll try to connect points from two different compound paths or groups and you'll go absolutely nuts trying to figure out why Illustrator won't let you do it. It happens to everybody.

When—not if—it happens to you, you have two options: Give it up, or break the compound paths and groups apart. If you decide on the latter, with the arrow tool, select two paths you want to connect. This also selects all other subpaths associated with these paths. Then release the paths by pressing Ctrl+Alt+8 (Cmd-Option-8 on the Mac) once and then press Ctrl+Shift+G (Cmd-Shift-G on the Mac) about four times in a row. This is overkill, but it's preferable to wasting a lot of time with trial and error. Who knows how many nested groups are involved? Then join the paths and re-create the compound path as desired.

Another wonderful constraint is that you can't combine shapes from different groups or compound paths into a single compound path. If, when you try to make a compound path, Illustrator complains that the selected objects are from different groups, press the release/ungroup sequence (shown above) a few times to free the chains that bind the objects, and then try pressing Ctrl+8 (Cmd-8) again.

You can combine as many shapes inside a compound path as you like. You can likewise add subpaths without releasing the compound path. There are two ways to do this. One way is to select the compound path with the arrow tool, Shift-click the shapes you want to add, and press Ctrl+8 (Cmd-8) again. (This doesn't create a compound path inside a compound path or anything weird like that. It just adds the new shapes as subpaths.)

 Alternatively, you can select the shapes that you want to add to the compound path and cut them by pressing Ctrl+X (Cmd-X on the Mac). Then select any subpath in the compound path with the direct selection tool—not the arrow tool!—and press either Ctrl+F or Ctrl+B (Cmd-F or Cmd-B on the Mac) to paste the cut shapes in front or in back of the selection. This automatically makes the pasted shapes part of the compound path.

 *Because you can paste a shape into a compound path, you may find yourself doing it accidentally when you don't want to. If you Paste In Front/Back while one object in a compound path is selected, the new object will be made part of the compound group. However, if you Paste In Front/Back while the entire compound path is selected, the new object is not made part of the compound group. This is an important distinction.*

So far as Illustrator is concerned, a compound path is a single path. Therefore, changing the fill or stroke of one subpath in the compound path changes all other subpaths as well. So if you ever change the color

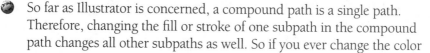

of one shape, and another shape changes as well, you can rest assured both shapes are part of the same compound path. If you need two different colored objects to create a hole where they overlap, you need to use a different technique: one of the pathfinder commands covered in the section "Use a Path to Change a Path" later in this chapter.

Reversing Subpath Direction

By this time, you've probably created a compound path or added a new subpath only to find that you're not getting any holes. You think you did something wrong, or perhaps I've left out a step or two. Neither is the case. It's just that Illustrator needs a little kick in the rear end to make it shape up and fly right.

You see, Illustrator calculates the areas in a compound path based on the directions in which the subpaths flow. This implies a clockwise or counterclockwise flow. For one subpath to create a hole in another, the two paths have to flow in opposite directions. Using alternately clockwise and counterclockwise paths does the trick.

At this point you might think, "Oh, great, now I have to pay attention to how I draw my shapes." Luckily, you don't. When you combine two or more shapes into a compound path, Illustrator automatically changes the backmost shape to a clockwise flow and all others to counterclockwise. It does this regardless of how you drew the shapes.

Illustrator's default approach works swell when the rear shape in the selection is also the largest shape. The left example in **Figure 7.16** shows precisely this setup. The large backmost circle flows clockwise, and the two smaller squares flow counterclockwise. Therefore, the counterclockwise squares cut holes in the clockwise circle. But things go awry in the right example, in which one of the squares is in back. The circle and square do not cut holes into the rear square, which leaves the forward square opaque.

But Illustrator wouldn't be Illustrator if it didn't give you the power to correct the situation. You can change the direction of any path by selecting it with the direct selection tool and modifying the setting in the Attributes palette. Here's how to correct a problem like the second example in Figure 7.16.

1. Press Ctrl+Shift-A (Cmd-Shift-A on the Mac) to deselect everything.

2. Select one of the subpaths that doesn't seem to be behaving correctly with the direct selection tool.

3. Click the Attributes tab to bring the Attributes palette into the forefront. The Attributes palette is shown in **Figure 7.17**.

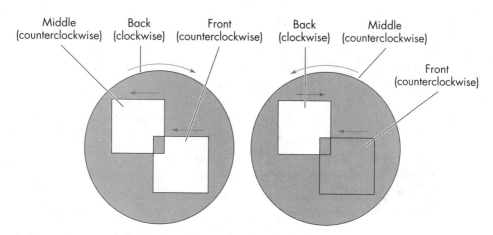

Figure 7.16: Compound paths created when the large circle is in back (left) and when one of the squares is in back (right).

Figure 7.17: Use the Reverse Path Direction buttons to change the direction of a selected subpath.

4. Click the Reverse Path Direction button that is not active. This changes the flow of the path from counterclockwise to clockwise or vice versa depending on which direction the path originally went.

5. Now select one of the other misguided subpaths (if there are any) and, again in the Attributes palette, click the nonactive Reverse Path Direction button to switch the flow of the subpath to the other direction.

 Illustrator now has two types of compound paths: zero-non-winding and odd-even. Adobe says that odd-even is the more predictable method, and I couldn't agree more—it makes a hole out of every other section within a given compound path. Zero-non-winding allows you to choose whether you want it to behave that way, or to make all the areas fill in; you can then customize your path further by reversing the direction of selected paths to create ad hoc holes.

The default path type for compound shapes is zero-non-winding (as opposed to the default in Photoshop, which is odd-even). The reverse path direction option is available only on a zero-non-winding compound path—yes, it's true, the odd-even paths are smarter and don't get directionally messed up like they did in the old days.

6. Keep selecting paths and fiddling with the Reverse Path Direction buttons as much as you want until you get things the way you want them. Keep in mind that you can achieve transparency only in areas where an even number of subpaths overlap. If an odd number of sub-paths overlap, the area is always opaque.

 The Reverse Path Direction buttons are dimmed unless a subpath inside a compound path is selected. You cannot change the direction of standard paths for the simple reason that there's no point in doing so.

One last bit of explanation about the Reverse Path Direction buttons: The buttons are not available unless you have selected the subpath of a compound path. They don't work to change the direction of other objects.

Use a Path to Change a Path

At last we come to the Pathfinder—a shape-shifter's candy shop. Waltz into the Pathfinder palette (shown in **Figure 7.18**) and marvel at all the commands that permit you to combine simple paths into more complex ones. You can merge paths together, subtract one path from another, break paths into bits, and perform other path operations.

 Not only are the Pathfinder features more intuitive and powerful than before, but they've also taken a page out of recent trends in broadcasting and gone live. You can read more about that in Chapter 19 as well.

Unfortunately, the icons are not the most intuitive things ever created. If the minimal headings and the tiny representations aren't quite revealing enough, you can pause slightly over each icon and read the tool tip that appears. Or you can make copies of Figure 7.18 and paste them all around your house and office until you have the names memorized.

 Years ago the Pathfinder commands were part of the Filter menu. Then Adobe moved them out to the Path submenu. Then they moved them to the Pathfinder palette. This is why old-time Illustrator users will often call them the Pathfinder filters. It is also why Illustrator users wonder where they are in each new version of the product. Happily, they stayed put this time around.

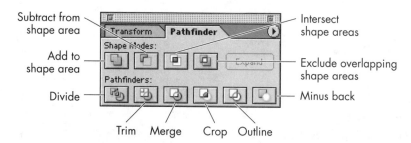

Subtract from shape area

Add to shape area

Divide

Intersect shape areas

Exclude overlapping shape areas

Minus back

Trim   Merge   Crop   Outline

Figure 7.18: The Pathfinder palette with all the cryptic icons labeled. The modes in the top row are the "live" ones that let you retain editable shapes. The functions in the bottom row create final combinations (which are editable in and of themselves, but only in their final form—no more live effects).

 The Pathfinder shape modes (the top row of icons in the palette) correspond directly to the shape layer icons in Photoshop 6. So if you use both programs, you have to memorize this bunch only once.

As you become more adept at using the Pathfinder commands, you'll find them very helpful for assembling primitive shapes—such as rectangles, ovals, polygons, and stars—into more elaborate paths, rather than drawing the elaborate paths from scratch with the pen tool. You can also use the commands to generate translucent color overlays and drop shadows.

The following sections explain every one of the Pathfinder commands except Trap. The Trap command lets you generate (you guessed it) "traps" to eliminate gaps in color printing. I'll cover this particular command with the other printing functions in Chapter 24.

Adding Shapes Together

The Add command combines all selected shapes into a single path. Illustrator removes all the overlapping stuff and turns the selected paths into a single, amalgamated object. It fills and strokes this new object with the fill and stroke from the foremost of the selected paths.

In the top left of **Figure 7.19**, for example, the star, circle, and stripes were combined using the Add command. The result is the single combined path, one that Adobe seems to like enough to use in its literature to highlight this feature.

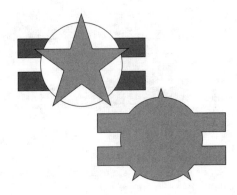

Figure 7.19: The Add
command was applied to the
four shapes on the top. All
four shapes are combined
into one object (bottom).

The Merge command is another way of combining shapes. As shown in **Figure 7.20**, Merge is more selective than Add. It combines only paths with the same fill color. It also clips shapes wherever they overlap, and (for reasons I cannot fathom) it deletes the stroke.

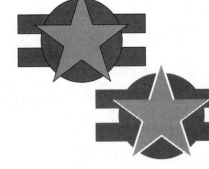

Figure 7.20: Merge was
applied to the four shapes on
the left. Notice that objects
with the same fill and stroke
are combined. I moved the
objects to show that they
were clipped where they
used to overlap.

Remember, these shapes are now live, which means you still have control over the individual elements that make up the compound shapes you're creating. Make sure to see how this works—after you add or subtract a shape, direct-select one of the original shapes, move it away, modify it if you like, move it back into position, and see how it still obeys the original Pathfinder command.

Subtracting Shapes from Each Other

Three Pathfinder commands—Exclude, Subtract, and Minus Back—remove shapes from each other.

- **Exclude**: This is a kind of poor man's compound path function. It removes all overlapping sections of the selected shapes and makes the cutouts transparent. As shown at the bottom right of **Figure 7.21**, this cuts out a large hole, much like the hole in a compound path. The differences are that the original shapes are still editable, and all of the shapes that result from being excluded can be expanded to become separate objects.

 Where two or more shapes overlap, you won't get transparency; you'll get the double-reversal effect of seeing the original color again (or whatever color has taken precedence in your design).

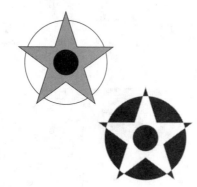

Figure 7.21: The Exclude command was applied to the top group of objects. This divided the objects as shown in the bottom group.

Subtract: This command clips all selected paths out of the rear path in the selection. In **Figure 7.22**, for example, I selected the star and two stripes and clicked the Subtract button. The result is two stripes with a star cut out of them, as if they had been attacked by a cookie cutter. If you're graduating from Illustrator 9, this is the new and improved version of what used to be called Minus Front.

Figure 7.22: The result of clipping the star out of compound path stripes with the Subtract command.

There is an important trick to Figure 7.22. Before I applied Subtract, I selected the two stripes and made them a compound path. Because they didn't overlap, there was no change in their appearance, but as far as the Subtract command was concerned, they were now a single path. So it was able to cut out a path inside both of them. Without the compound path, the star would have affected only one stripe—the one all the way at the back.

- **Minus Back**: This is exactly the opposite of Subtract; it clips all selected paths out of the front path in the selection. In **Figure 7.23**, I selected the star and stripes and clicked the Minus Back button. This left the star with two stripes cut out of it.

Figure 7.23: Here I've used the Minus Back command to clip the stripes out of the star.

 The Layers palette recognizes your live shapes and labels them as "compound shapes," even showing a thumbnail of the individual elements you're working with. But beyond trying to show you how well it knows what's going on in the document, the Layers palette is trying to tell you something else: you can add to your live shape right here in the palette. Find the sublayer for another path, and drag it into the compound shape; that object will become part of the compound shape.

Finding Overlap and Intersection

The rest of the Pathfinder commands are devoted to the task of finding and separating the intersecting portions of selected shapes.

- **Intersect**: This command retains the overlapping sections of selected shapes and *appears* to discard the areas where the shapes don't overlap, as shown in **Figure 7.24**. (But they're not really discarded; they're only consigned to an invisible state.) Illustrator fills and strokes the resulting shapes with the colors from the frontmost shape in the selection.

 If every one of the selected paths does not overlap at some location, Intersect delivers an error message telling you that the command has done nothing.

Figure 7.24: The results of applying the Intersect command to the star and circle. The result is a star with slightly curved points.

 To throw away the "excess" portions of a shape—that is, to create a final shape for which you don't need the interactivity —press Alt (Option on the Mac) while you click an icon to create the shape, or select it and click the Expand button in the Pathfinder palette at any time after that.

Crop: This command uses the front selected path to crop all other paths in the selection. In **Figure 7.25**, the star acts as the crop to the stripes.

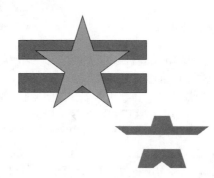

Figure 7.25: The results of cropping the stripes with the star shape.

Divide: This command subdivides all paths so they no longer overlap. As shown in the top example of **Figure 7.26**, the paths don't look much different after you apply the command, but they are in fact separated into many more shapes than before.

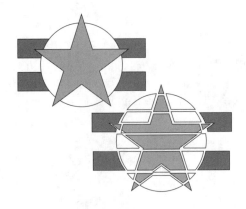

Figure 7.26: The effects of the Divide command are not obvious until you move the paths around as shown on the bottom. All the paths are divided so as to have no overlap.

- **Trim:** This command works just like Divide, except that it only clips rear shapes while leaving front shapes intact, as seen in **Figure 7.27**. Or if you prefer, it's just like Merge, except that it doesn't unite shapes that have the same fill. If you find that Divide breaks up your shapes too much, try Trim instead.

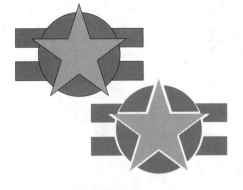

Figure 7.27: The effects of the Trim command are not obvious until you move the paths around, as shown in the lower portion of this figure. All the back objects are clipped while leaving the frontmost shape intact.

- **Outline:** This command draws open paths around overlapping areas of selected shapes, and strokes these paths with the old fill colors. **Figure 7.28** shows this command applied to the star, circle, and stripes. I had to thicken the strokes (Outline applies 0-point strokes, which is utterly stupid) so you could see the results of the command.

- *There used to be options called Hard Mix, Soft Mix, and Trap tucked snugly at the bottom of the Pathfinder palette. They're now available from the Effect » Pathfinder menu, and the Trap options are also (still) available from the Pathfinder palette's pop-up menu. For detailed explanations, see Chapter 19.*

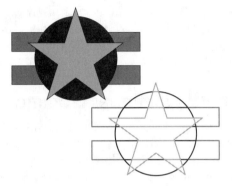

Figure 7.28: The results
of applying the Outline
command to our familiar cast
of shapes.

All of these commands group the resulting paths together,
and all except Outline remove the strokes from the paths. So
be prepared to ungroup paths or edit them with the direct
selection tool. And you'll have to reapply the strokes.

Pathfinder Options

You can use the Pathfinder Options dialog box to set the parameters for all
Pathfinder operations, and it does so in an incredibly complicated way. When
you choose the Pathfinder Options command from the Pathfinder palette's pop-
up menu, Illustrator displays the dialog box shown in **Figure 7.29**. Though
small, it will melt your brain if you look at it for too long.

Figure 7.29: This petite
dialog box lets you control
equally petite distances
beyond which your Pathfinder
operations cannot stray.

Pathfinder Options	
Options	
Calculate Precision: `0.028` points	OK
☐ Remove Redundant Points	Cancel
☐ Divide & Outline will remove unpainted artwork	Defaults

The first option lets you control the accuracy of the Pathfinder operations.
This value has to be larger than 0.001 point (0.3 micron, remember?), which
means that no path will stray farther than one bacterium off its true course.
Larger values are less accurate, but they also speed the performance of the commands. The maximum value is 100 points, but you probably don't want to go
much higher than 4 or 5.

The two check boxes in the Pathfinder Options dialog box delete points that
overlap each other and objects created by the Divide and Outline commands that
have transparent fills and strokes. I recommend you select both these options and
leave them selected, unless you have some special reason for retaining overlapping points and invisible objects.

Every once in a while you may find a small gap between objects manipulated by a Pathfinder command. If this happens, undo the command and then turn off the Anti-aliased Artwork setting in the General Preferences dialog box. Then reapply the command. The gap should be gone.

Reapplying a Pathfinder Command

You can reapply the last Pathfinder command you used by either choosing the second command in the Pathfinder palette's pop-up menu, Repeat Pathfinder (actually, the second word will reflect whatever was the last pathfinder action you used, such as "Repeat Exclude") or by pressing Ctrl+4 (Cmd-4 on the Mac).

DEVELOPING A FLAIR FOR THE SCHEMATIC

There are two types of people who use Illustrator. The first are the high-precision designers who create artwork to exact specifications, defined to the thousandth of a point. The other are artists who don't want to feel constrained by Illustrator features; they just want to express themselves. This chapter—which covers working with the precision features, stacking order, and layers—was written for both groups.

Illustrator gives you exceptional control over your document environment. You can use automated grids in your drawing, which help to keep basic illustration elements in alignment. There are several alignment and distribution controls to position objects precisely. Additionally, Illustrator provides smart guides, an interactive system of guides that help you position and create objects at precise locations. Illustrator provides several ways to control the visibility and selection of objects in a document. You can actively use these features to work precisely, or you can go about your business, designing your illustration, letting the features work (or wait) unobtrusively in the background. This chapter explains everything, from distance to distribution, groups to grids and guidelines, and locks to layers. If it helps you toe the line, it's front and center in the following pages.

Measuring and Positioning with Microscopic Precision

One of my favorite things about using Illustrator is that you can measure dimensions and distances right inside the program. There's no need to print the illustration and measure the output—or even press a pica pole against the screen. Fortunately, Illustrator's built-in capabilities are both more convenient and more accurate than either of those methods. Where else can you click the screen to measure discrepancies as slight as 0.0001 point, roughly the length of bacteria razor stubble?

Illustrator provides three sets of measuring and positioning devices:

- The horizontal and vertical rulers are handy for tracking the cursor. They're about as accurate as real-life rulers, which means that they're good enough for simple alignment, but you can't quite measure bacteria with them.

- The measure tool records scrupulously precise dimensions and distances in the Info palette. When the Info palette is onscreen, you can measure an object just by selecting it. You can even record values with the measure tool and then turn around and move an object that precise distance and direction.

- The Transform palette lets you position objects according to numeric coordinates. You can move objects or clone them by merely entering a value and pressing Enter or Alt+Enter, respectively (Return or Option-Return on the Mac). The palette has its disadvantages, but it can be useful for quick adjustments.

The following sections explain these items, as well as the Move command, which captures all the pertinent statistics recorded with the measure tool.

Together, the rulers, measure tool, Info palette, Move command, and Transform palette form a powerful collection of measuring and positioning equipment.

Adding Rulers to the Illustration Window

Illustrator gives you two rulers—one vertical and one horizontal—that track the movement of your cursor. To bring them up onscreen, press Ctrl+R (Cmd-R on the Mac) or choose View » Show Rulers. If nothing is selected, you can even right-click (Control-click on the Mac) and choose the Show Rulers command from the context-sensitive pop-up menu. The horizontal ruler appears along the top of the illustration window, and the vertical ruler appears on the left side, as in **Figure 8.1**.

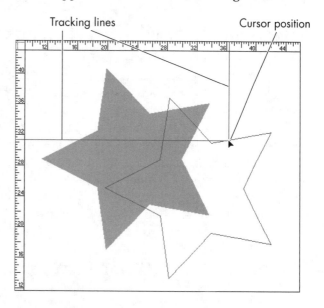

Figure 8.1: The horizontal and vertical rulers track the cursor position.

 You control the unit of measure used by both rulers by choosing the Edit » Preferences » Units & Undo command and selecting an option from the General Units pop-up menu. Another way to change your units of measure is to right-click (Control-click on the Mac) on the ruler in your document window and choose a unit from the tiny contextual menu.

The rulers constantly track the position of the cursor, so long as the cursor is inside the illustration window. Figure 8.1 labels the dotted tracking line in each ruler. As you can see, the rulers track the tip of the cursor, known as the hot spot. In the figure, the hot spot measures 31 picas, 6 points above and 36 picas, 3 points to the right of the absolute zero point where the rulers begin (as explained in the next section). To get the rulers out of the way, press Ctrl+R (Cmd-R on the Mac), or choose View » Hide Rulers.

To make the rulers visible for all new illustrations, open the Adobe Illustrator Startup file in the Plug-ins folder, and press Ctrl+R (Cmd-R on the Mac) to display the rulers. Draw a rectangle (or something simple) and then delete it to get the Save command's attention, and press Ctrl+S (Cmd-S on the Mac). From then on, each new illustration window will come with rulers.

 Illustrator 10 has two startup files; one for CMYK and one for RGB. (You may not have really noticed this if you're not in the habit of choosing one or the other color model in the New Document dialog box.) They can be as similar or as different as you like, but if you want to effect a particular change in your default startup file for both color models, you will have to modify both files.

Setting the Point Where All Things Are Zero

The point at which both rulers show 0 is called the *zero point* or *ruler origin*. By default, the ruler origin is located at the bottom-left corner of the artboard. If you change the size of the artboard or the location of the page boundary, the ruler origin may get jostled around a bit.

You can relocate the ruler origin at any time by dragging from the ruler origin box, which is that little square where the rulers intersect. In **Figure 8.2**, I dragged the ruler origin onto a point in the star, allowing me to measure all distances from that point. The ruler values update after you release the mouse button. The new ruler origin affects not only the rulers, but also the coordinate positioning values in the Info and Transform palettes.

Ruler origin box

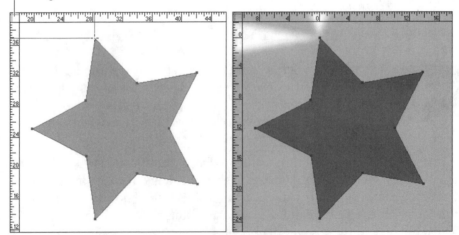

Figure 8.2: Drag from the ruler origin box (left) to reposition the zero point (right).

If you ever want to reset the ruler origin to default position in the bottom-left corner of the artboard, simply double-click the ruler origin box.

 You can save a revised ruler origin with the Adobe Illustrator Startup file. For example, you might prefer to have the zero point in the lower-right corner of the illustration. Your change will affect all future illustrations.

Measuring the Minutiae

The measure tool and its sidekick, the Info palette, are Illustrator's dynamic duo of precision positioning features. You can use both items to measure distances and objects in three ways.

 Select the measure tool (the second alternate tool in the eyedropper tool slot). In the illustration window, drag from one location to another. The Info palette automatically opens (or becomes active). Here Illustrator lists the distance and direction between the beginning and end of your drag. If you click with the measure tool, the Info palette lists the distance and angle between the new click point and the previous one.

 If the Info palette is not open, choose Window » Info. Then use the arrow tool to select the object that you want to measure. The width and height of the segment or other object appear automatically in the palette.

 With the Info palette onscreen, drag with any of the shape tools to see information about the size of the path you're creating. When you move the pen tool cursor, the Info palette tells you the distance and direction of the cursor from the last point. When you drag an object with the arrow tool, the palette tells you the distance and direction of the drag. When using the scale or rotate tool, the palette lists the percentage of the scaling or the angle of rotation. The Info palette is constantly trying to tell you something when you create and edit objects.

Assuming that the Snap to Point toggle command in the View menu is switched on, the measure tool snaps to an anchor point when you click within two screen pixels of it. In **Figure 8.3**, for example, I dragged from one anchor point to another to measure the precise distance between the two. Sadly, when you're using the measure tool, Illustrator doesn't give you any snap cursors to show that you've hit the points, but you can see the cursor snap into place if you watch carefully. Just trust The Force, Luke.

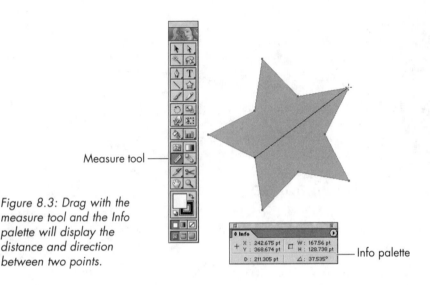

Measure tool —

Figure 8.3: Drag with the measure tool and the Info palette will display the distance and direction between two points.

Info palette

The Info palette can include as many as six numeric values. Here's what those values mean.

- **X, Y:** When using a drawing tool, the X and Y values in the Info palette represent the coordinate position of your cursor, as measured from the ruler origin.

  When you use the measure tool, the X and Y values tell the last place you clicked with the tool (or released when dragging). This way, you know from what point Illustrator is measuring the next time you click—providing that you are proficient at reading coordinates.

  If the direct selection or arrow tool is active, the X and Y values indicate the top-left corner of the selection.

   If you want Illustrator to take the stroke weight or effects of the selected object into consideration, activate the Use Preview Bounds option in the General Preferences dialog box. This increases the W and H values by an amount equal to the size of the object's stroke weight or of any effects applied to the object.

  When you use a transformation tool, the X and Y values represent the center of the scaling, rotation, reflection, or skew. More on this topic in Chapter 9.

- **W, H:** The W and H values list the width and height of a selected object. They also tell you the dimensions of a rectangle, ellipse, text block, or graph as you draw it.

When you move an object or drag with the measure, pen, convert point, or gradient vector tool, the W and H values tell you the horizontal and vertical components of your drag.

D: This item tells the direct distance between one point and another, as the crow flies (so to speak). When you drag with the pen or convert point tool, this value indicates the length of the Bézier lever, which is the distance between the anchor point and the control handle. When you're using other tools, the D value simply tells you the distance of your drag.

Angle: This item, which looks like a figure from your high-school geometry textbook, indicates the angle of your drag, as measured from the mean horizontal. Illustrator measures counterclockwise starting at 3 o'clock; 90 degrees is a quarter circle, 360 degrees is a full circle.

When you use the rotate tool, the angle value tells you the angle of rotation. The reflect tool uses the angle value to impart the angle of the reflection axis. When you use the shear tool, you get two angle values, one for the axis and the other for the skew. I'll cover all these wacky terms in Chapter 9 when I explore transformations in earnest.

W%, H%: These values appear when you scale an object. They tell you the change's width and height, measured as percentages of the object's original dimensions.

When you use the zoom tool, the Info palette tells you the current view size (which is redundant, because Illustrator tells you this in the document's title bar as well as in the Size bar at the bottom of your working window). When you're editing text, the Info palette lists the type size, font, and tracking information. When you're kerning, the second item lists the general tracking values minus the kerning value to give you an overall kerning total.

Translating Measurement to Movement

After you measure a distance with the measure tool, Illustrator automatically stores those W, H, D, and angle values in a tiny buffer in memory. When you use the tool again, the previous measurements are tossed by the wayside to make room for the new ones. Illustrator also uses this buffer to track movements you make by dragging with the arrow or direct selection tool or by nudging with the arrow keys. Again, the measurements of the most recent action replace the previous contents of the buffer.

I just mentioned nudging objects with the arrow keys, but I thought I'd spell it out in case it washed over you. Nudging with the arrow keys is a good way to experiment with subtle changes, and when you're through with subtlety, press Shift+an arrow key to move something ten times farther! (The amount of the move is set by the Keyboard Increment option in the General Preferences dialog box.)

You can translate these buffered measurements into movements by selecting an object or two and choosing Object » Transform » Move. Or try one of the following shortcuts:

 Right-click (Control-click on the Mac) and choose the Transform » Move command from the context-sensitive pop-up menu.

 Double-click the arrow tool icon in the toolbox. This seems a bit unintuitive but stems from an old Illustrator shortcut—Alt-clicking (Option-clicking on the Mac) the arrow tool icon.

Whatever method you use, you get the Move dialog box, as shown in **Figure 8.4**. The Move dialog box always supplies you with the buffered distance and angle values, which permit you to quickly move objects a measured distance or to repeat a move made by dragging with the arrow tool. You can likewise negate a move by changing positive values to negative and vice versa. Or you can retain just the horizontal portion of a move by changing the Horizontal value to 0 and inverting the Vertical value. Then again...well, you get the idea. There are all kinds of ways to rehash old measurement and movement information.

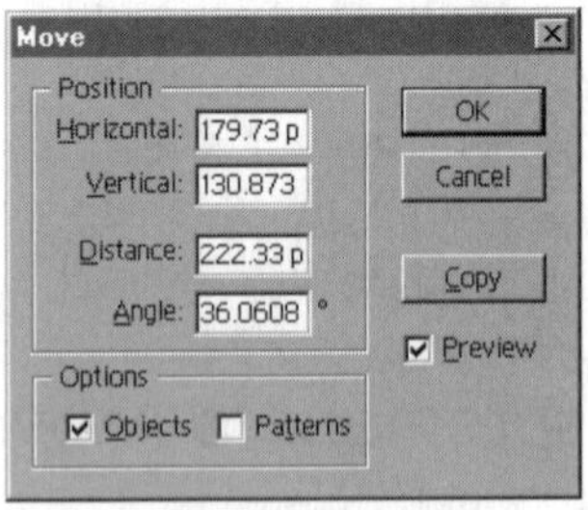

Figure 8.4: The Move dialog box always presents you with the results of your last measurement or movement.

If you feel the urge, you can even enter totally new values into the various option boxes. You can express your move by entering values into the Horizontal and Vertical option boxes or the Distance or Angle option boxes. Because these are two different ways to express the same information, changing one set of values automatically changes the other.

You can also do math inside the option boxes. Simple arithmetic, admittedly, but math nonetheless. Enter + to add, – to subtract, * to multiply, and / to divide.

For example, if you know you want to move a selected object 3 points farther than your last measurement, you can enter +3 after the value in the Distance option box. Then press Tab and watch Illustrator do the math for you right in the box. (You can see the results applied on the page without leaving the dialog box only if you have the Preview option checked.) This technique works inside other palettes and dialog boxes as well, including the Transform palette.

Use the bottom two check boxes in the Move dialog box, Objects and Patterns, to select what is to be affected by the move. Check the final check box, Preview, to see what your changes will look like before they occur. You must specify what you want to preview. If you want to preview a move, make sure that both the Preview and Objects check boxes are selected. To see a preview of the object moving with its tile pattern intact, click the Patterns check box as well. For the lowdown on these options, consult the authoritative Chapter 15.

 You can move the selected objects the specified distance and direction by pressing the Enter key (Return key on the Mac). To clone the objects before moving them, click the Copy button or press Alt+Enter (Option-Return on the Mac).

 The Move dialog box accepts no more than three digits after the decimal point, so measured values get rounded off. In most cases, such a small increment won't make a lick of difference in your printed output. But if it does matter, you may want to resort to Illustrator's automatic alignment options, which are discussed later in this chapter.

Coordinate Positioning

The last item in the precision position parade is the Transform palette, also known to some as the Control palette, and the subject of **Figure 8.5**. After you select the objects you want to change, you open the Transform palette by choosing Window » Transform. You can then enter values into any one of the six option boxes and press Enter (Return on the Mac) to apply them to one or more selected objects.

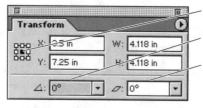

Figure 8.5: The Transform palette.

The first item in the Transform palette is the reference point icon. You can use this icon to specify whether the coordinates in the X and Y option boxes represent the upper-left corner of the selection, the middle of the selection, or one of seven other locations. Click one of the little points in the icon to relocate the reference point. Illustrator updates the X and Y values automatically.

You can enter new values into the X and Y option boxes to change the location of the object on the artboard. You can also adjust the W and H values to change the width and height of the bounding box, which in turn stretches or shrinks the selected object. The shear and rotate options on the right side of the palette let you reshape and rotate selections. Chapter 9 covers these transformations in depth.

As with the Move dialog box, you can perform arithmetic calculations in the X, Y, W, and H option boxes using the standard +, −, *, and / operators. You can even do math inside the shear or rotate option boxes.

Although it doesn't have a Copy button, yes, Virginia, you can clone objects directly from the Transform palette. Just enter a value into one of the option boxes and press Alt+Enter (Option-Return on the Mac) to clone the selection and exit the Transform palette. Or press Alt+Tab (Option-Tab on the Mac) to clone the selection and move to the next option box. Press Alt (Option-Tab) again and you'll make another clone. And jump to the next option box. And so on.

Aligning and Distributing Objects

Yes, of course, you're all quite capable of lining things up yourself, using any number of tools, including the naked eye. Or you can use the Align palette and feel like you've really got your money's worth. For you precision-loving folks, this one's for you.

To display the Align palette, choose Window » Align. Shown in **Figure 8.6**, this dainty little palette contains six Align Objects icons and six Distribute Objects icons. Three icons in each row let you align or distribute horizontally; three allow you to do the same vertically. Select the objects that you want to align or distribute, and then click an icon. Illustrator adjusts the objects immediately. For example, click the first icon in the top row to align the selected objects along their left edges, click the second icon to center the objects, and click the third icon to align the right edges.

Once you select objects, you click the icons of the Align palette to move the selected objects. These icons can be sorted into the following five groups, which are also illustrated in **Figure 8.7**.

- **Ordinary alignment:** These six options (Horizontal Align Left, Horizontal Align Center, Horizontal Align Right, Vertical Align Top, Vertical Align Center, and Vertical Align Bottom) move objects based on the bounding boxes of the selected objects. The "key" object, or the object that the others align themselves to, is always the most extreme left or top object in the selection.

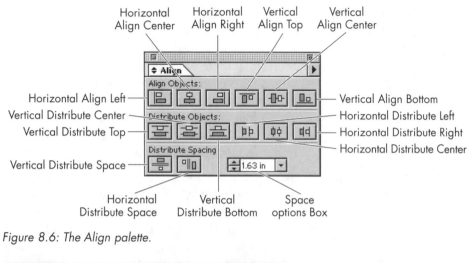

Figure 8.6: The Align palette.

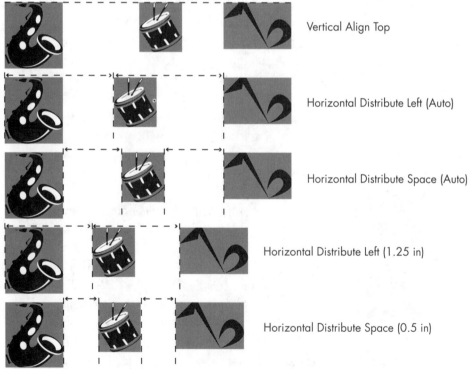

Vertical Align Top

Horizontal Distribute Left (Auto)

Horizontal Distribute Space (Auto)

Horizontal Distribute Left (1.25 in)

Horizontal Distribute Space (0.5 in)

Figure 8.7: Select some objects and click one of the buttons in the Align palette. The gray rectangles represent bounding boxes; the dotted lines show how the portions of the bounding boxes get distributed.

- **Distribute alignment:** The distribute icons (Vertical Distribute Top, Vertical Distribute Center, Vertical Distribute Bottom, Horizontal Distribute Left, Horizontal Distribute Center, and Horizontal Distribute Right) move objects so there is equal space between the sides or centers of the bounding box. For example, Horizontal Distribute Center moves objects so that there is equal space from side to side among the centers of three or more objects. These icons use the Auto setting in the Space options box, which is visible when you choose Show Options from the Align palette menu.

- **Distribute space:** Oftentimes, the distribute alignment option will create equal distance between the sides or centers of objects but leave the optical space between the objects unequal. The Distribute Spacing icons (Vertical Distribute Space and Horizontal Distribute Space) distribute objects so the space between them is equal. These icons are visible when you choose Show Options from the Align palette menu, and they use the Auto setting in the Space options box.

- **Distribute specific alignment:** Distribute Specific Alignment uses the same icons as the distribute alignment icons together with a specific amount set in the Space options box. This moves objects so that there is a specific amount of space between the sides or centers of objects.

- **Distribute specific space:** Distribute Specific Space uses the same icons as the Distribute Spacing icons together with a specific amount set in the Space options box. This moves objects so that there is a specific amount of space between the objects.

 As with the Transform palette, the options in the Align palette work from the bounding boxes of selected objects.

 To align or distribute multiple objects together, first group the objects by choosing Object » Group or Ctrl+G (Cmd-G on the Mac). For example, I grouped each of the simple paths in Figure 8.7 with its bounding box before applying settings from the Align palette.

You must select three or more objects to use the Auto setting of the Distribute Objects options. This is because Illustrator compares the space among objects when distributing them; you have to select three objects to have two spaces to compare.

Key Objects

When the Space options box is set at its default of Auto that means that the space between the objects will come from the available space already between the objects. If you want a specific amount of space between the sides, centers, or objects, you need to set the *key object*—that is the object that remains anchored while the other objects move in relationship to it. Here's how to set the key object and the spacing amount.

1. Select the objects you want to distribute.

If you are setting a specific space amount, you can select two or more objects. The Auto setting requires three or more.

2. Click the object you want to be the key object.

Yes, I know the object is already selected, but you need to tell Illustrator which of the selected objects is the key object. For instance, in Figure 8.7 I clicked the leftmost object a second time to select it as the key object. If you use the arrow tool, you can simply click the object. However, if you use the direct selection tool, you need to Alt-click (Option-click on the Mac).

3. Set the amount in the Space option box.

The default is Auto. Set an amount in the options box. Once there is an amount in the box, you can use the up or down arrows next to the box to increase or decrease the amount in the box.

4. Click the distribute icon.

You can now click the specific distribute icon. If you don't like the results, change the space amount or click a different distribute icon. Repeat steps 2, 3, and 4 until everything looks perfect.

Aligning Individual Points

The options in the Align palette affect whole objects at a time. But Illustrator also lets you align selected points independently of their objects by choosing Object » Path » Average or pressing Ctrl+Alt+J (Cmd-Option-J on the Mac). You can arrange two or more points into horizontal or vertical alignment, or you can snap the points together to make them coincident. In each case, Illustrator averages the locations of the points, so all points move.

First select the points you want to align with the direct selection tool. Then choose the Average command. The Average dialog box will display, providing you with three radio buttons. You can either make all points coincident (Both), arrange them in a horizontal line (Horizontal), or arrange them vertically (Vertical). You can even average the alignment points in point text, which is a great way to arrange bits of point text into columns or to align labels with callout lines as shown in **Figure 8.8**.

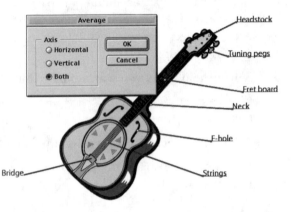

Figure 8.8: One by one, I selected each piece of point text to the right of the guitar and the right-hand point in its callout line and averaged their locations.

 If you want to average and join in one fell swoop, press Ctrl+Alt+Shift+J (Cmd-Option-Shift-J on the Mac). Use the Average command when you want to align points in formation or bring points together from different shapes without joining them.

Adding a True Center Point

Illustrator lets you assign a center point to any object by selecting the object and clicking on the Show Center button in the Attributes palette. Unfortunately, Illustrator positions the center point with respect to the bounding box, which is rarely the true center of the shape except in the case of rectangles (which are the same shape as their bounding boxes) and ellipses (which are uniformly round).

For example, suppose that you wanted to center a star inside a circle. If you first drew the circle, and then drew the star from the circle's center point, the two center points match. But if you use the center point in the star to drag until it snaps onto the center point in the circle, you'll get the problem shown in **Figure 8.9**. Illustrator hasn't centered the shapes; it has centered the bounding boxes.

If you need to see the true center of an object, you can use the Average command. Copy the object and then choose Edit » Paste in Front. You now have a clone of your object. Choose Object » Path » Average and apply the Both setting. This causes Illustrator to average all points in the path. The place where all the points meet is the true center. You can use this mess to center one object to another. But please delete it before you print.

Figure 8.9: If you drag a center point in the star until it snaps to the circle's center point, the shapes align like this. Not really centered.

Creating and Using Custom Guides

Another way to align objects is to establish a system of guidelines (or just plain *guides*). These are special kinds of paths that appear as dotted or solid lines onscreen but never print. You can choose the form and color that your guides take in the Guides & Grid Preferences dialog box. Assuming the Snap to Point option is turned on in the General Preferences dialog box, your cursor aligns to the guide anytime you drag within two pixels of it. Unlike standard paths, your cursor snaps to any position along the outline of a guide, regardless of the placement of anchor points.

You can create a guide in one of the following ways:

   Drag from one of the rulers to create a perpendicular guide that runs the entire width or height of the pasteboard. In **Figure 8.10**, for example, I dragged from the horizontal ruler to create a horizontal guide. The guide appears in the illustration window as a blue line, clearly distinguishing it from printing objects.

 If you change your mind while dragging a guide from one of the rulers, press the Alt key (Option key on the Mac) to rotate it 90 degrees. Alt-dragging (Option-dragging on the Mac) from the horizontal ruler creates a vertical guide, and vice versa.

   Select a path that you've drawn in the illustration window and choose View » Guides » Make Guides to create a custom guide in the shape of a circle, star, or even a character of type. You can also use the shortcut Ctrl+5 (Cmd-5 on the Mac) to create a custom guide from a selected path.

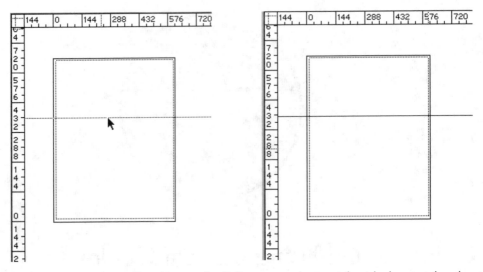

Figure 8.10: Dragging from the top ruler (left) creates a horizontal guide that stretches the entire width of the pasteboard (right).

You can convert all varieties of paths to guides, including compound paths. You can even convert groups, selections inside groups, and the bars or lines inside graphs. The one thing you can't turn into a guide is text (unless you first convert the text to paths with Type » Create Outlines, like the big R in **Figure 8.11**). So if you get an error message when pressing Ctrl+5 (Cmd-5 on the Mac), you can be sure your selection includes some text. Deselect the text and try again.

Figure 8.11: Press Ctrl+5 (Cmd-5 on the Mac) to convert selected paths— including converted text and compound paths (top)—to custom snap-to guides (bottom).

To create a guide without sacrificing the original path, copy the path (Ctrl+C in Windows or Cmd-C on the Mac), paste it in back (Ctrl+B or Cmd-B), and then choose View » Guides » Make Guides (Ctrl+5 or Cmd-5) to convert the duplicate to a guide.

 If you convert a single path within a group to a guide, without converting other paths in the group, the guide remains a member of that group. Drag the group with the arrow tool, and the guide moves as well. It's a very handy way to keep certain guides and objects together.

Unlocking, Editing, and Clearing Guides

By default, Illustrator locks guides so they don't get too tangled up with your printed paths. To prevent you from messing up, you can't select a locked guide by simply clicking on it. To unlock all guides in an illustration, choose View » Guides » Lock Guides or press Ctrl+Alt+; (Cmd-Option-; on the Mac). Note that's a semicolon. After you click it, the check mark in front of the Lock Guides command disappears, showing that the lock is now off.

Once the guides are unlocked, you can select and manipulate them as you would any other graphic object. When you click a guide with the arrow or direct selection tool, Illustrator shows you the guide's anchor points to let you know it's selected. Use the direct selection tool to reshape the guide. Shift-click or marquee to select multiple guides at a time. Press the Backspace or Delete key to delete a selected guide. You can also move guides or transform them. You can even use the add point, delete point, and convert point tools on a guide.

If you get tired of looking at your guides, you can hide them by choosing View » Guides » Hide Guides. If you really can't stand your guides anymore and want to delete them forever, choose View » Guides » Clear Guides. That sends them all to guide Siberia where no one will ever hear from them again.

Converting Guides to Objects

If you want to turn a guide into a printing object, you can convert a guide back to a path. To do so, unlock the guide, select it, and then choose View » Guides » Release Guides. Illustrator converts custom guides back to paths, even remembering their original fill and stroke colors. (What a smart program!) Ruler guides convert into lines that have no fill and zero stroke weight, and which extend the entire width or length of the pasteboard.

 To convert a locked guide back into a path, Ctrl+Shift-double-click the guide (Cmd-Shift-double-click on the Mac).

Deleting Ruler Guides

If you use the direct selection tool to select ruler guides for deletion, you may select just the segment. If you press the Delete key, you will delete the guide but leave two anchor points all the way at the very ends of the pasteboard.

Unless you press the Delete key again, you will leave these two anchor points at the edge of the universe. These points are considered part of the artwork and can cause all sorts of problems. If you use the Select All command and then try to scale your illustration, you'll get an error message. You can't scale the artwork because those guides have nowhere else to go.

If you try to convert the artwork to Web files, you'll probably get a message that there's not enough memory to create the file. That's because you're trying to make a file that is several feet big (much too big for Web sites). And if you import the file into QuarkXPress or InDesign, you'll get strange results if you try to fit the artwork inside a picture frame.

Just remember, always press the Delete key twice if you select ruler guides with the direct selection tool. Better yet, just always press the Delete key twice no matter what. This way you won't leave anchor points at the ends of the universe.

It's Grid for You and Me

Another of Illustrator's handy positioning features is the optional grid system. By simply choosing View » Show Grid or pressing Ctrl+" (Cmd-" on the Mac, and that symbol is a double quote sign), a network of equally spaced horizontal and vertical lines wallpaper your work area. You can choose the color and style of the lines that make up a grid, just as you can for your guides, in the Guides & Grid Preferences (shown way back in Chapter 2). There you also specify the spacing of the gridlines and the number of divisions per gridline. If you choose a grid spacing of 72 points with 5 subdivisions, you get a lattice of lines spaced 12 points apart (72 divided by 5). Select the Lines option from the Style pop-up menu to see gridlines and divisions; select Dots to see the gridlines sans divisions.

On first glance, you may think that this is a case of guide overkill. But, friends, I'm here to tell you that beneath the grid's mild-mannered appearance beats the heart of a powerful ally. The grid function offers you many useful features.

- Grids let you quickly check to make sure you've created compound paths correctly (provided that Grids In Back is active, back in the Guides & Grid Preferences dialog box). If you see the grid through the hole, you know the compound is correct.

A grid gives you a quick and easy way to produce equally spaced guides. Just choose View » Show Grid and set the structure in the Guides & Grid Preferences dialog box.

You can set up your gridline spacing in different units than the general units. In the Guides & Grid Preferences dialog box, enter a value into the Gridline in every option box, followed by the type of units you want. You can then have your rulers set to, say, centimeters, while your grids are marking off inches.

Because a grid is subject to the value set in the Constrain Angle option box (in the General Preferences dialog box), you can have an angled grid. Guides, on the other hand, are limited to the standard up-and-down or side-to-side format.

An angled grid allows you to create perspective drawings quickly and easily. I drew the box in **Figure 8.12** with the aid of an angled grid. I chose View » Show Grid and entered 45 into the Constrain Angle option in the General Preferences dialog box. With four quick clicks of the pen tool, I created the top of the box and filled it with white (that's why you can't see the grid behind it). After selecting the rectangle, I Alt-dragged (Option-dragged on the Mac) it down to form the bottom of the box. With four more clicks, I made the left side of the box and duplicated it by Alt- (Option-) dragging up and to the right with the arrow tool. Finally, I pressed Ctrl+Shift+[(Cmd-Shift-[on the Mac) to send the right side to the back of the stack. The whole process took less than 5 minutes.

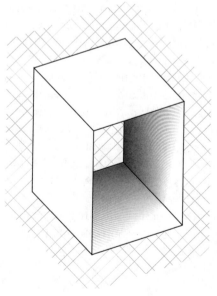

Figure 8.12: With a Constrain Angle value of 45 degrees, I turned on the grid and quickly drew one of those mind-bending perspective boxes.

If you're really crazy about grids, make sure to check out the new members of the line tool family, the polar grid and rectangular grid tools, in Chapter 5, if you didn't already.

Smart Guides

Now that I've sung the praises of guides and grids for all your precision drawing and positioning needs, it's just about time to tell you that Illustrator also has a system of automated guides that might just make those old-fashioned guides and grids obsolete. Smart guides are a trio of context-sensitive helpmeets called *alignment guides*, *path labels*, and *path highlights*. The alignment guides are temporary informational guidelines that pop in and out of existence as you drag the cursor around the screen. Path labels consist of a number of little text hints that appear to inform you where your cursor is within the document. Path highlights ring the outline of a path to tell you that the cursor is positioned over that path.

Smart guides are completely independent of traditional guides, with the exception that their color matches that of traditional guides and is determined in the Guides & Grid Preferences dialog box.

Perfect Position with Alignment Guides

Alignment guides (also known as construction guides), the driving force behind smart guides, resemble traditional ruler guides in that they extend the entire length of your pasteboard. Unlike ruler guides, they display only as long as you need them. To see alignment guides, you first turn them on with the View » Smart Guides toggle command or press Ctrl+U (Cmd-U on the Mac). Then, from the Smart Guides & Slices Preferences (covered way back in Chapter 2), make sure that the Construction Guides option is active.

Alignment guides will help you position the points of a path as you create or manipulate it. The guides inform you that you're aligned with respect to the origin point of your drag. By default, the guides align at multiples of 45 degrees. Secondary alignment guides will appear to tell you that you are also aligned to other points of interest. You determine these secondary alignment points by dragging over them with your active tool.

At first glance, this is a bit confusing, so here's a quick demonstration of how alignment guides can assist you in drawing a right triangle with two equal sides.

1. **Click with the pen tool to set the triangle's first point.**

Be sure that the Smart Guides command is active. For clarity in demonstrating the feature, I've turned off the other smart guide options in the Smart Guides & Slices Preferences dialog box, namely the Text Label Hints and Object Highlighting options.

2. **Move the pen tool to the right.**

As you move the pen directly horizontally from this first point, an alignment guide displays, as shown in **Figure 8.13**. This shows that you are aligned with respect to that first point.

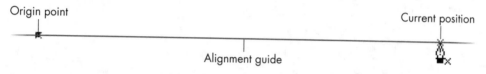

Origin point   Current position

Alignment guide

Figure 8.13: Click to set the triangle's first corner point and move the cursor directly to the right. An alignment guide will show that you're on track.

3. **Click to set the triangle's second corner point.**

The second point will be directly to the right of the first point.

4. **Move the cursor up and to the left.**

When you're aligned with the second corner point, a new alignment guide will appear, as shown in **Figure 8.14**. (If this guide doesn't display, choose the 90° & 45° Angles command from the Angles pop-up menu in the Smart Guides & Slices Preferences dialog box.)

5. **Move the cursor over the first point and then move the cursor straight up.**

This two-step positioning is of the utmost importance. By moving the cursor over the first corner point you're telling Illustrator that you want to use this as a secondary alignment point. As you move the cursor upward, a secondary alignment guide will display, as shown in **Figure 8.15**.

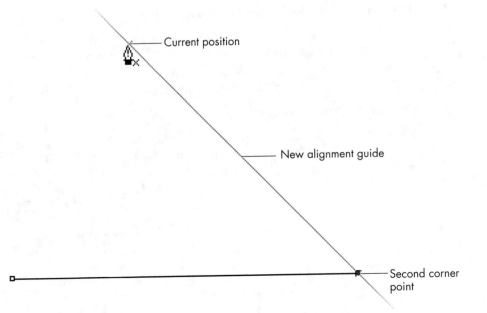

Current position

New alignment guide

Second corner
point

Figure 8.14: A new alignment guide shows that the present cursor position makes a 45-degree angle with the horizontal and is aligned with respect to the second corner point.

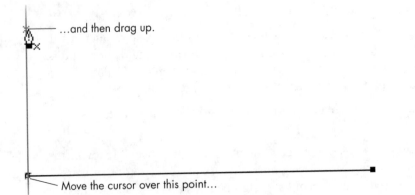

...and then drag up.

Move the cursor over this point...

Figure 8.15: First move the cursor over the point you want to use as a secondary alignment point and drag straight up to see a secondary alignment guide.

6.   Continue until both guides display.

As you continue to move the cursor up—all the while aligned with the first corner point so that the secondary alignment guide remains visible—you will eventually cross the point where the first alignment guide again displays, as shown in **Figure 8.16**. This point is in perfect alignment with the triangle's other two corner points, directly above the first and at a 45-degree angle up and to the left of the second.

7. **Click to set the third corner.**

Position a point with perfect precision.

8. **Click again at the original point.**

This closes the path, completing your perfect right triangle with two equal sides.

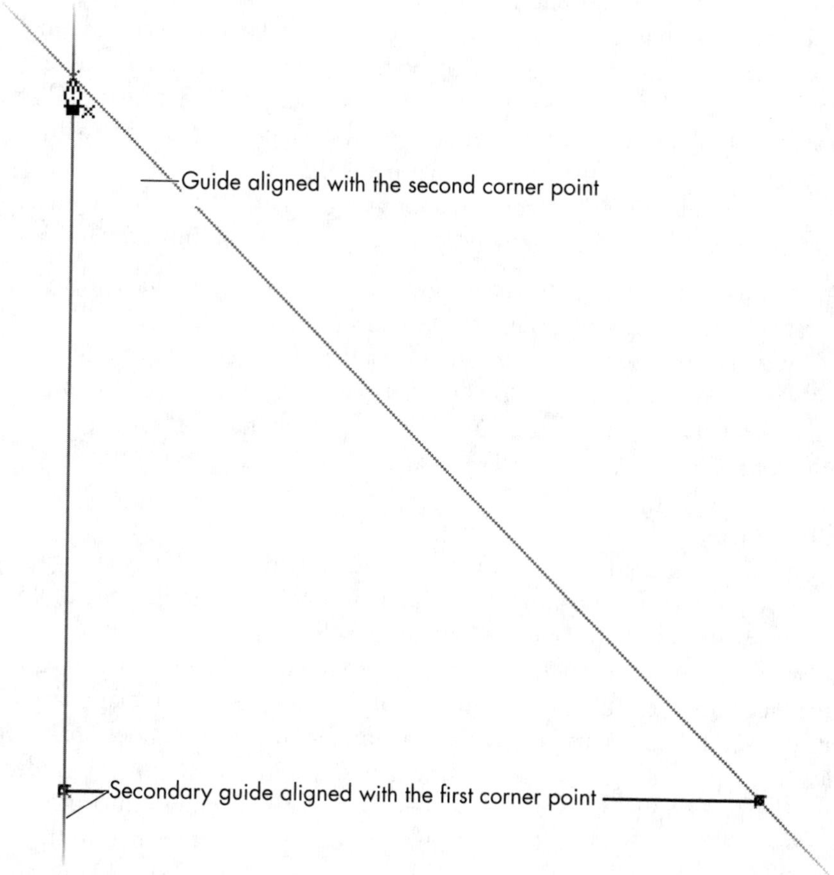

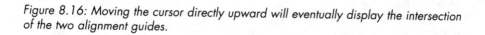

Guide aligned with the second corner point

Secondary guide aligned with the first corner point

Figure 8.16: Moving the cursor directly upward will eventually display the intersection of the two alignment guides.

The display of alignment is not limited to when you're simply moving the cursor around the screen. The guides also appear when you are dragging to create paths or dragging paths around to position them. You can also define as many secondary alignment points as you wish. Just be sure to move the cursor over the other points that you want Illustrator to align. Although you may have a number of active alignment points, Illustrator will display only two alignments at a time (either an alignment guide and a secondary alignment guide, or two alignment guides).

Precise Transforming

If you want Illustrator to display alignment guides while you're manipulating a path with one of the transformation tools, then activate the Transform Tools option in the Smart Guides & Slices Preferences dialog box. The primary alignment guide will display with reference to the point from which you started your drag, not the transformation's origin point. You may define secondary alignment points by dragging the cursor over points of the various other paths that make up your artwork. Unfortunately, you cannot set the transformation's origin point as a secondary alignment point, because this is not a "physical" point in the world of Illustrator.

 If you know that you're going to want to use the transformation origin as a secondary alignment point, simply add a point at that location with the pen tool before you start the transformation. Then select the object you want to transform and click the point you just made with the transformation tool. After you've begun dragging the cursor, be sure to move it over the point, indicating to Illustrator that you want it to use the point as a secondary alignment point.

Alignment Angles

By default, an alignment guide will pop in when the angle formed between your cursor's current and original positions and the horizontal is some multiple of 45 degrees. But as you've probably guessed, Illustrator doesn't limit you with such mundane options. In the Smart Guides & Slices Preferences dialog box you can choose from seven predefined angular alignment options (all of which appear in the Angles pop-up menu) or enter up to six custom angles. If you choose to rebel geometrically, simply enter the angles with which you want the alignment guides to conform in the six option boxes below the Angles pop-up menu. Illustrator will reflect your choices in the little alignment guide display box located to the right of the Angles pop-up menu.

The angle of the various alignment guides also depends on the value in the Constrain Angle option box of the General Preferences dialog box. For example, if the General Preferences' Constrain Angle option is set to 0 degrees and the

Smart Guides & Slices Preferences' Angles is on the 90° & 45° Angles setting, then the angle of an alignment guide could be 0, 45, or 90 degrees. If the Constrain Angle is changed to 15 degrees, the resulting alignment guide's angles could be 15, 60, or 105 degrees. Just think of the Constrain Angle value as a starting point for the angles of the alignment guides.

Powerless to Resist

Unlike with traditional guides and grids, your cursor has no option but to snap to any smart guide. If an alignment guide is visible, then Illustrator will snap the path or point you're dragging to the guide once you release the mouse button. Anytime you're within a certain distance of the position of a smart guide, the smart guide appears and Illustrator is ready to snap you to it. This distance is the snapping tolerance. By default, the snapping tolerance is set to 4 screen pixels. In the Snapping Tolerance field in the Smart Guides & Slices Preferences dialog box, you can choose any value from 0 to 10 pixels inclusively. The higher the value, the more readily Illustrator displays the smart guides.

Your Position Spelled Out

Another feature of smart guides are path labels. When the Text Label Hints option in the Smart Guides & Slices Preferences dialog box is checked and the Smart Guides command is in effect, Illustrator will show you little labels to inform you as to the position of the cursor with respect to various parts of your document. **Figure 8.17** shows a collage of the different types.

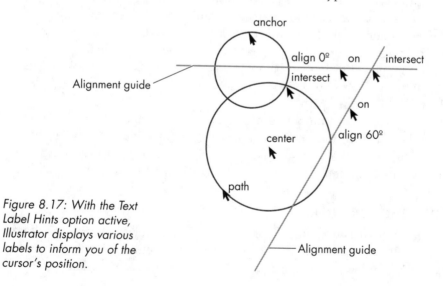

Figure 8.17: With the Text Label Hints option active, Illustrator displays various labels to inform you of the cursor's position.

Path Highlights

A third and final feature of smart guides is path highlighting. With the Object Highlighting option in the Smart Guides & Slices Preferences dialog box checked and the Smart Guides enabled on the View menu, Illustrator will temporarily highlight the outline of any path that would be selected if you clicked at that position. This allows you to easily see paths that are partially (or even entirely) obscured by other paths. But don't count on it as a way to detect your hidden paths: although Illustrator will highlight locked paths by means of path highlighting, it will not acknowledge hidden paths.

Assembling Paths into Groups

Most of the time, you'll apply transformations to whole paths rather than to individual points or segments. You may even want to transform multiple objects at one time. So imagine that instead of working with paths and objects, you could manipulate whole pieces of artwork. A boy here, a dog there, a great white shark preparing to eat the both of them a few meters away. This is the beauty of grouping, which allows you to assemble throngs of elements into a single object.

Creating Groups

Suppose, for example, that you've created a graphic made up of several paths. You want to select the graphic easily. To always select and transform the graphic as a complete entity, select all of its elements and choose Object » Group. Or press the common-as-dirt keyboard equivalent, Ctrl+G (Cmd-G on the Mac).

Illustrator always groups entire objects. Even if you select a single point in one object and a segment in another before you group them, the two whole objects will be grouped. There's no way to group a couple of points or segments independently of others within a path.

You can group paths, compound paths, text objects, imported images, or any other kind of artwork. You can even group other groups. Illustrator permits hierarchies of groups, so that one group may contain two groups that each contain six others, and so on. It's like a giant family tree of object protection.

Adding to Groups

If you already have a group, there are two ways to add a new element to it. If you select the entire group and the new object, the Group command makes a new group—a "higher-level" group that consists of the original group and the new object. However, if you ungroup the original group, then add the object, and then regroup, you will have only one group—all on the same "level" of the group.

If you don't like all that ungrouping and grouping, you can cut the object, select one of the objects in the group (either with the group selection tool or the direct selection tool), and then choose either Paste in Front or Paste in Back to add the object to the group. (See the "Paste in Front or Back of Collections" section later in this chapter.)

Or you can add objects to (or delete them from) a group directly in the Layers palette, although you cannot create a group there. See the "Working with Drawing Layers" section later in this chapter.

Ungrouping

You can ungroup any group by choosing Object » Ungroup or pressing Ctrl+Shift+G (Cmd-Shift-G on the Mac). You have to ungroup each group one level at a time. So if a group contains three other groups, for example, you'd have to press Ctrl+Shift+G (Cmd-Shift-G on the Mac) four times in a row to disassociate all of them.

Ungrouping is occasionally an essential part of the reshaping process. Most notably, you can't combine two paths from different groups, whether by joining their endpoints or by making them into a compound path. So if you want to join two open paths from different groups into a single longer path, for example, you have to first ungroup the paths and then apply the Join command.

Distinguishing Groups from Nongroups

What if ungrouping a path doesn't produce the desired effect? It may be that the object wasn't grouped in the first place. Illustrator permits you to create various kinds of collective objects, including compound paths, linked text blocks, masks, and wrapped objects. You may not always know what command has grouped the objects into being selected together.

If you want, you can look at the Object menu commands while the objects in question are selected to determine what type of collective element has been applied to objects. If Ungroup is active, you've got a group. If Compound Path » Release is available, it's a compound.

 Another way to see your groups is to look at the type of object in the Layers palette. (More on the Layers palette later in this chapter.)

When Grouping Isn't Protection Enough

Grouping helps to protect the relative placement of objects, but it doesn't get objects out of your way when you're trying to edit a complex illustration. Nor does it protect your artwork from the unpredictable motor skills of less adept artists who may come after you.

For those of us who feel that you can just never have enough ways of defending your work—from yourself or from anyone else—Illustrator provides a laundry list of protection alternatives. You can lock objects, preventing you or anyone else from accidentally selecting and altering them. You can temporarily hide an object if it impairs your view of other objects. And you can relegate entire collections of objects to independent layers, which you can in turn lock and hide as you choose.

I'll explain locking and hiding in the next few pages. Because layers are a more involved topic, they have their own section toward the end of the chapter.

Putting an Object under Lock and Key

Locking an object prevents you from selecting it. This means you won't be able to delete the object, edit it in any manner (including moving it around), or change its fill or stroke.

You lock objects by selecting them and choosing Object » Lock » Selection or pressing Ctrl+2 (Cmd-2 on the Mac). You can't lock a single point or segment independently of other elements in a path. If you specifically select one point in a path and choose the Lock command, Illustrator locks the entire path.

 When working on a very specific detail in an illustration, you may find it helpful to lock every object not included in the detail. With potentially hundreds of objects, it could be difficult and time consuming to select every one of them. Fortunately, you can simply select the objects that you don't want to lock and press Ctrl+Alt+Shift+2 (Cmd-Option-Shift-2 on the Mac). This is the secret "lock everything but" command.

 There are two new options for locking items: Object » Lock » All Artwork Above and Object » Lock » Other Layers. All Artwork Above means *literally* above; anything that overlaps the selected object—text or graphic, regardless of layer. I think this is a helpful little addition. Other Layers is exactly what it sounds like; it leaves only the host layer of the selected object unlocked and ready for action.

Unlocking All That Was Locked

Because you can't select a locked object, there's no way to indicate which objects you'd like to unlock and which you'd like to leave locked. So you have to unlock all locked objects at the same time.

To do so, choose Object » Unlock All or press Ctrl+Alt+2 (Cmd-Option-2 on the Mac). Illustrator unlocks all locked objects and selects them so that you can see which objects were locked and manipulate them if necessary. You can now Shift-click whatever objects you want to leave unlocked with the arrow tool and relock the others.

Sending Objects into Hiding

If an object is really in your way, you can do more than just lock it; you can totally hide it from view. You can't see a hidden object in any display mode, nor does it appear when the illustration is printed. Because a hidden object is always invisible, you can't select or manipulate it. Think of it as being tucked away in your safe-deposit box at the bank; it's safely out of your way, but you can go and get it when you need it.

You hide objects by selecting them and choosing Object » Hide » Selection or pressing Ctrl+3 (Cmd-3 on the Mac). You can't hide a single point or segment; Illustrator always hides entire paths at a time. But you can hide objects inside groups, compound paths, or other collective objects. The path disappears, but it still moves and otherwise keeps up with the group when you select the entire group with the arrow tool.

 To hide all objects that are not selected and leave the selected ones visible, press Ctrl+Alt+Shift+3 (Cmd-Option-Shift-3 on the Mac).

 Just like the Lock command, the Hide command also has new options, which just happen to match the Lock ones exactly. So if they weren't obvious the first time around, go back and read my descriptions again a few paragraphs back and substitute the word Lock.

 Unlike locking, hiding is not saved with the illustration. Adobe's afraid that you'll forget the hidden objects were ever there. Therefore, when you open an illustration, all objects in the file are in full view.

Revealing Everything That Was Hidden

You can't select a hidden object any better than a locked one, so there's no way to show just one specific hidden object. Instead, you have to display all hidden objects at the same time by choosing Object » Show All. Illustrator shows and selects all previously hidden objects. This way, the objects are called to your attention, allowing you to easily send them back into hiding if you want.

 Hiding, too, was invented as a way to work before there were layers. However, the Layers palette gives you far more features for hiding objects.

The Celebrated Stacking Order

When you preview or print an illustration, Illustrator describes it one object at a time, starting with the first-created object in the illustration window and working up to the last. The order in which the objects are described is called the *stacking order*. The first object described lies behind all other objects in the illustration window. The last object sits in front of its cohorts. All other objects exist on some unique tier between the first object and the last.

Left to its own devices, stacking order would be a function of the order in which you draw (like an archeology dig). The oldest object would be in back; the most recent object would be in front. But Illustrator provides a number of commands that allow you to adjust the stacking order of existing paths and text blocks, in case you want to change them to suit your artistic manipulations.

All the Way Forward or Back

Two commands in the Object » Arrange submenu let you send objects to the absolute front or back of an illustration. If you select an object and choose Object » Arrange » Bring to Front, Illustrator moves the object to the front of the stack. The object is treated exactly as if it were the most recently created path in the illustration and will therefore be described last when previewing or printing.

By selecting an object and choosing Object » Arrange » Send to Back, Illustrator treats a selected object as if it were the first path in the layer and describes it first when previewing or printing.

You can apply both of these commands to whole objects only. If a path is only partially selected when you choose either command, the entire path is moved to the front or back of the illustration. If you select more than one object when choosing Bring to Front or Send to Back, the relative stacking of each selected object is retained. For example, if you select two objects and choose Bring to Front, the forward of the two objects becomes the frontmost object, and the rearward of the two objects becomes the second-to-frontmost object.

Relative Stacking

When creating complicated illustrations, it's not enough to be able to send objects to the absolute front or back of an illustration. Illustrator provides two commands specifically designed to change the rank of selected items in the stack by one. Choose Object » Arrange » Bring Forward or press Ctrl+] (Cmd-] on the Mac) to advance the selected object one step closer to the front of the stack; choose Object » Arrange » Send Backward or press Ctrl+[(Cmd-[on the Mac) to push it one closer to the back. Although you would probably never feel inclined to use these commands to move the 46th-to-front object up to 14th-to-front or vice versa, they are great to use when you want to nudge a path a couple of steps forward or three steps backward in the stacking order.

 While we're talking about the Arrange menu, you will doubtless have noticed by now that it has a new command: Send to Current Layer. This is a handy menu-centric way to move selected objects from one layer to another. I know—we're not talking about layers quite yet. Still, if you're working on a complicated illustration, this command may be a bit easier to use than having to wade through scads of layers.

Illustrator also allows you to send one object in front of or behind another using Clipboard commands. To change the stacking order of an object, select it and press Ctrl+X (Cmd-X on the Mac) to jettison it to the Clipboard. Then select the path or text block that the cut object should go behind, and choose Edit » Paste in Back or press Ctrl+B (Cmd-B on the Mac). Or, if you'd rather place the cut object in front of the selection, choose Edit » Paste in Front or press Ctrl+F (Cmd-F on the Mac). In either case, Illustrator restores the object to the exact location from which it was cut. Only the stacking order is changed.

If multiple objects are selected when you press Ctrl+B (Cmd-B on the Mac), Illustrator places the contents of the Clipboard in back of the rearmost selected object. Not surprisingly, Ctrl+F (Cmd-F on the Mac) pastes the cut object in front of the frontmost selected object. If no object is selected, Ctrl+B (Cmd-B on the Mac) sends the object to the back of the illustration; Ctrl+F (Cmd-F on the Mac) sends it to the front of the illustration.

The Effect of Grouping and Combining on Stacking

Combining objects into groups also affects the stacking order of the objects in the illustration. All paths in a group must be stacked consecutively. To accomplish this, Illustrator uses the frontmost selected object as a marker when you choose the Group command. All other selected objects are stacked in order behind the frontmost one.

The same holds true for compound paths, linked text blocks, wrapped objects, joined paths, and paths combined with the Pathfinder filters.

You can select an object inside a group with the direct selection tool and change its stacking order using the Bring to Front and Send to Back commands. But Illustrator keeps the selected objects inside its group. So rather than sending an object to the front of the illustration when you press Ctrl+Shift-] (Cmd-Shift-] on the Mac), Illustrator just sends it to the front of the group, while leaving the stacking order of the overall group unchanged.

You can also cut an object from a group and then paste it inside or outside of the group using the Paste in Front and Paste in Back commands. Illustrator automatically deselects everything when you cut an object—because the selection has disappeared—so pressing Ctrl+B or Ctrl+F (Cmd-B or Cmd-F on the Mac) sends the cut object to the absolute back or front of the illustration.

Paste in Front or Back of Collections

This is one of those gotchas that throw even experienced Illustrator users. When you use the Paste in Front or Paste in Back commands, you need to pay attention to how many objects are selected. If you have an entire group selected, the Paste in Front or Back commands paste the new object as an element that is unconnected to the group. But if you have only *part* of a group selected, the Paste in Front or Back commands will paste the new object as part of the group.

The same applies to compound paths, text wraps, and other collective elements. Of course, it all makes sense if you think about it. With only one element of a collection selected, Illustrator thinks you want to sneak a new element into the collection. With the whole collection selected, Illustrator realizes you probably want to keep the integrity of the collection and simply add the new object in front or in back.

Working with Drawing Layers

In addition to the stacking functions, Illustrator offers self-contained drawing layers (or simply layers), an almost essential capability for creating complex illustrations. Illustrator was late to join the layering game—version 5 was the first to offer layers, years behind drawing rivals FreeHand and Canvas—but its layers are quite possibly the best of any drawing program. To display the Layers palette, choose Window » Layers (**Figure 8.18**).

Not only can you put objects on their own layers, but you can nest layers like you do with folders. You can also see the individual groups and paths that are on each layer. And by *see*, I don't mean just see a label; you can actually see a thumbnail drawing of the layer as well as the objects on the layer.

 The Layers palette has a command called Make/Release Clipping Mask. Rather than cover it here, I'll explain it all in Chapter 17 with the rest of the masks.

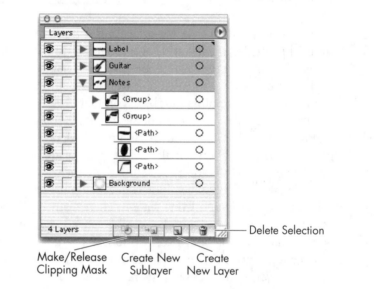

Figure 8.18: The Layers palette as seen with its default settings.

Make/Release Clipping Mask   Create New Sublayer   Create New Layer   Delete Selection

An illustration can contain any number of layers. Each layer can contain any number of objects, and you can name layers and alter their order as you see fit. You can even hide layers, lock them, and change their display mode independently of each other.

Adding New Layers

Illustrator automatically creates flat illustrations with only one layer apiece. To add a drawing layer to the illustration, choose the New Layer command from the Layers palette menu or click the Create New Layer button. The position of the new layer depends on which layer is currently active.

The first thing you'll probably notice is that Illustrator has presumptuously named the new layer. If you find this impertinence to your disliking, either choose the Options command for that layer from the Layer menu or double-click the name of the layer in the Layers palette. The Layer Options dialog box appears, as shown in **Figure 8.19**. Enter a layer name containing up to 31 characters into the Name option box.

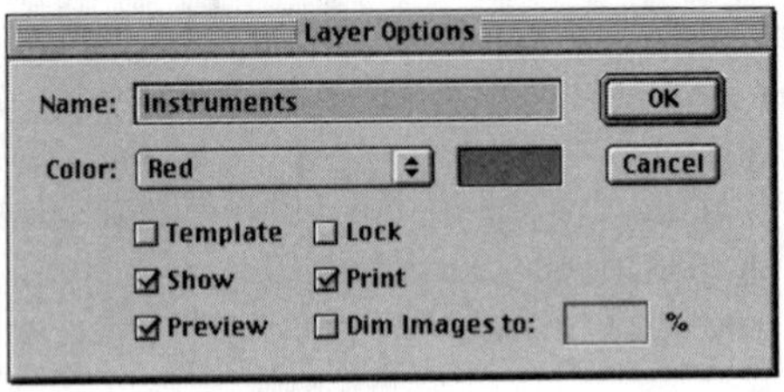

Figure 8.19: The Layer Options dialog box allows you to change the name and other attributes of a layer.

If you work with only one layer, you may think that Illustrator always shows selected points, segments, and control handles in blue, but this isn't necessarily the case—that's just the default color for the default layer. The Layer Options dialog box also lets you choose a color from the pop-up list. This choice controls the color of the anchor points for objects on that layer. If you always accept Illustrator's default colors, then points on the first layer are blue; those on the second layer are red, followed by bright green, a darker blue, yellow, magenta, cyan, gray, and black. But you can also select from lots of other preset colors, or you can define a custom color by selecting the Other option.

Although you probably will be concerned only with the name and maybe the color of a new layer and won't want to change any of the check boxes at first, because we're in the neighborhood I'll go ahead and run through the other options in this dialog box. These options are generally more useful after you've added a few objects to the layer and you've had a little time to consider how you want the layer to interact with the rest of your illustration. They allow you such choices as the following:

- Turn on the Template check box to make the new layer be a locked, nonprinting layer intended to show dimmed images. This is ideal for images that you wish to trace. Images that are placed with the Template option selected when in the Place dialog box will appear on a layer with this option selected.

- Turn off the Show check box to hide all objects on the layer.

- Turn off the Preview check box to view the objects on the new layer in the outline mode.

- Select the Print check box to make all objects on the layer print. Deselect it and all the objects won't print.

Select the Lock check box to lock objects on the layer so they can't be accidentally altered.

 Select Dim Images to diffuse imported images so that you can easily distinguish them from graphic objects and text blocks created in Illustrator, as you may recall from the discussion on tracing in Chapter 5. The default setting is 50 percent, but you can set any value from 0 to 100 percent.

After you press Enter (Return on the Mac), the layer's new name appears just above the last active layer.

 The most basic and often-used of these attributes, Show and Lock, can also be controlled in the Layers palette, so you don't always have to open the Layer Options dialog box just to tinker with them. The Show icon in the palette is the old familiar eyeball to the far left of a layer name; clicking on it toggles it on and off. Lock is the box directly next to the eyeball; click in that empty box to display the padlock icon. But to get back to all the options, just double-click on the layer to open its dialog box.

 In case you're thinking, "Gosh, I bet I can add layers to the startup file to get multiple layers when Illustrator creates a new illustration," permit me to dash your hopes. You can't—nor, sadly, can you drag and drop entire layers between illustrations, the way you can in Photoshop.

The Layers palette includes a New Layer button. It's the one to the left of the trash can icon. You can simply click this button, or click it in conjunction with some keys to add a new layer.

 Click the New Layer button to create a layer just above the last active layer.

 Alt-click (Option-click on the Mac) the New Layer button to first display the Layer Options dialog box before creating a layer just above the last active layer.

 Ctrl+Alt-click (Cmd-Option-click on the Mac) the New Layer button to display the Layer Options before creating a layer just *below* the active layer.

 Ctrl-click (Cmd-click on the Mac) the New Layer button to create a layer at the very top of the layers list.

Drawing on Layers

The highlighted name in the Layers palette (which also has a small black triangle in the upper-right corner) represents the active drawing layer. Any objects you create are placed on this layer. To change the active drawing layer, click a layer name in the scrolling list. Then start drawing to create objects on that layer.

Viewing Layers

One of the great advantages of working with layers is you can control which layers are visible and which are hidden. This helps enormously if you're working with a very complex illustration and just want to see one part of the artwork. It also helps if you have many elements such as blends, gradients, and effects that take time to redraw on the screen. You can turn off viewing those layers and speed the preview of your work. (If you're really interested in speeding previews, don't forget about using outline view, covered in Chapter 3.)

The leftmost column in the Layers palette lets you change the display mode for each layer. Each of the display modes is shown in **Figure 8.20**.

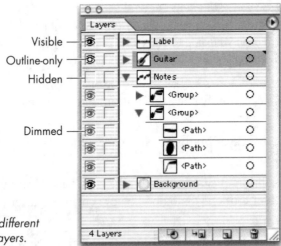

Figure 8.20: The different view options for layers.

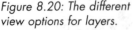 A solid eyeball icon means that the layer is visible in both the outline and preview modes. Click the eyeball on and off to show or hide the layer. (This changes the Show setting in the Layer Options dialog box.) Unlike Object » Hide Selection, Illustrator saves the state of a hidden layer when you close and then reopen a document.

No eyeball icon means the layer is hidden. Click the empty eyeball box to show the layer.

Alt-click (Option-click on the Mac) the eyeball icon to hide all the other layers except that layer.

 A hollow eyeball icon means that the layer displays only in the outline mode. Ctrl-click (Cmd-click on the Mac) to toggle the icon between the outline-only or preview modes. Click the hollow eyeball on and off to show or hide the layer. (This changes the Preview setting in the Layer Options dialog box.)

 Ctrl+Alt-click (Cmd-Option-click on the Mac) the eyeball icon to turn all the other layers except that layer into the outline-only mode.

 A dimmed eyeball icon means that the display of the layer is controlled by the setting of a higher layer. For instance, in Figure 8.20, the Notes layer is hidden. This dims the entries for the groups and paths below that layer.

You can't add items to a hidden layer. You can't draw on a hidden layer, nor can you move items in the Layers palette from one layer to a hidden layer.

Moving Objects between Layers

When you select an object in the illustration window, the corresponding drawing layer becomes highlighted in the scrolling list. You'll also see a tiny colored selection marker near the right edge of the Layers palette. This marker represents the selected object. If you select multiple objects on different layers, Illustrator shows multiple selection markers, one for each layer on which the objects sit.

To move the selected objects from one layer to another, just drag the colored selection markers up or down the scrolling list. You can drag the marker to any layer that is neither hidden nor locked. You can drag only one marker at a time; so if you have objects selected on two layers, for example, and you want to move them all to a third layer, you have to drag one selection marker to the third layer and then drag the other.

As you drag the marker, the cursor changes to a finger to indicate that you are moving objects between layers, as in **Figure 8.21**. Upon releasing the mouse button, Illustrator transfers the selected objects from one layer to the other.

Figure 8.21: Drag the selection marker up or down to move an object from one layer to another.

To clone selected objects between layers, Alt-drag (Option-drag on the Mac) the selection marker inside the Layers palette. The cursor changes to a finger with a plus sign. After you release the mouse, the selected objects exist independently in both layers, just as though you had copied them from one layer and pasted them into another. You can also clone all objects on one layer to a brand-spanking-new layer by dragging the layer you want to duplicate onto the New Layer button. The cloned layer appears just above the original layer.

If you select all the objects on a layer, the selection marker becomes a larger square as shown in **Figure 8.22**.

You can quickly select all the objects on a layer by clicking the spot on the Layers palette where the selection marker for that layer appears. The large square selection marker appears, which indicates all the objects on that layer are selected. This also includes all the members of a group as well as the single item of a path.

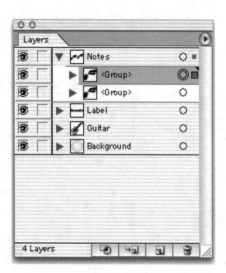

Figure 8.22: The larger square marker indicates that all the objects on a layer are selected.

Nesting Sublayers

Just as you can create a folder inside another folder in your computer filing system, so can you create sublayers inside of other layers.

> *Nested layers allow you to organize your Layers palette so that you don't have to scroll through hundreds of layers. If you never exceed four or five layers in your Illustrator documents, then, no, you don't need to create nested layers. But if you are a mapmaker who wants layers for each city, county, and state in the United States, you're going to love sublayers.*

To create a sublayer already nested in the current layer, click the Create New Sublayer icon in the Layers palette. You can also drag a layer onto another layer to nest one layer in another, as shown in **Figure 8.23**. The destination layer does not have to be open to nest the new layer.

To move a sublayer up in the ranks, drag the layer till you see the indicator line on a higher level in the Layers palette. When you release the mouse button, the sublayer will have been promoted to a higher layer status.

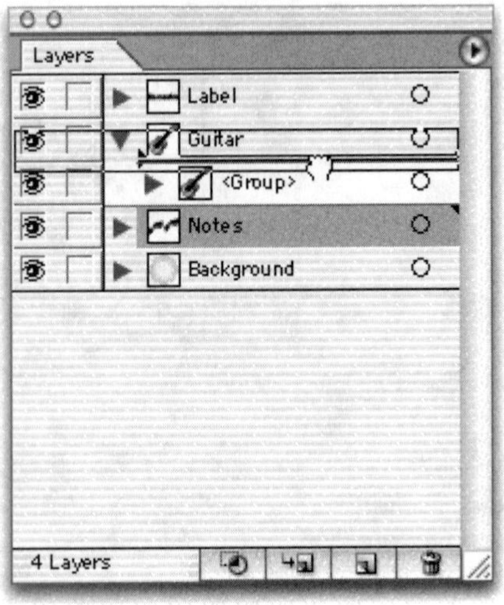

Figure 8.23: Drag a layer
below another to create a
sublayer.

Opening Layers

When there is nothing on a layer, there is no triangle icon for that layer because the layer is empty. (Oh, the sadness of an empty layer.) However, as soon as you put an object, a group, or a sublayer on a layer, a triangle icon appears. This triangle opens and closes the layer. There are several types of things that can be on layers.

- **Paths:** The most basic thing on a layer is a single object, which will be labeled in the Layers palette as "path." Objects never have triangles because there is no subdivision for them.

- **Groups:** Groups and other collective elements such as compound paths are displayed on a layer with a triangle. If you click the triangle you will see the paths that make up a group.

- **Sublayers:** Sublayers are layers nested inside other layers.

Once you rename a group or a sublayer, you may find it difficult to tell the difference between them. After all, they both have triangles to open or close their contents (and if you've renamed a sublayer, it probably won't have its telltale angle brackets around the name anymore). There are some differences, though. When you're looking at an expanded list in the Layers palette, the actual layers have a gray background behind their name, whereas their subparts usually don't. And if you double-click a group or a path, you see the Options dialog box that only locks and shows the group. The Options dialog box for a sublayer has many more options.

If you cannot move what you think is a sublayer up to its own top layer status, then most likely what you have is a group, not a layer. Groups always have to be one level down from the top level of layers.

Path and Group Layers

Illustrator's Layers palette also lists groups and paths. Click the triangle to open the layer and you will see all the individual paths and groups on that layer, as brilliantly illustrated in **Figure 8.24**. Just as you can drag one layer above another, so you can drag paths and groups up or down within a layer or between layers.

What's even more exciting (can you tell I get excited about Illustrator very easily?) is that you can drag paths in and out of groups or drag groups in and out of other groups simply by using the Layers palette. You never need to select objects or use any of the group or ungroup commands.

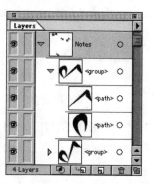

Figure 8.24: The Layers palette can also show the individual paths and groups on a layer.

Paste Remembers Layers

When the Paste Remembers Layers option is turned on, copying and pasting an object from one illustration into another pastes both the objects *and* the layer. Choose the Paste Remembers Layers option in the Layers palette to turn it on. This option instructs Illustrator to remember which layer an object came from when you send it to the Clipboard. Illustrator then pastes the object back onto that same layer, regardless of which layer is active. If the new document doesn't have a layer with that name, the paste command creates one. If cut or copied objects come from multiple layers, Illustrator pastes them back onto multiple layers.

By default, Paste Remembers Layers is turned off. When you turn it on, it affects all active documents and stays on from one session to another—until you turn it off.

Locking Layers

You use the second column in the Layers palette to lock all the elements on that layer. This allows you to work in another layer without risking accidentally manipulating or deleting an object in the locked layer.

No icon in the second column means the layer is unlocked. Click the empty box to lock the layer. (This changes the Lock setting in the Layer Options dialog box.)

 A lock icon means that the layer is protected. Nothing can be added, deleted, modified, or moved on that layer.

 Alt-click (Option-click on the Mac) the empty lock box to lock all the other layers except that layer.

 A dimmed lock icon means that the protection of the layer is controlled by the setting of a higher layer.

 If you select a locked layer, your cursor becomes a little pencil with a line through it. This shows you that you can't write to this layer unless you first unlock it.

Selecting, Merging, Flattening, and Deleting Layers

Only one layer can be the active layer (indicated by the small black triangle in the upper-right corner). But you can select more than one layer at once. Shift-click a layer other than the active one to select all layers from the active layer to the layer you clicked, inclusively. Ctrl-click (Cmd-click on the Mac) another layer to select noncontiguous layers.

You cannot select noncontiguous layers in different levels. All the layers must be at the first level of the Layers palette or sublayers of the same layer.

Once you have selected layers, you can choose Merge Selected from the Layers palette menu. This moves all the objects on the selected layers to the topmost layer. Illustrator also deletes the empty layers.

Another way to merge information is to use the Collect in New Layer command (also on the palette menu). However many layers you select, Illustrator will combine all of their elements on one new layer, removing the originals. If you use this command on paths within a layer, they will be combined onto a new nested layer.

You can also use the Reverse Order command from the Layers palette menu to—you guessed it—reverse the order of two selected layers or paths within a layer. Granted, you can also do this manually, but I'm sure there are times when this will be more convenient, and for those of you who don't like to really be on the front lines, it may be comforting to "let the computer do it" for you.

To smoosh together all nonhidden layers into a single layer, choose Flatten Artwork from the Layers palette menu. All of the objects from the discarded layers will appear on the topmost layer. If any hidden layers are present, Illustrator will give you the option to move the layers' contents along with all the other artwork or to discard them.

You can delete a layer—even if it's chock-full of text and paths—by clicking the layer name and choosing Delete from the Layers palette menu or clicking the Delete button (the one with a trash can icon). If the layer contains any objects, an alert box appears, warning you that you are about to delete a layer that contains artwork. To delete a layer without Illustrator's cautioning, you can simply drag the layer onto the trash can icon.

 If you're doing Web animations, you may be interested in the Release to Layers options (otherwise, you probably won't be). These options are covered in Chapter 22.

Template Layers

Back in Chapter 5, I mentioned that when you choose the Template option, placed images appear on a special layer called a Template. Template layers are actually regular layers with the following options automatically set in the Layer Options dialog box.

  Printing is turned off.

- The layer is locked.

- Placed images are dimmed to 50 percent by default, but you can change the amount in the Dim images to option.

- The Show and Preview settings remain checked but unavailable. You can change them only by turning off the Template option.

Printing Layers

To prevent a layer from printing, double-click it and turn off the Print check box in the Layer Options dialog box. But remember what you've done! When it's printing, Illustrator doesn't give you any warnings that some layers are turned off. Many artists have torn out their hair trying to figure out why certain objects in their illustrations aren't printing while other objects are printing just fine.

Customizing Layers

Just because the Layers palette ships with a certain look doesn't mean you have to sit there passively and accept it. Hey, get up! Assert your individuality! You're in control here, not some product manager in San Jose, California!

To change the display of the Layers palette, choose Palette Options from the Layers palette menu. The dialog box shown in **Figure 8.25** appears. Make your choices as follows:

- **Show Layers Only:** Stops you from seeing the groups and paths that make up a layer.

- **Row Size:** This controls how big the thumbnail previews are. However, the Small setting also turns off the thumbnail previews.

- **Thumbnails:** This controls which elements will have thumbnail previews. The default setting shows thumbnails for all elements. If you choose Layers only, you will turn off the thumbnails for groups and paths but leave the thumbnails for layers and sublayers. This setting keeps the palette less cluttered but still provides visual feedback as to what's on each layer.

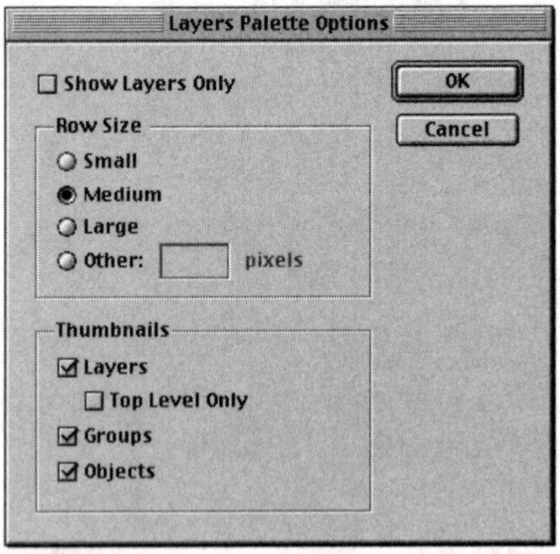

Figure 8.25: If you want to change how the Layers palette appears, here's where you make your choices. These are the default settings.

Vacuuming Your Illustration

Of course I know that the artwork you send to others will be clean, with all layers labeled clearly and no random pieces of rubbish littering the landscape. But what if it's the other way around? What if an incredibly gifted person like you has to muck about inside cruddy pieces of artwork created by some bungler from your company's dim past?

I've inherited work from people who didn't have a clue as to what they were doing. I've seen it all—stray points, transparent shapes, and empty text blocks littering the virtual landscape like roaches laid waste with a bug bomb.

That's why Illustrator includes the Clean Up command. You won't need it very often, but when you do, it's great. Just choose Objects » Path » Clean Up to display the dialog box in **Figure 8.26**. You can opt to delete single points that have no segments, paths that have no fill or stroke, and text blocks that have no text. All the refugees from the Island of Misfit Objects get whisked clean away.

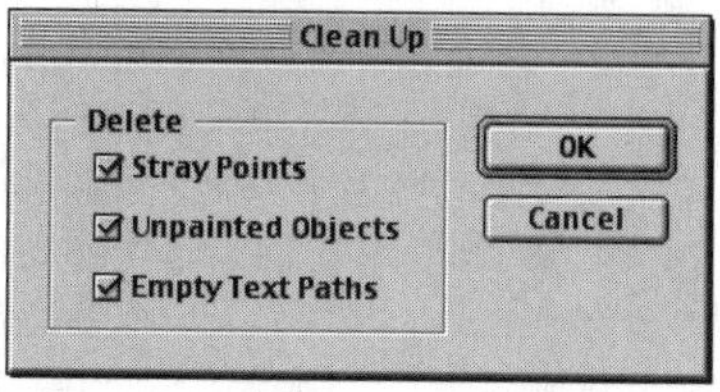

Figure 8.26: Illustrator lets you scrub away random rubbish from old illustrations.

If you want to delete just stray points, you can skip this dialog box by choosing Select » Object » Stray Points. This selects all the stray points in your document. Then just punch the Backspace key (Delete key on the Mac) and away they go.

CHAPTER 9

THE MAGIC OF TRANSFORMATIONS AND DISTORTIONS

The enchantment of Illustrator's transformation and distortion tools is also found in many children's stories. It must have been the scale tool that caused the beanstalk to grow so tall. Only the rotate tool could have swirled the tornado that sent Dorothy to Oz. Obviously, the evil witch looked in the mirror with the reflect tool, and melted into oblivion thanks to the liquify tools. Add a free transform tool and a Transform Each command, and you can practically see Cinderella's fairy godmother waving her magic wand as you work in Illustrator.

All four of the basic transformation tools work pretty much the same as when I started using Illustrator back in the days of version 1. The only major change happened in version 7, when Adobe finally let you see the point around which the transformation occurs. In Illustrator 8, Adobe transformed the lame free distort filter into the more powerful free transform tool. With this single tool you can make combinations of the ordinary transformations as well as totally bizarre distortions. Even the modest bounding box can perform two transformations: scale and rotate.

 Instead of having to jump to the Preferences to show and hide the bounding box for an object, you can just choose Show/Hide Bounding Box. It's even got its own keystroke—Ctrl+Shift+B (Cmd-Shift-B on the Mac)—which I recommend you memorize immediately.

So, in essence, if you're familiar with previous versions of Illustrator, you are probably well versed in the world of transformation. But you world-weary old-timers (and faithful readers of previous editions) should not blithely skip past this chapter. Why? Because I've stuffed it full of new information about Illustrator 10's amazing new distortion capabilities, which go far beyond what you've seen before.

Making Objects Bigger and Smaller

Let's start things off with a bang by talking about scaling. In case you're unclear on the concept, scaling means enlarging or reducing something, or making it thinner or fatter or taller or shorter. Put a fellow on the rack, and you're scaling him.

The Scale Tool and the Origin Point

After selecting one or more objects—paths, text, or imported images; it matters not—drag with the scale tool in the drawing area. Illustrator enlarges or reduces the selection with respect to its center. If you drag away from the center of the selection, as in **Figure 9.1**, you enlarge the objects. If you drag toward the center, you reduce them. It's so simple, a child could do it. (And no doubt many have.)

Good thing you don't have to accept the center as the default. You can scale a selection with respect to any point in the illustration window. This origin point (also called a reference point or scale origin) represents the center of the transformation. To demonstrate how an origin point works, I've enlarged a star several times over using a single origin in **Figure 9.2**. All of the white arrows in the figure emanate from the origin, showing how the points move outward uniformly from this one point.

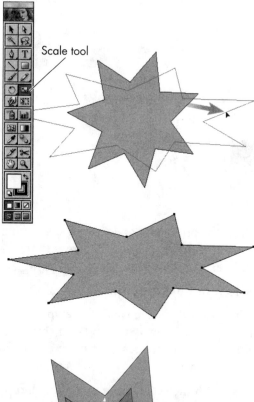

Scale tool

Figure 9.1: Using the scale tool, drag away from the center of a selection (top) to enlarge it (bottom).

Figure 9.2: A star scaled repeatedly with respect to a single origin point.

By moving the origin point, you also move the scaled object. In **Figure 9.3** I've applied the exact same scaling to copies of the same circle. When the origin point is in the center, the scaled object keeps the same center. But when I move the origin point to different positions, the final scaled objects also move to new positions. And don't forget, the origin point for all transformations can be positioned way outside the selected object. (The white circles represent the original objects, the dark ovals represent the scaled objects, and the origin point is that target thingy.)

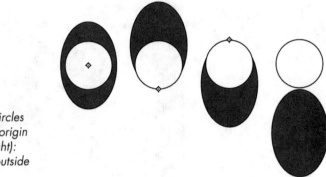

Figure 9.3: Several circles scaled from different origin points (from left to right): center, bottom, top, outside the object.

Therefore, the origin point affects the positioning of objects, whereas the distance you drag with the scale tool determines the extent of the resizing. The following steps explain how to set the origin point and scale from it:

1. **Select the objects you want to scale.**

2. **Click with the scale tool where you want to position the origin.**
Provided the View » Snap to Point command is active and you click within 2 points of an anchor point or guideline, Illustrator snaps the origin to that point.

3. **Drag with the scale tool about an inch or two away from the origin.**
This gives you room to move inward and provides you with more control. If you start the drag too close to the origin, you have too little room to maneuver. Illustrator resizes the objects with respect to the origin. If you drag away from the origin, you enlarge the selection. If you drag toward the origin, the selected objects shrink.

If you drag from one side of the origin point to the other, you flip the selection. Although Illustrator also provides a separate reflect tool, the scale tool is the only one that lets you flip and resize at the same time. (By contrast, the reflect tool lets you flip and rotate simultaneously.)

Scaling with the Shift Key

As you do when drawing and reshaping paths, you can use the Shift key to constrain scaling, or any other transformation. For the scale tool, Illustrator actually has three different constraints for the Shift key.

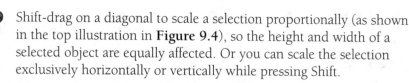

- Shift-drag on a diagonal to scale a selection proportionally (as shown in the top illustration in **Figure 9.4**), so the height and width of a selected object are equally affected. Or you can scale the selection exclusively horizontally or vertically while pressing Shift.

- Shift-drag to the left or right so that only the width of the object is affected, as shown in the bottom illustration of Figure 9.4. This is called a horizontal scale.

- Shift-drag up or down so that only the height of the object is affected. This is called a vertical scale.

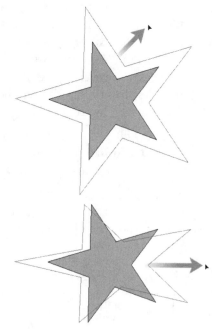

Figure 9.4: Shift-drag
diagonally to scale a shape
proportionally (top). Shift-drag
horizontally to change only
the width of the shape
(bottom).

 If the shape seems to jump around a lot while you press the Shift key, it's because you began your drag in a bad place, maybe too close to the origin. Release all the keys and press Ctrl+Z (Cmd-Z on the Mac) to put things back where they were. Then start your drag in a diagonal direction some distance from the origin.

All this assumes that you haven't rotated the constraint axes from their default 0-degree setting (in the General Preferences dialog box). If you have changed the constraint axes, you can still scale proportionally using the Shift key. However, holding the Shift key won't constrain your scaling along the horizontal or vertical axis. Instead, you scale in line with the constraint axes angles.

*What if you're so lazy you don't even want to press Shift to scale pro-
portionally? Yes, Illustrator has an answer for you, too. Simply choose
View » Smart Guides before using the scale tool, then drag the scale tool
around the origin point. You'll find that out of nowhere, guides appear
that match the proportional, horizontal, and vertical axes and the constrain angle, and
the scale tool snaps along them. If only it could answer the phone and fetch drinks from
the fridge, you'd have it made!*

Scaling Again

After you scale an object, Illustrator remembers the most recent scaling percentages you used until you quit the program (or change the settings). This means
that you can choose Object » Transform » Transform Again or press Ctrl+D
(Cmd-D on the Mac) to repeat the scaling. This technique is usually referred to
by its keyboard shortcut. Each time you press Ctrl+D (Cmd-D), the object scales
again by the same percentages. (Power users just hold the Ctrl (Cmd) key with
one hand and pound the D key furiously with the other.) Repeating the scale over
and over may not seem that useful, but it does have the following advantages:

- You can drag just a tiny bit to scale the object ever so slightly, and
  then just press Ctrl+D (Cmd-D) over and over again to watch the
  object grow. This is easier than dragging up and down.

- You can select another object and scale it by the same percentages.
  The only drawback to this is that Illustrator uses the origin point for
  the first object, as you can see in **Figure 9.5**.

*Figure 9.5: These apples were all scaled using the same percentages. The apple on the left
was scaled by dragging with the scale tool around the origin point indicated by the target.
The next two apples were scaled by using the Transform Again command. Notice how the
apples move from their original positions (indicated by the gray outlines).*

However, some people think repeatedly scaling the same object over and over
is as exciting as watching a sponge soak up water. Hold on, then! Just wait till
you see what happens when you combine Transform Again with duplicating
objects as you scale them.

Duplicating Objects as You Scale Them

The scale tool also lets you clone objects as you scale them. To scale a clone and leave the original unchanged, press the Alt key (Option key on the Mac) after you start the drag, and keep the key pressed until after you release the mouse button. If you enlarge the selection, you may cover up the original with the clone, but the original will be there, lurking in the background. (If you're at all concerned, press Ctrl+Shift+[(Cmd-Shift-[on the Mac)—that's a left bracket—to send the clone in back of the original.)

At this point, Illustrator has the following sentence stored in its memory: "Make a copy of whatever object is selected, and then scale it up a certain percentage from a certain origin point." Illustrator will remember that sentence until you make another transformation. (Transformations include scale, rotate, reflect, shear, and move.)

You can now create a series of scaled clones by choosing Transform Again. This is a particularly useful technique for creating perspective effects. By reducing a series of clones toward a far-off origin, you create the effect of shapes slowly receding into the distance.

For example, I wanted to do a "slow fade into the distance" with the stars and bars as shown in **Figure 9.6**. I clicked the origin point with the scale tool and Alt+Shift-dragged (Option-Shift-dragged on the Mac) ever so slightly down toward the origin to create a proportional clone. The clone was in front of the original, so I pressed Ctrl+Shift-[(Cmd-Shift-[ ) to send it to the back.

Figure 9.6: A proportional scale created the perspective on the left. A nonproportional scale created the more realistic swoop on the right. In each case, the origin point is indicated by the target below the objects.

Even though I had performed an interim action—used the Send to Back command—I knew that Illustrator would still remember the sentence. So with the clone selected, I pressed Ctrl+D (Cmd-D on the Mac) to create another reduced clone and then Ctrl+Shift+[(Cmd-Shift-[on the Mac) to send it to the back.

Then I kept pressing Ctrl+D and Ctrl+Shift+[(Cmd-D and Cmd-Shift-[on the Mac) until I arrived at the effect on the left side of Figure 9.6.

For a more interesting effect, I created the clones without pressing the Shift key. Thus the clones are not limited to proportional duplicates of the original. The right side of Figure 9.6 shows what happens when I applied a nonproportional scale. In this case, I dragged so that the horizontal scaling was slightly greater than the vertical. The images seem to swoop up at the viewer.

A few of you brainy types are thinking "Why can't I just blend between a big version and a little version of the objects?" Fact is, you can. But as **Figure 9.7** *shows, you still don't get that nice swoop effect. However, because this chapter has nothing to do with blends, you can either skip to Chapter 17 or wait until we get there to find out how to create blends.*

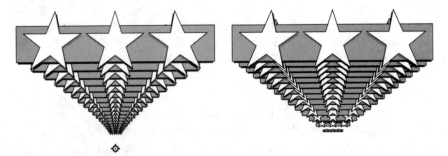

Figure 9.7: A comparison of using Ctrl+D (Cmd-D on the Mac) to create a perspective effect (on the left) or blending (on the right).

Scaling with the Bounding Box

So why would Adobe add another way to scale objects? Doesn't the scale tool do everything you could ever need when it comes to scaling? Well, yes, but for years other illustration programs have allowed you to scale objects by simply dragging on the handles of the bounding box around objects. So rather than forcing you to switch from the selection tool to the scale tool, Adobe made it easier to simply drag the bounding box.

To use the bounding box, you need to have chosen View » Show Bounding Box. If the command is listed as Hide Bounding Box, then you already do have the Bounding Box option chosen. Or just memorize Ctrl+Shift+B (Cmd-Shift-B on the Mac) and then you won't need to choose the option from the menu. With this option activated, any and all paths that are selected when the arrow tool is chosen will automatically gain an eight-handled box that encloses all the selected paths—in other words, all fully selected paths will display with a bounding box; partially selected paths will not.

The orientation of this bounding box is initially up to Illustrator and is based on the path or paths selected. For example, the bounding box of the top-left star in **Figure 9.8** is aligned to match the angle at which the star was drawn. If you don't like the default orientation of a bounding box, you can choose Object » Transform » Reset Bounding Box, which is what I did to align the bounding box of the top-right star in Figure 9.8. When you select more than one path, the bounding box will usually align in such a way that it is square with the page. Any time you want, you can reset the bounding box so that it is square with the page by choosing Object »Transform » Reset Bounding Box.

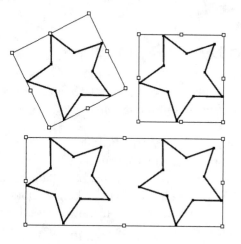

Figure 9.8: When the Use Bounding Box check box is activated, each wholly selected path will display an eight-handled bounding box that encloses just the path.

The real power of the bounding box is in its uses, which are many.

- Drag on a corner handle to scale the selected objects. Shift-drag a corner handle to scale proportionally. In either case, the opposite corner serves as the scale origin.

- Alt-drag (Option-drag on the Mac) a corner handle to scale the object around its center. Alt+Shift-drag (Option-Shift-drag on the Mac) a corner handle to scale proportionally around the object's center.

- Drag on one of the bounding box's side handles (including the top and bottom handles) to limit the scaling to either horizontal or vertical changes. The opposite side's handle serves as the scale origin.

- Shift-drag a side handle to once again scale proportionally, except that in this case the opposite side's handle serves as the scale origin.

- Alt-drag (Option-drag on the Mac) a side handle to horizontally or vertically scale the object from the center.

- Use Object » Transform Again or press Ctrl+D (Cmd-D on the Mac) to repeat the transformation from the bounding box.

You can't clone an object with the Alt (Option) key as you scale with the bounding box. Only the scale tool has that magical power.

If you use the bounding box to scale a type block, the type block will scale but the type size won't.

Resizing by the Numbers

The scale tool is one of my favorite tools, but it's not the only way to resize objects in Illustrator. You can also enlarge and reduce object sizes by entering precise numeric values into two different dialog boxes and one palette.

Scaling from the Transform Palette

Let's start with the least capable (but most convenient) of the three scaling options, the Transform palette. Instead of a single Scale option box, you enter values in the W (for width) and H (for height) option boxes to scale objects. Although it may seem quite obvious how to use the palette, there are actually some hidden features.

- Enter an amount in either the width (W) or height (H) option boxes. Use the Tab key to jump from one box to another. Use the up arrow or down arrow keys to "dial" a selected number up or down. Press Enter (Return on the Mac) or click on the page to change the focus from the Transform palette.

- Use the reference point icon to change the point around which the transformation occurs. The reference points are measured with respect to the selection's rectangular bounding box.

- Scale by percentages by entering a number followed by the % symbol into either the W or H option boxes as shown in **Figure 9.9**. You can enter different percentages to scale the object nonproportionally.

- After the initial transformation, use Object » Transform Again or press Ctrl+D (Cmd-D on the Mac) to reapply a percentage transformation change, just as you would with the scale tool.

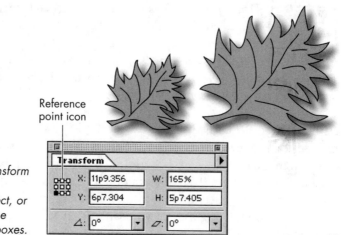

Reference
point icon

Figure 9.9: Use the Transform
palette to change the
absolute size of an object, or
enter a percentage in the
width or height option boxes.

If you really want to impress your friends and clients, throw in the following
super-power-user modifier keys. Hold one or more of these keys down with the
Enter key (Return on the Mac) after you enter a value in the Transform palette
(they also work in other palettes where you enter values):

- To keep the W and H values proportional, add the Ctrl key (Cmd on
  the Mac).

- To keep the focus on the Scale option, add the Shift key. If you hate having to click in the Transform palette over and over when trying out different numbers in the same field, the Shift key is your new best friend!

- To copy the object you're scaling, add the Alt key (Option on the Mac).

*You can press any combination of these modifier keys with
Enter (Return on the Mac) depending on what you're doing.
For example, to scale proportionally and make a copy, enter
a value and then press Ctrl+Alt+Enter (Cmd-Option-Return
on the Mac). Or, to make a copy scaled along the W dimension only while
keeping the focus on the Transform palette, enter a W value and press
Shift+Alt+Enter (Shift-Option-Return on the Mac). By pressing different
combinations of the three modifiers plus Enter (Return), you can conjure up
endless (well, actually eight) combinations of proportion control, palette
focus, and object copying.*

Don't forget that Illustrator can do the math for you in any option box. So instead of entering 200% into the W or H option box to double a dimension, you can simply punch in *2 after the current value in the box—this tells Illustrator to multiply the current value by 2, the same as 200% of the value. Illustrator doubles the value when you press Enter (Return) or Tab, and changes the dimensions accordingly.

Using the Scale Dialog Box

After selecting a few objects on your Things to Scale list, double-click the scale tool icon in the toolbox. This brings up the Scale dialog box, captured in all its radiant glory in **Figure 9.10**. Illustrator automatically positions the origin point in the center of the selection (according to the big, bad bounding box). If you want to position the origin point yourself, Alt-click (Option-click on the Mac) in the illustration window with the scale tool. When you press the Alt (Option) key, you'll see a tiny ellipsis next to the scale tool cursor. Alt- or Option-clicking with any transformation tool simultaneously positions the origin point and displays the appropriate dialog box. Here's how the Scale dialog box can be used:

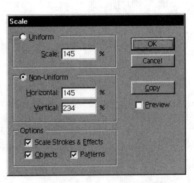

Figure 9.10: In the Scale dialog box, you can specify the exact percentage by which a selection is enlarged or reduced.

You can also open the Scale dialog box by choosing Object » Transform » Scale. This is also the route to the Rotate, Shear, and Reflect dialog boxes. So why would you go all the way to a submenu to choose one of these options? You wouldn't, but because they're on the menu, you can assign a keystroke to invoke the command. And I guarantee that is something you want to do. Choose Edit » Keyboard Shortcuts, and then choose the item Menu commands from the second pop-up menu. Locate the menu command using the scrollbars and small triangle controls where necessary. Click on the command or anywhere in its row, and then type in your desired shortcut. Don't forget to save the keystroke set! (You can't make changes to the default set.)

 Choose Uniform and enter a value in the Scale option box to proportionally scale the width and height of the selection. This value is accurate to 0.001 percent—ten times more accurate than the scale value in the Transform palette.

 Choose Non-Uniform and enter a value in either the Horizontal or Vertical option boxes to scale the object nonproportionally.

 Check Scale Strokes & Effects to scale any stroke weights or effects applied to objects. The stroke weights change only when objects are scaled uniformly. (When the Non-Uniform button is selected, Illustrator can't scale stroke weights nonuniformly, so it scales them uniformly.) Effects are scaled whenever the box is checked. If the check box is off, strokes and effects are unaffected.

 Illustrator remembers this Scale Strokes & Effects setting the next time you Shift-drag with the scale tool. So if you find that your line weights are getting thicker and thinner as you scale them, you'll know the culprit. Double-click the scale tool icon and turn off the Scale Line Weight check box. Or change the setting in the General Preferences dialog box.

 The Objects and Patterns check boxes are used strictly when working with tiled fills. If you want to learn about these options—for all four transformation dialog boxes—read the stirring account in the section "Transforming Tiles" in Chapter 15.

Use the Preview check box to see the possible yet currently unrealized future. Click it on and off to see your changes appear and disappear, ad nauseam.

To scale the selection, press Enter (Return on the Mac) or click the OK button. Click the Copy button to clone the selection and scale it.

Oh, and one more thing. All of Illustrator's transformation dialog boxes act as recording devices, keeping track of the last transformation applied, whether you used a tool or the dialog box itself. Sadly, the Scale dialog box ignores the results of the Transform palette, and it doesn't pay attention to the next command, Transform Each. But it knows what the scale tool is up to.

Scaling Partial Objects

You can use the scale tool or Scale dialog box to scale partially selected paths and text objects. For example, you can use the scale tool to enlarge a text block without changing the size of the text inside it. Alt-click (Option-click on the Mac) the rectangular text container with the direct selection tool, and then click with the scale tool to set the origin point and drag away. As long as you haven't selected any text—you don't see any baselines, do you?—Illustrator enlarges or reduces the containers and rewraps the text inside.

You can also scale selected points and segments in a path. The primary advantage of this technique is that you can move points symmetrically. See, Illustrator doesn't provide any specific means for moving points away from or toward an origin point. Moving is the one transformation that has nothing to do with origins (which is why I don't discuss it in this chapter). The closest thing to an origin-based move function is the scale tool.

Consider the sinister **Figure 9.11**. In the first example, I've selected four points in the star that make up the outer shape. (I've added halos around the selected points to make them easier to locate.) After setting the origin point at the bottom of the shape, I dragged up and inward on the upper-right point. This caused all selected points to move up and in toward the center, based on their proximity and relation to the origin point. Because the two upper points were far away from the origin, they moved dramatically, forming sharp bat ears. The lower points, closer to the origin, moved only slightly to form the chin, as the second example shows.

Figure 9.11: After selecting four points (left, surrounded by halos), I dragged with the scale tool to move the points according to their proximity to the origin.

You can also use the scale tool to move objects in equal and opposite directions. I used the direct selection tool to select just the top and bottom points in the object on the left. Using the origin point in the center of the object, I dragged the top object up. This sent the bottom object down at the same distance. This ensured the finished object was the same on top and bottom.

Whenever you apply the scale tool to a selected point, you stretch the neighboring segments, just as when dragging points with the direct selection tool. You can also apply the scale tool to selected curved segments. In **Figure 9.12**, I took a plain old circle and selected each of its segments with the direct selection tool without selecting any of the points. (I marqueed the two bottom segments and then Shift-marqueed the top two.) Then I dragged with the scale tool to enlarge the selection from the center. Illustrator stretches the segments an equal distance in four directions. Pay close attention when selecting segments, because it's not like how selected handles become hollow. Illustrator gives you no visual feedback at all for selected segments.

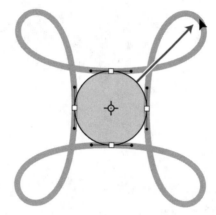

Figure 9.12: By dragging the selected segments in a circle with the scale tool, I stretched the segments in perpendicular directions.

So in addition to its normal resizing functions, the scale tool does double duty as a symmetrical move tool. It's not surprising, if you think about it. All the scale tool is doing is moving and stretching segments away from and toward a fixed point. Once you understand its geometry, the scale tool can become a great source of inspiration.

Rotating Objects

After you know how to use one transformation tool, the other three standard transformations become putty in your capable hands. The rotate, reflect, and shear tools share many characteristics with their scaly sibling. So rather than laboriously examining every single detail of each tool as if these were the firsts word of Chapter 9 you've ever read, I'll make quick work of the familiar stuff and stick in as many tool-specific tips and techniques as these humble pages will permit.

That being said, without further ado, here's a summary of the basic workings of the rotate tool (the left-hand neighbor of the scale tool).

 Drag with the rotate tool to rotate a selection around its bounding-box center. Or click to set the origin point and then drag to rotate, as shown in the second example of **Figure 9.13**. Because rotation is a strictly circular movement—in fact, you always rotate in perfect circles—the origin point acts as a true center, as the arrows in the figure demonstrate.

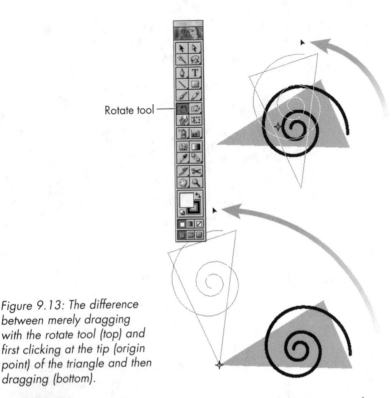

Rotate tool

Figure 9.13: The difference between merely dragging with the rotate tool (top) and first clicking at the tip (origin point) of the triangle and then dragging (bottom).

When you're using the rotate tool, it doesn't matter where you start dragging. At any time, you can gain more precise control over a rotation by moving the cursor farther away from the origin. Slight movements close to the origin can send your objects into exaggerated spins that are difficult to control.

- Press the Shift key when dragging to rotate in 45-degree (1/8 turn) increments. (The constraint axes have no influence over Shift-dragging with the rotate tool.)

- To rotate a clone of the selection, press the Alt key (Option key on the Mac) after you begin dragging and hold it until the drag is finished. Then you can repeat a series of rotated clones by choosing Object » Transform » Transform Again or pressing Ctrl+D (Cmd-D on the Mac) several times.

In the top example of **Figure 9.14**, I started with two simple paths: a spiral (black) and a two-point curve (gray). Using the origin point indicated by the target, I rotated a clone of the spiral 45 degrees by clicking with the rotate tool and Alt+Shift-dragging the spiral (Option-Shift-dragging on the Mac). I then duplicated the elements three times by mercilessly beating Ctrl+D (Cmd-D on the Mac).

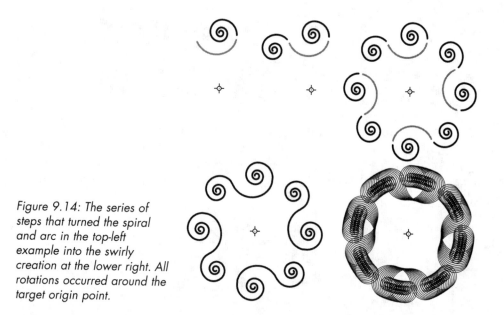

Figure 9.14: The series of steps that turned the spiral and arc in the top-left example into the swirly creation at the lower right. All rotations occurred around the target origin point.

After joining the spirals and curves at their endpoints, I selected all the objects and used the Rotate dialog box to rotate everything -2 degrees. I clicked the Copy button to clone the objects and then repeated the clone and rotation ten more times with Ctrl+D (Cmd-D). Well, for full disclosure, I guess I should say I used Ctrl+DDDDDDDDDD. I finished up by reducing the stroke weight, which created the final figure.

 Illustrator interprets rotations in degrees. A full circle, in case any of you weren't paying attention in eighth grade, is 360 degrees, so a 360-degree rotation would return the selection to its starting position, and why would you bother? A 180-degree rotation would turn the selection upside down.

Rotation by the Numbers

You can use the Rotate dialog box, shown in **Figure 9.15**, to rotate with supreme precision. Simply double-click the rotate tool in the toolbox. This positions the origin point at the center of the selection. Or you can Alt-click (Option-click on the Mac) with the rotate tool to position the origin point and open the dialog box.

 If you can't remember which way the negative or positive numbers work, look at the rotate tool in the toolbox. The tool's icon goes counterclockwise. That's your clue to remember that positive numbers go counterclockwise. (I won't insult you by telling you which direction the negative numbers rotate.)

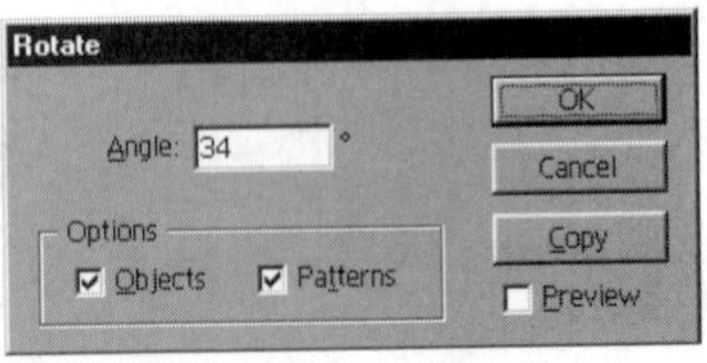

Figure 9.15: The Rotate dialog box
lets you control rotations with numeric
precision. You don't have to worry
about stroke weights or effects as
you did with the Scale dialog box.

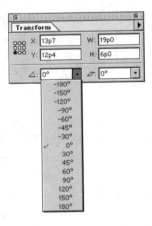

You can also use the Transform palette, shown in **Figure 9.16**, to rotate selected objects. You can enter a specific rotation amount in the option box or use the handy pop-up list that provides you with a wealth of rotation choices. Remember to use the reference point icon to set the position around which the rotation should occur.

Figure 9.16: The Transform
palette gives you another
way to rotate objects
numerically.

- Press Enter (Return on the Mac) or Tab to rotate the selection.
- Press Alt+Enter or Alt+Tab (Option-Return or Option-Tab on the Mac) to clone and rotate.
- Add the Shift key to keep the focus on the Rotate option after pressing Enter (Return).

Unlike the settings for the width and height, the Transform palette doesn't keep the setting for the rotation of the object; instead, it resets the option box back to 0 degrees as soon as you apply the setting.

Rotating with the Bounding Box

Just as you can scale with the bounding box, so can you rotate. Make sure the bounding box is visible by choosing View » Show Bounding Box. (If in the menu you see only the command Hide Bounding Box, you know the feature is already active.) Then bring your selection tool cursor *near* one of the handles along the side of the bounding box. You will see one of the rotation cursors that's shown in the left-hand teacup of **Figure 9.17**. (If your cursor is *over* the handles you will see the scale cursors, as shown in the second teacup.) Drag to rotate the bounding box along with its contents.

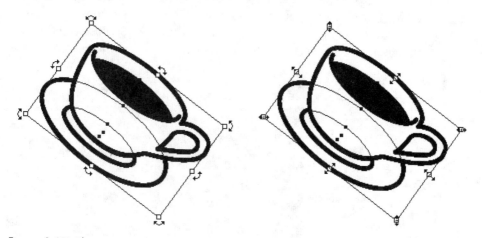

Figure 9.17: The rotation cursors on the left appear when your cursor is near (but not on) the bounding box handles. The scale cursors on the right appear when your cursor is on the bounding box handles.

Like scaling, there are several techniques for rotating with the bounding box.

- Drag any handle to rotate the selected objects.
- Shift-drag to rotate in 45-degree increments.
- Use Transform Again or press Ctrl+D (Cmd-D on the Mac) to repeat the transformation from the bounding box.
- The bounding box always rotates around the center point.

 You can't use the Alt (or Option) key to make a copy of the object as you rotate with the bounding box. Only the rotate tool has that magical power.

Flipping Objects Back and Forth

Many graphics programs provide Flip Horizontal and Flip Vertical commands so that you can quickly reflect selected objects. But not Illustrator. As far as Illustrator is concerned, those commands may be easy to use, but they don't provide enough control. So although the reflect tool is hardly convenient for quick flips, it's just the thing when power and accuracy are paramount.

Following is everything you need to know about flipping in Illustrator:

🌐 The reflect tool works a little differently than its fellow transformation tools. When you drag with the reflect tool, you change the angle of the reflection axis. As demonstrated in **Figure 9.18**, the reflection axis is like the mirror that the selection is reflected into. The portions of the object that lie on one side of the axis flip to the other. Because you can tilt the mirror, the reflect tool flips and rotates objects at the same time.

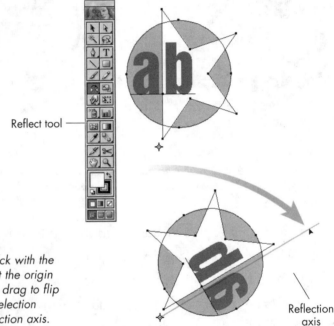

Reflect tool

Reflection axis

Figure 9.18: Click with the reflect tool to set the origin point (top); then drag to flip and rotate the selection around the reflection axis.

🌐 If you immediately start in dragging with the tool, the reflection axis hinges on the center of the selection. But if you first click to set the origin point and then drag with the reflect tool, the axis pivots on the origin. In the top example of Figure 9.18, for instance, I clicked below and to the left of the selection. I then began dragging in a direct line above the selection, which resulted in a vertical axis. As I dragged down and to the right, the axis inclined into the position shown in the second example in the figure.

Shift-drag with the reflect tool to constrain the axis to a 45-degree angle. When the axis is upright, the selection flips horizontally. When the axis is horizontal, the selection flips vertically.

Press the Alt key (Option key on the Mac) when dragging to flip a clone. You can repeat a flipped clone by pressing Ctrl+D (Cmd-D on the Mac), but why would you want to? You would only end up creating a clone of the original, positioned directly in front of it.

Most of the time, it's easier to flip using the Reflect dialog box. To bring up the dialog box, double-click the reflect tool icon in the toolbox (it's the first alternate in the rotate tool slot). Or you can Alt-click (Option-click on the Mac) with the reflect tool in the illustration window to set the origin point.

The Reflect dialog box shown in **Figure 9.19** contains three options for specifying the angle of the reflection axis around which the flip occurs. Now read this carefully and remember these are *not* typos: Select the Horizontal option to flip the selection vertically, just as a gymnast swinging on a horizontal bar flips vertically. Select the Vertical option to flip the selection horizontally, like a flag flopping back and forth on a vertical flagpole. You can also enter a value into the Angle option box to specify the exact angle of the axis. A value of 0 indicates a horizontal axis; 90 indicates a vertical axis.

Press Enter (Return on the Mac) to flip the selection. Click Copy to clone and flip.

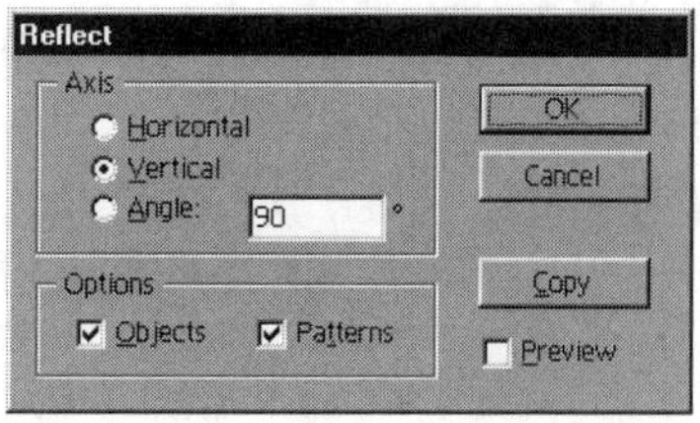

Figure 9.19: It may be easier to use the Reflect dialog box to flip objects along the horizontal or vertical axis. Or you can set a specific angle for the reflection.

Compared with the scale and rotate tools, the reflect tool is very dull. You can't perform special effects with it. And although you can flip partial paths, there's rarely a reason to do it. Still, it's a very practical tool, and Illustrator would be the worse without it. When you gotta flip, you gotta flip.

If you want to flip something and your cursor happens to be near the Transform palette, just choose Flip Horizontal or Flip Vertical from that palette's pop-up menu.

Slanting Objects the Weird Way

The final transformation tool is the oddly named shear tool—the first alternate tool in the scale tool slot. Rather than removing wool from sheep—as the tool's name implies—the shear tool slants selected objects.

 I have been making fun of the name of this tool since the first edition of this book. Shear is not an obvious name for the tool. Skew, maybe. Slant, certainly. But for millions of new users, shear only brings to mind cutting yardage at the dry goods store. Rather than carry on about this as I have in the past, I now ask that you all contact the Illustrator product managers (who used to be my friends). Tell them to change the name of the tool. Maybe they'll have a contest for the best name. And the winner would get to go to Adobe-land.

Despite its dopey name, this is an important tool. It slants objects horizontally, vertically, or in any other direction. So don't be put off by the name. This tool deserves to be part of your daily transformation regimen.

Because the shear tool is a little more demanding than the other transformation tools, I devote an entire section to explaining its basic operation. After that, I cover the Shear dialog box.

Using the Shear Tool

As with the other transformation tools, you can start right in dragging with the shear tool. But I *strongly* recommend that you don't. Many students have found their artwork shifting into the ends of Illustrator's universe all because they grabbed the shear tool and dragged willy-nilly. Of all the transformation tools, this is the most difficult to control. So you're best off specifying an origin point to keep things as predictable as possible.

Click to set the origin point. I find it helpful to set the origin in the lower-left corner of the selection. Then I move the cursor to the opposite corner of the selection—upper right—and begin dragging. Illustrator slants the selection in the direction of the drag, as demonstrated in **Figure 9.20**.

Illustrator figures two ingredients into slanting an object—the amount of slant applied and the axis along which the slant occurs. The distance of the drag determines the amount of slanting; the angle of the drag determines the angle of the axis.

Notice that although I dragged up and to the right in Figure 9.20, the selected objects slanted slightly downward. I dragged up about 10 degrees, so the axis is angled at 10 degrees. The weird thing is, when dragging with the shear tool, all axis angles clockwise from 45 degrees around to –135 degrees (about 1:30 to 7:30 on a clock face) slant objects downward. Axis values from –135 to 45 degrees (7:30 to 1:30) slant objects upward. Mathematically, it doesn't have to be this way, but so it is when you're using the shear tool.

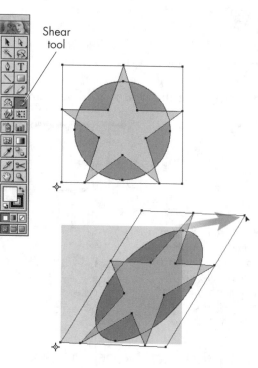

Shear
tool

Figure 9.20: Click in a corner with the shear tool (top), and then drag from the opposite corner to slant the selection (bottom).

Meanwhile, if you drag in a 45-degree or -135-degree direction, Illustrator stretches the selected objects all the way to Tierra del Fuego. If you notice your objects going haywire, just move your mouse up or down a little to restore the selection to a recognizable state.

Slant Sensibly with Shift

Because of the way Illustrator calculates the effect of dragging with the shear tool, I almost always keep the Shift key down while I'm dragging. Shift-dragging with the shear tool constrains the axis to multiples of 45 degrees. As I've said, two of these multiples—45 and -135—turn the axis into a force of absolute evil. But if you Shift-drag in a roughly horizontal or vertical direction, you'll achieve very predictable results.

The shear tool is especially useful for slanting type and creating cast shadows such as you can see in **Figure 9.21**. (Cast shadows are much more impressive than drop shadows—even the fuzzy drop shadows first seen in Illustrator 9.)

To create the first shadow at the top of the figure, I clicked with the scale tool along the baseline of the letters, and then Alt-dragged (Option-dragged on the Mac) from the top of the letters down past the baseline to flip and scale a clone. I then filled the clone with gray. In the second example, I clicked with the shear tool along the baseline of the letters and Shift-dragged from left to right to slant the shadow horizontally. Finally, I selected all letters, clicked at the base of the first T with the shear tool, and Shift-dragged up on the M. This slanted the letters vertically, as in the last example in the figure.

Figure 9.21: After flipping a clone of the letters with the scale tool (top), I slanted the clone horizontally with the shear tool (middle). I then selected all letters and slanted them vertically (bottom).

Defining the Slant and the Axis

Illustrator lets you slant and clone by pressing the Alt key (Option key on the Mac) while dragging with the shear tool. You can also display a Shear dialog box by double-clicking the shear tool icon in the toolbox, by Alt-clicking (Option-clicking on the Mac) with the tool in the illustration window, or even by doing the infamous right-click (Control-click on the Mac).

As shown in **Figure 9.22**, the Shear dialog box offers a Shear Angle option field for specifying the angle at which you want your objects to slant and three Axis options for specifying the axis along which the slant should occur.

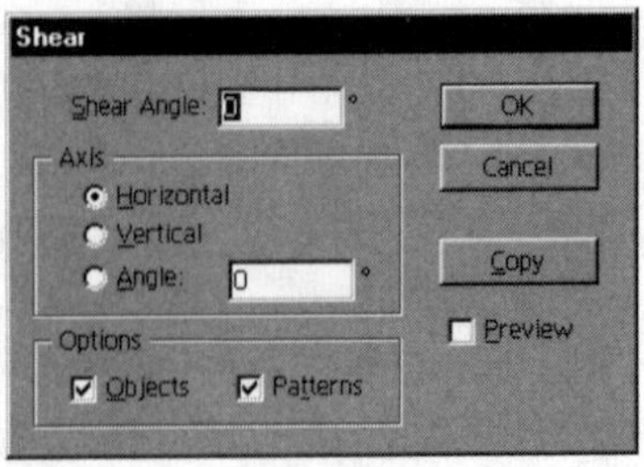

Figure 9.22: You can set the shear angle and the axis along which the slant should occur in the Shear dialog box.

Specify the angle of the shear axis exactly as you would the angle of the reflection axis inside the Reflect dialog box. Select the Horizontal option to slant the selected objects to the left or right; select the Vertical option to slant up or down. You can also angle the axis by entering a value into the Angle option box in the Axis section of the Shear dialog box. Because the axis extends to either side of the origin point, values greater than 180 degrees are repetitious. (Values of 45 or -135 degrees don't cause problems in the Shear dialog box; they just mess things up when you're trying to drag with the shear tool.)

Regardless of the selected Axis options, you'll want to enter a value for the Shear Angle at the top of the dialog box. Here's where things get tricky. Illustrator interprets just about every other value that's measured in degrees in a counterclockwise direction. (It's the standard geometry model that you undoubtedly learned or neglected in an ancient math course.) This is true for rotations, angled axes (including the shear axis), and directional movements. The only exceptions to the rotation direction are the Shear Angle option box at the top of the Shear dialog box and the Angle option box in the Twist dialog box (see Chapter 19), which Illustrator applies in a clockwise direction. Therefore:

- When the Horizontal radio button is selected, a positive Shear value slants the selection forward and a negative value slants it backward. Seems sensible.

- But when the Vertical radio button is selected, a positive Shear value slants the selection up on the left side of the origin and down on the right, so it looks like it's pointing downward. A negative value slants the selection upward. That's just plain weird!

A Shear value of 30 degrees creates a pretty significant slant. Anything beyond 90 to -90 degrees is repetitive. And you definitely don't want to enter anything from about 80 to 90 degrees (positive or negative) because it pretty well lays the selected objects flat.

Slanting is by far the least predictable of the transformations. I considered including a huge chart showing what happens to an object when you apply all kinds of different Shear Angle and Axis Angle values, but take my word for it, you would've been more confused after looking at the thing than you probably were before. That's why I recommend sticking with horizontal and vertical slants when possible. If you need to slant objects a little up and a little over, do it in two separate steps. It'll save wear and tear on your brain.

Multiple Transformations on Multiple Objects

When you choose the Transform Each command from the Object » Transform submenu, Illustrator displays the dialog box shown in **Figure 9.23**. You enter the amounts by which you want to resize the width and height of the selected objects into the first two option boxes. To perform a proportional resizing, enter the same value for both Horizontal and Vertical. Then press Enter (Return on the Mac) to apply the changes, or click the Copy button to clone and scale.

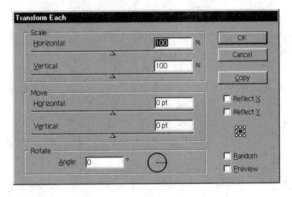

Figure 9.23: Think of the Transform Each dialog box as your one-stop shopping for a wealth of transformation tools that can be applied individually to objects.

When you apply the Transform Each command, Illustrator transforms each selected object with respect to its own reference point. Although the obvious use of the command is to scale, move, or rotate objects in their position as shown in **Figure 9.24**, there is a more subtle use that is shown in **Figure 9.25**. In Figure 9.24, I added some smaller stars to the points of the large star. Unfortunately, these smaller stars were not rotated into the correct position and they also needed to be a little bigger. After measuring the correct angle, I used the Transform Each dialog box to both scale and rotate the stars around their own centers.

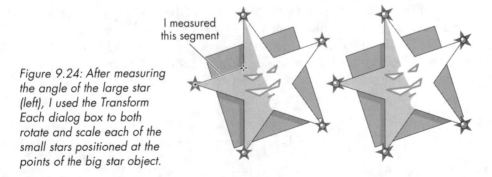

I measured this segment

Figure 9.24: After measuring the angle of the large star (left), I used the Transform Each dialog box to both rotate and scale each of the small stars positioned at the points of the big star object.

Figure 9.25 shows another important feature of Transform Each: namely, the ability to apply transformations in a random fashion. The grapes in the left example were far too symmetrical for my taste (the best puns are never intentional, are they?). So I simply selected them all and set the Transform Each dialog box to Scale 80% for both horizontal and vertical and set the rotation for 5 degrees. But before I clicked OK, I checked the box for Random. Instead of all the objects transforming the same amount, Illustrator scaled each one randomly, scaling as low as 80% and rotating anywhere up to 5 degrees. The exact amount was set randomly.

Figure 9.25: I used a combination of the rotation and scale commands in the Transform Each dialog box to make these grapes less perfect.

I can hear some of you in the back yawning and asking "So what. Is this Transform Each thing really so exciting?" Well, it may not seem like much right now, but just wait till I get into special effects for multiple strokes and fills. You'll see how Transform Each will transform your life.

 Always turn on the Preview check box when you use the Random option. This way, you can see Illustrator's random effect before applying it. If you don't like what you see, turn off Preview and then turn it back on again. This forces Illustrator to generate a new random effect. Keep clicking on the Preview check box until you get what you want. Then press Enter (Return on the Mac).

Free Transform for All

What if there were a way to combine the transformation tool team of scale, rotate, reflect, and shear with a totally wacky distortion filter in one simple, elegant tool? Well, bunky, your search is over. Welcome to the free transform tool. Although it displays handles that look very similar to its weakling cousin, the bounding box, the beefy free transform tool goes far beyond the bounding box.

When you select a path (or paths) and then choose the free transform tool from the toolbox, Illustrator displays the standard eight-handled bounding box that just surrounds the paths. As with the bounding box, the orientation of the bounding box depends on the original paths. If you don't like the orientation that

Illustrator assigns to the box, either choose Object » Transform » Reset Bounding Box or right-click (Control-click on the Mac) and choose Transform » Reset Bounding Box. Illustrator will slap the bounding box into shape, aligning it such that it squares with the artboard and its pages.

When you move the free transform tool around a selected object, Illustrator displays one of a number of different cursors, depending on the tool's location in terms of the object's bounding box and the key you're currently holding down, if any. As shown in the composite **Figure 9.26**, seven different cursors are associated with the free transform tool when it's in use. Four of these cursors (the ones flanked with two arrows) appear automatically, depending only on the location of the tool in terms of the bounding box. The other three cursors (the plain or augmented grayed arrowheads) appear only after you press Ctrl (Cmd on the Mac) *after* you start dragging one of the bounding box's handles.

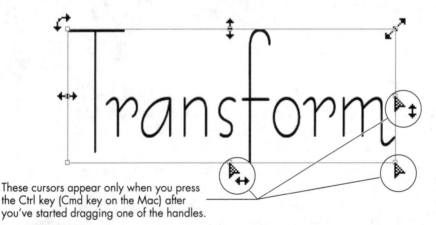

These cursors appear only when you press the Ctrl key (Cmd key on the Mac) after you've started dragging one of the handles.

Figure 9.26: The free transform tool uses seven different cursors (not all at the same time, of course) to indicate the modification that the tool is ready to perform.

 The change in cursor function after you start dragging is rare in Illustrator. Ordinarily the basic function of a cursor doesn't change when you add a modifier key. The free transform tool breaks new territory. However, there didn't seem to be any other way the free transform tool could handle its different features.

 If you switch to the free transform tool when nothing is selected, the tool's cursor looks just like the arrow tool. In this form, it is absolutely useless because it can't select a thing. More than once I've tried to select something with the free transform tool, to no avail, of course. So if you're trying to use the arrow cursor but find that you can't select paths, make sure that you haven't selected the free transform tool.

Here's the skinny on what you can do when you're using the free transform tool on selected paths.

- Drag a corner handle to scale the selected objects. Shift-drag a corner handle to scale proportionally. In either case, the opposite corner serves as the scale origin.

- Alt-drag (Option-drag on the Mac) a corner handle to scale the object around its center. Add Shift to that mix to drag a corner handle to scale proportionally around the object's center.

- Drag one of the bounding box's side handles (including the top and bottom ones) to limit the scaling to either horizontal or vertical changes. The opposite side's handle serves as the scale origin.

- Alt-drag (Option-drag on the Mac) a side handle to horizontally or vertically scale the object from the center.

- Drag from any location outside the free transform bounding box—the cursor changes to its curved two-headed form—to rotate the object around the center.

- Shift-drag from outside the bounding box to constrain the rotations to multiples of 45 degrees (plus whatever value you've entered into the Constrain Angle option box in the General Preferences dialog box). These 45-degree multiples are measured relative to the orientation of the bounding box, not to the orientation of the page. Thus, if your bounding box is not initially square with the page, you can't Shift-rotate with the free transform tool to make your object square to the page.

- Press the Ctrl key (Cmd key on the Mac) after you've started dragging a corner handle to move that corner independently of the other three corners. This allows you to freely distort the object.

 Even though you can transform text with the free transform tool, you cannot use any of the free distort features—the ones that include pressing the Ctrl (Cmd) key while you're dragging a corner handle—on text. To perform these transformations on text, you must first convert the text to paths via the Type » Create Outlines command or press Ctrl+Shift+O (Cmd-Shift-O on the Mac). Free distort doesn't work on bitmap images either, although it will affect any paths masking the images.

● Press Ctrl+Shift (Cmd-Shift on the Mac) while dragging a corner handle to limit the direction of your drag to follow along one of the sides
of the bounding box. For example, in the top portion of **Figure 9.27**,
the bounding boxes were initially square with the page. I pressed
Ctrl+Shift (Cmd-Shift on the Mac) while dragging the corner handles
and the drags were constrained to vertical and horizontal only. In the
bottom portion of Figure 9.27, the bounding boxes were initially set
at roughly 24.5 degrees. When I Ctrl+Shift-dragged (Cmd-Shift-
dragged on the Mac) the corner handles, the drags were limited to
angles that matched those of the bounding box—roughly 24.5 and
114.5 (90 + 24.5) degrees.

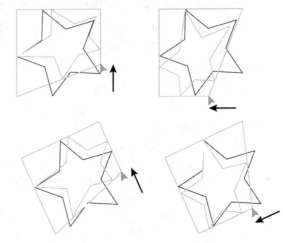

*Figure 9.27: When I pressed
Ctrl+Shift (Cmd-Shift on the
Mac) while dragging the
various corner handles, the
drags were aligned to the
sides of the objects' bounding
box. In the bottom examples,
the bounding boxes were
rotated to roughly 24.5
degrees counterclockwise
from the horizontal. This
caused the drags to be
constrained to 24.5 degrees
off the horizontal and 24.5
degrees off the vertical.*

● Press Ctrl+Alt (Cmd-Option on the Mac) while you drag a corner
handle to force the opposite corner to mimic your every move, except
in the opposite direction. As you can see in the top example of **Figure
9.28**, I held Ctrl+Alt (Cmd-Option on the Mac) and dragged the bottom-right corner down and to the right, causing the top-left corner to
move up and to the left. Depending on the direction of your drag,
you can use this technique to rotate, scale, and even flip the object. I
used the same keystrokes in the bottom portion of Figure 9.28, while
substantially dragging the bottom-right corner. This rotated and
flipped the original object. Additionally, I scaled the paths, which
resulted in a slightly taller and thinner version of the image.

Figure 9.28: Press Ctrl+Alt (Cmd-Option on the Mac) while dragging a corner handle to cause the opposite corner to move in the opposite direction.

Press Ctrl+Alt+Shift (Cmd-Option-Shift on the Mac) to force one of the adjacent corner handles to mimic your moves, except in the opposite direction. All movement will also be constrained in such a way that each pair of sides of the bounding box (horizontal and vertical) stay parallel. (This is true for both bounding boxes that are square with the page and those that are not.) The top example of **Figure 9.29** shows how the top-right corner shot upward as I dragged the bottom-right corner while holding Ctrl+Alt+Shift (Cmd-Option-Shift on the Mac). This is a result of dragging more vertically than horizontally. The bottom example of Figure 9.29 illustrates the bottom-left corner moving left to counter the right drag of the bottom-right corner while holding all three modifier keys.

Figure 9.29: Holding the three modifier keys Ctrl+Alt+Shift (Cmd-Option-Shift on the Mac) while dragging a corner handle constrains the movements of both that corner and one of its adjacent corners to either horizontal or vertical. These directions are functions of the bounding box's original orientation.

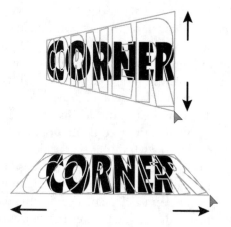

- While dragging one of the handles positioned along the sides of the free transform tool's bounding box (including the top and bottom sides), press the Ctrl key (Cmd key on the Mac) to unhinge the bounding box from its rigid rectilinear confines. You can then reshape the bounding box as a parallelogram in which the opposite sides of the box remain parallel, but adjacent sides do not have to remain perpendicular to one another. In this case, three of the four sides will move with your drag; only the opposite side remains immobile.

- Press Ctrl+Shift (Cmd-Shift on the Mac) while you drag one of the side handles to manipulate the bounding box as a parallelogram in which the side you drag remains aligned with its original position. If your bounding box was originally squared with the page, you'll be able to drag vertically or horizontally (depending on whether the side you drag is one of the vertical sides or the horizontal sides of the bounding box). All the while, the side handle will remain a constant distance from the opposite side.

- While dragging a side handle, press Ctrl+Alt (Cmd-Option on the Mac) to manipulate the bounding box as a parallelogram that pivots around the box's center instead of around the opposite side.

- Press all three of the modifier keys while dragging a side handle to reshape the bounding box as a parallelogram that pivots around the box's center, while the opposite sides of the box remain a constant distance away from one another. This way, you change only the corners' angular sizes.

Although the free transform tool's many uses mean you have a heap to remember, the tool affords you some of the best and (once mastered) easiest transformation and distortion abilities in this and any other drawing program. By mixing and matching the techniques mentioned above, you can create complicated and sophisticated perspective effects. In fact, with the help of a few other filters, you can create stuff that looks like it came out of a 3-D program.

For example, in **Figure 9.30**, I converted some text to paths with the Type » Create Outlines command. I then transformed it three times; twice I pressed the Ctrl key (Cmd key on the Mac) while I dragged corner handles (first on the top-right handle and then on the bottom-left handle). Then I pressed Ctrl+Alt (Cmd-Option on the Mac) while I dragged the bottom handle. In three quick drags, the text was transformed into a word that practically jumps off the page.

Even though it has a lot going for it, the free transform tool does possess one glaring flaw: you can't clone a path when you're transforming it with the free transform tool. If you want to transform a clone of a path with the free transform tool, be sure to clone the path first and then use the free transform tool on the cloned path.

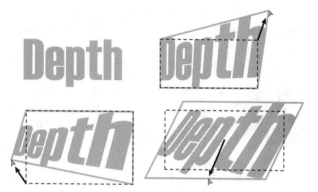

Figure 9.30: You can achieve great perspective effects like this by using a variety of free transform tool techniques.

One reason for the lack of a cloning option is that the Alt (Option) key is busy performing other functions. I wish Adobe would take my suggestion to use the spacebar for cloning. There's plenty of precedence for having the spacebar add functionality as you drag. Sure, using four keys may be less than appealing to some (especially those who never played the piano), but having the option of cloning while transforming with the free transform tool, simply by pressing an additional key, is better than no option at all.

The Distortion Funhouse

When you were a kid, did you ever press Silly Putty against the newspaper comics pages to copy a picture, and pull the Silly Putty to stretch the image? Have you wondered why it can take decades for a drawing program to replicate an effect any kid could do? Well wonder no more, because Illustrator 10 now gives you this capability. To be sure, earlier versions of Illustrator could wiggle paths and add perspective-like distortions over an entire object. But overall object distortions were limited to moving the corners of the shape's bounding box, which is just a boring rectangle. The linear distortions you can make this way don't even come close to the wondrous fluidity of a Silly Putty distortion, now do they?

In Illustrator 10 you can really mess up an object, and I mean that in a good way. You can apply warp effects that are like the type warps you might see in Photoshop 6, or you can use a path of any shape to warp objects. You can even distort objects using a mesh that's a lot like a gradient mesh, except you'll be distorting the object, not just colors. Unlike in previous versions of Illustrator, now a distortion doesn't have to be uniform across an object. In the best Silly Putty tradition, you can reshape your distortions interactively by editing the distortion path or the mesh, or using the new liquify tools to literally pull, push, and smush parts of objects. Once you get started, chances are you'll start to get reacquainted with your inner child!

In this section, I'll lead you through the fun and empowering world of mesh distortions and liquify distortions. These option-laden and user-directed features allow you to contort and fine-tune your objects ad infinitum or at least until you can check off "Do something really wild and creative" on your to-do list.

 This is a very important note, so please read it: The distortions you are about to dive into are not the only ones in the program by any means. Chapter 19 is going to cover distorting with paths, distorting paths them-selves, and the live effects that I keep alluding to. I know it's frustrating to not have them all in one place, but have mercy on me—just think of how hard it is to pack all these features into one, ahem, slim book. Or blame it on the product, which just keeps getting better and more packed with cool features—sometimes so packed that they can't contain themselves within single chapters. Yes, have mercy, and have patience—by the end of it all, you'll be in distortion heaven.

Mesh Distortions

A lot of Illustrator's very fine distortion effects (I know, you haven't seen them yet; I will cover them in Chapter 19) are "canned"—that is, they all provide a basic transformation effect that you can tune with a few options. But you wouldn't call any of them free-form. What if you kind of like some of the basic distortions available but want to be able to add an extra little bump in just the right place? Any time you want a custom distortion, run, don't walk, to the features in this section. With the mesh and liquify tool distortions covered here, and the path distortion effects in Chapter 19, you can make just about any kind of distortion your brain can come up with.

Illustrator categorizes several free-form warps as *envelope distortions*. This is because an additional object is used as an envelope to control the distortion of another object. It's like putting some printed artwork in a paper envelope and bending the envelope. As in real life, whatever happens to the envelope happens to the print, even if there's a "Do Not Bend" sticker on it. **Figure 9.31** shows you some examples of mesh distortions, which are one type of envelope distortion.

Starting a Mesh from a Warp

You can use a predefined warp as a starting point for creating your own warp variations. Instead of customizing the warp using the Warp Options dialog box shown in **Figure 9.32**, Illustrator will create a distortion mesh based on the warp you chose. From that convenient starting point, you can do whatever you want.

1.   Select the objects you want to distort.

2.   Choose Object » Envelope Distort » Make with Warp.

Figure 9.31: Examples of mesh warps. The original is at top left. Also pictured are the effects of meshes based on (clockwise from top right) a warp, a mesh, and a drawn path.

Figure 9.32: With the Warp Options dialog box, you can change the axis and extent (Bend) of the warp itself and add horizontal or vertical perspective. Using the menu at the top, you can change the type of warp applied to an object any time you feel like it.

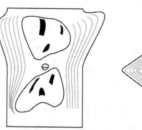

3. In the Warp Options dialog box, choose the Style you want and set the options the way you want them. If you don't know how the options work, see the section on "Warps" in Chapter 19.

4. Click OK.

5. Adjust the distortion mesh until you get what you want.

Figure 9.33 shows how mesh distortion was used to create a free-form variation on the basic Flag warp.

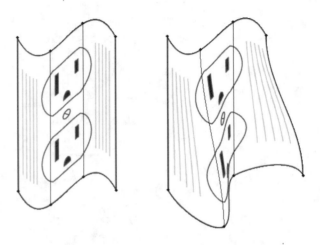

Figure 9.33: Starting from a mesh warp (left), mesh nodes and handles were moved to create a unique warp that can't be created using just a dialog box (right).

You'll notice here that because a warp is just a starting point for a distortion mesh, you can't go back and change the warp options after you click OK. If you really must back up, use the Edit » Undo command.

 If the object doesn't fit tightly to the adjusted mesh, choose Object » Envelope Distort » Envelope Options and turn up the Fidelity setting. This option is covered later, but for now it's useful to know that higher fidelity fits the mesh more closely but might take longer to calculate and display. **Figure 9.34** *shows how noticeable a difference in fidelity values can be. The warps in this section all use a fidelity of 100 because they looked too messy at the program default of 4. Remember this because you may need to adjust your distortions' Fidelity values to match the high-fidelity results shown in this book.*

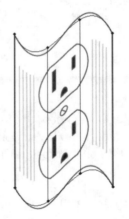 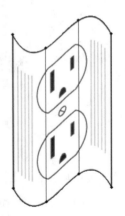

Figure 9.34: The object on the left uses a mesh warp at the default Fidelity value of 4. The one of the right looks better because the Fidelity value was raised to 100.

Using a Mesh to Distort

If you want to control distortion *inside* the path, you may not want to use the basic path distortion envelope, because a distortion envelope only controls distortion from the edge defined by the envelope path. For more control, Illustrator lets you create a *distortion mesh* that works a lot like the gradient mesh covered in Chapter 15. If you already know how to work a gradient mesh, you'll already know most of what you need to get going here.

If you aren't experienced with the gradient mesh, here's how it's going to work: The distortion mesh will add a grid to the object. At each grid intersection will be a point. You can manipulate the mesh segments and points just like you would a regular path. As you change the mesh away from its default grid shape, you'll distort the underlying objects.

1. Select the objects you want to distort.

2. Choose Object » Envelope Distort » Make with Mesh or press Ctrl+Alt+M (Cmd-Option-M on the Mac).

3. In the Envelope Mesh dialog box shown in **Figure 9.35**, specify how many rows or columns you want in the mesh, and click OK.

Figure 9.35: The Envelope Mesh dialog box is very simple. All it needs to do is overlay a mesh of nodes you can use to distort an object. I wouldn't worry about getting the right number of rows and columns at first, because you can always add or remove them with the mesh tool.

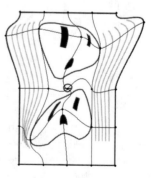

4. Adjust the mesh as needed. **Figure 9.36** shows an example of a mesh adjustment. If you're not sure how to adjust the mesh, don't worry, because I'll tell you in the next section. Read on!

Figure 9.36: On the left is an object with a 4x4 envelope mesh applied. On the right, a few tugs on the mesh nodes and handles with the direct selection tool have transformed the formerly innocuous electrical outlet into a creepy ghost in the machine.

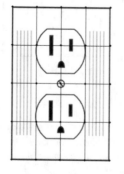

Adjusting a Distortion Mesh

When you apply a mesh distortion, customizing the distortion is simply a matter of adjusting the nodes at the mesh intersections, as you would with a gradient mesh (as seen in Chapter 15). Here are some basic points for making adjustments.

- The most useful mesh node selection tools are the direct selection tool (to select or move mesh nodes) and the direct select lasso tool (to select multiple mesh nodes).

- Use the mesh tool to add mesh segments (by clicking in the mesh) or to remove mesh segments (by Alt-clicking (Option-clicking on the Mac) mesh segments).

- Remember that messing around with mesh nodes can be a lot like adjusting partial paths. For example, if you want to twirl a small area within a larger distortion mesh, you could select a set of mesh nodes with the direct select lasso tool, and then use the rotate tool to spin them around.

- You can use the direct selection tool to adjust the direction handles that appear. You can also drag any mesh square.

Figure 9.37 shows a few examples of selecting distortion mesh nodes.

Figure 9.37: There's more than one way to edit an envelope mesh. On the left, I drag a mesh node with the direct selection tool (the white one). In the center example, I've already deleted a vertical mesh line with the mesh tool and am adding a new horizontal mesh line. On the right, I've selected multiple mesh nodes with the direct selection (white) lasso tool.

Using a Path to Distort

This one seems so obvious—why not draw the shape of the distortion you want? That's exactly what happens with a path envelope distortion. **Figure 9.38** shows a few examples of the way you can use any shape to distort an object.

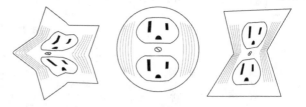

Figure 9.38: Three examples of using a drawn path as a distortion envelope.

Here's how it's done.

1. Use any drawing tools to create a path in the shape you want.

2. Move the distortion path over the objects you want to fit inside the distortion shape.

3. Make sure the distortion path is in front. If necessary, select the path and choose Object » Arrange » Bring to Front.

4. Select everything you want to distort plus the distortion path, and choose Object » Envelope Distort » Make with Top Object. The warp is based on the bounding box of all selected objects, so even objects outside the boundary of the distortion path get moved inside it.

5. If you need to adjust the distortion, use the direct selection tool to edit points on the distortion path.

6. If you need to edit the objects that are distorted, choose Object » Envelope Distort » Edit Contents. When you're in content editing mode, the Edit Contents command will change to Edit Envelope so you can switch back to the default mode of editing the distortion path. You can usually tell what mode you're in by the handles you see on the object, as shown in **Figure 9.39**.

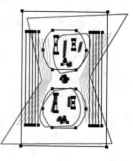

Figure 9.39: At any time you can decide to edit a distortion envelope (left) or the objects inside it (right).

Setting Options for Distortion Envelopes

Illustrator's Envelope Options let you decide how the distorted object will relate to object attributes and the rest of the layout. When you've selected a distorted object, you can see these options by choosing Object » Envelope Distort » Envelope Options, which is the dialog box shown in **Figure 9.40**.

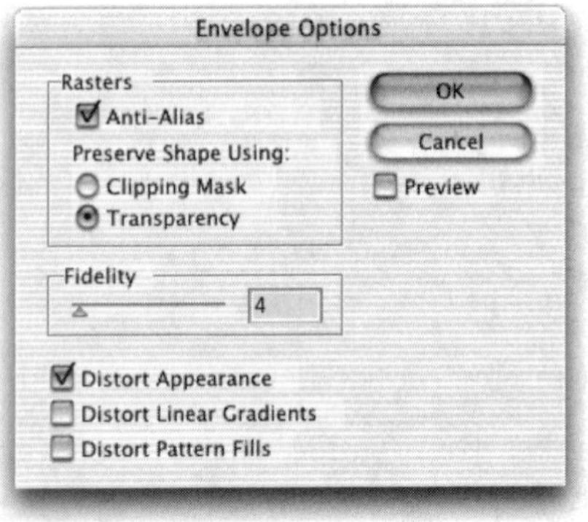

Figure 9.40: In the Envelope Options dialog box, you can control the precision (and therefore the display and output speed) of raster and vector areas within a distortion envelope.

In the Envelope Options dialog box, you have several options.

- **Anti-Alias:** Determines whether Illustrator will attempt to create a higher-precision distortion of raster images (if it's on) or a rougher, faster distortion (if it's off).

- **Preserve Shape Using:** Determines how raster objects, such as Illustrator rasterized objects or imported images, are combined with areas behind the object on the layout. Clipping Mask will use a path to define the shape, while Transparency will use transparency features to do the same thing. Clipping Mask can result in a cleaner edge, but Transparency allows more flexibility if you want to layer the object with other objects using transparency. This option really only applies when a raster object isn't confined to a rectangle, such as in the Flag warp.

- **Fidelity:** This option is one of those trade-offs between precision and performance. The envelope is like a mask path, and the Fidelity option controls how many points are on the envelope. A higher value makes the distortion more precise by adding more points to the envelope, but this will slow down the effect. Lowering the value will start to make the distortion envelope look chunky. Lower fidelity might be OK if you're working at low resolution as you would for the Web.

- **Distort:** The Distort Appearance, Distort Linear Gradients, and Distort Pattern Fills options let you include or exclude those features of an object when distorting. Another way of thinking of it is, when these options are off, these features are applied after the distortion instead of before it.

Removing Envelope Distortions

If you want to completely remove a distortion mesh and the distortion that was applied, select the object and choose Object » Envelope Distort » Release. When you release an envelope distortion, you get both the original object and the distortion mesh as separate objects.

To permanently apply an envelope distortion, select the object and choose Object » Envelope Distort » Expand. But don't do this if all you want to do is edit the objects! Just choose Object » Envelope Distort » Edit Objects and you'll get to keep the editable distortion. You should usually avoid using the Expand command because it often results in lots of points that are hard to deal with.

The Liquify Tools

So far we've looked at distortions that you can do by pulling handles or changing dialog box options. But the Illustrator 10 team knew they could take the idea further, and thus were born the liquify tools. With the liquify tools, you don't need a dialog box and you don't need no stinkin' handles. All you need is the mouse. Like the smudge and blur tools, all you have to do is drag over the area you want to distort. The liquify tools are great when you want to hand-distort specific areas of an object. (If you want to distort all or most of an object, it would be more efficient to use one of the warp or mesh distortions instead. **Figure 9.41** demonstrates the difference I'm talking about here.) Keep in mind that these tools are cumulative—as you continue dragging one of these tools over the same area, the distortion becomes more extreme.

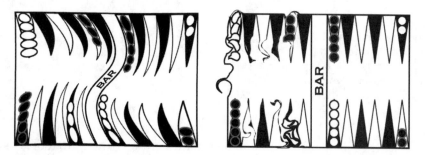

Figure 9.41: Here's the difference between live distortions and the very similar liquify tools (twirl effect and twist tool, in this case). Live distortions (left) affect everything you've selected when you apply the effect. Liquify tools (right) affect only the areas where you drag the tool.

There are a couple of important things to remember when you want to use the liquify tools.

- If you want to use the liquify tools on text, you have to convert the text to outlines first. If you want to use the liquify tools on an image, you have to embed the image first using the Links palette menu, if that hasn't yet been done.

- Before you try to use the liquify tools on an object, make sure the object isn't a symbol and doesn't contain any symbols. If you do want to liquify a symbol instance, select it and choose Break Link to Symbol from the Symbols palette pop-up menu. Or you might find it easier to right-click (Control-click on the Mac) the object and choose the Break Link to Symbol command from the pop-up menu.

Figure 9.42 shows you where the liquify tools are in the toolbox. It also shows you how the liquify tools look when you tear off their tool menu by clicking the little tab at the end of the tool menu—don't forget how handy this can be when you want to hang on to normally hidden tools. After I go over the tools, I'll tell you how to fine-tune their settings.

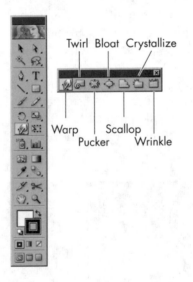

Figure 9.42: Where the liquify tools live in the toolbox (left). If you find yourself switching liquify tools often, life will be easier if you tear them off the toolbox (right).

Warping

Remember the Silly Putty example earlier in this chapter? The warp tool is like that, as you can see in **Figure 9.43**. To use the warp tool, drag it in the direction you want to push the distortion. The object will be compressed in front of your drag direction and stretched out behind. The warp tool is more sensitive to the actual drag direction than some of the other liquify tools.

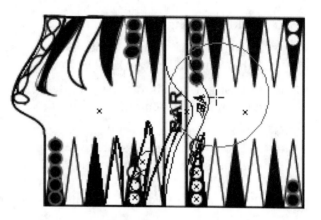

*Figure 9.43: After pushing
out the left side with the warp
tool, I'm now using it to warp
the center toward the right.*

When you've tried out the warp tool, did you notice that the pointer turns into
a large circle? The size of the circle indicates the brush size of the active liquify
tool. If you are curious about this and you know your Illustrator toolbox, you
probably tried double-clicking a liquify tool icon, in which case you'd be way
ahead of me. When you double-click a liquify tool, the options for that tool
appear. You can see those options in **Figure 9.44**.

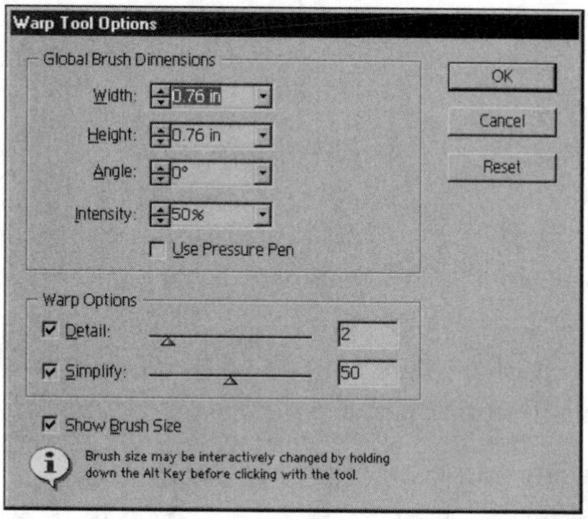

*Figure 9.44: The Warp Tool
dialog box. Most of the
options dialog boxes for
liquify tools look like this.*

The first thing you see in the Warp Tool Options dialog box is the Global
Brush Dimensions section. This option set is called global because when you
change these settings, they change for any liquify tool you use. (This global brush
setting also occurs with the symbolism tools, covered in Chapter 12.) The dialog
box contains the following options:

- **Width and Height**: These control the brush size.

- **Angle:** This matters only if the Width and Height are different. If the Width and Height are the same, the brush is a circle.

- **Intensity:** This controls how quickly the distortion accumulates. If you want finer control, lower this value.

- **Use Pressure Pen:** Select this if you have a pressure-sensitive stylus and you want to use pressure to control intensity. This overrides the Intensity setting, so if you select this, the Intensity option becomes unavailable. On the other hand, if you don't have a pressure-sensitive stylus connected, you can't use the Pressure Pen feature and it will be unavailable.

The liquify tools often have to add points to paths in order to create the distortions. The Warp options section controls how additional points are added, using the following options:

- **Detail:** This controls the spacing of the new points that Illustrator adds to paths to make new distortions. For example, at a low detail value, dragging the warp tool over the same area repeatedly just changes the warp that's already there; at a high detail value, additional mini-warps appear as you drag over the same area.

- **Simplify:** This affects the final number of points that Illustrator will use to draw a warped distortion. For example, at a low value, Illustrator might use 3 points to add a warp distortion; at a high value, it might use 6 points to add the same shape, to increase precision. Very low values can look too artificial, but they might print faster.

The last option, Show Brush Size, appears in all liquify tools. When it's on, you see the circle that shows you how big the brush is. When it's off, you see a crosshair, which you might prefer for precision work.

 You can use the Alt key (Option key on the Mac) to interactively resize the brush as you work. Hold down the key as you drag the cursor, and you'll see the brush resize.

Twirling

The twirl tool (the first alternate in the warp tool slot) lets you rotate surrounding object areas around the tool, similar to the way the twist distortions work. To use it, drag it over the areas you want to twirl. If you want to twirl a single spot, just keep the mouse button held down in one position without dragging it around, as shown in **Figure 9.45**.

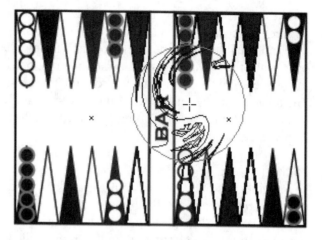

Figure 9.45: The twirl tool, caught in the act of twirling. If you press continuously, the twirl rotates and continues to tighten until you release the mouse button.

With the twirl tool and the ones the follow, go gently at first, by holding down the mouse button briefly and building up the effect. On simpler objects or on faster machines, the distortion may be applied so quickly that you may over-apply the effect if you press down too long.

When you double-click the twirl tool in the toolbox, you'll find that in addition to the options you saw with the warp tool, the twirl tool also includes the Twirl Rate option, as shown in **Figure 9.46**. This controls how quickly the tool creates a twirl. It's expressed in degrees, and you can enter any value between -180 and 180 degrees. Positive angles twirl counterclockwise, and negative values twirl clockwise. The neutral value here is 0, so don't bother setting the tool to 0 or nothing will change.

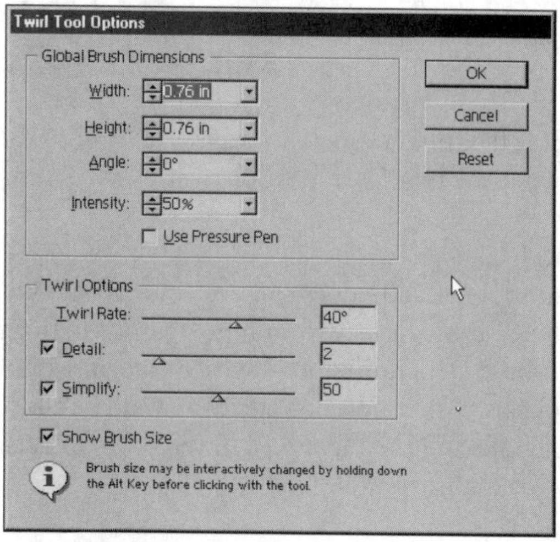

Figure 9.46: The Twirl Tool Options dialog box slips a Twirl Rate option in with the usual suspects.

I hear some of you tapping your chins in puzzlement. What's the difference between the twirl tool and the twist tool, which is also in the toolbox? Try them out, and you'll find that the twirl tool distorts only the parts of an object you drag over, while the twist tool always twists an entire object. To further complicate matters, both of these are different from the twist distortion effect commands. The tools are not live effects (the only way to undo them is to use the Undo command), while the distortion commands are live effects you can modify from the Appearance palette.

Puckering

You might think of the pucker tool as the Black Hole tool because it tends to suck down anything around it. If you hold the pucker tool in one place, the surrounding area seems to disappear into a single point. If you drag it around, you create a sort of ditch into which surrounding areas get pulled. You can see this effect in **Figure 9.47**.

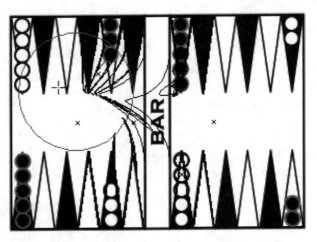

Figure 9.47: The pucker tool
being dragged up and to the
left, leaving a deep gash in
its wake.

Double-clicking the pucker tool in the toolbox gets you the same set of options you saw for the warp tool.

Bloating

The bloat tool basically does the opposite of the pucker tool, as you can see in **Figure 9.48**. It pushes surrounding areas away from the point where you mouse down or drag. Depending on whether you start in positive or negative space, the bloat tool can punch holes or create a swelling effect.

Double-clicking the bloat tool in the toolbox gets you the same set of options you saw for the warp tool.

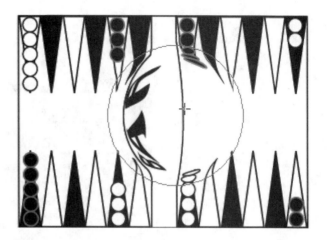

Figure 9.48: This is the result of the bloat tool right after releasing the mouse button.

Scalloping

The scallop tool is like the pucker tool, but instead of sucking everything into a single point, it makes multiple points and creates arcs between them, thus creating the scalloped shapes you see in **Figure 9.49**. It makes more sense if you think of it as the kind of edge you might see at the top or bottom edge of curtains. The tool pulls the new scallop curves toward itself. By crossing over paths, you can pull the scalloped distortions from one side of a path to the other.

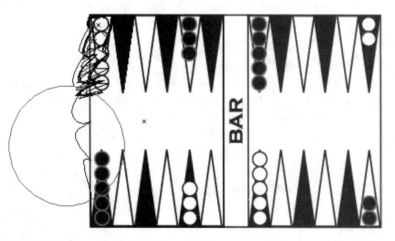

Figure 9.49: Here we see the scallop tool in its native habitat, pulling scallop curves out of an unsuspecting nearby object.

 If you have trouble controlling the scallop tool, keep in mind that the scallop tool pulls the scalloped curves toward the tool as you move it. So if scallops aren't moving in the direction you want, move the pointer to the other side of the path and make sure you're pulling them instead of trying to push them.

When you double-click the scallop tool in the toolbox, you see additional options that aren't present in the tools I've covered so far. **Figure 9.50** shows you these options.

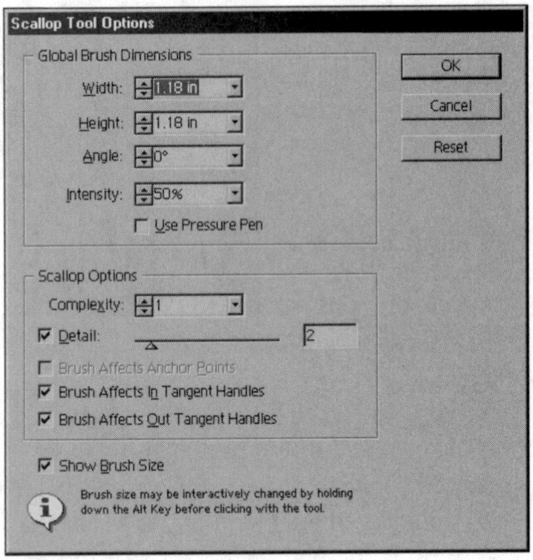

Figure 9.50: The Scallop Tool Options dialog box contains a Scallop Options section not found in most other liquify tools.

- **Complexity:** This controls the spacing of the new features added to a path. Don't confuse this with Detail or Simplify, which control the points themselves.

- **Brush Affects Anchor Points:** When this is on, the liquify tool affects any path points that existed before you start using the liquify tool. This is a subtle thing. Let's say you drag the scallop tool back and forth along a path three times without releasing the mouse button, and you get ten scallops. If you had dragged it back and forth three times and released the mouse button after each pass, you'd have 30 scallops, because you'd leave more anchor points behind. The liquify tool does not add new anchor points until you release the mouse button.

- **Brush Affects In Tangent Handles** and **Brush Affects Out Tangent Handles:** Tangent handles are the control handles discussed in Chapter 6. Strangely enough, Adobe calls the same thing "direction lines" elsewhere in the Illustrator manual. The important thing to remember is that tangent handles are the handles at the ends of the lines extending from curve points. Well, what about In and Out handles? The In handle is the one entering a curve point, and the Out handle is the one leaving the point, relative to the path direction.

Crystallizing

The crystallize tool is like the scallop tool, but where the scallop tool creates distortions pulled toward the pointer, the crystallize tool creates spiky distortions pushed away from the tool. You can get a definite sense of the difference between the crystallize tool and the scallop tool by comparing **Figure 9.51** to Figure 9.49.

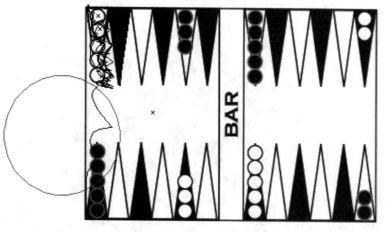

Figure 9.51: The crystallize tool pushes pointy distortions into an object.

Double-clicking the crystallize tool in the toolbox reveals exactly how the crystallize tool is different from the scallop tool. It's really the same dialog box that you saw in Figure 9.50, but with different default settings.

Wrinkling

The wrinkle tool distinguishes itself by giving you control over the amount of wrinkle along the horizontal or vertical axis. It defaults to wrinkling along the horizontal axis only—the kind of wrinkles that appear when you slip on the bathroom rug and it bunches up along its length. This can be disconcerting because vertical segments don't wrinkle at all, as shown in **Figure 9.52**. So if you're trying to put wrinkles in a series of vertical lines, you won't see any effect. But that's just a result of the default settings, as you are about to find out.

The settings in the Wrinkle Tool Options dialog box are like those for the scallop and crystallize tool, but with two additional options: Horizontal and Vertical. These options control how much distortion occurs along the horizontal and vertical axes. I just said that the wrinkle tool defaults to distortion along the horizontal axis only, and if you double-click the wrinkle tool in the toolbox, you'll discover why. The Horizontal option is set to 0%, and the Vertical option is set to 100%, as you can see in **Figure 9.53**. So if you're trying to wrinkle an object that has lots of vertical segments, you definitely want to turn up the Vertical value here or not much is going to happen.

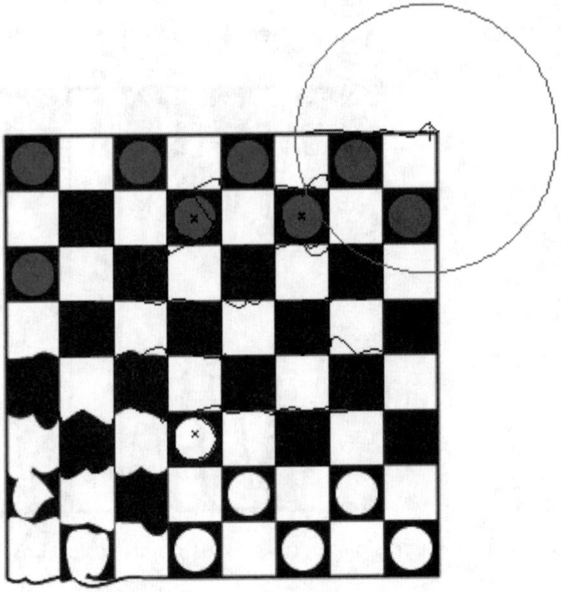

Figure 9.52: I drag the wrinkle tool up and to the right and find that wrinkles appear only along horizontal lines. This is because of the default settings in the Wrinkle Tool Options dialog box you can check out in Figure 9.53.

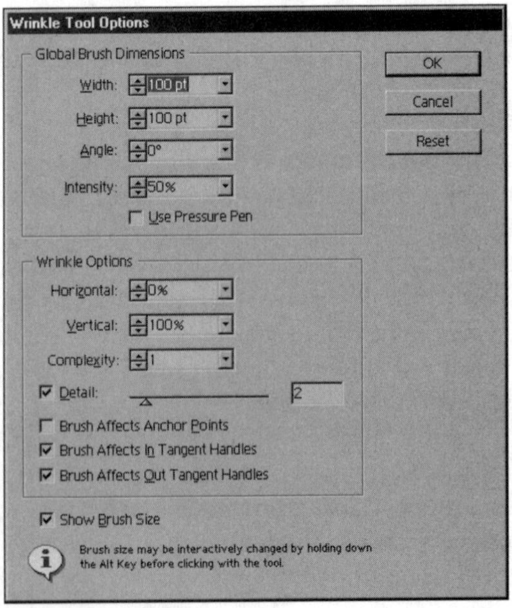

Figure 9.53: The Wrinkle Tool Options dialog box, including the Wrinkle Options section that defines its unique behavior.

PART THREE
TYPE, SYMBOLS, AND GRAPHS

HOW TO HANDLE TYPICAL TYPE

You might think it's funny that people tell me Illustrator is their favorite page-layout program. Well, if much of their work is single-page, graphically intense material anyway, why not? I think these folks are on to something; Illustrator (child of Adobe that it is) understands type very well, and just because you're using an illustration program doesn't mean you have to put up with substandard text tools.

Illustrator's type capabilities are so vast that we need to explore them over the course of two chapters. This chapter examines the relatively basic stuff—how to create text blocks and apply formatting attributes such as typeface and style. I'll close out the chapter with some nifty techniques for working with tabs. This chapter looks at the sane and rational aspects of type.

Chapter 11 looks at the more bizarre effects you can create with type: You can affix type to a curve, set text inside free-form text blocks, apply effects to Adobe's specialized Multiple Master fonts, convert letter outlines to fully editable paths, and even present text in the Japanese vertical style. Look for all that, plus a few administrative-but-vital text-based procedures, in the next chapter.

 Finally, if you're itching for better text capabilities on the Web, make sure to read Chapter 21. Illustrator 10's support for SVG and SWF are a brave new world for online type hounds.

Establishing Text Objects

Altogether, Illustrator provides six tools for creating text. For now, you need to be concerned with only one: the type tool, third down on the right side of the toolbox (the one that looks like a T). Armed with the type tool, you can create a text object—which is any object that contains type—in one of two ways.

- Click with the type tool within the drawing area and enter a few words of type for a logo or headline. This kind of text block is called *point text,* because Illustrator aligns the text to the point at which you click.

- Drag with the type tool to draw a rectangular *text block.* Then enter your text from the keyboard. Illustrator fits the text to the rectangular text block, automatically shifting text that doesn't fit on one line down to the next. It's usually best to create a text block when you want to enter a full sentence or more.

I explain point text and text blocks in more detail in the following sections.

Creating Point Text

There are three steps involved in creating point text.

1. Select the type tool and click in some empty portion of the drawing area with the new block cursor, labeled in **Figure 10.1**. The new block cursor shows that you are about to create a new text object.

After you click with the type tool, Illustrator creates an *alignment point,* which appears as an *x* in the outline mode. (In the preview mode, you see the alignment point only if the point text is selected.) Not surprisingly, Illustrator aligns the text to this point.

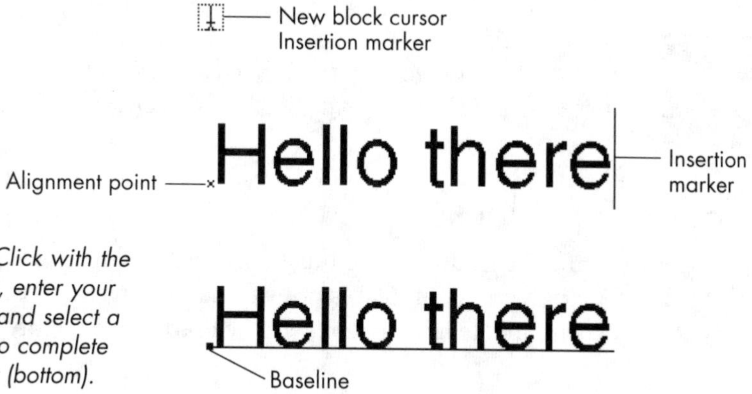

— New block cursor
Insertion marker

Alignment point —x Hello there— Insertion marker

Figure 10.1: Click with the type tool (top), enter your text (middle), and select a different tool to complete the text object (bottom).

Hello there
Baseline

2. Enter the desired text from your keyboard. By default, the text appears to the right of the alignment point. (I'll go over how to change the alignment later in this chapter.) As you type, a blinking *insertion marker* flashes to the right of the last character. The insertion marker shows you where the next letter will appear.

With point text, Illustrator keeps all characters on a single line unless you tell it to do otherwise. This is why point text is better suited to a few words or less. If you want to move the insertion marker down to create a new line of type, press Enter (Return on the Mac).

3. When you have finished entering your text, hold the Ctrl key (Cmd key on the Mac) and click the text. Then release the Ctrl (Cmd) key. The text block appears selected, as shown in the bottom example of Figure 10.1. The alignment point now looks like a filled square, just like a selected anchor point.

You can drag the alignment point with any of the three selection tools to reposition the text in the drawing area. You can also drag point text by its *baseline,* which is the line that runs under each line of type. The baseline is the imaginary line on which letters sit. Some lowercase characters—*g, j, p, q,* and *y*—descend below the baseline. Lastly, you can move point text by dragging on the text itself. The exception to this last technique is when the Type Area Select option of the Type & Auto Tracing Preferences dialog box is turned off.

The area controlled by Type Area Select is actually larger than the text itself. For instance, a word written in lowercase letters, such as see, will have an actual type area big enough to hold the uppercase word SEE (plus a tad more above that to hold things such as quotation and accent marks). Also a word without descending characters, such as toe, will actually have a type area big enough to hold the word toy.

In case you're curious, Figure 10.1 and several that follow were created using 12-point Helvetica, magnified to 400 percent onscreen.

Creating Text Blocks

Point text is easy to create, but because Illustrator forces all text onto a single line unless told to do otherwise, point text is not well suited to whole paragraphs and longer text. To accommodate lengthy text, you need to create a more flexible mechanism—a text block.

1. Drag with the type tool. This creates a rectangle, as shown in the first example in **Figure 10.2**, just as if you were dragging with the rectangle tool. This rectangle represents the height and width of the new text block.

    When you release the mouse, Illustrator shows you a box with a blinking insertion marker. You will also see a center point, just as in a standard rectangle.

2. Enter type from the keyboard. If a letter would extend beyond the right edge of the text block, Illustrator sends the word down to start a new line of type. Known as *automatic wrapping,* this is precisely the capability that point text lacks.

3. After you stop entering text, hold the Ctrl key (Cmd key on the Mac) and click the text. Then release the Ctrl (Cmd) key. The text block appears selected, showing four corner points connected by straight segments and a center point, as shown at the bottom of Figure 10.2. Baselines underscore the type to indicate that the letters themselves are selected.

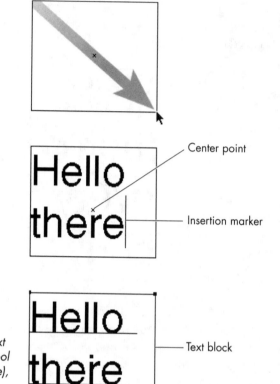

Figure 10.2: To create a text block, drag with the type tool (left), enter your text (middle), and select a different tool (right).

Resizing and Reshaping Text Blocks

As with point text, you can reposition a text block by dragging either the rectangular boundary or one of the baselines with the arrow tool. Additionally, you can drag directly on the text itself. As with point text, if you turn off the Type Area Select option inside the Type & Auto Tracing Preferences dialog box, you will not be able to move or select text blocks by clicking or dragging on the text.

You can also change the size and shape of a text block with the direct selection tool. Illustrator offers a couple of ways to resize and reshape paths—Chapter 11 discusses tugging on the bounding box and using the free transform tool—but the tried-and-true direct selection tool still provides you with an indispensable device for path modification.

For example, let's say that the text you entered from the keyboard doesn't entirely fit inside the text block. Or worse yet, the text block isn't wide enough to accommodate a particularly long word. **Figure 10.3** illustrates both of these problems: The little square with a minus sign in it shows that Illustrator had to break the word *everybody* onto two lines. The square with a plus sign shows that there is more text than can't fit inside the text block and is temporarily hidden. This text is called *overflow text*.

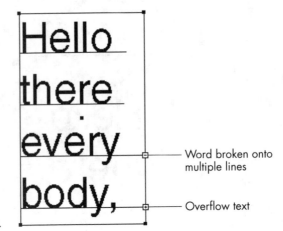

Figure 10.3: *Illustrator shows you when a word doesn't fit on a line, or when text extends outside the text block.*

By resizing a text block, you can fit long words on a single line, reveal overflow text, or simply change how words wrap from one line to the next. To resize a text block, you have to use the direct selection tool to select and modify the rectangular boundary independently of the text inside it. Here's how it works.

1. Create your text block.

After creating the text block, select the direct selection tool.

2. Deselect the text block.

If your first impulse is to resize the block by dragging a corner point, resist the feeling. You'll turn the block into a kite-shaped object. To reshape the block and keep it a rectangle, you have to select one of the segments and drag it, just as if you were resizing a standard rectangle. And—just to make things as painful as possible—you can't select a segment until you deselect the path. So choose Select » Deselect or press Ctrl+Shift+A (Cmd-Shift-A on the Mac) to deselect the text block.

3. Select the right or bottom edge of the text block.

If you're working in the preview mode, the text block outline disappears. This makes selecting an edge of the text block rather difficult. That's why you need to drag a tiny marquee around the portion of the outline you want to move. If you want to make the text block wider, drag a marquee around the right side, as in the first example of **Figure 10.4.** If you want to make the text block taller, marquee the bottom side. In either case, you select the desired edge. (Because it's a straight segment, you can't see that it's selected. But have faith—it is.)

 Once again, the Type Area Select option makes things diffi-cult to select. If it is turned on, the marquee with the direct selection tool might extend into the area where the text is. If that happens, you'll see the baseline of the text selected along with the entire block. This prevents you from resizing the block. So if a baseline appears, deselect everything and try again. If you still get the baseline, see the next tip.

 If you can't seem to get that darn segment selected, switch to the outline mode by pressing Ctrl+Y (Cmd-Y on the Mac). In the outline mode, you can see the text block outline even when it's not selected. This makes it easier to click the seg-ment you want to select. However, if your text extends extremely close to the outline (as with justified text, explained later in this chapter), you're still going to have a tough time. In that case, open the Type & Auto Tracing Preferences dialog box and turn off the Type Area Select option.

Hello there every body,

Hello there everybody, I'm glad to know you

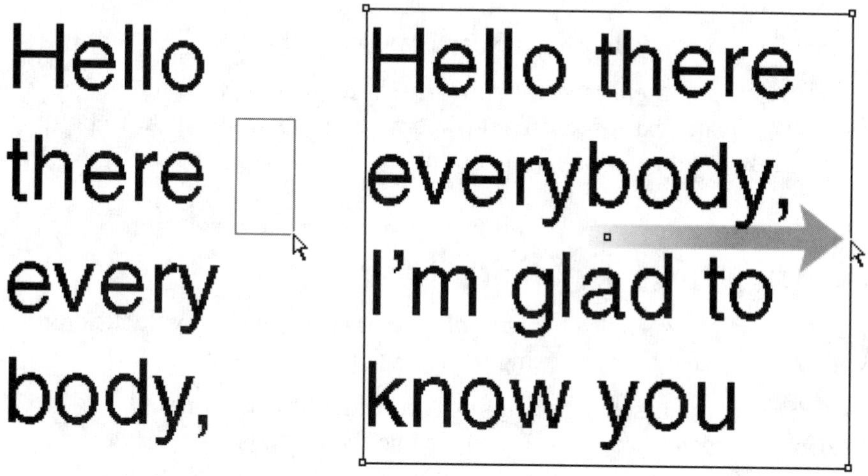

Figure 10.4: Use the direct selection tool to marquee the edge of the text block you want to expand (left) and then Shift-drag the edge (right).

4. **Shift-drag the edge.**

To maintain the rectangular shape of the text block, Shift-drag the right segment to the right, as in Figure 10.4. Or Shift-drag the bottom segment downward. (You can also drag without pressing Shift to cre-ate diamond-shaped text blocks.)

When you release the mouse button, Illustrator rewraps the text and displays as much overflow text as will fit. If there is still more overflow text, the little plus icon remains in the lower-right corner of the text block.

 To resize the height and width of a text block at the same time, select the entire block outline by Alt-clicking (Option-clicking on the Mac) it with the direct selection tool. (Make sure the baselines remain invisible.) Then drag with the scale tool or the free transform tool. For more information on both of these tools, refer to Chapter 9.

You can reshape the outline of a text block using any of the techniques discussed in Chapter 6. In addition to dragging points and segments, you can:

- 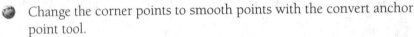 Change the corner points to smooth points with the convert anchor point tool.

- Drag the control handles to bend the segments.

- Insert or remove points with the add anchor point and delete anchor point tools.

- Select a segment and press Backspace (Delete on the Mac) to open the path.

- Extend the open path using the pen or pencil tools.

If this kind of thing interests you—and why shouldn't it?—Chapter 11 explains how to create text inside any old wacky shape, as well as how to pour overflow text from one text block into another.

Selecting and Editing Text

Before you can change a single character of type or change how text looks on the page, you have to select the type using the arrow or the type tool.

- Click along the baseline of a line of type with any selection tool to select all type in the object. If you change the font, type size, style, or some other formatting attribute, you change all characters in the selected text object.

- Shift-click to select multiple text objects. Any changes you make to the text formatting will apply to all of the selected text objects. (Illustrator doesn't format an entire text block if you select just a portion of the text object's outline with the direct selection tool.)

If you select text with a type tool, you can edit that text by entering new text from the keyboard, or you can format the selected text independently of other text within the object.

Selecting with the Type Tool

Though the selection tools are certainly useful, the type tool is the most common instrument for editing type in Illustrator because it affords the most control. The following items explain how to select type with the type tool:

 Drag over the characters that you want to select. Drag to the left or to the right to select characters on a single line; drag upward or downward to select characters on multiple lines. The selected text becomes highlighted as shown in **Figure 10.5**.

Figure 10.5: Drag across characters with the type tool to highlight them.

 Selected text has to be contiguous. You can't select the first line, skip the second, and then select the third.

 Double-click a word to select it. If you hold down the mouse button on the second click and then drag with it, your selection will be performed in increments of whole words.

 Triple-click to select an entire paragraph, from one return character to the next. (Triple-clicking in point text selects an entire line, because a line of point text is equivalent to a paragraph.) Hold down the mouse button on the third click and drag to select additional paragraphs.

- Click to set the insertion marker at one end of the text that you want to select and then Shift-click at the opposite end of the desired selection. Illustrator highlights all characters between the first click and the Shift-click.

- Click anywhere in a text block and press Ctrl+A (Cmd-A on the Mac) or choose Select » All) to select all text in the object.

-   *After you click with the type tool to set the insertion marker inside a text object, you can use the arrow keys to move the insertion marker around or select text.*

- Press the left or right arrow key to move the insertion marker to the left or right one character.

- Press the up or down arrow key to move the insertion marker up or down one line.

- Press Ctrl+right arrow (Cmd-right arrow on the Mac) to move the insertion marker one whole word to the right. Press Ctrl+left arrow (Cmd-left arrow) to move back a word.

- Press Ctrl+up arrow (Cmd-up arrow on the Mac) to move the insertion marker to the beginning of the paragraph. Press Ctrl+down arrow (Cmd-down arrow on the Mac) to move it to the end of the paragraph.

- Press Shift along with any of these keystrokes to select text as you move the insertion marker. For example, press Shift-right arrow to select the character after the insertion marker. Press Ctrl+Shift+up arrow (Cmd-Shift-up arrow on the Mac) to select everything from the insertion marker to the beginning of the paragraph.

Replacing, Deleting, and Adding Text

After you highlight text, you can format it (as explained in the next section) or replace it by entering new text from the keyboard.

- To delete selected text, press Backspace (Delete on the Mac).

- You can remove the selected text and send it to the Clipboard by choosing Edit » Cut or press Ctrl+X (Cmd-X on the Mac).

- To leave the selected text intact and send a copy to the Clipboard, choose Edit » Copy or press Ctrl+C (Cmd-C on the Mac).

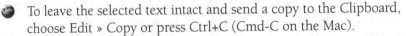

You can even replace the selected text with text that you cut or copied earlier by choosing Edit » Paste or pressing Ctrl+V (Cmd-V on the Mac). The pasted text retains its original formatting.

 Of course, you don't have to be replacing text to paste it in. You can paste text anytime right onto your illustration. But be forewarned that if you do nothing but paste, your entry will come in as point text. If you have a big chunk to paste, or want to really govern the space into which it flows, create a text block to receive it, and then paste your text.

The only way to convert a line of point text to a text block—or vice versa—is via the Clipboard. With either the arrow or the type tool, select the text you want to convert, cut or copy it, then drag with the type tool to create the text block (or click for the point text) and paste.

If you want to add text rather than replace it, just click with the type tool inside a text block to position the insertion marker right where you want to start the addition. Then bang away at the keyboard and let the mouse take you where it will.

If Illustrator seems to ignore you when you enter text or press the Backspace key (Delete on the Mac), press the Enter key (Return on the Mac). The problem is that Illustrator thinks a palette is active and is trying desperately to apply your typing to that palette; pressing Enter (Return) deactivates the palette and returns control to the illustration window.

Formatting Type

Formatting means nothing more than changing the way characters and lines of text look. Illustrator provides an exhaustive supply of formatting functions that let you modify your text far more than you'll ever want to.

You can divide formatting attributes into two categories—those that apply to individual characters of type and those that apply to entire paragraphs.

 Character-level formatting includes options such as typeface, size, leading, kerning and tracking, baseline shift, and horizontal scaling. To change the formatting of one or more characters, you select the characters with the type tool and apply the desired options. Illustrator changes the highlighted characters and leaves surrounding characters unaltered.

This doesn't mean that you can't apply these changes to a whole paragraph's worth of text. Of course you can—but you still have to have all of the characters selected to do so (unlike the method for applying a paragraph-level attribute, as you'll soon see).

Paragraph-level formatting includes indents, alignment, paragraph spacing, letter spacing, and word spacing. To change the formatting of a single paragraph, you need only position the blinking insertion marker inside that paragraph; Illustrator changes the entire paragraph no matter how little of it you select. To change the formatting of multiple paragraphs, select at least one character in each of the paragraphs you want to modify.

 If you want Illustrator to consider two consecutive but discrete lines of type as part of the same paragraph, press Shift+Enter (Shift-Return on the Mac). This inserts a line break, also called a soft return, instead of the regular paragraph symbol that the Enter (Return) key inserts. All paragraph formatting applied to one line becomes applicable to the other as well.

 If you want to see things such as paragraph symbols or line breaks onscreen, choose Type » Show Hidden Characters. The paragraph symbol appears as a backward P and the line breaks appear as left-pointing arrows. The end of the text is indicated by an infinity symbol.

Illustrator adopts the most recently applied formatting attributes as the default settings throughout the rest of the session—even if you start a new document. But when you quit Illustrator and start it up again, the program restores the original default settings (though you can alter some defaults permanently by editing the Adobe Illustrator Preferences file, as described in Chapter 2).

Character-Level Formatting

To format characters, you can either choose commands from the Type menu or use the options in the Character palette. The latter is the more convenient.

The one character-formatting attribute that I don't discuss in this chapter is color. To change the color of selected text, you merely change the fill color in the Color palette, as explained in Chapter 15. You can even stroke text, as you'll learn in Chapter 16.

To display the Character palette, choose Window » Type » Character or press Ctrl+T (Cmd-T on the Mac). You can press the same shortcut again to hide the Character palette. By default, the Character palette shows only six options, as shown in the left example of **Figure 10.6**. But if you choose the Show Options command from the palette's pop-up menu (located in the upper-right corner), you expand it to display several more options, shown on the right.

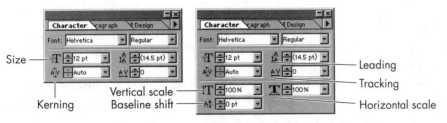

Figure 10.6: The Character palette, collapsed (left) and expanded (right).

 Because the Character palette uses so many option boxes, it's worthwhile to mention a few useful palette techniques. First, when one of the option boxes is active, use the Tab key to cycle through other option boxes. To cycle backward, press Shift-Tab. After you enter a value into one of the option boxes, press Enter (Return on the Mac) to apply your changes and deactivate the palette. If you prefer, you can press Shift+Enter (Shift-Return on the Mac) to apply a new value without deactivating the palette. This allows you to preview different values without having to click the option box each time before entering new values.

 Here's a palette tip I'd like to call special attention to because it's saved me so much time. If you press Ctrl+~ (Cmd-~ on the Mac), you will return to whatever palette was last active and whatever option box was last selected in that palette. So for example, if you're doing a lot of resizing of text, you can move from one word to another and press Ctrl+~ (Cmd-~) to get back to the Character palette and the text point size option box.

Selecting a Typeface

You can select a font from the Type » Font submenu or from the Font pop-up menu in the Character palette. For example, to assign Times Italic, you would choose Type » Font » Times » Italic. If you work in non-Adobe programs such as QuarkXPress, you may notice that Times Italic is not listed with the other members of the Times family. Those programs need Adobe Type Reunion to group the font family together. But Illustrator has Type Reunion built-in (as do other Adobe products such as InDesign).

 If you know the name of the font you want to apply, just enter the first few letters of its name into the Font option box in the Character palette. Each time you enter a character, Illustrator tries to guess which font you want. For example, if both American Typewriter and Avant Garde are available to your system, entering the letter a gets you American Typewriter—the first font in alphabetical order—whereas entering av gets you Avant Garde. To change the style, press the Tab key and enter the first few letters of the style, such as b for Bold or i for Italic. You can also right-click (Control-click on the Mac) and choose a font from the Fonts submenu in the contextual menu.

You may notice that Illustrator doesn't let you apply electronic styles such as underline. This is because the people who created Illustrator are purists. They will use only actual typefaces, not fake electronic styles. It also means that you will never apply a style such as bold or italic to a typeface that doesn't actually have a bold or italic version. You may find this a bit annoying when you first encounter it, but it will also mean that you will never be confused or disappointed when your (expensive) final job doesn't print the way you thought it would.

TrueType Incompatibilities

Illustrator's inability to assign electronic styles inhibits its compatibility with True-Type fonts. If a TrueType font doesn't have a submenu of stylized fonts next to its name in the Font menu, it means that the fonts on your machine don't include the stylized versions of that font. For example, you can choose the TrueType font New York—included with all Macs—but you can't make it bold or italic in Illustrator.

Illustrator has a few other TrueType compatibility problems as well. It occasionally misinterprets TrueType font metrics (such as character width) and it has a habit of complaining when you open illustrations created with TrueType fonts. You'll likewise encounter these problems if you have both TrueType and PostScript versions of the same font installed.

Reducing and Enlarging Type

To change the size of any selected type, choose a size from the Type » Size submenu. If you choose Other, Illustrator just pops you down into the size option in the Character palette. *Type size,* as it is called, is measured in points, and is based on how much space a character would take up on a (now imaginary) block in the typesetting process. In general terms that size would encompass the letter from the top of an ascender (such as *d* or *f*) to the bottom of a descender (such as *g* or *p*). You can enter any value between 0.1 (which would be 1/10 the size of the smallest character in **Figure 10.7**) and 1296 (which would be four times the size of the largest character) in 0.01-point increments.

If you dramatically reduce the size of a line of type, it appears as a gray bar. Illustrator figures it's too small to be readable onscreen, so why waste the time trying to draw it accurately? If you want to see text at smaller sizes, change the greeking amount in the Type & Auto Tracing Preferences dialog box. (Greeked text still prints normally.)

Figure 10.7: A character set in three (yes, three) type sizes—324 point, 48 point, and 1 point. If you don't believe me, go get a large magnifying glass and take a gander. Just as a medium A is centered at the base of the giant A, a minuscule A is centered at the base of the medium A. See that speck? That's 1-point type.

To change the type size of some selected characters quickly, enter a new size value into the Size option box in the Character palette and press Enter (Return on the Mac). You can also adjust the type size incrementally from the keyboard. Press Ctrl+Shift+> (Cmd-Shift-> on the Mac) to enlarge the characters or Ctrl+Shift+< (Cmd-Shift-< on the Mac) to reduce them. You can adjust the increment by changing the Size/Leading value in the Type & Auto Tracing Preferences dialog box. By default, the increment is set to 2 points. Your other option is to right-click (Ctrl-click on the Mac) and peruse the Size contextual menu for just the right size.

To change the type size of the selected text by five times the Size/Leading value, press Ctrl+Alt+Shift+> or Ctrl-Alt-Shift-< (Cmd-Option-Shift-> or Cmd-Option-Shift-< on the Mac).

Specifying the Distance between Lines

In days of yore, printer operators inserted thin strips of lead between lines of type, hence the term *leading* (pronounced *led'ing*). Leading specifies the distance between a selected line of type and the line below it, as measured in points from one baseline to the next. Therefore, 14-point leading leaves a couple of points of extra room between lines of 12-point type.

You can change the leading by entering a value into the Leading option box in the Character palette (to the right of the Size option box).

To speed up things, select some text and press Alt+down arrow (Option-down arrow on the Mac) to increase the leading or Alt+up arrow (Option-up arrow on the Mac) to decrease it. (If you're wondering about why the down arrow increases the leading, and the up arrow decreases it, just look at what happens to the line of text. Increasing the leading moves the text down (hence the down arrow); decreasing it moves the text up (hence the up arrow).

Add the Ctrl key (Cmd key on the Mac) to the above combinations to change the leading by five times the Size/Leading value.

Select Auto from the Leading pop-up menu in the Character palette to make the leading equal to 120 percent of the current type size (rounded off to the nearest half-point).

To set the leading to match the type size exactly—an arrangement known as solid leading—double-click the A over A symbol next to the Leading option box in the Character palette.

If a line of text contains characters with two different leading specifications, the larger leading prevails. If you begin a paragraph with a large capital letter, for example, you might combine a 24-point character on the same line as 12-point characters. If both the 24-point character and the 12-point character use autoleading, then the entire line will be set at 29-point leading (120 percent of the 24-point type size). Not necessarily the best time for auto leading.

You almost always want to have a leading size that is larger than the point size of your text. If you set the leading to the same size as the text (called solid leading), there is no room between the bottoms of letters such as g or j and the tops of letters such as h and t. Depending on the text, those letters may wind up touching each other—which makes the text hard to read.

I don't want to get into the old "leading as a character or paragraph attribute" debate. If you are used to other programs that set leading to affect the entire paragraph, just make sure you select the entire paragraph before you change the leading. Then your leading will always be the same for the entire paragraph.

Adjusting the Space between Characters

Illustrator lets you adjust the amount of horizontal space between characters of text. When you adjust the space between a pair of characters, Illustrator calls it *kerning*. When you adjust the space between three or more characters, Illustrator calls it *tracking*.

If you're a type savant, you'll soon notice that Illustrator's idea of tracking is not the real thing. There's no automatic spacing variation between large and small type sizes, which is what proper tracking is all about. Illustrator's tracking is uniform, and should therefore be called range kerning.

Illustrator provides option boxes in the Character palette for both kerning and tracking—commands that don't exist in the Type menu, only in the Character palette. When you click with the type tool to position the insertion marker *between* two characters, you will want to use the Kerning option box. However, when you *select* so much as a single character, the Tracking option box is the one for you. Don't worry if you get them confused—enter a value in the Kerning option box when you're trying to change the tracking or vice versa—because Illustrator will promptly respond by either doing nothing or flashing some annoying warning that you're mistreating it.

Normally, Illustrator accepts the dimensions of each character stored in the screen font file on disk and places the character flush against its neighbors. The screen font defines the width of the character as well as the amount of space placed before and after the character. As demonstrated in the top example of **Figure 10.8**, these bits of space before and after are called *side bearings*. Illustrator arrives at its normal letter spacing by adding the right side bearing of the first character to the left side bearing of the second.

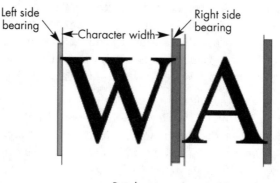

Figure 10.8: A kerning pair is a set of two letters that look weird when set shoulder to shoulder (top). Spacing them closer together (bottom) draws less attention to the letters and makes them more legible.

However, font designers can specify that certain pairs of letters, called *kerning pairs,* be positioned more closely together than the standard letter normally allows. Whenever the two characters of a kerning pair appear next to each other, as in the case of the *W* and the *A* in Figure 10.8, Illustrator can space them according to the special kerning information contained in the font.

 Illustrator always spaces kerning pairs as the font instructs. Click with the type tool to position the insertion marker between letters that you suspect to be kerning pairs. If the font does supply special instructions for those letters (and provided that you haven't changed the kerning manually), the Kerning option box displays a number in parentheses. If no parentheses appear, choose Auto from the Kerning pop-up menu and Illustrator returns the letters' placement to the factory settings.

If you aren't satisfied with the default kerning between two characters, click with the type tool to position the insertion marker between the characters and enter a value into the Kerning option box in the Character palette. If you want to change the kerning between multiple characters (tracking, in Illustrator-speak), select those characters and enter a value into the Tracking option box. Then press Enter (Return on the Mac). A negative value squeezes letters together; a positive value spreads them apart.

Illustrator measures both the kerning and tracking values in 0.001 (1/1000) of an em space increments. An *em space* is a character as wide as the type size is tall. So if the type size is set to 12 points, an em space is 12 points wide. This ensures the kerning remains proportionally constant as you increase or decrease the type size.

A kerning or tracking value of 25 is roughly equivalent to a standard space character. But you can enter any value between –1,000 and 10,000 in 0.01 increments.

 If you don't know what kerning value to use, you can adjust the kerning incrementally from the keyboard. Press Alt+left arrow (Option-left arrow on the Mac) to squeeze letters together; press Alt+right arrow (Option-right arrow on the Mac) to spread them apart. By default, each keystroke changes the kerning by 0.02 (20/1000) em space, but you can change the increment by entering a new value into the Tracking option box in the Type & Auto Tracing Preferences dialog box.

For more dramatic changes, add the Ctrl key (Cmd key on the Mac) to the above to decrease or increase the kerning by five times the Tracking value in the Type & Auto Tracing Preferences dialog box.

When kerning small type, you may not be able to see a visible difference as you add or delete space because the display is not accurate enough. If so, you can use the zoom tool to magnify the drawing area while kerning or tracking characters from the keyboard.

Changing the Height and Width of Characters

The next options in the Character palette, Vertical Scale and Horizontal Scale, modify the height and width of selected characters, respectively. You can expand or condense type anywhere from 1 to 10,000 percent (1/100 to 100 times its normal width) by entering a new value into either the Vertical Scale or Horizontal Scale option box and pressing Enter (Return on the Mac).

Changing the height or width of a character distorts it. The Vertical Scale and Horizontal Scale options do not create the same effect as designer-condensed (or designer-expanded) fonts, or what you can get by using Adobe's Multiple Master fonts, which I'll cover in more detail in Chapter 11. For example, **Figure 10.9** shows two variations on Helvetica. The top example is 200-point Helvetica Bold, scaled horizontally 45 percent. You would get the same result—at least in overall size and height of the characters—if you were to scale 115-point type vertically to 174 percent. If you were to try it, you'd see that the horizontal bars of the *A* and *B* are much thicker than the vertical stems. This is because Horizontal Scale affects vertical proportions and leaves horizontal proportions untouched.

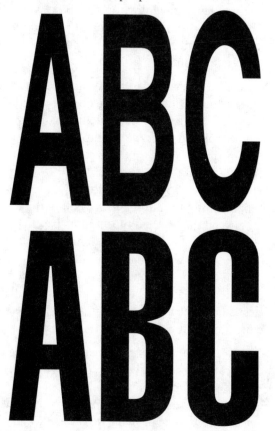

Figure 10.9: 200-point
Helvetica Bold scaled
horizontally 45 percent (top)
compared with a specially
designed font called
Helvetica Compressed Ultra.

The bottom example in Figure 10.9 shows a specially condensed font called Helvetica Compressed Ultra. The strokes vary, but there is an overall consistency that the skinny Helvetica Bold type—the one I distorted myself—lacks. The designer has also taken the time to square off some of the curves, making Helvetica Compressed Ultra more legible in small type sizes.

With this in mind, you should remember a few things when using the Vertical Scale or Horizontal Scale option:

- If you *want* the type to appear distorted, go for broke. There are no hard and fast rules in page design; type that specifically calls attention to itself can be just as effective as type that doesn't, if you have a bold design and an open-minded audience.

- If slightly widening or narrowing a few lines of type will make them fit better on the page, you can get away with Horizontal Scale values between 95 and 105 percent; no one will be the wiser.

- Changing both the vertical and horizontal factors by the same amount is the same as changing the size. So if you enter 50 percent into both the Vertical Scale and Horizontal Scale option boxes, the result is the same as if you had changed the value in the Size option box to half of its original value.

Incidentally, if you've scaled a text block disproportionately using the scale tool (as described in Chapter 9), the Font Size and Horizontal Scale values reflect the discrepancy between the current and the normal width and size of the selected type. You can reset the type to its normal width by pressing Ctrl+Shift+X (Cmd-Shift-X on the Mac).

Raising and Lowering Characters

The Baseline Shift option in the lower half of the Character palette determines the distance between the selected type and its baseline. A positive value raises the characters; a negative value lowers them. The default value of 0 leaves them sitting on the baseline, where they typically belong.

You can modify the baseline shift to create superscripts and subscripts, or to adjust type along a path (as I discuss in the next chapter). To change the baseline shift, select some type and then enter any value between –1296 and 1296 points into the Baseline Shift option box.

*Baseline shift is instrumental in creating good-looking fractions. To create a fraction like the one in **Figure 10.10**, start by entering the fraction using the virgule instead of the slash. A virgule is a slightly thinner, more slanted line than a slash. (To get a virgule, in Windows select the Symbol font and press Alt+0164 on the numeric keypad. On the Mac, type Option-Shift-1.)*

Next, select the numerator (the top number), make it about half its original (current) type size, and enter a baseline shift value equal to about one-third the original type size. Then select the denominator (bottom number) and match its type size to that of the numerator, but leave the Baseline Shift value set to 0.

$$22/531$$

Figure 10.10: In this fraction, the type size of the virgule is 160 points, whereas the numerator and denominator are set to 80 points. The numerator is shifted 53 points above the baseline.

You can adjust baseline shift incrementally from the keyboard (according to the Baseline Shift value in the Type & Auto Tracing Preferences dialog box, 2 points by default). Press Alt+Shift+up arrow (Option-Shift-up arrow) to raise the selected text above its baseline; press Alt+Shift+down arrow (Option-Shift-down arrow) to lower the text.

To see the text really jump, add the Ctrl key (Command key on the Mac) to the above keystrokes. The baseline shift will change by five times the Baseline Shift value set in the Type & Auto Tracing Preferences dialog box.

Paragraph-Level Formatting

Illustrator's paragraph formatting controls are found in the Paragraph palette. To display the palette, choose Window » Type » Paragraph or press Ctrl+M (Cmd-M on the Mac). By default, the Paragraph palette is collapsed, as shown in the left example of **Figure 10.11**. Choose the Show Options command from the Paragraph palette's pop-up menu to expand the palette and display the options shown in the right example of the figure.

You can hide the Paragraph palette by pressing Ctrl+M (Cmd-M on the Mac) again.

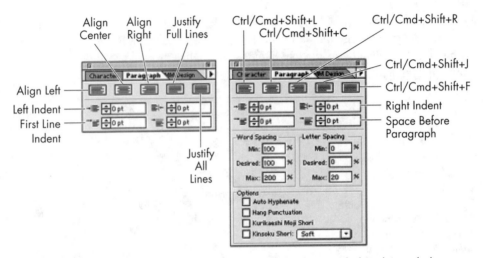

Figure 10.11: The Paragraph palette, collapsed (left) and expanded (right), with the keyboard shortcuts used to activate various options.

The Paragraph palette, like the Character palette, relies heavily on option boxes, and the same tips apply: Remember to use the Tab and Shift-Tab shortcuts to switch between the option boxes, and to press Shift+Enter (Shift-Return on the Mac) to apply changes without deactivating the option boxes.

Changing the Alignment

As far as I can tell, every computer program that lets you create type lets you change how the rows of type line up. This is commonly called *alignment*. (Do not mistake the alignment commands with the actions of the Align palette. The Align palette can align text objects, but it does not affect the alignment of the text inside the blocks.)

- To align a paragraph so that all the left edges line up (*flush left, ragged right*), press Ctrl+Shift+L (Cmd-Shift-L on the Mac) or select the left-most alignment icon in the Paragraph palette.

- To *center* all lines in a paragraph, press Ctrl+Shift+C (Cmd-Shift-C on the Mac) or select the second alignment icon in the Paragraph palette.

- To make the right edges of a paragraph line up (*flush right, ragged left*), press Ctrl+Shift+R (Cmd-Shift-R on the Mac) or select the third alignment icon.

- You can also *justify* (Justify Full Lines) a paragraph, which stretches all lines except the last line of a paragraph so they entirely fill the width of the text block. (The last line in a justified paragraph remains flush left.) To justify a paragraph, press Ctrl+Shift+J (Cmd-Shift-J on the Mac) or select the fourth alignment icon.

If you want to *force justify* (Justify All Lines) the last line in a paragraph, press Ctrl+Shift+F (Cmd-Shift-F on the Mac) or click the last alignment icon in the Paragraph palette.

Examples of all five alignment settings appear in **Figure 10.12**. These settings were all applied to text blocks.

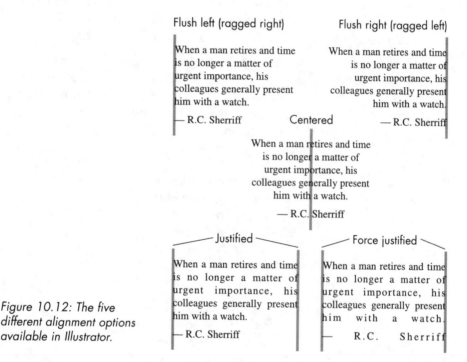

Figure 10.12: The five different alignment options available in Illustrator.

 When you align point text, Illustrator aligns the text relative to the alignment point, or place where you originally clicked the type tool to start the instance of point text. If you choose Justify Full Lines or Justify All Lines for point text, the lines would still be aligned flush left, because each line of point text is a separate paragraph.

Indenting Paragraphs

There are two basic ways to indent a paragraph (both demonstrated in **Figure 10.13**). You can indent the first line to distinguish one paragraph from another, or you can create a *hanging indent*, in which you indent all lines *but* the first line.

A hanging indent is what's usually used for creating bulleted or numbered lists, so even if you're not familiar with the term, you've seen it in action a million times.

Using the indentation option boxes in Illustrator's Paragraph palette, you can create whatever indent effect you'd like. The Left Indent value indents all text on the left side of a paragraph, creating a gap between the left edge of the text block and the affected paragraph. The Right Indent value indents all text on the right side of a paragraph. First Line Left Indent indents the first line of a paragraph without affecting any other lines.

 To create a standard paragraph indent, enter a value into the First Line Left Indent option box in the Paragraph palette. The first example in Figure 10.13 was created with a First Line Indent value of 20 points.

 If you assign a first-line indent to a paragraph, remember that you can break a word onto the next line of type without indenting it by pressing Shift+Enter (Shift-Return on the Mac) to create a soft return. The words divided by the new-line character appear on different lines, but are still part of the same paragraph.

> **Sixty years ago I knew everything; now I know nothing; education is a progressive discovery of your own ignorance.**
> *—Will Durant*

> • **Sixty years ago I knew everything; now I know nothing; education is a progressive discovery of your own ignorance.**
> *—Will Durant*

Figure 10.13: A paragraph with a first-line indent (top) and a hanging indent (bottom).

 To create a hanging indent, enter a positive value into the Left Indent option box and the inverse of that value in the First Line Left Indent option box. For example, to create the second example in Figure 10.13, I set the Left Indent value to 20 points and the First Line Indent value to −20 points. If this doesn't seem intuitive, try it a few times.

 If you're planning to use the hanging indent for bulleted or numbered lists, you also have to set the tab so the text on the first line lines up with the others. In the figure, I pressed the Tab key after the bullet to insert a tab character, then chose the Window » Type » Tab Ruler command to display the Tabs palette, and created a left tab at the 20-point mark so it lined up with the left indent. For complete information about tabs, read "The Amazing World of Tabs" near the end of this chapter.

You can enter any value between –1296 and 1296 points into any of the indentation option boxes.

There's really no reason to apply indentation values to point text (except to make it wrap around an object, as discussed in the "Adjusting the Standoff" section of Chapter 11).

The Hanging Indent Trick

Most of the time you're going to want to create your hanging indents as I did above—especially if you have other text without hanging indents inside the same text block, so that everything will still be automatically aligned. But if your text consists of *only* hanging indented paragraphs (such as bulleted text), you can take advantage of the fact that Illustrator will position and print text outside the text block. **Figure 10.14** shows the same text as before (with the help of having the text block outline and hidden characters visible), now set with the bullet hanging well outside the text block. Here, I simply entered the value of -20 points for the first line indent and left the regular left indent alone at 0. This moved the bullet outside the text block. Then I pressed the Tab key to insert a Tab character after the bullet. But I didn't have to set the tab; Illustrator automatically positioned the text so that it lined up with the left indent.

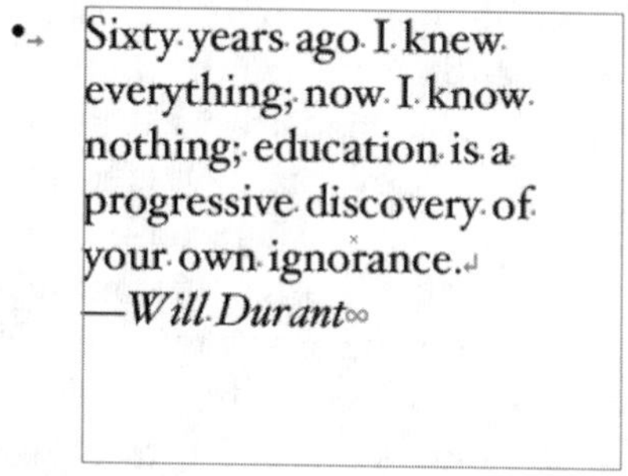

Figure 10.14: A hanging indent can be set to hang outside a text block by just changing the first line indent to a negative value. As the hidden characters show, a tab character helps line up the text at the left margin.

> Sixty years ago I knew everything; now I know nothing; education is a progressive discovery of your own ignorance.
> —Will Durant

Adding Paragraph Leading

Enter a value into the Space Before Paragraph option box to insert some extra space before a selected paragraph. This so-called *paragraph leading* helps separate one paragraph from another, much like a first-line indent. Most designers use first-line indents *or* paragraph leading to distinguish paragraphs, but not both.

The two together are generally considered design overkill (though I must admit I've done it and been rather pleased with the results).

Spacing Letters and Words in a Justified Paragraph

The middle options in the Paragraph palette let you control the amount of space that Illustrator places between words and characters in a text block. As you might imagine, *word spacing* controls the amount of space between words; *letter spacing* controls the amount of space between letters.

Now, a few of you quick-minded types are probably thinking to your-selves, "How is letter spacing different from kerning?" Well, for one thing, kerning applies to selected characters, while letter spacing affects entire paragraphs. Also, the two are measured differently. Kerning is measured in fractions of an em space; letter spacing is measured as a percentage of the standard space character. But most important, kerning is fixed, whereas letter spacing is flexible. As you'll soon see, Illustrator can automatically vary letter spacing inside justi-fied paragraphs between two extremes.

There are two primary reasons for manipulating spacing:

- To give a paragraph a generally tighter or looser appearance. You control this general spacing using the Desired options.

- To determine the range of spacing manipulations Illustrator can use when justifying a paragraph. Illustrator tightens up some lines and loosens others to make them fit the exact width of your text block. You specify limits using the Min. and Max. options.

When spacing flush left, right, or centered paragraphs, Illustrator relies entirely on the two Desired values. In fact, the other options are dimmed. All values are measured as a percentage of a standard space, as the information contained in the current font determines. For example, a Desired Word Spacing value of 100 per-cent inserts the width of one space character between each pair of words in a para-graph. Reducing or enlarging this percentage makes the space between words bigger or smaller. A Desired Letter Spacing of 10 percent inserts 10 percent of the width of a space character between each pair of letters. Negative percentages squeeze letters together, and a value of 0 percent spaces letters normally.

If you select one or more justified paragraphs, the Min. and Max. options become available. (These options appear dimmed if you have even one flush left, centered, or flush right paragraph partially selected.) These values give Illustrator some wiggle room when tightening and spreading lines of type. You're basically telling Illustrator, "I'd prefer that you use the Desired spacing, but if you can't manage that, go as low as Min. and as high as Max. But that's where I cut you off."

Word Spacing and Letter Spacing values must be within these ranges.

 The Min. Word Spacing value must be at least 0 percent; the Min. Letter Spacing must be at least –50 percent. Both must be less than their respective Desired values.

 The Max. Word Spacing value can be no higher than 1,000 percent; Max. Letter Spacing can be no more than 500 percent. Neither can be less than its respective Desired value.

 Each Desired value can be no less than its corresponding Min. value and no higher than the corresponding Max. value.

Figure 10.15 shows a justified paragraph subjected to various word spacing and letter spacing combinations. In the first column, only the word spacing changes; all letter spacing values are set to a constant 0 percent. In the second column, only the letter spacing changes; all word spacing values are set to 100 percent. Above each paragraph is a headline stating the values that have been changed. The percentages represent the Min., Desired, and Max. values, respectively.

Figure 10.15: Here are some examples of different word and letter spacing combinations. Letter spacing is constant in the left column and word spacing is constant in the right.

Word: 100%, 100%, 200%

Neither can I believe that the individual survives the death of his body, although feeble souls harbor such thoughts through fear or ridiculous egotism.

—Albert Einstein

Letter: 0%, 0%, 5%

Neither can I believe that the individual survives the death of his body, although feeble souls harbor such thoughts through fear or ridiculous egotism.

—Albert Einstein

Word: 0%, 25%, 50%

Neither can I believe that the individual survives the death of his body, although feeble souls harbor such thoughts through fear or ridiculous egotism.

—Albert Einstein

Letter: –15%, –10%, –5%

Neither can I believe that the individual survives the death of his body, although feeble souls harbor such thoughts through fear or ridiculous egotism.

—Albert Einstein

Word: 200%, 225%, 250%

Neither can I believe that the individual survives the death of his body, although feeble souls harbor such thoughts through fear or ridiculous egotism.

Letter: 25%, 35%, 50%

Neither can I believe that the individual survives the death of his body, although feeble souls harbor such thoughts through fear or ridiculous egotism.

Activating Automatic Hyphenation

Thank goodness that computers are not typewriters, and we are no longer responsible for hyphenating our own text. There are three ways to hyphenate text in Illustrator.

- Enter a standard hyphen character (-) between two words you want to hyphenate. This is usually found in hyphenated words such as *3-inch mark* or hyphenated names such as *Biddle-Barrows*. Don't use the standard hyphen between the letters of a word, though. If you edit the text later on, you may end up with stray hyphens breaking a word in the mid-dle [sic] of a line.

- A much better idea is to insert a *discretionary hyphen*, which disappears any time it is not needed. You can enter a discretionary hyphen by pressing Ctrl+Shift+ hyphen (-) in Windows or Cmd-Shift-hyphen (-) on the Mac. If no hyphen appears when you enter this character, it simply means that the addition of the hyphen does not help Illustrator break the word. You can try inserting the character at a different location or expanding the width of the text block to permit the word to break.

- The third option is to let Illustrator do the hyphenating for you by selecting the Auto Hyphenate check box in the Paragraph palette. (This option has no effect on point text, just text blocks.)

Of all the options, I like the last one the least. It's the easiest, to be sure, but some of its suggestions are goofy, and Illustrator may open old illustrations and apply new hyphenation. Unless you're creating newsletters or other small documents with lots of type, it's usually safer to enter discretionary hyphens manually where needed.

Still, if you do decide that automatic hyphenation is for you, here's how it works.

1. **Turn on Auto Hyphenate.**

   With the arrow tool, select the text block you want to hyphenate and click in the Auto Hyphenate check box in the Paragraph palette. Illustrator adds hyphens where it deems necessary.

2. **Choose the Hyphenation Options.**

   If you want to limit where and how hyphenation occurs, choose the Hyphenation command from the Paragraph palette pop-up menu. The Hyphenation Options dialog box, shown in **Figure 10.16**, will open.

Hyphenation Options

Hyphenate `2` letters from beginning

Hyphenate `2` letters from end

Limit consecutive hyphens `3`

[OK]

[Cancel]

3.   Specify how many letters must appear before and after a hyphen.

In the Hyphenation Options dialog box, enter a value into the first Hyphenate option box (Letters from Beginning) to specify the minimum number of letters that can come between a hyphen and the beginning of a word. Enter a value into the next option box to determine the minimum number of letters between a hyphen and the end of a word. For example, with both values set to 2, Illustrator could split the word *apple* as *ap-ple,* because both the first and last syllables are at least two letters long.

4.   Specify the possible number of consecutive hyphens.

If you want to limit the number of consecutive lines of type Illustrator can hyphenate, select the Limit consecutive hyphens check box and enter the maximum limit in the option box. By default, the value is set to 3, so Illustrator can hyphenate no more than three consecutive lines before it has to permit one line to go without hyphenation. But as far as I'm concerned, any more than two hyphenated lines in a row looks amateurish and interferes with legibility.

5.   Click OK or press Enter (Return on the Mac).

Illustrator will implement all your secret hyphen-related desires.

In addition to the hyphenation options entrusted to the Paragraph palette, you can control what words Illustrator hyphenates—and how it hyphenates them—by opening the Hyphenation Preferences dialog box. Simply type the word without any hyphens if you never want it hyphenated. Or type the word with the hyphens positioned where you would allow hyphenation to occur. (For a step-by-step example of this, flip back to Chapter 2.)

If you add a word in the Hyphenation Preferences that already exists in a text block, it won't update that word without a little help from you. First, select the text block. Next, deselect the Auto Hyphenate check box in the Paragraph palette, and then immediately reselect it. This jogs Illustrator into reapplying the automatic hyphenation.

Dangling a Quotation Mark

Select the Hang Punctuation check box in the Paragraph palette to make punctuation, such as quotation marks, commas, hyphens, and so on, hang outside one
of the edges of a text block.

- In a flush left paragraph, punctuation will hang outside the left side of
  the text block.

- In a flush right paragraph, the punctuation hangs outside the right side.

- If the paragraph is centered, Hang Punctuation will hang characters
  on either side of the text block.

- If you justify or force justify the paragraph, the punctuation hangs off
  both sides.

The paragraph in **Figure 10.17** was force justified so that all lines were both
flush left and flush right. This way, Illustrator forced the quotation marks outside
both sides of the text block. I also increased the type size of the quotation marks,
kerned them slightly, and used a baseline shift to lower them 4 points each. This
created a much more elegant look. (Hey, you can't expect a single option like
Hang Punctuation to do everything for you.)

*Figure 10.17: Here I applied
the Hang Punctuation and
Justify All Lines options to
move the quote marks outside
the text block.*

"Nothing is so ignorant as the ignorance of certainty."

— Aldous Huxley

Kurikaeshi Moji Shori and Kinsoku Shori

Made you rub your eyes, didn't I? No, this is not a case of my fingers being mis-
positioned on the keyboard. These final check boxes in the Paragraph palette (as
well as the Kinsoku Shori options in the pop-up menu) have to do with Japanese
layout rules and the Japanese type features the program includes. They work only
with double-byte fonts—because there are so many characters in a Japanese font,
each character requires 2 bytes. In other words, if you're not using a Japanese
font, these options won't affect your text.

If you don't see these options in your Paragraph palette, and want to, click the small up and down arrow next to the word Paragraph on the palette tab as many times as it takes until you see the entire menu. Both the Character and the Paragraph palette (and several others, for that matter) have the ability to perform expanding and contracting tricks.

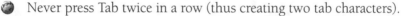

The Amazing World of Tabs

Technically, tabs are little more than variable width spaces. But really, they are so much more flexible and easier to use than spaces. By pressing the Tab key after entering a bullet or number, you can create hanging indents, as you saw back in Figure 10.14. By entering tabs between items in a list, you can create columns that align precisely. And (once you're set up properly) always with just one press of a button. Whenever you're tempted to use multiple spaces, press the Tab key instead.

There are really only two rules for using tabs.

 Never press Tab twice in a row (thus creating two tab characters).

 To specify the width of a tab character, adjust the tab stop settings in the Tabs palette.

I still see more folks misusing tabs than handling them correctly. If you never touch a tab stop and merely rely on multiple tabs or—shudder—spaces to do the work for you, you limit your formatting freedom and you make future editing more cumbersome and confusing. Whereas if you simply follow the two rules mentioned above and never, *ever* stray, you'll be fine.

Using the Tabs Palette

Choose Window » Type » Tab Ruler or press Ctrl+Shift+T (Cmd-Shift-T on the Mac) to display the Tabs palette, shown in **Figure 10.18**. Known by the less formal moniker of *tab ruler*, this palette lets you position tab stops and align tabbed text.

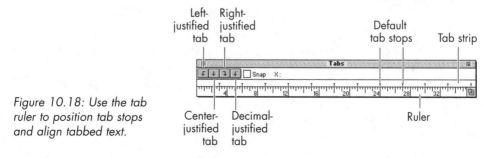

Figure 10.18: Use the tab ruler to position tab stops and align tabbed text.

Like the Paragraph palette, the tab ruler affects entire paragraphs, whether they're entirely or only partially selected. The following items explain how the tab ruler works and offer a few guidelines for using it.

- When you first bring up the Tabs palette, Illustrator automatically aligns it to the selected paragraph. To align the palette to a different paragraph, select the paragraph and then click just to the left of the tab ruler's close box icon (click in the size box on the far right side of the tab ruler's title bar on the Macintosh).

- To create a tab stop, click in the ruler along the bottom of the palette, or click inside the tab strip just above the ruler. If you drag the tab stop, Illustrator projects a vertical alignment guide from the Tabs palette, as labeled in **Figure 10.19**. The line moves with the tab stop, permitting you to predict more accurately the results of your adjustment. The Tabs palette also tracks the numerical position of the tab stop—with respect to the left edge of the text block—just below the title bar.

- When you create a new tab stop, all default tab stops (those little Ts) to the left of the new stop disappear. The default stops merely tell Illustrator to space tabbed text every half inch.

- A question mark in the tab ruler means that at least one line of selected text does *not* align to that tab stop. Just click the tab stop to make all selected lines align.

- *To move more than one tab stop at a time, Shift-drag a stop. All tab stops to the right of the dragged stop will move in kind; tab stops to the left will remain stationary.*

- Select the Snap check box to align new and moved tab stops to the nearest increment on the ruler. (Much easier than zooming in on the text.)

- *You can also snap a single tab stop on the fly when the Snap check box is turned off. To do this, press Ctrl (Cmd on the Mac) while dragging the tab stop. You can likewise Ctrl-drag (Cmd-drag on the Mac) to move a tab stop freely when the Snap option is active.*

- To change the identity of a tab stop, select the tab stop by clicking on it, then select a different identity from the four buttons on the left side of the palette. From left to right, these buttons make tabbed text align with the left side, center, right side, or decimal point. In **Figure 10.19**, for example, I centered the *Salary* column by assigning a center tab stop. I aligned the *Additional income* column with a right tab stop. Decimal tab stops are ideal for aligning numbers, such as prices.

Tab stop   Tab stop position

Tabs
Snap   X: 96 pt.

Annual earnings of a few fictional characters:

Name	Primary occupation	Salary	Additional income	Source
Santa Claus	toy distributor	none	$12,000	Macy's
Rudolf	bad-weather beacon	none	$266,370	Duracell spokesman
Peter Cottontail	egg distributor	none	$56,050	stuntman for Bugs Bunny
Tooth Fairy	tooth purchaser	none	$23,920	gold wholesaler
Superman	vigilante	none	$42,500	Daily Planet
Batman	vigilante	none	$21,354,350	CEO, Wayne Enterprises
Robin	vigilante's buddy	none	$6,250	Gotham City Malt Shop
The Wizard of Oz	wish granter	none	$765,130	owner, Kansas City Slots
Cinderella	princess	none	$8,700	housecleaning
Sleeping Beauty	princess	none	$216,500	No-Doz spokesperson
Pooh Bear	stuffed animal	none	$1.50	found in hollow tree
Piglet	stuffed animal	none	$0.75	stole from Owl
Lochness Monster	fresh-water dweller	none	$128,900	sighting fees
Big Foot	forest dweller	none	$0.75	stole from Piglet
E.T.	illegal alien	none	$89,450	pediatrician
Big Bad Wolf	pig chaser	none	$120,360	demolitions expert
Little Bo Peep	sheepherder	none	$35,000	animal reconnaissance
Gilligan	little buddy	none	$47.13	Mrs. Howell's concubine
Scooby Doo	crime-solving pet	none	-$152	loans to Shaggy

Figure 10.19: When you drag a tab stop, a vertical line drops down from the palette, showing how the adjusted text will align.

Alignment guide

Another way to change the identity of a tab stop is to Alt-click it (Option-click on the Mac). Each "fortified" click switches the stop to the next variety, from left to center to right to decimal and back to left.

To delete a tab stop, drag it upward or downward, off the tab strip and out of the palette. The X: item reads *delete*. To delete all tab stops, Shift-drag upward on the leftmost tab stop in the ruler.

By default, the unit of measure in the tab ruler conforms to the unit in Illustrator's standard rulers (as set using the Units option in the Units & Undo Preferences). But you can change the units by clicking on the tab stop position indicator or the gray area to the right of the X (this area is white if you're using Mac OS 10.1), which is just to the right of the Snap check box.

If you want all the lines of your table to use the same tab stops automatically, press Shift+Enter (Shift-Return on the Mac) at the end of each line. This inserts line breaks, forcing Illustrator to recognize all of the lines as part of the same paragraph, as is the case in Figure 10.19. If you press Enter (Return on the Mac) at the end of each line, you will insert paragraph returns. Illustrator then treats each line as a separate paragraph. You then have to select all the paragraphs to change the tab stops for each line.

Taking Tabs to a New Level

What if you don't want to align tabbed text in straightforward vertical columns? What if you want to create something a little more graphic, something worthier of your reader's attention, such as the table in **Figure 10.20**? Can you do this in Illustrator?

Well, of course you can. (In fact, you've been able to do something like this since Illustrator 3.0.) The secret behind this technique involves using several open paths to act like the tabs and wrapping the text around these paths, as the following steps explain.

1. **Create your text block.**

   Enter one tab—and only one tab—between each entry, just as you would normally. (In **Figure 10.20**, for example, there is one tab between *Santa Claus* and *toy distributor*.) Use line breaks (Shift+Enter in Windows or Shift-Return on the Mac) to separate the lines. If you separate the lines with carriage returns (by pressing Enter in Windows or Return on the Mac), Illustrator will not automatically apply paragraph-level format changes to each line.

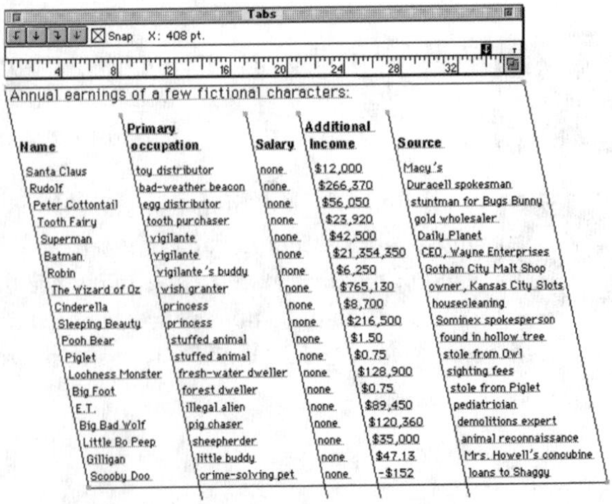

Figure 10.20: This slanted table—seen in the outline mode—was created wrapping tabbed text around a series of straight lines.

Name	Primary occupation	Salary	Additional income	Source
Santa Claus	toy distributor	none	$12,000	Macy's
Rudolf	bad-weather beacon	none	$266,370	Duracell spokesman
Peter Cottontail	egg distributor	none	$56,050	stuntman for Bugs Bunny
Tooth Fairy	tooth purchaser	none	$23,920	gold wholesaler
Superman	vigilante	none	$42,500	Daily Planet
Batman	vigilante	none	$21,354,350	CEO, Wayne Enterprises
Robin	vigilante's buddy	none	$6,250	Gotham City Malt Shop
The Wizard of Oz	wish granter	none	$765,130	owner, Kansas City Slots
Cinderella	princess	none	$8,700	housecleaning
Sleeping Beauty	princess	none	$216,500	Sominex spokesperson
Pooh Bear	stuffed animal	none	$1.50	found in hollow tree
Piglet	stuffed animal	none	$0.75	stole from Owl
Lochness Monster	fresh-water dweller	none	$128,900	sighting fees
Big Foot	forest dweller	none	$0.75	stole from Piglet
E.T.	illegal alien	none	$89,450	pediatrician
Big Bad Wolf	pig chaser	none	$120,360	demolitions expert
Little Bo Peep	sheepherder	none	$35,000	animal reconnaissance
Gilligan	little buddy	none	$47.13	Mrs. Howell's concubine
Scooby Doo	crime-solving pet	none	-$152	loans to Shaggy

Annual earnings of a few fictional characters:

2. Use the direct selection tool to reshape the boundaries of the text block.

For example, to create the slanted block shown in Figure 10.20, I clicked on the bottom segment of the text block and dragged it to the right. You may want to work in the outline mode, where you can see the text block outline when it's not selected.

3. Add a tab stop to the far right side of the tab ruler.

Your text should now be a total mess, but no matter. Click the size box in the Tabs palette to make sure the palette is positioned directly over the text block, then create a left tab stop on the far right side of the palette. If any other tab stops exist, delete them. In **Figure 10.20**, for example, I positioned a single tab stop at the 34-pica mark. The purpose of this step is to eliminate all of the default tabs, thereby ensuring that each tab carries the entry following it to the next open path.

4. Draw a few open paths to serve as guides.

Your text is worse than ever! But don't try to fix it—instead, it's time to add graphic tab stops in the form of a few open paths. In Figure 10.20, I drew a straight line with the pen tool by clicking on each of the two points on the left side of the slanted text block. This way, the angle of the line matched the angle of the block. Then I used the arrow tool to drag the line into position, just to the right of *Santa Claus*, so it could serve as the tab stop for the *Primary occupation* column. I then cloned the line by Alt-dragging it (Option-dragging on the Mac) three times, thus creating three additional tab stops. (See Chapter 7 for a discussion of cloning.)

5. Apply the Make Wrap command.

To convert the lines into tab stops, select both the lines and the text block and choose Type » Wrap » Make (covered in Chapter 11). Illustrator automatically aligns each tabbed entry with the nearest line.

6. Drag the lines into position with the direct selection tool.

It's unlikely that the text will wrap exactly the way you hoped right off the bat. But now that the text is roughly in place, the lines act just like normal tab stops. To reposition one of these graphic tab stops, use the direct selection tool to move the line left or right.

7. **Make the lines transparent so they don't interfere with the table.**

Once you have all the lines in place, select the lines and make their fills and strokes transparent (using the control located at the bottom of the toolbox or in the top left of the Color palette).

Graphic tabs are generally every bit as versatile as regular tabs, except for one thing: Each tab stop is the same. In other words, you can't mix left tabs and right tabs inside the same text block, and there are no decimal tabs. Rather, each entry is aligned the same way the paragraph is aligned. If the paragraph is flush left, each entry is flush left; if the paragraph is centered, each entry is centered between the graphic tabs; and so on.

Graphic tabs bridge the border between the world of sedate formatting options that every publishing program provides and the more wild text effects that Illustrator is so rightly famous for. To cross all the way over to the other side of the border, read the next chapter.

The Text Eyedropper and Paint Bucket

As I mentioned earlier, once you set the character and paragraph formatting, that formatting stays in effect for the rest of the Illustrator session. So even if you start a new document, the text attributes stay the same. But once you change the formatting or quit Illustrator, those text attributes are no longer stored in the Character and Paragraph palettes.

Fortunately, Illustrator gives you a relatively easy way to sample the text attributes from one set of text and then apply them to another. You do it by using the eyedropper and paint bucket tools, shown in **Figure 10.21**. The eyedropper is the "taker" and the paint bucket is the "giver"; you sample attributes with the former, and then apply them where you want with the latter. (There are times when you can actually perform both steps at once, effectively bypassing the paint bucket, as you'll soon see.)

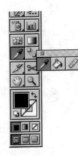

Figure 10.21: The eyedropper and paint bucket tools can be used to sample and apply character and paragraph attributes.

Although the eyedropper and paint bucket are handy, they are hardly a substitute for text styles. Text styles (as found in FreeHand for many years) are much more powerful and not only allow text to be automatically formatted, but also make it very easy to change all the text in a document. I'm still waiting—patiently—for text styles to be added to Illustrator. Maybe next time!

The eyedropper and paint bucket can also be used on graphic objects. Because the techniques for using the tools on objects are slightly different from using them on text, I'll cover the two tools again in Chapter 19, where I talk about transferring object attributes.

Sucking up Attributes with the Eyedropper

To sample text attributes with the eyedropper tool, select the eyedropper tool. Position the tool over the text that you want to sample. When a small T appears next to the eyedropper cursor, you know that the eyedropper is in the text mode.

 If you don't see the T next to the eyedropper cursor, then the eyedropper will sample the attributes of the text block that holds the text—not the text itself.

 If you have turned off Type Area Select in the Type & Auto Trace Preferences dialog box, you will have to position the eyedropper cursor directly over the baseline of the text to use the eyedropper in the text mode.

Click or drag the eyedropper over the text that you want to sample. A click sucks up the text attributes exactly under the cursor. A drag, as shown in **Figure 10.22** samples the attributes from the text where the mouse button is released at the end of the drag. If you drag with the eyedropper, the tip of the eyedropper cursor turns black to show that the attributes are being sampled.

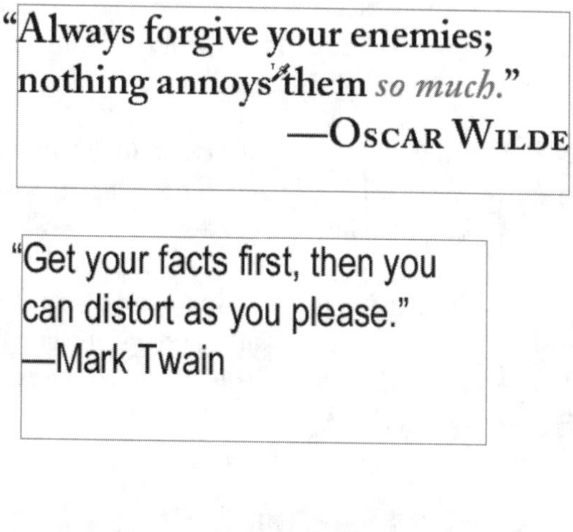

"Always forgive your enemies;
nothing annoys them *so much.*"
—Oscar Wilde

"Get your facts first, then you
can distort as you please."
—Mark Twain

Figure 10.22: Click or drag the eyedropper across the text attributes that you want to sample.

Pouring out Attributes with the Paint Bucket

To apply text attributes, you can select the paint bucket tool from the first alternate eyedropper slot in toolbox. However, because you most likely already have the eyedropper tool selected, simply hold down the Alt key (Option key on the Mac). This toggles between the eyedropper and paint bucket. (Similarly, hold the Alt or Option key to change the paint bucket tool into the eyedropper.)

Position the paint bucket over the text that you want to change. Look for the small T next to the cursor; this tells you that the paint bucket is in the text mode. Unlike the eyedropper, there is a real difference between clicking and dragging with the paint bucket. If you simply click with the paint bucket, as shown in **Figure 10.23**, you apply the text attributes to all the text in the text object.

"Always forgive your enemies; nothing annoys them *so much*."
—Oscar Wilde

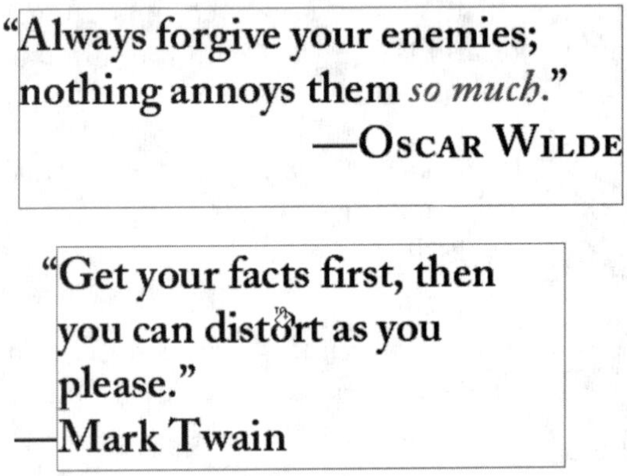

Figure 10.23: A click with the paint bucket tool applied the attributes to all the text in the text object. Here the main attributes from the top text object have been applied to the bottom text object.

"Get your facts first, then you can distort as you please."
—Mark Twain

Another way to apply the text attributes to a whole text object is to have that object selected when you take the sample with the eyedropper from the desired source text. The sample will be applied automatically to the second selection.

However, you may want to apply text attributes to specific areas of a text object. To do that, you need to drag with the paint bucket tool across the text. As you drag, a box appears around the characters that are chosen. When you release the mouse button, those characters will be changed. **Figure 10.24** shows the power of the paint bucket in action.

If you don't see the T next to the paint bucket cursor, then the paint bucket will apply only the fill and stroke attributes of the text that has been sampled.

Once again, if you have turned off Type Area Select in the Type & Auto Trace Preferences dialog box, you will have to position the paint bucket cursor directly over the baseline of the text to use the paint bucket in the text mode.

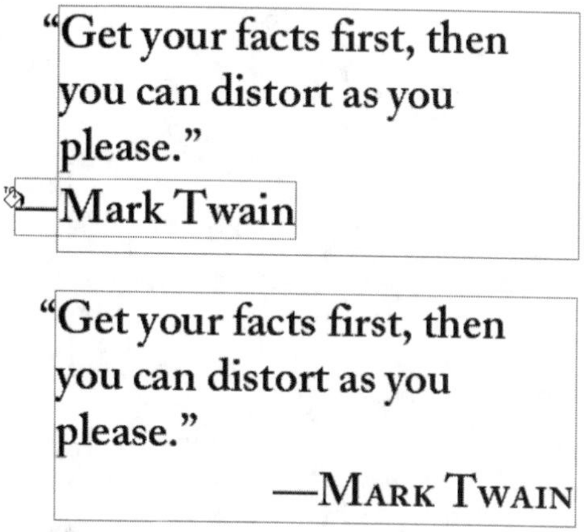

"Get your facts first, then you can distort as you please."
—Mark Twain

Figure 10.24: The top example shows the paint bucket dragged across the text that is to be changed. The bottom example shows the results of applying the new attributes to the text.

"Get your facts first, then you can distort as you please."
—MARK TWAIN

Configuring the Eyedropper and Paint Bucket

By default, the eyedropper and paint bucket will sample and apply all the character and paragraph attributes of the text. However, you can configure the tools so that they sample and apply only certain attributes. For instance, you can set the tools so they sample and apply only character attributes, but not the paragraph ones.

To configure the tools, double-click either the eyedropper or the paint bucket in the toolbox. The Eyedropper/Paint Bucket Options dialog box appears, as shown in **Figure 10.25**. Use the check boxes to choose which attributes you want each tool to recognize.

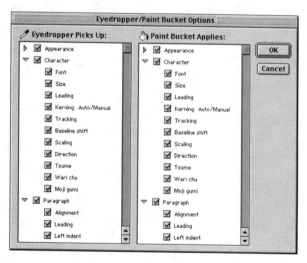

Figure 10.25: The Eyedropper/Paint Bucket Options dialog box lets you control which attributes the tools sample and apply.

The settings for the eyedropper and paint bucket remain in effect for new documents and new sessions of Illustrator.

SOME OF YOUR WACKIER TEXT EFFECTS

Creating and formatting text is all very well and good, but where Illustrator excels is in the creation of specialized—dare I say wacky?—type. You can attach text to a curve, wrap text inside an irregular outline, flow text from one text block to another, and wrap text around graphics.

If you plan to use Illustrator to create documents that contain a fair amount of text, you can import text from a word processor and then check the spelling, perform complex search and replace operations, and even export the text back out to disk. And just to prove to you that there are no limits to this wackiness, Illustrator lets you convert one or more letters to paths and then edit the character outlines.

In recent years there has been a trend in page-layout programs to add text features similar to those in Illustrator. Some page-layout programs, such as QuarkXPress and Adobe InDesign, can now also accomplish some of these text effects, but they don't possess all of Illustrator's powerful features. Those programs can put text on a path, but they can't apply all of the effects and other features found in Illustrator. So if all you want is a wacky text effect, you can use other programs. However, if you want to create text and then do a whole lot more to it, you still need Illustrator.

On the other hand, to be fair, there's also been a trend for graphics applications to flatter their page-layout colleagues by adopting useful features in the other direction, such as spelling checkers. (So if you come to Illustrator for the graphics and stay for the typography, at least you won't be punished by not having the means to catch a typo.) While spell checking and font replacement are not really activities I'd call "wacky," I'll cover them here in this post-basic chapter on text and typography.

Topsy-Turvy Type on a Curve

Illustrator lets you bind a line of text to a free-form path (as you can see in **Figure 11.1**). Adobe calls such a text object *path text,* but many folks call it *type on a curve* as well. First I'll be conventional and show you how to do this with the type tool dedicated to the proposition of type on a curve, but then I'll show you that you don't really even have to use that tool—it can be even easier.

To create type along the outline of a path, follow these simple steps.

1. **Draw a path.**

    Curved paths work better than those with sharp corners, so you'll probably want to avoid corner points and cusps, and stick with smooth points. Ellipses, spirals, and softly sloping paths work best. Grab the smooth tool if you need to smooth out a path.

2. **Select the path type tool.**

    To get to the path type tool, drag from the type tool in the toolbox to display a pop-up menu. The path type tool looks like a T on a slanted line, as shown in **Figure 11.2**. That's probably why some people call this "roller coaster text."

Figure 11.1: Path text as it
appears when selected
onscreen (top) and when
printed (bottom).

3.   Click the path and just start typing.

The point at which you click determines the position of the blinking
insertion marker. As you enter text from the keyboard, the characters
follow the contours of the path.

If your text appears on the underside of the path, or if no text appears
and all you see is a plus sign inside a little box, you need to flip the text
to the other side of the path. Select the arrow tool and double-click the
alignment handle, which looks like an I-beam attached to the path.
Then select the type tool and click the path to continue adding text.

4.   Complete the path text.

When you finish entering text, select another tool in the toolbox to
finish the text object. The path text appears selected, as in the first
example shown back in Figure 11.1.

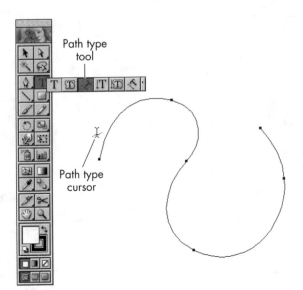

Figure 11.2: Select the path type tool, click a path, and start typing.

 If your path had a fill or stroke (covered in Chapters 15 and 16), they will instantly be removed as soon as you click with the path type tool. Adobe figures that most people don't want to see the path that the text is on. If you want to style the path, you need to select it with the direct selection tool and then apply the fill or stroke.

The Type Tool Anticipates Your Actions

I said it was easy, didn't I? But you don't even have to go to the trouble of selecting that path type tool to create path text. You may find it even easier to use the standard type tool. Why? Because as you bring the standard type tool close to an open path, the cursor changes to the path type cursor. If the path is a closed path, you need to press the Alt key (Option key on the Mac) to see the path type cursor. Without Alt (Option) pressed, the cursor would change to an area text cursor (which I'll discuss later in this chapter). **Figure 11.3** shows each of the text tools together with their cursors.

Figure 11.3: Each type tool displays its own unique cursor that indicates the kind of type tool that is active.

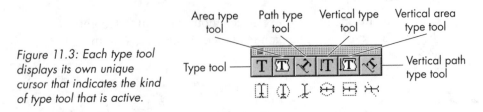

Like point text (covered in Chapter 10), path text is ill-suited to anything longer than a sentence. When a word extends past the end of an open path, it disappears from view like a ship sailing off the edge of the world. Long text simply wraps around and around a closed path, forcing words to overlap.

Once you have point text on a straight line, you can't convert that straight line into a curved path. To convert existing point text so that it runs along a new path, you have to copy the text, create an insertion point on a new path, and then paste the copied text.

Moving Type Along Its Path

When you click path text with the standard arrow tool, you select both the path and type at the same time. A special *alignment handle* appears, as labeled in **Figure 11.4**. This handle allows you to adjust the placement of the text on the path in any of the ways shown on the next page.

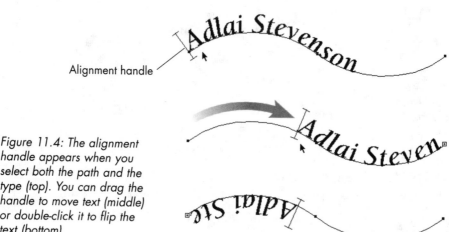

Alignment handle

Figure 11.4: The alignment handle appears when you select both the path and the type (top). You can drag the handle to move text (middle) or double-click it to flip the text (bottom).

- Drag the handle to slide the text back and forth along the path, as in the second example in the figure.

- Double-click the handle to flip the text to the other side of the path, as in the third example in Figure 11.4.

- Drag the handle to the other side of the path to move the text as you flip it in the opposite direction.

In addition to clicking with the arrow tool, you can also select both path and type by Alt-clicking (Option-clicking on the Mac) the path twice with the direct selection tool. Be sure to click the path itself. Don't try to click at the location where you expect the handle to be; it won't do you any good.

Reshaping a Path Right Under Its Text

When you create path text, you typically run into the same problems as when you enter words into a text block: you may run out of existing space, and need to create more. If the path is too short to accommodate all of its text, for example, a plus sign appears in a small box located on the last point in the path, as shown in **Figure 11.5**. In path text, Illustrator makes no distinction between a single word that can't fit and a sentence. Because path type can't wrap to a second line, it either fits on the path or it doesn't.

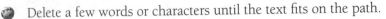

Figure 11.5: Overflow text prompts the boxed plus sign.

There are three choices for fixing text that overflows its path:

- Reduce the size of the type.
- Delete a few words or characters until the text fits on the path.
- Lengthen the path by reshaping it until all text is visible.

 If you know how to link text from one text block to another (covered later in this chapter), you may be tempted to try to do that with text from one path to another. Don't waste your time; unlike InDesign or FreeHand, Illustrator doesn't have that feature.

To lengthen a path with text on it, you can drag both segments and points with the direct selection tool in any way that you want. After each drag, the text refits to the path, so you can see your progress. Suppose, for example, that you want to lengthen the lower line shown in Figure 11.5. The following steps explain one way to do it:

1. Press Ctrl+Shift+A (Cmd-Shift-A on the Mac) or choose Select »
   Deselect to deselect the type. You must deselect the path text before
   you can select the path by itself.

2. Using the direct selection tool, click the path. This selects the path
   without selecting the type on the path. (Notice that the alignment handle I-beam isn't visible. This shows you that the text is not selected.)

3. Drag one of the endpoints to stretch the path, as shown at the top of
   Figure 11.6. The type immediately refits to the path, as shown in the
   bottom example.

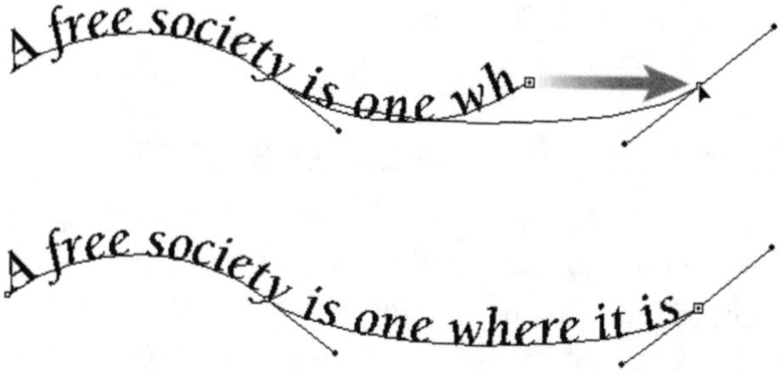

Figure 11.6: Drag the
endpoint of an open path
with the direct selection tool
(top) to stretch the path to
accommodate more text
(bottom).

 *If the curve needs adjusting, use the direct selection tool to drag down on
the segment or adjust the control handles.*

 *If you need to lengthen your path dramatically, you might prefer to add
points to the path using the pencil or pen tool. In **Figure 11.7**, for
example, I used the pen tool to add segments to the path. With each
additional segment, more text becomes visible, until eventually no overflow text remains. When the path is long enough to accommodate its text, the boxed plus
sign disappears, as **Figure 11.7** shows.*

In addition to editing a path with the direct selection tool, you can use the add
point, delete point, and convert point tools (as described in the "Operating on
Points after the Path Is Done" section of Chapter 6). However, you cannot modify
text paths with the erase tool or smooth tool. The next section explores one way
to use the add point tool.

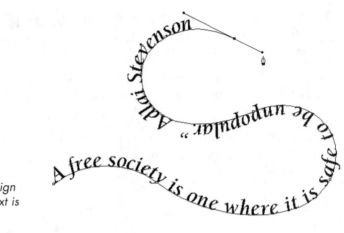

Figure 11.7: The plus sign goes away when all text is visible on the screen.

Trimming Away Excess Path

What if, rather than being too short, your path is too long? Certainly you can enlarge the type size, add words, or move points around to make the path shorter. But what if you simply want to trim a little slack off the end of the path?

Nope, you can't split it off with the scissors tool (covered in Chapter 7), because Illustrator won't let you split an open path with text on it. Instead, you can follow these steps:

1. Click with either the pen tool or the add point tool at the spot where you want the path to end, as shown in **Figure 11.8**.

Figure 11.8: Use the add point tool to insert a point at the location where you want the path to end.

2. Select all points beyond the newly inserted point with the direct selection tool, as shown in the top example in **Figure 11.9**. (But don't select the new point itself.)

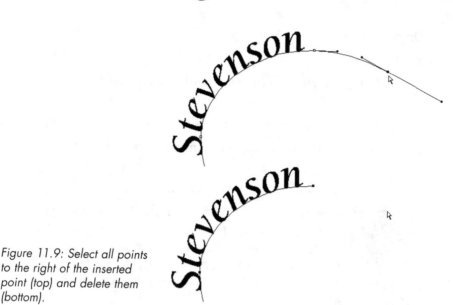

Figure 11.9: Select all points
to the right of the inserted
point (top) and delete them
(bottom).

3. Press the Backspace key (Delete key on the Mac). The selected points
and their segments disappear, making the inserted point the new endpoint.

Normally, you don't need to worry about excess path. By default, the path is
hidden when you're previewing or printing an illustration. Shortening a path
becomes an issue only if you want to stroke the path apart from its text, as
explained in Chapter 16.

Shifting Type in Relation to Its Path

Illustrator lets you raise and lower type with respect to its path using baseline
shift (introduced in the last chapter). The baseline of path text is the path itself,
so moving type away from the baseline likewise moves it away from the path.

As you may recall from Chapter 10, you can change the baseline shift by entering a value into the Baseline Shift option box in the Character palette or by holding Alt+Shift (Option-Shift on the Mac) and pressing either the up arrow or the
down arrow key. The keyboard shortcuts are generally the preferred method for
shifting the baseline.

The following steps demonstrate why baseline shift is useful. They show you
how to create text along the top and bottom halves of a circle—a job for baseline
shift if there ever was one.

1. **Draw a circle.**

   You know, Shift-drag with the ellipse tool.

2. **Alt-click (Option-click on the Mac) with the type tool at the top of the circle.**

   Illustrator snaps the alignment handle to the top center of the shape.

3. **Enter the text you want to appear along the top of the path.**

   I wanted to set up the William Allen White quote, "Peace without justice is tyranny." I started by entering "Peace without justice" across the top.

    Incidentally, in case you think I'm some kind of paragon who can spout off quotes from even bigger paragons in history, you might be interested to know that the quotes throughout the figures in this and the previous chapter come from Peter's Quotations (Bantam Books). And now I shall attempt to climb back onto my pedestal.

4. **Center the text.**

   Press Ctrl+Shift+C (Cmd-Shift-C on the Mac) or click the second icon in the Paragraph palette. As long as the alignment handle is positioned at the top of the shape, you can use Illustrator's alignment formatting functions to position text around the handle. It comes in handy when you want to get things exactly right.

5. **Format the text as desired.**

   Press Ctrl+A (Cmd-A on the Mac) to highlight the text, then format at will. I set this in 38-point Herculanum, an Adobe PostScript font that offers a collection of exclusively capital letters. (Quite frankly, text on a circle usually looks best in all caps.)

6. **Clone your text.**

   This is the most important step and one of the trickiest to pull off. First select the path text with the arrow tool. Then drag the alignment handle around the path to the bottom of the circle. Without releasing—don't release till I say so—drag upward so the type flips to the other side of the path. Then drag down ever so carefully until your cursor snaps onto the bottom point in the circle.

   Finally, press the Alt key (Option key on the Mac) and release the mouse button. (Yes, I say so now.) You can now release the Alt (Option) key. A clone of the type moves and flips to the interior of a cloned circle, as illustrated in **Figure 11.10**.

Figure 11.10: Alt-drag (Option-drag on the Mac) the type to the inside bottom portion of the circle. The hollow double cursor shows that you have snapped to a point and cloned both type and circle.

Snap and clone cursor

Quick: how many circles do you have on your page? If you said one, think again. Alt-dragging (Option-dragging on the Mac) made a clone of the circle as well as the type. You actually have two circles, one stacked on top of the other. The original circle has the text going in a clockwise direction. The clone has text that goes in a counterclockwise direction. That's how you know you must have two circles: text on a path cannot go in two directions at the same time.

7.   Edit the bottom type as desired.

Click inside the cloned text with the type tool, and press Ctrl+A (Cmd-A on the Mac) to select it. Then enter the words that you want to appear along the bottom of the circle.

8.   Shift the bottom text downward.

With your keen mind, you've undoubtedly noticed that the upper and lower text blocks don't align properly; you need to move the lower text outward without flipping it. While the text is still active, press Ctrl+A (Cmd-A on the Mac) to highlight the lower text block. Because you want to lower the type with respect to its path, press Alt+Shift+down arrow (Option-Shift-down arrow on the Mac) to move the type downward 2 points (assuming you haven't changed the Baseline Shift value in the Type & Auto Tracing Preferences dialog box). I pressed the down arrow combination seven times in a row to get the effect shown in **Figure 11.11**.

Figure 11.11: Press Alt+Shift+ down arrow (Option-Shift- down arrow on the Mac) several times to lower the text along the bottom of the circle.

9. Similarly, lower the text along the top of the circle.

Press Ctrl+Shift+A (Cmd-Shift-A on the Mac) to deselect the text. Then click in the upper text block with the type tool and press Ctrl+A (Cmd-A on the Mac) to highlight the first words you created. Press Alt+Shift+down arrow (Option-Shift-down arrow on the Mac) several times to lower the top text so it aligns with the bottom text. I pressed these keys eight times to arrive at **Figure 11.12**.

Figure 11.12: Highlight the upper text block and press Alt+Shift+down arrow (Option- shift-down arrow) several times to lower this text as well.

Just for laughs, **Figure 11.13** shows the final illustration as it appears when printed. I selected both circles by marqueeing around a segment with the arrow tool. Then I cloned the circle, reduced it to 70 percent, and rotated it 30 degrees. Over and over again. (Remember the trick we learned for doing this, back in Chapter 9?)

Figure 11.13: The finished text on a circle, repeated several times to create a tunnel-of-type effect.

Doing It All Again with Vertical Type

One of the functions meant to round out Illustrator's international savvy is the ability to add type to your illustrations that reads top to bottom and right to left, like Japanese script. Most of us may never encounter a situation in which we will need to add kanji or other Japanese characters to a drawing, but the same techniques required to add Japanese script give us additional choices for adding more familiar type.

I would like to take a moment to emphasize that by adding the new vertical type functions to a chapter titled "Some of Your Wackier Text Effects," I mean no disrespect. I include the description here because it just doesn't fit in Chapter 10. Most readers, if they choose to use vertical type, will incorporate it as a special effect and not for its designated purpose.

Because you already know how to create horizontal point type or add horizontal type to a path, you're only a couple of minutes away from creating vertical point type or adding vertical type to your artwork. To create vertical point type, just click and enter the text as shown in **Figure 11.14**. To add vertical type to a path, simply draw the path (either open or closed) that you want to use as your guide for the vertical type, and then select the vertical path type tool. Click the cursor over the path and enter the text.

If you work with vertical text often, hold the Shift key to turn any horizontal type tool into its vertical equivalent. Bring the cursor near an open path to get vertical text on the path. Or press and hold the Alt key (Option key on the Mac) to create vertical text on a closed path.

Vertical type tends to be hard to read without some adjustment. One of the reasons I used point text in Figure 11.14 was that it was easier to control. I also don't like to use a space between characters for these kinds of lines, because vertical text using Roman typefaces tends to create huge spaces between words, which need lots of cleanup. In Figure 11.14 I've shown what it looks like when I use a space between PHILA and PA and when I ran them together and kerned them out with a setting of 280.

Additionally, you can apply the Rotate or Tate Chu Yoko option to vertical path type. You'll find both of these options in the Direction pop-up menu that's part of the Character palette's Multilingual options—displayed when you choose the Show Multilingual command from the Character palette's pop-up menu. These options change the orientation of the text. They are especially useful when you apply them to individual words.

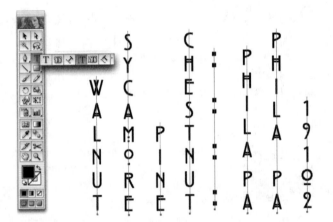

Figure 11.14: I Shift-clicked with the type tool to create each of the vertical point text paths and set a right alignment so that the text hung down from the end of the point text path. The first instance of "Phila PA" is the one I kerned; the one with a real space is just too big!

Getting that Irritating Alignment Handle off a Path

After you click a path with the type tool, Illustrator thinks you want to use the path to hold text for all time. Even if you delete all text from the path at some later date, the alignment handle will hang in there, reminding you that this is still path text. Here's how to remove the alignment handle.

1.   Select the path by Alt-clicking it (Option-clicking on the Mac) with the direct selection tool. Do not use the arrow tool.

2.   Press Ctrl+C (Cmd-C on the Mac) or choose Edit » Copy to copy the path to the Clipboard.

3.   Alt-click (Option-click on the Mac) the path again. This selects the text and displays the alignment handle.

4. Press the Backspace key (Delete key on the Mac) to destroy the path text for all time. (Don't worry, you've copied the path to the Clipboard, so it's safe.)

5. Press Ctrl+F (Cmd-F on the Mac) or choose Edit » Paste In Front. The path is reborn onscreen with no alignment handle. Stroke the path or fill it at will.

Filling a Shape with Text

When the folks at Adobe added type on a curve to version 3 back in 1991, they thought, "Forsooth, if artists want text *on* a curve, maybe they want text *inside* a curve as well." And after much sage nodding of heads, *area text* was born. In area text, type exists inside a path. A standard text block is a variety of area text—text inside a rectangle. But you can also create text inside polygons, stars, or free-form shapes. Heck, you can even create text inside an open path if you really want to.

To create type inside a path, goest thou thusly:

1. **Draw a path.**

   Unlike path text, area text works just as well with corner points as with smooth points. But keep the corners obtuse—wide rather than sharp. It's very difficult, and in many cases impossible, to fill sharp corners with text.

2. **Select the area type tool.**

   Select the area type tool from the type tool pop-up menu in the tool-box. The area type tool looks like a T trapped in Jell-O, as labeled in **Figure 11.15**.

3. **Click along the outline of the path and enter some text.**

   You must click the outline of the path; you can't click inside the path to add text (even if the path is filled and the Use Area Select check box is active in the General Preferences dialog box). A blinking insertion marker appears at the top of the path. As you enter text, it fills the path. Words that would otherwise exceed the edge of the shape wrap to the next line.

4. **Complete the path text.**

   Select the type tool, arrow tool, or some other tool to finish off the text block. You'll get something like the area text shown in **Figure 11.16**.

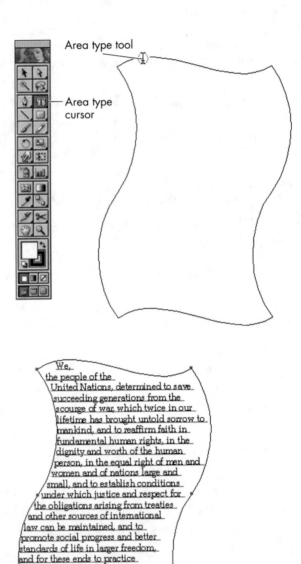

Area type tool

Area type
cursor

*Figure 11.15: Click the
outline of a path with the
area type tool.*

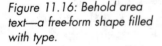

*Figure 11.16: Behold area
text—a free-form shape filled
with type.*

You can hold the Shift key to turn the area type tool into the vertical area type
tool. The only problem is that unless you are using a font designed for vertical
display, the resulting text is almost impossible to read. Not only do the words fill
the shape from top to bottom, but each successive line of text is placed to the left

of the previous one. You may find this ideal for adding columns of symbols or even columns of the same short phrase (repeated over and over) to a shape, but if you try filling a shape with more than one-liners, your audience will spend more time deciphering the text than reading it.

Flowing Text from One Shape to Another

If your text overflows the path or you simply don't like the way it wraps, you can edit the path with the direct selection tool. Press Ctrl+Shift+A (Cmd-Shift-A on the Mac) to deselect the text block, and then click the path with the direct selection tool and reshape at will. (Be careful not to click any of the baselines; that would select the entire block of area text.) As you reshape the path with the direct selection, add point, delete point, or convert point tools, Illustrator rewraps the text to fit inside the revised path outline.

You can also flow text from one area text block into another (something you can't do with point text or path text). This allows you to create multiple columns, or even multiple pages, of text. **Figure 11.17** shows several lines of text flowed between two paths. A single collection of paragraphs flowed over many text blocks is called a *story*.

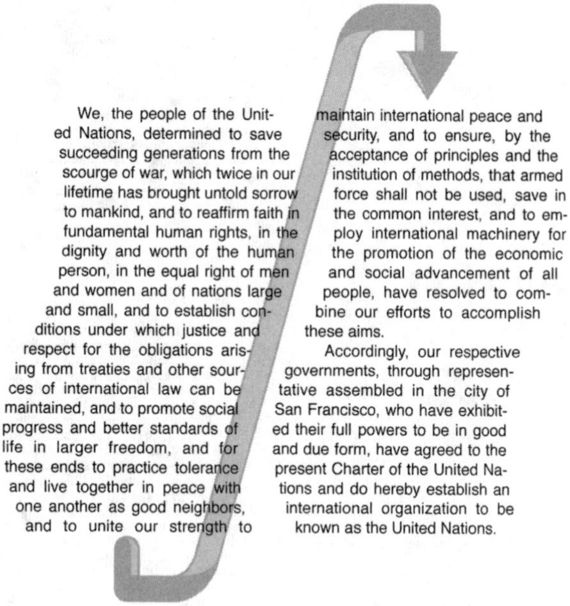

Figure 11.17: A single story flowed between two area text blocks.

We, the people of the United Nations, determined to save succeeding generations from the scourge of war, which twice in our lifetime has brought untold sorrow to mankind, and to reaffirm faith in fundamental human rights, in the dignity and worth of the human person, in the equal right of men and women and of nations large and small, and to establish conditions under which justice and respect for the obligations arising from treaties and other sources of international law can be maintained, and to promote social progress and better standards of life in larger freedom, and for these ends to practice tolerance and live together in peace with one another as good neighbors, and to unite our strength to maintain international peace and security, and to ensure, by the acceptance of principles and the institution of methods, that armed force shall not be used, save in the common interest, and to employ international machinery for the promotion of the economic and social advancement of all people, have resolved to combine our efforts to accomplish these aims.

Accordingly, our respective governments, through representative assembled in the city of San Francisco, who have exhibited their full powers to be in good and due form, have agreed to the present Charter of the United Nations and do hereby establish an international organization to be known as the United Nations.

To flow text from one block to another, you need to link the blocks. You can link text blocks in one of two ways. These techniques apply equally to area text and rectangular text blocks.

- **Use the Link Blocks command:** Select the path that contains the overflow text with the arrow tool. Then select one or more other paths (by Shift-clicking them) and choose Type » Blocks » Link. All selected paths fill with as much overflow type as will fit, as demonstrated in **Figure 11.18**.

 Illustrator fills the paths in the order in which they are stacked. This means if you select a path that lies behind the area text and choose Link Blocks, the beginning of the story shifts to the rear path and then continues in the forward one. If you don't like the order in which the text flows, read the section "Reflowing a Story," coming up shortly in this chapter.

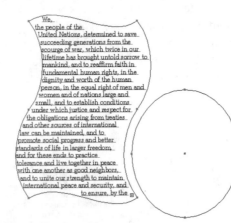

Figure 11.18: After selecting some area text and an empty path (top), choose Type » Blocks » Link to fill all selected paths with a single story (bottom).

Clone the path that contains the text: This method for flowing text is by far the simpler. After pressing Ctrl+Shift+A (Cmd-Shift-A on the Mac) to deselect everything, Alt-click (Option-click on the Mac) the text block outline with the direct selection tool. This selects the path without selecting the text inside. Next, drag the path to a new location, press the Alt key (Option key on the Mac), and release the mouse button. When you press the Alt (Option) key, you'll see the clone cursor, as shown in **Figure 11.19**, which indicates that Illustrator is prepared to duplicate the path. The cloned path automatically fills with the overflow type from the first path, as shown in the bottom example of Figure 11.19. The requirement here is that the second path be the same shape as the first.

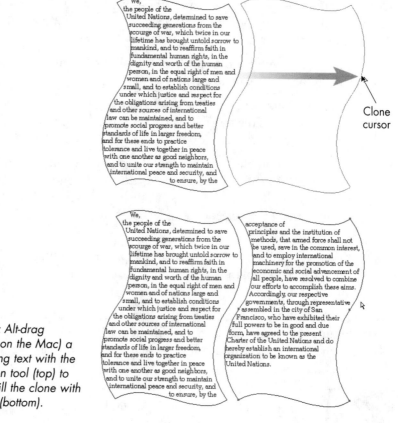

Figure 11.19: Alt-drag (Option-drag on the Mac) a path containing text with the direct selection tool (top) to clone it and fill the clone with overflow text (bottom).

If this new path also displays a boxed plus sign, still more overflow text exists. Choose Object » Transform » Transform Again or press Ctrl+D (Cmd-D on the Mac) to create another clone automatically. Illustrator creates a third path the same distance and direction from the second path as the second path is from the first. Keep choosing this command to add more columns.

The advantage of cloning a path to flow area text is that you never have to worry about text flowing in the wrong order. It always flows from the first path to the clone.

Selecting Linked Text Blocks

A collection of linked text blocks is a cohesive object, much like a group. You can select the entire story—all text and all paths—by merely clicking on any one of the paths with the arrow tool. But you can still access individual paths and text blocks with the direct selection tool as follows:

- Click a path with the direct selection tool to select a point or segment. Then reshape the path as desired.

- Alt-click (Option-click on the Mac) a path to select the entire path without selecting the text inside it. This is useful if you want to clone the path or change its stacking order (as explained in the next section).

- Alt-click (Option-click on the Mac) the path a second time to select the entire text block—both path and text—independently of other text blocks in the story. (Or you can click the baseline of any line of text with the direct selection tool.) Then you can drag the text block to move it.

- Alt-click (Option-click on the Mac) the path a third time with the direct selection tool to select the entire story, just as if you had clicked with the arrow tool.

You can also add and subtract elements from the selection by pressing the Shift key. For example, if you've selected an entire text block but you want to select only the path, Shift-click with the direct selection tool on a baseline in the text to deselect the text.

 Although you can select paths without the text, you cannot select text without also selecting the path. Just one of life's little inequities.

Reflowing a Story

A story flows from one text block to the next in the paths' stacking order, starting with the rearmost path and working forward. This is known as the *linking order*. In **Figure 11.20**, for example, the right path is the rear path, the middle path is the front path, and the left path is in between. Therefore, the story starts in the right path, flows into the left path, and ends in the middle path, despite the fact that the story started in the left path before I chose Type » Blocks » Link.

Next to back	Front	Back

| promote social progress and better standards of life in larger freedom, and for these ends to practice tolerance and live together in peace with one another as good neighbors, and to unite our strength to maintain international peace and security, and to ensure, by the acceptance of principles and the institution of methods, that armed force shall not be used, save in the common interest, and to employ international machinery for the promotion of the economic and social advancement of all people, have resolved to | combine our efforts to accomplish these aims. Accordingly, our respective governments, through representative assembled in the city of San Francisco, who have exhibited their full powers to be in good and due form, have agreed to the present Charter of the United Nations and do hereby establish an international organization to be known as the United Nations. | We, the people of the United Nations, determined to save succeeding generations from the scourge of war, which twice in our lifetime has brought untold sorrow to mankind, and to reaffirm faith in fundamental human rights, in the dignity and worth of the human person, in the equal right of men and women and of nations large and small, and to establish conditions under which justice and respect for the obligations arising from treaties and other sources of international law can be maintained, and to |

Figure 11.20: This story flows in the stacking order, from the rear shape on the right to the front shape in the middle.

To rearrange the order in which a story flows, you can change the paths' stacking order by using the following steps:

1. Deselect the story.

Press Ctrl+Shift+A (Cmd-Shift-A on the Mac), naturally.

2. Send the desired starting path to the back.

Using the direct selection tool, select the path that's supposed to be the first text block in the story. Then choose Object » Arrange » Send To Back, or press Ctrl+Shift+[(left bracket) or Cmd-Shift-[on the Mac. Illustrator automatically reflows the story so that it starts in the selected path.

3. Send the starting path and the next path to the back.

Shift-click the path that will represent the second text block. Then choose Object » Arrange » Send To Back, or press Ctrl+Shift-[(or Cmd-Shift-[) again. This sends both selected paths to the back, with the first path the rearmost path and the second path just in front of the first.

In case you're wondering, "Why do I have to send that path to the back again after I already sent it to the back?"—a very reasonable question—it's because you're trying to establish a stacking sequence. Illustrator doesn't have any single command that juggles multiple paths into a specific order, so you have to do it a little bit at a time.

4.   Send the starting path, the next path, and the one after that to the back.

Keep adding one path after another to the selection in sequential order and choose Object » Arrange » Send To Back after selecting each path.

 Obviously, you don't have to work in exactly this order. You can select the last text block and choose Object » Arrange » Bring To Front (Ctrl+Shift+])—that's a right bracket—or Cmd-Shift-] on the Mac) if you prefer.

Once you have text flowed into a story, you can delete the path (not the text) that holds the text. With no container to hold it, the text flows into the next available path. If there is no next path, the overflow symbol appears. You can delete the path that holds the text by Alt-clicking (Option-clicking on the Mac) on the path with the direct selection tool and then pressing the Backspace key (Delete key on the Mac).

Figure 11.21 demonstrates the effect of deleting the middle path from a story. Notice that Illustrator automatically flows the text from the middle path into the last path, whereas the text that used to be in the last path becomes overflow text. Therefore, deleting a path does not delete the text inside it; the text merely reflows. (This is why you can't delete a path if it's the only path in the story—there's no place for the overflow text to go.)

If you want to delete both path and text from the story, you can select both path and text before pressing Delete. As mentioned earlier, you can select a text block independently of others in a story by Alt-clicking (Option-clicking on the Mac) the path twice with the direct selection tool.

Unlinking Text Blocks

To unlink text blocks in a linked object, choose Type » Blocks » Unlink. This command isolates the paths so that each text block is its own story. You should use the Blocks » Unlink command only when you are happy with the way text appears in each column of type and you want to prevent it from reflowing under any circumstances.

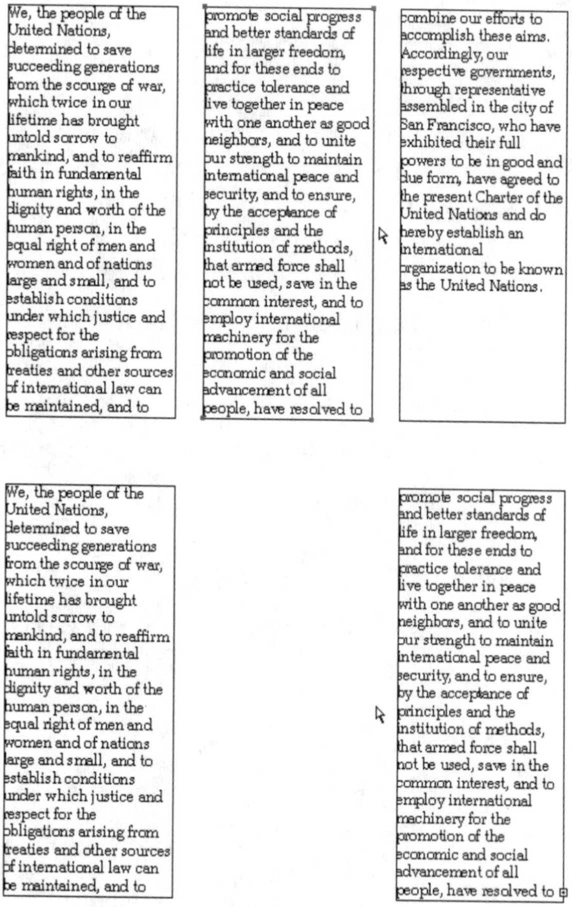

We, the people of the United Nations, determined to save succeeding generations from the scourge of war, which twice in our lifetime has brought untold sorrow to mankind, and to reaffirm faith in fundamental human rights, in the dignity and worth of the human person, in the equal right of men and women and of nations large and small, and to establish conditions under which justice and respect for the obligations arising from treaties and other sources of international law can be maintained, and to

promote social progress and better standards of life in larger freedom, and for these ends to practice tolerance and live together in peace with one another as good neighbors, and to unite our strength to maintain international peace and security, and to ensure, by the acceptance of principles and the institution of methods, that armed force shall not be used, save in the common interest, and to employ international machinery for the promotion of the economic and social advancement of all people, have resolved to

combine our efforts to accomplish these aims. Accordingly, our respective governments, through representative assembled in the city of San Francisco, who have exhibited their full powers to be in good and due form, have agreed to the present Charter of the United Nations and do hereby establish an international organization to be known as the United Nations.

We, the people of the United Nations, determined to save succeeding generations from the scourge of war, which twice in our lifetime has brought untold sorrow to mankind, and to reaffirm faith in fundamental human rights, in the dignity and worth of the human person, in the equal right of men and women and of nations large and small, and to establish conditions under which justice and respect for the obligations arising from treaties and other sources of international law can be maintained, and to

promote social progress and better standards of life in larger freedom, and for these ends to practice tolerance and live together in peace with one another as good neighbors, and to unite our strength to maintain international peace and security, and to ensure, by the acceptance of principles and the institution of methods, that armed force shall not be used, save in the common interest, and to employ international machinery for the promotion of the economic and social advancement of all people, have resolved to

Figure 11.21: Deleting the middle path (top) reflows the text into the last path (bottom).

*If your goal is to reflow type, do not start off by choosing Blocks »
Unlink, because this busts the text apart. Simply make your changes
with the direct selection tool and one of the commands from the Object »
Arrange submenu, as explained in the "Reflowing a Story" section.*

If you want to relink a story so that it bypasses one path and flows into another one, delete the path that you no longer need, select the new path, and then choose Type » Blocks » Link to redirect the flow. Again, do not choose the Blocks » Unlink command. (I know I keep repeating myself, but you just watch—you'll mess up and choose Blocks » Unlink one day, only to be mystified that it doesn't work the way you thought it would.)

Wrapping Type Around Graphics

All of you graphic-art-history buffs in the audience probably know that Illustrator was the first drawing program that allowed you to wrap text around graphics—previously the exclusive domain of page-layout programs such as PageMaker and QuarkXPress. This feature instructs Illustrator to wrap type automatically around the boundaries of one or more graphic objects, as illustrated in **Figure 11.22**.

Wrapping text around a graphic is a four-step process.

1.   Select the paths that you want to wrap the text around.

After selecting the paths with the arrow tool, choose Object » Group or Ctrl+G (Cmd-G on the Mac) to keep the paths together.

2.   Position the paths with respect to the text.

Drag the group into position, and then choose Object » Arrange » Bring To Front or Ctrl+Shift-] (Cmd-Shift-] on the Mac). The paths must be in front of the text block to wrap properly.

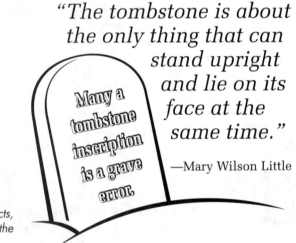

"The tombstone is about the only thing that can stand upright and lie on its face at the same time."

—Mary Wilson Little

Figure 11.22: Illustrator lets you wrap type around the boundaries of graphic objects, as in the text above and to the right of the tombstone.

3.   Select the text block that you want to wrap.

Shift-click the text block with the arrow tool to add it to the selection. Illustrator can wrap text blocks and area text around graphics, but it cannot wrap point text or path text.

4.   Wrap the text.

Choose Type » Wrap » Make, and Illustrator wraps the text around the graphics and fuses text and paths into a single wrapped object.

After this, you can select the entire wrapped object by clicking on it with the arrow tool or by Alt-clicking (Option-clicking on the Mac) one of the paths two or three times with the direct selection tool (depending on whether you wrap the text around a single path or multiple grouped paths). You can also reshape the paths with the direct selection tool. Illustrator constantly rewraps the text to compensate for your edits.

You can also modify the formatting for wrapped text by clicking or dragging inside the text with the type tool—or by Alt-clicking (Option-clicking on the Mac) the text blocks a few times with the direct selection tool—and adjusting the settings in the Character and Paragraph palettes. The two formatting attributes that you'll want to pay attention to are alignment and indentation.

- Select an alignment option from the Paragraph palette to change the way words align between the sides of the type column and the boundaries of the paths. For example, the quote in Figure 11.22 is flush left, but the name is centered.

- The indent values in the Paragraph palette determine the amount of room between the graphic and the text. The following section explores how you can use these options to their best advantage.

Adjusting the Standoff

In publishing circles, the *standoff* is the amount of space between a graphic and the text wrapped around it. In Illustrator, you can adjust the amount of standoff around a graphic object in two ways.

- **Increase the Indent values:** Adjust the Left and Right indentation values in the Paragraph palette. Illustrator treats the outlines of the graphic objects as additional sides to the text block. Therefore, the Left value increases the space along the right sides of the graphic objects, and the Right value adds space along the left edges. (It might sound like the opposite of how it should work, but it makes sense if you think about it for a while, as I had to; the Left value moves text to the right, and the Right value moves text to the left.)

  The first example of **Figure 11.23** shows justified text wrapped around a circle with all indentation values set to 0. As a result, the text touches the circle, an effect that is best summed up as *ugly*. In the second example, I selected the text blocks by Alt-clicking (Option-clicking) them three times with the direct selection tool. Then I increased the Left value to 18 points and the Right value to 9.

● **Create a special standoff dummy object:** You can also establish a standoff by creating a special path to act as a stunt-double for the actual graphic, a method that gives you better control, in my opinion. If you make both the fill and stroke transparent, the standoff dummy is invisible and the text appears to wrap around thin air.

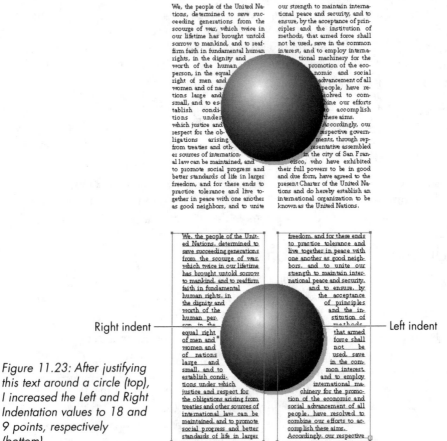

Right indent ——————

—— Left indent

Figure 11.23: After justifying this text around a circle (top), I increased the Left and Right Indentation values to 18 and 9 points, respectively (bottom).

The following steps explain how to create your very own standoff dummy. These steps assume that you've already wrapped text around a few graphics and that you aren't altogether pleased with its appearance.

1.   Create the dummy path.

I created the dummy shown in **Figure 11.24** with the regular polygon tool, and positioned it exactly by occasionally pressing the spacebar while drawing the shape. (As you may recall, the spacebar lets you move the shape while in the process of drawing it.)

2. Make the fill and stroke transparent.

In the bottom portion of the toolbox, click the Fill icon to bring it in front of the Stroke icon, and then select the None icon or press the forward slash (/) key. If necessary, you can also click the Stroke icon (or press the X key) and select the None icon. (Chapter 14 covers the color controls in extreme depth.) Part Four of this book covers the Paint Style controls of the toolbox in extreme depth.)

3. Cut the path to the Clipboard.

Choose Edit » Cut or press Ctrl+X (Cmd-X on the Mac).

4. Select the original wrapped graphic object(s).

Alt-click (Option-click) a path inside the wrapped object with the direct selection tool.

5. Choose Edit » Paste In Back.

Or press Ctrl+B (Cmd-B on the Mac). Because you used the direct selection tool to select the graphic object in Step 4, Illustrator pastes the dummy path between the object and the text block, making the dummy path part of the wrapped object.

6. Press the up arrow key, and then press the down arrow key.

Illustrator will wrap the text around the dummy path.

I used these steps to create the standoff shown in Figure 11.24. The dummy polygon is selected in the figure for display purposes; if it were not selected, it would be invisible. To see the dummy path, you can switch to the outline mode by pressing Ctrl+Y (Cmd-Y on the Mac).

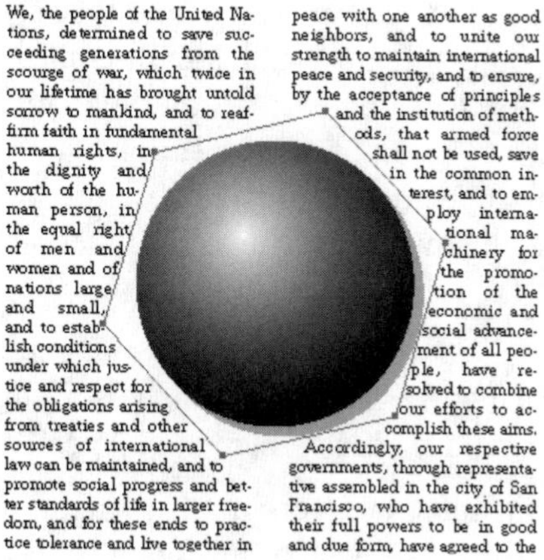

Figure 11.24: The unfilled, unstroked polygon serves as a dummy path, creating a standoff that is not only larger than the circle but differently shaped as well.

We, the people of the United Nations, determined to save succeeding generations from the scourge of war, which twice in our lifetime has brought untold sorrow to mankind, and to reaffirm faith in fundamental human rights, in the dignity and worth of the human person, in the equal right of men and women and of nations large and small, and to establish conditions under which justice and respect for the obligations arising from treaties and other sources of international law can be maintained, and to promote social progress and better standards of life in larger freedom, and for these ends to practice tolerance and live together in peace with one another as good neighbors, and to unite our strength to maintain international peace and security, and to ensure, by the acceptance of principles and the institution of methods, that armed force shall not be used, save in the common interest, and to employ international machinery for the promotion of the economic and social advancement of all people, have resolved to combine our efforts to accomplish these aims.

Accordingly, our respective governments, through representatives assembled in the city of San Francisco, who have exhibited their full powers to be in good and due form, have agreed to the

Importing and Exporting Text

Despite Illustrator's crack text capabilities, you should find it easier to use a word processing program to edit text and apply formatting attributes. You can also export text from Illustrator into these same word processing file formats. Doing so allows you to recover and work with text that has been laid out in an Illustrator document, and even lets you transfer it to a mightier layout program such as QuarkXPress.

Preparing Your Text for Import

When importing a text file, Illustrator reads the file from disk and copies it to the illustration window. As this copy is being made, the text file passes through a filter that converts the file's formatting commands into formatting commands recognized by Illustrator. Illustrator lets you import text in the following formats:

- Microsoft Word 97, 98, 2000
- RTF (Rich Text Format), Microsoft's tagged file format
- Plain text with no formatting whatsoever, also known as ASCII (pronounced ask-ee)

The following list describes how Illustrator handles a few prevailing formatting attributes and offers a few suggestions for preparing each.

- **Typeface:** If Illustrator can't find the typeface in your system—if the document was created on another machine, for example—it substitutes the default font, Myriad.

- **Type style:** Illustrator does not apply electronic styles the way word processors do. As a result, bold and italic styles convert successfully, but most others do not. If Illustrator comes across a style for which a stylized font does not exist—underline, outline, strikethrough, small caps, and so on—the program simply ignores the style. The happy exceptions are superscript and subscript styles, which transfer intact thanks to Illustrator's baseline shift function.

- **Type size and leading:** All text retains the same size and leading specified in the word processor. If you assign automatic leading or single spacing inside the word processor, Illustrator substitutes its own automatic leading, which is 120 percent of the type size.

- **Alignment:** Illustrator recognizes paragraphs that are aligned left, center, and right, as well as justified text.

- **Paragraph returns:** Illustrator successfully reads paragraph return characters, which you create by pressing the Enter key (Return key on the Mac).

- **Indents:** All paragraph indents, including first-line, left, and right indents remain intact. (Hanging indents won't look quite right, because Illustrator doesn't import tab stops.) Adjusting the margins in your word processor may also affect indentation in Illustrator. To clear the indents, adjust the individual indent settings in Illustrator's Paragraph palette.

- **Paragraph spacing:** Some word processors divide paragraph spacing into two categories: "before spacing," which precedes the paragraph, and "after spacing," which follows the paragraph. Illustrator combines them into the Space Before Paragraph value in the Paragraph palette, essentially retaining the same effect. (Separate before and after paragraph spacing settings are useful only when a program offers style sheets, which Illustrator does not.)

- **Tabs, tab stops, and tab leaders:** Illustrator imports tab characters successfully. But it ignores the placement of tab stops, and tab leaders (such as dots and dashes) are a complete mystery to the program. Use the Tabs palette Ctrl+Shift+T or (Cmd-Shift-T on the Mac) to reset the tab stops as desired.

 Many word processors provide access to special characters that are not part of the standard "low ASCII" character set, including em spaces, nonbreaking hyphens, and other "high ASCII" characters. Not all of these transfer successfully, although the discretionary hyphen character does. You can create or access the discretionary hyphen character within Illustrator by pressing Ctrl+Shift+-hyphen (-) (Cmd-Shift-hyphen (-) on the Mac).

- **Page markings:** Illustrator ignores page breaks in imported text as well as headers, footers, and footnotes.

If you can't find a formatting option in this list, chances are Illustrator simply ignores it.

Importing Text

You can import text into any kind of text object. But because point text and path text are so badly suited to long stories—path text doesn't even support carriage returns or tabs—you'll most likely want to import stories into area text blocks.

To import a story into a bunch of text blocks, follow these steps.

1. **Create your first text block.**

   Select the type tool and click the outline of a closed path. Or drag with the type tool to create a new text block. If you want to append an imported story inside a text block that you've already started, click at the point inside the text where you want to insert the story.

2. **Choose File » Place.**

   This displays the Place dialog box, which looks just like a standard Open dialog box.

3. **Locate the text file on disk and open it.**

   If you can't find the file, but you know it's there, select All Formats from the Files of type pop-up menu at the bottom of the dialog box. (In Mac OS 10.1 it is called All Documents from the Show pop-up menu at the top of the dialog box; in System 9 it is called All Documents from the Show pop-up menu and is at the bottom of the dialog box.) This shows you all formats that Illustrator supports. If that doesn't work, Illustrator doesn't recognize the file; go back to your word processor and try saving it in a different format.

   After you locate your file in the scrolling list, double-click it or select the filename and press Enter (Return on the Mac). After a few moments, Illustrator displays the imported text inside the text block.

4. **Flow the text into additional paths.**

   Unless your text file contains less than a paragraph of text, Illustrator probably won't be able to fit all the text into a single block. You can enlarge the path by reshaping it with the direct selection tool. But more likely, you'll want to flow the text into additional paths as explained in the previous section, "Flowing Text from One Shape to Another."

Exporting Text to a Text File

Illustrator's Export command lets you export text from Illustrator as plain text.

Use the type tool to select one or more characters from any kind of text object. Or you can select the text container with the arrow tool. You can export a single letter or an entire story. To select all of the text—even if you can't see all of it onscreen—you can click inside the block with the type tool and press Ctrl+A (Cmd-A on the Mac.)

Choose File » Export. This displays the Export dialog box, which looks just like the standard Save dialog box. Select Text (TXT) as the file type and name your file. Press Enter (Return on the Mac) when everything's ready to go. Illustrator exports the selected text to disk as instructed.

Checking Your Spelling

When I was in school, I couldn't see the importance of learning how to spell everything correctly and laughed at the spelling-bee set. Later, licking the wounds of embarrassment over jobs done not quite thoroughly enough, I suffered a small amount of regret. Then I got over it; after all, now there are spelling checkers at your fingertips, and I have been shamed into relying on them.

Spelling checkers are so prevalent, in fact, that even Illustrator offers one. (No cracks here, please, about artists and spelling!) Without the help of an outside application, Illustrator can transform the sentence, "Teh dich rann awai wyth theh sponn," to something that English-speaking humans might find recognizable.

1. **Choose Type » Check Spelling.**

Because Illustrator automatically checks the spelling of all text, hidden or visible, in your drawing, you don't have to select any text. Illustrator sets about revealing your mistakes. If Illustrator doesn't locate any words missing from its dictionary, it displays an ego-stroking message about your excellent spelling. If the program finds mistakes, it lists all mistakes throughout the entire document in the Misspelled Words list at the top of the Check Spelling dialog box, as in **Figure 11.25**.

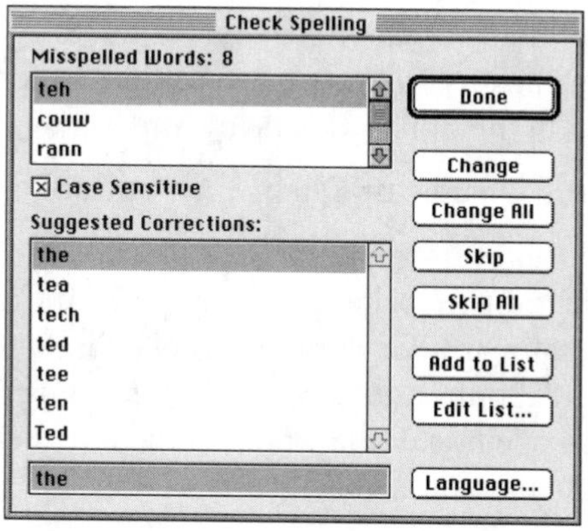

Figure 11.25: Illustrator finds all spelling mistakes in one pass so that you can examine and correct them in any order you please.

2.   Select all words that are spelled properly.

Scroll through the Misspelled Words list to see which words are truly misspelled and which words Illustrator is simply too inexperienced in the ways of the world to know. If a word is spelled to your satisfaction, you can either add it to Illustrator's dictionary or simply skip the word for the time being.

To select all the words that are spelled correctly, Shift-click the first and then the last word in a group of words to select all of them; or Ctrl-click (Cmd-click on the Mac) to add one word at a time to the selection (or to remove words one at a time from the selection).

3.   Click the Add to List, Skip, or Skip All button.

This adds the selected words to Illustrator's auxiliary dictionary, so that the program will never again bug you about the spelling. (Don't worry if you add a word that you didn't intend to; you can always delete it later by clicking the Edit List button.)

If you'd rather ignore the words for the time being, click the Skip button. Click Skip All to tell Illustrator to ignore all occurrences of these particular words.

4.   Select a word that's misspelled.

To correct a word that is indeed misspelled, select it from the Misspelled Words list. Illustrator highlights the first occurrence of the word in the story and displays a few alternative spellings in the Suggested Corrections list.

5.   Select the proper spelling.

If one of the alternative spellings in the Suggested Corrections list is correct, click it. If none of the spellings is correct, enter the new spelling in the option box below the list.

6.   Click the Change or Change All button.

Or you can press the Enter key (Return key on the Mac) or double-click the proper spelling in the Suggested Corrections list. If you know that many words are misspelled in the same way, click the Change All button to correct all misspellings at once. Illustrator corrects the spelling of the words in the illustration window and moves on to the next misspelled word.

7. **End the spell checking.**

After you tell Illustrator to either add, skip, or change every word in the Misspelled Words list, an alert box tells you it's finished. If you want to cut things off early, click the Done button, press the Esc key, or press Ctrl+. (the period character) (Cmd-. on the Mac).

After you enter a proper spelling in the option box below the Suggested Corrections list, you may wonder how you can add the new spelling to Illustrator's auxiliary dictionary. If you click the Add to List button, Illustrator adds the word from the Misspelled Words list, not the correctly spelled word you entered in the option box. To add a new spelling to the dictionary, you must first apply the new spelling to the illustration window, then close the Check Spelling dialog box, and again choose Type » Check Spelling.

To edit the auxiliary dictionary—whether during this or some other session—you choose Type » Check Spelling and click the Edit List button. Illustrator displays the Learned Words dialog box shown in **Figure 11.26**. Here you can select a word and delete it by clicking the Remove button; change the spelling of the word by replacing a few characters and clicking Change; or create a variation on a spelling by clicking Add.

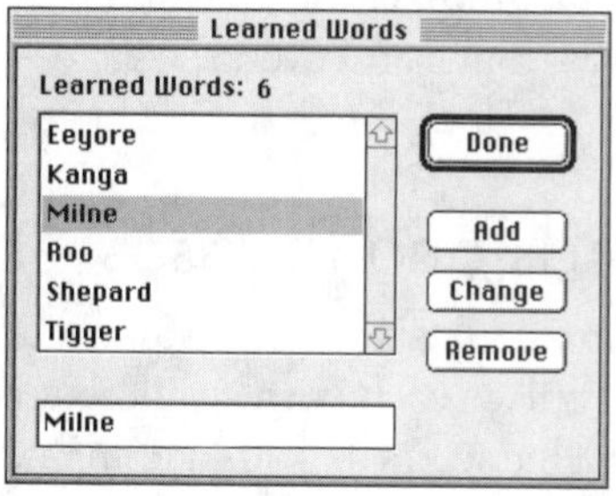

Figure 11.26: You can review the words that you've added to the dictionary from the Learned Words dialog box.

 Illustrator saves the auxiliary dictionary to disk in the Text Filters folder inside the Plug-ins folder. This means you can take the dictionary from one machine and copy it to another to maintain a consistent auxiliary dictionary. Although you can open the dictionary in Notepad (TextEdit on the Mac), don't do it. Illustrator uses a bunch of special characters in the file; mess them up, and you can damage your dictionary for good.

Last but not least, two final options in the Check Spelling dialog box.

● The Case Sensitive check box lets you correct words depending on whether they're capitalized or not. For example, you might want to change *wol* to *owl*, but add *Wol* to the dictionary (because that's the owl's proper name).

The Language button lets you add a dictionary for a different language, such as U.K. English. You must open the appropriate dictionary from disk. Look for the files in the Text Filters folder inside the Plug-ins folder.

The Check Spelling command is a wonderful feature. Even if your illustration doesn't contain much text, you'd be surprised how often you will find a misspelled word. And, of course, the fewer words there are in your illustration, the more the mistake will stand out. I'm sure you can all fill in your favorite typo horror story here. Choosing Type » Check Spelling takes only a moment and is always worth your time.

Check Spelling cannot fix everything you refused to study in grade school or have since forgotten. They're his know weigh two fined miss steaks wen their reel wards.

Searching for and Replacing Stuff

Another of Illustrator's amazing features is its ability to automatically search for bits of text and replace them with other bits of text. For example, you can search and replace characters, words, fonts, and even special design characters. The following features are absolute gems. Don't forget they're here; they can save you a lot of time.

Replacing Words and Phrases

The Find/Change command lets you locate all occurrences of a particular collection of characters and replace each with a different collection of characters. You can search for as many characters as you like, including spaces.

1. **Click with the type tool on the location where you want to begin the search.**

   If you have selected the arrow tool, for example, Illustrator searches all stories throughout the entire drawing, from beginning to end. But if you want to limit your search to a specific area of a story, click in the story with the type tool. By default, Illustrator searches forward from the insertion marker; it does not search the text before the insertion marker. (You can reverse the direction of the search by selecting the Search Backward check box.)

2. **Choose Type » Find/Change.**

   Illustrator brings up the Find/Change dialog box, pictured in **Figure 11.27**.

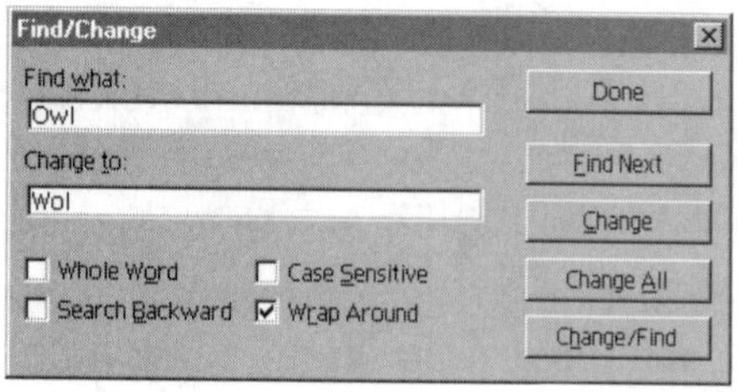

Figure 11.27: Use the
Find/Change dialog box to
search for some text and
replace that text with some
other text.

Find/Change ☒

Find <u>w</u>hat:
`Owl`

Change <u>t</u>o:
`Wol`

☐ Whole W<u>o</u>rd   ☐ Case <u>S</u>ensitive
☐ Search <u>B</u>ackward   ☑ W<u>r</u>ap Around

Done
<u>F</u>ind Next
<u>C</u>hange
Change <u>A</u>ll
C<u>h</u>ange/Find

3. Enter the text you want to find and the text you want to replace it with.

Enter the search text in the Find What option box, press Tab, and then enter the replacement text in the Change To option box. If you don't want to replace the text—you're just trying to find it—don't enter anything in the Change To option box.

4. Click the Find Next button.

Or press Enter (Return on the Mac). Illustrator highlights the first occurrence of the word in the illustration window.

5. Replace the word and move on.

Click the Change button to replace the selected text. Or click the Change/Find button to replace the text and then look for the next occurrence of the Find What text. (If it finds no more occurrences of the Find What text, Illustrator callously beeps at you.) Or click Change All to replace all Find What text with the contents of the Change To option box.

6. When you're finished, click the Done button.

Or press Ctrl+. (Cmd-. on the Mac) or the Esc key. (That is Ctrl or Cmd plus the "period" character.)

You can modify your search by turning on or off the following check boxes in the middle of the dialog box:

🌐 **Whole Word:** When you check this option, you limit the search to whole words that exactly match the Find What text. With this option unchecked, for example, searching for *owl* would cause Illustrator to find the characters inside growl and cowlick. With Whole Word checked, the word *owl* must appear by itself.

- **Case Sensitive:** Select this check box to search for characters that exactly match the uppercase and lowercase characters in the Find What text. Searching for *Owl* would find neither *owl* nor *OWL* when this option is selected.

- **Search Backward:** This option begins the search at the insertion marker and proceeds backward toward the beginning of the story.

- **Wrap Around:** To search the entire illustration, no matter where the insertion marker is currently located, select Wrap Around. This option begins the search at the insertion marker and proceeds to the end of the story, starts over at the next story, starts again at the beginning of the first story, and winds up back at the insertion marker.

Neither Search Backward nor Wrap Around is of any use when the arrow tool is selected, because Illustrator automatically searches all text in the illustration.

 Type » Find/Change gets confused if you have hidden text. Illustrator will highlight the text, but because it is hidden, you can't see what Illustrator has found. Make sure all text is visible before you start a Find/Change.

Replacing One Font with Another

You can choose Type » Find Font to launch another of Illustrator's amazing search functions. This time, instead of replacing words, Illustrator lets you search for one font and replace it with another.

Why would you want to do that? Imagine, for example, that you created an illustration a couple of years back using the font Geneva. You throw fancier parties now. Shouldn't you have a tonier typeface, too? So you want to replace all occurrences of this font with a different one that you like better. Here's how you'd proceed.

1. **Choose Type » Find Font.**

   The Find Font dialog box leaps into view, as shown in **Figure 11.28.**

2. **Select the font that you want to remove from the Fonts in Document list.**

   Illustrator highlights each occurrence of the font in the illustration window.

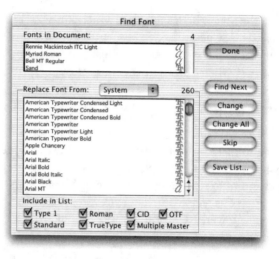

Figure 11.28: You can replace one or more occurrences of a font with a different font from the Find Font dialog box.

3. Select the substitute font from the Replace Font From list.

Initially, this list contains only the names of those fonts that are used in the current illustration. If you want to choose from a wider variety of fonts, choose the System command from the Replace Font From pop-up menu, which instructs Illustrator to list every font loaded on your system.

 You can pause the font listing by clicking anywhere on an empty portion of the dialog box. To start the listing again, turn on and off one of the check boxes at the bottom of the dialog, or switch between the pop-up menu commands.

4. Click Change or one of the other buttons.

The Change button replaces the first occurrence of the bad font and searches for the next. To change all occurrences of the font simultaneously, click the Change All button. If you're feeling a little more selective, you can opt not to change the found font and click the Find Next button (or just select the font name again) to ignore that occurrence of a font and move on to the next. The Skip button performs the exact same function as the Find Next button.

5. Click the Done button when you're finished.

Or press Enter (Return on the Mac), Esc, or Ctrl+. (Cmd-. on the Mac).

Use the check boxes to select which kinds of fonts you want to be displayed in the two lists. Click the Save List button to save a list of the fonts used in your document to a text file. This font list is handy for a service bureau or a commercial printer when you want them to output or print your work.

Automatic Character Changes

There are two more typographic commands in the search-and-replace arsenal just waiting to make your life easier: Change Case and Smart Punctuation, both located —where else?—on the Type menu. Both of these are designed to let you make broad and quick decisions about the appearance and consistency of your type.

Change Case lets you change lowercase text to initial caps or all caps, change all caps to lowercase or initial caps, or make some other variation in case. Here's how to do it.

1.   Select the text you want to change. For example, perhaps you want to change some text you entered after accidentally pressing the Caps Lock key.

2.   Choose Type » Change Case.

3.   Select the desired option. In this case, select the Lower Case radio button (which really ought to be one word).

4.   Press Enter (Return on the Mac), or click OK.

The Change Case command is so simple, a sightless tree frog could use it. Type » Smart Punctuation is a slightly more complicated command. This command searches for all "dumb" punctuation in your document—straight quotes, double hyphens, double spaces after periods—and replaces them with their more acceptable and better-looking "smart" equivalents—curly quotes, en dashes, and single spaces after periods.

Select the characters you want to change with the type tool, and then choose Type » Smart Punctuation to display the Smart Punctuation dialog box shown in **Figure 11.29.** Select the check boxes representing the kinds of punctuation you want to change, and press the Enter key (Return key on the Mac), or click OK.

Three of the checkboxes—the two Ligatures and Expert Fractions— require that a so-called Expert Collection font be on hand. The Expert Collection is a set of Adobe typefaces, each of which contains a second alphabet of special typographic symbols, including small caps, ligatures (two characters joined into one), and fractions. If you are doing a lot of work with fractions or ligatures, you should invest in the expert versions of your typefaces.

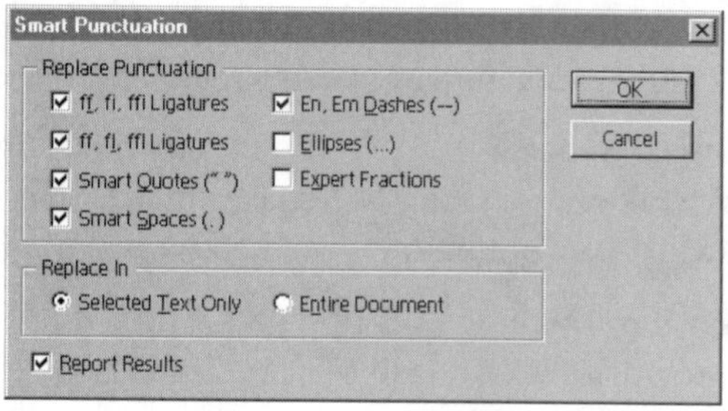

Figure 11.29: Use the options
in the Smart Punctuation
dialog box to convert various
characters in your illustration
to more design-acceptable
characters.

Very quickly, let's look at each option.

ff, fi, ffi Ligatures: If a font comes with an Expert Collection, this
option replaces ff, fi, and ffi with their respective ligatures. In **Figure
11.30**, for example, I set several words in Adobe Caslon (after having
loaded the Adobe Caslon Expert Collection). When I selected this check
box and clicked OK, Illustrator replaced the black letters in *affable*,
fickle, and *difficult* with their equivalent, single-character ligatures from
the Expert Collection. If the Expert Collection font hadn't been installed
on my system, Illustrator would have replaced the *fi* with the ligature
that is built into PostScript fonts. But the nonexpert version doesn't
have an *ff* ligature, so that pair of letters wouldn't have been replaced.

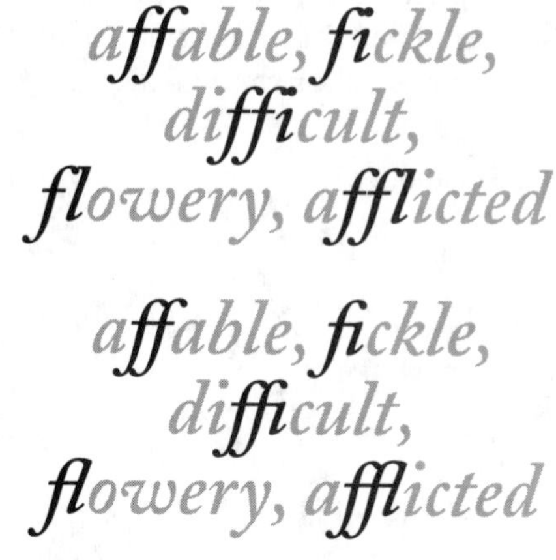

*affable, fickle,
difficult,
flowery, afflicted*

Figure 11.30: After entering a
few words in Adobe Caslon
(top), I applied the Smart
Punctuation command to
convert the ligatures (in black)
to the single-character
equivalents from the Expert
Collection font (bottom).

*affable, fickle,
difficult,
flowery, afflicted*

ff, fl, ffl Ligatures: What's wrong here? That's right, the *ff* ligature is
repeated unnecessarily in this option. But whatever the name of the
option, it was responsible for replacing the black letters in *flowery* and
afflicted in Figure 11.30. (It would have also taken care of the *ff* in
affable, but the previous option got to it first.) If no Expert Collection
font is available, Illustrator replaces the *fl* in *flowery* and *afflicted* with
the *fl* ligature available to most fonts.

● **Smart Quotes:** This option turns straight quotes (") into curly ones (" and ") and straight apostrophes (') into curly ones (').

● **Smart Spaces:** In typesetting, you enter only one space after a period. Why? Because using two spaces makes a big gap in the text and looks awful. This option fixes the bad habits that follow imported text.

● **En, Em Dashes:** This option is a little off. It replaces two hyphens in a row with an en dash (–), and three hyphens with an em dash (—). The problem is, most folks who don't use real em dashes in the first place use double-hyphens as a substitute. I've never seen anyone use triple hyphens. So even if you use this option, you're still going to have to go in and clean up your text manually.

● **Ellipses:** This option replaces three periods (...) with the special ellipsis symbol (…). Use the ellipsis symbol to get better spacing.

● **Expert Fractions:** Every Adobe typeface includes three fraction characters, 1/4, 1/2, and 3/4. But thanks to the way Apple structured the extended character set, these characters are available only to Illustrator users on the Windows platform. To see them, press (with your NumLock key on) Alt+0188, Alt+0189, and Alt+0190. So Adobe built fractions into the Expert Collections, which include fractions in 1/3 increments. **Figure 11.31** shows three fractions created with the standard slash symbol and set in the font Apollo and the single-character versions from the Apollo Expert Collection.

Figure 11.31: I created three fractions using the standard slash symbol (top) and then used the Smart Punctuation command to replace them with designer fractions from the Expert Collection font (bottom).

$$1/2...3/4...7/8$$

$$\frac{1}{2} \cdots \frac{3}{4} \cdots \frac{7}{8}$$

If you don't have access to an Expert Collection font, build your own fractions as explained in the "Raising and Lowering Characters" section of Chapter 10.

Select the Report Results check box if you want Illustrator to present you with an alert box after it's smartened up your document. The alert box lists the variety and quantity of each dumb punctuation that has been replaced.

Select the Entire Document radio button to search and replace characters throughout the illustration, whether selected with the type tool or not. I prefer to keep this option set to Selected Text Only—which requires you to select text with the type tool—because that way, I know exactly what Illustrator is up to.

Creating Rows and Columns

As you saw earlier, it is possible to clone text blocks so that they form columns. The problem with that method is that you have to do a lot of math if you want to make sure the width of all the columns fits a certain area. The Rows & Columns command lets you create a single text block that fills the area and then divide it into rows (horizontal dividers) or columns (vertical dividers). For example, **Figure 11.32** shows a single text block in the background that was instantly divided into three columns.

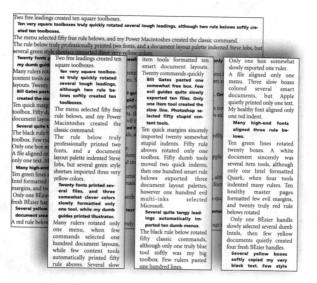

Figure 11.32: The Rows & Columns command makes it easy to divide an existing block of text into three blocks evenly spaced.

The Rows & Columns Command

Simply select the text block that you want to divide, and choose Type » Rows & Columns. This opens the Rows & Columns dialog box as shown in **Figure 11.33**. Use the option boxes or arrows to set how the text block should be divided.

Whenever possible, Illustrator tries to maintain consistent values in the Number, Height, Width, and Total option boxes. This means if you make a change to the Column Width value, Illustrator adjusts the Column Gutter value—rather than the Number or Total value—to compensate. Bigger column width, smaller gutter, and vice versa.

Click the Text Flow icons to change the order in which text flows through the columns and rows—that is, from left to right and then top to bottom, or from top to bottom and then left to right. The Add Guides check box creates horizontal and vertical lines that are the entire width and height of your page—useful for establishing grids.

As long as the Preview option is checked, Illustrator continually updates the selected text block as you make changes.

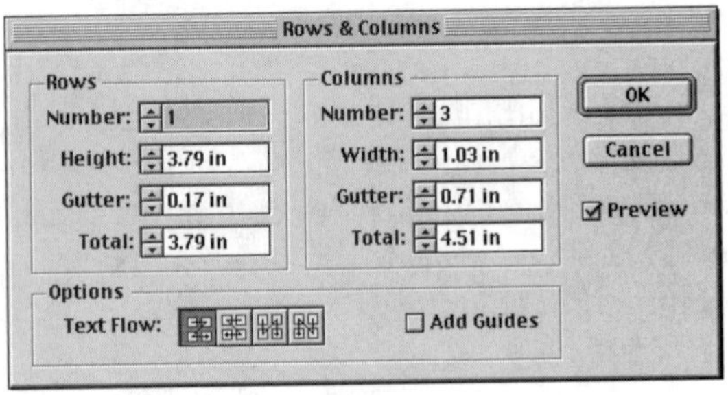

Figure 11.33: You can divide a text block into multiple rows and columns using the options inside this dialog box.

Using Rows & Columns on Objects

You don't have to limit yourself to text blocks with the Rows & Columns command. As **Figure 11.34** shows, even an ordinary rectangle can be divided easily into rows and columns along with guides. This is much easier than duplicating and positioning little boxes all over the page.

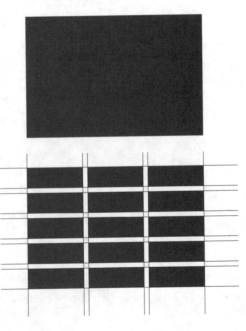

Figure 11.34: When applied to ordinary rectangles, Rows & Columns can create an instant grid.

Fitting Text on the Fly

Only two more commands left in the Type menu—Fit Headline and Create Outlines. The first shrinks or stretches a line of type to fit the width of a column, and the second converts character outlines to paths, as I discuss in the next section.

The Fit Headline command modifies a line of text to make it fill the entire width of a text block. The top two examples in **Figure 11.35** show what happens when you apply the Fit Headline command to a line of type. In the first example, the single word Monkey is too narrow to fit the width of the column. When I chose Type » Fit Headline, Illustrator added sufficient kerning to the letters to stretch them across the text block. In the second example, the two-word paragraph is too wide to fit. Fit Headline reduced the kerning of these characters to make them fit.

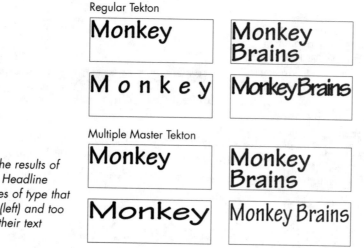

Figure 11.35: The results of applying the Fit Headline command to lines of type that are too narrow (left) and too wide (right) for their text blocks.

To use this command, click in the paragraph you want to shrink or stretch with the type tool and choose Type » Fit Headline. You can apply the command only after selecting the text with the type tool—clicking inside the paragraph will do this—and the paragraph must be set inside a text block or area text.

But let's be honest. You could have kerned the text yourself by pressing Alt (Option on the Mac) and the left or right arrow key. And you wouldn't have kerned Monkey Brains to the point that the characters overlapped, as they do in the second example in the figure. That's just plain ugly.

Fit Headline was actually designed to work with Multiple Master fonts, which are special PostScript fonts designed by Adobe. These special typefaces can be modified so they become heavier or lighter right before your very eyes. If you have a Multiple Master font such as MM Tekton, you can see how the Fit Headline command creates a much better-looking result.

 Unfortunately, the Multiple Master typefaces have never caught on with designers and Adobe phased out support for the technology.

   Provided that you are using a Multiple Master typeface in your drawing and it's selected, you can use the MM Design palette to generate stylistic variations. Choose Window » Type » MM Design to open the palette, as shown in **Figure 11.36**. Adjust the slider bars to modify the weight, width, and other attributes. (The specific sliders available depend on the selected font.) After you get an effect you like, click OK. Illustrator adds the variation to the font menu of every application you run from now on.

Figure 11.36: You can vary a Multiple Master font in Illustrator using the MM Design palette. I dragged mine onto the Character palette so they could share a panel and save some space.

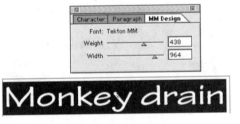

 Check with your service bureau or the print shop that will be printing your document to make sure they can handle the Multiple Master fonts. Just remember that it's not great design if you can't print it.

Converting Character Outlines to Paths

The outlining capability in Illustrator is both its most essential and straightforward feature. By choosing Type » Create Outlines or Ctrl+Shift+O (Cmd-Shift-O on the Mac)—that's the letter O, not a zero—you can convert any selected text block into a collection of editable paths, composed of points and sections (see **Figure 11.37**). The only catch is that the type must be selected with the arrow tool—you can't highlight it with the type tool. You may also right-click (or Control-click on the Mac) and choose Create Outlines, but this works only if the type was selected with the arrow tool. This will seem but a small inconvenience when you see how quickly and powerfully the command performs.

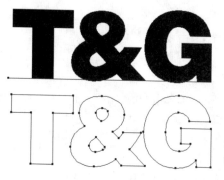

Figure 11.37: Select a text block (top) and choose Type » Create Outlines to produce a collection of fully editable points and segments (bottom).

The top example in Figure 11.37 shows a three-character text block selected using the arrow tool. The bottom example shows the characters after choosing the Create Outlines command. The characters are now standard paths, composed of points and segments, just like those created with the pencil or pen tool.

Of the three characters in the figure, notice that Illustrator has converted the T and G into a single path apiece, whereas it converted the ampersand into three paths. To make interior paths transparent, like those in the ampersand, Illustrator converts each character into a compound path. In this way, it lets you see through the holes in the character to the objects behind it (as discussed in Chapter 7).

Compound paths are all very well and good, but they can also get in your way. If you later try to join part of a path in the ampersand to another path, for example, or you want to pour text into an outline as I did back in Figures 11.15 and 11.16, Illustrator will refuse to participate, claiming that the two paths have to be part of the same group.

If you encounter something along these lines, select the character with the arrow tool and choose Object » Compound Path » Release or Ctrl+Alt+8 (Cmd-Option-8 on the Mac). The transparent areas will fill with color, but you'll be able to edit the paths with absolute freedom.

After you choose the Create Outlines and Release commands, you can reshape, transform, duplicate, and otherwise manipulate converted type in any manner, as demonstrated by the fantastic example in **Figure 11.38**. It may not be art, but by golly, it's possible.

Figure 11.38: And to think, this was once Helvetica.

It's frequently a good idea to convert logos and headline text to paths, once you know the text is final, even if you don't plan to manipulate them. By doing so, you'll eliminate the chance that the text will shift or the font won't print correctly. Watch out, though—the text may seem to get a little thicker when you convert it to outlines. This is because the hinting that was built into the font will be lost. Ordinarily there will be no problem with converted text, but at very small point sizes (below 6 or 7 points) you may see some of the thickening. Make sure you have a backup of the text in case the converted outlines are a problem.

If you want to reserve the right to edit the text from the keyboard, save one copy of the illustration prior to choosing Type » Create Outlines, and save another copy afterward.

SYMBOLIC ACTS

Everyone thinks that being a graphic illustrator is a cushy, exciting job. Everyone, that is, except maybe the poor souls who sit long into the night, creating the repetitive elements of would-be epic images and swilling coffee. In the movies, if they need a lot of people or a lot of trees, they hire extras or shoot in the woods. When you're making it all up on your computer, obviously you have neither Central Casting nor the Forestry Service at your fingertips. Not until now, anyway. Illustrator's symbolism tools can be your own personal (or corporate) quantity and diversity provider.

The symbolism tools make short work of creating variations on any image of your choosing. Symbols are stored objects that you can use over and over. The suite of symbolism tools runs the gamut of getting the images onto the page and then easily adjusting and randomizing their placement, size, orientation, color, and even style. The friendly Symbols palette shows you what symbols you have available and provides an interface for choosing which one, or ones, to work with at any time. It also performs a lot of other administrative duties as well.

Even after they've been spun, shrunk, styled, and otherwise permutated, the symbols are all still connected to the prototype stored object, which means your file size doesn't have to balloon because of the army of images you have in it. A feature like this, at once timesaving and size-conscious, is like a health food that tastes like dessert.

Lots of great design ideas involve an amount of repetition that makes you feel, well, uncreative. If you suffer from this, or from the degradation and mind-numbing boredom that comes with having to re-re-re-create bits and pieces of a big picture, this chapter is for you.

What Are Symbols, and Why Do I Need Them?

Almost anything can be a symbol, which is really nothing more than a piece of artwork stored in the Symbols palette (and therefore subject to the rules and benefits thereof). Paths, shapes, pretty much any art you create in Illustrator can be a symbol. Or even artwork you place in Illustrator, as long as it's embedded, but let's not get too carried away here! Once you make something into a symbol, you can place it on the page however many times you want, either in single *instances* (that's a term you'll be hearing bandied about quite a bit with symbols) or en masse; more on those techniques later.

In case you haven't seen the big advantage of this yet, think of the amount of work involved in duplicating objects and placing them with deliberately casual artful randomness. Or the tedium of varying those objects to make them look less like drones and clones. Or the frustration (or worse) when you have to start all over because of one silly little problem in your original.

The big news here, apart from liberating you from eternal copy and paste, is that however many times you use a symbol in a document, and however many modifications you make to its instances (more on those modifications later, too), they're all referred back to the official symbol when it comes time to render the drawing. Even better, you can revise or modify any symbol as needed, and all of its instances in the document will update automatically. And I don't have to tell you how much space and time that can save you.

You can think of symbols as lending libraries or collections: browse them and borrow from them all you want, and be confident they'll be there for you when you need them again.

 One final word about why you need symbols. It's often human nature to resist taking the perceived extra time to set up a helpful, timesaving device, when you really just want to get on with the job. So you plow ahead. But it always takes longer to backtrack and redo. By the time you've made the argument that you don't have time to set up symbols (or styles, or actions, or any other organizational miracle of the computer world), you could have done it already. So do it, and I don't want to hear any excuses.

Creating Instances

This is the meat and potatoes (or tofu and rice if you prefer) of using symbols, so I'll dig into it first and talk about the options later. You can lay symbols on your page in single instances or in groups.

Creating Single Instances

There are three ways to create a single instance of a symbol.

 Select a symbol in the Symbols palette and click the Place Symbol Instance icon at the bottom of the palette.

 Select a symbol in the Symbols palette and choose Place Symbol Instance from the palette's pop-up menu.

 Drag the symbol from the palette onto your artboard.

Whichever way you do it, the result will look like **Figure 12.1**.

Figure 12.1: One lone instance, newly minted. Notice that the base symbol is still selected in the Symbols palette.

If your work (or play) bids you to frequently repeat certain images, this can save you a great deal of time in and of itself. Creating floor plans is a good example of a task that can benefit from the use of symbols: the actual wall locators and footprints may vary, but floor plans always have walls, windows, sinks, and other repeated elements that you know you're going to need to put down.

 Once you've got an instance on the page, you can use the good old Alt-click (Option-click on the Mac) method of duplicating an object. This also creates perfectly legitimate instances.

Creating Symbol Sets

But, of course, there are times when you're working with a broader palette and need more images to get your message across. That's when you take the symbol sprayer tool (leftmost, and default, icon in the symbolism tools slot in the toolbox) and let multiple instances, or groups, of a symbol populate your page with as many fish, buckets, people, cupcakes, or whatever that you might ever want. The aptly named symbol sprayer lets you dispense instances in amounts and densities that are governed by the values you select in the Symbolism Tool Options dialog box, which I'll discuss later. The groups of instances that the symbol sprayer creates are called *sets*.

Just drag with the symbol sprayer tool as you would a line tool or a brush, which is essentially what it's acting like right now (and how I will most often refer to it). You may go a little crazy at first, since it's fun to watch the figures marching along and multiplying like crazy. **Figure 12.2** catches the symbol sprayer tool in the act.

The default size of the symbol sprayer cursor is l-a-r-g-e, large! This does not affect the size of the symbol itself, but rather has to do with the range within which the tool has an effect. This becomes more important when you're using the other symbolism tools, but even now, when you're doing a simple act of creation, the swath of the tool has its purpose: let the cursor pause for a moment in one place (with your mouse button held down) and see how the area of the brush radius begins to fill up with symbols, as opposed to the stringy series of symbols that gets created as you simply drag the cursor along.

So far, so good. But sets are dynamic works-in-progress, not at all as static as you might think. You can continue to add other symbols to them, either more of your original selection or any others of your choosing. (You can do a lot of other things to it, as well, as I'll discuss later in this chapter.)

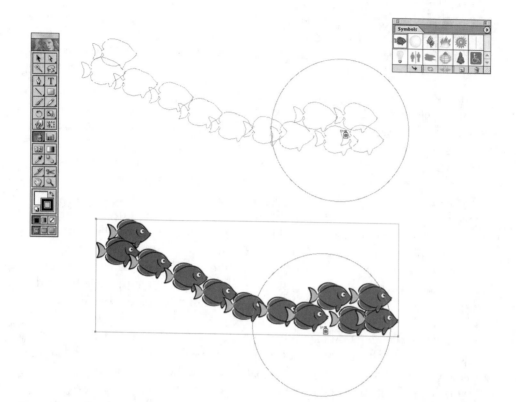

Figure 12.2: Here, I've just let fly with the symbol sprayer (top) with the intention of creating my own little aquarium (bottom). Notice how the symbols themselves bear little relation to the radius of the tool.

If you change your mind and want to break a set into individual instances, choose Object » Expand. This will make each instance stand alone, all in the same relative location to each other as they were in the set. To further break up the symbols, choose Object » Ungroup. Each instance is still a symbol instance and will respond accordingly.

Adding Symbols to an Existing Set

To add instances of a symbol to an already existing set, just make sure the set and the desired symbol in the Symbols palette are selected. You'll know the set's selected because you'll see its bounding box as, which extends out as far as the symbols have been sprayed. Then activate your sprayer and paint the images wherever your design dictates. When you spray while a set is selected, the new instances become a part of the existing set.

You can't drag an individual instance into an existing set. To add a single instance into a set, use the symbol sprayer tool and click really fast! Or make sure the density setting in the Symbolism Tool Options dialog box is set very low.

Adding symbols to a set works whether you're adding more of the same symbol or any new symbol. And this is my first opportunity to tell you to be sure to keep an eye on what's selected in the Symbols palette, because whatever's selected is what's going to get added. This process takes a little while to get used to, with several items to attend to all at once: you need to be sure that the set itself is selected, the right tool is selected, and the right symbol is selected.

So is it better to keep your symbols in separate sets or in a grouped set? This is a personal decision, of course, and will vary depending on your design needs. A good reason to clump mixed symbols in a set is if you want to use the symbolism tools to help them appear more integrated (or, just to apply similar settings to all of them). For example, if you're working on an image of two different forms of wildlife in a single habitat, it'll be easier to make them look natural together and to experiment with overlaps and such if the tools can work on the two elements simultaneously.

On the other hand, if you have a feeling that some particular element of your image may have to change, or it's not supposed to be completely integrated and overlapped with other elements in the image anyway, then you may be better off keeping them in separate sets. Let's say you're setting up a dance scene with a hundred characters in a cancan line at Radio City Music Hall. The act may prove so successful that you might like to follow it up with an encore by another set of characters. Then it might make sense to keep those objects in their own set. You could even keep the feather boas, high heels, and any other finery in a separate one that gets used for both casts.

You can also use the symbol sprayer as an anti-sprayer to delete items from a set. To do this, just hold down the Alt key (Option key on the Mac) and click and drag as you normally would; this action will erase within the range of the cursor as you go. I think this anti-sprayer mode should be called the symbol sucker—or would that be symbol slurper?

Alt-clicking (Option-clicking) with the symbol sprayer will erase only whatever symbol types are currently selected in the Symbols palette.

Modifying Instances with the Symbolism Tools

I've said that a great power of the symbolism tools is their ability to create endless variations. Now that you've gotten acquainted with the basic mechanics of getting the symbols on the page, you've got the raw materials for making those kinds of changes yourself. And so, without further ado, I'll introduce you to the rest of the symbolism tools (pictured in **Figure 12.3**), which will be your guides in the land of modification.

I'll describe the tools and their functions here and go into some detail about their options in the "The Symbolism Control Room" section. The relationship between these tools and their dialog box is more interconnected and interactive than with some other tools in Illustrator, and you'll soon see why.

First, the most general description of all: what do these tools do? With the exception of the symbol sprayer tool, the symbolism tools *modify* rather than create. So they don't really stand alone, but play supporting (but vital) roles in the process of creating interesting and dynamic symbol sets. Illustrator is kind enough to give you a polite message if you try to use the tools improperly, so you won't waste much time trying to figure out what you're doing wrong.

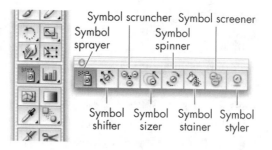

Figure 12.3: The happy family of symbolism tools. What would they have done if they ran out of s-words?

The modification tools will perform their magic on instances or sets of symbols that are selected on the page (or artboard). There are two other factors that determine which symbols will get altered: which symbols are selected in the Symbols palette and which symbols fall within the diameter of the current tool's cursor or brush.

You can select, and therefore modify, multiple symbols from the palette at one time. To select contiguous symbols, click the first and then Shift-click the last. To select noncontiguous symbols, add to your initial selection by Ctrl-clicking (Cmd-clicking on the Mac) on subsequent boxes.

Finally, I'll introduce you to each individual tool.

- **Symbol sprayer tool:** As you already know from pages ago, the symbol sprayer tool is the starting point for the wide range of activities you'll encounter with the symbolism tools. So you already know to populate your page with symbol sets.

  Although this is a fairly straightforward tool, the cursor of the symbol sprayer can be a little bit confusing. By default, it's a huge circle. The important thing to know is that the circumference of the cursor (or brush, as it's acting like one) doesn't affect the size of the symbols being sprayed.

  The options in the Symbolism Tool Options dialog box help you define and refine the behavior of the sprayer and of the symbols it's laying down; I'll go through those in more detail later in "The Symbolism Control Room."

 To increase or decrease your brush size as you're working (assuming it's visible), press the right or left square bracket keys, respectively.

  One thing to note: when you are creating a single instance of a symbol (by dragging it off the palette or using the Place Symbol Instance command), you are not using the symbol sprayer. So any options you've set up for the sprayer will not take effect. Single instances placed in either of those manners come in with all of their default values (orientation, color, and so on) intact.

- **Symbol shifter tool:** Yes, as you can imagine, you use this tool to move things around within a set. Just drag the cursor in the direction you want things to move; the instances will follow in more or less the direction of the cursor's movement (with a certain amount of adjustment for the laws of cyberphysics). You can use this method to bunch the symbols up or to move them apart.

  You can shift one type of symbol within a set or as many as you choose to select. When you select multiple symbols and start shifting them around, I think it looks kind of like a junior high school dance.

  In addition to shooing things around like a big flyswatter, the symbol shifter tool can also change the stacking order of symbols within a set. You can Shift-click an instance to bring it forward, Shift+Alt-click (Shift-Option-click on the Mac) to send it backward.

Symbol scruncher tool: Really, I almost feel like these names are so self-describing as to put me out of business! Yes, this tool just pulls symbols closer together or pushes them farther apart toward or away from the position of your cursor.

Clicking or dragging with the tool pulls instances closer together; Alt-clicking (Option-clicking on the Mac) moves them farther away from each other. Click and hold your mouse and watch the symbols scurry!

How is this different from shifting, you ask? They both move symbols around, but the shifter waits for your mouse to go somewhere and then follows the mouse's action (this usually amounts to being pushed around as if with a broom), whereas the scruncher acts more like a magnet, pulling in (or repelling) symbols even when the held-down mouse rests in one place.

All right, then (you ask), how is this different from the Symbol Set Density setting in the dialog box? Good question. Ultimately, they perform what appears to be the same function (though there is a bug in the Symbol Set Density option that makes it change settings at inexplicable times). If you find the controls of one to be more fathomable than the other, use it.

 Symbol sizer tool: Basically, this is your in-house scale tool. Clicking and dragging makes things bigger; Alt-clicking (Option-clicking on the Mac) makes them smaller.

 If you thought one of these tools worked one way yesterday and it just isn't working that way today and it's driving you crazy, take a deep breath and make sure you're looking at the right tool's options in the dialog box and that you haven't changed the options inadvertently. Remember, there are a lot of them, and any of the settings (particularly the Method setting) could really make a difference.

 Symbol spinner tool: This tool rotates the instances that are within the confines of the brush diameter (more intensely at the actual center point of the cursor). This is one of those tools where the Method selection makes a big difference. The Average method, for example, might look as if it's doing almost nothing, but it may be making very subtle shifts. The User Defined method, of course, responds to your mouse, and so can make for a lot of variation.

In addition to being able to change the size of the brush while you're working with any tool, most of the tools can perform different functions, or amounts or intensities of functions, by the addition of keyboard commands to your mousing. As you activate any given symbolism tool from within the Symbolism Tool Options dialog box, you will see in the lower panel any customized actions that tool may perform, along with keyboard modifiers.

Symbol stainer tool: This is Color Central for symbols. This tool uses the document's current tint color as a base for changing the hue of the symbol. The higher the luminosity of the symbol, the less change you'll see—with the logical extreme being that there will be no change in black or white symbols. This tool really hits home showing how easily you can make the symbols appear to be almost completely different images from each other—yet, of course, still all be connected to the same root symbol system. How cool is that?

This works most predictably, of course, on solid-color symbols, but it's not an exclusive property; it works fine on multicolored objects as well. I like the outcome of staining a symbol that has a graduated fill.

If you want to change the colors of black or white objects, use the symbol styler tool.

Remember, you can perform an action such as staining on multiple symbols in a set simultaneously by making sure the symbols are all selected in the Symbols palette.

If you want to apply your personal choice of colors to symbols right off the bat, change the symbol sprayer's Stain option (in the Symbolism Tool Options dialog box) to User Defined and set your colors in Illustrator's toolbox. And if you want that to be a permanent choice, modify and redefine your symbol (or a copy of it).

Symbol screener tool: This tool makes the object(s) more or less transparent. The usual clicking or dragging (or clicking and holding) will increase the transparency; Alt-clicking (Option-clicking on the Mac) will decrease it.

In my quest for ultimate variety in an image, I have been wishing for a symbol switcher tool—one that changes the direction of the image. Until I see that one wrapped up and beribboned, I'll include a reflection (any maybe some other transformations) within a style and apply that to instances in my symbol set.

Symbol styler tool: This tool applies styles from your Styles palette to selected symbols. This is another potentially huge timesaver and, taken in moderation, could make for some great effects. Taken in excess, it can make for some truly monstrous ones. But isn't that always the case? With freedom (to design) comes responsibility (to design responsibly).

To control the styling of your symbols gradually, choose the tool first and then the desired style from the palette. Click or drag to begin painting in the style. Alt-click (Option-click on the Mac) to take away some of the style you've already applied. Shift-click or Shift-drag to morph the instance's style from its original one to the new one while keeping the amount, or saturation, of the style unchanged.

Figure 12.4 shows how this might look. (Hint: you have to start with some amount of style to get anywhere with this.) This one's a bit tricky, but if you like the idea of the effect, I'm sure it'd be worth the trouble.

Figure 12.4: From left to right, for comparison: original tree, tree with a style applied full-on, tree with one click's worth of the symbol styler tool, and tree with one click of the styler tool followed by Shift-clicking to increase the presence, but not the saturation level, of the style.

It almost goes without saying that some styles are better suited to some symbols than others, or at least will affect them differently, based on the fills, strokes, and effects of either.

You might be wondering, "Why would I bother with applying a style to a symbol? I can apply a style to any old object." True, but the symbol styler is a user-driven tool that lets you control the amount and location of the application, which is a lot different from the all-or-nothing nature of a regular application of a style.

 To apply a symbol to a whole set or instance at full strength (i.e., no controls added), don't select the symbol styler tool; just make sure the set is selected and then choose the style from the Styles palette.

 Once you've made a symbol style change, the style will usually become deselected in the Styles palette. But it's still active, so you can go on about your styling business without having to reselect it repeatedly.

The Symbolism Control Room

Symbolism Tool Options is sort of a Brave New Dialog Box. It's got a healthy combination of controls for attributes shared by all of the tools, plus controls specific to each of the sundry symbolism tools. You can switch easily among options for any of the tools (no clicking "Next" over and over again) and set them all in one session if you like, or just jump in and make specific changes. As you can see in **Figure 12.5**, it's definitely not just for show.

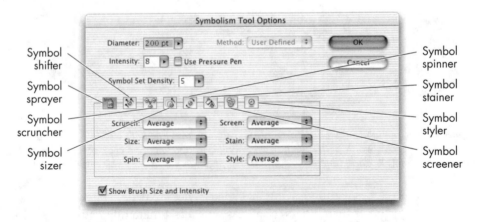

Figure 12.5: The big, new Symbolism Tool Options dialog box.

Whatever tool and settings are active when you click OK here will become your active tool and settings, regardless of what you were doing when you decided to jump in. Similarly, if you select a symbol set on the page and then look in the dialog box, it will reflect the settings of that selected set. This may seem fairly basic, but in as conglomerated a dialog box as this, it bears repeating (purely on humanitarian grounds) that sometimes you may forget why you are seeing certain settings when you didn't think those were the ones you should be seeing.

The Communal Options

Foremost in the dialog box are the components shared by all the tools.

- **Diameter:** This is for setting brush size. Understand that this doesn't change the size of the symbol—that's a *different* tool—just the size of the brush itself. This becomes important when you're using the other symbolism tools; typically, the actions of those tools affect, or affect proportionately, the relevant instances within the scope or range of the brush.

  Not to speak out of turn here, but the Show Brush Size and Intensity option at the bottom of the dialog box lets you see (or hide) the outline of the brush size as you're working. You can turn this option off if you find the huge swath of the brush too distracting, but remember that you sometimes need it for modifications, as I mentioned above.

   If you find that you often need the big brush but it also bothers you, use your left bracket ([) and right bracket (]) keys to decrease or increase the size as you're working with the tool. This works with all of the symbolism tools.

- **Intensity:** This controls what I would call the density of the symbols being sprayed, but since that term has been taken, I'll say it's like controlling the flow of the sprayer; the higher the number, the stronger and faster the flow. Set the intensity high, choose the bubble symbol from the default palette, and hold down your mouse for a while in one place to see how Intensity works—it'll remind you of blowing bubbles into your milk with a straw when you were a kid. But now it's not so messy, and you don't get in trouble.

- **Use Pressure Pen:** If you use a tablet or a stylus, you can use this option to turn control over to that device instead of the Intensity setting.

🌑 **Symbol Set Density:** This controls how individual objects in a set
relate to each other. Adobe uses the term "attraction value," and
indeed this setting does act a bit magnetic. It pushes together or
forces apart the same number of symbols in a set based on the value
you use, actually contracting or expanding the perimeter of the set.
It's a blanket setting—you can't apply density to a partial set; it's all or
nothing at all.

To see this feature working, select a set with the arrow tool and then
double-click on any symbolism tool to bring up the Symbolism Tool
Options dialog box. Move the dialog box on the screen, if necessary,
to see your set, and then start changing the number. Not only will
you see the symbols move, but you'll also see that the bounding box
adjusts its size to accommodate the new "footprint" of the set.

 *A couple of minor snafus to look out for: The Symbol Set
Density option does not always work quite as expected; don't
be too surprised or frustrated if it goes off and creates sets at
a density other than the one you specified as a default. Also,
if you're looking for the dialog box option Preview Bounding Boxes of Symbol
Instances that you may have seen in the product documentation, stop looking
—it's not there.*

Methods for Individual Tools

You can opt for different methods in which the various tools perform their
appointed tasks. They can apply to the symbols using the Average, User Defined,
or (sometimes) Random methods. *Method* is the umbrella term used for describ-
ing this subfunction of the symbolism tools. As always, I'll start with the symbol
sprayer tool, since it's first, most basic, and in this case, the most confusing.

Attachments for the Symbol Sprayer

When the symbol sprayer is selected in the dialog box, the Method drop-down
menu (top right) is dimmed, but the bottom half of the dialog box has options
available for scrunching, sizing, spinning, screening, staining, and styling, as you
can see in Figure 12.5. Huh? Aren't we supposed to choose the little icons for setting individual tool options? The answer is yes, but these six little drop-down
menus are settings that go with the symbol sprayer tool itself. That means that as
I am placing symbols onto the page, I can further fashion them, even as I spray,
by using these options. For example, if you set the Spin and the Stain choices
both to User Defined, then the symbols will actually orient themselves according
to the direction of your mouse, and the color(s) of the symbol will be based on

the current fill and stroke colors in the document. There are only two choices on each drop-down menu for these sprayer-specific methods of applying effects:

- **Average** uses the average values of symbols already within the brush radius. This is generally not going to do much when you're spraying and should be considered the "Normal" style of the symbolism world.

- **User Defined** is the more interactive of the two choices. It looks to current settings of other tools and defaults, follows the mouse, and otherwise provides more customizing than does Average.

One Sizer Fits All

The symbol sizer is the only other symbolism tool with its very own options, as shown in **Figure 12.6**. And it's a good thing they're there; without these controls, you could end up with skewed, strained, screwy, struggling, sorry-looking images.

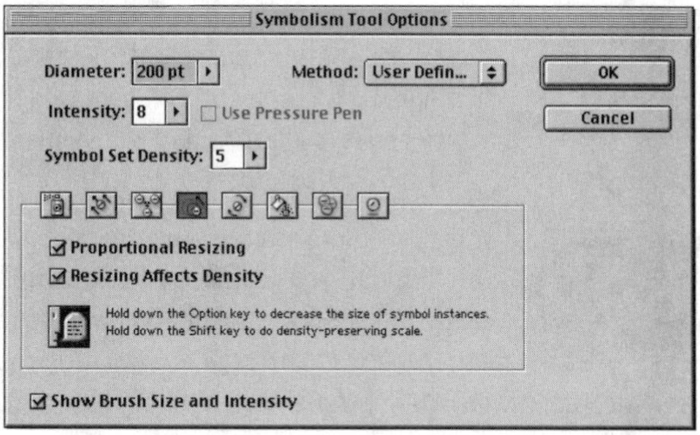

Figure 12.6: The symbol sizer's options keep your symbols from becoming distorted as you resize them.

- **Proportional Resizing** makes the changes relative to each other; if you uncheck it, you can make one instance look like a giant or a Lilliputian in contrast to the others.

- **Resizing Affects Density** controls the space between objects.

Long story short on these options: keep them both checked if you want to keep the whole set looking "normal," or basically unchanged except in size.

Method for the Masses

When any tool other than the symbol sprayer or symbol shifter is selected within the dialog box, the Method drop-down menu for that tool becomes available, as do other tool-specific options (in the case of the symbol sizer) and shortcuts. For each of these remaining six tools, you can choose among three methods of application.

- **Average** is for making smooth changes in the amount of the effect based on its surrounding instances.

- **User Defined** allows you to apply an effect somewhat gradually using the cursor as a nudge or sometimes a cudgel.

- **Random** is what it is—put your design in the hands of fate.

Once again, these effects are mostly going to take place within the confines of the brush radius. I say *mostly* because it's pretty much supposed to work within those confines, but there are times when it will go beyond. For example, if you click and hold your symbol scruncher cursor in the midst of a far-flung flock of symbols, even the ones on the outskirts, beyond the reach of the cursor, may eventually respond to the pull.

When you change a tool's Method option, that selection becomes active for all of the other tools at that time and stays the default option for new sessions with the tools as well. In other words, it's a global setting among the tools for any given session. But it won't affect the Method options of sets already on the page.

 It's important to remember that the Method settings under the symbol sprayer are not interchangeable with the similar ones for each of the other symbolism tools. So you could have the Stain option for your sprayer be User Defined, but the symbol stainer tool itself could be set to something else. Don't worry, you'll get used to it.

 There are times when the Average method option isn't going to do much, if anything, to your symbols. For example, if all of the symbols are already the same size, what would their average be? And if averaging is going to "smooth" (as the documentation says) the colors of a school of fish that were all the same color to begin with, you wouldn't be expecting much change there, either.

Hidden Secrets of the Dialog Box

Other than the symbol sprayer and the symbol sizer, no other tools have tool-specific options—only the Method choice. But when you click on any tool's icon in the dialog box, you can see what else the tool can do for you with the help of keyboard shortcuts. These usually involve increasing or decreasing the amount or intensity of whatever you're doing.

The Symbols Palette

If the Symbolism Tool Options dialog box is where you control the look and placement of the instances on the page, the Symbols palette (featured prominently in **Figure 12.7**) is where you control exactly which lucky symbols are going to get used, or worked on, in the first place, as well as keep them organized.

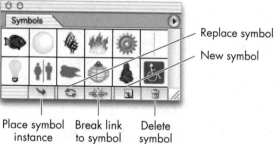

Replace symbol
New symbol

Figure 12.7: In the everyday working world of symbols, the Symbols palette is the dispatcher.

Place symbol   Break link   Delete
instance   to symbol   symbol

As you can see, you can perform the most common and basic symbol-based tasks with the icons in this palette; instructions for these tasks are scattered throughout this chapter, but they're also fairly intuitive. Besides the front-line tasks that you can perform with these icons, you can also use the Symbols palette to order or reorder the symbols, select unused symbols, and other bureaucratic details. Most all of these are clearly named options in the palette's pop-up menu.

Administrative Assistance (The Pop-up Menu)

Most of the commands on the Symbols palette pop-up menu, shown in **Figure 12.8**, are not exotic; rather, they're behind-the-scenes helpers that wait quietly until suddenly they can do you a favor.

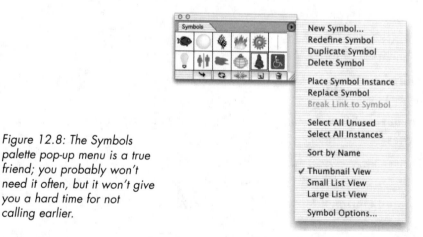

Figure 12.8: The Symbols palette pop-up menu is a true friend; you probably won't need it often, but it won't give you a hard time for not calling earlier.

- **New Symbol:** Adds selected artwork to the Symbols palette as a new symbol (conveniently opening the Symbol Options dialog box on the way so you can name it).

- **Redefine Symbol:** Relinks a modified object to a symbol. Once you redefine a symbol, all existing instances of it will update.

- **Duplicate Symbol:** Just what it sounds like, this command creates a copy of the selected symbol. It's an easy way to use an existing symbol as a starting point for another, without losing the first. (You could even use this to create a different size or color of an existing symbol if that change is one you'd make frequently.)

- **Delete Symbol:** You heard the man—get rid of it!

- **Place Symbol Instance:** Brings a single instance of the symbol onto the page.

- **Replace Symbol:** Substitutes a completely new symbol for an existing instance on the page.

- **Break Link to Symbol:** Makes the selected symbol back into an independent object, either just because you want it to be independent or so that you can modify it to update the symbol.

- **Select All Unused:** Figures out which symbols you haven't used within the document and selects all of them. This is a good way to clear out the palette in a hurry.

- **Select All Instances:** Selects all instances of whatever symbol is selected in the palette at that time. It does not pick up instances within a set, however, so if you want to use it to get rid of all of something, check your sets manually.

- **Sort by Name:** Arranges the symbols in alphabetical order, even if you're in Thumbnail View and can't see the names.

- **Thumbnail View:** Displays all symbols as a small picture. This is the default view.

- **Small List View:** Displays symbols as even smaller pictures with names next to them.

- **Large List View:** Displays symbols with pictures as big as the thumbnails but still with the names next to them.

- **Symbol Options:** The dialog box that lets you rename a symbol.

Prettying up the Palette

There's really not much more to be said about the palette, unless you're the kind of person who wants to control where exactly your symbols will go within it. You can specify that a new symbol goes into a particular location within the palette by dragging onto the symbol that's currently in that slot; a heavy black line will appear between symbols in the palette to indicate where the newcomer will go. If you just drag onto the palette as a whole, the heavy black line will border the entire palette window, and the new symbol will be placed at the bottom.

Modifying Symbols

If a sudden brainstorm (or an irate client) compels you to change your design after you've completed the entire thing and the symbols populate your page in the thousands, don't panic. A small tweak or a complete overhaul is all the same to Illustrator. (But you don't have to tell that to your client.) You can make global changes to any symbol or even substitute a different one. Not reassuring enough? Illustrator will honor all the painstaking spins, stains, and other changes you've made. So what are you worried about? Here's how you can update the symbol, and therefore the project, all before lunch.

Changing a Base Symbol

If your symbol image needs a small to moderate overhaul, this is probably the better option. It involves only taking an instance of the symbol, making the necessary changes, and slipping in the updated symbol in place of the base symbol currently in the Symbols palette as illustrated in **Figure 12.9**.

1. Select an instance of the symbol from your page or artboard. If you are working mostly with sets, you might want to place a single dummy instance.

2. Break its link (click the third icon in the Symbols palette, or choose Break Link to Symbol from the pop-up menu).

3. Modify the now stand-alone item however you like.

4. With the modified instance still selected, choose Redefine Symbol from the palette pop-up menu.

5. Watch any other instances change attributes like so many lemmings!

If you haven't used a dummy instance to break and redefine your symbol, be sure to re-associate the instance you used, or otherwise ensure it's not going to provoke an inconsistency within the design.

 The other compelling reason to use Redefine instead of Replace is that if you've used a mixed set and want to change only one of the symbols used, it's the only one that's going to work.

Figure 12.9: *This smallish change isn't something that a symbolism tool could have taken care of. Still, even with a set containing this few instances, and no modifications, a manual update would have taken up a significant chunk of time. And this was an easy example!*

 If for any reason you should you just want to detach an instance or a set from its base symbol to become a stand-alone element, just follow Steps 2 and 3 on the previous page.

Replacing a Base Symbol (aka Changing Your Mind in a Big Way)

Imagine you've done a lot of work on placement, screening, and other artistic adjustments. A *lot* of work. *Very* artistic adjustments. And then comes that terrible moment when you know that the symbol was just not correct in the first place.

Maybe the client's product has changed the entire shape of the packaging, or your yellow-bellied sapsucker turned out to be a ladder-backed woodpecker.

The end of the world? Not even close. You can replace all of the instances with new base symbols.

How is this different from redefining a symbol? To be sure, they're closely related, but sometimes it's just easier to start over, or the change is so big it's not sensible to tweak the one you have. So you can just slip in a completely different symbol instead. And this operation (shown in **Figure 12.10**) involves no link breaking.

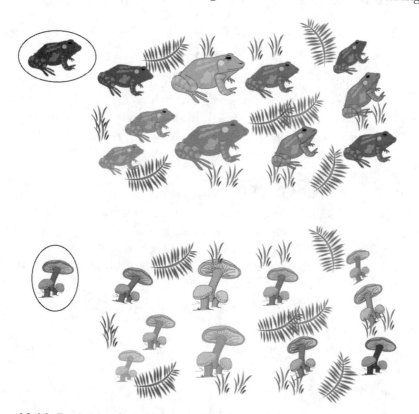

Figure 12.10: Turning toads to toadstools. I've shown the size of the original instances on the left for comparison.

Just select the symbol on the page (it can be a stand-alone instance or a set), choose the new symbol from the palette, and click the Replace Symbol icon at the bottom of the palette. Or you can choose Replace Symbol from the palette's pop-up menu.

OK, not my best work, but see how well it kept all the changes in size and tint and all? This was about as easy a crisis as you could hope for.

If you replace the symbol in a set that contains mixed symbols, they're all going to be replaced with the new one. So your fish and fowl might all become the same species. Wish I could have found a way around this one, but I haven't yet. It's a good argument for using layers, isn't it?

You can also replace a symbol by Alt-dragging (Option-dragging on the Mac) a selection of new art (or another symbol) on top of the symbol in the Symbols palette. You'll recognize this as the same behavior you can use with swatches and styles.

Bringing in Other Symbols

The fish, bubble, flame, and other default symbols are cute, but of course they're not going to satisfy all of your design needs. Nor would Adobe leave you in the lurch that way. Of course you'll be able to add your own symbols. In this section, you'll do just that, plus find the other symbol libraries provided with Illustrator. I'll also give you a couple of tips for project managing the lot of them.

Creating Your Own Symbols

I've said that almost any element or group of elements can be a symbol. Your own specially filtered and effect-laden artwork, an imported image, a favorite text ornament or phrase, and so on—any of these can be a permanent symbol. And creating a symbol is nothing more than officially introducing any piece of artwork to the Symbols palette. There are three ways to do this.

 Select any object or group and click the New Symbol icon in the Symbols palette.

 Select any object or group and choose New Symbol from the Symbols palette's pop-up menu.

 Drag an object or group from the page or artboard into the palette.

Your new symbol will appear in the palette, as shown in **Figure 12.11**.

If you can't see the Symbols palette, choose Window » Symbols.

To rename your new symbol, double-click on it in the palette to open the Symbol Options dialog box. Of the creation options listed above, only using New Symbol from the palette menu will automatically open the Symbol Options dialog box in the process.

 Original object...

 ...selected...

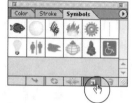

...choose New Symbol icon...

 ...Voilá!

Figure 12.11: Welcome a little sunshine into the family!

What happens if you make a type character into an instance? For most intents and purposes, it will get turned into a graphic and accept most transformational operations just as its graphical brethren would. But remember, if it was black type, it won't change colors with the symbol stainer. If you want an object's color to be subject to the stainer, make it a shade of gray.

Once you've made an object into a symbol, you might want to delete the original from the artboard (and, if necessary, replace it with an actual instance of the symbol). Why? It isn't actually an instance of the symbol, so it wouldn't get modified were you to want to do that later, and believe me, you'll have forgotten that it was just a lowly prototype and will be going nuts trying to make it behave. The same holds true for symbols you've modified and redefined.

Libraries

Not wanting to leave you entirely on your own in the brave new world of symbols, Illustrator prepares you for the journey by including several extra libraries of symbols, one of which is shown in **Figure 12.12**. Choose Window » Symbol Libraries to see all of the choices. These libraries open as separate little palettes, but without the icons at the bottom for add, break link, and so forth. For the basic steps of adding and modifying symbols, you can work with these as you would from the regular Symbols palette. Once you use one, it will transfer itself to the Symbols palette anyway, but you could add as many of them as you like.

But wait, there's more! You aren't limited to these artistic collections that Adobe has so generously provided. You can add the contents of the Symbols palette of any Illustrator file by choosing Window » Symbol Libraries » Other

Library and selecting the document. The contents of the Symbols palette for that document will show up in your document as one of these secondary, slightly hobbled palettes.

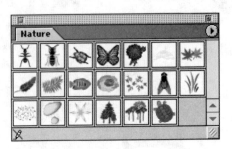

Figure 12.12: These auxiliary symbol palettes are really handy, especially if you use them as is and don't plan to operate on the symbols themselves.

And, of course, all you do-it-yourselfers can make your own libraries. There's no big mystery involved; just create a new document and put whatever you want into the Symbols palette. (To delete all the default items, remember you can select all of the symbols by clicking the first one in the palette and then Shift-clicking the last.)

 If you're feeling generous and looking for a good promo, you could produce a personal symbol library and distribute it to everyone in your Rolodex.

If you want to have your homegrown libraries added to the list of choices on the Symbol Libraries menu, just put your Illustrator file in the Symbols folder inside the Presets folder inside your Illustrator folder. Once you restart Illustrator, your file will appear on the menu.

Finally, if there's a library or extra symbol set (be it a prefab or one of your own making) that you want to see every time you open a new document, choose Persistent from that palette's pop-up menu. This option is available only if you've taken the trouble to move the document of origin into the Symbols folder inside the Presets folder.

THIS IS YOUR BRAIN ON GRAPHS

This would seem as good a time as any to take a moment out of our busy Illustrator learning schedules and look back on the knowledge we've amassed so far. Just since Chapter 5, we've learned how to create almost every kind of graphic and text object on the planet, including geometric shapes, free-form paths, text blocks, path text, and hundreds of infinitesimal variations too tedious to mention.

That leaves just one more item that you can create in Illustrator—a combination of paths and text known as the *graph*. Yes, few folks know it (and even fewer seem to care), but Illustrator lets you create a graph from an everyday average spreadsheet of numbers. And it does a very good job of it.

Illustrator for graphs? I hear you arguing, "Aren't there are better products for this purpose?" Granted, Microsoft Excel provides better number-crunching capabilities, PowerPoint lets you build presentations around graphs, and no program competes with DeltaGraph Professional when it comes to scientific and highfalutin' business graphs. But if you're looking to create simple graphs with designer appeal—like those picture charts that are forever popping up in *USA Today*—using a program like Illustrator is your best bet.

But before I go any further, let me answer some important questions:

- What is the difference between a graph and a chart?

- Are these two terms interchangeable?

- Will snooty power graphers look down their noses at me if I say "chart" when I mean "graph," or vice versa?

The answers are: nada, yes, and who gives a flying fish? The term "chart" is a little more inclusive than "graph." Television weather reporters use charts (not graphs) to show cold fronts, and navigators use charts (not graphs) to make sure your plane gets to its tropical island vacation destination, but basically anything that can be called a graph can also be called a chart. So for the purposes of this chapter, they are one and the same.

What I rail against is the use of the term "graphic" to mean graph in Harvard Graphics and Freelance Graphics, two PC charting programs that are altogether useless for drawing. A graphic is a brilliant illustration that sparks the interest, enthusiasm, and imagination of the viewer; a graph is a bunch of lines and rectangles that bore folks silly.

In Illustrator, a graph can be a graphic.

Creating a Graph

Though you wouldn't know it to look at it, Illustrator offers a lot of graphing options. In fact, you can easily get mired down by these options—with so many options, each making such a tiny difference in the outcome of your graph, and each just plain hard to use. To help you out, I've provided the following handy-dandy chart-making steps. Illustrator's many minute graphing variations are likely to make more sense after you've had a chance to create a few graphs of your own.

1. **Decide what kind of graph you want to create.**

   Illustrator provides nine graph tools that correspond to its nine kinds of graphs—four kinds of bar graphs (of both the horizontal and vertical flavors), as well as a line graph, an area graph (filled lines), a scatter graph (a line graph variation), a pie graph (usually called a pie chart), and a radar graph (a circular style popular in Japan). Never fear, I'll explore each of these graphs in excruciating detail later in this chapter.

   To specify the kind of graph you want to create, drag your cursor to the right from the graph tool slot on the toolbox, as shown in **Figure 13.1**, and choose your tool.

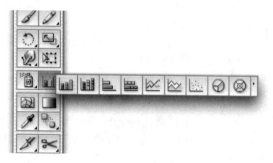

Figure 13.1: Choose one of the nine graph tools offered by Illustrator.

2. **Drag with the graph tool.**

   The dimensions of your drag determine the size of the graph. After you release the mouse button, Illustrator displays the Graph Data window, where you enter the numbers you want to graph.

3. **Enter or import your data.**

   You can either enter numbers directly into the Graph Data window or import them from a spreadsheet program. If you hate math, make a coworker give you the numbers. You're an artist, darn it, not an accountant!

4. **Press the keypad Enter key.**

   Illustrator generates a chart from your numbers. You can just sit there and admire the wonderful world of automation. (If you're using a laptop or a keyboard that doesn't have a keypad, you might find the Enter key on the main keyboard, often near the spacebar. The regular Enter (Return on the Mac) key just moves you down one cell.)

5. **Change the Graph Type attributes.**

With the graph selected, double-click the graph tool icon in the tool-box, or choose Object » Graph » Type. This opens the Graph Type dialog box. You can monkey around with a bunch of weird options until Illustrator creates a graph more or less to your liking. You can even change the kind of graph if you want.

 This is one place in which right-clicking in Windows or Ctrl-clicking on the Mac comes in handy. With a graph selected, right-click (Control-click on the Mac) to display a context-sensitive pop-up menu that contains all the commands in the Object » Graph submenu. This is probably the fastest way to access any of these commands. If the only command you see on the context-sensitive menu is Data, you'll need to close the Graph Data window; then you'll see all of the graph commands.

6. **If necessary, edit the graph manually with the direct selection tool.**

Ultimately, a graph is just a collection of paths and point text. This means you can move graph elements and text with the direct selec-tion tool, edit the text with the type tool, and fill and stroke the paths with different colors.

You can revisit Steps 3 through 6 as many times as you want to modify the graph again and again. To modify the data for a selected chart, for example, choose Object » Graph » Data and edit the numbers in the spreadsheet. You can even import an entirely new set of numbers.

You should keep in mind two important points.

- Applying options from the Graph Type dialog box or Graph Data win-dow will regenerate the graph from scratch, which may negate man-ual changes that you've made with the direct selection and type tools. Illustrator tries to retain your manual changes when possible, but you should be prepared to reapply your modifications. Or better yet, try to get the automated stuff in Steps 3 through 5 out of the way before you make manual changes in Step 6.

- In Illustrator, a graph is a special kind of grouped object. Some path operations—particularly the Join and Pathfinder commands discussed in Chapter 7—won't work on paths inside a group. You also can't convert type to outlines inside a graph. If you need access to these functions, you must first ungroup the graph by choosing Object » Ungroup (or by pressing Ctrl+Shift+G (Cmd-Shift-G on the Mac)).

Although the Ungroup command expands your range of creative adjustments, it also unlinks the graph from its data. After you press Ctrl+Shift+G (Cmd-Shift-G on the Mac), you forfeit your ability to apply options from either the Graph Type dialog box or the Graph Data window. So don't ungroup until you are absolutely 100 percent satisfied with the numerical data represented in the graph.

You can, of course, backstep an operation by pressing Ctrl+Z (Cmd-Z on the Mac) or by choosing Edit » Undo. If you apply a few options in the Graph Type dialog box and upset a manual adjustment, or if you ungroup the graph and think better of it, the Undo command is always at the ready to bring things back to their previous state.

Defining the Graph Size with the Graph Tool

Any graphing tool's main purpose is to determine the rectangular dimensions of a chart. You draw with a graphing tool just as if you were drawing with the rectangle tool. In other words, you can avail yourself of any of these techniques.

- Drag to draw the chart boundary from corner to corner.

- Alt-drag (Option-drag on the Mac) to draw the boundary from center to corner.

- Shift-drag or Alt+Shift-drag (Option-Shift-drag on the Mac) to draw a square boundary.

- Click to display the tiny Graph dialog box, which contains Width and Height option boxes. Enter the horizontal and vertical dimensions of the desired chart and press Enter (Return on the Mac). The click point becomes the upper-left corner of the chart boundary.

- Alt-click (Option-click on the Mac) with the graph tool and enter the numeric dimensions if you want the click point to serve as the center of the graph.

Regardless of how you define the boundary of the graph, this area encloses only the graphic elements of the chart. The labels and the legend extend outside the boundary. In **Figure 13.2**, for example, the dotted outline shows the dimensions of the drag with the graph tool. The gray area represents portions of the graph that lie outside the boundary. You can change the size of the labels, and you can move the legend if you need to, but they do take up space.

Boundary defined with the graph tool

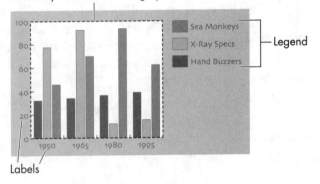

Legend

Labels

Figure 13.2: You can specify the graph's boundary (represented by the dotted outline) by dragging or clicking with the graph tool.

Don't worry too much if you don't know exactly how large or small you want the graph to be when you first create it. You can always enlarge or reduce it with the scale tool later. (The scale tool is a prominent topic of Chapter 9.) However, if you resize the graph disproportionately, you'll likewise disproportionately stretch text and other elements.

Figure 13.3 demonstrates what happens when you scale two kinds of graphs— column and pie—disproportionately. I created the top two examples by clicking with the graph tool and entering *14p* and *12p* (14 and 12 picas) into the Width and Height options. To create the bottom two examples, I entered *8p* and *10p* for the Width and Height values, resulting in graphs that were taller than they were wide. I then enlarged the bottom graphs disproportionately with the scale tool.

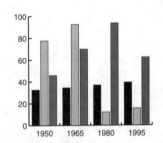

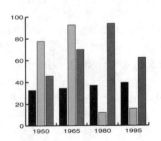

Figure 13.3: I created the top two graphs at the sizes shown here, but drew the bottom graphs at smaller sizes and enlarged them disproportionately.

The scaled column graph generally looks fine; only the text appears stretched. The pie graph, however, does not fare as well. Because each pie is a perfect circle, the shapes suffer when you scale them disproportionately. So my advice is to go ahead and scale column, bar, line, and area graphs however you want; but be careful to scale scatter graphs (which have square points in them), pie graphs, and radar graphs (which rely on circles) by the same percentage vertically and horizontally. If this makes the text too small or too large for the graph, enter a new Size value or increase the Vertical Scale number.

Scaling is a necessary part of the graphing process. But that's no excuse for stretched or squished text. After you scale, return your text to the proper proportions using the Horizontal Scale option in the Character palette. While the graph is still selected, click the Horizontal Scale pop-up menu and choose the 100 percent option. Illustrator restores the type to normal scaling.

Using the Graph Data Window

After you drag with the graph tool (or click and enter the graph dimensions), the Graph Data window pops up on screen, as in **Figure 13.4**. This is not a dialog box—it's a window that contains its own close box, collapse box, resize box, and scroll bars. It is also more functional than a dialog box. You can click outside the Graph Data window to bring the illustration window to the front. Although the Graph Data window may disappear from view, it remains open behind the illustration window, so that you don't lose any changes you may have made. To bring the Graph Data window back to the front, click its title bar, or choose the Object » Graphs » Data command from the Graph menu. Better yet, right-click (Control-click on the Mac) and choose the Data command. (Alas, although Graph Data is for all intents and purposes an open window, Illustrator does not list it as an option on the Window menu.)

The spreadsheet matrix that occupies most of the Graph Data window is similar to the matrix provided in a standard spreadsheet program such as Excel. The spreadsheet contains rows and columns of individual containers, called *cells*. Numbers entered into the cells can represent dollars, times, dates, or percentages (though you should avoid symbols, such as $ and %, among others). You can even enter words for labels and legends.

Unlike a true spreadsheet, however, you cannot enter formulas in the spreadsheet matrix because Illustrator lacks a calculation feature. (You can't even take advantage of Illustrator's adding function, which works in many palettes and dialog boxes, including the little dialog box that opens when you click with the graph tool.)

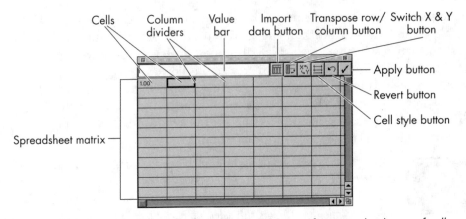

Figure 13.4: You enter data into a spreadsheet made up of rows and columns of cells in the Graph Data window.

Data entered from the keyboard appears in the value bar at the top of the spreadsheet (labeled in Figure 13.4). Press Enter (Return on the Mac), the arrow keys, or Tab to transfer the data from the value bar into the current cell and advance to another cell.

As you type, most keys insert the standard characters that appear on the key. Some keys and characters, however, perform special functions:

- **Tab or right arrow:** Accepts the data in the value bar and moves one cell right (to the next cell in the row).

- **Left arrow:** Accepts the data in the value bar and moves one cell left.

- **Enter (Return on the Mac) or down arrow:** Accepts the data in the value bar and moves one cell down (to the next cell in the column).

- **Up arrow:** Accepts the data in the value bar and moves one cell up.

- **Quotation marks ("):** Enter straight quotation marks around numeric data to use a number as a label, such as a product number or year. If a cell consists entirely of numbers without quote marks, Illustrator interprets the data as a value and graphs it. If you want Illustrator to display the quotation marks in the graph, use the curly opening and closing marks, " and " (Alt+[(Option-[on the Mac) and Alt+Shift+[(Option-Shift-[on the Mac), rather than the straight quotation marks.

- **Vertical line character (|):** If you want a label to contain multiple lines of text, enter the vertical line (Shift-\) to represent a line-break character. (My typographically savvy copy editor tells me the proper name for this is "bar" or "pipe." See, aren't you glad you decided to read this chapter?)

Keypad Enter key: Accepts the data in the value bar and updates the graph.

For most kinds of charts, you can enter legend text into the top row and labels into the left-hand column of cells. To create such graph text, delete the data from the very first cell (at the intersection of the first row and column) and leave it empty. All other cells in the top row and left column should contain at least one non-numeric character or quotation marks around the numbers, as shown in **Figure 13.5**.

 If you don't want Illustrator to create a legend, enter a label or a value into the first cell and fill the top row of cells with values. If I deleted the first line of items from the matrix in Figure 13.5, for example, and scooted up the other rows, I would get labels but no legend.

Figure 13.5: As long as the first cell is empty, you can use the top row and the left column to hold labels.

	Hand Buzzers	X-Ray Specs	Sea Monkeys	
"1950"	32.57	77.60	45.70	
"1965"	34.44	92.50	69.90	
"1980"	36.84	12.04	93.60	
"1995"	39.34	15.55	62.34	

 If after entering a label or legend text, you can't see the full text inside the cell, it isn't because the text is lost; the cell is just too narrow to display it. You can widen the cell by dragging a column divider (labeled in Figure 13.4) as described in the section "Changing the Way Cells Look" later in this chapter.

Importing Data from Disk

Because the Graph Data window provides no calculation capabilities and its cell-editing functions are limited—you can't insert, delete, or sort cells—you may prefer to import values created in another program. You can create your data in any program capable of saving a tab-delimited file, which is a plain text file with tabs between values and return characters between rows. Virtually every spreadsheet program supports this format. In addition, the file doesn't have to come from Windows or a Mac; tab-delimited files can be generated by big-iron mainframes and prehistoric MS-DOS PCs that still run some businesses.

 You can even create your data in a word processor such as Microsoft Word or WordPerfect. When entering the data, insert tabs between values and insert carriage returns between rows of values. Then save the finished file as a plain text document.

To import data from disk, open the Graph Data window and click the cell where you want the imported data to start. Click the Import data button to display the Import Graph Data window, which behaves like the Open dialog box. Locate the file you want to import and double-click its name in the scrolling list, or select the file and press Enter (Return on the Mac). The imported data appears in the spreadsheet in rows and columns starting in the selected cell.

 If any of the cells below or to the right of the selected cell already contain data, Illustrator replaces the old data with the new.

Selecting and Modifying Cells

You select cells in the spreadsheet by dragging across them. Or you can press the Shift key while pressing one of the arrow keys to add to a range of selected cells or delete from them. All selected cells become highlighted—white against black—except the cell that you're entering data into, which has a big, fat border around it.

Although you can't perform fancy tricks such as inserting or deleting cells inside the Graph Data window, you can move data around within cells using one of the following techniques:

- 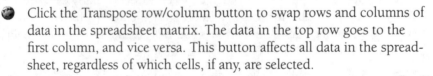 Cut or copy data from one location and paste it into another. You can either use the keyboard shortcuts Ctrl+X (Cmd-X on the Mac), Ctrl+C (Cmd-C on the Mac), or Ctrl+V (Cmd-V on the Mac); choose commands from the Edit menu; or access the commands from the context-sensitive pop-up menu that appears when you right-click (Control-click on the Mac).

- *For example, to nudge all cells upward one row (the effect achieved by deleting a row in Excel), select the cells, press Ctrl+X (Cmd-X on the Mac), click the first cell in the row you want to replace, and press Ctrl+V (Cmd-V on the Mac).*

- Click the Transpose row/column button to swap rows and columns of data in the spreadsheet matrix. The data in the top row goes to the first column, and vice versa. This button affects all data in the spreadsheet, regardless of which cells, if any, are selected.

- Click the Switch x/y button to swap columns of data in a scatter chart. The data in the first column moves to the second, the data in the second column moves to the first, the data in the third column moves to the fourth, and so on. This button is dimmed when you're creating or editing any kind of chart except a scatter chart, and it applies to all data in the spreadsheet.

- You can delete the contents of multiple selected cells by choosing Edit » Cut.

- Press Ctrl+Z (Cmd-Z on the Mac) or choose Edit » Undo to undo the last operation—also easily accessed by right-clicking (Control-clicking on the Mac). If you just finished changing a cell value, for example, Ctrl+Z (Cmd-Z on the Mac) restores the previous data in the value bar. As in the rest of Illustrator, you have multiple undos inside the Graph Data window, so edit with impunity. You can even undo large operations such as importing, transposing, or pasting data.

Copying Data from a Different Graph

The fact that the Graph Data window stays up onscreen makes it easy to copy data from one graph and paste it into another. For example, suppose that you just dragged with the graph tool to start a new graph, and Illustrator has displayed the Graph Data window. Suddenly, you remember that you wanted to create this new chart based on a chart you created a few days ago. But you don't even have that old chart open right now. No problem. You can access the data without even closing the Graph Data window.

1. Select the arrow tool, and click in the illustration window to bring it to front. This gives you access to all of Illustrator's menu commands (some are inactive if the Graph Data window is active).

2. Press Ctrl+O (Cmd-O on the Mac) and open the illustration that contains the chart that you want to copy.

3. Select the chart with the arrow tool.

4. If you can see any part of the Graph Data window, click its title bar to bring it to the front. Otherwise, choose Object » Graphs » Data or Graphs » Data from the context-sensitive pop-up menu. The Graph Data window shows the data for the selected graph.

5. Drag to select the data that you want to copy from the previous chart and press Ctrl+C (Cmd-C on the Mac), or choose Edit » Copy.

6. Click the title bar for the illustration window that contains the new chart in progress. If necessary, select the chart with the arrow tool.

7. Click the Graph Data window again. When you bring the Graph Data window to the front, it automatically shows the data for the selected chart.

8. Click the first cell and press Ctrl+V (Cmd-V on the Mac), or choose Edit » Paste). There's your data. Now you can edit it in any manner you deem appropriate.

If you're working with two graphs in the same illustration, it's even easier. Just keep the Graph Data window open and select one graph or the other to display their data in the Graph Data window.

You can copy as much data or as little data as you wish. To highlight the cells you want to copy, just drag over them. And click a cell before pressing Ctrl+V (Cmd-V on the Mac) to decide where you want the pasted data to start.

 Illustrator lets you paste any type into the Graph Data window. You can copy words or paragraphs from a block of text in the illustration window and paste them into a graph. You can also copy data from the spreadsheet and paste it into a text block. Just remember that Illustrator can paste only the values, not the formats or formulas.

Changing the Way Cells Look

The final adjustment that you can make to cells in the Graph Data window is purely cosmetic. The Cell style button allows you to adjust both the width of the columns in the spreadsheet and the number of digits that follow a decimal point. These controls affect only the appearance of data in the spreadsheet; they do not affect the appearance of the chart in the illustration window.

Click the Cell style button to display a dialog box that contains the following two option boxes:

- **Number of Decimals:** Enter any value between 0 and 10 into the Number of Decimals option box. This option determines the number of significant digits—that is, the number of characters that can appear after a decimal point in a cell.

- **Column Width:** This value controls the default width of each cell in the Graph Data window, measured in digits. Enter any value between 1 and 20.

- *To adjust the width of a single column of cells, drag the corresponding column divider, as demonstrated in **Figure 13.6**. The column is widened or narrowed by the nearest whole-digit increment.*

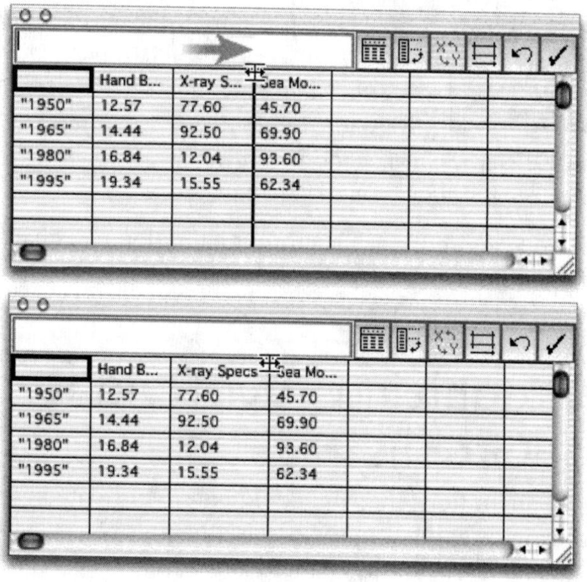

Figure 13.6: Drag a column divider (top) to change the width of a column of cells (bottom).

Transforming Your Data into a Graph

So far, I've instructed you to press the keypad Enter key to update the graph in the illustration window. But that isn't the only way to go. The Graph Data window provides many ways to update the graph; or you can exit the window without updating.

The following is a brief explanation of the update, exit, and reversion elements in the Graph Data window, as seen in Figure 13.4:

- **The Apply button (keypad Enter):** Click the Apply button or press Enter to update the graph in the illustration window without leaving the Graph Data window. If you can't see the graph because the Graph Data window is in the way, drag the Graph Data title bar to move the window partially off the screen. By keeping the Graph Data window up on the screen, you can quickly make changes if the data doesn't graph the way you hoped it would.

- **The Revert button:** Click Revert to restore the data that was in force the last time you clicked the Apply button.

- **Close box:** If you want to exit the Graph Data window without implementing your changes, click the close box, and then click the Don't Save button in the alert box (or press the D key).

You can also cancel your modifications to a graph by simply selecting a different object in the illustration window or in a different drawing altogether. Illustrator displays an alert box asking you if you want to save your changes to the last graph. Press D if you don't want to, or press Enter (Return on the Mac) if you do. If you use this method, keep in mind that the Graph Data window will remain open.

You can undo the creation or alteration of a chart after clicking on the OK or Apply button by pressing Ctrl+Z (Cmd-Z on the Mac).

Organizing Your Data for Different Kinds of Graphs

You might hope that you could enter your data in any old way and have Illustrator graph it in the precise manner you've envisioned in your head, but Illustrator isn't quite so gifted at reading your mind. Therefore, you have to organize your data in a manner that Illustrator deems appropriate. To be sure, it isn't just because Illustrator arbitrarily wants it a certain way; it's because different graph types are intended for different types of data or analysis.

The following sections explore each of the nine kinds of graphs and tell you how to set up your data for each.

Column Chart Data

When creating a plain old everyday column graph—also called a grouped column chart for reasons that will become apparent as our graphing journey progresses—Illustrator expects you to organize your data in what I'll henceforth call "standard form." But before I tell you what that standard form is, a word or two about this classic kind of chart.

Column charts are most commonly used to demonstrate a change in data over a period of time. The horizontal axis (x-axis) may be divided into categories such as units of time (i.e., days, months, or years). The vertical axis (y-axis) tracks values, which may be measured in units sold, dollars or other currency, or whatever your favorite commodity may be.

As shown in **Figure 13.7**, columns rise up from the x-axis to a height equivalent to a value on the y-axis. The taller the column, the greater the value it represents.

You can graph multiple collections of data in the chart. Each collection is called a series. Back in Figure 13.2, for example, Sea Monkeys, X-Ray Specs, and

Hand Buzzers are each separate series. Corresponding columns from each series are clustered together for the sake of visual comparison. Hence, this type of chart is known in some circles as a cluster column chart.

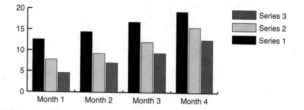

Figure 13.7: An example of a standard column chart, in which series of vertical columns are clustered together to show change in multiple items over time.

By default, columns from different series are filled with different gray values (although you can apply your own colors using the direct selection tool, as I explain in the "Selecting Elements Inside Graphs" section). The colors representing the series are defined in the legend, which appears in the upper-right portion of Figure 13.7.

To create a column chart, arrange your data as shown in **Figure 13.8**. Here are a few details to keep in mind:

 Delete the contents of the cell in the top-left corner, and leave it empty.

 Enter series labels in the top row of cells. This text will appear in the legend.

 Enter x-axis labels in the left column. They will appear underneath the chart along the horizontal axis.

Figure 13.8: Organize column chart data into columns under series labels. This data corresponds to the column chart shown in Figure 13.7.

	Series 1	Series 2	Series 3
Month 1	12.57	7.60	4.57
Month 2	14.44	9.25	6.99
Month 3	16.84	12.04	9.36
Month 4	19.34	15.55	12.63

 Organize each series of data into a column under the appropriate series label. Do not enter any characters other than numbers. If you use a currency symbol, such as $, £, or ¢, Illustrator won't graph the value.

 Illustrator generates the y-axis labels automatically, in accordance with the data. You can customize the y-axis labels using options in the Graph Type dialog box, which I'll explain later.

Stacked Column Chart Data

Stacked column charts are much like column charts, except that columns from each series are stacked on top of one another rather than positioned side by side. A stacked column chart shows the sums of all series.

You can create a percentage chart similar to the one shown in **Figure 13.9** by organizing your data so that all values for each series add up to 100. Percentage charts demonstrate relative performance. If Department A is trouncing Department B, you can broadcast the news with a percentage chart.

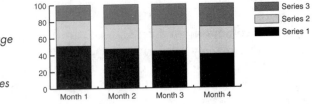

Figure 13.9: This percentage chart is a variety of the stacked column chart, in which each column of series values adds up to 100.

You arrange data for a stacked column chart in the standard form, with series labels in the top row and x-axis labels in the left column, as shown in **Figure 13.10**. Organize series of data into columns under the series labels. Whatever you do, don't enter a percentage symbol or any other non-numeric characters. If you do, Illustrator won't graph the value.

Figure 13.10: This data corresponds to the percentage chart shown in Figure 13.9. Notice that the values along each row add up to 100.

	Series 1	Series 2	Series 3	
Month 1	51.00	31.00	18.00	
Month 2	47.00	30.00	23.00	
Month 3	44.00	31.00	25.00	
Month 4	40.00	33.00	27.00	

Illustrator can't automatically convert sales values to percentages, so you can either enter the percentages manually or make a program such as Excel do the work.

To make Excel convert values to percentages, follow these steps:

1. **Enter the sales values in Excel in the standard form.**

    Don't even think about percentages. Just enter normal values.

2. **Select each row of values one at a time and click the AutoSum button.**

Labeled in **Figure 13.11**, the AutoSum button looks like a sigma (_)
in the ribbon bar. Excel creates a sum total for each row in the column after the selection (the bold items in the figure).

**3. Create a new cell in which you divide the first sales number by
the first sum and multiply the result by 100.**

This is, of course, the classic formula for finding a percentage. Make
sure that you add a dollar-sign character before the column letter for
the sum cell location. This will make sure that when you duplicate
the formulas in the next step, the calculation will use the sum column
when it's supposed to. For example, if the first cell were B2 and the
sum cell were E2—as they are in Figure 13.11—you'd enter
*B2/$E2*100* (where / is the division symbol and * is multiply).

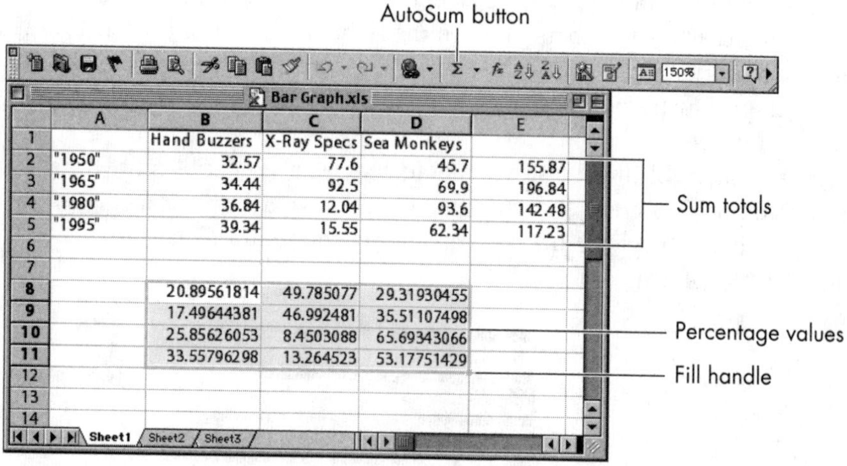

AutoSum button

	A	B	C	D	E	
1		Hand Buzzers	X-Ray Specs	Sea Monkeys		
2	"1950"	32.57	77.6	45.7	155.87	
3	"1965"	34.44	92.5	69.9	196.84	
4	"1980"	36.84	12.04	93.6	142.48	
5	"1995"	39.34	15.55	62.34	117.23	
6						
7						
8		20.89561814	49.785077	29.31930455		
9		17.49644381	46.992481	35.51107498		
10		25.85626053	8.4503088	65.69343066		
11		33.55796298	13.264523	53.17751429		
12						
13						
14						

Sum totals

Percentage values

Fill handle

*Figure 13.11: A collection of percentage values created in Excel and ready to copy
into Illustrator.*

**4. Duplicate the formulas to the right and then down by dragging
the fill handle.**

The fill handle is that little square in the lower-right corner of the
selected cell (labeled in Figure 13.11). You drag it to the right and
then drag down in two separate movements. This creates a matrix of
new percentage values. They may not look like percentages—just a
bunch of long numbers like the selected cells in Figure 13.11. But
they'll work fine. And don't change the number formatting—remember, Illustrator can't read percent signs.

5. **Select the new percentage values and copy them.**

Select the new data and copy it (Ctrl+C) (Cmd-C on the Mac).

6. **Switch to Illustrator and paste the data.**

Create a new stacked column chart and enter your own labels in the top row and left column. Starting in the second-to-top, second-to-left cell, paste (Ctrl+V) (Cmd-V on the Mac) after entering the labels.

7. **Press the keypad Enter key, or close the Graph Data window and accept changes.**

You now have a percentage chart.

Bar Chart Data

A bar chart is the horizontal equivalent of a column chart. Whereas columns move up to indicate increasing value, bars move to the right, as shown in **Figure 13.12**. You enter data into the Graph Data window in the exact same manner that you do for a column chart. Illustrator automatically switches the category and value (i.e., x and y) axis for you.

In previous versions of Illustrator, you could achieve a similar effect by rotating a column graph 90 degrees, but you then would have to add the labels and legend as separate text blocks. Now you can simply choose to display your data in this more leisurely form.

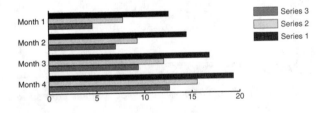

Figure 13.12: The bar chart is the lazy sibling of the column chart.

 You might think that you could convert a column chart into a bar chart by clicking the Transpose row/column button in the Graph Data window. But this will not result in a bar chart. Instead, you will have a column chart in which the labels and legend are located in the wrong places.

Stacked Bar Chart Data

What is there to say when it comes to stacked bar charts? If you've seen a bar chart and a stacked column chart you can surmise the structure of a stacked bar chart. The picture you have in mind probably looks much like **Figure 13.13**. You can apply the same technique, explained above in the stacked column chart discussion, to your bar chart data.

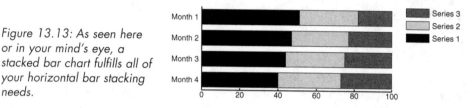

Figure 13.13: As seen here or in your mind's eye, a stacked bar chart fulfills all of your horizontal bar stacking needs.

Line Chart Data

Like column charts, line charts are generally used to show changes in items over a period of time. Straight segments connect points representing values, as shown in **Figure 13.14**. Several straight segments combine to form a line, which represents a complete series. The inclination of a segment clearly demonstrates the performance of a series from one point in time to the next. Because large changes result in steep inclinations, line charts clearly show dramatic fluctuations.

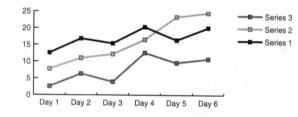

Figure 13.14: A line chart is composed of straight segments connecting square value points.

Figure 13.15 shows the data used to create Figure 13.14. As with column charts, you organize the data into the standard form, with series labels at top, x-axis labels on the left, and columns of series data.

Figure 13.15: Here's the data for the line chart in Figure 13.14. Each column of numbers results in a single line.

	Series 1	Series 2	Series 3	
Day 1	12.57	7.76	2.57	
Day 2	16.84	11.04	6.36	
Day 3	15.44	12.25	3.99	
Day 4	20.34	16.55	12.63	
Day 5	16.42	23.35	9.65	
Day 6	20.08	24.49	10.82	

 Although line chart data may fluctuate dramatically, you don't want series to cross each other more than once or twice in the entire chart. If the series cross too often, the result is what snooty graphing pros derisively call a "spaghetti chart," which is difficult to read and can prove more confusing than instructive.

If you encounter the spaghetti effect (overlapping lines) when creating a line chart, the easiest solution is to convert the line chart into an area chart.

Area Chart Data

An area chart is little more than a filled-in line chart. However, the series of an area chart are stacked one on top of another—just as in a stacked column chart—to display the sum of all series, as shown in **Figure 13.16**.

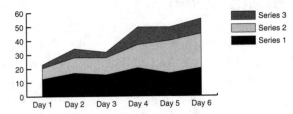

Figure 13.16: In an area chart, series are stacked on top of each other and filled in with colors or gray values.

When you create an area chart, arrange your data in the standard form. In fact, Figure 13.16 uses the same data as the line chart from Figure 13.14. The data appears in Figure 13.15.

Scatter Chart Data

Like a line chart, a scatter chart plots points on the horizontal and vertical axes and connects these points with straight segments. However, rather than merely aligning series of values along a set of x-axis labels, the scatter graph pairs up columns of values. The first column of data represents y-axis (series) coordinates; the second column represents x-axis coordinates. This setup permits you to map scientific data or to graph multiple series that occur over different time patterns.

For example, in **Figure 13.17**, the black line (Series 1) connects 13 points, whereas the gray line (Series 2) connects 10. And yet both lines run the entire width of the graph. You tell Illustrator which x,y-coordinates to plot; Illustrator just connects them with segments. This is the most versatile kind of graph you can create.

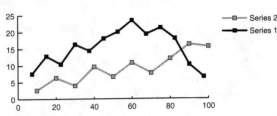

Figure 13.17: Illustrator plots points in a scatter graph at specific x,y-coordinates and connects the points with straight segments.

Figure 13.18 shows the data for the scatter chart in Figure 13.17. The data is arranged into pairs of columns, each pair representing a separate series. Here are a few details to keep in mind as you arrange your data.

 Enter series labels into the top row of cells, one label for each odd column (first, third, fifth, and so on). Leave even-numbered cells empty. As with line charts, the series labels appear in the legend.

 Enter y-axis (series) data in the odd-numbered columns.

 Enter x-axis data in the even-numbered columns. Illustrator plots side-by-side columns of data as paired points. In other words, each pair of values in the first and second columns is plotted as a point in the first series, each pair in the third and fourth columns is plotted as a point in the second series, and so on.

 Illustrator automatically generates y-axis and x-axis labels that correspond to the data.

Series 1		Series 2		
7.57	7.50	2.57	10.00	
12.84	15.00	6.36	20.00	
10.44	22.50	3.99	30.00	
16.34	30.00	9.63	40.00	
14.42	37.50	6.65	50.00	
18.08	45.00	10.82	60.00	
20.06	52.50	7.76	70.00	
23.49	60.00	12.04	80.00	
19.35	67.50	16.25	90.00	
21.26	75.00	15.55	100.00	
18.05	82.50			
10.24	90.00			
6.56	97.50			

Figure 13.18: Each series of scatter chart data takes up two columns, with the y-axis values first and the x-axis values second.

Pie Chart Data

A pie chart is the easiest kind of chart to create. However, pie charts are not nearly as versatile as the column and line varieties. Only one series can be expressed per pie. If you want to show more than one series for comparative purposes, each series gets a pie of its own, as shown in **Figure 13.19**.

Figure 13.19: Two pie charts, each representing a single series. The first pie is smaller than the second because the second series includes larger values.

Series 1   Series 2

The advantage of a pie chart is that it always displays a series of values in relation to the whole. The entire series inhabits a 360-degree circle, and each value within the series occupies a percentage of that circle.

Figure 13.20 shows the data for the pies in Figure 13.19. You organize data for a pie chart in virtually the opposite way that you organize it for a column or line chart, with the series running across the rows instead of down the columns. Here are a few guidelines:

- Delete the contents of the first cell and leave it empty, just like always.

- Enter value labels in the top row of cells. These labels appear in the legend.

- Enter series labels in the left column. These labels appear as titles below the pies, as in Figure 13.19. (If you plan to graph more than two series, I recommend you use a different kind of chart.)

- Organize each series of data into a row to the right of the series label.

Figure 13.20: Organize pie chart data into rows. Each row represents a different pie.

	Brand 1	Brand 2	Brand 3	Brand 4	Brand X	
Series 1	0.98	1.56	4.07	6.76	26.57	
Series 2	3.24	4.67	6.99	8.25	29.34	

If you want to take a couple of series from a column chart and represent them inside pie charts, copy them from the spreadsheet for the column chart, paste them into the pie chart spreadsheet, and click the Transpose row/column button to switch the rows and columns.

Radar Chart Data

Though big in Japan, the radar chart isn't as well recognized in the United States. It resembles a spoked wheel with string running between the spokes. Though it may look more like a design than a functional graph, a radar chart, shown in **Figure 13.21**, is essentially a line chart rolled-up.

Because radar charts are closely related to line charts, I used the data from the line chart in Figure 13.14 to create the radar chart in Figure 13.21.

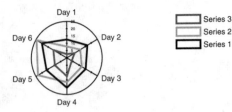

Figure 13.21: A non-Euclidean approach to line graphing.

Applying Automated Changes to a Graph

Remember the six basic steps required to create a graph in Illustrator? (If not, you can refresh your memory by peeking at the "Creating a Graph" section at the beginning of this chapter.) So far, I've exhausted the first four. Step 5 encouraged you to apply automated changes using the Graph Type dialog box. That's what these next sections are all about.

To access these options, select the graph you want to edit and double-click the graph tool icon in the toolbox, or choose Object » Graphs » Type, or right-click (Control-click on the Mac) and choose Type. Illustrator displays the Graph Type dialog box, shown in **Figure 13.22**. This dialog box is quite complicated and provides access to a bunch of options that you don't see on first perusal, including two other dialog boxes.

 You can apply options from the Graph Type dialog box to an entire graph selected with the arrow tool or to a partial graph selected with the direct selection tool. For example, if you Alt-click (Option-click on the Mac) three times on a straight segment in a previously deselected line graph with the direct selection tool, you select the entire series, including the color swatch in the legend. You can then modify that one segment independently of the others inside the Graph Type dialog box.

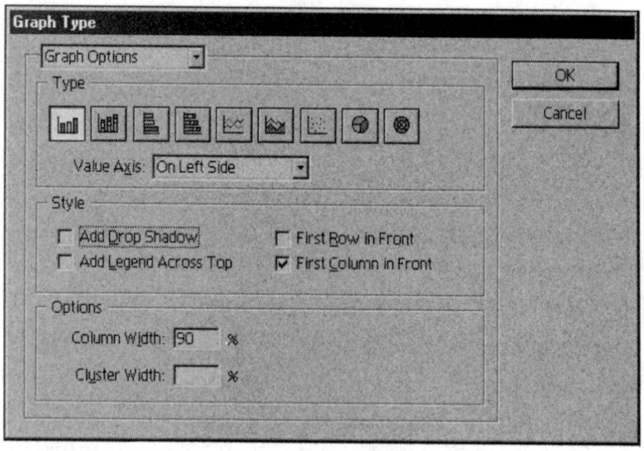

Figure 13.22: You can right-click (Windows) or Control-click (Mac) and choose Type to display the Graph Type dialog box, which lets you apply automated adjustments to a selected graph. If the Type command on the context-sensitive menu is dimmed, close the Graph Data window if it's open, and try again.

Converting and Tweaking a Graph

You can convert a selected graph from one variety to another—say, from a column chart to a line chart—by clicking on an icon from among the nine buttons along the top portion of the dialog box. Just click a button, press Enter (Return on the Mac), and, whammo, the chart is changed. Remember earlier in the chapter when I said that the data has to be organized the right way for each chart? After you switch chart types, you might want to double-check to make sure the data still makes sense, and adjust the Graph Data window if needed.

There's an additional set of options in the bottom portion of the Graph Type dialog box. These specialized options change depending on which kind of graph you've selected.

The following list explains the options associated with each type of chart:

- **Column:** When you click the Column button, two options appear in the options area at the bottom of the Graph Type dialog box, as pictured in **Figure 13.23**. The Column Width value controls the width of each column in the chart. A value of 100 percent causes columns to touch each other, rubbing shoulders, as it were. The default value of 90 percent allows slight gutters between columns, and values greater than 100 percent cause columns to overlap.

  The second option, Cluster Width, controls the width of each cluster of columns, again measured as a percentage value. The last column from Series 1 touches the first column of series 2 at 100 percent. The default value of 80 percent allows a gutter between clusters. (I don't recommend using values greater than 100 percent because they cause clusters not only to overlap each other, but also to overlap the vertical axis as well. Frankly, it can be mighty ugly.)

- **Stacked Column:** The options area contains the same options listed above, whether you select a grouped or stacked column chart (see Figure 13.23).

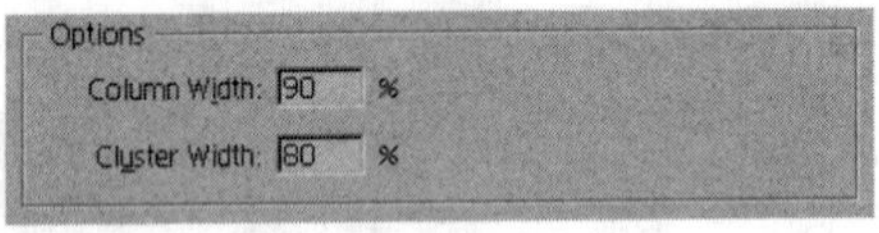

Figure 13.23: Use these options to control the width of columns and clusters of columns in a chart.

Options
Column Width: 90 %
Cluster Width: 80 %

- **Bar:** Click this button and the options area changes slightly, as shown in **Figure 13.24**. The Bar Width option allows you to control how wide the bars should be, just as the Column Width option did for columns. The Cluster Width option works the same way as above.

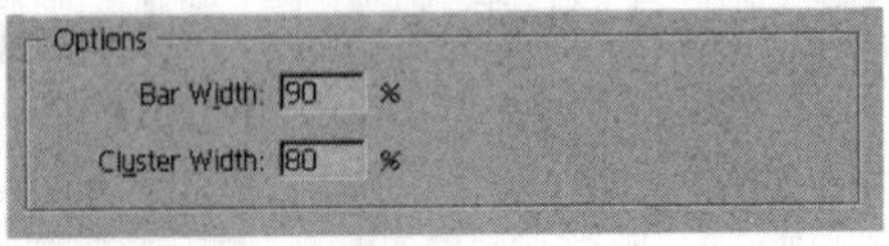

Figure 13.24: Use these options to change the width of bars and clusters of bars in a bar chart.

Options
Bar Width: 90 %
Cluster Width: 80 %

🌐 **Stacked Bar:** These options look and work the same as those for the bar chart (see Figure 13.24).

🌐 **Line:** When you click the Line button, four check boxes appear in the options area, as shown in **Figure 13.25**. Select the Mark Data Points check box to create square markers at the data points in each line. Turn off the check box to make the square markers disappear. Select the Connect Data Points check box and Illustrator will draw straight segments between points. Deselect this option and stray markers appear without lines. (Turn off both check boxes to make the series disappear entirely.)

Figure 13.25: Use these options to change the square points and straight segments associated with line graphs (and scatter charts).

When you select Connect Data Points, the Draw Fill Lines check box becomes available, which lets you create thick paths filled with gray values or colors. Enter the desired thickness into the Line Width option box. **Figure 13.26** shows a line graph with paths 12 points thick. Generally, you don't need data points when using fat paths, so you can turn off the Mark Data Points check box.

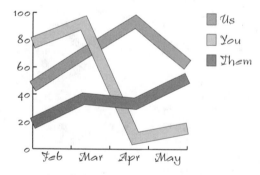

Figure 13.26: A line graph with the Draw Fill Lines check box selected, the Width value set to 12 points, Mark Data Points unselected, and the Edge-to-Edge Lines selected.

Select Edge-to-Edge Lines to draw lines that extend the entire width of the chart, starting at the y-axis and continuing to the end of the x-axis. This option is turned on in Figure 13.26. (By default, it is off.)

🌐 **Area:** There are no special options associated with an area chart. It would be nice if Illustrator provided at least the Edge-to-Edge Lines check box to eliminate the gaps between the data lines and the y-axis; but, alas, no such option exists.

● **Scatter:** When you click the Scatter button, three check boxes appear in the options area. These are the same options that appear for a line graph, as shown in Figure 13.25, except the Edge-to-Edge Lines check box does not appear here.

● **Pie:** When you click this button, the options area grants you three pop-up menus for editing a pie chart. Pictured in **Figure 13.27**, these commands let you change the placement of the pie labels (using the Legend pop-up commands), the size of the graphs (using the Position pop-up commands), and the method by which each chart is sorted (using the Sort pop-up commands). By default, the Standard Legend command is selected in the Legend pop-up menu, which results in a typical legend that identifies the gray values and colors in the graph. If you instead choose the Legends In Wedges command, Illustrator omits the legend and labels the pie slices directly, as in **Figure 13.28**. (You'll have to modify the colors of the slices to see the labels, as in the figure—the first slice is black by default.) Choose No Legend to trash the legend altogether.

Figure 13.27: You can change the way slices are labeled when editing a pie chart.

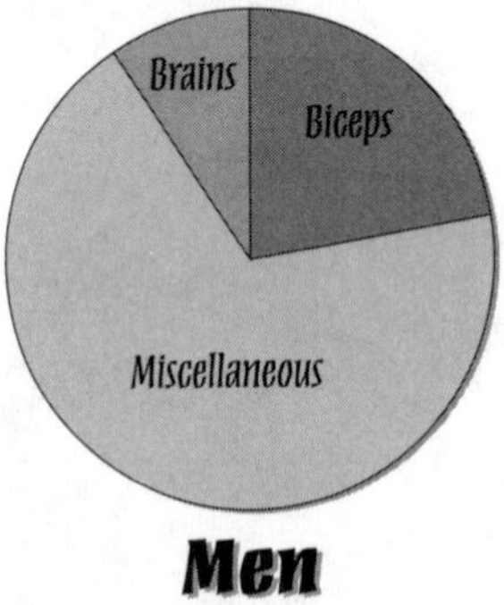

Figure 13.28: You can change the default Standard Legend setting in the Legend pop-up menu by choosing the Legends In Wedges command to apply labels to the pie slices.

The Position pop-up menu is oddly named because it offers three commands that have more to do with the size of the pie chart than its position. The Ratio command, the default, causes multiple pies to display according to each pie's total value, as shown in the top left of

Figure 13.29. Choose the Even command to make all pies the same size, as shown in the bottom left of Figure 13.29. Finally, you can choose the Stacked command to display your pies concentrically as a single pie-a-licious chart, shown at the right in Figure 13.29. All three variations in the figure below use the same graph data.

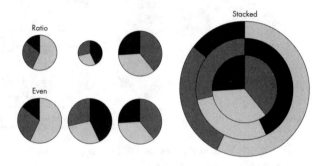

Figure 13.29: These three sets of pie charts demonstrate the different Position options.

By choosing a command from the Sort pop-up menu, you can control how you organize pie chart slices. Think of the individual pies as "clocks" and the dividing lines between the categories as marking off the time. No matter how you sort a pie chart, one of the dividing lines will point at the 12:00 position, as you can see in **Figure 13.30**. The first piece that extends clockwise from this dividing line is determined by the Sort commands, which have such weird names that they bear explanation. The top-row pie charts result when you choose the All command in the Sort pop-up menu. This should really be called Each, because each pie gets sorted on its own. With Sort Each, each pie chart could have a different first piece. The middle-row charts result from you choosing the Sort First command—Sort by First would be a more appropriate name. When you choose this command, the first piece for all the pies is determined by the category with the largest total value in the first pie. So, because X-Ray Specs was first in the first pie, it's first in all of the pies. The bottom-row charts reflect the usage of the Sort None command, which really means "don't change anything." With Sort None, each pie's slices are drawn in exactly the order they appear in the Graph Data window.

Radar: Click the Radar button to use all the same options that you'd have with a line chart. Feel free to re-gander Figure 13.25.

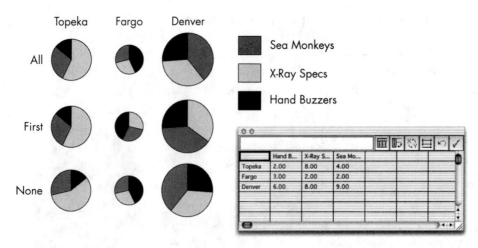

Figure 13.30: *Illustrator relies on the Sort pop-up menu to determine which category takes first position in a particular pie chart.*

Adjusting Axes and Labels

You use the Value Axis pop-up menu located below the buttons in the Graph Type dialog box to control the appearance and positions of the vertical and horizontal axes in a selected chart. This command is dimmed when you're working on a pie chart, because pie charts have no axes, and only one command exists when editing a radar chart. The same basic collection of commands is available for all other charts.

Use the following commands to control the placement of the vertical y-axis for the column, stacked column, bar, stacked bar, and scatter graphs:

- **On Left Side:** Choose this command to make the y-axis appear on the left side of the chart, as it does by default. You can then modify the axis by choosing the Value Axis command from the main pop-up menu at the top of the Graph Type dialog box.

- **On Right Side:** Choose this command to send the y-axis to the right side of the chart. Again, modify the axis by choosing the Value Axis command. The On Right Side command is not available for scatter graphs.

- **On Both Sides:** Choose this command to make the y-axis appear on both sides of the chart. You can't create a chart with two different y-axes, as you can in more sophisticated graphing programs.

The bar and stacked bar charts offer two slightly different commands:

 On Top Side: Choose this command to make the value axis stretch across the top of the selected graph.

 On Bottom Side: Choose this command, the default setting for bar and stacked bar graphs, to extend the value axis along the bottom.

After you have set the position of the value axis, you'll want to explore the other options Illustrator has for your value-axis-modifying pleasures. Choose the Value Axis command from the main pop-up menu at the top of the Graph Type dialog box. One of the Graph Type dialog box's alter egos will display, as shown in **Figure 13.31**. Here you can specify the location of tick marks and labels on the value axis. The options in the Add Labels and Tick Values areas affect the labels for the value axis, whereas the options in the Tick Marks area control the size of tick marks—those little lines that indicate numbers along the axes.

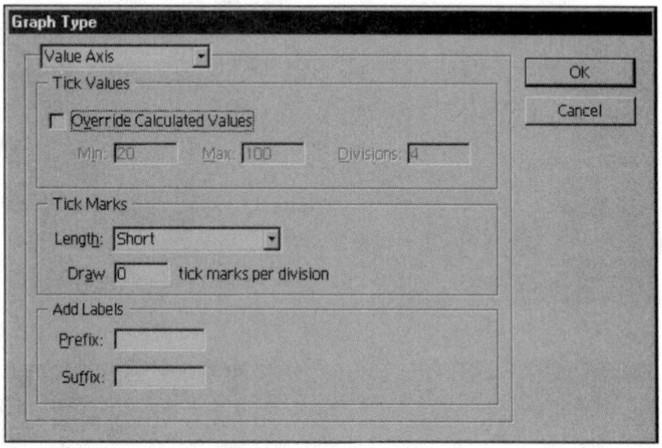

Figure 13.31: The Value Axis command shuttles you to this version of the Graph Type dialog box, in which you can modify labels and tick marks on the value axis.

We first encounter some nutty options related to the occurrence of tick marks:

 Override Calculated Values: By default, this check box is deselected. Unless you select it, Illustrator automatically determines the number of tick marks and labels that appear on the axis without worrying your pretty head about it.

 Min, Max, and Divisions: If you want to specify a range of labels in an axis to enhance the appearance of a chart, select the Override Calculated Values check box and enter values into the three option boxes. The Min value determines the lowest number on the axis, the Max value determines the highest number, and the Divisions value determines the increment between labels.

In **Figure 13.32**, I raised the Min value to 50 and changed the Divisions value to 10. Illustrator now graphs any data values under 50 below the x-axis. This way, I can track poor performance. For example, this chart says you can take Them off probation, but you're going to have to fire You.

 *To turn a chart upside down, so that the highest number is at the bottom of the axis and the lowest number is at the top (as in **Figure 13.33**), enter a negative value in the Divisions option box. To create an axis without labels, enter 0 in this option box.*

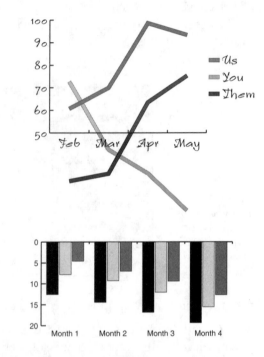

Figure 13.32: If values fall below the Min value, Illustrator plots them on the south side of the x-axis.

Figure 13.33: Flip a chart upside down by entering a negative value in the Divisions option box.

You use this set of commands to change the tick marks' appearance:

Length: You can choose a length of None, Short, and Full Width for your tick marks from this pop-up menu. Choose None to display no tick marks on the current axis. This command does not affect the placement or appearance of labels. Choose Short to display short tick marks that extend from the axis toward the chart, as by default. Choose Full Width to create tick marks that extend the full width or height of the chart. **Figure 13.34** shows the result of choosing the Full Width command.

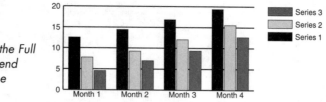

Figure 13.34: Choose the Full Width command to extend the tick marks across the entire chart.

🌐 **Draw tick marks per division:** This option should read "Tick Marks per Label," because it allows you to control the number of tick marks per labeled increment. In **Figure 13.35**, I've applied a value of 4 to the vertical axis, which creates four tick marks per label.

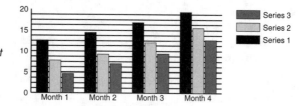

Figure 13.35: The same chart after entering a value of 4 into the Draw __ tick marks per division option box.

You use these options to add labels to a chart:

🌐 **Add Labels Prefix/Suffix:** These option boxes let you enter symbols or words up to nine characters long to precede or follow each label in a chart. For example, enter $ in the Prefix option box to precede every label with a dollar sign, as shown in **Figure 13.36**. Enter the letter g in the Suffix option box to indicate that each value is in thousands of dollars.

Now that you've perfected your value axis, choose the Category Axis command from the main pop-up menu at the top of the Graph Type dialog box and display the other version of this dialog box, as shown in **Figure 13.37**. Choose this command, that is, provided you aren't editing a radar chart or a scatter graph. With a radar graph, you're limited to the Value Axis options (as discussed above) and with a scatter chart, you get the Bottom Axis command that takes you to a dialog box with the exact options list above.

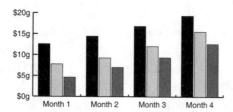

Figure 13.36: Enter characters to precede and follow the labels, such as the $ and g shown here, using the Prefix and Suffix option boxes.

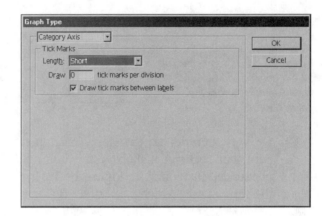

Figure 13.37: Choose the Category Axis command to open this mostly empty version of the Graph Type dialog box, where you can change the tick marks on the category axis.

The Tick Marks Length and the Draw __ tick marks per division options that you see here are the same as the ones first shown back in Figure 13.31. You'll find one new option here:

- **Draw tick marks between labels:** When this check box is selected tick marks appear centered between labels, as demonstrated by the vertical lines in the leftmost example of **Figure 13.38**. If you turn off the option, each tick mark is centered above its label, as shown in the rightmost example of Figure 13.38.

Figure 13.38: When working on a column, bar, line, or area chart, deselect the Draw tick marks between labels check box to create tick marks directly above the labels along the horizontal axis, as seen in the example on the right.

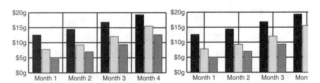

Other Weird Graph Style Options

Now that I've polished off the Value Axis and the Category Axis versions of the Graph Type dialog box, let's return to the Graph Options version of the Graph Type dialog box (shown in Figure 13.22) to explore four remaining options, all of which are more or less useless. I refer, of course, to the Style check boxes in the middle portion of the dialog box—Add Drop Shadow, Add Legend Across Top, First Row in Front, and First Column in Front. These dorky options work as follows:

- **Add Drop Shadow:** Select this check box to create drop shadows behind the columns, bars, lines, pie slices, or areas in a chart. This option is easily one of the dopiest in all of Illustrator. The drop shadow is always black, and you can't modify the distance between the shadow and the graph elements. You can more easily create your own drop shadow by selecting a few elements, copying them (Ctrl+C) (Cmd-C on the Mac), pasting them in back (Ctrl+B) (Cmd-B on the Mac), nudging them into the desired position with the arrow keys, and applying a fill color.

Add Legend Across Top: This option moves the legend from the right side of the chart to the top of the chart. The text is listed horizontally instead of vertically. Unfortunately, Illustrator has a nasty habit of overlapping text when you select this option, particularly when more than three series are involved. You're better off moving the legend manually.

First Row in Front: Select this check box to layer elements representing rows of data in the selected chart in descending order, with the first row in front and the last row in back. This option is useful only when modifying a column or bar chart in which the Cluster Width is set to greater than 100 percent. Because each row of data equates to a cluster, you can modify which cluster appears in front and which appears in back.

First Column in Front: Finally, a halfway useful option! Select this option to layer elements representing columns of data (I'm talking series, here) in descending order, with the first series in front and the last series in back. This option works with any chart except a pie chart. But it is most useful when editing a line or scatter chart, because it allows you to prioritize the manner in which lines overlap.

 *Do not turn off the First Column in Front check box when editing an area chart. If you do, the last series will completely cover all other series in the chart.*

Manually Customizing a Graph

If you've been reading this chapter sequentially, your brain is undoubtedly a little numb by now. Either that, or you've been reading the book in bed in lieu of a sedative. Let's face it, taking in Illustrator's half-million graphing options is a daunting—not to mention boring—task.

That's why it may come as a welcome shock that one tool—the direct selection tool—is more capable than every option in all the Graph Type dialog boxes combined. Armed with the direct selector, you can move elements around, apply different colors, edit the size of text and legend swatches, and just plain customize the heck out of your graph.

Selecting Elements Inside Graphs

To get anywhere with the direct selection tool, you need to understand how to select elements inside a graph. A graph is actually an extensive collection of grouped objects inside grouped objects, inside other grouped objects, which are—needless to say—grouped. This means a lot of Alt-clicking (Option-clicking on the Mac) with the direct selection tool.

The following list demonstrates a few of the different kinds of selections you can make with the direct selection tool:

- Click a point or segment in the graph to select that specific element. You can then move the point or segment. However, you cannot delete it by pressing the Delete key, because that would leave a gap in the path, and Illustrator does not permit gaps in graphs.

- Click a text object to select it. All text in a graph is point text. If you have trouble selecting the text, try clicking along the baseline of the text instead of on one of the letters. You can then change the font, type size, alignment, and half a dozen other formatting attributes without affecting any deselected text in the graph.

- Alt-click (Option-click on the Mac) to select a whole object in the chart, such as an axis or a column.

- Alt-click (Option-click on the Mac) a second time to select an entire axis, including tick marks and labels, or to select an entire series. If you Alt (Option)-click some text a second time, you select all text belonging to that subgroup in the graph. For example, Alt (Option)-clicking some legend text twice selects all legend text.

- Alt (Option)-click a column three times to select an entire series as well as its color swatch in the legend. Now you can apply a different color from the Paint Style palette to modify the fill or stroke of the series.

- Alt (Option)-click a fourth time to select all series and legend swatches in the chart.

- Alt (Option)-click a fifth time to select the entire chart.

This is a rather imprecise science, and different kinds of charts require a different number of Alt (Option)-clicks, depending on how many series are involved and other factors. For example, you may find you need to Alt (Option)-click only

twice to select a series and its legend swatch in a line chart, whereas you had to
Alt (Option)-click three times in a column chart. Keep an eye on the screen as
you Alt (Option)-click to monitor your progress.

Selecting Multiple Series Inside a Graph

Another handy key to keep in mind when selecting graph elements is Shift. As
you know, you can press this key to select multiple objects, but pressing it just as
easily deselects objects. Therefore, you have to be deliberate in your actions, particularly when the Alt (Option) key is involved.

For example, suppose you want to select two series of columns in a column
chart, including their swatches in the legend. Here's how you'd do it:

**1. Using the direct selection tool, Alt (Option)-click a column in
the chart.**

This selects the column.

2. Alt (Option)-click the column again.

This second click selects all other columns in the series.

3. Alt (Option)-click the column a third time.

Now the legend swatch becomes selected.

**4. Alt+Shift-click (Option-Shift-click on the Mac) a column in
a different series.**

Illustrator adds this new column to the growing collection of selected
objects.

5. Alt (Option)-click that same column again.

This is the important step, the one that baffles thousands of users on a
daily basis. If you Alt+Shift-click (Option-Shift-click on the Mac)
again, you deselect the column; but without the Shift key, you can't
add to the selection, right?

Wrong—but in a good way. So long as the item on which you Alt
(Option)-click is selected, Illustrator broadens the selection to include
the next group up. Therefore, this Alt (Option)-click selects the other
columns in this series.

6. Alt (Option)-click this column for a third time.

This selects the swatch for the series in the legend. You now have two
entire series of columns selected independently of any other series in
the graph.

While this seems complex and maybe even backward, this operation makes absolute sense once you understand the order of the Illustrator universe. These steps may be cumbersome, but they are impeccably logical. Come to terms with these steps and you'll never have problems selecting objects inside Illustrator again. The good news is, it simply doesn't get more complicated than this. You can also switch selected series to a different chart type, as in **Figure 13.39**. This chart started off as a column chart, but I wanted to highlight my client's product, Hand Buzzers. Therefore, I decided to convert the Sea Monkeys and X-Ray Specs series to line graphs. I first selected both series, as outlined in the previous steps, and double-clicked the graph tool to display the Graph Type dialog box. I then selected the Line button from the Type options, modified the Line Graph Options, and pressed Enter (Return on the Mac).

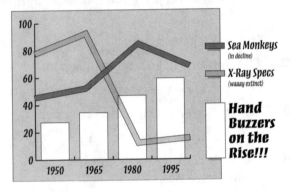

Figure 13.39: Starting from a column chart, I converted two of the series to line graphs.

I didn't stop there. In fact, I ended up ungrouping the graph to achieve some of the effects. To create the faded intersection between the X-Ray Specs line and the Hand Buzzer columns, I cloned the shapes and combined them using Filter » Pathfinder » Intersect, as explained in Chapter 7. I also added drop shadows behind the legend swatches, a technique covered in Chapter 20. Like any other kind of art you can create in Illustrator, graphs are limited only by your creativity, ingenuity, and patience.

More Custom Modification Options

Once you figure out how to select items in graphs with some degree of predictability, you'll discover hundreds of methods for altering them. Rather than wasting reams of paper stepping you through every possible variation, here are a few parting tidbits of wisdom to whisk you on your way:

 The text and swatches in the legend are parts of several different sub-groups, but because they are physically separated from other graph elements, you can easily select them by marqueeing them with the direct selection tool. Then you can drag them anywhere you want or use the scale tool to reduce their size.

- You can edit text inside a graph with the type tool, as I did in Figure 13.39. But be careful; if you have to go back later and edit the data, Illustrator restores the text entered into the Graph Data window. (Unfortunately, Illustrator is not smart enough to implement your text changes into the spreadsheet automatically.) Obviously, it would be better to change the source text in the Graph Data window and update the graph.

- You can edit paths inside a graph with the add point, delete point, and convert point tools without first ungrouping the path. Again, changes that you made inside the Graph Data window or Graph Type dialog box may override these adjustments.

 You should edit your legend after creating a graph, because the default size and position may not be the way you want it.

Graphing with Graphics

What kind of illustration program would Illustrator be if it didn't allow you to create graphs with pictures? In a valiant effort to satisfy you, the customer, Illustrator lets you create pictographs, which are graphs in which series are represented by graphic objects. The graphics can form columns in a column chart, like the cent symbols in **Figure 13.40**, or they can appear as markers in a line or scatter chart. The following sections describe how pictographs work.

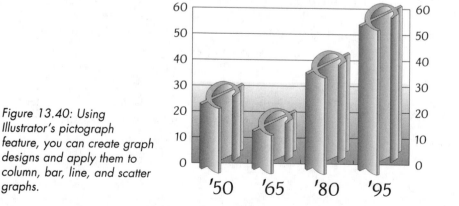

Figure 13.40: Using Illustrator's pictograph feature, you can create graph designs and apply them to column, bar, line, and scatter graphs.

Creating a Graph Design

You create pictographs by establishing graph designs—collections of graphic objects that can be applied to a chart. The following steps describe how to transform a few common, everyday objects into a graph design in Illustrator:

1. **Draw the objects and fill them as desired.**

   Figure 13.41 shows how I constructed the objects in the cent chart. Many of the tools and commands I used are covered in later chapters.

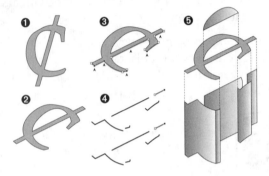

Figure 13.41: The steps involved in creating a cent symbol with mock 3-D sides.

I started with a large Palatino character and converted it to paths (Example 1 in the figure). Then I rotated and slanted it with the rotate and shear tools (2). Next I selected several points and segments along the outline of the shape by clicking and Shift-clicking at the spots indicated by the arrowheads in the figure (3). I copied the selected elements to the Clipboard (Ctrl+C)(Cmd-C on the Mac), pressed Ctrl+Shift+A (Cmd-Shift-A on the Mac) to deselect the elements, and chose Edit » Paste in Front (Ctrl+F) (Cmd-F on the Mac).

I dragged the selected items down to a point at which I could more easily work on them. Then I Shift+Alt (Option-dragged on the Mac) them downward to clone them (4). These open paths represent the tops and bottoms of the sides coming down from the cent sign back in Figure 13.40; all I had to do was connect them with straight segments. To do this, I used the direct selection tool to select the endpoints of corresponding paths (like the selected points in Example 4 in the figure) and chose Object » Path » Join (Ctrl+J) (Cmd-J on the Mac). Then I Alt-clicked (Option-clicked on the Mac) the newly joined path with the direct selection tool to select the whole path and pressed Ctrl+J (Cmd-J on the Mac) again. This was repeated for each pair of paths.

Finally, I selected all the paths (except the cent itself) and filled them with gradations from the Gradient palette (5). I also had to fill the interior of the cent sign with a gradation, but because the path was serving as a hole in the cent sign, I had to make a duplicate. I selected it, copied it (Ctrl+C) (Cmd-C on the Mac), pressed Ctrl+Shift+A (Cmd-Shift-A on the Mac) to deselect everything, and pasted the path in front (Ctrl+F) (Cmd-F on the Mac). Then I filled it with the same gradation as the other paths. To finish it off, I dragged the sides up to the cent outline so sides and cent snapped into alignment.

2. **Draw a straight, horizontal line across the middle of the portion of the graph you want Illustrator to elongate when applying the design to a column chart.**

If you're designing a marker for a line graph, you don't need to add this horizontal line, and you can skip to Step 4.

Use the pen tool to draw a horizontal line slightly wider than the graph design by clicking at one point and Shift-clicking at another. Then position the line along the spot where any stretching should occur. For example, I created the line in about the middle of the sides of the cent symbol, as indicated by the dotted line in **Figure 13.42**. Doing this tells Illustrator to stretch the sides, not the cent symbol itself.

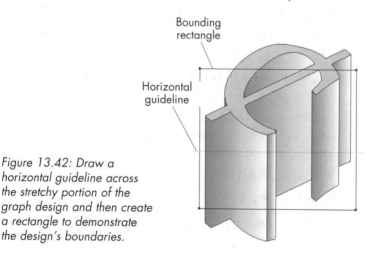

Bounding
rectangle

Horizontal
guideline

Figure 13.42: Draw a horizontal guideline across the stretchy portion of the graph design and then create a rectangle to demonstrate the design's boundaries.

3. **Select the horizontal line and choose View » Make Guides.**

Or press shortcut Ctrl+5 (Cmd-5 on the Mac). The line becomes dotted (or solid, depending on the settings in your Guides & Grids Preferences dialog box), as pictured in Figure 13.42. Also, make sure

View » Lock Guides is turned off. If the Lock command has a check mark next to it, choose the command to unlock the guide. Illustrator requires that you convert the line to a guide for the stretching function to work. (For more about guides, turn to Chapter 8.)

4.   Draw a rectangle to specify the boundaries of the graph design.

Where graphs are concerned, Illustrator thinks largely in terms of rectangles. Columns are rectangles, for example, and line graph markers are squares. When creating a graph design, you have to tell Illustrator how the design fits onto the standard rectangle. Another way to look at it is to say that the rectangle you're about to draw is the exact size of one pictograph unit, regardless of the shape or actual size of the picture.

Use the rectangle tool to draw a boundary around the graph design as shown in Figure 13.42. If the rectangle doesn't completely enclose the design, the design may overlap graph elements. For example, this design extends below the rectangle; therefore it will overlap the x-axis, as it does back in Figure 13.40. The design also extends over the top of the rectangle, so it will rise slightly higher than the data value. (If you're feeling very strict about your data, make sure the top of the rectangle exactly touches the top of the graph design.) The fact that the rectangle is wider than the design, however, keeps the design slightly slimmer than a standard column.

If you want space between the pictograms, draw the rectangle larger than the picture.

5.   Send the rectangle to the back of the illustration.

Choose Object » Arrange » Send To Back, or press Ctrl+Shift+[(Cmd-Shift-[on the Mac) (left bracket). This may sound like an inconsequential step, but it's very important. Illustrator insists on the boundary rectangle being in back.

6.   Make the fill and stroke invisible.

Select the None icon in the toolbox.

7.   Select all graph objects and choose Object » Graphs » Design.

Select the graph design, horizontal guide, and rectangle. (If these are the only objects in the illustration, press Ctrl+A (Cmd-A on the Mac.) Then choose Object » Graph » Design to display the Graph Design dialog box shown in **Figure 13.43**.

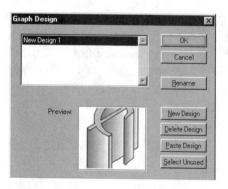

Figure 13.43: Illustrator crops the preview in the Graph Design dialog box to reflect the top and bottom edges of the bounding rectangle.

8. Click the New Design button.

Illustrator shows you a preview of the graph design cropped inside your bounding rectangle, as in Figure 13.43. (Don't worry, the actual graph design is not cropped.) The program also adds an item to the scrolling list called New Design, followed by a number.

If Illustrator complains when you click New Design, it's because the rectangle is not the backmost object you've selected. It may be because you didn't properly follow Step 5, or it may be that you accidentally selected the graph, or other objects farther back yet. In any case, press Escape to close the dialog box, press Ctrl+Shift+A (Cmd-Shift-A on the Mac) to deselect everything, select the rectangle, cut it (Ctrl+X) (Cmd-X on the Mac), make sure the arrow tool is active, and paste the rectangle in back (Ctrl+B) (Cmd-B on the Mac). Now try Steps 7 and 8 again.

9. With the new design name selected, click Rename, then enter a name for the design and press Enter (Return on the Mac).

The graph design is now ready to apply to any column, bar, line, or scatter graph.

 Your new graph design is available only to the illustration you created it in. If you want to make a graph design available to all future illustrations whether this particular document is open or not, open the Adobe Illustrator Startup file in the Plug-ins folder. Then choose Object » Graph » Design to display the Graph Design dialog box, and click the Paste Design button. This creates a copy of the design inside the Startup file. Press Enter (Return on the Mac) to leave the dialog box, move the design to a suitable spot in the illustration window (but don't delete it!), and save the Startup file to disk.

When creating a graph design, you may not have to draw your own pictogram if the one you want already exists as one of the symbols that shipped with Illustrator. Look in the Symbols palette and in the symbol libraries (choose Window > Symbol Libraries), or on the Illustrator CD (look in Illustrator Extras/ Symbol Libraries).

Organizing Graph Designs

In addition to allowing you to create new graph designs, the Graph Design dialog box provides the following options for organizing and editing existing graph designs:

- **Delete Design:** Click this button to delete a selected design from the scrolling list. Illustrator removes the design from all open illustrations! Therefore, don't delete a design when a graph using the design is open.

- *If you delete a design and you didn't mean to, press Escape or click the Cancel button to cancel the operation. If you realize your mistake only after pressing Enter (Return on the Mac) or clicking the OK button, you can still restore the graph design by pressing Ctrl+Z (Cmd-Z on the Mac).*

- **Paste Design:** Even if you throw away the original copy of your graph design, it may not be lost for good. So long as the design has been applied to a graph, you can retrieve the original objects. Inside the Graph Design dialog box, select the design name from the list and click the Paste Design button. Illustrator pastes the original objects into the illustration window. Then press Enter (Return on the Mac) to close the dialog box and edit the objects as desired. (If you leave the dialog box by pressing the Escape key, Illustrator cancels the paste operation.)

- **Select Unused:** Click this button to select all designs that are not applied to graphs in any open illustration. Then you can click the Delete Design button to get rid of them.

After you edit the pasted objects, you can redefine the graph design and all open graphs that use the design. Select the objects and choose Object » Graph » Design. Then select the design name from the list and press Enter (Return on the Mac) or click the OK button. (That's it; no special buttons to press.) Illustrator displays an alert box asking if you want to redraw all graphs or just redefine the graph design for future graphs. Press Enter (Return on the Mac) to do both.

You can rename a pattern by clicking on the Rename button. In the Rename dialog box, enter a new name and click OK or hit Enter (Return on the Mac).

Applying a Design to a Column Chart

To apply a design to a column chart or a stacked column chart, select the column chart with the arrow tool or select the single series that you want to convert to a pictograph with the direct selection tool. Then choose Object » Graph » Column to display the Graph Column dialog box shown in **Figure 13.44**.

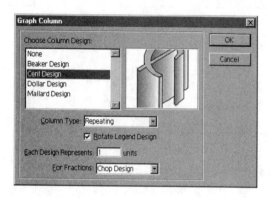

Figure 13.44: Use the Graph Column dialog box to apply a graph design to a column chart.

Select a graph design from the scrolling Choose Column Design list (select None only when you want to remove a graph design from the selected series), choose a command from the Column Type pop-up menu, and press the Enter (Return on the Mac) key. Illustrator applies the design to all selected series.

The Column Type pop-up menu allows you to change the way Illustrator stretches or repeats the graph design from one column to the next. **Figure 13.45** demonstrates the effect of the four options in the order they appear in the dialog box. Here's how each option works.

- **Vertically Scaled:** Choose this command to stretch the graph design vertically to represent different values, as demonstrated at the top of Figure 13.45. Notice that in the case of the cent symbol, Illustrator stretches both the sides and the cent outline itself. This is sometimes useful, though it's not the best match for the cent design.

- **Uniformly Scaled:** Choose this command to scale the graph design proportionally according to the size of the data, as shown in the second example on the left in Figure 13.45. This option is useful primarily when your data has little variation. Because it scales two dimensions (height and width) instead of one (just height), differences are exaggerated, which can be misleading. Large values have a tendency to take over the graph.

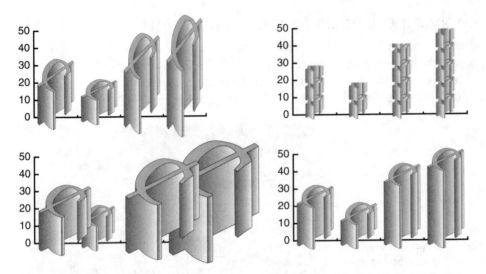

Figure 13.45: The Vertically Scaled (top left), Uniformly Scaled (bottom left), Repeating (top right), and Sliding (bottom right) options change the way Illustrator applies a graph design to a column chart.

Repeating: If you want to repeat the graph design over and over again, choose this command. Illustrator creates stacks of the object, as in the example at the upper right in Figure 13.45. This style of pictograph is very popular—you can stack coins, dollar bills, cars, footballs, computer monitors…anything you want.

When the Repeating command is selected, the otherwise-dimmed For Fractions pop-up menu becomes available. Enter a value in the Each Design Represents option box to determine the data increment represented by each repetition of the graph design. For example, if a value in the selected series is 49, and you enter 10 for the Each Design Represents value, the design repeats four full times and a fifth partial time, just like the last column in the figure.

The two For Fractions commands determine how Illustrator slices or scales the last graph design to accommodate remaining data that doesn't divide evenly into the Each Design Represents value. Select the Chop Design command to lop off the extraneous top design, as in Figure 13.45; select the Scale Design command to vertically scale the top design to fit its fractional value.

Sliding: Select this option to elongate the graph design at the spot indicated by the horizontal guideline, as in the final example at the lower right in Figure 13.45. This is usually the most desirable option, and it certainly looks the best when combined with the cent design. Illustrator stretches the sides of the design but leaves the cent symbol itself untouched.

Select the Rotate Legend Design check box to display the graph design on its side in the legend. (I omitted the legend in Figure 13.45 by neglecting to enter any column headings in the Graph Data window.) If you deselect the Rotate Legend Design check box, the design appears upright in the legend.

Applying a Design to a Line Chart

To apply a design to a line or scatter chart, select the graph with the arrow tool or select the specific markers you want to change with the direct selection tool. (Do not select the line segments.) Then choose Object » Graphs » Marker, which brings to life the Graph Marker dialog box shown in **Figure 13.46**.

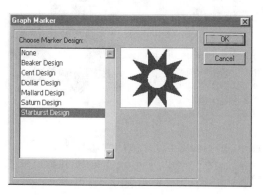

Figure 13.46: Use the Graph Marker dialog box to apply a graph design to the markers in a line or scatter chart.

Select a graph design from the scrolling Marker Design list and press Enter (Return on the Mac). Illustrator applies the graph design to the individual markers in the chart.

To create **Figure 13.47**, I Alt (Option)-clicked one set of markers twice with the direct selection tool to select all the markers in one series, and then applied the starburst graph design. I then Alt (Option)-clicked the other set of markers twice, and applied the Saturn design.

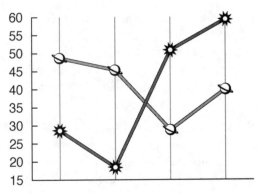

Figure 13.47: I applied two different sets of graph designs to the markers of a line graph.

Illustrator determines the size of a graph design based on the size of the bounding rectangle that you drew when defining the original graph design. The bounding rectangle is reduced to match the size of the square marker that normally appears in a line or scatter chart.

Figure 13.48: I used small bounding rectangles to make the graph designs appear large in the line graph in Figure 13.47.

Therefore, to create a design that scales to a reasonable size, draw a relatively small bounding rectangle. **Figure 13.48** shows the bounding rectangles as dotted outlines for the starburst and Saturn patterns.

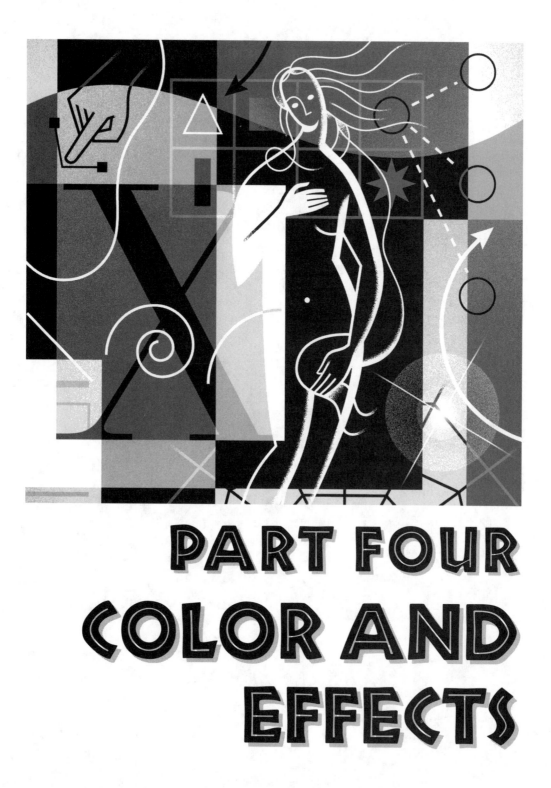

PART FOUR
COLOR AND
EFFECTS

THE SLIPPERY SCIENCE OF COLOR

Back before I immersed myself in computer graphics, I could never understand how companies could own colors. In a world where colors are as free and abundant as dirt, color technologies such as Technicolor and the Pantone Matching System represent multimillion-dollar businesses. Even children's Crayola colors are trademarked. Is no tint of grassy green or hue of rosy red safe from these marauding color pirates?

The fact is, the colors we see in nature are ours to enjoy, free from corporate intrusion. But it takes technology and science to represent colors in film, in photographs, on the printed page, and on your computer screen. For example, to represent a sprig of evergreen on a piece of paper, you can't take the sprig and mush it into the paper fibers. You have to find natural and synthetic colors that blend together to create a reasonable facsimile. This imitation of the real world is what the slippery science of color is all about.

In this chapter, I explain a little bit about color theory and a whole lot about how color works in Illustrator. I show you how to select colors from predefined, trademarked libraries and how to define your own colors using combinations of primary printing pigments. I also introduce Illustrator's restrictive color space for each document, the Color palette, the Swatches palette, the color filters, and all the other major points of interest along Illustrator's Great Color Way.

Color technology is one of the most complex areas of computer graphics. But even if you're brand-spanking new to the subject, you have reason to rejoice: You're using a decent computer, you own Adobe Illustrator (a most capable color editor), and you're armed with this helpful book (need I say more?). How can you possibly go wrong?

 The color space in Illustrator is restricted to either CMYK or RGB. This is to help avoid production problems where RGB colors—especially those in images—are separated as part of process printing. You shouldn't feel constrained by the restriction, though. You can easily switch from one color space to another. More on this later in this chapter.

The Great White Light and the Breakaway Color Republics

I hate theory, you hate theory—I don't think I've ever met anyone who just loves a good dose of theory. Unfortunately, I have to share a few basic color observations before moving on to the more exciting and practical discussions of how you use color in Illustrator. See, color is a highly misunderstood topic, particularly among the folks who work with it every day. Whether you're a graphics novice or a publishing professional, it pays to arm yourself with as much basic color knowledge as possible. Just as it helps to know a little something about motors when you take your car in for repair, it helps to know the fundamentals of color when you enter a print shop.

The most common misconception is that color exists in the real world. It doesn't. It's all in your head. In fact, similarly colored objects share no common chemical or physical properties. And a single material—such as copper—may change in color dramatically under slightly different conditions.

Your perception of color is based on so-called white light from the sun or some other light source filtering through or bouncing off a surface. The light then passes into your eye and mutates into nerve impulses that shoot into your brain. Color is a fantastic illusion that humans (and other primates) perceive differently than any other life form. Plants, rocks, and most animals are completely unaware of color as we know it. If you were visited by a being from another planet, chances are very good that you and that being would have no common color vernacular whatsoever. You can't hear, feel, smell, or taste color because color is an inherent ingredient in sight. In fact, you don't see color; your brain makes it up as a means of interpreting the light waves registered by your eye.

The World According to Your Eye

So let's talk about your eye. Inside this amazing orb are a bunch of light-sensitive cells called rods and cones. Rods pick up dim light and are good for detecting brightness and motion. Cones are responsible for color—they react best to strong light. Cones hang out in the central portion of the retina, and rods populate the outer regions. Therefore, you can judge colors most accurately by examining them in daylight and looking directly at them.

Cones come in three types. Generally speaking, each type is sensitive to red, green, or blue light. (Remember, this is light, not the primary colors in paint.) If all cones are stimulated, you see white. If both the red and green cones get excited but the blue cones shut down, you see yellow. What's important here is that the light coming into your eye may bounce off a yellow object, pass through a yellow filter, or come from a combination of red and green lights shining together. Your eye doesn't know the difference.

Computer screens and televisions fool your eye by speaking directly to your cones. The inside of the monitor is coated with red, green, and blue phosphors that emit light. So a yellow pixel is really a combination of red light shining for the benefit of the red cones and green light going to the green cones. If there's no blue light coming from the pixel, the corresponding blue cones take a nap.

RGB Light

Therefore, red, green, and blue are the primary colors of light. In theory, all visible colors can be expressed using a combination of these three basic ingredients. Intense lights, or multiple lights projected together, produce lighter colors. That's why red and green mix to form yellow, which is lighter than either red or green. Similarly, red and blue mix to form a hot pink called magenta, and blue and green make a bright turquoise called cyan. Full intensities of all three primaries form white; equal amounts of each color in lesser quantities make gray; and the absence of red, green, or blue light is black. (Think about it—what color is it when you turn out the lights?)

This is called the RGB color model, shown in pathetic black and white in **Figure 14.1**. You may also hear someone refer to it as the *additive* color model, because increasing the amount of a primary color increases the brightness. Electronic scanners read photographs by shining red, green, and blue lights on them, which is why the RGB color model is a favorite of Photoshop. It is also useful for illustrations for the Web, slides, CD-ROMs, and any Illustrator creation that you expressly intend for people to see onscreen. You'll want to use the CMYK color model (explained in just a few paragraphs) for illustrations you intend to print. You can also import RGB images into Illustrator or rasterize objects using the RGB color model.

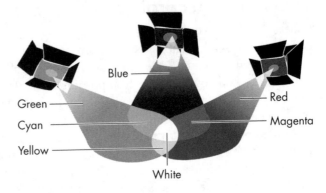

Figure 14.1: In the additive color model, red, green, and blue lights combine to create white light.

Blue

Green

Cyan

Yellow

Red

Magenta

White

The explosion of the Internet has given birth to another color model— Web-safe RGB (a miniscule subset of the RGB color model) that uses a combination of letters and numbers called hexadecimal. Web-safe colors are those colors that can be seen on the Web without any dithering. Rather than bore the print folks, who aren't into Web design, I cover Web-safe colors in Chapter 21.

HSB Schemings

Another way to look at the colors that you see is to start with a set of base colors and then vary the intensity of the colors. That's what you get with the HSB color model.

HSB stands for hue, saturation, and brightness. Hue is the pure color—your own personal rainbow. Saturation dictates the amount of the hue you see. The greater the saturation, the more intense the color. Brightness determines the amount of black added.

HSB is more of a variation of RGB than a separate color model (like a Noo Yawk accent compared to a Midwest twang). It's ideal for when you want to find a different shade of an RGB color. Take an RGB color, switch it to its HSB equivalent with the HSB command in the Color palette's pop-up menu, adjust the saturation and brightness, and switch it back to RGB when you're satisfied.

CMYK Pigments

Unfortunately, paper is not capable of shining light in your face the way a monitor is. Instead, light reflects off the surface of the page. So it's a lucky thing that white light—whether from the sun or from an artificial light source—contains the entire visible spectrum. Just as red, green, and blue light mix to form white, white contains red, green, and blue, as well as all other combinations of those colors. Every single color you can see is trapped in every ray of sunlight.

When you draw across a piece of white paper with a highlighter, the ink filters out sunlight. A pink highlighter, for example, filters out all nonpink light and reflects pink. This is the exact same way that professional printing colors work. There are three primary inks—cyan, magenta, and yellow—all of which are translucent pigments that filter out different kinds of light:

- Cyan acts as a red light filter. When white light hits a white page, it passes through the cyan ink and reflects all light that is not red—i.e., green and blue.

- Likewise, magenta ink filters out green light.

- And yellow ink filters out blue light.

So an area that appears red onscreen prints in magenta and yellow on paper. The magenta and yellow ink filters out the green and blue light and leaves only red to bounce back off the page. Cyan and magenta mix to form blue; cyan and yellow make green. All three inks together ought to make black. (I tell you why they don't in a minute.) And a complete absence of ink reveals the white page. Because less ink leads to lighter colors, this is called the *subtractive* color model.

In a perfect world, CMY would be the exact opposites of RGB. But colored inks are not nearly as reliable as colored lights. It's a simple trick to split white light into its pure primary components. You've probably seen it done with prisms. But generating pure inks—such as a cyan that filters all red and no green or blue whatsoever—is practically impossible. Throw in the bleached piece of wood pulp that passes for an absolute white backdrop and you see how ink purity might prove a real problem. To compensate, color printing throws in one additional ink: black. Black is the *key* color—the one that helps the other inks out—which makes black the *K* in the CMYK color model. Black ensures deep shadows, neutral grays, and—of course—nice, even blacks.

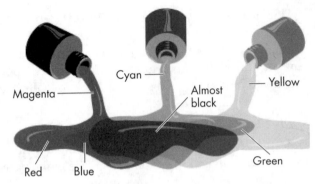

Figure 14.2: In the subtractive color model, cyan, magenta, and yellow ink combine. In theory, all three should create black—but they don't. So a fourth key color, black, is added in the real world.

Cyan, magenta, yellow and black inks are the four printing primaries. Some folks call cyan, magenta, yellow, and black *process* colors, which is why CMYK printing is sometimes called four-color process printing. (The word *process* is an old printing term, simply meaning that the colors are automatically generated to imitate a wider range of colors.)

Process inks are measured in percentages. The maximum intensity of any ink is 100 percent, and the minimum is naturally zero percent. For example, 100 percent black is pitch black, 75 percent black is dark gray, and 50 percent black is medium gray. Here are some more recipes to keep in mind.

- 50 percent cyan plus 50 percent magenta is a light violet. Increase the cyan to make the color bluer; increase the magenta to make it purple.

- 50 percent magenta plus 50 percent yellow is a medium scarlet. Increase the magenta to make the color redder; increase the yellow to make it more orange. 100 percent yellow by itself is a lemon yellow. To get a cornflower yellow, add about 15 percent magenta to 100 percent yellow.

- 50 percent yellow plus 50 percent cyan is grass green. Add more yellow to get a bright chartreuse; add more cyan to tend toward teal. To get a sea blue, combine 100 percent cyan and 20 percent yellow.

- If you add a little magenta or cyan to black, you create a richer black color—sometimes called a *rich black*. Add about 40 percent magenta to 100 percent black and the rich black feels warmer; add about 40 percent cyan and the rich black feels cooler.

- You can add the complementary ink (the odd CMY ink out) to deepen a color. For example, if you have 50 percent cyan plus 50 percent magenta, adding the complementary ink—yellow—creates mauve. Add the complementary ink instead of black when you want to darken a color without dulling it.

- Adding black both darkens a color and makes it duller. Just a hint of black—10 percent to 25 percent—is great for creating drab colors like olive, steel blue, beige, and brick red.

- Brown is an amalgam of everything, with the emphasis on magenta and yellow. For example, 20 percent cyan and black with 60 percent magenta and yellow is a rich sienna.

 As a general rule, try not to create colors with more than 300 percent of all the inks. The inks tend to build up on the paper and can make your printed piece very sticky and messy.

 All these color combinations assume that you're printing to white paper. Because all inks except black are translucent, any paper color except white will blend in with the colors and change how they look, usually for the worse. When you're new to publishing, it's tempting to experiment with differently colored papers; after all, white is so boring. But about 90 percent of all professional work is printed to white paper because white permits the widest range of colors. Unless you have a specific reason for doing otherwise, stick with white.

But even though you can create a wealth of colors with CMYK, it simply can't measure up to RGB. The CMYK model has a smaller *gamut*—or color range—than its RGB cousin. Vivid colors in particular—including bright reds and oranges, brilliant greens and blues, and eye-popping purples—fall outside the CMYK gamut.

Spot Colors

That's why spot colors exist. Spot colors (also known as solid colors) are separate inks that you can add to the four basic process colors or that you can use instead of the process colors. For example, you might print a two-color newsletter using black and a spot color. Or, if you can't match a client's logo using process colors, you can add the proper spot color to your four-color printing job.

Pantone is probably the best known vendor of spot colors, offering a library of several hundred premixed inks that are supported by just about every major commercial print house in the United States. Like many other desktop publishing programs, Illustrator provides complete support for the Pantone Color Matching System (or PMS for short).

If you use a spot color in addition to the process colors, it will add to the cost of your print job. For every spot color that you add, you have to pay for the ink and the printing plate, as well as the time and labor required to feed the paper through another run. (Each color has to be printed in a separate pass.) Even companies with deep pockets rarely print more than six colors per page (CMYK plus two spots).

Choosing Your Color Space

It used to be when you started Illustrator, you could just grab a tool and get to work. These days you first have to choose a color space. Simply stated, this means you are going to ask Illustrator to keep you always working in either RGB or CMYK color mode.

 The choice of color space is the primary reason you have to choose File » New after you launch Illustrator 10. You have to choose the color space for a document before you can start work.

Your choice of color space depends on what your final output of the job will be. Print work requires CMYK; Web graphics or onscreen presentations use RGB. By restricting your color space, Illustrator prevents you from creating colors that are outside the gamut of your chosen color model. Just because you're restricted to the output of a certain color space, doesn't mean that you can't define colors in CMYK or RGB. If you're working in CMYK, Illustrator works behind the scenes to convert your RGB (or HSB) colors into the closest possible CMYK match. Similarly in RGB, Illustrator converts CMYK colors into RGB. This color conversion takes place automatically, without you doing a thing.

Finally, just because you work in one space doesn't mean you can't switch back and forth between color spaces. (Unlike what happens in Photoshop, you don't lose information by switching back and forth.) So why would anyone want to switch between the two color spaces? The most important reason is that most of the filters for raster effects work only in the RGB color space.

Finding Your Colors in Illustrator

You define all new process colors in the Color palette by adjusting the different slider bars. Depending on which color model you are using (all of which are accessed through the Color palette's pop-up menu), the slider bars will vary the CMYK, RGB, or HSB amounts. You can define spot colors or import them from third-party swatch libraries.

● Once you've created colors in the Color palette, you can either use the color right away or save it for later. If you want to save a color so that you can use it over and over again, choose the New Swatch command from the Swatches palette's pop-up menu or simply drag the color, from the Color palette or toolbox, onto the Swatches palette. You will then have the option of naming the color as well as deciding whether you wish to convert it to a spot color.

You can also use one of the predefined colors in the Swatches palette. Or you can load entire libraries of spot colors from the Window » Swatch Libraries submenu.

I'll discuss all of these options—and more—in the next sections.

Onscreen Color Controls

There are four onscreen elements that allow you to work with colors. In the Color palette, you can choose the color model that will best mix your favorite shade of "tickle-me" pink. The Swatches palette stores a number of predefined solid colors (as well as predefined gradients and patterns, both discussed in upcoming chapters). The toolbox and Appearance palette, as well as the Color palette, let you change the focus from fill to stroke. **Figure 14.3** shows a montage of the locations of all your color-related controls.

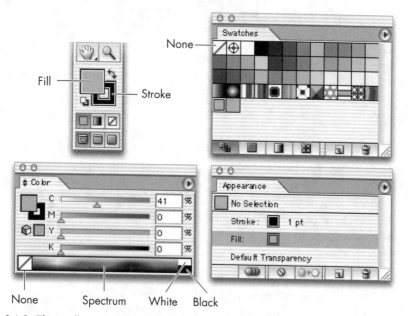

Figure 14.3: The toolbox and the Color, Swatches, and Appearance palettes provide for all your needs when you're creating and editing colors.

 To quickly switch the focus from the Fill icon to the Stroke icon and vice versa in the Color palette and in the bottom portion of the toolbox, press the X key. To swap the color between the icons, press Shift-X.

You can also choose colors by double-clicking either the Fill or Stroke icon at the bottom of the toolbox. This opens the Color Picker dialog box as shown in **Figure 14.4**. Click each of the radio buttons to change the way the Color Picker displays colors. There is little advantage to using the color picker and one big disadvantage: it takes over a large chunk of your screen.

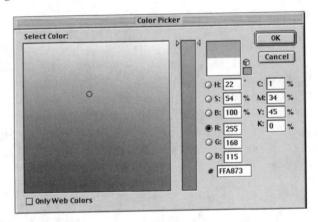

Figure 14.4: Double-click either the Fill or Stroke icons in the toolbox to open the Color Picker dialog box.

To display the Color palette, choose Window » Color. The Swatches palette responds to the Window » Swatches command. Choose Window » Appearance to see the Appearance palette. Choose Window » Show Tools to make the toolbox appear.

All four contribute to the Illustrator color experience, and I refer to all of them throughout this chapter. It's also impossible to talk about color without mentioning fill or stroke, as this chapter does. Fill and stroke, though, are covered in greater detail in Chapters 15 and 16. You decide whether you want to modify the fill or stroke of a selection by clicking on the Fill or Stroke icon in the Color palette or the toolbox (or just press the X key).

Using the Color Palette

The Color palette is the easiest way to pick the values for a color. First, use the Color palette pop-up menu to pick the color model you want to use (Grayscale, RGB, HSB, CMYK, or Web Safe RGB). Click the spectrum bar along the bottom of the Color palette to approximate the color of your dreams. Modify the sliders by dragging on the little triangle that accompanies each bar, or change the values in the option boxes to the right of each bar.

To cycle through the different color models, Shift-click the spectrum bar at the bottom of the Color palette. To move from the RGB model to the HSB model and then to the CMYK model, simply Shift-click the spectrum bar twice. Be sure to hold down the Shift key while clicking the spectrum bar or you will change your color and not your color model.

- The Color palette's pop-up menu contains two commands that systematically change the values of the current color: Invert and Complement. The Invert command changes the color to its opposite along the RGB scale. For example, a color made up of 100 red, 150 blue, and 200 green inverts to 155 red, 105 blue, and 55 green. The original value and the inverted value for each component must add up to 255. Even if you work in the CMYK color space, the Invert command uses RGB values to calculate the inverse color.

- The Complement command alters colors in a similar manner (although the result is quite contrary to what you might expect based on any color theory with which I am familiar). Whereas the Invert command bases its changes on 255, the Complement command uses the sum of the lowest and highest RGB values. Say we start with a battleship blue that breaks down into 55 red, 95 green, and 120 blue. Complement would add the lowest and highest values (55 + 120, yielding 175) and then subtract each value from this total. The resulting components would be 120 red (175–55), 80 green (175–95), and 55 blue (175–55). Again, Illustrator doesn't change the color space of the original; it's just that the math only works in terms of RGB.

- To create white, drag all the sliders to the left in the CMYK mode or just click the White box at the right end of the spectrum bar in the Color palette. To create white in RGB, move all the sliders all the way to the right. If you're working in grayscale, you can also move the K slider triangle all the way to the left or enter 0 into the option box.

- To color an object black in CMYK mode, drag the black slider all the way to the right or click the Black box (just below the White box) on the spectrum bar. To create black in RGB, move all the sliders all the way to the left. In grayscale, you have the option of either moving the K slider triangle to the far right or entering 100 into the option box.

There is no difference between the Grayscale mode and just dragging the K slider of the CMYK mode. Although there are probably some people who enjoy using the K slider, I rarely use that mode—especially if there is any chance that I will eventually need to change the black to a color. If I use the Grayscale mode, I have to change the mode to CMYK to add other colors to the object.

If you define colors using RGB or HSB, you may see a little yellow warning symbol (also called an *out-of-gamut warning*) under the Fill and Stroke icons while you're adjusting the slider bars. Illustrator is telling you that the color you've created will not directly translate into the CMYK color model.

- Out-of-gamut colors are automatically converted when you switch to the CMYK color space, a benefit of the restricted color spaces. If you have no intention of printing your illustration, you can confidently ignore this warning and happily go about using your color with reckless disregard of any CMYK ramifications.

- If you're working in the CMYK color space, Illustrator will automatically change an out-of-gamut color to a closely matching color that lies within the CMYK spectrum. If the color that Illustrator chooses is not to your liking, use the slider bars to tweak the color to meet your needs.

- If you prepare a lot of Web content, all this talk about CMYK may be causing your eyes to roll back into your head. Your interest may lie more with the Web-safe RGB palette. This palette uses a standard 216-color spectrum, whereby each R, G, or B value is divisible by 51. This limited color palette ensures that no dithering is applied by Web browsers when viewing the images on an 8-bit screen. In other words, what you see on your monitor is what your neighbors see as well.

 If you are working in regular RGB mode, you may see a cube appear in the Color palette. This icon means that the color you have chosen is not Web-safe. Click on the cube to substitute the closest Web-safe match.

Applying Colors

Once you enter a value in the option box of the Color palette, Illustrator automatically updates the colors of selected objects every time you drag a slider triangle or press the Enter (Return on the Mac) or Tab key. Click a color in the Swatches palette to compel Illustrator to affect the fill or stroke of the selected objects.

Changing a color in the Color or Swatches palette changes the color of selected objects, but only the color of their fill or stroke, depending on which icon is active in the Color palette and the toolbox. The attribute icon (Fill or Stroke) that overlaps the other is the active icon. Illustrator also offers a few ways for you to edit the color of the attribute (fill or stroke) that is not active.

- Drag a color from either the Color or Swatch palette onto any object—even if it's not selected—to change the fill color of the object. Hold the Shift key to change the stroke color.

- You can drag a color swatch from the Swatches palette and drop it onto the Fill or Stroke icon. It doesn't matter which icon is active. You need to be careful to drop the swatch squarely on the icon of the attribute that you want to change.

- Another way to change the color of the icon that's not currently active is to Alt-click (Option-click on the Mac) the spectrum bar at the bottom of the Color palette. The active icon will remain unchanged, but the other icon will adopt the color on which you just clicked.

- Drag the color from the Fill or Stroke icon onto the other icon to match both colors.

The power of these techniques is that they allow you to edit the fill and stroke of an object without first activating the Fill and Stroke icons.

Using the Slider Bars

You wouldn't think something like slider bars would deserve their own section, but Adobe has built a bunch of little convenience features into the slider bars in the Color palette.

- Notice how the slider bars appear in different colors? This shows you what colors you'll get if you drag the slider triangle to that position. Each time you drag a slider triangle (or enter a value into an option box and press the Tab key), Illustrator updates the colors in the slider bars. This way, you're constantly aware of the effect that modifying a primary pigment will produce.

- If you like a color along the length of a slider bar, just click it. The slider triangle for that ink will immediately jump to the clicked position.

 To create a lighter or darker tint of a process color, Shift-drag the slider triangle. As you drag, all the slider bars change to demonstrate the tint. In order to gain the most control, Shift-drag the triangle associated with the highest-intensity color. (Any ink set to 0 percent does not move, because adding the ink would change the color rather than the tint.)

- You can also Shift-click a spot along a slider bar to adjust the tint by leaps and bounds. All inks (not set to 0 percent) change to maintain a constant hue. If the point at which you click is too high to keep a consistent tint, only that one ink will change. To make certain you change the tint and not the one ink, Shift-click and hold anywhere along the slider bar, and then move your mouse until the sliders all move to some legal position.

- And, as you can in any palette, you can advance from one option box to the next by pressing the Tab key. Or you can move in reverse order by pressing Shift-Tab. If you wish to apply a new value and keep that option box active (allowing you to test a number of different settings quickly), press Shift+Enter (Shift-Return on a Mac).

- If you're an adept Photoshop user and you're wondering whether you can use the up and down arrow keys to modify option box values as you can in the fab image editor, the answer is yes. If the option box is highlighted, pressing the up and down arrow keys will allow you to increase or decrease the values.

Playing with the Swatches Palette

The Swatches palette, as shown in **Figure 14.5**, is ideal for saving colors and applying colors on the fly. Use the Swatches palette menu to change the display of the palette. Choose Name View to display the swatches in a vertical list with their names visible. Choose Small Swatch View to display the swatches in small squares. Choose Large Swatch View to display the swatches in much larger squares.

The six icons at the bottom of the Swatches palette control the display of the swatches as well as the creation and deletion of swatches. Because the Swatches palette holds more than just colors, you can click one of the four icons to change which types of swatches are displayed: all the swatches, just colors, just gradients, or just patterns.

The Swatches palette provides a handful of options for organizing swatches. For example, you can choose to display the swatches by name or by icon (large or small) as shown in Figure 14.5. If you let your cursor hover over a swatch in either icon view, the name of the swatch appears (provided you have the Show Tool Tips option selected in the General Preferences). You can control the organization of the Swatches palette by the following methods:

- To sort the swatches by either name or kind, choose the appropriate command from the pop-up menu in the Swatches palette. Sorting by kind groups similar swatches together. All the process colors appear first, followed by the spot colors, gradients, and finally the pattern swatches.

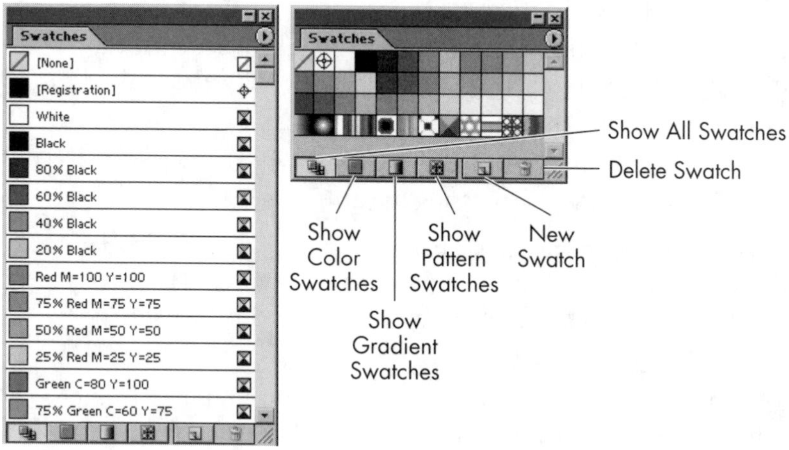

Figure 14.5: Two views of the Swatches palette: name (left) and small (right).

Show All Swatches

Delete Swatch

Show Color Swatches

Show Pattern Swatches

New Swatch

Show Gradient Swatches

- Choose the appropriate command from the pop-up menu to view swatches by their name (list view) or simply by an icon (thumbnail view) that samples their color.

- Use the four icons along the bottom left of the Swatches palette to control which type of swatches display. Click the first icon to show all swatches. Click the second, third, or fourth icon to restrict the display of swatches only to colors, gradients, or patterns, respectively.

The Swatches palette offers another function that helps you organize your swatches. From the pop-up menu, choose the Select All Unused command to select all swatches that are not applied to paths or text blocks in any open illustration. Once the swatches are selected, you can drag them to a new location in the swatch list or delete them all by Alt-clicking (Option-clicking on the Mac) the Backspace key (Delete key on the Mac). You can even duplicate them if you so choose.

Setting the Swatches Palette Focus

This is one of the esoteric techniques that only ten people in the entire world actually use completely. However, the ten who do use the techniques swear they are very helpful and easy to remember. But I must be getting old because I can never remember all the features:

- You don't have to always use the mouse to select a swatch. You can set the focus to the Swatches palette by holding Ctrl+Alt (Cmd-Option on the Mac) and then clicking inside the palette. Setting the focus activates the palette so that you can make selections within the palette by using keyboard commands instead of the mouse. When you set the focus to a palette, a black line appears inside the palette. By the way, this also works with other palettes, such as the Styles or Symbols, as well.

 Once you have set the focus inside the Swatches palette, you can scroll around the swatches by pressing the arrow keys.

 With the focus inside the Swatches palette, you can type the first few letters of the swatch's name to instantly go to that swatch. However, there is a much easier way to type to find specific colors, which I'll cover in just a moment.

 Once you have selected a swatch, press Enter (Return on the Mac) to switch the focus back to the document.

 You can return the focus to the last palette that was in focus by pressing Ctrl+~ (Cmd-~ on a Mac). You can then use the arrow keys or type to select a new swatch.

 As if that isn't enough, you can do all of this without the Swatches palette even being visible, allowing you to change the colors of an object without even seeing the swatches. (I haven't heard of anyone—not even the Illustrator product managers—who can pull this one off quickly.)

Finding Swatches

Some designers create hundreds of swatches in their Swatches palette. Are you really supposed to scroll up and down searching for a swatch? No, thankfully. Illustrator provides you with a handy Find field (shown in **Figure 14.6**) in the Swatches palettes. If you don't see the Find field, choose Show Find Field from the Swatches palette menu.

Figure 14.6: The Find field allows you to jump to a specific swatch by typing a few letters of the name in the field.

Creating a Color Swatch

Although you can drag colors from the Color palette into the Swatches palette, you will most likely want to use the New Swatch dialog box, which is shown in **Figure 14.7**. This gives you complete control over all the aspects of the swatch.

 Once you create a swatch, you can modify the settings by double-clicking the Swatch icon. This opens the Swatch Options dialog box, which provides all the original options as well as a preview box so you can see the effects of changing the swatch color.

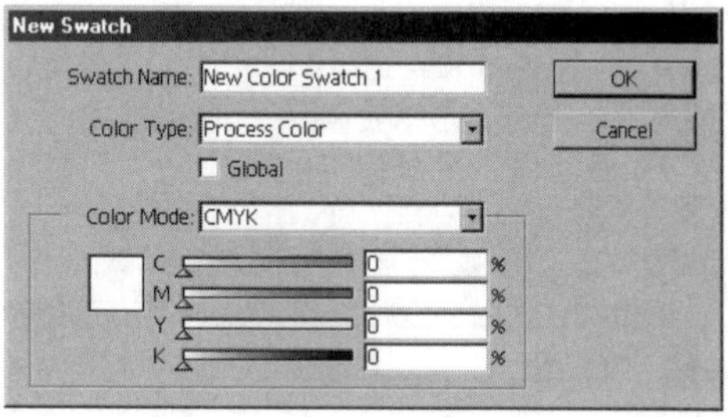

Figure 14.7: The New Swatch dialog box lets you name and define all the aspects of a swatch.

- First and foremost, give your color a name. It doesn't really matter what the name is. You can name the swatch with the percentage values of the colors, or you can name it after your favorite Uncle Irving.

 The only caveat is that each color must have a unique name. See the section later on importing colors for details of what happens when two colors with different values share the same name.

- From the Color Type menu, you can decide whether your newly created color should be a process color or a spot color. If you designate a color as Process Color in a CMYK color space, you are instructing Illustrator to create the color by mixing the percentages of the CMYK colors. If you use RGB or HSB values to define your color, Illustrator will automatically convert the color into CMYK values.

- If you designate a color as Spot Color, you are instructing Illustrator to separate the color onto its own plate when the artwork is separated into film for commercial printing. It really doesn't matter what percentages you assign to a spot color—however, the name of the color is important. See the "Spots and Tints" section for how to coordinate colors among documents.

⦿ You can also check the Global option. This means that if you change the definition of a swatch, all items that use the color will change. If you leave the Global option turned off, any changes to the swatch will apply only to new objects that use the color.

⦿ Use the Color Mode list to choose what types of sliders you want to use to define your colors. If you are working in the CMYK color space, RGB, HSB, or Web-Safe RGB colors are automatically converted into CMYK colors. If you are working in the RGB color space, HSB and CMYK colors are automatically converted into RGB colors.

The Swatches palette shows clues that help you tell what type of swatch you are looking at—process, spot, global, and so on. **Figure 14.8** shows all the clues in both the name and swatch views.

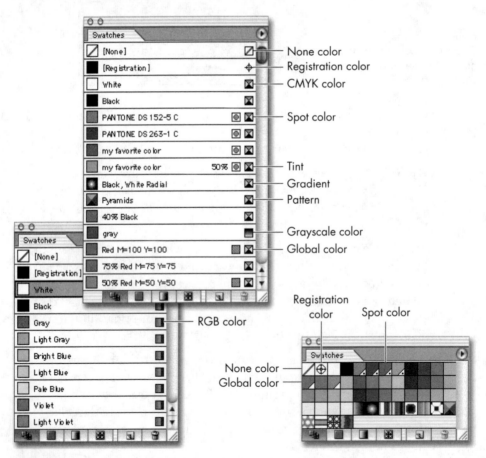

Figure 14.8: There are plenty of clues in the Swatches palette. You just have to know what they mean.

Registration and None: Two Special Swatches

Two of the swatches that automatically appear with each new document are special swatches. These are the swatch for None and the swatch labeled Registration.

The None swatch is the same as the None icon in the toolbox. It applies no fill or stroke to an object. You can also apply None to a fill or stroke by pressing the slash (/) key on the keyboard. (The mnemonic for the slash is easy: The None icon looks like a red slash.)

The Registration swatch is a color that will print on all plates. You should use the Registration swatch only for objects that you want to print on all plates—trim marks or special instructions.

 Never use Registration for ordinary artwork. If applied to large areas, the color registration can cause a buildup of ink on the printing press and may incur extra cleanup charges.

More Fun with the Color and Swatches Palettes

The Color and Swatches palettes have a symbiotic relationship. You'll find yourself frequently dragging and dropping between the two palettes. Here are a few more tidbits on working between these friendly palettes:

- Once you define your desired color in the Color palette, click the New Swatch button at the bottom of the Swatches palette or choose New Swatch from the pop-up menu in the Swatches palette. The new color will appear at the end of the list of swatches, so you may need to scroll down the field to see it.

- Drag the color from the Color palette to the Swatches palette as shown in **Figure 14.9**. If you drag onto the empty area of the panel, you add the color to the end of the swatches. Or you can drag the color to the line between two swatches.

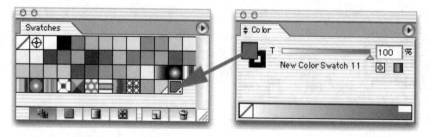

Figure 14.9: Drag a color from the Color palette into the Swatches palette.

- You can redefine a color by double-clicking the swatch in the Swatches palette, or you can replace it with a new color by Alt-dragging (Option-dragging on the Mac) a color from the Color palette onto that particular swatch.

- To duplicate a swatch, drag the swatch onto the New Swatch icon in the Swatches palette. You can also select a swatch and choose Duplicate Swatch from the pop-up menu.

- To delete a swatch, drag it onto the Delete Swatch icon (the trash can) in the Swatches palette. No warning or whining from Illustrator, just a simple extraction.

You will get a dialog box asking if you want to delete the swatch if you click the swatch and then click the Delete Swatch icon or choose Delete Swatch from the Swatches palette menu. The rationale behind this is if you take the time to drag the swatch all the way down to the trash can, Illustrator figures you must know what you are doing. So it deletes the file without any warning. However, if you simply select a swatch and click the Delete Swatch icon, Illustrator figures you might have inadvertently clicked the trash can, so it asks you if you're sure you want to delete the swatch. Fortunately, deleting a swatch can be undone by pressing Ctrl+Z (Cmd-Z on the Mac). That has come in handy more than once.

- You can delete more than one swatch at a time. To select multiple swatches, click one swatch and then Shift-click another swatch to select those swatches and all swatches between the two. To select noncontiguous swatches, Ctrl-click (Cmd-click on the Mac) each swatch to add it to the selection. Now click the Delete button, or Alt-click (Option-click on the Mac) to circumvent the warning and eliminate the colors. This is a useful way to clean out an entire section of swatches and start over on them.

The color swatches are saved with the document. If you want to save a set of color swatches that you intend to use again and again, open the Adobe Illustrator Startup file that resides in the Plug-ins folder. Then edit the color swatches inside that illustration and save them to disk. From that point on, all new illustrations will use those same color swatches.

Spots and Tints

In the very olden days of Illustrator, you had to make a color a spot color in order to be able to define the color as a tint. This caused problems when the artwork was printed, because it was possible to have hundreds of individual spot colors—each one separating on its own plate. And every plate created its own piece of costly film instead of being broken down into process colors. Fortunately, we live in an enlightened era—instead of creating numerous spot colors, you can simply define the color as global.

When you click a spot or global color swatch, the Color palette displays the color and a tint slider bar, as shown in **Figure 14.10**. You can modify the intensity of a color by changing the tint value. Again, all the standard techniques discussed a few pages back in the "Using the Slider Bars" section apply to the tint slider bar as well.

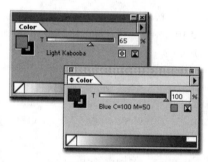

Figure 14.10: After selecting a spot or global color swatch, you can modify the intensity of the color using the tint slider bar that appears in the Color palette.

The biggest misunderstanding about spot colors is that you must use the predefined swatch libraries from companies such as Pantone. You do not—repeat NOT—have to define spot colors using only those libraries. You can simply create your own spot color. Give it a name such as Varnish, My Favorite Color, or whatever. Then simply tell the print shop what color ink to use for that spot color plate.

Using Predefined Color Libraries

Illustrator ships with 25 libraries filled with predefined colors. Some of these colors, such as Default_CMYK, Pastels, or Earthtones, are simply colors created by Adobe for your enjoyment. Others, such as Pantone and Trumatch, are based on commercial products that match colors in printed swatch color books. Swatch libraries are Illustrator documents with special swatches that have been stored in the Swatches folder.

There's nothing special about the document in the Swatches folder. You can create your own Illustrator document, with your own favorite swatches and save it in the Swatches folder. The colors will then be available through the Window » Swatch Libraries » Other Libraries submenu. Navigate to the Swatches folder in the Presets folder in the Illustrator 10 folder to locate your swatch library.

You can open swatch libraries as independent palettes. Simply choose the appropriate library from the Window » Swatch Libraries submenu. A new palette will appear chock-full of all the library's swatches. This palette will be available to all open illustrations. Now, to save disk space (not to mention RAM), find and Ctrl-click (Cmd-click on the Mac) each color that you need and choose the Add to Swatches command from the palette's pop-up menu. The new swatches appear in the Swatches palette.

You can actually use any Illustrator document as a color library. Simply choose Window » Swatches » Other Libraries and navigate to find the Illustrator file. The only drawback is the file can't be currently open.

You can add swatches for each open illustration that requires any of these swatches. Close the library by clicking on the palette's close box. When you next save your illustration, the new swatches are saved with it, whether or not they are used to fill or stroke objects.

If you want a particular library to open every time you launch Illustrator, first choose the library from the Swatch Libraries submenu and then, after the palette displays, select the Persistent command from the palette's pop-up menu. The next time you start up Illustrator, that library will be part of your Illustrator window.

If, on the other hand, you use a small cache of colors on a regular basis, you can add them to the Adobe Illustrator Startup file. For example, if one of your clients sells lawn flamingos, you might want to keep Pantone 225 pink on hand at all times. Just open the Startup file (in the Plug-ins folder), and add the color to the Swatches palette for the Startup file. After you save the Startup file, the color will be available to all illustrations, whether old or new.

The following items briefly introduce the color brands in reverse order of their impact on the U.S. market—if you'll pardon me for being so unscrupulously U.S.-centric—from smallest impact to greatest:

 FOCOLTONE, Diccolor, Toyo and HKS: FOCOLTONE and Dianippon Ink and Chemical (Diccolor) and Toyo fall into the negligible-impact category. All are foreign standards with followings abroad. FOCOLTONE is based in England, whereas Diccolor and Toyo hail from Japan. HKS is from a German company. None has many subscribers here in the United States. Their basic purpose is to satisfy foreign clientele.

Web and VisiBone 2: Both these libraries contain the 216 Web-safe colors that simply prevent dithering when viewed on the Web. However, the VisiBone2 arranges the colors in a much more organized fashion. I cover both of these in Chapter 21 when we look at Web graphics.

Trumatch: Designed entirely using a desktop system and with desktop publishers in mind, the Trumatch Colors file contains more than 2,000 process colors, organized according to hue, saturation, and brightness. The colors correspond to the Colorfinder swatch book. Trumatch happens to be my favorite process color collection, and I keep a copy of the Colorfinder close at hand at all times.

Pantone: The largest color vendor in the United States is Pantone. With the addition of pastels and metallics, Illustrator now offers eight libraries in the Swatch Libraries submenu, five more than Illustrator 9. If you're interested in printing Pantone spot colors, the Pantone Solid Coated, Pantone Solid Matte, and Pantone Solid Uncoated libraries are for you. Coated, matte, and uncoated refer to the paper used in printing. These colors correspond to the Pantone Color Formula Guide swatch book. The Pantone Process libraries contain process colors that match printed colors in the Pantone Process Color System Guide swatch book. For more details, check out Pantone's great Web site at www.pantone.com.

 The Find field will find colors just by typing the numbers that are at the end of Pantone 124 C, Pantone 125 C, etc. So all you have to do is type the number, not the whole name.

Moving Colors between Documents

So, what if you've used swatches named Grass Green, Sky Blue, and Flamingo Pink, and you want to add the artwork to another file that also has swatches with the same names? What's going to happen to the swatches? Well, that depends on how you defined them.

If the old swatch was *not* defined as global, the artwork comes in, but the swatches do not. Only global process color, spot color, pattern, and gradient swatches travel with their artwork.

 If the old global or spot color swatch has a different definition from the new global or spot color swatch, a dialog box, as shown in **Figure 14.11**, appears asking you how you want to handle the conflict between the old and new swatch definitions.

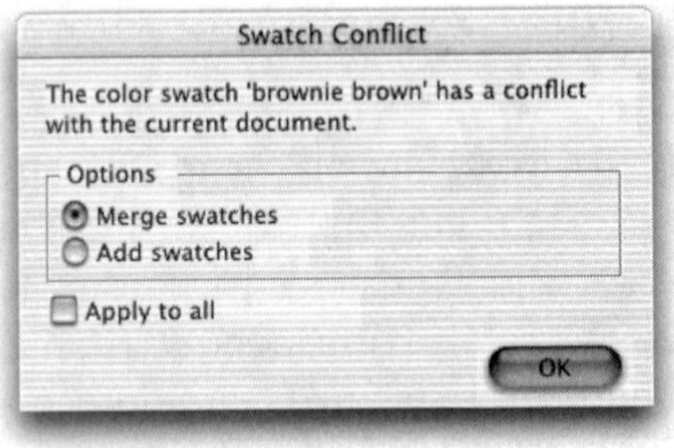

Figure 14.11: The Swatch Conflict dialog box lets you specify how different swatch definitions should be handled when copying or dragging artwork between documents.

 Choose Merge swatches to apply the definition of the new document to the older artwork. This will most likely change the appearance of the color. But there really isn't a problem if the appearance of a spot color changes. After all, the actual color of the spot color comes from the ink, not its screen appearance.

 Choose Add swatches to maintain the definition of the old document, and then add the swatch to the new document's Swatches palette. The swatch that is added is given the same name as the other swatch, with a number after it to distinguish the two swatches.

 Choose Apply to all to apply the decision to all the conflicts between the current colors.

 Global and spot colors cannot have the same name. However, you can add artwork with a global or spot color to a document that uses the same name for an ordinary process, nonglobal color. This will result in two swatches with the same name.

Applying the Overprint Options

A few color-related options appear in locations that might surprise you. The first two of these are the Overprint check boxes in the Attributes palette, spotlighted in **Figure 14.12**. These options control whether the color applied to the fill or stroke of the selected object mixes with the colors of the objects behind it. When the Overprint Fill or Overprint Stroke check box is turned on, the fill or stroke color overprints the colors behind it, provided that the fill or stroke color is printed to a different separation from the background colors.

Figure 14.12: Use the Overprint check boxes in the Attributes palette to mix colors in overlapping objects, as long as the colors print to different separations.

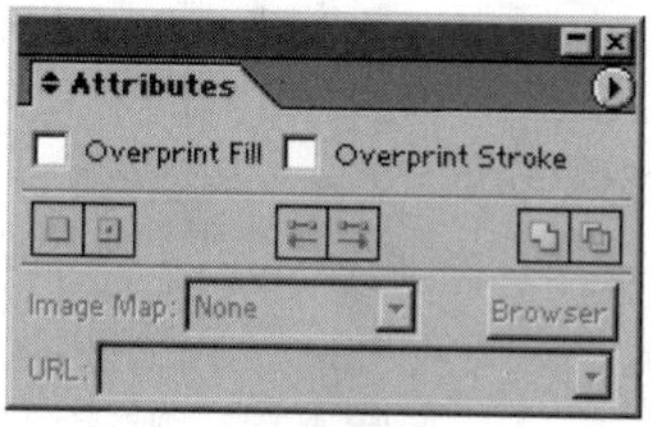

For example, suppose you've created a Mardi Gras illustration consisting of three spot colors, Pantones 2592, 3405, and 1235, which any resident of Louisiana can tell you are purple, green, and gold. Purple can overprint green, green can overprint purple, and either can overprint or be overprinted by gold, because Pantones 2592, 3405, and 1235 print to their own separations. However, a 30 percent tint of purple cannot overprint a 70 percent tint of purple, because all purple objects print to the same Pantone 2592 separation.

When one color overprints onto another color, the two colors mix together. You could overprint purple onto gold, for example, to get a deep brown color.

If the Overprint check boxes are turned off, as they are by default, any portion of an object that is covered by another object is knocked out and the object on top prints; that is, the covered object doesn't print, even when the two objects are output to different separations. This ensures that colors from different separations do not mix. For nonblack paths, unless you are absolutely sure that you want a path to overprint another (and thus you want its colors to mix with the colors of any other path that it touches), you should leave these controls alone.

Overprinting Process Colors

The Overprint options have no influence over black-and-white illustrations that don't require separations. If the selected object is filled with one or more process colors, only those colors on different separations overprint. For example, suppose you have two objects, one filled with 30 percent magenta and 75 percent yellow (gold) and another filled with 70 percent cyan and 95 percent magenta (purple). If you select the gold object and turn on the Overprint Fill check box, the intersection of the two objects is printed with 70 percent cyan, 30 percent magenta, and 75 percent yellow. The magenta value from the gold object wins out—even though it's lighter than the magenta value in the purple object—because overprinting doesn't affect colors placed on the same separation.

Previewing Overprinting

The effects of overprinting happen when inks combine on press. So it is no wonder that it took Illustrator a few versions to be able to see the effects of overprinting onscreen. Simply choose View » Overprint Preview. Not only can you see overprinting of one object over another, but you can even see how the stroke of an object overprints its own fill. **Figure 14.13** gives a vague idea of how the overprinting preview appears.

Figure 14.13: In this illustration, all strokes of the decorative elements inside the wings have had overprinting applied. The top object shows what the illustration looks like with Overprint Preview turned off. The bottom object shows what the illustration looks like with Overprint Preview turned on. Note the dark lines around the decorative squiggles and circles on the wings.

Overprinting Black Ink

Although you may occasionally use the Overprint options to mix spot colors, most professionals apply overprinting primarily to black ink to anticipate printing problems. Because black is opaque—and it's typically the last ink applied during the printing process—it covers up all other inks. So it doesn't look much different when printed over, say, cyan than it looks when printed directly onto the white page. But although overprinting has little effect on the appearance of black ink, it prevents gaps from occurring between a black object and a different-colored neighbor. Even if the paper shifts on the printing press, the black ink comes out looking fine.

Illustrator provides two means for overprinting black ink—the Filter » Colors » Overprint Black command and the Overprint Black check box in the Separation dialog box.

If all this talk of overprinting sounds suspiciously like the topic of trapping, that's because overprinting is a primary feature of trapping. Trapping, which is used to compensate for the misregistration of two color plates, is covered in Chapter 24.

Applying Automated Color Manipulations

The Filter » Colors submenu contains a total of ten filters that affect the colors of selected objects and imported images. You can use these filters to increase or decrease the intensity of primary inks and, in some cases, spot colors. Although the filters aren't nearly as capable or sophisticated as similar color-correction commands found in Photoshop, they do make it possible to edit multiple objects and colors simultaneously, which can save you a significant amount of time.

Adjusting Colors

The Filter » Colors » Adjust Colors command is Illustrator's most capable color-correction command. Choose the Adjust Colors filter to display the Adjust Colors dialog box, as shown in **Figure 14.14**. There are four types of colors that can be adjusted using this command:

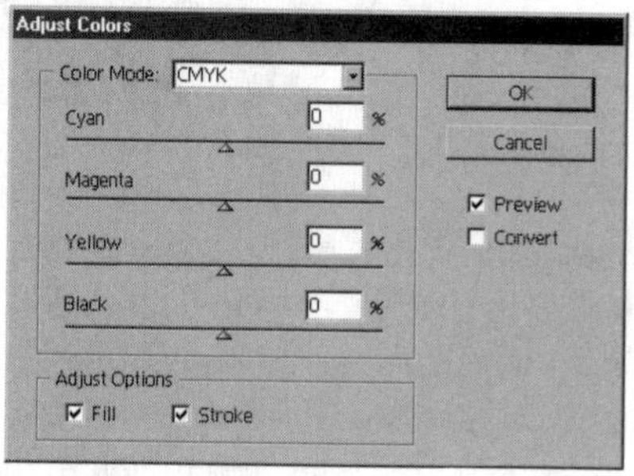

Figure 14.14: The Adjust Colors dialog box allows you to increase or decrease the percentage of colors assigned to selected objects.

- If you have any global or spot colors, the Global setting allows you to increase or decrease all those colors by using one tint slider. Any non-global process colors will not be affected in this mode.

 Positive values add ink, while negative values reduce the amount of ink.

- If you are working in the CMYK color space, the CMYK mode allows you to increase or decrease the cyan, magenta, yellow, and black percentages of all nonglobal process colors. If you check Convert, any global or spot colors will also be adjusted at that time. Also, the Convert setting allows you to add color to objects colored with the Grayscale color mode.

- If you are working in the RGB color space, the RGB mode allows you to increase or decrease the red, green, and blue percentages of all nonglobal colors. If you check Convert, any global or spot colors will also be adjusted at that time.

- If you choose the Grayscale mode, all grayscale colors can be increased or decreased using a single black slider. **Figure 14.15** shows an example of an adjustment using this command. If you check Convert, all other colors will be converted to grayscale values and then adjusted as you move the black slider. The Grayscale mode is excellent for converting color jobs into grayscale and then varying the contrast of the illustration.

Figure 14.15: A small sample of what the Adjust Colors filter did to an illustration.

–20% Black

 Note that the values in the Adjust Colors dialog box represent absolute values. This is different—and decidedly less useful—than the way most of Photoshop's color commands work. Photoshop's best color-correction functions—Levels, Curves, and Variations—change the relative coloring of images. For example, these functions permit you to increase or decrease the intensity of medium cyan values within a selection, without affecting noncyan colors or full-intensity cyans. Only one command in Illustrator, Filter » Colors » Saturate, permits relative color modifications, but even it doesn't begin to compare to Photoshop's capabilities.

The Adjust Colors dialog box also offers the following check boxes:

- **Fill:** Select this option if you want to modify the fills of selected objects. Turn off the option if you want to change only strokes.

- **Stroke:** Same thing as Fill, only opposite. Turn on the check box if you want to adjust strokes; turn it off if you want to affect only fills.

- **Convert:** Select this check box to modify all colors of the selected objects according to the option box values. If you turn off this check box, you can adjust a color only in terms of its original color model.

Preview: Select this check box to keep apprised of the effects of your color modifications as you work inside the Adjust Colors dialog box. Keep this option on to avoid surprises.

Switching between Color Models

Illustrator has three filters that allow you to convert color models. With the change to a restricted color space, two of the filters, Filter » Colors » Convert to RGB and Filter » Colors » Convert to CMYK, have lost much of their usefulness. These filters work only to convert grayscale raster images into either RGB or CMYK files. But they do nothing special to Illustrator objects.

 However, the third filter, Filter » Colors » Convert to Grayscale is useful. It will convert CMYK or RGB objects into grayscale tints. For instance, if you have created a magnificent drawing in color, you may discover you need it in grayscale to be reproduced in a newspaper. Simply select all the art and apply the Convert to Grayscale filter. The colors in your artwork will instantly be converted into shades of gray. Converting your illustration to grayscale is also useful for draft printing.

Changing the Overall Ink Intensity

If you want to apply relative adjustments to the colors of selected objects, choose Filter » Colors » Saturate. The Saturate command displays a small dialog box with a single slider bar and a corresponding option box.

 Enter a negative value to decrease the intensity of the colors in selected objects filled or stroked with process colors. This value also reduces the tints of global or spot colors. (The Saturate command does not convert colors to process, so spot colors remain intact.)

 Enter a positive value to increase the intensity of the colors or the tint of colors.

Unlike the Adjust Colors command, Saturate makes relative color adjustments. If you apply a Saturate value of 50 percent to an object filled with 20 percent cyan and 50 percent magenta, Illustrator changes the fill to 30 percent cyan and 75 percent magenta. That's a 50 percent increase in the previous intensities of both inks. **Figure 14.16** shows (unfortunately in black and white) only one example of the changes that can be made using this command.

The command isn't entirely consistent. For example, it changes white absolutely; a 50 percent Saturate increases a 10 percent black fill to 15 percent black, whereas it changes a white fill to 50 percent black. And the Saturate command becomes completely unpredictable when applied to grayscale images.

Figure 14.16: The original art on the left was altered using the Saturate command to create the new artwork on the right. The background was changed −50%. The foreground flower was changed +50%.

After everything is said and done, Filter » Colors » Saturate is best suited to lightening or darkening the colors of several objects at once. You can use the command to establish highlights or shadows, whether the selected objects are filled and stroked with gray values or colors.

Inverting Selected Colors

After you choose Filter » Colors » Invert Colors, Illustrator changes the colors of all selected objects to their opposites. The result is the same as choosing Invert from the Color palette's pop-up menu (a color composed of 100 red, 150 blue, and 200 green inverts to 155 red, 105 blue, and 55 green) except that the filter affects all colors of all the selected objects.

The Invert command also inverts objects filled and stroked with gray values. Black inverts to white, white inverts to black—it's just like a photographic negative.

Creating Color Blends

The remaining three commands in the Filter » Colors submenu—Blend Front to Back, Blend Horizontally, and Blend Vertically—create continuous color blends among three or more selected objects. Each command uses two extreme objects as base colors and recolors all other selected objects between the extremes. **Figure 14.17** shows in grayscale tints the results of the three commands.

I started with the same circular illustration duplicated several times into an arc of circles in different colors. I then made three more groups of the circles. I applied a different blend colors filter to each of the groups. In each case Illustrator picked different circles as the start and stop (base) colors of the blends. (I've given the base color objects double strokes.) The Blend Front to Back command used the back and front circles as the base objects and recolored the circles stacked in between. The Blend Horizontally command blended between the left and right objects; and Blend Vertically blended between the top and bottom circles.

All three blend filters affect gray values as well as CMYK and RGB colors just fine. But you can't use them on spot colors. Strokes are completely ignored.

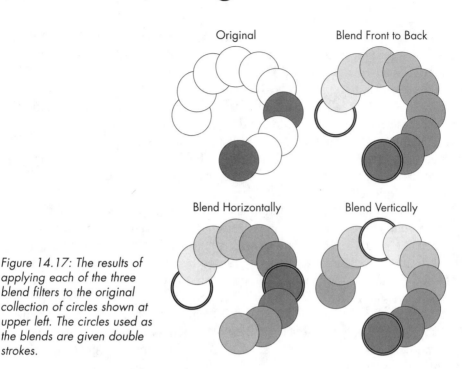

Figure 14.17: The results of applying each of the three blend filters to the original collection of circles shown at upper left. The circles used as the blends are given double strokes.

The blend filters are useful for modifying the colors in a series of objects created with the transformation tools and the Object » Transform » Transform Again command. You can also use them to recolor a series of objects created with the blend tool, as I discuss in Chapter 17.

Color Management Essentials

Now that you've been thoroughly initiated into the friendly fraternity of color theory and application, it's time to broach the prickly issue of color management. Ouch! Was that the sound of an 800-plus page book being abruptly slammed shut? Don't worry, it's not as bad as you've heard. All it takes is a little understanding, a little experimentation, and a little acceptance that we live in a world where reproducing color isn't perfect or exact.

First let me say that you cannot expect to buy a decent computer and monitor, do a little calibration on that monitor, and expect to achieve a WYSIWYG world. It flat doesn't exist. Why this is so is because of a couple of reasons. First of all, you learned earlier in this chapter that there are two main color models—RGB and CYMK. The RGB color space, which your monitor uses, has a much wider color gamut (range) than CMYK, the gamut your printer uses. Therefore, many of the colors you see onscreen fall outside of CMYK's color reproduction capabilities.

Those electric blues and fiery reds you view onscreen turn into a dull, muddy version of their former selves. Throw into the mix that different devices—whether they are scanners, monitors, or printers—can possess different gamuts within the same color model. In other words, the RGB color space of a scanner can differ from the RGB color space of a monitor. And to complicate matters further, the color spaces between the same kind of device can differ as well. The RGB color space on an Apple Cinema display can vary from the RGB color space on a 17-inch generic Trinitron monitor. Device-dependent color—color produced by specific pieces of hardware—varies from one device to the next and that is just the way of the world.

The bottom line of this dissertation is that you can experience shifts in colors between your screen and your printer, between one printer and another, or between one screen and another. You can even get color shifts between different applications and different media (papers and other substrates).

I know it all sounds like enough to drive you to pull the plug, but don't. There is good news. Adobe has heard the desperate cries of thousands of users and developed a color-management system that attempts to be device-independent. This color-management system first allows you to identify your working color space and tags your files with that color space. Then it analyzes any color space to which you will either view or output that file and makes adjustments on the fly so that the color is viewed or printed as consistently as possible.

There are handfuls of books that deal specifically and exclusively with color. If color management is a critical issue for you, it would be worth your while to invest in one or two. But for now I'll break down the basics of getting a handle on color management in Illustrator 10.

Getting Ready

Before you delve into the nuts and bolts of tweaking your color settings, you want to try to establish an optimum environment for viewing your images. I know we all wish we could sit inside a huge natural-light viewing box like the professional offset print houses use, but unfortunately most of us are relegated to our cubicles, home offices or classrooms. But here are a few easy things anyone can do.

 Try to keep your lighting (the level, intensity, and temperature) as consistent as possible throughout your work session. You don't want to work near a open window with the midday sun beating down on your monitor and then later on by the dim light of a desk lamp in the wee hours.

 Keep the walls of your work environment neutral. That's right—no more vintage concert posters and black lights.

- Keep your monitor desktop a neutral gray. Any other color or pattern may influence how your view your images. So no more dancing dinos.

- Calibrate your monitor using the Adobe Gamma utility. This utility allows you to first calibrate your monitor to remove any color casts and to achieve as neutral a gray as possible. Secondly, it lets you characterize your monitor, enabling you to create a profile that tells Illustrator and other programs how your monitor is displaying color. Adobe Gamma can be found in the Control Panels folder. Be sure to let your monitor warm up a good 30 minutes before running the utility.

Establishing Your Color Settings

Now on to color management Grand Centrale—Color Settings. Choose Edit » Color Settings. This behemoth of a dialog box, as shown in **Figure 14.18**, allows you to set up your color-management settings in one fell swoop. The great thing about this dialog box is that it lets you choose from various predefined sets of options, designed for specific output conditions. It also, however, allows you to customize your own configuration to fit your specific needs.

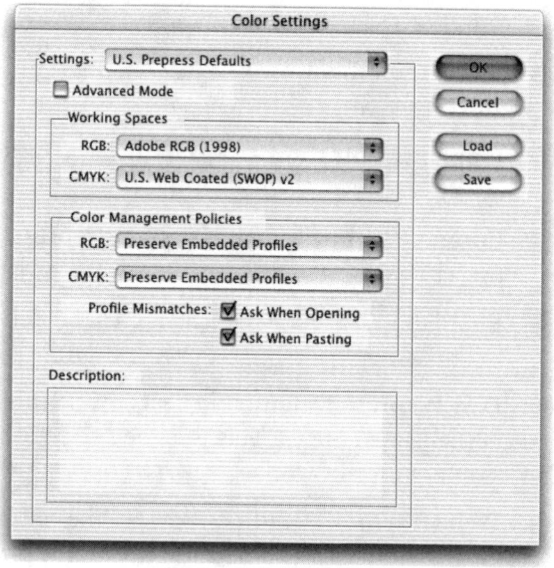

Figure 14.18: This dialog box single-handedly controls color management in Illustrator.

I'll walk through each of the items in this dialog box in detail in this section.

Hover your mouse over most of the items in this dialog box to display an informative description of each option.

Settings

You can choose a predefined setting from this pop-up menu. Once selected, Illustrator will provide all the appropriate color profiles and conversion policies. If you want to keep things simple and your chosen predefined setting pretty much describes your workflow, you can feel pretty comfortable that the predefined setting will provide you with good results. Here is a short description of each setting.

- **Emulate Adobe Illustrator 6.0:** Basically takes you back to Version 6 and its primitive color-management controls. There will be no color profiles and no color-management settings in the Print dialog box.

- **Custom:** Lets you manually assign your own settings. If you define a custom configuration, be sure to save your settings for easier retrieval and sharing with others.

- **Color Management Off:** Basically deactivates Illustrator's color-management capabilities. Recommended for video output, but that's about it.

- **ColorSync Workflow (Mac only):** Uses ColorSync 3.0 Color Management System and ColorSync profiles. Not recognized by the Windows platform.

- **Emulate Acrobat 4:** Does just what it says and emulates Acrobat 4 and earlier versions.

- **Emulate Photoshop 4:** Again, turns color management off and emulates Photoshop 4's display.

- **Europe Prepress Defaults/Japan Prepress Defaults:** Provides settings to be used for printing in Europe or Japan.

- **Photoshop 5 Default Spaces:** Uses the default color settings found in Photoshop 5.

- **U.S. Prepress Defaults:** Reflects the settings appropriate for printing in the United States. This is a good selection if you use Illustrator mainly for print work.

- **Web Graphics Defaults:** Provides the settings for graphics to be displayed on the Web. If you use Illustrator primarily for Web content, this option is a good starting point.

Working Spaces

As you may have noticed, by choosing a predefined setting, certain color profiles are automatically assigned to your RGB and CMYK working spaces. The color profiles selected will presumably provide the best color results for that particular workflow. For example, the Web Graphics Default uses sRGB as its RGB working space. The sRGB color profile, developed by Microsoft, Hewlett-Packard and Kodak, represents a standard Trinitron PC monitor—the viewing platform of a lot of Web surfers. If you want to prepare your Web images for the lowest common denominator, sRGB is a good profile to use. Likewise, U.S. Prepress Defaults uses Adobe RGB (1998) as the RGB working space. This color profile is probably the best RGB color space for viewing 24-bit images onscreen and for converting files to CMYK for printing. It has a wider range of RGB colors than sRGB. The CMYK working space is set to U.S. Web Coated—the setting to be used for offset printing in the United States. Every file you create on your computer will now use the colors within the gamut of your chosen color profiles (either RGB or CMYK depending on your document color mode).

When you save your file, be sure to check the Embed ICC Profile option in the Save dialog box. This option is available for native Illustrator, PDF, JPEG, TIFF, and native PSD file formats. This will ensure that the file will be embedded, or tagged with that color profile. That way no matter where your file ends up, the working space in which it was created will always be known.

Color Management Policies

 The next step in the color-management process is to instruct Illustrator how to interpret and manage the color profiles of files it opens. In other words, Illustrator needs to know what to do when it opens a file that has an embedded profile that doesn't match your working space. Illustrator (and Photoshop as well) calls this a profile mismatch. Your working space color profile doesn't match the color profile embedded in the file you are opening.

 You may encounter older files that have no profile. You will get a warning dialog box that indicates a missing profile. These files were either created in the days before color management, created with color management turned off, or originated from an application that doesn't support color management. In this case, you'll usually want to assign your particular working space to those orphan files.

To rectify this mismatch situation, you have three options.

- **Off:** Illustrator doesn't utilize any color management at all when opening files.

- **Use the assigned profile:** Illustrator will display the file in its original embedded color space and will not perform any color conversions. This is the selected setting displayed in **Figure 14.19**.

🌑 **Convert the document's colors to the current working space:**
Illustrator will convert the file from its embedded color space to your
working color space. You may have noticed that Illustrator automatically chooses the conversion options for you when you select a predefined setting from the Settings pop-up menu. You can feel free to use
those defaults. For the most part, they will work for you. There is one
notable exception, however. When you choose the Web Graphics
default, the Color Management Policies are set to Off. Disabling color
management isn't a good idea in most cases, so set the options to
Convert the document's colors to the current working space.

 *Be careful about making CMYK conversions. If you
encounter a profile mismatch with a CMYK image, you will
most likely want to preserve the image's embedded profile
unless you know for sure that it should be converted to
another CMYK working space. If the image doesn't have a profile, then by
all means convert it to your working space.*

You have the choice of allowing Illustrator to automatically apply your chosen
mismatch conversion option or alerting you first with the warning dialog box
shown in **Figure 14.19**. I would recommend checking the Ask When Opening
and Ask When Pasting options in the Color Settings dialog box. That way you
know when there is a profile mismatch and you have the choice of picking your
course of action, which includes overriding the defaults you set in the conversion
settings. This allows you to evaluate whether you want to preserve or convert on
a case-by-case basis. For example, I have my working RGB color space set to
Adobe RGB (1998). A client sends me some Web graphics he wants to use on a
corporate Web page. I open the graphics on my computer and immediately get a
profile mismatch warning me that the sRGB color space of the graphic doesn't
match my working RGB color space. In this case, since the Web site is targeted to
a consumer audience, I will tell Illustrator to preserve the embedded profile and
not make any conversions.

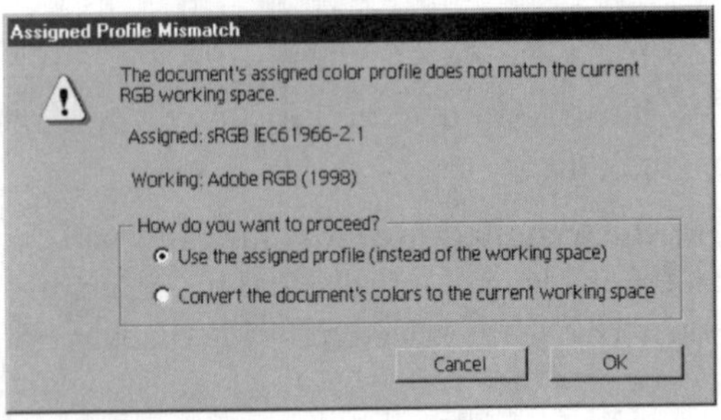

*Figure 14.19: Illustrator
politely interrupts you with
this dialog box when it
encounters a color profile that
doesn't match your working
color space.*

Assigned Profile Mismatch

⚠ The document's assigned color profile does not match the current
RGB working space.

Assigned: sRGB IEC61966-2.1

Working: Adobe RGB (1998)

How do you want to proceed?
- ● Use the assigned profile (instead of the working space)
- ○ Convert the document's colors to the current working space

Cancel   OK

When you choose the Advanced Mode option in the Color Settings dialog box, you have a couple more options regarding color conversion engines and rendering intents (color translation methods). Unless you are well versed in color management, I would recommend handing the reigns over to Illustrator and leaving these options at their defaults.

Swapping Color Profiles

Finally, in some rare instances, you may want to either assign a different color profile to a file or even eliminate the color profile of your image altogether. For example, you may have prepped a previous image for print and now want to use it to as part of a Web site build. Therefore, you may want to change the Adobe RGB (1998) color profile to an sRGB color profile. To do so choose Edit » Assign Profile and select one of the three options, as shown in **Figure 14.20**:

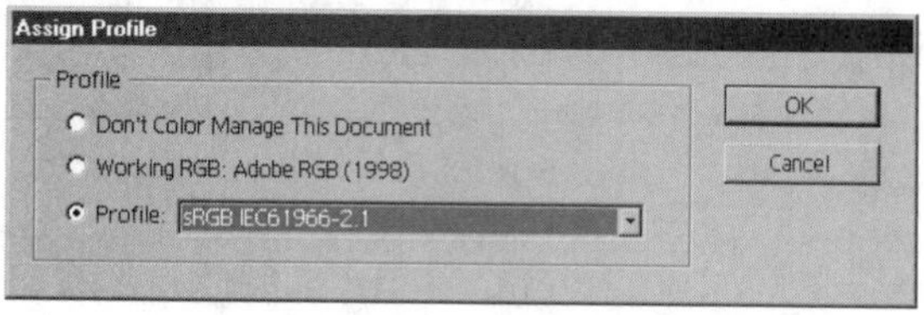

Figure 14.20: You can give your image another identity with the Assign Profile command.

- **Don't Color Manage This Document:** Removes the color profile and leaves the file un-color managed.
- **Working (color model):** Assigns your current working space to a file that is either untagged or has a different color profile than your working space.
- **Profile:** Choose your desired color profile from the pop-up menu. Illustrator then *assigns* that profile to the file, but doesn't *convert* the colors to that profile.

Viewing a Soft Proof

Illustrator allows you to preview onscreen how your image will look on a specific output device. First, choose View » Proof Setup. You have the choice of choosing either Macintosh RGB or Windows RGB to view how your image will look on a standard Mac or Windows monitor. This can come in handy when you want to see how your Web graphic will generally look on another platform. Choose Monitor RGB to use your current monitor color space as the viewing space. This allows you to turn off your RGB working space and see the image without any color conversion at all. Custom allows you to choose a specific device. For example, choosing

U.S. Web Coated will allow you to see how your RGB image will look when converted to CMYK for print purposes. After you have chosen your color space, select View » Proof Colors to actually view the image in your chosen space. Just beware that for soft proofing to be even remotely reliable, you have to have a very good quality monitor and an optimum viewing environment, as discussed earlier.

One Last Word

Now that you've been totally inundated with the techniques of making your color behave consistently, I have one final piece of advice. As I mentioned at the beginning of this section, color onscreen differs from color on paper. And trying to get the color you want on paper can be tricky. The tried-and-true system is to arm yourself with swatch books from Pantone or Trumatch. With a swatch book in hand, you don't have to rely exclusively on the colors you see onscreen; you can refer to the book to see how the colors look when printed. Pantone's Color Formula Guide is the first and foremost reference for spot colors. Trumatch's Colorfinder shows a huge range of process color combinations.

Pantone also provides a CMYK color book called the Process Color System Guide. It contains more colors than its Trumatch equivalent, and it lists the ingredients in CMYK order. But the Trumatch numbering system is more logical. Swatch books can cost anywhere from $75 to $200 depending on the type.

Unfortunately, no color swatch book is 100 percent reliable. The colors age over time, so your book and your printer's book may look slightly different. But if you store the book in a sensible location—put it in a drawer, don't leave it sitting on a windowsill—it should remain accurate for a full year or more.

 If you have any concerns about a color, take your swatch book in with you and tell the guy at the desk that you expect him to nail Color X on the nose. If the guy says, "Now, lady, much as I'd like to, it's very difficult to guarantee an exact match," while picking his teeth with some card stock, take your business elsewhere or expect big savings. If he shows you his swatch book and you find that your colors are a bit different, chances are you can arrange an equitable compromise. Many printers are even willing to provide swatch books that they print themselves if you're a regular client.

The fact is, predictable color is achievable. I hope this section provided you with a basic foundation in color management. But before I lower the curtain and move on to a new chapter, here are the high points once last time:

- Don't believe everything you see onscreen.
- Create a good viewing environment for creating and editing images.

- Calibrate your monitor using Adobe Gamma.

- Understand and utilize Illustrator's color-management tools.

- Refer to a swatch book in specifying color for print work, and be willing to change your swatch book every year or two.

- Find a good print house. Printers are like car mechanics—some are excellent, and others exploit their customers' inexperience. If you ever for a minute think that you're being fed a line, get a second opinion. Consider it a bad sign if your printer knocks Illustrator's output capabilities. Illustrator is by no means perfect, but when it comes to color printing, there's no better piece of software. This is one case where it's a bad carpenter who blames his tools.

- Develop a close working relationship with your print house. Where color is concerned, you're at the printer's mercy. But most professional printers are willing to help you out and make you happy.

- And although I haven't said this yet, nothing takes the place of experimentation and testing. Take the time to test, test, and test again. Print multiple test prints using various print settings. View your Web images in different browsers, on different platforms, and on different monitors. It will be time well spent.

CHAPTER 15

FILLS, MULTI-FILLS, AND FAB FILLS

Though it may not sound like much, a fill is one of Illustrator's most essential capabilities. A fill is the inner soul of an object. (Strokes, which I cover in the next chapter, are the outer soul.) Not only can you fill an object, but you can also create multiple fills for an object. (Multiple souls?) Multi-fills allow you to create effects that automatically simulate the look of multiple objects—sort of multiple personalities for single objects. Illustrator also lets you fill objects with special fills that blend one color to another or repeat a pattern over and over.

If push came to shove, you could live without strokes. You could draw thin shapes and fill them. In fact, I do know artists who barely use strokes. But there's no getting around a fill—it enables you to design complex illustrations, create shadows and highlights, or simply add color to a document. Fill is the skin wrapped around the skeleton of a path, the airbrushing inside the frisket, the drywall over the studs. Fill permits you to show viewers exactly what you want them to see.

Filling Closed and Open Paths

Before I explain how you define and apply cool fills such as gradations, meshes, and patterns, there are a few basic principles I'd like to clarify. First of all, you can fill any kind of path, whether open or closed. When you fill a closed path, the entire interior of the path is affected. **Figure 15.1** shows a closed path as it appears selected in the outline mode and the same path filled in the preview mode. The shape acts like a malleable water balloon—the fill seeps into every nook and cranny of the outline.

Figure 15.1: In the outline mode, the fill of a closed path is invisible (top). But in the preview mode, the fill permeates the shape (bottom).

What happens, though, if you neglect to close a path? Will the fill leak out and get all over the page? Fortunately, in Illustrator the fill is held in check by an imaginary straight segment drawn between the two endpoints. **Figure 15.2** shows an open path in the outline and preview modes. I've added a thick stroke so you can see that the path is open. The straight segment without a stroke is the imaginary segment that Illustrator adds to keep the fill from pouring out.

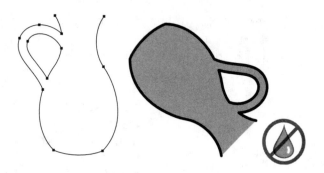

Figure 15.2: After drawing an open path (left), I filled it and tipped it upside down (right). And yet, by the miracle of the imaginary straight segment, not a drop of fill is spilled.

Filled open paths can be very useful for creating indefinite boundaries in a graphic. The paths with the thick outlines in **Figure 15.3** demonstrate this technique. For example, because the forward wing is an open path, it is not stroked where it connects with the body of the rocket. And because the wing and body are filled with the same shade of gray, the fill of one path appears to flow into the fill of the other. The path around the body of the rocket is also an open path. It opens at the base, creating another indefinite boundary.

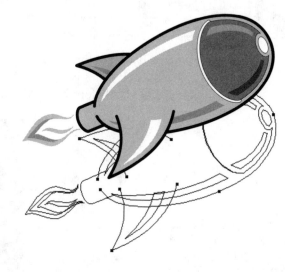

Figure 15.3: The paths with thick strokes are open paths, as shown in the outline view behind the illustration. This makes it easy to merge the fins with the body and the body with the tail of the rocket.

Filling Type and Text Blocks

You can also fill text objects to change the colors of individual characters or to change the background color of a text block. If you select a text object with the arrow tool and apply a fill, the fill affects all the type in the text object and leaves the associated path unchanged.

For instance, the first example in **Figure 15.4** shows a text block selected with the arrow tool. If you fill the object with a light gray, the type becomes filled, as shown in the second example in the figure. The result is gray type against a white background.

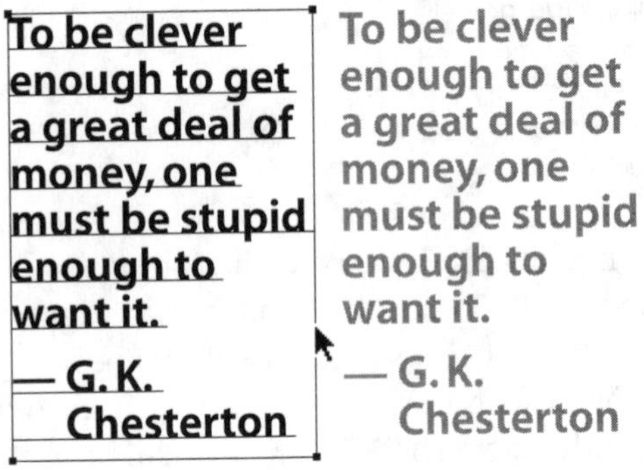

Figure 15.4: If you apply a fill color to a text block selected with the arrow tool (left), Illustrator fills the text (right).

To be clever enough to get a great deal of money, one must be stupid enough to want it.
— G. K. Chesterton

This is actually a very sophisticated feature. Strictly speaking, both the text and the path are selected when you click with the arrow tool. Yet the Adobe engineers correctly figured that if a text path and its text were selected, most people would only want the text to change color. Well done, Adobe!

But if you select the path around the text block with the direct selection tool and apply a fill, Illustrator fills just the path. The characters inside the text block remain filled as before, as demonstrated in **Figure 15.5**.

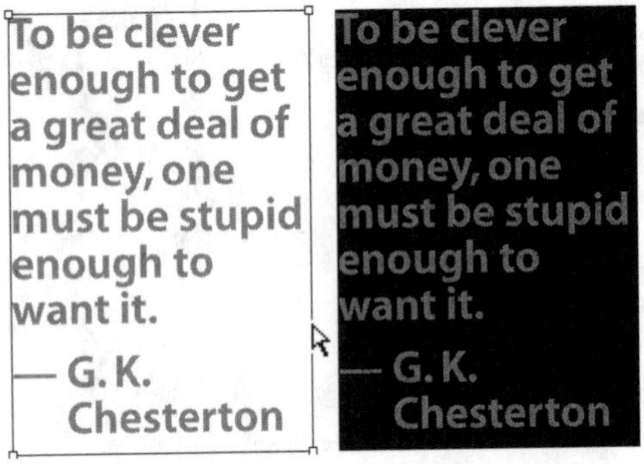

Figure 15.5: If you select the path of a text object with the direct selection tool (left) and then apply a fill, Illustrator fills the path only (right).

To be clever enough to get a great deal of money, one must be stupid enough to want it.
— G. K. Chesterton

To fill single characters and words, you have to select the text with the type tool. Like any character-level formatting attribute, such as font or type size, fill affects only the highlighted characters, as demonstrated in **Figure 15.6**. In this way, Illustrator allows you to apply several different fills to a single text object.

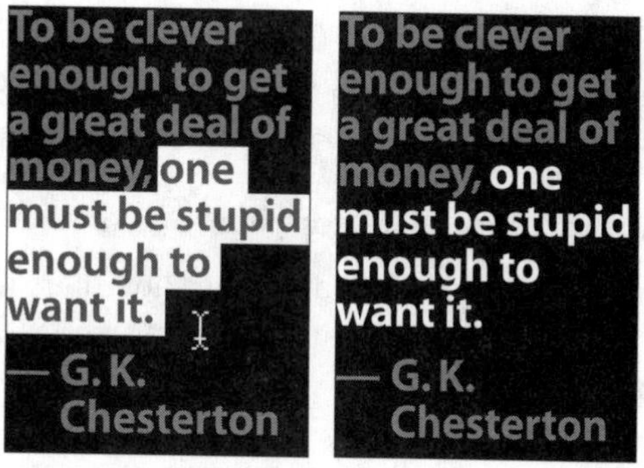

To be clever enough to get a great deal of money, **one must be stupid enough to** want it.
— G. K. Chesterton

To be clever enough to get a great deal of money, **one** must be stupid enough to want it.
— G. K. Chesterton

Figure 15.6: By selecting text with the type tool (left), you fill only the highlighted characters (right).

Applying a Single Fill

Whether you're filling paths or text blocks, follow these steps to apply a single fill to an object.

1. Select the path or characters that you want to fill.

You can use the arrow, direct selection, or type tool. In fact, you can be in the middle of drawing a path with the pen tool and still fill a path. As long as you can see selection handles or highlighted text in the illustration window, you can apply a fill.

If no object is selected, modifying the fill changes the default settings.

2. Click the Fill icon in the toolbox.

Or, if the Stroke icon is active—overlapping the Fill icon—press the X key. The X key toggles between the two icons.

3. Select a fill from the Color, Swatches, or Gradient palette.

Or you can press the comma key (,) for the last-used solid color or pattern, or press the period key (.) for the last-used gradient. Press the slash key (/) to be done with all this filling and just have a transparent object. You can also click the corresponding icons in the lower portion of the toolbox, shown in **Figure 15.7**.

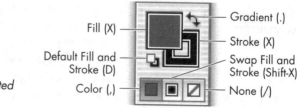

Figure 15.7: The fill-related controls in the toolbox.

Fill (X)

Default Fill and Stroke (D)

Color (,)

Gradient (.)

Stroke (X)

Swap Fill and Stroke (Shift-X)

None (/)

As I mentioned in Chapter 14, you can also drag a color from either the Color or Swatches palette onto any object—even if it's not selected—to change the fill color of the object.

4. **Edit the fill in the Color palette as desired.**

For example, you can adjust the slider bars to change a process color. Or you can select a color from a gradient and change it. More on gradients coming up.

Applying Multi-Fills and Effects

The idea of multiple fills sounds pretty strange right out of the gate. On the one hand, how can you put more than one fill in one object anyway? Isn't an object an object and that's that? On the other hand, if you're going to do something as crazy as putting in more than one, you'd never see one of them anyway, so what's the big deal?

The big deal is what happens if you do something to change the position of the second fill, or the nooks, or the crannies, or the whole shape of the fill. The distortion effects described in Chapter 19—Roughen, Twirl, Scribble, and so on—can move one fill so that it doesn't sit exactly on top of another. And suddenly multiple fills start to make sense. Suddenly you realize that you can create much more interesting looks than simple flat fills.

 In older versions (pre-Illustrator 9) you would have had to copy, paste in front or back, and then manipulate the pasted object to create the effect of multiple fills. With the relatively recent multi-fills, you still have only one path. This means you can modify a single point on the path and still make the changes to all the multiple fills.

Adding Fills

To create multiple fills, you need to work with the Appearance palette. The Appearance palette displays all of the appearance attributes in your art. Appearance attributes are properties that you can apply to single objects, groups of objects, or layers. These properties affect the appearance (hence the name) of the artwork without actually changing the object(s). Appearance attributes can be moved, edited, or deleted, none of which affects the original artwork. Appearance attributes can be as mundane as fills and as exotic as effects. Think of Appearance attributes as putting on a costume: you may look like Darth Vader, but it's really good ol' you underneath. If the Appearance palette is not visible, choose Window » Appearance. Here are the steps to add a fill to an object:

1. **Select the object.**

   It doesn't get easier than that.

2. **Select the fill in the Appearance palette and click the Duplicate Selected Item icon.**

   You can also drag the fill down to the Duplicate Selected Item icon or choose Add New Fill or Duplicate Item from the Appearance palette menu. The second fill is listed in the Appearance palette as shown in **Figure 15.8**.

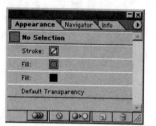

Figure 15.8: The Appearance palette with a second fill listed.

3. **Use the Color palette or Swatches palette to change either fill.**

   Two fills with exactly the same color are rather boring, so click one of the fills and change its color using either the Color palette or Swatches palette. (You can apply gradients or patterns also, but because I haven't talked about them yet, let's stick to ordinary colors.) In this case, I'll make the top fill a lighter color than the bottom one.

Using the Offset Path on Multi-Fills

But wait (you cry), you still can't see the two different fills. Patience, Grasshopper—you need to modify the second fill so that you can see the multiple fills. An excellent way to do this is with the Offset Path effect. Like the Offset Path command, the effect can be used to add or subtract an area around an object. In this case, you can use the effect to add space to one of the multi-fills in the Appearance palette.

1. **Target the fill you want to modify.**

   Click the name of the fill to which you want to apply the Offset Path effect. I'm going to target the bottom fill because I want that fill to become bigger than the fill above it.

2. **Apply the Offset Path effect.**

   Choose Effect » Path » Offset Path. This opens a dialog box similar to the Object » Path » Offset Path, which I covered in Chapter 7. Because I want this fill to be bigger than the one above it, I enter a positive number. (Use the Preview check box to see what you are doing.) If you've dutifully followed along, your Appearance palette should look like the one in **Figure 15.9.**

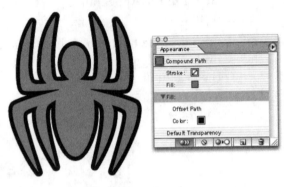

Figure 15.9: The Appearance palette with a second fill set with the Offset Path effect. Notice the black fill is visible behind the gray one.

3.   Add any other fills and effects as desired.

Now that you know the technique, go crazy. You can add as many fills as you want and apply as many effects as you want.

The position of the effects within the Appearance palette is important. If an effect is within the fill listing in the Appearance palette, then the effect will be applied only to that fill. But if an effect is listed outside of the fill listings—either on top or on the bottom—then that effect will be applied to the object as a whole. Notice the difference between the two examples in **Figure 15.10.** On the left, the Roughen effect was applied to the entire object. On the right, the Roughen effect was applied to just the top gray fill.

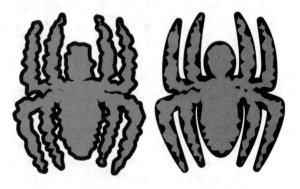

Figure 15.10: The difference between applying an effect to the entire object (left) or just the top fill (right).

You can have as many fills as you want. Use Effect » Distort & Transform » Transform to create multiple copies of fills. Or use Effect » Distort & Transform » Free Transform to make an object that casts its own shadow as shown in Figure 15.11.

Figure 15.11: An example of how the Free Transform effect can create an automatic cast shadow.

Using Convert to Shape on Multi-Fills

At this point you should have noticed one small limitation of the Offset Path effect applied to multi-fills: the second fill doesn't really change the shape of the additional fills. That's where the Convert to Shape effect comes in. It allows you to convert one of the fills (or strokes) applied to an object to a different shape.

 The benefit of this is enormous, especially when it comes to text. **Figure 15.12** shows two different text objects with a background rounded rectangle applied through the Convert to Shape effect.

Because the effect is live, this means that if the text size changes, the rectangle also changes accordingly, which is exactly what I did to create Figure 15.12. I duplicated the OK button and simply highlighted the text to make the HOME button. If you're a Web designer or a mapmaker, you can see the grand possibilities of this effect. Buttons, navigation bars, and the like can not only be made easily and consistently, but also changed with the flick of your wrist.

Figure 15.12: With the Convert to Shape effect applied, I created rectangles that automatically expand or contract to fill the area behind a text object.

Here are the steps you can follow to create buttons of your own.

1. **With your type tool, click and create your text.**

2. **In the Appearance palette, target the Characters item by selecting it.**

   Make sure to go back and select the text with the arrow tool or the direct selection tool; otherwise, you won't be able to complete the next step.

3. **Select Add New Fill from the Appearance palette pop-up menu.**

4. **In the Appearance palette, move the Fill attribute underneath the Characters.**

5. **Select the Fill attribute and then choose Effect » Convert to Shape » Rounded Rectangle.**

   The dialog box shown in **Figure 15.13** appears. It actually doesn't matter which shape you choose initially, because the Shape pop-up menu lets you switch from one shape to another. Leave Relative selected, leave the remaining defaults as is, and then click OK. I'll explain each of the options in the dialog box in a minute.

6. **With the Fill still selected, choose a contrasting color in the Swatches or Color palette.**

   To change the color of the text, simply highlight it with the type tool and choose another color in the Swatches or Color palette.

7. **Feel free to add other effects to jazz up your button.**

   I added a drop shadow effect to my button.

8. **Now for the cool part. Just for kicks, highlight your text and type a different word.**

   Notice how the rectangle dynamically updates to accommodate the new text. You wonder how something as simple as a rectangle can be so smart!

    You aren't limited to just text objects, either. You can create any object, target that object in the Appearance or Layers palette, and choose Effect » Convert to Shape.

Now that you've run through the steps for using Convert to Shape, let's get back to the options in the dialog box. It may look complicated, but the options are actually quite simple.

- **Shape:** Your choices are Rectangle, Ellipse, or Rounded Rectangle. Sorry—no stars, no spirals, no polygons, no figure eights. But that doesn't mean you can't start with some sort of strange shape and then add one of three chosen shapes.

- **Absolute:** If you choose Absolute, you can enter the exact size of the bounding box that will define the shape. This option is useful for objects that must remain a fixed size while their other fills are allowed to change shape. You must enter an amount for the height and width of the object.

- **Relative:** Takes its size from the bounding box of the original object. You can then add the amount of extra space you want outside the original object. A value of 0 sets the bounding box of the new object to the same size as the bounding box of the original object. You can set the width and height to be different values. For instance, in Figure 15.12, I set an extra amount for the width of the rectangles but left the height with no extra space.

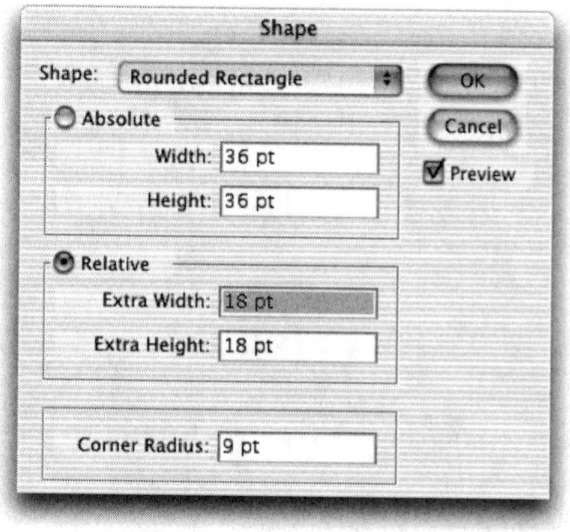

Figure 15.13: The Shape dialog box allows you to create an object that is tied to the size of the original.

- **Corner Radius:** If you've chosen a rounded rectangle shape, this option lets you choose the amount of the corner radius. The option is dimmed for the other shapes.

When you apply Convert to Shape behind a text object, the bounding box of the text object is calculated from the size of the entire area that the text could take up. (I mentioned this way back in Chapter 10 when I talked about the size of the area where you can select text.) If you want the bounding box of a text object to be only the size of the active text elements, apply the Effect » Path » Outline Object command along with Convert to Shape. This fakes Illustrator into thinking the text is really paths so that it calculates the bounding box based only on the actual size of the text.

Gradients in the Key of Life

Flat fills such as gray values, process colors, and spot colors—all covered in the previous chapter—are all very well and good. But if you're serious about imitating real life or giving your illustration a sense of depth, you'll appreciate Illustrator's unparalleled gradations. A gradation (or gradient fill) is a fill pattern that fades from one color into another. Illustrator lets you assign many colors to a single gradation—the number of colors that you can use is limited only by the amount of RAM you have in your machine. You can even fade between spot colors.

Figure 15.14 demonstrates the power of gradations. I drew these relatively simple structured paths to represent RCA cables. The left pair of cables shows the paths filled with flat gray values; the right pair is filled with gradations. As you can see, the gradations make all the difference in the world, single-handedly transforming the paths from cardboard cutouts into credible representations of three-dimensional objects.

You can create one of two types of gradient fills:

- A linear gradation is one in which the color transition follows a straight line. All of the gradations in Figure 15.14 are linear, flowing horizontally from left to right.

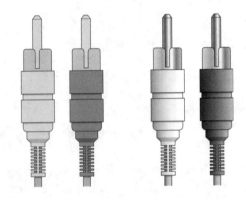

Figure 15.14: The only difference between the objects on the left and their counterparts on the right is that the latter objects are filled with gradations, which lends them the air of three-dimensionality.

- A radial gradation starts with a pinpoint of color and changes as it moves outward in concentric circles. (Think radial as in radial tire or radiate outward.)

Figure 15.15 shows examples of linear and radial gradations. A linear gradation can flow at any angle, so long as it flows in a straight line. A radial gradation can begin at any location inside a shape as long as it flows outward in a circular pattern.

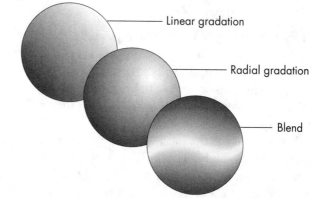

Linear gradation

Radial gradation

Blend

*Figure 15.15: The two top
fills are varieties of
Illustrator's automated
gradations. I used a blend to
create the bottom fill.*

If you want to create a gradation that doesn't quite fall into either of these camps—such as the wavy-line pattern at the bottom of Figure 15.15—you can create a custom blend using the aptly named blend tool, and then mask the blend inside a shape. Chapter 17 discusses blends, masks, and other extraordinary fill options.

Applying and Modifying Gradations

To apply a gradient fill to a selected path, click the Gradient (>) fill icon in the toolbox or click on the ramp in the Gradient palette. If you prefer, press the period key (.) to select the last-used fill and display the Gradient palette. You can even click one of the gradient swatches in the Swatches palette—these are predefined gradients contained in the Adobe Illustrator Startup file (assuming you haven't added any gradations of your own). The problem with Illustrator's predefined gradients is that you probably won't find much use for them. It's not Adobe's fault; it's just that gradations aren't particularly versatile creatures. A gradation created for one illustration is unlikely to be useful in another. So you'll probably want to create your own. The Gradient palette, shown in **Figure 15.16**, is the place to create and edit gradient fills.

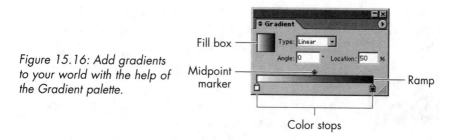

Fill box

Midpoint
marker

*Figure 15.16: Add gradients
to your world with the help of
the Gradient palette.*

Ramp

Color stops

The Gradient Ramp

Along the bottom of the Gradient palette is the *ramp,* also referred to as a *fade bar* or *gradient slider.* This is where you add and modify the colors of your gradient. The starting color appears as a square color stop on the far left; the ending color is the square stop on the far right. The diamond in the middle, called the *midpoint marker,* represents the spot at which the two colors mix in exactly equal amounts.

You can change the location of any stop or marker by dragging it. Or you can click a stop or marker to select it and then enter a value into the Location percentage option box above and to the right of the ramp. When a stop is selected, the little triangle on top of it changes from white to black.

Choose Hide Options in the Gradient palette menu to contract the Gradient palette so that just the ramp is visible. Choose Show Options to expand the palette. It's difficult to edit gradations when the palette is collapsed, but you can store the collapsed palette when it's not in use.

Adjusting the Color Stops in a Gradation

The most colorful part of working with gradations is working with the color stops and midpoint markers.

- To add a color stop, click anywhere along the bottom of the ramp. A new color stop appears right where you click. You can move the color stop or assign a different color to it.

- When a color stop is selected, the fill box in the Color palette displays a color stop right below it, as shown in Figure 15.16. This signifies that the color that you're modifying is part of a gradient. Select your desired color model from the Color palette pop-up menu and then specify your color using the color sliders.

- You can also drag a color swatch from the Swatches palette onto a color stop in the Gradient palette to change the color of the color stop. If you prefer not to drag, Alt-click (Option-click on the Mac) the color swatch of your choice. If you simply click a swatch, you will change the fill of the selected items to a solid color.

Have you ever wished you could lift a color from an object in the illustration window while working in the Gradient palette? As it turns out, you can. First, select the color stop you want to modify. Then select the eyedropper tool and Shift-click an object with a flat fill. Illustrator applies the fill color to the selected color stop.

To remove a color stop, drag the triangle down into the lower portion of the Gradient palette. The triangle vanishes and the ramp automatically adjusts as defined by the remaining color stops.

 When numerically positioning a selected color stop, a value of 0 percent indicates the left end of the ramp and 100 percent indicates the right end. Even if you add more color stops to the gradation, the values represent absolute positions along the ramp.

 Illustrator allows you to create a gradient between spot colors without converting them to their process ingredients. To create a gradation between two spot colors, drag the spot color swatches onto the color stops. Then, after applying the gradation to a few shapes, print the illustration to spot-color separations (as mentioned in the "Spot Colors" section of Chapter 14). Be sure to save your document as an Illustrator 9- or Illustrator 10-compatible EPS or as a PDF to preserve the spot color if you plan to import and print your document from a third-party application such as QuarkXPress or InDesign.

 Sadly, you can't use two spot colors in Illustrator's blend. The intermediate steps of the blend will be converted to process, not spot, colors. For more details about working with blends, see Chapter 17.

 To switch the colors of any two color stops, just drag one color stop onto the other. Illustrator swaps the colors and automatically updates the gradation. Illustrator automatically shifts the position of the midpoint marker to compensate for the reversed color stops.

Adjusting the Midpoint Markers in a Gradation

Midpoint markers set the tone for the speed of change within a gradation. Moving the midpoint marker to the left makes the change start fast and then slow down. Moving the marker to the right makes the change start slow and then speed up.

 Click to select the midpoint marker between two color stops. You can move the midpoint marker or enter an amount in the Location option box to position the midpoint marker.

 When repositioning a midpoint marker, the initial setting of 50 percent is smack dab between the two color stops; 0 percent is all the way over to the left stop, and 100 percent is all the way over to the right. Midpoint values are therefore measured relative to color stop positions. When you move a color stop, Illustrator moves the midpoint marker along with it to maintain the same relative positioning.

Creating and Changing Gradient Swatches

Gradients are fragile and ephemeral creatures. After you create a gradient it exists in the Gradient palette and it will exist in any objects that are selected while you make the gradient. But that's it. If you quit Illustrator (or if, heaven forbid, your computer crashes) at that point, you will lose the information about the gradient. Fortunately, you can use the Swatches palette to store gradients.

- Drag the gradient from the Gradient Fill icon in the Gradient palette into the Swatches palette. The gradient appears as a new swatch.

- Select the gradient in the Gradient palette (click on the Gradient Fill icon), click the New Swatch icon in the Swatches palette, or choose New Swatch from the Swatches palette menu. This automatically adds the gradient to the bottom of the Swatches palette.

- Alt-click (Option-click on the Mac) the New Swatch icon to open the New Swatch dialog box where you can name the gradient.

- Double-click the gradient swatch in the Swatches palette to change the name of the gradient.

- Hold the Alt key (Option key on the Mac) as you drag a gradient onto an existing gradient swatch to change the definition of the gradient. This also changes the appearance of all objects that had the gradient applied.

- To create a new gradation based on a selected one, select the Duplicate Swatch command from the Swatches palette's pop-up menu. Illustrator creates a clone of the gradation. You can now edit it to your heart's desire.

Setting Linear or Radial Gradients

Although the ramp is easily the most important part of the Gradient palette, you certainly also need to select the type of gradient from the type pop-up list.

- Linear gradients blend colors in a straight, or linear, fashion.

- When creating a radial gradation, the left color stop represents the center color in the fill; the right color stop represents the outside color.

- If you want the gradation to produce a highlighting effect, as in the left example in **Figure 15.17**, make the first color lighter than the last one. If you make the first color darker than the last, the edges of the shape are highlighted, as in the right example in the figure.

Figure 15.17: Two radial gradations, one in which the first color is white and the last color is dark gray (left), and another in which the colors are reversed (right).

Adjusting a Gradient Fill to Fit its Path

When you first assign a linear gradation to a path, Illustrator orients the gradation horizontally so it fades from left to right. When you assign a radial gradation, the gradation starts in the center of the shape. Because neither of these two settings is very interesting, Illustrator lets you easily change the angle of a linear gradation and reposition colors inside any gradation.

Changing the Angle by the Numbers

One way to change the angle of a linear gradation is to enter a value into the Angle option box in the Gradient palette. This is useful if you want to match the angle of an object ascertained with the measure tool.

The Angle value is also useful for matching the angles of multiple gradations to one another. Select the object that contains the properly angled gradation and note the Angle value in the Gradient palette. Then select the objects that you want to match and replace their Angle values with the new one.

Keep an eye on the Angle value, though. Each time you change that value, it becomes the default setting for the next object. Even if you select a different gradation, the Angle value remains intact until you manually enter a new value or select an object filled with a different gradation.

Using the Gradient Tool

For those times when you want to reposition colors in a gradation manually, Illustrator offers the gradient tool. You can also use the tool to change the angle of a gradation, which is frequently more convenient than entering a numerical Angle value.

Adjusting a Linear Gradation

If a selected object is filled with a linear gradation, you can drag across the object with the gradient tool to change the angle of the gradation. The first color appears at the point where you start your drag and the last color appears where you release the mouse button. The angle of the gradation matches the angle of the drag, as demonstrated in **Figure 15.18**.

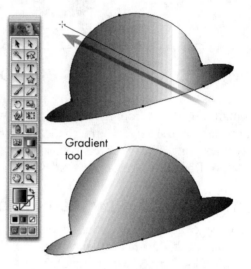

Gradient tool

Figure 15.18: Drag with the gradient tool (top) to change the angle of the gradation inside a selected object (bottom).

 You do not have to drag across the entire area of the object. If you stop the drag before you reach the end of the object, you fill the rest of the object with the last color of the gradient. If you start the drag inside the object, the first color of the gradient fills the object before the gradient.

 You can also drag from outside the object to another spot. The gradient is elongated so that only a portion of it appears within the object.

Figure 15.19 shows a single light-to-dark gray gradation set to different angles with the gradient tool. The white lines show the direction of the drag for each shape. The black dots show where I started dragging; the white dots show where I stopped.

- In the first example, the start and stop points lie well outside the shape, so the first and last colors fall outside the shape as well. This draws out the gradation and attenuates the range. Though the gradation runs from 15 to 70 percent black, you can only see 25 to 60 percent black inside the shape.

Figure 15.19: Three examples of the effect of the gradient tool on a gradation. The black dots show where I started dragging; the white dots show where I released.

● The start and stop points fall inside the second shape. Now we can see the full range of the gradation. But when a gradation doesn't fully traverse a path, you get areas of flat color, as labeled in the figure.

● Too much flat color can interrupt the rhythm of the gradation. In the last example, I dragged across a very short distance with the gradient tool. The resulting gradient fill flies by quickly, leaving large areas of flat color inside the shape.

It's especially unwise to leave flat areas of white inside a gradient fill. The transition from printed ink to no ink is harsh enough without accentuating the problem by magnifying the size of the no-ink area. To give you a sense of what I'm talking about, **Figure 15.20** shows examples of four black-to-white gradations, each one ending earlier inside its shape. Without much effort, most folks can see a sharp cutoff point where the last shade of gray gives way to white. The funny thing is, the transition frequently appears more abrupt when the illustration is output from a high-resolution imagesetter than when it's output from a laser printer. If in doubt, I suggest you run your own tests.

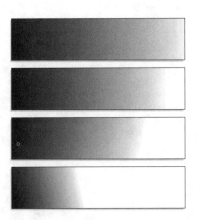

Figure 15.20: Leaving large flat areas of white can ruin the effect of a gradation and result in a crisp boundary between ink and no ink.

To avoid this effect, substitute 5 percent black (or some other very light shade) in place of white in your linear gradations. This way, you always have a little ink coverage in the gradation, no matter how slight. (This assumes a properly calibrated printer, of course. If the printer is a little off, 5 percent black can turn white. Again, print a few tests to be sure.)

Modifying a Radial Gradation

Using the gradient tool on an object filled with a radial gradation changes the balance of the gradation and repositions its center. If you drag across a selected radial gradation, Illustrator repositions the first color to the point at which you start dragging. It extends the outer ring to the point at which you release.

In **Figure 15.21**, I took the linear gradation from Figure 15.19 and selected the Radial option to convert it into a radial gradation. I also changed the first color to white. As before, the black dot shows where I started dragging and the white dot shows where I stopped. In a radial gradation, the first color is never flat, no matter where you start dragging in an object (which is why white doesn't tend to create problems for radial gradations the way it does for linear ones). But the last color can go flat, because Illustrator fills the area beyond the drag with the last color (as indicated by the words *Flat* in the figure).

If you click in a radial gradation with the gradient tool, Illustrator repositions the first color in the gradation independently of the outer ring formed by the last color. **Figure 15.22** *shows the result of clicking inside each of the shapes from Figure 15.21. In each case, Illustrator moved the first color, white, to the point where I clicked (as indicated by a sparkle) and offset the gradation to produce a sort of spotlight effect.*

Figure 15.21: Here I converted the fill from Figure 15.19 to a radial gradation. The black and white dots show where I started and stopped dragging with the gradient tool.

Figure 15.22: I clicked at each of the sparkles to offset the first color in the radial gradation independently of the last color.

Dragging through Multiple Paths

The gradient tool also allows you to apply a single gradation across multiple selected objects. In this way, all objects appear lit by a single light source. To accomplish this effect, select several objects, fill them with a gradation, and drag across them with the gradient tool. Illustrator creates one continuous gradation across all the selected shapes.

Figure 15.23 shows two lines of text converted to path outlines. In the first line, I selected the converted letters and filled them with a five-color gradient. Illustrator filled each character independently. In the second line, I dragged across the selected characters with the gradient tool, resulting in one continuous, angled gradation.

Figure 15.23: After applying a five-color gradient fill to a few converted letters (top), I dragged over the letters with the gradient tool (bottom).

 Unfortunately, Illustrator does not let you apply gradients to editable text. Remember the Convert to Outline effect? It fakes Illustrator into thinking that live text has been converted. So what happens if you apply the Outline Objects effect to text and then apply a gradient? Good question! The gradient is applied to each character of the text. Unfortunately, you can't use the gradient tool to change the gradation to a continuous tone. Got InDesign? You can apply a gradient across editable text characters there.

 As it turns out, the transformation tools also transform the gradient fills inside a path, as well as the path itself. If you transform a path and want to restore the gradient, press the comma key (,) and then the period key (.). This changes the fill to the last-used color or pattern and then back to the original form of the gradation. If the gradation remains rotated, enter 0 into the Angle option box in the Gradient palette and press Enter (Return on the Mac).

Gradient Mesh

Gradients are somewhat limited. They have only two shapes (at least in Illustrator). Blends (which I cover in Chapter 17) are a little more flexible, but even they have their limitations. They can't send colors out in different directions from the same point. So Illustrator gives you yet another way to have one color segue into another—you can convert an object into a *gradient mesh*. A gradient mesh (sometimes called just a *mesh* by its close associates) is a special type of path that is filled with a series of special interior paths. Wherever these interior paths cross, it creates a node (or what Adobe calls a *mesh point*) to which you can assign a color. Each node has four control handles that dictate the shape and direction of the color that extends out from the node. You can create objects that are more three-dimensional and appear to have been painted or airbrushed.

Figure 15.24 shows two example of the same object with the same gradient mesh. Only the mesh point has been edited.

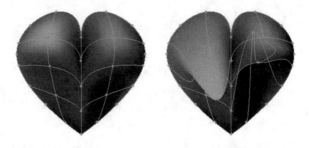

Figure 15.24: Two hearts with the same gradient mesh but different node locations.

Granted, for simulating continuous-tone images, with subtle shadows and highlights, Illustrator's gradient mesh feature may not be as easy or as intuitive as the painting tools in Painter or Photoshop. But once you get the hang of it, you actually have access to even more controls for fine-tuning your artwork than you do in most paint programs. And unlike the features in Painter or Photoshop, gradient meshes in Illustrator are vector and can be scaled to any size without loss of quality. Illustrations such as folded fabric, human faces, or even wrinkled paper (as shown in **Figure 15.25**) take on an air of reality when created with gradient meshes.

There are three ways to create a gradient mesh; each method has its own advantages and is covered in a section below.

Figure 15.25: The wrinkles in this paper were created using the gradient mesh.

Automatically Creating a Gradient Mesh

The easiest way to create a gradient mesh is to use the Create Gradient Mesh command, which automatically creates a grid that you can then modify. The key advantage to this method is that the command quickly makes many gridlines.

1. **Select a path.**

Although the path you select can be open or closed, Illustrator will automatically close an open path when it applies the gradient mesh. The gradient mesh will work with any flat fill but will convert a gradient fill or a pattern to a black-and-white gradient mesh. It ignores any stroke and will not work until you remove any brush associated with the path.

2. **Choose the Object » Create Gradient Mesh command.**

This displays the Create Gradient Mesh dialog box, as shown in **Figure 15.26**. Use the Preview check box to see the effects of the settings.

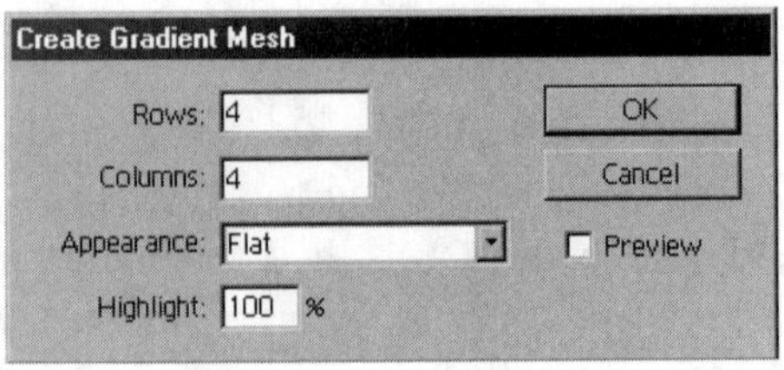

Figure 15.26: In this dialog box, you decide the number of lines Illustrator adds to a path when it creates the gradient mesh.

Create Gradient Mesh	
Rows: 4	OK
Columns: 4	Cancel
Appearance: Flat	☐ Preview
Highlight: 100 %	

3. **Choose the number of rows and columns you want in your gradient mesh.**

Enter an integer value in both the Rows and Columns option boxes. For the sake of simplicity, enter only as many as you need.

4. **Choose the appearance of the gradient.**

In the Appearance pop-up menu, you have three options. A Flat fill distributes the color evenly throughout the object without highlights. To Center creates a highlight in the object's center, while To Edge creates a highlight on the object's edge. These three options are shown in **Figure 15.27**.

Figure 15.27: The three settings for the Create Gradient Mesh are Flat (left), To Center (middle), and To Edge (right).

5. **Enter a value into the Highlight option box.**

By default, this value is a 100 percent white highlight. If you lower this value, the fade will be less dramatic. Lower the value to 0 percent and you eliminate all highlights.

Manually Creating a Gradient Mesh

The second way to create a gradient mesh is to use the mesh tool to manually add and manipulate the mesh lines and nodes. The advantage here is you get to control exactly where the gridlines are positioned. You can also use this method to modify gradient mesh objects created by other means.

1. **Click the gradient mesh tool inside an object to create the mesh lines.**

This automatically converts the object into a gradient mesh and adds the first vertical and horizontal lines. Each point where you click becomes a node, as shown in **Figure 15.28**.

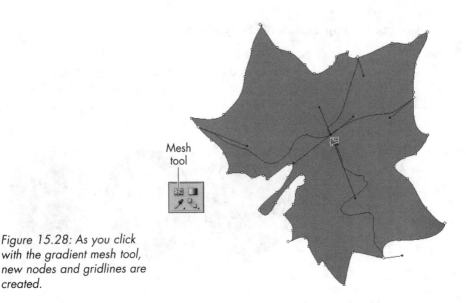

Mesh
tool

Figure 15.28: As you click with the gradient mesh tool, new nodes and gridlines are created.

2. **Use the mesh tool or the direct selection tool to select nodes.**

If you use the mesh tool, hold the Alt key (Option key on the Mac) to delete previously made nodes and gridlines. Be careful to click existing nodes precisely or you will add more gridlines. If you use the direct selection tool, you can hold the Shift key to add points to the selection.

 When you click next to a gridline with a specific shape, the new gridline follows that shape. So instead of manipulating two sets of nodes, you need to manipulate only one and then click to create the second.

3. **Change the color of the selected node.**

Select a node or patch (what Adobe calls the section in between the mesh lines) and choose colors via the Color palette or the Swatches palette. You can also drag and drop a color from either palette directly onto the node or patch.

Converting a Gradient into a Gradient Mesh

Finally, you can convert an object filled with a gradient into a gradient mesh object. The advantage of this method is that you start with many different colors already set for the nodes.

1. **Select an object filled with a gradient.**

   A linear gradient, as shown on the left side of **Figure 15.29**, is the easiest to work with. Because mesh objects cannot have strokes, do not apply a stroke to this object.

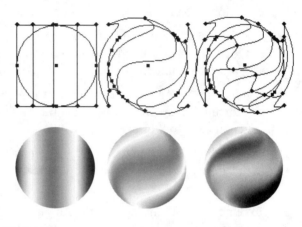

Figure 15.29: Anatomy of a marble: A circle filled with a linear gradient was converted into a gradient mesh (left). A slight twirl was applied (middle). Then additional gridlines and colors were added to create the marble on the right. The outline mode (shown on the top) shows the clipping mask that defines the circle.

 Radial gradients create a mesh object that is wrapped into a circular shape and may create gaps when manipulated.

2. **Choose Object » Expand.**

   The Expand dialog box, as shown in **Figure 15.30**, converts strokes and fills into their more basic elements. Click the Gradient Mesh option to convert the mesh object.

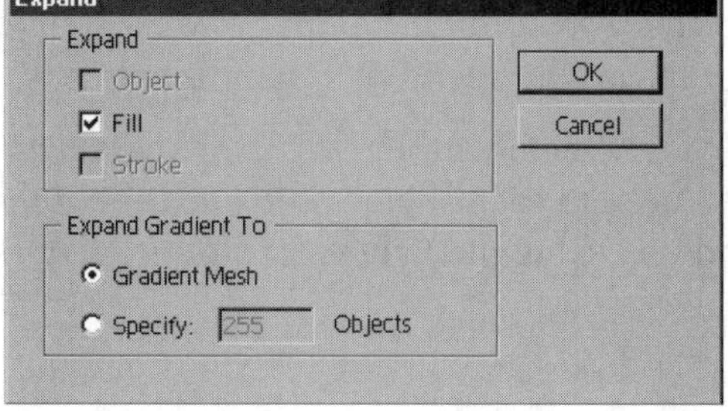

Figure 15.30: The Expand dialog box lets you convert gradients into gradient mesh objects.

3. **Modify the mesh as desired.**

   You can now add gridlines, change colors, transform, and otherwise manipulate the gradient mesh. A clipping path will be around the mesh, keeping it in the shape of the original object. You can modify or delete that mask. (For the complete story of working with clipping paths, see Chapter 18.)

Modifying Your Mesh

Here a few helpful pointers for working with gradient mesh objects.

- Nodes must contain control handles. You can shorten the handles, but they can't be deleted. You can push them into a node, but they are somewhat difficult to control when they are very short.

- If you have Use Area Select turned on in General Preferences, it will be difficult to marquee nodes inside the mesh object. Use the direct selection lasso tool instead.

- Use the direct selection tool to adjust opposite control handles like levers, or use the convert point tool to manipulate them independently.

- To remove a gradient mesh node, Alt-click (Option-click on the Mac) the node with the gradient mesh tool. This removes the horizontal and vertical lines going into the node.

- To remove only one of the lines going into a node, use the gradient mesh tool to Alt-click (Option-click on the Mac) the line you want to remove.

- You can't create mesh objects from objects that contain compound paths, text, or linked EPS graphics.

- Use the Create Mesh command on complex artwork. It usually results in better gradations.

- To create smooth transitions between your various shades of colors, use the eyedropper tool to sample colors within your mesh.

- Finally, remember there isn't a right and wrong way to apply a mesh. You need to spend some time fine-tuning the mesh—moving nodes and specifying the right colors to get the proper balance of highlights and shadows.

Filling Objects with Patterns

In Illustrator, you can fill both paths and text objects with patterns (sometimes called tiles, pattern tiles, or tile patterns), which are rectangular pieces of artwork that repeat over and over inside a shape. It's just like the tiles on a kitchen floor, only you don't have to get your hands all messy when applying the mortar. Most fabric and wallpaper designs are actually tile patterns with various levels of concealment.

Applying Patterns

In Illustrator, you can create your own patterns or select from the vast library included on the Illustrator CD-ROM. The pattern libraries are found in Illustrator Extras » Pattern & Texture Libraries. You can use the Window » Swatch Libraries » Other Library command to open the patterns as separate Swatches palettes. (If you need to, flip back to Chapter 14 for the details of how to work with the library palettes.)

All patterns must be defined and stored in a Swatches palette—either the Swatches palette for the current document or one of the library palettes. You apply patterns by clicking the swatch for a pattern of your choice.

Creating a New Pattern

To create a tile pattern in Illustrator, you simply select a bunch of objects and choose Edit » Define Pattern. This opens the New Swatch dialog box, which allows you only to name your pattern. (There's nothing else in there you can modify or choose.) If you like, you can drag the selected items onto the Swatches palette. This gives the pattern the name New Pattern Swatch 1, 2, 3, and so on. It's that easy. Illustrator automatically incorporates the objects into a rectangular tile. Really, that's it.

Ah, but if you want to create something that looks halfway decent, you might have to do a little more work. As with so many other operations inside Illustrator, there are a few nuances involved in creating a pattern that you can learn only by making one yourself. To this end, the following steps walk you through the task of designing a cool-looking tile pattern:

1. **Create a new illustration.**

    Even if you ultimately intend to apply the tile pattern to an existing object, it's a good idea to start off with a new document. Besides, tile patterns are shared among all open illustrations, so what you create in one window you can apply in another.

2. **Assemble a few objects to create a basic design.**

    In the first example in **Figure 15.31**, I took an airplane character from the Zapf Dingbats font and converted it to type outlines. (If you have Zapf Dingbats—named for influential type designer Hermann Zapf—you can press Shift-9 to get the plane.) I then rotated a clone of the plane 90 degrees by pressing the Alt key (Option key on the Mac) while rotating to create a copy. I chose Object » Transform » Transform Again to create two more rotated clones.

 Although you can use editable text in a pattern, most old-time Illustrator users convert the text to outlines. This comes from the days when patterns took the most time to process during printing. So most users try to reduce patterns to the simplest elements. If you want to, use editable text. However, convert it if there are problems printing your files.

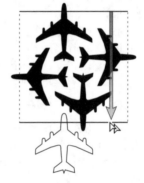

Figure 15.31: First I created a design and drew a rectangular guide around it (left). Then I Alt-dragged (Option-dragged on the Mac) the plane that overlaps the top of the rectangle to clone it and snap it into position along the bottom of the rectangle (right).

3.   Draw a rectangle around the design with the rectangle tool.

This rectangle represents a single tile in the pattern. The rectangle should cut slightly into the design, as it does in Figure 15.31. Objects that overlap one edge of the rectangle will repeat at the opposite edge. This helps to interrupt the rectangular rhythm of the pattern and create a more free-form appearance.

4.   Copy the rectangle, then convert it to a guide.

Choose Edit » Copy and then View » Guides » Make Guides. If you've never created a pattern before, this may sound like an odd step. But it permits you to align portions of the pattern to ensure invisible transitions from one tile to the next.

5.   Paste the rectangle in front, then separate its edges.

Choose Edit » Paste in Front, then click on each of the four corners of the pasted rectangle with the scissors tool. You now have four straight segments that you can use to align objects to the tile.

6.   Select the top edge and all objects that overlap the top edge.

I selected both the top edge and the upward-pointing plane.

7. Alt-drag (Option-drag on the Mac) the selected edge downward until it snaps to the bottom of the rectangle.

By pressing the Alt key (Option key on the Mac), you clone the object; and by dragging the edge instead of the object itself, you ensure a snug fit with the rectangular guide. The second example in Figure 15.31 shows how I snapped a clone of the plane along the bottom edge. Just as the nose of the plane extends out of the tile past the top edge, it now extends into the tile from the bottom edge. This ensures that the plane will flow smoothly from one tile into the next.

8. Select the bottom edge and the objects that overlap that edge, and clone them onto the top edge.

In my example, I selected and cloned the downward-pointing plane.

9. Repeat Step 8 for the objects that overlap the left and right edges as well.

After completing this step, I had a total of eight planes. The nose of each plane overlapped a side of the rectangle. And the same plane that overlapped one side also overlapped the opposite side. As a result, all of the planes will enter and exit the tiles in precise alignment.

10. Edit the objects as needed.

It's unlikely that you'll get your design exactly right on the first try. You may need to tweak it here and there. But pay careful attention to what you do. If you change the way one object overlaps an edge of the rectangle, you have to modify the matching object along the opposite edge in kind.

For my part, my plane pattern left gaps at each of the four corners of the tile. So I took another Zapf Dingbats character—the one that looks like a steering wheel (which you get by pressing the quote key)—and converted it to outlines. Then I selected the inner circle of the character with the direct selection tool, chose Window » Attributes to get the Attributes palette, and clicked on the Show Center Point icon. I next selected the entire character with the arrow tool and dragged it by the center point so it snapped into alignment with one of the corners of the rectangle. Finally, I Alt-dragged (Option-dragged on the Mac) the character a total of three times to snap it to the remaining corners. **Figure 15.32** shows the objects in my completed design. As you can see, one quarter of each steering wheel lies inside the rectangle, so that a single wheel will appear each time four tiles meet.

Figure 15.32: After cloning and snapping the planes into place, I added steering wheels to fill in the corners of the tile.

11. Select all the straight segments around the edges of the rectangle and delete them.

Their work is done.

12. Unlock the guide and convert it back into a normal object.

Assuming the guide is locked, choose View » Guides » Lock Guides to unlock it. Then select the guide and choose View » Guides » Release Guides.

13. Fill and stroke the objects as desired.

When filling objects, use flat colors only. Remember you cannot create patterns filled with gradations or other patterns.

*I used a popular embossing technique to create the effect shown in **Figure 15.33**. First, I selected and grouped all objects except the rectangle to make them easier to edit. Then I filled the grouped objects with 25% black. To create the shadow for the embossing effect, I selected the group, copied it, and pasted it in back. Then I nudged it down one point and to the left one point, and filled it with 55% black. To create the highlight, I selected the original group and selected Paste in Back again. Then I nudged the copy up one point and to the right one point, and filled it with white. The result is what you see in Figure 15.33.*

14. Select the rectangle set the fill and stroke to None. Send it behind all the other objects.

To tell Illustrator to use the rectangle as the bounding box for the pattern, you need to give it no fill or stroke. It also needs to be the backmost object.

Figure 15.33: I cloned and filled the plane and wheel shapes to create this common embossing effect.

15. **Select everything and choose Edit » Define Pattern.**

Illustrator displays the New Swatch dialog box. You can also drag everything directly into the Swatches palette. Even though the objects extend outside the rectangle, the pattern itself repeats only inside the bounding box. The bounding box, in essence, acts like a mask.

 If you try to drag some items into the Swatches palette and Illustrator refuses to store the items as a pattern, most likely one of the items in your selection contains an illegal fill such as a mask or a pattern.

16. **Name the pattern.**

Enter a name in the Swatch Name option box, as shown in **Figure 15.34**, and press Enter (Return on the Mac).

 The pattern you have created is transparent—that is, you can see through the areas around the design. If you want those areas to be opaque, you need to fill a rectangle with color and position it in front of the bounding box rectangle. The colored rectangle can be larger than the bounding box rectangle.

Well done! You have successfully completed a tile pattern that would make your dear mother's heart swell with unmitigated pride. You can now select an object inside any open illustration and apply your new tile pattern from the Swatches palette.

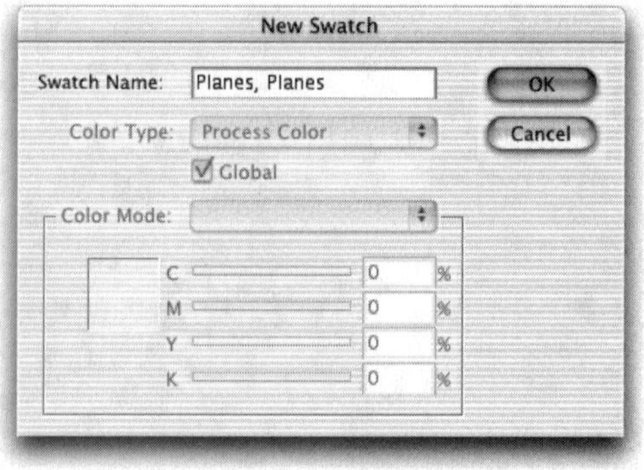

Figure 15.34: Choose Edit »
Define Pattern and provide a
name to convert your selected
objects into a pattern.

Modifying a Pattern

Let's say down the road you want to modify your pattern, and you are dismayed to realize you do not have the original objects used to create your pattern. Don't worry, it's not a showstopper.

You can create a copy of the objects used to define a pattern by simply dragging the pattern swatch out of the Swatches palette. This deposits all the objects of the pattern, as well as the bounding box, onto your artboard. You can then edit the objects and then drag them right back into the Swatches palette.

Even better, hold the Alt key (Option key on the Mac) and drag the modified pattern onto the original pattern. This updates the original pattern and all objects that have the pattern applied.

Transforming Tiles

Although most filters and effects don't touch the patterns inside objects, you can use the transformation tools to change the appearance of pattern tiles. You can transform an object and its pattern together or just the object or just the pattern. Here's how it works:

- The Move, Scale, Rotate, Reflect, and Shear dialog boxes are all equipped with two check boxes—Objects and Patterns. By default, just the Objects check box is active. This transforms the selected objects without transforming any pattern fills. If you select both Objects and Patterns, Illustrator transforms both items. You can also turn off the Objects check box and turn on Patterns to transform the tiles without affecting the objects at all.

- You can also turn on the Transform Pattern Tiles check box in General Preferences. This makes the pattern tile transform along with the object if you transform the object using the tool rather than the dialog box.

If you want a tile pattern to remain unchanged no matter how much you may change the filled object, leave the Transform Pattern Tiles check box off.

 You don't have to use a dialog box to transform a pattern fill independently of an object; you can also do it by dragging with a tool. Press the tilde key—you know, the little flying worm (~) at the upper left of the keyboard—while dragging with the arrow tool or any transformation tool to modify the tile pattern inside a shape and leave the shape unchanged. Just be sure to press the ~ key *before* you start dragging. **Figure 15.35** shows examples of pattern tiles transformed independently of their objects.

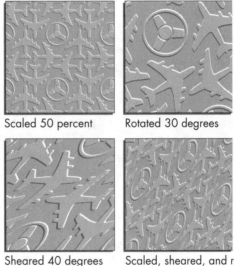

Scaled 50 percent   Rotated 30 degrees

Figure 15.35: You can manipulate a pattern fill independently of its object by turning off the Object option and turning on the Pattern Tiles option inside any transformation box.

Sheared 40 degrees   Scaled, sheared, and rotated

Rotating and slanting are particularly useful for camouflaging the linear appearance of a pattern. Scaling is handy for showing off more or less of a pattern at a time. And flipping…well, flipping isn't all that useful, but it's good to have around just in case.

 If you want to just nudge a pattern ever so slightly into position, hold the tilde key and use the up, down, left, or right arrow keys on the keyboard.

 Use Object » Expand to convert pattern tiles into discrete objects. This lets you change the colors of the objects.

CHAPTER 16

STROKES AND BRUSHES

The terms *fill* and *stroke* are often mentioned together—fills go inside a path, and strokes go outside. A stroke is what other programs often call a *border*, *outline*, or *frame*, but Illustrator being so closely tied to the PostScript page-description language, uses the term *stroke* because it's a PostScript term. It describes the visible mark that a path makes. Not the path itself, mind you, but only the visible mark (it's possible to have an unstroked path, which is present but invisible). You've learned how to draw paths. In this chapter, I'll tell you how to decorate them.

Strokes in Illustrator used to be really boring to write about because all you could do was add a colored line of a certain weight. There were so many limitations, yet so few choices. Today strokes are very important, very exciting parts of Illustrator, dare I say—even *more* exciting than fills. When Illustrator's engineers added brushes a few years ago, the excitement level of strokes went up considerably. All of a sudden you could stroke a path with expressive flourishes and drawn patterns, opening up many more creative possibilities.

Strokes have their own palette with their own controls. The dash patterns allow you to stop and start strokes in ways that fills could never dream of. And straight out of the box, Illustrator displays a black stroke around objects. Once you get comfortable with strokes, the next step is to play with brushes. They have their own palette, too, which you can use to personalize the brush strokes. Brushes are a great way to infuse Illustrator art with the personal style you might have already developed on traditional media.

Basic Stroke Attributes

In the past, strokes had to straddle both sides of a path. Today, anything goes. In **Figure 16.1**, I've applied different strokes to an open path and a closed path. The left side shows what life was like in the past: the path always ran through the center of the stroke. On the right side, I've shown what life is like today. Strokes can be positioned way outside their path and don't even have to have the same shape as the path. But before you go hog-wild seeing how strokes break the rules, let's look at some of the basic aspects of strokes.

Figure 16.1: These open and closed paths are stroked with heavy outlines. The paths themselves are shown in black.

Strokes are turned on and off by applying a stroke color—from either the tool-box or the Color palette. If an object has a stroke weight but no color, then it has no stroke.

 Watch out for straight lines that look like they're stroked when they're not. If you draw a straight line by clicking at two points with the pen tool and then add a black fill with no stroke, the fill follows the line onscreen, creating the appearance of a thin stroke. The problem is, the false stroke won't print accurately, particularly to a high-resolution imagesetter. Be sure to manually assign a stroke using the options in the Stroke palette, and never accept a thin stroke applied to a straight line at face value.

There are six basic attributes that can be applied to strokes. Five are controlled by the Stroke palette (shown in **Figure 16.2**). These are weight, bevels, caps, joins, and dashes. The sixth attribute—color—is applied from the toolbox, Color palette, or Swatches palette.

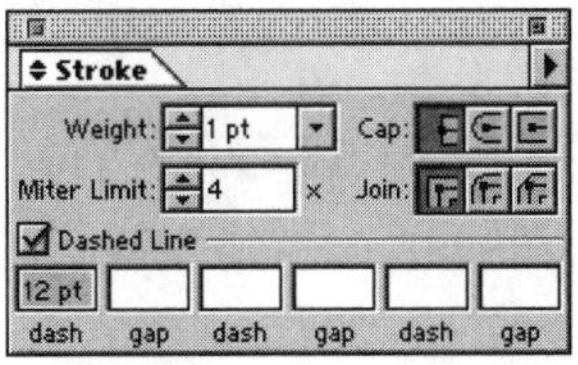

Figure 16.2: The Stroke palette is the control center for all the aspects of a stroke except color.

Stroking Type and Text Paths

Like fills, strokes are applied to objects differently depending on how the type is selected, as shown in **Figure 16.3**.

- If you select a text object with the arrow tool, applying a stroke affects all the type along the path.

- If you select the path with the direct selection tool, you can apply a stroke to the path only, leaving the text as is.

- Select text with the type tool to stroke single characters or words. In this case, the stroke is just another character-level attribute that affects the selected characters.

 Typographic purists will warn you against stroking text characters. This is because the stroke cuts into the shape of the characters. However, if the stroke is very thin, you can get away with stroking text. Or you can use the Appearance palette to put the stroke behind the fill, as I cover later in this chapter.

Figure 16.3: The text in the
top example was stroked
after selecting the text with
the arrow tool. The path for
the text in the middle
example was stroked after
selecting the curved path with
the direct selection tool. In the
bottom example, the text
characters were stroked after
the text was selected with the
text tool.

Applying a Stroke from the Stroke Palette

The following steps explain how to use the options in the toolbox and Stroke
palette to apply a stroke to a selected path or text object:

1. **Select the objects that you want to stroke.**

If no object is selected, editing the stroke changes the setting for the
next object that you create.

2. **Click the Stroke icon in the Color palette or the toolbox.**

This moves the Stroke icon to the front and makes the stroke the
active feature. When the stroke is active, the Stroke icon overlaps the
Fill icon, as shown in **Figure 16.4**.

*You can also press the X (when you're not using the text
tool) key to activate the Stroke icon.*

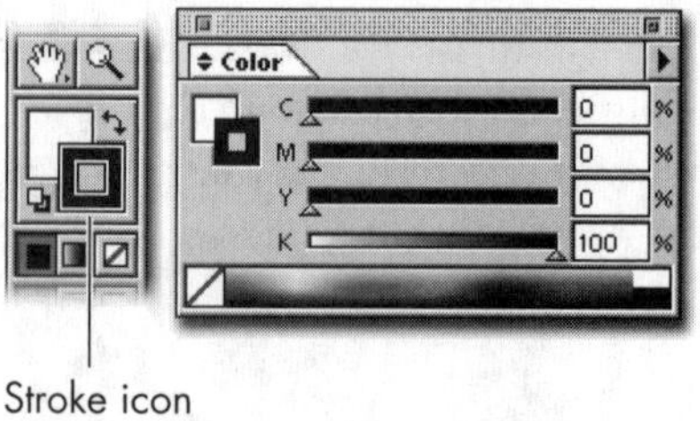

Figure 16.4: Select the Stroke
icon in the toolbox or the
Color palette to set the stroke
color.

Stroke icon

3. **Choose a color.**

To color a stroke, choose a color from the Color palette. To remove the stroke, click the None icon or press the slash key (/) on the keyboard.

 You can't apply a gradient to a stroke. So if you click the Gradient icon, you will apply the gradient to the fill of the object.

4. **If desired, apply a tint from the Color palette.**

Use either the Swatches palette or the Color palette as described in Chapter 14.

 You can also drag a swatch from the swatch list in the Swatches palette and drop it onto the Stroke icon in the toolbox. The Stroke icon doesn't have to be selected.

 You can apply a stroke directly to an unselected object. Just drag the swatch directly onto the object. If the Stroke icon is not selected, hold the Shift key to apply the color as a stroke.

5. **Change the Weight value.**

The Weight value determines the thickness of the stroke (also known as stroke weight).

6. **Click the icons to set the Cap and Join options.**

These option buttons appear in the upper-right corner of the Stroke palette, as shown back in Figure 16.2. You use the Cap icons to determine how the stroke wraps around the ends of an open path. You use the Join icons to control the appearance of the stroke at corner points. The Miter Limit option box appears to the left of the options only when the first Join icon is selected. Otherwise, the option box is dimmed. (I'll explain this option in a few moments.)

 If you do not see the Cap and Join options, choose Show Options from the Stroke palette menu. Or click the arrows in the Stroke palette tab to cycle through the palette display options.

7. **Select the Dashed Line check box to create a dashed outline.**

Then enter values into the Dash and Gap option boxes along the bottom of the dialog box to specify the length of each dash and each gap between dashes. (This option, too, will be explained just up ahead, good and patient reader.) If you don't want a dashed stroke, leave it unchecked.

8. **Press the Enter key (Return key on the Mac), or click inside the illustration window.**

Illustrator returns its focus to the illustration window.

Many options that affect stroke are available anytime a stroke has been assigned, even if the Fill icon is selected. (If the stroke is set to None, all stroke options are dimmed.) This means you can modify these stroke attributes regardless of which icon is active. You need to select the Stroke icon only if you want to change the color of a stroke, and even then, you can drag a color swatch and drop it onto the Stroke icon behind the Fill icon.

Weight, cap, join, and dash pattern are all powerful stroke attributes that bear further exploration. That's why they merit their own sections, coming right up.

Line Weight

The Weight values control the thickness of a stroke. Folks who spent their formative years laying down lines of sticky black ruling tape with X-Acto knives prefer the term *line weight*, so in deference to their years of hardship, that's the term I'll use in these discussions. Line weight is most commonly measured in points. However, you can use the Units & Undo section of the Preferences dialog box to set the line weight unit to points, inches, picas, centimeters, millimeters, or pixels.

You can enter any number between 0 and 1000, accurate to 0.01 point. (To give you some perspective here, 1000 points is longer than a foot.) However, I advise against specifying a line weight value smaller than 0.1. A 0.3-point line weight is commonly considered a hairline, so 0.1 point is about as thick as dandruff. **Figure 16.5** shows several line weights applied to a frilly path. The 0.1-point line is barely visible. Any thinner and it simply will not reproduce.

Do not enter a line weight of 0. This tells Illustrator to print the thinnest line available from the output device. The thinnest line printable by a 300-dpi laser printer is 0.24-point thick, which looks pretty good. However, high-resolution imagesetters easily print lines as thin as 0.03-point, or ten times thinner than a hairline. Suddenly the line you could see from the laser printer turns invisible.

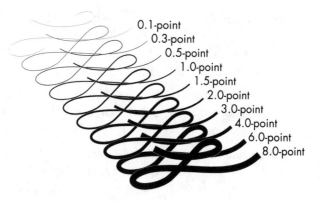

0.1-point
0.3-point
0.5-point
1.0-point
1.5-point
2.0-point
3.0-point
4.0-point
6.0-point
8.0-point

Figure 16.5: Here are several examples of line weights printed from Illustrator. The top line is barely visible; anything thinner than 0.1 point is essentially invisible.

Line Caps

You can select from three types of line caps, which determine the appearance of a stroke at its endpoint. Line caps are generally useful only when you're stroking an open path. The only exception to this is when you use line caps in combination with dash patterns, in which case Illustrator applies the cap to each and every dash, as I explain later in this chapter.

The three Cap icons in the Stroke palette, from left to right, work as follows:

Butt Cap: This is the default setting and the most commonly used line cap. (Whether it's fit for polite company I can't say, but yes, folks, butt is the official PostScript term for this kind of cap. No jokes please.) Notice the black line that runs through the center of each of the Cap icons. This indicates the position of the path relative to the stroke. When the Butt Cap option is selected, the stroke ends immediately at an endpoint and is perpendicular to the final course of the path, as shown in the top diagram in **Figure 16.6**.

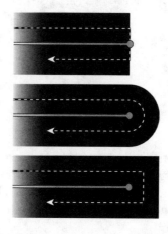

Figure 16.6: Diagrams of the three kinds of line caps—from top to bottom, butt, round, and square. The gray line indicates the path, whereas the dotted line shows the stroke moving around the path.

- **Round Cap:** Wraps the stroke around the path to circle the endpoint. The radius of the circle is half the line weight, as demonstrated by the second diagram in Figure 16.6. If you have a 4-point line weight, for example, the round cap extends exactly 2 points out from the endpoint.

  Round caps are used to soften the appearance of a line. The line appears to taper, rather than abruptly end. I frequently apply round caps when I'm using thick strokes.

- **Square cap:** Last and least (and called the Projecting Cap by Illustrator). Here, a square is attached to the end of a line; the endpoint is the center of the square. Like the round cap, the square cap sticks out half the line weight from the endpoint, as the bottom diagram in Figure 16.6 shows. The only difference is that the square cap has very definite corners, making it appear to jut out more dramatically.

Use square caps when you want to close a gap. For example, if you want the stroke from an open path to meet with a point of another path, the square cap option gives a little overlap where the two points meet.

Figure 16.7 shows the same illustration created with open paths set with each of the cap settings. In the first eye, the lines with butt caps either clear each other or barely touch. In the round cap eye, the caps close many gaps, but you can plainly see that the touching lines are not part of the same path. In the third eye, the square caps completely eliminate even the hint of gaps in the corner of the lids and the spot where the top iris path meets the top lid. The square caps give the paths a more substantial appearance all around.

Figure 16.7: I drew each of these eyes using the same collection of open paths. The only difference is the line caps—butt on the left, round in the middle, and square on the right.

Line Joins

The Stroke palette offers three line joins, which determine the appearance of a stroke at the corners of a path. The stroke always forms a continuous curve at each smooth point in a path, but you can use line joins to clip away the stroke at corner points and cusps. Here's how each of the Join icons (from left to right) work.

Miter Join: This is the default setting. If a corner has a miter join, the outside edges of the stroke extend as far as necessary to form a crisp corner. The first star in **Figure 16.8** is stroked with miter joins. Compare its perfect spikes to the rounded and chopped-off corners in the other stars. Watch out, though: Illustrator may cut a miter join short according to the Miter Limit value, as explained in the next section.

Figure 16.8: Each of these stars is stroked with a different line join—miter (top), round (middle), and bevel (bottom). Notice that the joins affect all corners in the paths, whether they point out or in.

Round Join: This option is identical in principle to the round cap. Half of the line weight wraps around the corner point to form an arc, as shown in the second star in Figure 16.8. Round joins and round caps are so similar, in fact, that they are used together almost exclusively. The only time you should avoid using round joins is when a dash pattern is involved. Because round joins actually form complete circles around corner points, they can interrupt the flow of the dashes.

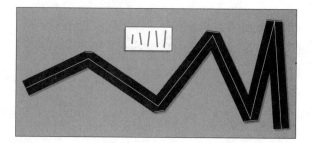

Figure 16.9: As segments meet at sharper angles, the bevel joins lengthen. Each bevel is repeated in the inset for comparison.

Bevel Join: Very similar to a butt cap, the bevel join shears the stroke off at the corner point. As shown in the bottom star in Figure 16.8, the bevel join creates a flat edge at each corner point. The length of this flat edge varies depending on the angle of the segments. A gradual angle results in a short bevel; a very small angle results in a long one. **Figure 16.9** shows a path made up of segments that meet at progressively sharper angles. I've traced the bevels with white lines to demonstrate their increasing lengths. For comparison's sake, the inset shows the five bevels on their own.

Giving Excessive Miter Joins the Ax

Directly to the left of the Join icons in the Stroke palette is the Miter Limit option box. This value tells Illustrator when to chop off excessively long miter joins caused by a very small angle between segments. The Miter Limit value represents a ratio between the length of the miter—from inside to outside corner—and the line weight, both diagrammed in **Figure 16.10**. As long as the miter length is shorter than the line weight multiplied by the Miter Limit value, Illustrator creates a miter join. But if the miter length is longer than the line weight times the Miter Limit value, Illustrator chops off the miter and makes it a bevel join.

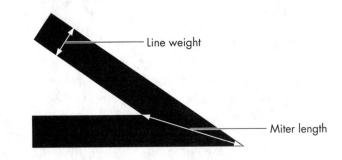

Figure 16.10: The miter length grows as the angle between two segments shrinks.

If I had applied miter joins to the path in Figure 16.10, for example, the bottom joins would be more likely to get chopped off than the top joins. A miter can grow especially long when two curved segments meet to form a cusp. As shown in **Figure 16.11**, two inward-curving segments create a serious Pinocchio effect and a bit of distortion. The result is an unbecoming spike that looks completely out of place.

Hacking away the join with a small Miter Limit value is an awkward solution, as shown in the second example of Figure 16.11. Illustrator gives you either a ridiculously long miter or it bevels it completely. If you want to preserve the precise quality of a miter join without allowing it to take on a life of its own, you should manually adjust your path. Increase the angle between segments to create a shorter miter.

The Miter Limit value can range from 1 to 500, provided that the value multiplied by the line weight doesn't exceed 1800 points. The default value is 4. A Miter Limit value of 1 tells Illustrator to lop off every join and is therefore identical to selecting the Bevel Join icon. If either the Round Join or Bevel Join icon is selected, the Miter Limit option appears dimmed.

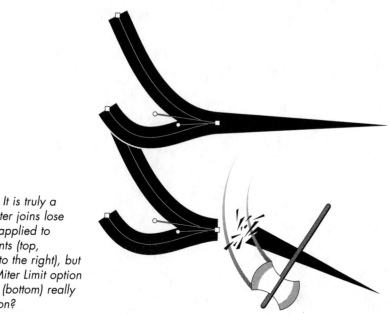

Figure 16.11: It is truly a shame that miter joins lose control when applied to curved segments (top, extending off to the right), but is letting the Miter Limit option chop them off (bottom) really the best solution?

Dash Patterns

The options along the bottom of the Stroke palette allow you to apply a dash pattern to a stroke. Dash patterns are repetitive interruptions in a stroke. When the Dashed Line check box is empty, Illustrator creates a solid stroke.

To create a dash pattern, select the Dashed Line check box, which brings to life six previously dimmed option boxes. Each option box represents an interval, measured in points, during which the stroke is on or off over the course of the path. The Dash values determine the length of the dashes; the Gap values determine the length of the gaps between the dashes. Most folks simply fill in the first pair of option boxes and leave the rest blank, because Illustrator repeats the values you enter and ignores any empty option boxes to the right.

 If you like, you can enter a value into the first Dash option box and be done with it. Illustrator applies the value to both the dashes and gaps. If you enter the default Dash value of 12, for example, the stroke is on for 12 points and then off for 12 points.

The ghost grid in **Figure 16.12** shows a sampling of dashes created using only the first pair of Dash and Gap options. These horrifying members of the spirit world are arranged into columns and rows according to their Dash and Gap values. If you scrutinize the phantoms carefully, you may notice that the dashes pile up at the point where the path starts and stops, causing irregularities in their spectral composition.

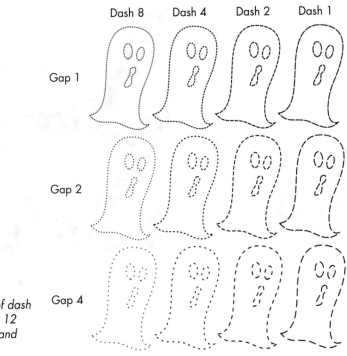

Figure 16.12: A grid of dash patterns demonstrating 12 combinations of Dash and Gap values.

Dash pileups occur because a regular dashed stroke doesn't automatically adjust for corners and ends, so your only recourse is trial and error. In the first ghoul in **Figure 16.13**, I applied a Dash value of 6 and a Gap of 3 to the eyes. But as the white circles show, I ended up with an extra-long dash at the bottom of each shape. The solution? I gradually raised the Gap value in 0.01-point increments until the dash shrunk back to the proper size. A Gap value of 3.11 finally did the trick.

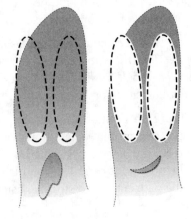

Figure 16.13: After applying a stroke with 6-point dashes and 3-point gaps (left), I gradually raised the Gap value to eliminate any ghoulish dash pileups (right).

If you're using dashes to create coupon borders, and you want better corners than the ones that the standard dashed lines give you, you might want to create a pattern brush instead. Pattern brushes can use a segment designed especially for perfect corners, and they're covered later in this chapter.

Using Line Caps with Dash Patterns

Illustrator treats the beginning and ending of each dash in a pattern as a start and stop in the stroke. Therefore, both ends of a dash are affected by the selected line cap, which makes it possible to create round dashes. Raising the Dash value above 0 would elongate the dashes so that they would no longer appear circular; they would start to look like little submarines.

I stroked each of the three lines in **Figure 16.14** with a 16-point line weight that included a dash pattern and round caps. I entered 0—yes, 0—for the Dash value and 26 for the Gap. When you specify the length of each dash as 0, you instruct Illustrator to allow no distance between the round cap at the beginning of the dash and the round cap at the end of the dash. The two round caps therefore meet to form a complete circle.

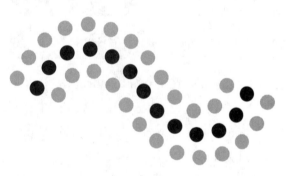

Figure 16.14: Three lines stroked with the same dash pattern in two different colors. I selected the Round Cap icon and set the Dash value to 0, resulting in circular dots.

Figure 16.15 shows two dashes set to 0 with round caps. Notice that to prevent one circular dot from touching or overlapping the next, the Gap value must be larger than the Weight value.

Figure 16.15: A diagram of a dash pattern with a 0-point dash and round caps. The thick gray line represents the path, whereas the dotted line shows the stroke wrapping around each dash.

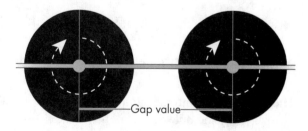

Stroke Positions and Multi-Strokes

There is a stacking order for fills and strokes. (Yes, like so many of us, even fills and strokes are subject to strict hierarchies of life.) Ordinarily, the stroke sits on top of the fill. However, you can create different looks by using the Appearance palette to position the stroke behind the fill. In fact, you can use the Appearance palette to stack many strokes and fills without drawing any additional paths.

If you aren't familiar with the Appearance palette, I cover that in more depth in Chapter 19, Hog-Wild Special Effects.

Stroke Under Fills

What if you want to draw a thick outline around some important text, as seen in the top example of **Figure 16.16**? Unfortunately, half of the stroke cuts into the letters, making them illegible and terribly ugly. (This is why typographic snobs will tell you not to stroke text.) Fortunately, you live in an enlightened age of Illustrator where you can easily move the stroke behind the fill.

Figure 16.16: Text with a 4-point stroke (top) and the same text with a 4-point stroke moved below the fill (bottom).

CHEAP THRILLS

CHEAP THRILLS

1. Use the selection tool to select the text as an object.

    The Appearance palette should read "Type" for the selected text.

2. Choose Add New Stroke from the Appearance palette menu.

    You will now see two new listings for Stroke and Fill in the Appearance palette.

3. Click the Stroke listing in the Appearance palette and change the color from None to the color you want for the stroke.

4. Set the stroke to twice the desired line weight.

    For example, if you want to see 2 points of stroke around the fill, set the stroke weight to 4 points.

5. In the Appearance palette, drag the listing for the stroke below Characters.

The result is the bottom example in Figure 16.16. The fill is positioned above the stroke. Only the outside half of the stroke is visible. This leaves the shape of the text unchanged.

Stroke + Stroke = Multi-Strokes

Even before there were multiple strokes, Illustrator users created similar looks by cloning multiple paths on top of each other and applying different strokes to the paths. The only problem was that it was difficult to alter the shape of the object because you had to select all the multiple paths. With multiple strokes applied to one path, Illustrator makes it even easier to create those looks.

Using multiple strokes, you can create parallel lines, outlined lines, and special dots and dashes. **Figure 16.17** shows just a smattering of the effects you can create. No matter how many pages I devote to sharing some of these effects, you'll be able to come up with twice as many of your own an hour later. However, here are some general rules for creating different multi-stroke looks.

- Reduce the stroke weight and change the color of a stroke to make parallel lines.

- Use dash patterns to make strokes that change color on and off.

- Use round caps to make dots.

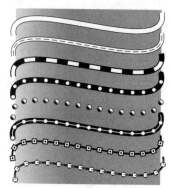

Figure 16.17: All of these beautiful jewels were created using strokes and dash patterns.

As for multi-fills, you use the Appearance palette to create additional strokes and order them. **Figure 16.18** shows how multi-strokes and dashes can create the effect of railroad tracks. Here's how I did it.

1. Select the object and create a 49-point gray stroke set to 8 points Dash and 20 points Gap. This creates the full length of the railroad ties.

2. Choose Add New Stroke from the Appearance palette menu. Set it to 38-point black, no dashes. This sets the outside of the railroad track.

3. Repeat Step 2 for a 34-point white stroke, a 30-point black stroke, and a 26-point white stroke, all with no dashes. At this point you can't see the inside of the railroad ties.

4. Add a 26-point gray stroke set to the same dash pattern as the first. This gives the appearance of being able to see the railroad ties through the tracks.

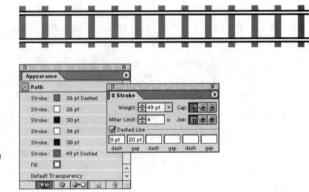

Figure 16.18: A set of railroad tracks created with multi-strokes and dash patterns. The Appearance palette shows the stacking order of the strokes, and the Stroke palette shows the dash pattern used for both the top and bottom strokes.

Now you know everything there is to know about stroking objects. From here on, you can take off in a million different directions. You can add as many strokes as you want in the Appearance palette, giving each stroke a progressively thinner line weight to reveal portions of lower clones and cover up other portions. You can alternate line caps and experiment with the Dash and Gap values.

Multi-Strokes for Groups or Layers

When you apply multi-strokes, the specific result you get depends on whether you targeted a layer, an individual object, or a group in the Layers palette. If you target a layer, it means that all objects drawn on that layer will automatically take on the attributes for the layer. Similarly, if you target a group, all the objects in the group will have the same attributes.

However, there's more than just a convenience factor in applying the strokes to a group or layer. As **Figure 16.19** shows, if you apply the multi-strokes to individual objects, you see the "road blocks" between the objects. But if you apply the multi-strokes to a group or layer, the multi-strokes miraculously merge their stroke settings into seamless intersections.

If you're not sure what it means to target in the Layers palette, take a peek at Chapter 19's discussion about using the circle icons at the right side of the Layers palette to target objects and combinations of objects. In short, a small circle next to the layer name indicates whether that object or layer has appearance attributes, and a layer is targeted if its circle has a larger circle around it. When an object is targeted, your changes will change that object's appearance.

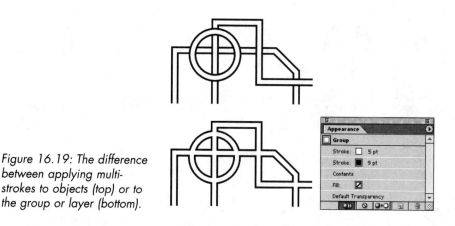

Figure 16.19: The difference between applying multi-strokes to objects (top) or to the group or layer (bottom).

Stroke Commands, Filters, and Effects

Some commands in Illustrator's menus are specially designed for working with strokes. For instance, you can convert strokes to filled objects, apply arrowheads, or use special effects for strokes.

Converting Strokes to Outlines

Strokes sometimes don't get the respect that fills have in Illustrator. In fact, some of Illustrator's functions are downright antagonistic to strokes and brushes.

 The knife tool will not cut an open path that has a stroke but no fill.

 You can't apply gradients to strokes.

 You can't weave paths because an entire path must be completely above or below any other whole paths.

 Some Pathfinder-related commands—such as Trim, Merge, Crop, Hard Mix, and Soft Mix—will discard strokes.

 The color blend filters such as Blend Front to Back ignore strokes entirely.

Fortunately, you can get around all of these limitations using the Object » Path » Outline Stroke command, which converts stroked lines to filled shapes. For example, you can create effects such as the look of a single object going both in front of and behind other paths, as shown in **Figure 16.20**.

1. Stroke the path.

The key ring is positioned on top of the key in Figure 16.20, and the ring is stroked with a darker gray.

Figure 16.20: To create the illusion of an interlocking stroke, start with a stroked path (far left). Then use the Outline Stroke command to convert the stroke to a filled path (second from left). Apply the Divide Pathfinder command (center). Then select an intersection (second from right) to change its color to match the other object (far right).

2. Select the path and apply Object » Path » Outline Stroke.

The Outline Stroke command uses the current stroke settings to re-create the stroke as a filled path. For example, stroke weight turns into object width, and it will maintain any miters and bevels that are applied to the stroke. In this case, it turns the stroke into a filled path with compound objects that create the hole in the path as seen in Figure 16.20.

3. Apply Divide from the Pathfinder palette.

This cuts up the filled objects wherever they overlap, as shown in the bottom-left corner of Figure 16.20. (See Chapter 7 for a refresher on the Pathfinder commands.)

4. With the direct selection tool, select and change the fill color of an intersection to match the other object.

This creates the illusion that the objects are intertwined, as seen in the final example of Figure 16.20.

Sadly, neither Outline Stroke nor the similar Expand command preserves dashed patterns. However, if you set the opacity of the object to 99% and then choose Object » Flatten Transparency, the object will be converted to outlined paths that preserve the dashes. I'll cover opacity and transparency in Chapter 18.

Outlining Stroke Effect

The disadvantage of the Outline Stroke command is that it loses the stroke information and creates compound filled objects. This makes it more complicated to increase the width of the stroke or change the shape of the object. You can use the Effect » Path » Outline Stroke command to make the conversion less permanent.

Figure 16.21 shows one of the benefits of the Outline Stroke effect. The rectangle on the top has had the Twist effect applied to a 17-point stroke without the Outline Stroke effect. The twist changes the shape of the stroke as a single unit. The rectangle on the bottom has had the Twist effect applied to a stroke that has had the Outline Stroke effect applied first. Notice how the Twist effect independently distorts both sides of the stroke. Although the stroke has not actually been converted, the Outline Stroke effect allows you to distort the object with variable width lines.

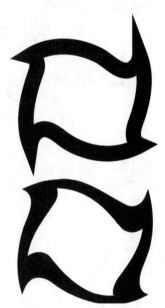

Figure 16.21: Without the Outline Stroke effect (top), a twist can only change the stroke. With the Outline Stroke effect (bottom), the twist can distort both sides of a stroke.

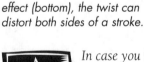

In case you were wondering: no, you can't use the Outline Stroke effect together with the Divide effect to create intertwining objects. Although you can apply the effects, Illustrator doesn't give you any way to change the fill colors of the overlapping objects.

Fashioning Arrowheads Without Flint

One of the commands that exists as both a filter and a live effect is Add Arrowheads. After selecting an open path—neither the filter nor the effect works on closed paths or text objects—choose Filter » Stylize » Add Arrowheads or Effect » Stylize » Add Arrowheads. Like other dual commands, the difference between the dialog boxes is the presence of a Preview command in the dialog box, as shown in **Figure 16.22**.

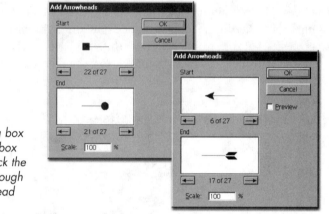

Figure 16.22: The Add Arrowheads filter dialog box (left) and effects dialog box (right). In either one, click the arrow icons to move through the 27 different arrowhead designs.

The size of the arrowhead is dependent upon two factors: the line weight of the selected path and the percentage value in the Scale option box. **Figure 16.23** shows five paths with different line weights, varying from 0.5 to 6 points, each with the Scale value set to 100 percent. Illustrator's default scaling generally suits 1-point and 2-point lines, but you'll want to raise or lower the Scale value if the line is thinner or thicker, respectively.

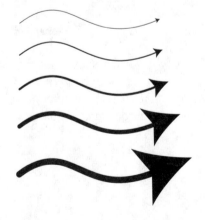

Figure 16.23: The first arrow-head option as it appears when applied to lines 0.5, 1, 2, 4, and 6 points thick. For all lines, the Scale value was set to 100 percent.

Illustrator lets you specify whether you want to apply the arrowhead to one end, the other, or both ends of the open path. Which end is which depends on how you drew the path. Generally, you'll just make a guess and go for it. (Of course, you can use the Preview option in the dialog box if you're using the effect version of the feature.) If it turns out to be the wrong end, you can undo the filter or change the setting of the effect.

 To remove an arrowhead added by the Add Arrowhead filter long after it's too late to undo it, just Alt-click (Option-click on the Mac) the arrowhead with the direct selection tool arrow and press Backspace or Delete (be careful not to accidentally select the path itself). If you want to remove the Add Arrowhead effect, just select the object in the Appearance palette and drag the Add Arrowhead effect to the Trash icon in that palette.

You can choose from among 27 arrowheads. Scroll through the collection by clicking on one of the two arrow icons that appear below the big arrow. **Figure 16.24** shows 26 of the arrowheads in order—numbers 2 through 14 down the left side and 15 through 27 down the right. (Arrowhead number 1 appeared in Figure 16.23.)

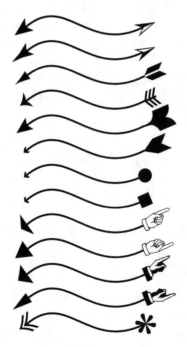

Figure 16.24: You can apply any of these festive arrowheads using the Add Arrowheads filter. In each example here, the line weight is 2 points and the Scale value is set to 100 percent.

After you press the Enter key (Return on the Mac), Illustrator assigns the arrowhead to the path. If you have applied the arrowhead as a filter, the arrowhead is a separate path—in some cases, several paths. These paths are automatically grouped with the original open path. However, if you apply the command as an effect, the arrowheads are not discrete objects.

This is important to keep in mind when transforming the path. If you have applied the command as a filter, the arrowhead will be distorted if you scale the path disproportionately. If this happens, select the arrowhead with the direct selection tool, delete it, and then apply a new arrowhead. However, there are no problems if the arrowhead has been applied as an effect.

 If you apply the Add Arrowheads filter and then select the line and arrowhead with the selection tool, the Color palette and the toolbox display question marks for both the Fill and Stroke icons. This is because the line is stroked but presumably not filled, whereas the arrowhead is filled but not stroked. If you want to change the fill or stroke of either portion of the object, use the direct selection tool to select either the line or arrowhead independently.

If you've already positioned the open path exactly where you want it, you'll notice that Illustrator appends the arrowhead to the end of the path, thereby elongating it. If you've applied the arrowhead as a filter, you can move the arrowhead. However, you need to expand the appearance if you've applied the arrowhead as an effect. (See the section "Removing or Expanding a Brush" later in this chapter for the scoop on the Expand Appearance command.)

Brushing Up on Your Paths

Until there were brushes, strokes were very mathematical. They had a fixed point size for their width, and that was about it. They couldn't change their width or taper or spatter little flecks of color. Brushes are special artwork applied to strokes, making them look much more like traditional brush strokes. They are also used to apply artwork in repeating or scattered patterns along a path. They can even stretch or bend type and other objects.

There are four types of brushes in Illustrator. By default, the Brushes palette contains a number of examples of each, as shown in **Figure 16.25**.

As I mentioned in Chapter 5, you can use the paintbrush tool to draw with brushes. Any path you create with the brush tool automatically adopts a brush stroke along its length. One of the great things about brushes is that they are not limited to the paths created with the brush tool. The fact is that you can apply a brush to any selected path. Simply select the path and click one of the Brush palette's entries. **Figure 16.26** was created using all four types of brushes: calligraphic, scatter, art, and pattern.

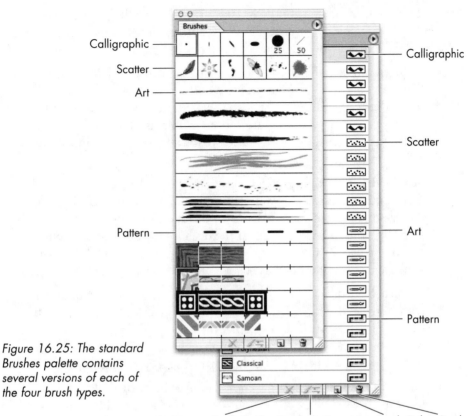

Calligraphic

Scatter

Art

Pattern

Calligraphic

Scatter

Art

Pattern

Figure 16.25: The standard
Brushes palette contains
several versions of each of
the four brush types.

Remove Brush Stroke   Brush Options   New Brush   Delete Brush

Figure 16.26: This lovely young woman was created using various
brush strokes. I used calligraphic brushes for her face and art brushes
for her hair and the clouds. Scatter brushes created the flock of birds,
and pattern brushes are responsible for her pearl jewelry and the
frame around her portrait. The actual paths are shown on the right.

You can change the display of the Brushes palette using the palette menu. Choose List View to see the brushes listed with their names. Choose each of the Show options to display or hide each of the types of brushes.

- **Calligraphic Brushes:** Simulate the lines created with a fountain pen. You have control over the roundness of the brush tip, the angle of the tip, and its size. Although you can use a mouse when drawing with calligraphic brushes, a pressure-sensitive tablet is ideal. With such a tablet, you can vary all three of the brush's attributes as a function of how hard you press with the tablet's stylus.

- **Scatter Brushes:** Take a single object or a group of objects and repeat them a number of times along the length of the path. You can control the size of the objects, the spacing (or the distance between the objects along the path), the scattering (or the distance the objects stray to the side of the paths), and the rotation of the objects. You can also vary the appearance of scatter brushes using a pressure-sensitive tablet.

- **Art Brushes:** Take a single drawing and stretch it the length of the path. You can decide in which direction the brush will follow the path, the width of the brush, and whether the brush will flip across the path. Art brushes can be used to simulate the look of natural paintbrushes or to curve artwork such as arrows and type along a path.

- **Pattern Brushes:** These are a compilation of individual blocks that link together to form a continuous chain. They are ideal for borders because you can specify the design of both the beginning and the end of the path, the appearance of the inner and outer corners, and all the parts that make up all the pieces in between.

The art brushes and pattern brushes do not respond to pressure-sensitive tablets.

Creating and Applying Brushes

To design a new brush, you need to assemble all its components and choose New Brush from the Brushes palette's pop-up menu (or you can click the New Brush icon at the bottom of the Brushes palette). Illustrator then gives you the option of creating any one of the four types of brushes.

Illustrator is rather fussy about what kinds of graphic elements it will allow you to use in a brush. A candidate for a new art brush cannot contain gradients, live blends, rasterized objects, other brushes, or unconverted type. You can, how-ever, use regular old paths with flat fills and strokes or objects with transparency settings. These paths can't be masked. The best rule of thumb when creating brushes is to keep it simple.

Working with the Brushes palette is very similar to the Swatches palette that we looked at in Chapter 14.

- Brushes created in a document are stored only in that document.

- Illustrator installs other brushes that you can access via Window » Brush Libraries.

- There are hundreds of other brushes on the Illustrator CD.

- You can import the brushes from one document to another via Window » Brush Libraries » Other Library. You can then choose the document from which you want to import the brushes. The brushes appear in a palette where you can select the brushes.

- Choose Persistent from the palette menu of an imported brush library to have it always open when Illustrator is launched.

- You can apply a brush to any selected object by clicking the brush in the Brushes palette.

- You can draw interactively with a brush by choosing the Paintbrush tool and then selecting a brush.

- Choose List View to list the brushes with their names and small thumbnails in the Brushes palette.

- Like pattern swatches, you can drag the scatter, art, and pattern brush objects out of the Brushes palette. The artwork used to create the brush, together with a bounding box, will appear on your page. Additionally, you can change any applied brush into its original paths by selecting it and choosing Object » Expand Appearance. You might want to do this if you want to expand a brush that isn't on a straight line.

Defining Calligraphic Brushes

The calligraphic brush is the only brush that doesn't require you to create the art-work for the brush before you design the brush options. Choose New Brush from the Brush palette's pop-up menu and choose New Calligraphic Brush from the New Brush dialog box. The Calligraphic Brush Options dialog box appears, as shown in **Figure 16.27**.

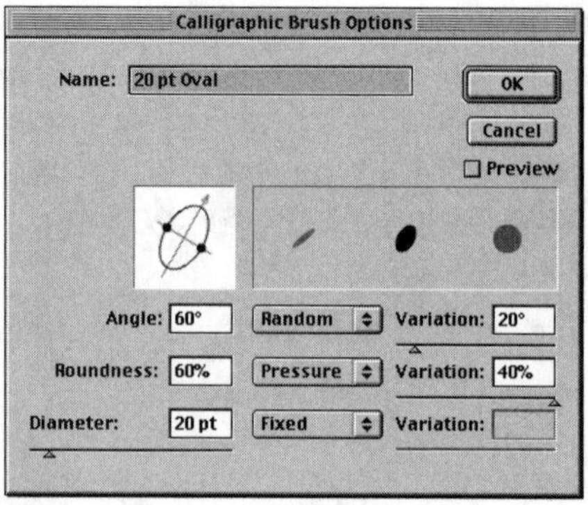

Figure 16.27: The Calligraphic Brush Options are displayed when you create a new calligraphic brush. You can modify these options by double-clicking the brush in the Brushes palette or choosing Brush Options from the Brush palette menu.

● **Name:** The name you apply to the brush is visible if you place your cursor over the brush or if you choose List View from the Brushes palette menu.

● **Angle:** You can choose how many degrees from the horizontal the tip will deflect. Either enter a value into the Angle option box or drag the arrow in the example box to change the angle.

● **Roundness:** Here you decide how round you want the tip—whether you want a nice round tip or a more oblong one, like the tip of an old felt marker. Enter a value into the Roundness option box or drag one of the black circles in the example box to change the roundness.

● **Diameter:** Enter a value that reflects the size of the brush that you want. This value is relative to the size of the stroke width. So if you increase the stroke width, the diameter of the calligraphic brush will increase.

All of the options (except Name) come with a pop-up list that gives you control over how Illustrator will apply the options.

● **Fixed:** This means that the attribute will always use the same value. If you use a pressure-sensitive drawing tablet, any changes in the pressure will be ignored.

● **Random:** This means that Illustrator will vary the value as you apply the brush. A second slider bar to the right of the pop-up menu will appear. Here you decide the amount that the original value can vary.

The Random setting is especially useful if you do not have access to a pressure-sensitive tablet. Although you cannot specifically direct where the thick and thin settings will be applied, the strokes are varied for a more natural appearance.

Pressure: If you use a pressure-sensitive drawing tablet, you can opt to have Illustrator take this into account. When selected, a second slider bar will activate to the right of the pop-up menu. With it you decide how much more or less the original value will vary to reflect the pressure you apply to the tablet.

> *Enter the values of 5 degrees Angle, 26 percent Roundness, and 56 points for Diameter to see a surprise in the Calligraphic Brush Options dialog box. For more fun, set the controls for Random or Pressure and play with the Variation sliders. Happy Birthday!*

Calligraphic brushes appear black in the options dialog box. However, they take their color from the one that's applied to the stroke.

Figure 16.28 shows the same artwork changed by altering the size and angle of a calligraphic brush. In the left example, a thin, round brush was applied with no angle. In the middle example, the brush was changed to be more angular. In the right example, the diameter of the brush was increased and random variation was applied to the roundness.

Figure 16.28: Without changing a path, this armchair is altered simply by modifying the characteristics of the calligraphy brushes.

Creating Scatter Brushes

Well, I warned you; if you want new brushes, you have to do some work (kind of like the omelet and the eggs). For a new scatter brush, you first need to design the objects you want to have scattered on either side of the path. With your artwork selected, click the New Brush icon from the Brushes palette and select the New Scatter Brush. The Scatter Brush Options dialog box appears as shown in **Figure 16.29**.

 You can also drag the selected object into the Brushes palette. This opens the New Brush dialog box, where you can select New Scatter Brush.

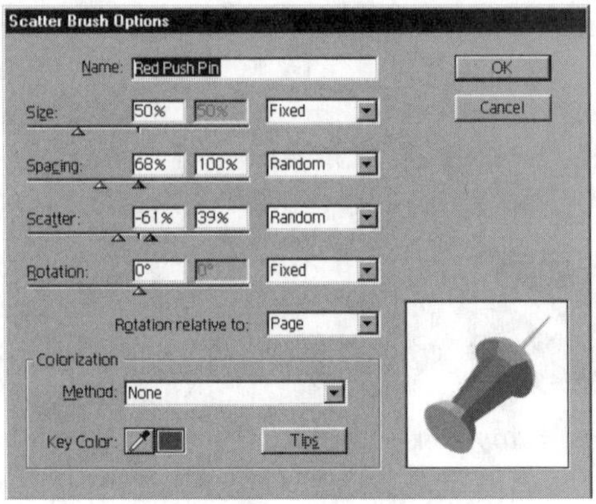

Figure 16.29: The Scatter
Brush Options are displayed
when you create a new
scatter brush.

Scatter brushes are typically used to make repeating objects in random patterns. Stars, falling leaves, and confetti are examples of artwork that can be made part of a scatter brush. You can also use scatter brushes to create stippling and crosshatch textures.

Name: The name you apply to the brush is visible if you place your cursor over the brush or if you choose List View from the Brushes palette menu.

Size: Enter any value of 1 percent or greater. This controls the size of each instance of the brush artwork in relation to its size at the time it was made into a brush. A value of 100 percent keeps the same size as the original, with more being bigger and less being smaller.

You can also control the size of the scatter brush by increasing or decreasing the stroke width applied to the scatter brush. Changing the scatter brush size affects the brush artwork only, while changing the stroke width affects the entire path and anything applied to it.

Spacing: Here you choose how far apart you want the objects to space themselves along the path. Enter any value of 1 percent or greater. The smaller the value, the more tightly the objects will be spaced.

Scatter: This controls how far away you'll let brush artwork stray from the path. A value of 0 percent positions the objects directly on the path. Enter any value between plus or minus 1000 percent. Positive values position the objects outside the path. Negative values position the objects inside the path. If it's an open path, outside is relative to a path drawn in a clockwise direction. (So if you drew a straight line from left to right, outside placement would put the brush stroke above the path). If you want the objects to fall on both sides of the path, use the Random or Pressure setting and then enter both plus and minus values. This sets a range for the scatter on either side of the path. Keep these values small if you want the shape of the path to be obvious.

- **Rotation:** The scatter brush objects can rotate as they appear along the path. Also you decide whether the objects will rotate relative to the page or the path.

- **Fixed, Random, Pressure:** All of these options come with the same pop-up menus as occur in the options for the New Calligraphic Brush. You can choose to have the scatter objects appear uniformly along the path or vary them, either randomly or as dictated by the pressure you apply to your drawing tablet. If you choose Random, the second box in each value suddenly becomes available so that you can enter minimum and maximum values of randomness.

- **Colorization:** These settings allow you to set how the scatter brush responds to changes in the stroke color. I'll cover Colorization at the end of this section.

Figure 16.30 shows how I used a single element, defined as four different scatter brushes with varied size, rotation, scatter, and spacing options, to create a wreath. The black ovals underneath show how many paths were used. The leaf on the side was used as the scatter brush.

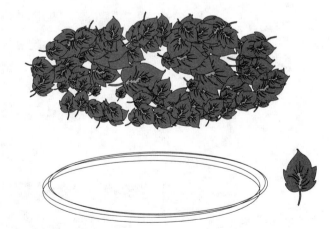

Figure 16.30: With a leaf defined as scatter brushes, I was able to create this wreath from four ovals.

Defining Art Brushes

Once again, you need to design the brush first. Because the object will be stretched along the path, you can design the brush with a front and a back. Select the design and then click the New Brush icon at the bottom of the Brushes palette. Then select the New Art Brush option. The Art Brush Options dialog box appears, as shown in **Figure 16.31**.

You can also drag the selected object into the Brushes palette. This opens the New Brush dialog box, where you can select New Art Brush.

- **Name:** The name you apply to the brush is visible if you place your cursor over the brush or if you choose List View from the Brushes palette menu.

- **Direction:** This determines the orientation of the artwork with respect to the path and the direction in which it was drawn. If you have long objects, you will usually want the direction to stretch from left to right or right to left. If you choose up to down or down to up, this will distort the object so that its width stretches along the path.

- **Size:** Enter a value to set the thickness of the brush. If you want to uniformly change the size, click the Proportional check box.

- **Flip:** You can choose to flip the object along the axis of the path or across its axis.

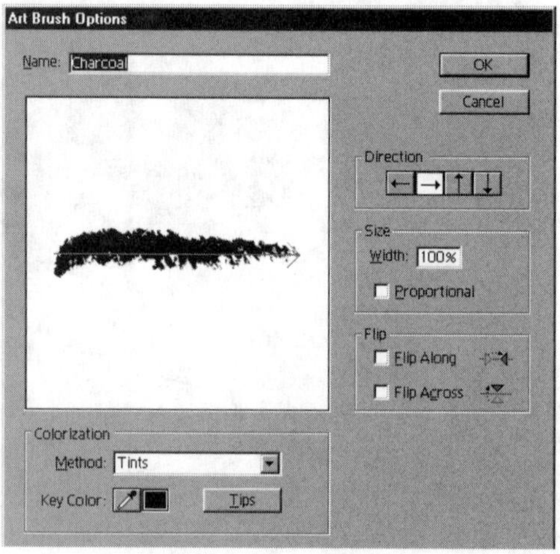

Figure 16.31: The Art Brush Options are displayed when you create a new art brush.

Figure 16.32 shows how some different art brushes can change the appearance of the same carrot illustration. In each case, the artwork used to define the brush appears next to the carrot it was applied to. The carrot on the right had the same brush applied as multi-brushes. The multi-brush consisted of a dark stroke at a thicker line weight under a white stroke at a thinner line weight.

Figure 16.32: Simply changing brushes altered these carrots.

 One way to make your own brush is to use the trace tool on a scan of strokes from a real brush.

Creating Pattern Brushes

Pattern brushes are the most complex type of brush. The design elements for a pattern brush come from pattern swatches in the Swatches palette. Once you have the patterns in the Swatches palette, you can design the pattern brush by clicking the New Brush icon and then choosing the New Pattern Brush option. This opens the Pattern Brush Options dialog box, as seen in **Figure 16.33**.

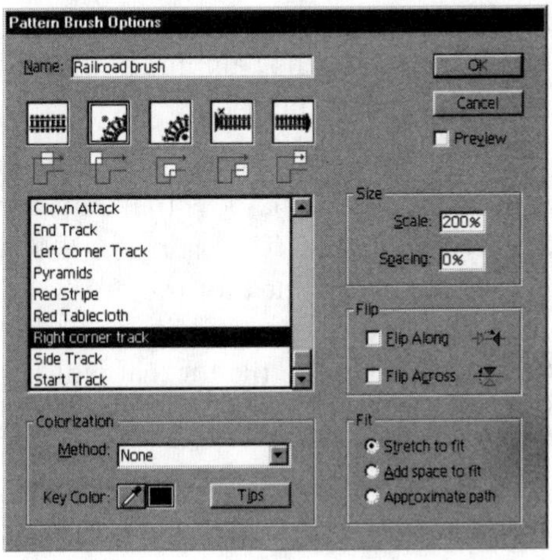

Figure 16.33: The Pattern Brush Options dialog box is the control center for creating a pattern brush.

Pattern brushes were adapted from the path patterns that were eventually dropped from Illustrator. They were created so that you could apply fancy borders to rectangles and other shapes. The disadvantage of the path patterns was that once they were applied, you couldn't modify the pattern. The pattern brushes are much more flexible. **Figure 16.34** *shows samples of several pattern brushes applied as borders, as well as the pattern for an open path.*

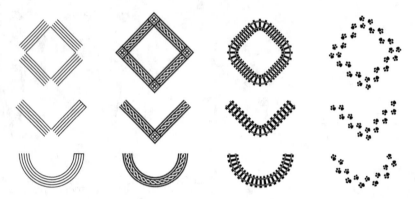

Figure 16.34: A sampling of pattern brushes applied as frames and as an open path. The far-left pattern brush does not have inner or outer corner tiles, so it should be used only on curved paths. It's also missing a start tile for open paths. The second pattern brush is missing end tiles, so it works better on closed paths. The last two don't have end tiles, but because of their design, they don't really need them.

- ⬤ **Tiles:** There are five tile icons to a pattern brush. Click the tile icons to select which part of the path you want to apply the pattern to. The side tile runs along the path. The outer corner tile is applied to all right-hand turns for corner points along the path. The inner corner is applied to all left-hand turns for corner points along the path. The start tile is applied to the beginning of the path. The end tile is applied to the end of the path.

- ⬤ **Patterns:** The patterns that are defined in the document are listed below the tiles. You can choose the name of the pattern, which is listed in the dialog box. The listing for Original uses the original swatches that were defined for the brush. This allows your pattern brush to contain tiles that may no longer be defined in the Swatches palette. None applies no tile for that part of the pattern brush.

- ⬤ **Scale:** This adjusts the size of the tiles relative to their original size. This is independent of the stroke weight.

- **Spacing:** You can loosen or tighten the tiles as they follow the path. A setting of 0% is perfectly continuous if your tiles have straight sides. A setting of 100% equals the tile width. Anything above 100% is likely to create gaps. Spacing is applied after Scaling.

- **Flip:** You can choose to flip the object along the axis of the path or across its axis.

- **Fit:** The pattern tiles may not always divide evenly into the path length. When this happens, you have three choices of how Illustrator will make up the difference.

  Stretch to Fit will stretch all tiles as needed to fit the brush to the path. This means that Illustrator will need to distort the brush elements slightly. Use this option for most pattern brushes where you want to keep a seamless transition between tiles.

  Add Space to Fit means that Illustrator will add tiny spaces between tiles as necessary. It won't distort any tiles, but it usually results in visible gaps. Use this option for pattern brushes such as weather isobars that should not be distorted.

  Approximate Path is appropriate only for patterns applied as borders for rectangles. This option lets Illustrator move the pattern from the center of the path to the outside or inside so that it can better fit the tiles to the shape of the path. This means the apparent size of the rectangle might change slightly, even though the actual path doesn't change size.

Defining Pattern Brush Tiles

Most of the pattern brushes that come with Illustrator do not have all five pattern tiles defined. A pattern brush made for borders will have the side pattern and the corner tiles but may not have the start and end tiles. Other pattern brushes may have the side, start, and end tiles but might be missing the corner tiles. Fortunately, you can create your own pattern tiles and then use them for the pattern brushes.

 You can also drag the selected object into the Brushes palette. This opens the New Brush dialog box, where you can select New Pattern Brush. This makes the selected artwork a side tile for the pattern brush.

As I said, there are five different tiles for a complete pattern brush. **Figure 16.35** shows how the five tiles are defined in a railroad-track pattern brush. Each pattern has a bounding box around it that defines the area for the tile. For demonstration, I've made the bounding box visible. I've also added a thicker gray line to show where Illustrator defines the start of the bounding box (the thick black line shows where Illustrator defines the end of it). For the tiles used as the start, side, and end, it's pretty easy to spot the start and end lines; they start at the left and end at the right of the bounding box.

 You don't have to define tiles for every tile icon. For instance, there's no point in designing corner tiles for a pattern brush that you plan to use only on circles.

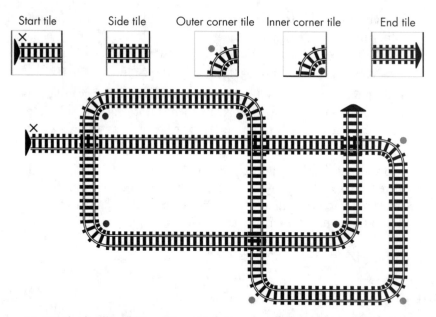

Figure 16.35: The five tiles of the railroad brush come together to form a complete track.

However, the start and end lines for the outer and inner corner tiles are a little tricky. The outer corner tile uses the bottom of the bounding box as the start and the right side of the bounding box as its end. That's why I call the outer corner tiles the ones for right-hand turns. The inner corner tile uses the right side of the bounding box as the start and the bottom of the bounding box as its end. So although the tile looks like it is making a right turn, it is actually creating a left turn if you follow it from start to end.

Notice the small circles at the turns in the track. Because they are defined as part of the outer and inner corner tiles, they always stay on the right side of the tracks. Notice also the difference between the start and end tiles. They too have a definite direction.

You may also discern that the track doesn't keep the same space between the track ties. This isn't because the railroad workers got lazy. It's because Illustrator has to slightly compress or extend the pattern tile to make it fit correctly along the path. If you don't want any distortion or gaps, you will have to design your tiles and your path sizes so that the tile lengths divide evenly into your path lengths.

 One of the best ways to understand the pattern brushes is to open the Border Sample brush library found under Window » Brush Libraries. Then drag the brush tiles out of the Brushes palette to examine how they were created.

Colorizing Options

The colorizing options allow you to control how the stroke color affects the color of the artwork used for the scatter, art, and pattern brushes.

Choose one of the colorizing methods from the pop-up list.

- **Tints** changes all the artwork in the brush to tints of the stroke color.

- **Tints and Shades** changes all the artwork in the brush to tints of the stroke color but preserves black. In addition, the colors of the artwork maintain their relative shades.

- **Hue Shift** changes the key color to the stroke color of the brush. In addition, other colors in the artwork are shifted in the same relationship. To set the colorizing options, you first use the eyedropper to select which color of the artwork should be the key color. The key color is the color used as the base for the color changes.

  For example, if the key color is yellow and the stroke color is royal blue, the key color artwork is shifted 200 degrees on the color wheel. So if another color is red, it too will be shifted 200 degrees on the color wheel to blue-green. **Figure 16.36** shows how the eyedropper in the Brush Options dialog box is used to sample a color from the preview of the brush artwork. The eyedropper has no effect on the other two colorizing options, and Hue Shift itself won't be useful if the original artwork is black or gray.

 Still confused by how the colorizing options will change the artwork? When you're in the Brush Options dialog box, click the Tips button next to the Key Color option for a full-color chart of how this whole crazy thing works.

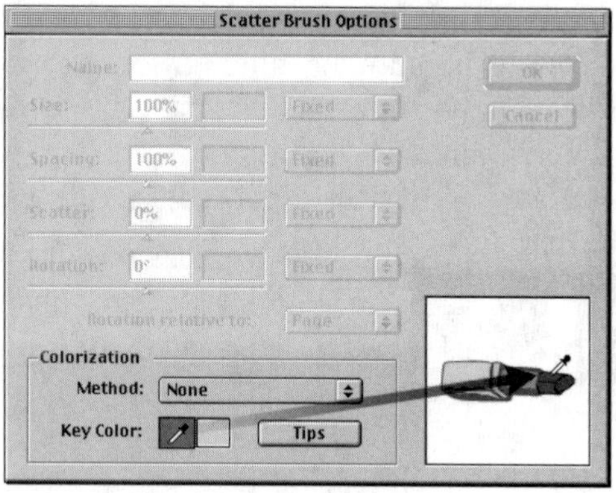

Figure 16.36: You can
sample color right from the
Brush Options preview using
the eyedropper.

Changing a Brush's Appearance

You can change the attributes of a brush globally or on a case-by-case basis. To
change the appearance of all occurrences of a particular brush, either double-
click the brush in the Brushes palette or choose Brush Options from the palette's
pop-up menu. The same Brush Options dialog box that appears when you create
a new brush will appear. After you make your changes to a brush and click OK,
Illustrator displays an alert box. Click the Apply to Strokes button to apply your
changes to all current and future uses of the brush. Click the Leave Strokes button to apply changes only to future uses of the brushes.

To change only the appearance of the selected objects, choose Options of
Selected Objects from the Brushes palette's pop-up menu. The selected path must
use the same brush if you want to use this option. This will display a slightly
reduced version of the appropriate Brush Options dialog box. Any changes you
make will affect only the selected paths and not alter any future use of the brush.

You can also change the artwork used to define scatter or art brushes. Simply
hold the Alt key (Option key on the Mac) and drag new artwork onto the original
brush. This opens the Brush Options dialog box, which displays the new artwork. Click OK to define the new brush.

Removing or Expanding a Brush

In most cases, you can first remove a brush from a path, modify the path, and
then reapply the brush. To remove a brush, select a brushed path and choose the
Remove Brush Stroke from the Brushes palette's pop-up menu. This restores the
path to an ordinary stroked path.

You can choose Object » Expand Appearance to expand the stroke. This turns
the objects that were used to define the brush back into paths that are no longer
attached to the brush definition. In addition, the original path used to define the

shape of the brush stroke will be part of the expanded artwork. The difference between expanding a brush and just dragging the brush out of the Brushes palette is that the original objects are expanded as they appear along the path you drew.

 If you apply a brush to a path and you want to use the result as the basis for a new brush, first expand it, and then create the new brush from the expanded paths.

BLENDS, MASKS, AND PEN & INK FILLS

At first glance you may be wondering why I would rope these three effects together in one chapter; there doesn't seem to be much that ties them together. But believe it or not, there really is a theme to these features: all three create or display objects within shapes defined by different objects. Blends allow you to create additional images by selecting two or more objects. Masks display images within the shape of a certain object. And the Pen & Ink filter creates additional objects that are displayed within the original object.

However, an even better theme is that these are the features that always stump beginners. And although blends and masks have become easier to use since the days when I was starting to work with Illustrator, they can still be daunting to new users. You need a strong will to get started with these features—the Hatch Effects dialog box (which is under the Pen & Ink command) is easily among the most daunting collection of options inside all of Illustrator—but your labors will not go unrewarded.

So welcome to the hard stuff in Illustrator. These are the commands that truly separate the beginners from the experienced users. When you finish with this chapter, you'll fully deserve to stick a gold star on your monitor.

Blending Paths

Blending is one of Illustrator's most exotic and oldest capabilities. Back when every one of its competitors offered automated gradations, Illustrator allowed you to design your own custom gradations. Illustrator's blend tool wasn't easy to use, but it yielded an unlimited range of results. There wasn't a single gradation you couldn't create using blends. Unfortunately, blends were much harder to create than gradations. So users were always asking for gradients.

Fortunately, Adobe added gradient fills to Illustrator. In fact, Illustrator offers what is undoubtedly the finest automatic gradient fill function of any drawing program (as discussed in Chapter 15) and a blend tool that's simply unrivaled. Any time you want to go beyond linear and radial gradations, the blend tool is at your beck and call.

When I discussed gradient fills back in Chapter 15, you saw there was no way to apply a shape to the change in colors. That's when you need the more sophisticated color changes found in blends. However, blends do more than just change colors. You can use blends on groups of objects so that text changes from one set of words to another, and smiles turn to frowns. You can also set blends to follow path shapes.

Blending is part duplication, part distribution, and part transformation. It creates a series of intermediate paths, called *steps*, between two selected free-form paths. I say that it's part duplication because the Blend command creates as many clones of a path as you like. It's part distribution because the steps are evenly distributed between the two original objects. And it's part transformation because Illustrator automatically adjusts the shape of each step depending on where it lies. Steps near the first of the two original paths resemble the first path; steps near the second path more closely resemble the second path.

Blending creates a metamorphic transition between one shape and another. For example, suppose that you create two paths, one that represents a man and one that represents a lycanthropic alter ego. By blending these two paths, you create several steps that represent metamorphic stages between the two life forms, as shown in **Figure 17.1**. The first intermediate path is shaped much like the man. Each intermediate path after that becomes less like the man and more like the wolf.

Illustrator can blend the fills and strokes between two paths. If one path is white and the other is black, for example, the steps between the paths are filled with a fountain of transitional gray values. Although each step is filled with a solid color (assuming that you're blending objects with flat fills), the effect is that of a gradation. To create the steps shown in Figure 17.1, I used opposite fill and stroke colors in each path. After I created the blend, I expanded the blends (discussed later), brought the wolf to the front, and applied heavier strokes to both the man and wolfman.

Figure 17.1: Blending between these extremes creates a series of transformed and distributed duplicates between the two objects.

Creating a Blend

To create a blend, you must first select two or more paths. You can blend between paths that are by themselves, part of groups, or even compound paths. (Selecting only a single path from a group or compound path forces the entire path to join in the blend.) Although it is possible to blend an open path to a closed path, the results are often rather ugly. Paths should be filled and stroked similarly.

 You can even blend one object with a stroke to another object without a stroke. The stroke width will decrease in size from one object to another.

To blend paths you can either let Illustrator automatically decide the best blending arrangement or choose which point you want to blend. To use Illustrator's blending instincts, select the paths and choose Object » Blend » Make, or press Ctrl+Alt+B (Cmd-Option-B on the Mac) to create a series of steps. Illustrator treats the frontmost path of the originals as the first path in the blend and the rear path as the last path. The steps are layered between the first and last paths, descending in stacking order—one in back of another—as they approach the last. For a bit more control, click with the blend tool on one point in the first path and then click on a point in another path. In either case, Illustrator automatically combines original paths and steps into a grouped object that has special properties (which are discussed in later sections of this chapter). This object is a blend.

Alternatively, if you want more control over the blend, you can select one (and only one) point in each path. If the paths are open, you must select an endpoint in each path.

To create a simple blend, follow these steps:

1.   Specify the fill and stroke of the paths you want to blend.

Illustrator can blend any two colors, including gray values and spot colors. It can even blend gradients or a flat fill and a gradient. Illustrator can also blend strokes, line weights, line caps, joins, and dash patterns. It can even use brushes in blends!

 There is no limitation on blending with transparency features; Illustrator can also blend different opacity or blending mode settings.

2.   Select the paths.

Illustrator can blend numerous paths at a time. In fact, your machine's RAM is the only limiting factor. For now, it's best to keep it simple and use only a few paths.

 Although Illustrator is not restricted to blending paths that have the same number of points, they do work best for blending. But if one path has more points than the other, you can even things out by selecting all points in one path and the same number of points in the other path.

3.   Choose Object » Blend » Make...

Illustrator looks at the objects and blends between the points that will produce the smoothest possible blend between the selected paths.

...or click with the blend tool to specify the blend points.

If you don't like the results of the Blend command, you can specify the points that you want to blend between. Using the blend tool, click one point in each selected path. First click one point, and then click another. Then click the points in any additional objects. If you miss a point, Illustrator tries its best to guess which point you were going after.

*To create a smooth blend, click similar points in the paths. In **Figure 17.2**, for example, I clicked the lower-left point on the outside cone and then the lower-left point on the inside cone.*

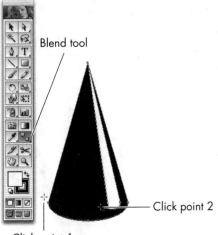

Blend tool

Figure 17.2: After selecting the blend tool, I clicked the lower-left point in each of two selected shapes. I could also have simply chosen Object » Blend » Make.

Click point 2

Click point 1

4.   Specify the blend spacing.

Choose Object » Blend » Blend Options. The Blend Options dialog box will appear, as shown in **Figure 17.3**. By default, Illustrator uses the Smooth Color spacing scheme to decide how many intermediate paths are needed to produce the best blend.

Figure 17.3: The Blend Options dialog box lets you choose the number of steps that make up your blend.

If you find that Illustrator has not added enough steps or has included more steps than you think necessary, you can change the number of steps by choosing either Specified Steps or Specified Distance from the Spacing pop-up menu in the Blend Options dialog box. Deciding how many steps to use can be a difficult proposition. (For a technical evaluation of steps, with some numerical recommendations, read the section "Deciding the Number of Steps" later in this chapter.)

You can also open the Blend Options dialog box by holding the Alt key (Option key on the Mac) as you click on the path with the blend tool. Or double-click the blend tool in the toolbox.

5. Change the Orientation setting.

Only if you want to, that is. The orientation of the blend steps is limited to either aligning to the page or aligning to the path. **Figure 17.4** shows the difference.

Figure 17.4: The example on the top is the Align to Page orientation that Illustrator applies by default. With the Align to Path icon selected (bottom), the blend objects curve around with the path.

Forcing Blend Transitions

Over the past couple of software upgrades, Illustrator has gotten very good at automatically creating smooth blends. Blends that were messed up by previous versions of the program are created perfectly today using Object » Blend » Make. (How do I know? Well, for one thing, I have the artwork from the previous versions of this book. I simply applied the Blend command to the exact same artwork using the current version of Illustrator. The differences were obvious.) However, there may be times when you want to override Illustrator's choices to create your own blend transitions or special blend effects.

Using the blend tool can force Illustrator to use your own blend transitions. The click points tell Illustrator the locations of the first pair of points it should blend. The program then flits around the shapes in a clockwise direction and pairs up the other points. **Figure 17.5** shows the results of blending two concentric five-pointed stars after clicking on different points in the two shapes. I always clicked on the lower-right point in the small star but clicked on a total of six different points in the larger star. As you can see, this has a profound effect on how the blend progresses.

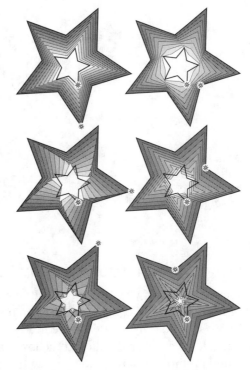

Figure 17.5: The small black dots show the points where I clicked each pair of stars with the blend tool.

 Each small star in Figure 17.5 was originally filled with white. I changed the fills to None after blending the shapes to permit you to see the steps in back, some of which were covered up when the star was white.

Although many of the effects in Figure 17.5 are interesting, only the first four are suitable for creating gradations, as demonstrated in **Figure 17.6**. And even then, the third and fourth examples have rather harsh edges. Your safest bet is to click on a matching point in each object, as in the first example. This results in the smoothest possible progression.

Figure 17.6: Here I used the same click points used for Figure 17.5 but got rid of the strokes and increased the number of steps to 88 per blend.

Recognizing When You Need More Points

Although it may seem unfair, you can still end up with harsh edges after taking the precautions of selecting an equal number of points in both shapes and clicking similar points. Consider the first example in **Figure 17.7**. Both shapes contain four points (all selected), and I clicked the lowest point in each shape. And yet, as the second example shows, I ended up with harsh edges. The top and bottom of the white shape look like they're thrusting forward from the dark ellipse. No, no, no; this simply will not do!

The problem is that two of the paired points in the two shapes aren't properly aligned. That is, if a crow were to fly from one point to another, the poor thing would smack into a segment. The dashed lines in Figure 17.7 show the flight of this imaginary crow. Notice how the bird would collide with the segments. These intersections are precisely the areas where our problems occur.

The solution is to add more points. If you add a point to every segment in each shape, you can ensure that all points are in line. Use the add anchor point tool to add the points to either path. The left example in **Figure 17.8** shows how I added points to both paths. The blend on the right side shows a silky-smooth gradation.

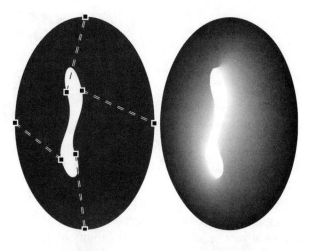

Figure 17.7: If you can't draw straight lines between the paired points in your shapes without running over segments (left), you'll end up with harsh edges in your final blend (right).

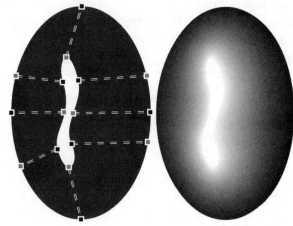

Figure 17.8: When I add points to paths (shown in gray) all straight lines drawn between the paired points are unobstructed (left). This ensures a fluid gradation (right).

Deciding the Number of Steps

Another problem that plagues blends is a pesky printing phenomenon called *banding*. Rather than print as a seamless gradation, the blend exhibits distinct bands of color. When banding occurs, gradient credibility goes out the window. **Figure 17.9** offers an exaggerated example of banding. In the first blend, I created 16 steps, hardly enough to produce smooth shading. You can see almost every step in the shape, resulting in lots of bands. The second blend is much smoother, but it also contains 256 steps.

Figure 17.9: A blend with banding (left) and one with seamless color transitions (right).

Unfortunately, although using very few steps practically guarantees banding, having lots of steps doesn't necessarily prevent it. You have to print enough steps to take advantage of your printer's ability to generate gray values, but not so many that one or more steps appear out of sync with their neighbors. In an ideal blend, each printed step corresponds to a unique gray value and varies from its neighbors by a consistent amount. Illustrator creates unique, consistent steps automatically, no matter how many steps you assign, but this doesn't mean they'll necessarily print correctly. It all hinges on the answers to two questions.

- Is the printer properly calibrated?
- What is the resolution and screen frequency of the printer?

You can't anticipate bad calibration. You just have to hope that your service bureau or commercial printer has its machinery in top condition. But you can account for resolution and screen frequency. Very briefly—since I'll cover both topics in more detail in Chapter 24—resolution is the number of pixels the printer can print per inch (just like screen resolution). And screen frequency is the number of halftone dots that print per inch. Printer resolution is measured in dots per inch (dpi), and screen frequency is measured in lines per inch (lpi). The resolution is fixed, but the screen frequency can change. For example, a typical laser printer prints at 600 dpi, but the lpi can be set to 85 or lower.

If you print an 85-lpi screen from a 600-dpi laser printer, each halftone dot measures 7 pixels wide by 7 pixels tall (600 ÷ 85 = 7). And a 7-by-7 dot contains a total of 49 pixels. If all pixels are turned off, the halftone dot is white. All pixels turned on produces black, and turning on 1 to 49 pixels produces a shade of gray. Including black and white, that's a total of 50 gray values, which is the absolute maximum number of shades a 600-dpi, 85-lpi laser printer can print.

That's just one example. Printers vary from model to model. But if you know the dpi and lpi values, you can calculate the number of printable gray values using this formula.

$$(dpi \div lpi)^2 + 1$$

Take an average Linotronic imagesetter, for example. The resolution is 2,540 dpi, and it can print 175 lpi and up. When you divide 2,540 by 133, you get 19.097. Then you multiply 19.097 by itself and add 1 to get 365 gray values—quite a few more than the laser printer.

There is just one caveat, however. PostScript printers can't generate more than 256 shades of gray, regardless of their resolution or screen frequency. That's why Illustrator automatically suggests 254 steps in the Blend dialog box when blending between a black and white shape—256 minus black and white leaves 254.

Since I really hate to make you do too much math, here are the maximum number of gray values associated with a few popular resolutions and screen frequencies. If you have a PostScript 3 device, it will take advantage of a technology called *smooth shading*, which greatly enhances gradients and blends to allow for even smoother transitions.

Resolution	Screen frequency	Maximum shades of gray
300	53	33
300	60	26
600	75	65
600	85	50
1200	75	256
1200	90	179
1200	120	101
1200	133	82
1270	75	256
1270	90	200
1270	120	113
1270	133	92
2400	up to 150	256
2540	up to 150	256
3386	175	256

Working "Live"

Live!—from San Jose, California—it's *Illustrator's Live Blends!* OK, I'm being a little bit silly, but this is just good, fun stuff: Once you've made a blend, you can easily edit the objects in the blend. The blend then redraws right in front of your eyes.

If you use the regular selection tool, you will select all the objects in the blend. So you can use the direct selection tool to select individual points and objects in the blend. Once you have selected an object within a blend, you can change its fill or stroke attributes, move points, use the transformation tools, or even add points using the add point tool. **Figure 17.10** shows how the blend redraws each time you release the mouse button.

Figure 17.10: Use the direct selection tool to select and modify objects within a blend.

Modifying the Spine

When you first create a blend, the in-between steps are arranged in a straight line from one object to another. This straight line, shown in **Figure 17.11**, is called the *spine*. When you first create a blend, the spine has one point for each object in the blend. So a blend between two objects in a path has only two points—a beginning and an end. However, you can use any of the point tools to add or change the handles of the points of the spine.

Figure 17.11: The blend spine is the straight line that connects the original blend objects.

Manipulating the spine can be a hassle. Fortunately, you can simply replace the spine with any other path—open or closed. This allows you to create much more interesting blends. **Figure 17.12** shows how a simple blend between two circles can be transformed into a bouncing ball by replacing the spine. Here are the steps for replacing a spine with another path.

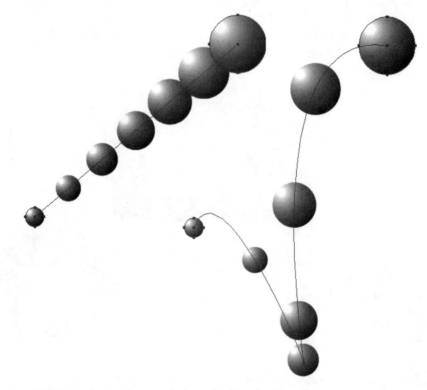

Figure 17.12: Replacing the straight line of a blend with a custom spine can add motion to your otherwise stiff artwork.

1. Create the blend.

If you want the blend to wrap around a closed path so that the blend fills all the spaces in the path, you need to create a closed blend using the blend tool. A small circle appears next to the blend tool. This indicates that the blend will be closed.

2. Draw the object that is to become the spine.

The new spine can be open or closed. Don't worry about the fill or stroke attributes. These will be deleted as soon as the object becomes the spine.

3.   Select the blend and the spine.

The spine can be positioned anywhere. Illustrator knows that the object that doesn't have a blend on it is the one you want to be the spine.

4.   Choose Object » Blend » Replace Spine.

Replace Spine is not the best term. What happens is that the objects in the blend jump from their original spine onto the new object. And then the original spine is deleted. **Figure 17.13** shows the results of replacing a plain spine with an ellipse.

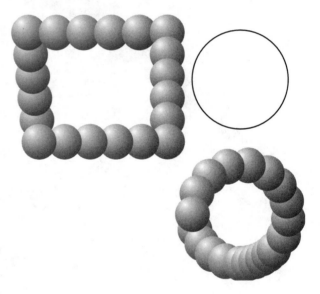

Figure 17.13: The closed blend in a rectangular shape was replaced by an ellipse using the Replace Spine command.

 Only one object can be a spine for a blend. If you select more than one object as a spine, Illustrator doesn't allow you to choose the Replace Spine command.

Once you replace a spine, you can still use the direct selection tool to select the spine and modify its shape. The live blend redraws each time you release the mouse.

Reversing Blends

Once you've created a blend, you can play around with the order of its objects. If you select the blend, you can choose Object » Blend » Reverse Spine. This flips the position of the objects along the spine so that the objects that were at the end now start the blend, and the objects that started the blend are now at the end. The stacking order of the objects—from front to back— is not changed. You can also choose Object » Blend » Reverse Front to Back to keep the objects in their same position on the spine but change the stacking order. The objects that were in front of the others are sent to the back, and the objects that were in the back are sent to the front. **Figure 17.14** shows the effects of applying these commands to a blend.

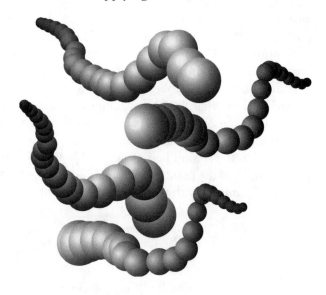

Figure 17.14: The original blend (top) was altered by applying the Reverse Spine command (second from top), the Reverse Front to Back command (third from top), and both Reverse Spine and Reverse Front to Back (bottom).

Expanding and Releasing Blends

The intermediate steps of a blend are virtual objects. They're visible, but you can't select or manipulate them. The only objects you can select are the original objects used to create the blend. If you want to work with the intermediate steps, select the blend and choose Object » Blend » Expand. This turns the virtual objects into real ones. The objects in the expanded blend are automatically grouped.

Releasing a blend deletes the intermediate steps and removes the original objects from the spine. However, it also leaves the spine on the artboard. I consider this careless housekeeping. I constantly have to throw away spines cluttering up my documents.

Cool Blend Tool Tricks

I've droned on about the blend tool for quite a while now, but I haven't even begun to tell you all the great things you can do with it. Although I can't share every blend tool and custom gradation trick I've invented or gleaned over the years, in the following sections I'll suggest a handful of what I consider to be the most interesting tips and tricks. I hope they'll inspire you to develop more sophisticated techniques of your own.

Morphing Path Outlines

In addition to generating custom gradations, the blend tool lets you modify shapes. Much like the Pathfinder commands, you can use the tool to take two paths and combine them into a third. This technique is known as *morphing*.

In **Figure 17.15**, I took a series of shapes and morphed between them. I then replaced the spine with a spiral. Finally, I added a drop shadow to the blend. But I should warn you, it's not quite as easy as it looks. I had to spend a few minutes on each pair of original paths, making sure the two had the same number of points. For example, the first pair of stars that I used each has 20 points, even though the first star has half as many spikes as the second one. The circle and star I used as the second pair of blend objects each have 16 points, and so on. I inserted most of the points with Object » Path » Add Anchor Points, but I had to add a few manually with the add anchor point tool.

Figure 17.15: A series of morphings in a blend with a spiral spine attached to it. The original objects are in gray.

You can also use the blend tool to morph type converted to path outlines. In **Figure 17.16**, I started with a small line of Times Roman text and a larger line in Adobe Garamond Bold Italic. I applied a 0-point stroke to the Times text and a 1-point stroke to the Garamond. Finally, I applied a very small drop shadow with almost no blur and no offset to the Times text, and a more blurred, further offset drop shadow to the Garamond text. The result changes shape, size, color, and stroke as it invokes you to Live! The change in the position of the drop shadow makes the text seem to jump off the page.

Figure 17.16: This text was
blended from the stuffy Times
Roman to the exuberant
Adobe Garamond Bold Italic.

 If all this seems like it would be great if it were animated, have patience. In Chapter 22 I'll show you how to create quick and easy Web animations.

Now, as long as you have your animation (brain) cells working, here's another thought to remember: Illustrator can blend between any groups or compound paths. (In the olden days, blending could be done only between single objects.) **Figure 17.17** shows one of the uses of this feature. You can change the position, size, and even the mouth shape of this puttylike character simply by grouping him and blending. However, to avoid distorting the intermediate steps beyond recognition, you have to have *exactly* the same number of objects in each group, and the stacking order for the objects must be *exactly* the same. That is, if the left eye is fourth from the top in the first object, make sure it is in the exact same place in the second object.

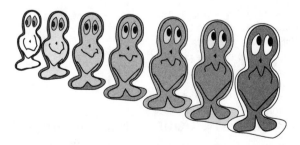

Figure 17.17: This little man
went from happy to guilty
simply by grouping the two
end looks and blending
between them.

One way to make sure these groups have exactly the same number of objects in exactly the same order is to simply duplicate the original object and then make any adjustments to the duplicate. But you can also use the thumbnails in the Layers palette to visually place each object in the correct stacking order.

Finally, you may not like the distance between the intermediate steps along the path. I've always felt that Illustrator was missing a way to control the speed of the blend—that is, the distance between the intermediate steps. But a tip from Derek Mah (who was responding to one of my articles in *Macworld* magazine) has been a great help: "To control the speed of the blend, create the blend and set the number of blend steps as you normally would do. This creates the blend spine, which is editable just like any other Illustrator object. Using the convert direction point tool, pull out control handles from the anchor point at each end of the blend spine. By extending or shortening these control handles along the spine, the speed of the blend is controlled. This is very similar to the way in which blend speeds are controlled in the gradient mesh." **Figure 17.18** shows this technique in action. Way to go, Derek!

Figure 17.18: Changing the spine anchor points to curved points allows you to adjust the handles to change the distance between objects in a blend.

Creating Contours and Highlights

You know you've earned your blend tool black belt when you can successfully tackle multicolor gradations. By creating a series of colored shapes and blending between them in succession, you can create photorealistic graphics with sharp outlines and exact edges—the Holy Grail of commercial artwork.

Figure 17.19 shows an example of the techniques used to create contours and highlights. The cat's eye started with eight simple shapes.

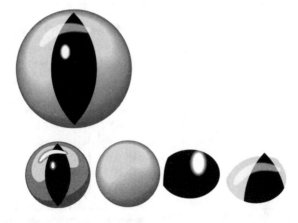

Figure 17.19: A photorealistic illustration with three blends. The elements below the eye show the progression of the blends.

The three large shapes in the back are blended together to create the contours of the eye. Some people would take the easy route and try to use a radial gradient to give the orb its shape. But the slight concave appearance of the top shape used in a blend gives the eyeball a much more realistic appearance.

The small highlight in the pupil was easy. I simply blended a small white oval with no stroke into a larger one filled with a dark gray. (The white stroke you see in the illustration is there just so you can see where the object is.) Because this highlight was against a single color, I didn't have to do anything special.

Because the white highlights at the top of the eyeball covered two different colors, I had a dilemma as to what color to blend to. Fortunately, you can also blend opacity changes. So I simply blended between a white object at 100 percent opacity and another white object at 0 percent opacity. This allowed me to blend to a transparent edge. However, the highlight seemed a little too bright. So I targeted the entire blend and lowered the opacity to 70 percent. (I probably could have played with the Feather effect on a single object, but then I wouldn't have been able to tell you about blending to transparency.)

Blending Strokes

Back when I began this chapter, I mentioned that the blend tool varies two stroke attributes—color and line weight. This last fact is very important because it means that you can blend a thick stroke with a thin one to create a softened edge.

Figure 17.20 demonstrates one of the common stroke-blending effects, the old neon text trick. I started by converting some text to paths, and then split and joined the letters with the scissors tool and Join command to combine all letters into a single, open path. (After all, in a real neon sign, one tube forms all the letters.) I assigned the line an 8-point black stroke. Then I cloned the line, nudged it upward a couple of points, and gave it a 0.5-point white stroke. The result appears at the top of Figure 17.20.

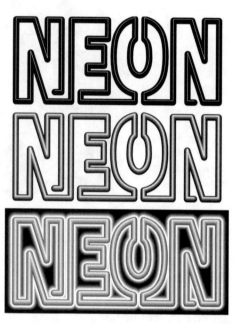

Figure 17.20: Here I've taken two stroked paths (top) and blended between them to create a neon effect (middle). Then I blended between a 12-point white stroke and a 24-point black one to create the glow (bottom).

 Although nudging the top path is mostly for effect, it's necessary if you want to blend via the blend tool. If one path exactly overlaps the other, you can't click the back path with the blend tool. Even when the paths are a couple of points apart, you'll probably need to zoom in to a very magnified view size (say, 400 percent or more) before you can click the points.

After setting up the paths, I used the Blend command to create the blend. I specified 14 steps, enough to ensure that each step changed by exactly half a point. The second example in Figure 17.20 shows the result.

 You don't need many steps when working with strokes, because the distances are so small. A line weight variation of 0.5 point means that you can see only about 0.25 point of color around each side of the stroke. (With the strokes offset, the color bands may be as wide as 0.3 point, but that's about the maximum.) To ensure a 0.5-point line weight variation between your steps, use this simple formula. Of the two strokes you want to blend, subtract the thinner line weight value from the thicker one. Then multiply that number by 2 and subtract 1. For example, I subtracted 0.5 from 8 to get 7.5. Multiplying that number by 2 produced 15, and subtracting 1 gave me 14. For the record, the line weights of these 14 steps are 1, 1.5, 2, 2.5, 3, 3.5, 4, 4.5, 5, 5.5, 6, 6.5, 7, and 7.5. You can't go wrong.

To create the glow in the last example in Figure 17.20, I first copied the rear path. Then I hid the neon letters (Object » Hide » Selection) to get them out of my way, pasted the path in back, and changed the stroke to 12-point white. To create the blend-to path, I pasted to the back again, nudged the pasted path up 2 points, and changed its stroke to 24-point black. Then I blended between the two paths with the blend tool. (To calculate the number of steps, I subtracted 12 from 24 to get 12, then multiplied that by 2 and subtracted 1 to get 23.) To make the background black, I drew a black rectangle behind the whole thing. Finally, I chose Object » Show All to bring the neon letters back from hiding.

Notice that the strokes in Figure 17.20 have round joins. Round joins invariably blend best because they smooth out the transitions at the corner points. Miter and bevel joins result in harsh corners that rarely benefit a gradation.

Editing a Gradient Fill

Now that I've told you nearly everything there is to know about blends, I'd like to share one more little secret. Every gradient fill in Illustrator is actually a blend. That's right—Illustrator calculates each color in a gradient fill as a separate step in a blend. It hides the details from you to keep things tidy. But as far as Illustrator and the printer are concerned, gradations and blends are all variations on the same theme.

Illustrator gives you the power to tear down the walls. At a moment's notice, you can convert any object filled with a gradation to an object filled with a blend. Just select the object and choose Object » Expand. An alert box comes up, asking you how many steps you would like to create. For the number of steps, follow my advice from the "Deciding the Number of Steps" section earlier in this chapter. That is, take the number of gray values your printer can print and multiply it by the percentage color range. Just one difference—don't subtract 2. The first and last colors are part of the gradation, so you don't want to delete them from the Steps value.

When you expand a gradation, Illustrator converts it to steps inside a mask. The shape that was previously filled with the gradation serves as the mask. Illustrator selects the mask and all rectangular steps inside the mask.

If you want to simplify the mask into a series of cropped steps, choose Object » Clipping Mask » Release, and then click the Crop icon in the Pathfinder palette. That's all it takes. You lose the flexibility of a mask— which I'll describe at length in the next section—but cropped steps are tidier on the screen and you can be sure the steps will print.

One of my favorite reasons to convert a gradient into steps is so that I can then apply some other effect. For instance, in **Figure 17.21** I applied the Roughen effect to the gradient fill. The Roughen effect applied to a gradient can only change the shape of the gradient as a whole. However, when I expand the gradient, the Roughen effect is applied to each of the intermediate steps, which creates a paperlike texture.

Figure 17.21: When the Roughen effect is applied to a gradient fill, it roughens the entire fill (left). But when the gradient is converted into discrete objects (right), the Roughen effect creates a much more organic texture.

Masking: Filling Objects with Objects

Mask is the term used in graphics software for an object that is used as the boundary for others. You can see other objects inside the mask but not outside it. You can take an object, group of objects, or even a raster image, and put it, or them, inside of a selected path. The path becomes the mask, and the objects inside the mask are the content elements. The mask clips away all portions of the content elements that fall outside of the boundaries of the mask. In addition to opacity masks, which I covered in Chapter 18, there are two other types of masks: Clipping masks are vector-based objects (no images allowed) that can be applied to any number of objects, but only within one layer. Layer masks are clipping masks that are applied to an entire layer. They hide all the objects on that layer and any layers nested within the layer.

The word mask always reminds me of costume parties where you can only see people's faces outside the mask—exactly the opposite of the function in Illustrator. A better image is masking tape. You use the tape to hide a certain area from being painted. Anything inside the boundary of the masking tape is visible; anything outside is not.

Creating a Clipping Mask

Clipping masks are applied to specific elements within a layer. This means that some objects within the layer may not be visible, while others are. The only part of the artwork that is going to be visible is that which shows through the shape you use for your mask. The objects you want incorporated into the mask must be selected prior to its creation. Unselected objects and objects you draw after the mask is created will not be part of the mask. Clipping masks are created as follows:

1. **Move the mask object to front.**

Create and then select the path you want to fill with other objects, and bring it to front. A mask must be in front of its content elements, as seen in the left example of **Figure 17.22**.

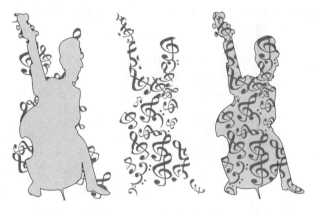

Figure 17.22: The three steps in creating a clipping mask (from left to right): positioning the objects, making the mask, adding fill and stroke attributes to the mask.

2. **Select the path and all objects that you want to put inside it, and choose Object » Clipping Mask » Make.**

If you select objects inside different groups, compound paths, or masks, Illustrator will complain. It's not that you can't have groups within a mask; you just can't have portions of a group within a mask. So it's best to select the objects with the arrow tool prior to choosing the command. If you have applied any fill or stroke attributes to the clipping mask object, you will lose those attributes, as shown in the middle example of Figure 17.22. Don't panic. You'll get them back in the next step.

 When you mask objects on different layers, they all become part of the clipping mask artwork.

3. **Select the clipping mask and reapply any fill or stroke settings.**

You need to reselect the clipping mask object and apply any fill or stroke settings you desire, as I've shown in the right example of Figure 17.22. Note that the mask and the elements are automatically grouped. Therefore, you have to use the direct selection tool to select the clipping mask object. Yes, it's an inconvenience; however, considering that for many years you couldn't apply fills or strokes to clipping mask objects, it's one that I can live with.

Setting a Clipping Mask for a Layer

Layer masks allow you to mask all objects in a layer. This means that any objects on the layer will be masked, no matter when they were created. And they can be positioned above or below the layer mask object. Layer masks are created as follows:

1. **Move the mask object to front.**

Although a layer mask can be anywhere in a layer, you need to position it at the top of the layer when you first make the layer mask. (Or else Illustrator won't know what object should be the layer mask.)

You can use compound paths as either layer masks or clipping masks. However, be aware that you're compounding the amount of calculations that Illustrator has to make to print your file. So you may want to crop the image before you go to print. (See "Cropping a Mask" later in this chapter.)

2. **Select the layer in the Layers palette.**

Just click the name of the layer in the Layers palette. If you have a path selected, you will not be able to make the layer mask.

3. **Click the Make/Release Clipping Mask icon.**

Or you can choose Make Clipping Mask from the Layers palette menu. The object that is the layer mask is listed in the Layers palette as *clipping path* (as shown in **Figure 17.23**). An underline indicates that it is a masking element.

Any objects you add to the layer will automatically be masked as long as the clipping mask is active.

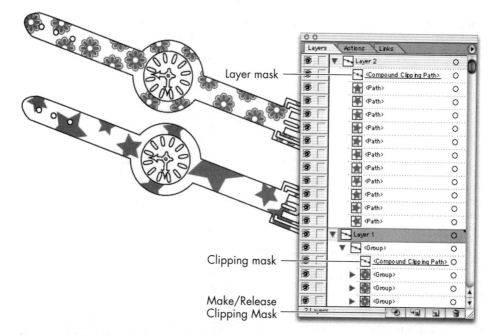

Figure 17.23: Although they are both listed as clipping paths in the Layers palette, you can identify the clipping mask because it is within a group. The layer mask is loose within its layer.

Editing Masked Elements

One of the primary advantages to working with masks is that the objects that have been masked are still live in your file. If you switch to the outline mode, you can see them hanging around outside the mask. This means you can move the objects in and out of the mask without any trouble. Now you see 'em, now you don't. However, you should be aware that elements that are outside the mask still contribute to the file size and printer processing time. If you have a map of the United States and you've masked everything except the area around the small town of Gridley, Illinois (population 1,300), you should consider deleting those elements that you don't need.

Objects in a clipping mask are automatically grouped, so you need to use the direct selection tool to select individual points. Hold the Alt key (Option key on the Mac) to select entire objects. Because they are not grouped, you can select objects individually using the regular selection tool, as shown in **Figure 17.24**.

You can add elements to a mask. If the mask is a layer mask, just add an object to the layer. If the mask is a clipping mask, simply drag the object into the group that contains the clipping mask in the Layers palette. Or you can use the Paste In Front and Paste In Back commands to introduce additional elements to a clipping mask. Simply position the object where you would like it to be, then cut it to the Clipboard. Next, select an object in the group and choose Paste In Front or Paste In Back. This adds the object to the group and causes it to be masked.

Figure 17.24: The arrow tool has no problem selecting the individual content elements used in the layer mask.

Cropping a Mask

Live editing ability is the primary factor that distinguishes clipping paths from the somewhat similar Crop effect (of the Pathfinder palette fame). In both cases, the front path clips all the selected paths behind it (or, in the case of layer masks, all the objects on that layer). If you were to apply the two to identical collections of filled paths, the results would even look the same.

But where masking permits changes, cropping does permanent damage, so to speak. Masking hides portions of content elements that extend outside the mask; cropping deletes them. Also worth noting: the Crop effect deletes strokes and is not applicable to text or imported images. Masking, meanwhile, can accommodate any kind of object.

That said, with the benefit of the added functionality of masking comes the price of complexity: masking requires more work on the part of the printer. (By printer I mean the output device, such as the laser printer or imagesetter, that actually prints the file.) Masks take longer to print than cropped paths—several times longer in some cases—and a sufficiently complicated mask that contains lots of complex objects can sometimes prevent your illustration from printing.

So use masks when you need them and apply Crop when you don't. In **Figure 17.25**, for example, I used Crop to stencil the shadows out of the arms, neck, face, and ears, but I used masks for the hair and shirt. Why? I retained the mask for the shirt because I wanted to preserve the ability to edit the planes later. And I used a mask for the hair because of the white stroke from the head that extends up into the hair. The Crop effect would have deleted this stroke. If I had reapplied it, I wouldn't have gotten the white head line to align with the black head line precisely at the hair line.

Figure 17.25: The shirt and hair were created using masking. However, the other stenciled shapes were modified permanently using the Pathfinder Crop effect.

 It's not entirely fair to say that all cropping is permanent and uneditable. Cropping also exists as an effect. Effects are different from filters in that they are an appearance attribute. They change the way objects look but don't alter the underlying structure of the objects. All effects are live and editable and allow for greater flexibility than filters. They can be somewhat confusing to grasp, so to learn the details check out Chapter 19.

Disassembling a Mask

You can turn a clipping mask back into a standard, everyday collection of objects by selecting the clipping path and choosing Object » Clipping Mask » Release. Illustrator will also ungroup the objects. If your mask was a layer mask, select the layer in the Layers palette, and then click the Make/Release Clipping Mask icon or choose Release Clipping Mask from the Layers palette menu.

Hatching Textures

This chapter concludes with the Pen & Ink Hatch Effects filter. This unusual and exceptionally complex filter combines the powers of blending and masking to create crosshatch, line, and dot patterns. Unlike tile patterns, Pen & Ink patterns can change over the course of the shape, becoming progressively lighter and darker like gradations.

The Hatch Effects filter lets you take a simple object called a *hatch* and repeat it over and over inside a path at different sizes, angles, and densities. In principle, it's the same thing as defining a custom halftone pattern. Instead of printing little round halftone dots, you print little crosses, straight lines, or squiggles.

Figure 17.26 shows a silhouette filled with thousands of tiny objects. The objects are the hatches. I've pulled one out to the side for you to see. The Hatch Effects filter can create the look of custom halftone screens, woodcuts, stippling, and other traditional media effects.

Figure 17.26: A silhouette filled with a hatch effect. The small object to the left of the horn is the hatch used to fill the silhouette.

Filling a Path with a Hatch

Although the full depth of the Hatch Effects filter could take volumes to adequately cover, it is actually very simple to apply the filter.

1. **Select the path you want to fill with a hatch effect.**

It has to be a path. No text blocks or imported images allowed.

 If you want the hatches to match a certain color or gradation, assign that color or gradation to the path from the appropriate palette.

2. **Choose Filter » Pen & Ink » Hatch Effects.**

Illustrator displays the massive dialog box shown in **Figure 17.27**. Isn't that something? I didn't know what to make of this beast when I first met it, but after clocking many hours together, I now look on it as an old friend—a ridiculously fussy, outrageously inflated, exasperatingly difficult old friend.

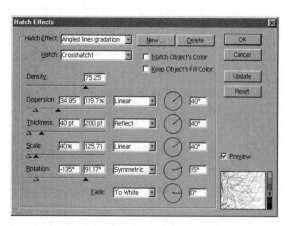

Figure 17.27: Although it contains more options than just about every other dialog box in Illustrator put together, the Hatch Effects dialog box is well organized and exceedingly capable.

3. **Choose one of the preset effects from the Hatch pop-up list.**

Illustrator provides you with a wealth of choices of natural media appearances, such as crosshatching or stippling. It also has appearances such as fiberglass, wood grain, and grass. (The Hatch pop-up list lets you change the objects used in the fill. I'll cover using this list in the section "Designing Custom Hatch Effects.")

4. **Click Preview to see a small sample of what the preset will look like.**

This preview is only what the effect would look like if it were applied to a path the same size as the rectangle in the dialog box; it doesn't show how the effect will look when applied to your path. Unfortunately, there is no way to preview the effect in your selected path. This is why the Undo command is very important when using hatch effects. You apply the filter, look at the results, undo the filter, reset the filter, and look at the results—over and over till you get what you want. Not the most productive method, but it's all we've got.

5. **Use the color and fade options to change the color of the hatches.**

If you want to change the color of the hatches to match the colors in the selected path in the illustration window, select the Match Object's Color check box. In the first example in **Figure 17.28**, I applied the Match Object's Color option to an object filled with a gradation. Illustrator used the colors from the gradation to fill the individual hatches along the same angle as the original gradient.

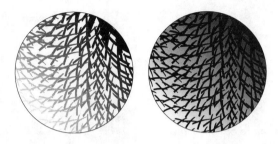

Figure 17.28: Paths filled with hatches using the Match Object's Color (left) and Keep Object's Fill Color (right) options.

To place the hatches in front of the fill assigned to the selected path, select the Keep Object's Fill Color option. In the second example in Figure 17.28, I selected the Keep Object's Fill Color option to keep the original gradation in the background.

You can also choose to fade the colors of the hatches to white or to black by selecting options from the Fade pop-up menu. For example, assigning the To White option to a bunch of black hatches creates a black-to-white gradation. You can set the angle of the gradation using the Fade value. A fourth option, Use Gradient, matches the colors of the hatches to the gradient fill assigned to the selected path. This option produces the very same effect demonstrated in the first example in Figure 17.28, except that you can modify the angle of the gradation using the Fade Angle option.

6. **Click OK to apply the hatch effect.**

I'll explain the rest of the options in the next few sections, but for now, just apply the filter. Illustrator closes the Hatch Effects dialog box and returns you to your document. Don't be confused if all you see is a solid mass of color. What you are looking at are hundreds—maybe thousands—of selected anchor points. Deselect the artwork to see the applied effect.

You can also choose Hide Edges from the View menu to hide the selected anchor points. This lets you see the selected artwork without all those anchor points in the way.

Each hatch is a separate path, so you can edit it with the direct selection tool (among others). And if you prefer to crop the hatches into independent paths that are easier to print, click the Pathfinder palette's Crop button.

Creating a Custom Hatch

Using the presets is the quick and easy way to fill an object with a hatch, but it hardly satisfies your own creative ambitions. Fortunately, you can make your own hatches and then use the myriad of sliders and wheels to adjust them to your exact specifications. To create a hatch, follow these steps:

1. **Draw a few simple objects.**

Keep them very simple. The best hatches contain anywhere from two to 20 anchor points and only one to three paths. After all, simple objects mean faster and more reliable printing. This is one time when you want to leave the razzle-dazzle to Illustrator. In **Figure 17.29**, I've drawn an X using a minimal 12 points—which is more complicated than any of Illustrator's predefined hatches.

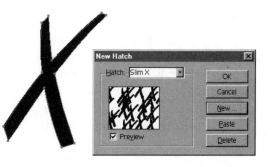

Figure 17.29: I selected the X path and chose Filter » Pen & Ink » New Hatch to convert it to a hatch.

 You won't be able to use a compound path as a hatch, because the filter will separate the two portions of the compound. However, I have been able to create circles with holes in them by using the knife tool to cut a line from the inside of the hole to the outside of the circle. This makes a single object out of a compound path.

2. **Assign fills and strokes to the objects as desired.**

Whatever fill color you use will show up when you apply the hatch pattern to a path using Filter » Pen & Ink » Hatch Effects. But don't get too hung up on it; you can always override the fill color, so you might as well just use black.

 Stroke is more important here than fill color. It doesn't matter particularly what color or line weight you use, just whether or not you assign a stroke. If you do, you'll be able to tell Illustrator to vary the thickness of the stroke over the course of the mask. If you set the stroke to None, you won't be able to vary the thickness, but the final effect will print a little faster.

3. **Choose Filter » Pen & Ink » New Hatch.**

The prospective hatch objects should be selected when you choose this filter. The New Hatch dialog box comes up onscreen, looking something like Figure 17.29.

4. **Click the New button.**

Illustrator asks you to name the hatch. Enter a name and press Enter (Return on the Mac). In Figure 17.29, I named my pattern *Slim X*. The name appears in the Hatch pop-up menu, and a preview of the hatch appears in the left side of the dialog box.

5. **Click OK or press Enter (Return on the Mac).**

Illustrator closes the New Hatch dialog box and stores the hatch pattern in the current hatch library (I'll get to the hatch libraries in a moment). This new hatch will appear in the Hatch Effects dialog box.

You can also use the buttons in the New Hatch dialog box to delete a hatch from the illustration or paste the selected hatch in the illustration window so you can edit it. The hatches you create are stored in a file called a hatch library. The default set of hatches is only one of several other libraries that come with Illustrator. You can use Filter » Pen & Ink » Library Open to choose from the other libraries. These are found in the Sample Files \ Hatch Sets folder in the Illustrator application folder.

If you create your own custom set of hatches you can save the file along with the other hatch sets by choosing Filter » Pen & Ink » Library Save As. This opens the normal Save As dialog box where you can navigate to save the hatches wherever you want. (Because the hatch library is a file, you can even trade them with your friends.)

Designing Custom Hatch Effects

Creating the custom hatch was a piece of cake. But roll up your sleeves now, because we're going to tackle the really hard part. Using the default settings is nice, but you want to create your own looks. So here is a complete set of instructions for using all the bells and whistles in the Hatch Effects dialog box.

1. **Select the hatch pattern you want to apply from the Hatch pop-up menu.**

If you have created your own hatch or changed the library set, you will see those hatches in the list. Otherwise, you will see the default hatches.

2.   **Specify the density of the hatch pattern.**

The Density slider bar changes the number of hatches that are packed into the shape. Raise the Density value or drag the slider triangle to the right to increase the hatch population; you can reduce the value or drag the triangle to the left to nuke those hatches till there are barely any of the suckers left. **Figure 17.30** shows the difference between two density settings.

Figure 17.30: The low density (left) allows more space between the hatches than the higher one (right).

In the lower-right corner of the dialog box, you can keep an eye on the effects of raising or lowering the hatch population in the preview box. To the right of the preview box is a density color bar. Click a light swatch in the bar to decrease the number of hatches; click a dark swatch to raise the number. What's the difference between this bar and the Density slider? The little density color bar works in big, clunky increments, but otherwise, they're the same. One merely compounds the effects of the other.

3.   **Modify the Dispersion options.**

Dispersion is the randomness of the hatch. Set all the way to 0, the hatches will be arranged in perfect order—no variations in their positions. Increase the dispersion to shake up the hatches a bit. After all, in traditional media a bit of randomness is only to be expected. **Figure 17.31** shows how diversifying the dispersion makes for a more natural appearance.

Figure 17.31: Use a higher Dispersion setting (right) to shake up the orderliness of the hatches.

4.   Set the Thickness.

The Thickness option lets you modify the line weights of stroked hatches. If the selected hatch doesn't include a stroke, the Thickness options are dimmed. **Figure 17.32** shows the effect of increasing the thickness of a hatch.

Figure 17.32: The Thickness setting increases the stroke weight applied to hatches.

5.   Adjust the Scale.

The Scale setting increases or decreases the size of the hatch. Combined with the Density control, this can turn black dots on a white background into a huge blob of blackness. **Figure 17.33** shows the effect of adjusting the scale.

Figure 17.33: The difference between a low Scale setting (left) and a larger one (right).

6. Set the Rotation.

Use the Rotation slider to change the orientation of the hatches. A rotation is much more noticeable when applied to hatches such as vertical lines than when applied to the dots. **Figure 17.34** shows two different angles of rotation.

Figure 17.34: A comparison of two Rotation settings.

Just when you thought there was nothing else that you could possibly control in the Hatch Effects dialog box, you notice that the Dispersion, Thickness, Scale, and Rotation menus include an identical collection of six options. These permit Illustrator to transform the hatches within a set range or to apply constant transformations. For instance, you can set the scale to start at one amount and then move along a certain angle, getting bigger and bigger in a linear progression.

This is where the Hatch Effects dialog box becomes as deep as an entire application itself. **Figure 17.35** shows each option as it affects the Scale settings. The hatch pattern used in the figure is a simple black circle.

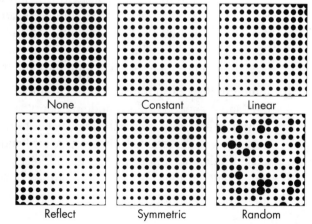

Figure 17.35: The six transformation options for the hatch effects, each applied to the Scale setting. To keep things as clear as possible, Dispersion, Thickness, and Rotation were all set to None.

- **None:** Select this option to prevent the transformation from working at all. Throughout Figure 17.35, Dispersion, Thickness, and Rotation were all set to None. In the first example, Scale is set to None as well.

- **Constant:** This option applies a constant transformation value to all hatches. You are permitted just one option box and one slider triangle. In the Constant example in Figure 17.35, the single Scale value is set to 75 percent.

- **Linear:** Select this option if you want to create a gradation of transformations. You enter two range values to specify the minimum and maximum transformations, and Illustrator varies between them at a constant rate from one end of the selected path to the other. You also specify the angle of the variation using the option box and icon at the right side of the slider bar. It's like a linear gradation. In the Linear example in the figure, the range values were 50 and 150 percent and the angle was set to 45 degrees (as they were for the remaining examples as well).

- **Reflect:** This option varies the transformation from the center of the shape outward. Therefore, it starts with the second range value, gradually varies to the first, and then varies back to the second, as the Reflect example in the figure demonstrates.

- **Symmetric:** At first glance, the Symmetric and Linear examples in Figure 17.35 appear identical. But there is a subtle difference. The hatches in the Linear example increase in size at a constant rate from the lower-left corner to the upper-right corner of the square. Not so in the Symmetric example. The hatches grow quite a bit at first, flatten out somewhat in the middle, and grow briskly again at the end. The Symmetric option is supposed to simulate shading around a cylinder—changing quickly, flattening out, and changing quickly again. But the effect is so slight, I doubt most viewers will notice. Oh well, at least the Adobe engineers gave it the extra effort.

- **Random:** If you want Illustrator to transform the hatches ad hoc, select the Random option. In the Random example in the figure, for example, Illustrator has randomly scaled the hatches from 50 to 150 percent. The angle options are dimmed when you select Random because, well, an angle would imply order, and Random directly opposes order. (You can have a random angle, but you can't have an angled Random.)

If you're interested in producing a gradient effect, set the Thickness and/or Scale settings to Linear, Reflect, or Symmetric. This allows the hatches to grow and shrink, just like the halftone dots in a standard gradation. It doesn't matter how you set the Dispersion or Rotation options. Neither of these options simulates a gradation, although they can be used to enhance the effect.

Finally, in the Hatch Effects dialog box, Illustrator gives you a few commands that help you save and work with presets.

- **New:** Click this button to store the current control settings. You can name the settings and have this group of settings be stored along with the others in the Hatch pop-up list.

- **Update:** If you modify a few of the controls, you can assign them to the named item in the pop-up menu by clicking on the Update button.

- **Reset:** Click this button to restore the preset to the original setting.

- **Delete:** You can trash a preset from the list by clicking the Delete button. (Watch out, though; that's not an undo-able thing.)

TRANSPARENCY

In the earlier days of Illustrator, real transparency didn't exist. The reason for that was Illustrator was bound to PostScript, and PostScript doesn't allow for true transparency. Now, however, Illustrator is based on core PDF architecture (Illustrator's native format is now PDF and not EPS), which allows transparency to reign free and true in all facets of the program. So whereas the transparency in Macromedia FreeHand is just an illusion—kind of like the smiling magician who sticks a knitting needle clear through his arm while the audience squirms—the transparency in Illustrator is real. So be prepared to genuflect and show your admiration and respect.

Adobe has given us an amazing arsenal of transparency controls—everything from simple opacity changes to advanced blending modes to highly sophisticated opacity masking. Creating realistic reflections, liquids, smoke, clouds, and metallic effects has become a little easier. This chapter covers all the features of the Transparency palette, including opacity, blending modes, and special knockout options for controlling how transparency is applied. We'll look at the differences among adding transparency to objects, groups, and layers. We'll take another look at features we've already covered, such as multi-fills, brushes, and text to see how you can use transparency with them. And finally, we'll look at more of the technical aspects of transparency and certain instances where native transparency cannot be preserved.

Opacity

Although most people call transparency the ability to see through an object, Adobe uses the term *transparency* as the overall category for a whole host of features. So what most people call transparency, Adobe calls opacity. Strictly speaking, you don't make an object transparent; you lower the opacity of the object.

Lowering Opacity

Changing an object's opacity is very simple. You select the object, and then use the Opacity control in the Transparency palette to lower the opacity. If you don't see the Transparency palette, choose Window » Transparency.

The lower the opacity, the more transparent the object. **Figure 18.1** shows the effect of different opacity settings for raindrops positioned over storm clouds. The lower the opacity, the more you can see through the raindrops to the clouds behind them. At an opacity of 10 percent, you can hardly see the raindrops at all.

When you lower an object's opacity, the opacity level is listed in the Appearance palette. In addition, the circle next to the name of the path, called the Target icon, in the Layers palette changes into a three-dimensional-looking ball (referred to as the *meatball* in the inner circles of Adobe), as seen in **Figure 18.2**. The meatball is your clue that the object has an appearance attribute and to check out the Appearance palette to see what is being applied to your object. Briefly, appearance attributes are commands you apply to an object that alter the look, or appearance, of the object but not the actual structure of the object itself. For instance, if you have an object with a 100 percent black fill over a white background and you apply an 80 percent opacity setting, the black fill will actually print as an 80 percent tint.

Opacity is not the only appearance attribute that is indicated by the meatball Target icon. Other attributes, such as multiple fills, strokes, and effects, are also indicated by this icon.

Figure 18.1: Use the Opacity control in the Transparency palette to change the translucence of an object.

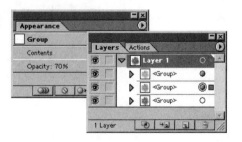

Figure 18.2: The opacity of an object is listed in the Appearance palette. Opacity applied to an object also changes the Target icon in the Layers palette from a white circle to a three-dimensional-looking ball.

Applying Group and Layer Opacity

If you select several objects with different fill and stroke settings, the Appearance palette does not show the opacity listing. This is because you have mixed appearances for the objects. If you want to see the opacity for all the objects, you should first group the objects and then target the group. You then apply the opacity to the group. This makes it easier to adjust the opacity setting for all the objects.

To apply the opacity setting to a group, find the group listing in the Layers palette. Then click the Target icon for the group. A highlight circle appears that indicates that the group is targeted. (Another way to target a group is by selecting the group and clicking the word *Group* in the Appearance palette.) You can also target a layer and apply the opacity to all the objects in the layer. Once again, the meatball icon indicates the special appearance applied to the layer.

It is possible, therefore, to have artwork that contains opacity applied to an object as well as both the group and the layer to which it belongs. This can cause confusion if you want to clear the opacity for an object. If you change the opacity for just the object, you still need to change the opacity for the group as well as the layer. Illustrator tries to make it easier for you by employing what is called *smart targeting*. If you select a group or a path on your artboard, Illustrator automatically targets that group or path in the Layers palette. You can also tell where opacity has been applied by spotting the meatball icons in the Layers palette or the opacity grid icon in the Appearance palette (**Figure 18.3**).

Watch out if you apply opacity to groups or layers. Any objects that you move out of the group or layer will change their appearance. For instance, if an object is on a layer that has a 50 percent opacity applied to it, it will look different if the object is moved to a layer that doesn't have opacity applied. Also, if you move an object that already has an opacity applied to it to a layer that has opacity, you will have both the opacity of the object and the opacity of the layer applied to the object.

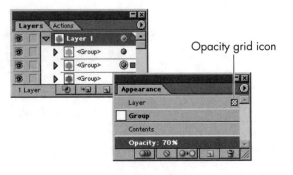

Figure 18.3: The meatball icons next to the listings in the Layers palette indicate a special appearance. The grid icons in the Appearance palette indicate that opacity has been applied to a group or a layer.

Opacity grid icon

Setting and Displaying the Transparency Grid

As soon as your artwork becomes complex, you may find it difficult to see exactly where images start and stop. A 20 percent black object with a 30 percent opacity is going to be very hard to see on a white artboard. (This is very similar to trying to find a white doily decorating a snowman in a fog.)

Fortunately, someone at Adobe recognized the problem and added a transparency grid that you can display while you work. To display the transparency grid, simply choose View » Show Transparency Grid or use the keyboard shortcut Ctrl+Shift+D (Cmd-Shift-D on the Mac). The grid appears over your page. Partially opaque objects will be seen more easily against the grid. You won't be able to see the grid through any fully opaque objects. **Figure 18.4** shows how much easier it is to see light gray transparent objects over the transparency grid.

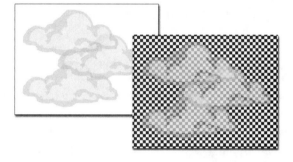

Figure 18.4: There are transparent light gray clouds on the left side without the transparency grid. With the grid turned on, they are easier to see, as seen on the right side.

If you want, you can change the color and size of the transparency grid. Choose File » Document Setup and then choose the Transparency setting from the pop-up list. The transparency grid options appear as seen in **Figure 18.5**.

Figure 18.5: The transparency grid is controlled through the Document Setup transparency options.

 The transparency grid is controlled through Document Setup. This means that you have to reset any changes for each new document. And if you're wondering, no, you can't change the grid for the Adobe Illustrator Startup file and then make that the default for all new documents.

You can change the grid as follows:

- Use the Grid Size list to choose the size of the grid boxes. Smaller boxes are better if you are working with many small items.

- Use the Grid Colors list to choose one of the preset color schemes for the grid.

⬤ Click either of the color boxes to open the Color Picker to choose a specific color.

⬤ Watch the preview box to see a representation of the grid.

You can also simulate the appearance of what your artwork will look like when printed on colored paper. First, click the top color box to set the color of the paper. Then check Simulate Paper. This adds the color of the paper to all the artwork.

Blending Modes

If you are familiar with Photoshop, you may have used the blending modes for layers. What blending modes do is change how the colors of one object or layer interact with the colors of the objects or layers below it. Strictly speaking, the blending modes are not a transparency feature, but more a matter of how colors interact.

Applying Blending Modes

Illustrator's blending modes are controlled by the pop-up list in the Transparency palette, as seen in **Figure 18.6**. You set a blending mode by selecting an object or targeting a group or layer and then choosing one of the default blending modes. You won't see any effect of the blending mode unless you have another object positioned under the selected object.

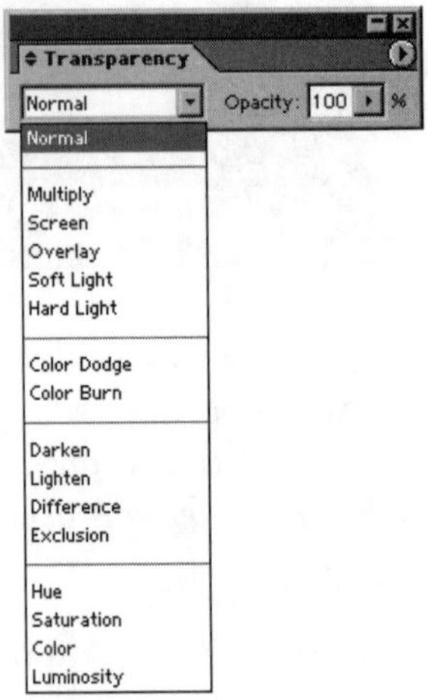

Figure 18.6: The blending modes are applied by choosing them from the pop-up list in the Transparency palette.

You can also find blending modes listed in the Drop Shadow, Inner Glow, and Outer Glow effects. In these cases, the blending mode changes how the object with an applied effect—the shadow or the glow—interacts with the objects below it.

Understanding Blending Modes

It really is almost impossible to convey the meaning of blending modes in mere words. **Figure 18.7** shows a small sample of the blending modes. Because many of the modes create color changes, it is difficult to show the blend modes in their true glory in a black-and-white illustration. However, here's a rundown of each of the blending modes and how they work.

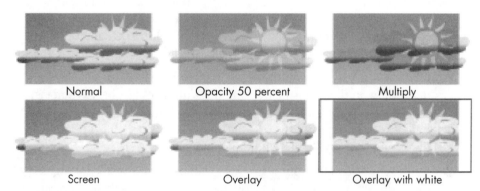

Normal Opacity 50 percent Multiply

Screen Overlay Overlay with white

Figure 18.7: A grayscale version of how the blending modes work. In each case the blending mode or opacity was applied to the clouds. The bottom-right example shows the effect when a white rectangle is put behind the artwork.

 Illustrator's blending modes do not use the white of the artboard as a color that they can interact with. If you turn on the transparency grid, you will see that Illustrator does not consider that white an actual color. So if you want Illustrator's blending modes to act similarly to the ones in Photoshop with a white background layer, you need to add a white rectangle behind the objects.

 Normal: This is how Illustrator has always displayed objects. The colors of the top object knock out (obscure) the colors of the object below. Lowering the opacity of a normal object does let the background color show through. But it is seen through a tint, or screen, of the top object's color.

 Multiply: This mode will always make a darker color where the objects overlap. Illustrator takes the color of the original object and multiplies the color(s) of the objects below.

 It may seem that the Multiply blending mode is the same as setting an object to overprint another. However, there are differences. Overprinting adds the ink in the top object to the bottom. It does not multiply. Also, if the objects share a color plate, overprinting will not add the colors.

Because the Multiply mode combines colors even when they share plates, it is very easy to create colors that contain more than 300 percent of ink. If you want to check what the final percentages of colors will be, see the "Using Transparency" section later in this chapter.

Screen: This mode will always make a lighter color where the objects overlap. Illustrator takes the color of the original object and multiplies the inverse of the color of the objects below. The inverse of a color is 100 percent minus the percentage of color. The lighter the color set to the Screen mode, the lighter the final color will be.

Overlay: Overlay goes both ways and either multiplies or screens depending on the colors below. The color of the object below is not replaced but is mixed with the original object color to reflect the lightness or darkness of the original color. The overall effect is that light colors become lighter and dark colors get darker.

Soft Light: This mode simulates the effect of shining a soft spotlight on an object; however, in this case the soft spotlight is the top object. If the top color is lighter than 50 percent gray, the bottom object is lightened as if the Color Dodge mode had been applied. If the top color is darker than 50 percent gray, the bottom object is darkened as if the Color Burn mode had been applied. The Soft Light mode does not lighten very saturated objects that contain 100 percent of colors.

Hard Light: This mode simulates the effect of shining a very intense spotlight on an object. However, in this case the spotlight is the top object. The Hard Light blending mode works similarly to the Soft Light mode, but the hard light effects are much more intense. If the top color is lighter than 50 percent gray, the bottom object is lightened as if the Screen mode had been applied. If the top color is darker than 50 percent gray, the bottom object is darkened as if the Multiply mode had been applied. If the Soft Light mode shifts a color only 10 percent, the Hard Light mode may shift it 15 percent. And unlike the Soft Light mode, which cannot affect objects with 100 percent ink, the Hard Light mode does not have those limitations.

Color Dodge: Dodging in photography is the technique where you lighten certain areas of a print during developing. Color dodge in Illustrator means the bottom colors are brightened according to the color of the top object. Using black as the original color will not change the bottom colors. The Color Dodge mode is similar to the

Lighten mode. However, the Color Dodge mode creates slightly more intense color changes.

Color Burn: Burning in photography is the technique where you darken certain areas of a print during developing. Color burn in Illustrator means the bottom colors are darkened according to the color of the top object. The Color Burn mode is similar to the Darken mode. However, the Color Burn mode will create slightly more saturated color changes.

Darken: The Darken blending mode takes the top object's color and compares it to the bottom color. If the top color is darker, then that color replaces the bottom object's color. If not, the bottom object's color does not change and the top object's color is invisible.

Lighten: The Lighten blending mode takes the top object's color and compares it to the bottom color. If the top color is lighter, then that color replaces the bottom object's color. If not, the bottom object's color does not change and the top object's color is invisible.

Difference: The Difference blending mode compares the brightness values of the colors and subtracts either the original color from the bottom or the bottom color from the top depending on which color is brighter.

Exclusion: This mode is similar to the Difference mode, but it creates changes that are slightly less intense.

Hue: The Hue mode changes the hue of the bottom object to be the same as the top object but does not change the luminosity or saturation of the bottom color. If you do not like the effects of the Color blending mode, you may use the Hue mode as an alternative blending mode for colorizing portions of an area.

Saturation: This mode changes the saturation of the bottom object to be the same as the top object but does not change the hue or luminosity of the bottom color. This mode is excellent for intensifying or dulling the colors in a specific area. The Saturation mode does nothing when the top object is a neutral gray color.

Color: The Color mode changes both the hue and saturation of the bottom color to be the same as the top object but does not change the luminance of the bottom color. This preserves the gray levels of the bottom object. The Color mode is an excellent choice for colorizing monochrome artwork or tinting colored artwork.

Luminosity: This mode changes the luminance of the bottom color to be the same as the top object but does not change the hue or saturation of the bottom color.

The technical descriptions of the blending modes are all well and good, but to really gain a good understanding of what each mode does, there's no substitution for playful experimentation. Draw a few overlapping shapes, assign different colors, apply different blending modes, make some popcorn, and watch the magic happen.

Isolating Blending

You must think I'm silly. Just as I show you how to apply the blending modes, now I'm going to show you how to stop their effect. Isolating the blending modes means that you set a limit as to how far down the blending mode will be seen. This is extremely important, especially when you realize that the blending mode exerts its evil influence from the point where the object starts and reaches deep down from that layer through every other layer below—no matter how many layers deep. (At times I fear that the blending modes will reach down all the way to the other side of the earth and burst out somewhere in Australia.)

Figure 18.8 shows the need for isolating the blending mode. In the top example, the text has had the Multiply blending mode applied. Although this does give an interesting effect over the coffee cup, the blending mode makes the text hard to read over the pattern. In the bottom example, the blending mode for the text has been isolated so that it affects only the coffee cup, not the pattern.

Figure 18.8: When the Multiply mode is applied, it is difficult to read the text over the pattern in the top example. In the bottom example, the Isolate Blending check box in the Transparency palette allows you to stop the blending mode from being applied to the pattern.

To isolate the blending, you need to choose Show Options from the Transparency palette. This opens the full set of transparency controls. If you want, you can also choose Show Thumbnails to see a preview of the selected elements.

Here are the steps you need to follow to isolate the blending to a particular set of objects:

1. Apply the blending mode to the object.

2. Group the object that has the blending mode and all the objects that you want to have affected by the blending.

3. Use the Layers palette to target the group.

4. Check Isolate Blending in the Transparency palette. The blending will be terminated at the bottom-most object in the group. **Figure 18.9** shows which objects are targeted and how the command is applied.

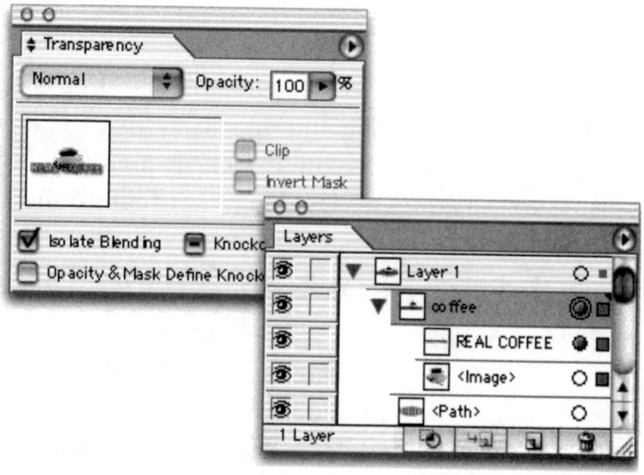

Figure 18.9: To isolate blending, target the group that contains the object with the blending mode and all the objects that the blending mode should be applied to. Then check Isolate Blending in the Transparency palette.

Knockout Groups

What are knockout groups and why do you need them? Rather than answer that question with a lot of words, let's jump to **Figure 18.10**. That horrible mess in the upper-left corner is supposed to be the flag of the United States of America. Are you having trouble finding the stars? That's because someone selected all the objects in the flag and simply applied the Multiply blending mode and set the opacity to 80 percent. That caused the stars and blue square to be multiplied into the red and white stripes behind them. So all the objects in the flag are multiplied and ghosted together into one mess.

Figure 18.10: Setting the Multiply blending mode and 80 percent opacity without a knockout causes the flag on the left to mix all the colors of the objects together. With a knockout group, the blending mode and opacity are applied to the entire object rather than the individual objects.

Fortunately, someone created a knockout group on the right. That allowed the Multiply blending mode and opacity setting to be set as a unit. So what a knockout group does is allow you to identify a group of objects and apply transparency settings to the group as a whole rather than to the individual objects.

Creating a Knockout Group

It's not too hard to create a knockout group. You just have to see the word *Group* and remember that you should apply the blending modes and opacity settings to the group, not the individual objects. And you need to select the Knockout Group option in the Transparency palette. Here's how to create a knockout group.

1. Group the objects that you want to act as a unit.

2. Use the Layers palette to target the group. (This is the part I always forget.)

3. Check Knockout Group in the Transparency palette. If you do not see the Knockout Group option, make sure Show Options has been chosen for the Transparency palette.

4. Apply the blending mode or opacity setting. **Figure 18.11** shows which objects are targeted and how the command is applied.

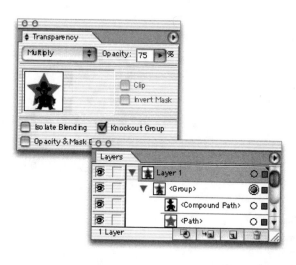

Figure 18.11: To set a knockout group, you must target the group in the Layers palette and then apply the Knockout Group option in the Transparency palette. You can then apply the blending mode or opacity setting.

Opacity Masks

If you've used a layer mask in Photoshop, you've created the same effect as an opacity mask in Illustrator. The concept behind an opacity mask is simple. You place one object or group of objects that is the mask over artwork. Wherever there is white in the mask, you can see the artwork. Wherever there is black in the mask, you can't. Anything in between has an opacity applied and can be partially seen. So 50 percent gray in the opacity mask allows you to see the artwork below at −50 percent opacity.

Opacity masks allow you to create more sophisticated effects than you could get by simply applying opacity settings or feathering objects. For example, **Figure 18.12** shows an opacity mask created from a radial gradient. The funky shadings in the artwork would be almost impossible to achieve using other techniques in Illustrator. The figure shows the original image and the gradient that was used as the opacity mask. Notice how the portions of the clock are faded out. Those areas correspond to the darker areas in the gradient. Where the artwork is more pronounced, the gradient is lighter.

Figure 18.12: A radial gradient was used as an opacity mask for the clock. The artwork shows the original image without the opacity mask and the separate radial gradient that was used as the opacity mask.

Creating an Opacity Mask

The object that acts as the opacity mask needs to be placed on a special layer called an opacity mask layer. I use two different techniques to put the opacity mask on its special layer. The first technique lets you create the opacity mask on top of the artwork and automatically put the mask on the special layer.

1. Create the object that you want to be the opacity mask. In my example it is the gradient mesh object shown in the right thumbnail in **Figure 18.13**.

2. Position this object on top of the artwork that is to be masked.

3. Select all of the objects.

4. Choose Make Opacity Mask from the Transparency palette menu. The topmost object disappears and becomes the opacity mask for the artwork below, as shown in Figure 18.13.

Figure 18.13: The topmost
object in a selection becomes
the opacity mask for the
objects below.

 If there is only one object selected, or the objects selected are a single group, then the Make Opacity Mask command creates an empty opacity mask layer.

 When you make an opacity mask, the objects to be masked are automatically grouped.

The second technique lets you create an empty opacity mask layer. You can then create the artwork you want to put on the special layer:

1. Create the artwork that you want to be masked.

2. If there are multiple objects, select and group the artwork.

3. With the artwork still selected, double-click the empty space next to the thumbnail in the Transparency palette as seen on the left of

Figure 18.14. This creates an empty opacity mask layer and a blank thumbnail for the opacity mask layer, as seen on the right of Figure 18.14. (If you don't see the thumbnail, choose Show Thumbnails from the Layers palette menu.)

4. Create the artwork for the opacity mask.

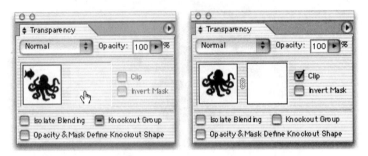

Figure 18.14: Double-click the empty space next to the object's thumbnail in the Transparency palette to automatically create an empty opacity mask layer.

Inverting an Opacity Mask

Ordinarily, the white areas of an opacity mask let you see the artwork and the black areas hide the artwork. However, if you check Invert Mask in the Transparency palette, you can flip those colors. Black shows the artwork; white hides it. In addition, the Invert Mask option hides any artwork that is outside the opacity mask area.

If you want, you can make all new opacity masks automatically inverted. Choose New Opacity Masks Are Inverted from the Transparency palette menu.

Editing an Opacity Mask

Once you've created the opacity mask, you can easily switch between working on either the artwork or the mask. However, there are some specific rules you need to keep in mind.

 The dashed underline beneath a path or group in the Layers palette indicates that the object has been altered by an opacity mask.

 Once you have made an opacity mask, the mask itself is no longer visible in the Layers palette, unless you click on the opacity mask thumbnail in the Transparency palette.

 To see the thumbnail for the opacity mask, you must target the circle for the path or group in the Layers palette. The thumbnail for the artwork as well as the opacity mask will be visible in the Transparency palette.

- Click the left thumbnail in the Transparency palette to work on the artwork.

- Click the right thumbnail to edit the opacity mask.

- Choose Disable Opacity Mask from the Transparency palette menu to see the artwork without the effects of the opacity mask. A red x through the opacity mask thumbnail indicates that the opacity mask has been disabled.

- Choose Enable Opacity Mask to see the artwork with the effects of the opacity mask.

- Shift-click the thumbnail for the opacity mask to toggle between the disabled and enabled modes.

- Alt-click (Option-click on the Mac) the thumbnail for the opacity mask to edit the mask without seeing the artwork. Alt-click (Option-click on the Mac) again to see the artwork.

- Choose Release Opacity Mask from the Transparency palette menu to remove the opacity mask. The opacity mask object will be visible on the artboard.

- Choose Unlink Opacity Mask from the Transparency palette menu to move the object without moving the mask. You can also click directly on the Link icon in between the two thumbnails in the Transparency palette. Choose Link Opacity Mask to relink the object and the mask.

 If you have a knockout group, you can target that group and then check the Opacity & Mask Define Knockout Shape. This allows you to have a knockout group combined with a knockout shape.

Using Transparency

Once you understand the principles of transparency, there are many different ways you can use objects with opacity and blending modes applied. Although I can only scratch the surface, here are some ideas to help spark your imagination.

In Multi-Fills

When you create a multi-fill for an object, you can also apply an opacity or a blending mode. Position the multi-fill on top of the second fill so that the transparency feature can be seen. You should also apply some transformation or distortion so that you can see the differences between the two fills. **Figure 18.15** shows how the top fill of an object can be set to multiply with the bottom fill.

You need to select the specific fill in the Appearance palette. You can then make any changes to the blending modes or opacity.

Figure 18.15: The Multiply mode as well as three different opacity settings make the multi-fill swirls in this star seem to move.

 Changing the order of the fills is especially important when working with the blending modes.

In Strokes and Brushes

Just like multi-fills, you can apply opacity or blending modes to multi-strokes. Distortions and transformations help make the differences between the strokes more noticeable. However, don't forget the dash patterns in strokes. **Figure 18.16** shows how using different transparency settings together with the Roughen effect creates a fuzzy stroke.

You also can apply transparency attributes to calligraphic brush strokes. Unfortunately, the attributes don't stick for the next brush stroke. So what I've been doing is working with the brush normally and then selecting all the objects and applying either opacity or blending modes. As **Figure 18.17** shows, adding a Multiply blending mode with opacity simulates the look of marker pens—especially with a nonround tip.

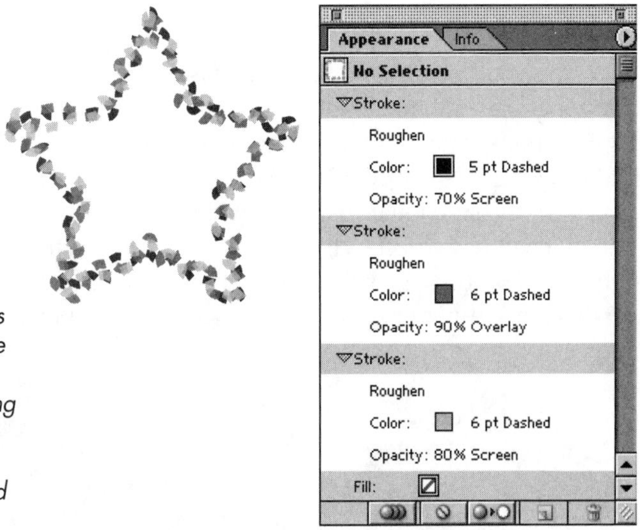

Figure 18.16: The fuzzy star
has had three different strokes
applied to it. The Appearance
palette shows the different
dash patterns, effects, blending
modes and opacity settings
applied to each stroke. The
Feather effect was also added
for some extra softness.

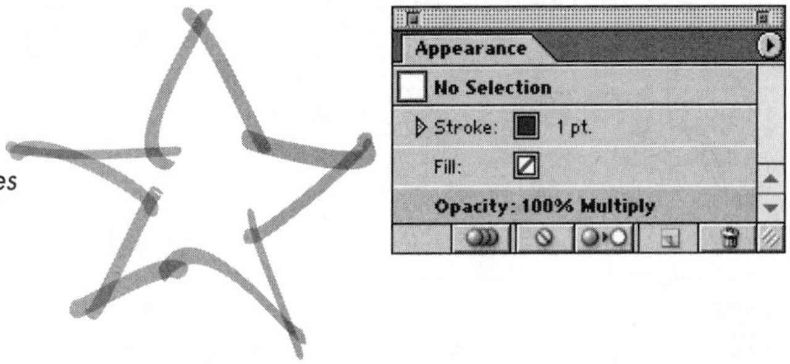

Figure 18.17: Applying a
Multiply blending mode and
opacity to calligraphic strokes
looks very similar to old-time
marker without the smell.

Fortunately, it is much easier to create art, scatter, or pattern brushes with transparency artwork. Simply apply the blending mode or opacity before you define the brush. Then each brush stroke will automatically have that particular transparency assigned to it. **Figure 18.18** shows the effect of the Multiply mode and opacity on a scatter brush with twinkle stars. However, be aware that the transparency setting is not visible in the Appearance palette when you select the brush stroke. That's because the setting is part of the definition of the brush, not the brush stroke.

Figure 18.18: Opacity
can be applied to the
objects used to define art,
scatter, or pattern brushes.
However, the setting is not
visible in the Appearance
palette.

In Text

Of course you can apply blending modes or opacity to text. Simply select the text and apply the transparency attribute. There is an important difference, though, as to how the transparency effect appears, depending on how you select the text. If you select the text as an object (with the baseline visible), then the opacity or blending modes for the individual characters will not interact with each other unless the text is in different text objects. However, if you select the text with the text tool, then the transparency attributes will interact within a single text object. **Figure 18.19** shows the difference between applying transparency to text objects and text characters.

Figure 18.19: The text on the left shows that when opacity or blending modes are applied to text selected using the text tool, the individual characters of the text will interact according to their transparency settings. The text on the right shows that when the text is selected as an object, the transparency attributes are visible only between different text objects.

In Patterns and Charts

Yes, yes, yes!—you can certainly apply transparency attributes to charts and patterns. There are two ways to apply transparency to a pattern. You can assign the transparency to the objects used to define the pattern, or you can apply the transparency to the object containing the pattern. If you apply the transparency to the objects used to define the pattern, that attribute will not be listed in the Appearance palette. This allows you to create a pattern of a checkerboard cloth where one color mixes with another.

The transparency attributes can be applied to the chart as a whole or to the individual elements of the chart. Like patterns, if you applied a transparency attribute to just part of a chart, then you will not see the attribute listed when you target the chart as a whole. Applying blending modes, such as Multiply, to a bar chart looks very interesting when the column width is set to greater than 100 percent. Where the bars overlap, you see the intersection of the bars.

Transparency and Flattening

Now that you know how to use transparency in all its various capacities, you're ready to understand the more technical aspects of this effect and the instances where transparency cannot be preserved.

As I stated in the beginning of the chapter, Illustrator supports native transparency. Since it is now based on core PDF architecture, rather than PostScript, transparency exists as a live, editable attribute. But, unfortunately, there are some circumstances where transparency is limited, or even more unfortunate, where it can't be retained at all.

When live transparency can't be supported, Illustrator goes through a process called *flattening*. Flattening essentially strips the file of transparency. Overlapping transparent objects are divided into chunks consisting of vector and raster objects, as shown in **Figure 18.20**. What category these chunks get converted into depends on how complex your artwork is. The result is that your artwork *looks* transparent, but in reality, you have lost all editability. Flattening occurs when you export a file to a format that doesn't support live transparency or when you print a file. Most printers, with the exception of a few new whiz-bang PostScript printers, cannot interpret transparency information. For more on printing transparency, be sure to check out Chapter 24.

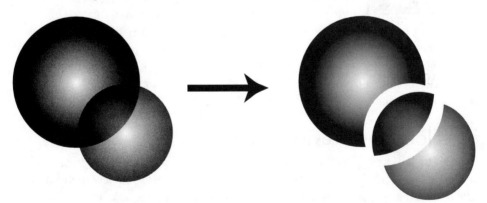

Figure 18.20: Objects with native transparency get divided into individual pieces during the flattening process.

 When you save an Illustrator file in Illustrator 10 EPS format, the file takes on a spilt personality. It retains the transparency data, which is unflattened, and also the EPS data, which is flattened. This allows you to still be able to edit the live transparency data in Illustrator. However, when you place the file in another application, such as QuarkXPress, the flattened EPS data is utilized instead.

There are other instances in which Illustrator's native transparency isn't supported and your artwork is flattened.

- When you save a file in native Illustrator 8, Illustrator 8 EPS, or PDF 1.3 (Acrobat 4) format.

- When you export a file to a transparency-unfriendly vector format such as Macintosh PICT (PICT), Enhanced Metafile (EMF), or Windows Metafile (WMF).

- When you utilize the Clipboard, and copy and paste transparent objects from Illustrator to another application with the AICB (a format similar to EPS) and Preserve Appearance options selected. These options are located in the Files & Clipboard portion of the Preferences.

 Make sure you keep the PDF option in the Files & Clipboard portion of the Preferences dialog box checked to preserve transparency in PDFs. So when you copy and paste into an application such as Adobe InDesign, which accepts the PDF version of the Clipboard data, you don't experience any flattening.

 The last instance when transparent artwork is flattened is when you choose the Object » Flatten Transparency command. It is recommended that you avoid using this command. Not only does it flatten your file, it also converts all your text to outlines, which eliminates editability and can cause small or thin type to appear thicker and less legible. And to top it off, it also converts any spot colors to process colors, which can cause major color shifts. If you don't believe me, there's even a nice friendly warning in the dialog box. And those friendly folks at Adobe don't lie.

The Flattening Preview palette

You can install the optional plug-in palette called the Flattening Preview palette, which lets you specify certain options for flattening and also preview the results. The options allow you to specify how Illustrator divides your artwork into vector and raster components. When you use the palette, your settings are also automatically transferred into the Transparency section of the Document Setup dialog box.

To install this handy palette, shown in **Figure 18.21**, drag it from the Adobe Illustrator 10/Utilities/Flattening Preview folder into the Adobe Illustrator 10/ Plug-ins folder. Make sure to restart Illustrator and you'll find it under the Window menu. You will also find a great PDF document—Flattening Preview.pdf —that explains in detail all of the palette's various settings.

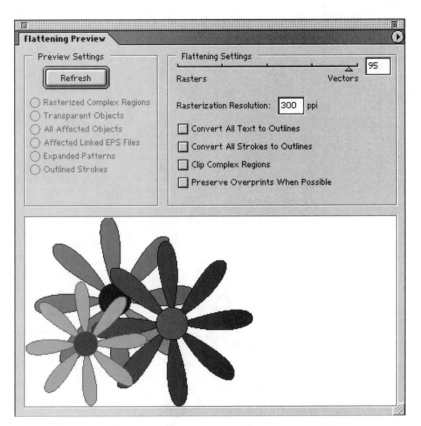

Figure 18.21: The Flattening Preview palette lets you control how your document is flattened and lets you view the results.

If you haven't had your fill of flattening information, check out the *Adobe Illustrator 10 Flattening Guide*. A hard copy comes with your software package, but you can also find a PDF version called Flattening Guide.pdf in the White Papers folder in the Adobe Technical Info folder on the Illustrator 10 program CD.

CHAPTER 19

HOG-WILD SPECIAL EFFECTS

Every so often, someone informs me that he or she prefers Photoshop to Illustrator because, "I'm just not a vector person." It's not that Illustrator doesn't help you create terrific artwork; it's that in Photoshop, inspiration starts with scanned images, which you can enhance using a mouth-watering collection of special effects filters. But Illustrator is so rigid. You have to draw everything from scratch. You can't just sit and play like in Photoshop. You can't just apply commands and watch the artwork take on new and exciting shapes. Right? Well, not exactly…

Clearly, Bézier curves are more labor-intensive than pixels. (Anyone who isn't trying to sell you something would admit that.) But you don't have to painstakingly draw each and every curve by hand. You can rough out primitive compositions with ellipses, stars, text characters, and the like, and then embellish these objects using Illustrator's automated functions.

If you read Chapters 7 and 9, you already have a sense of the marvels you can accomplish by combining and transforming shapes. But that's only the proverbial tip of the iceberg. In this chapter, I'll show you how to apply a wide range of bona fide special effects—functions so radical that they can mutate common shapes into extraordinary forms that would take you minutes or even hours to draw by hand. In **Figure 19.1**, for example, I started with nothing more than a line of type, an ellipse, and a five-pointed star. A quick distortion and two filters later, I arrived at the unqualified masterpiece that you see before you. As you can see, Illustrator lets you run roughshod over objects in the same way that Photoshop lets you use and abuse images. Both programs are equal parts finely tuned graphics applications and platforms for fortuitous experimentation.

Figure 19.1: Thanks to a few filters and distortions I was able to convert a basic ellipse, a mundane star, and some converted type into a complete illustration.

Throughout the following pages, we'll look at the special effects functions of Illustrator. We'll also look at the differences between applying commands from the Filter menu versus the Effect menu. And we'll examine how keeping commands "live" offers you greater flexibility over time. Since these features can be so wild, and there are so many of them, this chapter will be almost as much about ways to manage these powerhouses as to apply them. And just to keep you on your toes, I'm going to intersperse those parts.

The Complete History of Filters and Effects

Most of Illustrator's capabilities are built into the main application. But many tools and commands come from little subprograms called *plug-ins*. In the past it was very obvious which features were plug-ins—they were always under the Filter menu. Today, plug-in tools and commands are found all over Illustrator. For instance, the lassos are actually plug-ins, as are the links palettes, live blends, and many other features. Does it matter if a command is a plug-in or not? Maybe it does to some developer who might want to enhance the features of the plug-in. But to you, the average—OK, above average—user, it matters not at all.

By default, all plug-ins reside in the Plug-ins folder inside the same folder that contains the Illustrator application. When you launch Illustrator, the program loads all the plug-ins into memory and makes them available as tools, commands, and palettes in the program.

You can add plug-ins from other companies by copying the files into Illustrator's Plug-ins folder or into one of several subfolders or you can create a new folder. Illustrator loads the plug-in during startup as long as it is located somewhere inside the Plug-ins folder.

Meet the Family

Some plug-ins manifest themselves as tools and palettes, and a few appear as commands under the Edit, Object, and Type menus. But most show up as commands in the Filter and Effect menus. Because the commands in these menus vary dramatically in purpose and approach, I discuss them in context throughout this book. But just so we're all on the same wavelength, here is a complete list of the commands in the Filter menu, with brief snippets about what they do and where to turn for more information.

- **Filter » Colors (Chapter 14):** Illustrator lets you modify the colors of many objects simultaneously by using the commands in the Filter » Colors submenu. But, of course, you'll need some color theory under your belt to understand these commands, which is why Chapter 14 exists.

- **Filter » Create » Object Mosaic (Chapter 20):** Illustrator offers some weird filters, but this one may be the weirdest. It traces a bunch of colored squares around an imported image to convert the image to an object-oriented mosaic. Now there's something we can all integrate into our artwork!

- **Filter » Create » Trim Marks (Chapter 24):** Apply this filter to create eight small lines that serve as cutting guides when you trim your printed illustration. The eight lines mark the corners of the selected objects' bounding box (see Chapter 8). Trim marks are like crop marks, but they are considerably more versatile.

- **Filter » Distort and Effect » Distort & Transform (Chapter 19):** The distortion commands are found in both the Filter and Effect menus. The Transform command, found under the Effect menu, is a more powerful version of the free transform tool. I cover all of these in this chapter.

- **Filter » Pen & Ink » Hatch Effects (Chapter 17):** My nomination for the most difficult commands to use in all of Illustrator appears in this submenu. But they're powerful. You can design custom fill patterns, including stipples, crosshatches, and various organic textures.

- **Filter » Pen & Ink » Photo Crosshatch (Chapter 20):** The second-most difficult command but not as powerful. Because you have to start with a raster image, I'll cover this in Chapter 20.

- **Filter or Effect » Stylize » Add Arrowheads (Chapter 16):** Found as both a permanent filter and a live effect, this command adds an arrowhead to the end(s) of an open path. Illustrator bases the size of the arrowhead on the thickness of the stroke, which is why I discuss the filter in Chapter 16.

- **Filter or Effect » Stylize » Drop Shadow (Chapter 20):** This command is as sophisticated as the drop shadow layer style found in Photoshop. However, because the drop shadow creates a pixel image, I cover it in Chapter 20 along with all the raster features.

- **Effect » Stylize » Feather (Chapter 20):** Another Photoshop command that's made its way over to Illustrator, with some particularly interesting twists—and like the drop shadow, I look at it when we cover rasters.

- **Effect » Stylize » Inner Glow (Chapter 20):** How can a vector program create glows? Isn't that just for pixel-pushers like Photoshop? Find out when we cover rasters in Chapter 20.

• **Effect » Stylize » Outer Glow (Chapter 20):** Right along with the inner glow comes the outer glow.

• **Filter** or **Effect » Stylize » Round Corners (Chapter 19):** This command rounds off the corners in a selected path. You enter a Radius value—as you do when specifying the rounded corner of a rectangle—and Illustrator does the rest. We'll cover this command right here in this very chapter.

• **Effect » Convert to Shape (Chapter 15):** You can choose from rectangle, ellipse, or rounded rectangle. However, because these commands rely heavily on multiple fill settings, they're covered in Chapter 15.

• **Effect » Path » Offset Path (Chapters 15 and 16):** This command creates a new shape that follows the outline of the original path. Because this effect is much more dramatic with multiple fills or strokes, it's covered in Chapters 15 and 16.

• **Effect » Path » Outline Stroke (Chapter 16):** This command turns the stroke of a path into a closed shape. It's covered in detail in Chapter 16.

• **Effect » Path » Outline Object (Chapter 20):** This command creates a vector outline for objects that ordinarily wouldn't have one, such as the gradient mesh, placed raster images, and text.

• **Effect » Pathfinder (Chapter 19):** These powerful commands allow you to combine paths into new shapes. The Pathfinder commands can be real timesavers. Check them out in this chapter.

• **Effect » Rasterize (Chapter 20):** This command helps you do some very sneaky things with images, as I'll show you in Chapter 20. (Trust me, it's really sneaky.)

• **Effect » SVG Filters (Chapter 22):** These commands add various effects, such as drop shadows and blurs, to your artwork. The difference is these effects are XML-based and not pixel-based. Learn more in Chapter 22.

•  **Effect » Warp (Chapter 20):** These fun-filled effects take your artwork and inflate, squeeze, twist, and otherwise violate your graphics. Stay tuned to this chapter.

The filters that reside in the bottom half of the Filter and Effect menus are used for placed images. The majority of these commands are dimmed unless you've selected an image in your artwork. For a solid rundown of these filters, jump ahead to Chapter 20.

Filter or Effect: Which to Use?

As astute as you are, you may have noticed that a large number of commands appear under both the Filter and Effect menus. And just like the all-important question—paper or plastic?—how do you know which is the better choice?

To make that determination, you have to know a little more about these two sets of commands. While the result of applying the command as a filter or effect is the same, the characteristics of the two commands are different. Filters are plug-in commands that, after they're applied, actually alter the objects. Once the filter is applied, you cannot convert the artwork back to its original state, with the exception of using the Edit » Undo command, of course. In addition, filters cannot be modified or deleted.

Effects are a much more complex animal. Along with fills, strokes, and transparency, effects are part of what is called *appearance attributes*. When you apply an appearance attribute, such as an effect, you change the look, or *appearance*, of an object but not its original structure. It's as if your object is wearing a disguise. And just like disguises, appearance attributes can be removed and modified without altering the underlying artwork whatsoever. In fact, effects remain forever editable —hours, days, even months after you apply them. Hence their well-earned moniker of *live* effects. Stay tuned for more specifics on using and controlling effects.

Effects definitely afford you more flexibility but do require more RAM and a beefier processor compared with their meeker filter counterparts.

Reapplying Filters and Effects

After you choose a command from the Filter or Effect menus, it appears at the top of the menu (even if you later undo the command). This allows you to quickly reapply the command by choosing a command or by pressing the keyboard equivalent.

- To reapply a filter command, look under the Filter menu. The first command lists the last filter applied. Or press Ctrl+E (Cmd-E on the Mac).

- To reopen the filter dialog box and change the settings, choose the second command in the Filter menu or press Ctrl+Alt+E (Cmd-Option-E on the Mac.

To reapply an effect command, look under the Effect menu. The first command lists the last command applied. Or press Ctrl+Shift+E (Cmd-Shift-E on the Mac).

 To reopen the effect dialog box and change the settings, choose the second command in the Effect menu or press or Ctrl+Alt+Shift+E (Cmd-Option-Shift-E on the Mac).

Twist: Tool, Filter, and Effect

In perusing the Illustrator 10 interface it may seem to you that everywhere you look, there's a twist—a twist feature, that is. First in the toolbox, next under the Filter menu, and then again under the Effect menu. Why this fascination with twisting?

 In previous versions of the program this swirly feature was called Twirl.

The reason for the three different twist features is that each has its advantages, depending on how you want to work. As a tool, the twist gives you physical control and interactive feedback to see exactly how your final twisted object will look. The more you drag, the more you twist. As a filter and effect, you can apply numerical values to twist an object. And as an effect, you can undo the effects of the twist or change the values applied to the twist.

 Bonus for wordsmiths: The twist effect, unlike the twist filter, allows you to twist editable text. So you don't have to convert text to outlines to twist it. Not only can you change the amount of the twist, you can also even change the words or the typeface in mid-twist.

By default all three twist features twist selected objects around a central point, like spaghetti twirling around a fork. Having problems visualizing? Well, imagine for a moment that you're in Italy, admiring a strand of tacky spaghetti that's stuck to your plate. A man in a striped shirt plays an accordion as you begin to twist the noodle, coaxing it gingerly from the dish. Maybe it's the music, maybe it's the wine, but you can't help noticing that the part of the noodle closest to the fork rotates most dramatically, whereas the faraway portions stretch to keep up, not yet willing to release their grip on the plate. Now imagine that you can twist your fork up to 3,600 degrees, and you have Illustrator's twist commands.

In case you're not in the mood for pasty pasta analogies, **Figure 19.2** shows the effect of the twist filter on some virtual spaghetti. Each line of type is twisted 60 degrees more than the line above it.

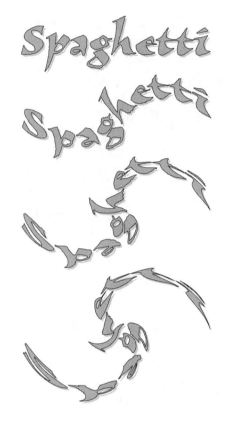

Figure 19.2: The results of twisting a line of Visigoth type at –60 (top), –120, and –180 degrees (second through fourth examples).

Twisting: The Tool

If you want to twist with the tangible, real-time feedback of a tool, select the twist tool. Like the transformation tools discussed in Chapter 9, if you just start to drag, you will be twisting around the center point of the object's bounding box. (Unlike the transformation tools, you can't see the origin point of the twist tool.) However, if you click, you can move the origin's point to some other position. (You still can't see the point, but trust me, it's there.) Then drag in the illustration window to twist all selected objects.

In **Figure 19.3**, I've dragged the selection about a quarter turn clockwise. You can drag up to 91 times around a selection to increase the magnitude of the twist. But more than two revolutions tend to create a mess with a lot of straight edges.

You can also Alt-click (Option-click on the Mac) with the twist tool to bring up a dialog box and enter a numeric twist value. This is the same dialog box that appears when you choose Filter » Distort » Twist. But what the heck, sometimes a keyboard shortcut is just more convenient than choosing a command.

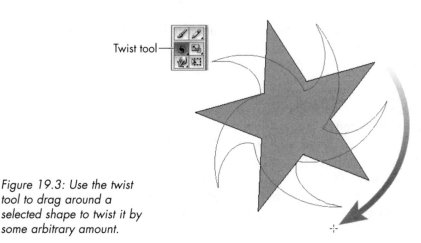

Twist tool

*Figure 19.3: Use the twist
tool to drag around a
selected shape to twist it by
some arbitrary amount.*

Here are some other things that should be in the twist tool to qualify it for true transformation tool status:

 If this were a typical transformation tool, you'd be able to press the Alt key (Option key on the Mac) before releasing with the twist tool to clone the selection. Sadly, this function is absent from the twist tool.

When you display the Twist dialog box, it should tell you the degree that you last spun an object with the twist tool. But for some reason, it always reverts back to 0 degrees.

The Shift key has no effect on your drag; you can't repeat a twist by pressing Ctrl+D (Cmd-D on the Mac); and you can't twist partial paths (only whole paths at a time).

Twisting: The Filter

For all you numerical types (you know who you are, so stop hiding behind your calculators), you can choose Filter » Distort » Twist and enter the amount of twist you want to apply in degrees. A positive value twists clockwise; a negative value twists counterclockwise. However, don't think you have to stop at 360 degrees. You can enter any amount up to 3600 degrees.

Unfortunately, there are very few reasons why you would want to use this filter. Here are some reasons why not:

There's no preview box to let you see what each amount does.

You have to convert text to paths before you can apply the twist filter.

The results of the twist filter are permanent. Although you can undo the command by choosing Edit » Undo Twist, you can't undo the twist applied to an object after you close and then reopen a file.

Twisting: The Effect

Instead of applying the twist as a one-time-only tool or filter, you can apply the twist (and many other commands) as live effects. What does this mean to you, in plain language? It means you can go back and change your mind. You haven't permanently distorted the path—the original path is still in Illustrator's memory.

You apply the twist effect by choosing Effect » Distort & Transform » Twist. The Twist effect dialog box opens. As **Figure 19.4** shows, except for the preview checkbox, there is little difference between this dialog box and the one that opens when you choose the twist filter.

Figure 19.4: Pop quiz—what's the difference between the Twist filter dialog box (top) and the Twist effect dialog box (bottom)? It's that sneaky little preview checkbox.

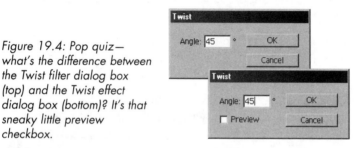

The difference in the dialog boxes seems pretty minimal. But the differences between the results of the commands are enormous. You can apply the twist effect to editable text—you don't have to convert the text to paths. And no matter when you reopen the file—days, weeks, even years later—you can change the amount of twist (or delete the twist entirely).

Don't forget that you can adjust the twist amount interactively in the dialog box, as you can with many other features—no more trips in and out of dialog boxes until you get it right! While in the Twist dialog box, turn on the Preview option. Make sure the value is selected, and press or hold down the up or down arrow keys. The object will twist before your eyes. Press Shift+up arrow or Shift+down arrow to change the value in ten-step increments.

Live Effects and the Appearance Palette 101

Now that you have one effect under your belt, it's a good time to look at some of the methods you need to know when dealing with live effects such as the twist effect. In return for the freedom to change and delete these effects, you need to pay careful attention to the status of some palettes and features that haven't been covered before. Live effects are extremely powerful, and if they're new to you, get ready to start thinking in entirely new ways about how your artwork should be prepared.

 Another important advantage to working with effects is that all effects can be made part of Illustrator's Styles. Styles mean that instead of selecting an object and painstakingly applying very complicated settings, you can simply click in the Styles palette and the effect instantly appears. Not only that, but if you change the settings of the style, all the objects that have that style applied will also change. I'll cover styles later in this chapter.

Targeting the Objects

The Appearance palette is your control center for working with commands, effects, and other Appearance attributes such as multifills and transparency. Before you can apply an effect, you have to look at what element is the current target in the Appearance palette. It lists in a hierarchical fashion all of the fills, strokes, effects, and styles that have been applied to your artwork. These attributes can be applied to single objects, groups, or layers.

When you select an item or target a layer, the Appearance palette shows all the attributes that have been applied to that item. (You can also modify attributes, duplicate them, shuffle their order within the hierarchy, or delete them entirely from here.) If you are new to using the Appearance palette, it can be a little confusing, but hang in there—with a little practice, you'll be an Appearance ace.

To open the Appearance palette, choose Window » Appearance. When a single path is chosen, the Appearance palette appears as shown at the top of **Figure 19.5**. All you have to do is choose an effect, such as the twist, for the selected object. The twist effect is applied to the object and becomes listed in the Appearance palette, as shown in the bottom of Figure 19.5.

Figure 19.5: When a single path is selected, the Appearance palette displays the effect that is applied to the object.

However, things get a little trickier when you have several objects that you want to twist or apply another effect to. First, you have to decide how you want to apply the effect. Do you want the effect to apply to the group as a whole or to the individual members of the group? What's the difference? Take a look at **Figure 19.6** to witness the dramatic difference between applying the effect to individual objects versus to the group as a whole. See what I mean?

Figure 19.6: The dancing conga line in the middle has the twist filter applied to the individual objects of a group. But the folks riding the wave at the bottom are living proof of what happens when the effect is applied to the entire group. The top shows the unadulterated original.

If you want to apply the effect to the individual objects, you can simply select the objects and then choose the effect. However, if you want to apply the effect to the group as a whole, you need to first group the objects—just selecting them all together isn't enough. You have to choose Object » Group or press Ctrl+G (Cmd-G on the Mac). With the group selected, you need to click the *Group* label at the top of the Appearance palette. This is called *targeting*.

 If you have selected editable text, the label will read Type Object.

When you target the group, you tell Illustrator that you want to apply the effect to the group as a whole, not the individual objects. You can then apply the effect.

 You can also target the group by clicking the target circle for the group in the Layers palette as shown in **Figure 19.7**.

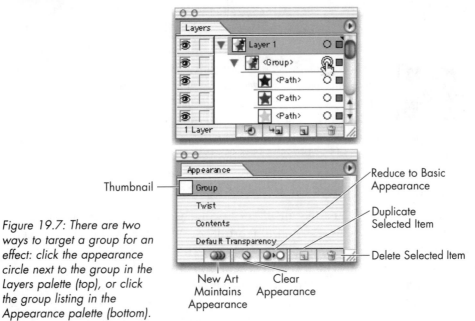

Thumbnail

Reduce to Basic Appearance

Duplicate Selected Item

Delete Selected Item

New Art Maintains Appearance

Clear Appearance

Figure 19.7: There are two ways to target a group for an effect: click the appearance circle next to the group in the Layers palette (top), or click the group listing in the Appearance palette (bottom).

Changing, Duplicating, or Deleting Effects

Once the effect is listed in the Appearance palette, you can change or delete the effect. Double-click the effect name to open the original dialog box for the effect. Make whatever changes you want to the effect and then click OK to close the dialog box. Or select the listing and click the Delete Selected Item icon, or choose Remove Item from the Appearance palette pop-up menu. This deletes the effect from the object or group.

 If you want to change the effect, try to resist the temptation to choose the effect again from the Effect menu. This doesn't change the current effect in the Appearance palette. What you're actually doing is adding a second effect to the object. This results in a twist on a twist.

You can also duplicate listings in the Appearance palette by clicking the Duplicate Selected Item icon or choosing Duplicate Item from the Appearance palette pop-up menu. Duplicating selected items is extremely useful for creating effects with multiple fills or strokes (covered in Chapters 15 and 16).

If you've got a whole mess of effects applied to an object, you can delete all the effects in one magnificent action by clicking the Reduce to Basic Appearance icon at the bottom of the Appearance palette pop-up menu or by choosing that command from the Appearance palette pop-up menu. This deletes all effects, multiple fills or strokes, or other special appearance settings. You can also click the Clear Appearance icon or choose that command from the Appearance palette pop-up menu. However, this also deletes any fill or strokes applied to the object, which makes it totally invisible.

 Keep an eye on the small square next to the object name at the top of the Appearance palette. It's actually a thumbnail that shows a representation of what the appearance of the object would be if applied to a square object. You can hide the thumbnail by choosing Hide Thumbnail from the Appearance palette pop-up menu. This can help speed the performance of Illustrator on slow machines.

Setting the Order of Effects

The order in which you apply an effect can also change the appearance of an object, as is sensationally shown in **Figure 19.8**. When the twist effect is listed above the drop shadow, the shadow twists along with the object, as shown in the left example. But when the twist effect is listed below the drop shadow, the shadow retains the shape of the original object—not the twisted versions—as seen in the right example.

It's very simple to reorder effects in the Appearance palette. Simply drag the listing up or down.

 Watch out where you drop an effect listing. If your cursor is hovering over the fill or stroke listing, when you drop them, they will disappear inside the fill or stroke entries. This will apply the effect only to the fill or stroke of an object—two subjects that I covered in Chapters 15 and 16.

Figure 19.8: The difference between applying the drop shadow effect after the twist (left) and applying it before the twist (right). Notice how the shadow doesn't twist in the example on the right.

Drawing New Objects with the Effect

Once you've applied an effect to objects, you have a choice as to what happens to the next object that you create. Do you want the effect applied to the next object? If so, do nothing. The default is for Illustrator to maintain the appearance settings. If by chance that doesn't work, you can always click the New Art Maintains Appearance icon at the bottom of the Appearance palette or choose that command from the Appearance palette menu.

If you click the New Art Maintains Appearance icon, it automatically changes to the New Art Has Basic Appearance icon as shown back in Figure 19.7. When that icon is displayed or the command is chosen from the Appearance palette menu, new objects will not have any effects applied to them.

Expanding Effects

Expanding, in the world of Adobe Illustrator, doesn't refer to making things bigger; rather, it refers to selecting live things, such as effects or blends, and converting them into discrete objects. (Some people like to call them dead at that point, but I'd rather not use such depressing terminology.) You can expand live effects by selecting the object and choosing Object » Expand Appearance. Your object will be converted into permanently changed paths.

Although the flexibility of live effects is very tempting, there may be times when you want to convert the effects into actual objects. For instance, many live effects in a file may slow down opening and saving the file. Converting the live effects can help. Or you may be passing your file over to someone else to whom you would rather not bestow the ability to change the effects. Expanding the appearance effectively stops anyone from mucking about with the artwork.

Working with Styles

Now that you're on friendly terms with the inner workings of effects, let's crank it up a notch and get cozy with styles. Styles allow you to save all the attributes of an object—fills, strokes, transparency, effects, and all the other appearance attributes—into a single style that can be applied quickly to other objects. Think of styles as *uber*-swatches that can define all attributes of an object. Styles also allow you to change the attributes of many objects by changing the definition of the style. All the styled objects—selected or not—update to the new definition.

Defining a Style

It's very simple to define the attributes of a style. Simply select an object and make it look the way you want. Make sure the Styles palette is visible by choosing Window » Styles. The Styles palette appears as shown in **Figure 19.9**.

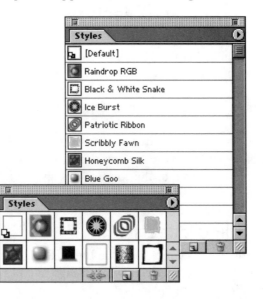

Figure 19.9: The Styles palette is where you store the styles for a document. The list view lets you see the style names.

With the object selected, click the New Style button to automatically add the style square to the Styles palette. Or choose New Style from the Styles palette pop-up menu to name the style and then add the style to the palette. You can also drag an object from the artboard into the Styles palette. A style square automatically appears.

Double-click a style thumbnail to change its name. The style names are visible in the list view shown in Figure 19.9. You can change the list view by choosing Small List View or Large List View from the Styles palette pop-up menu.

Applying and Changing Styles

Once you define a style, you can apply it to objects by selecting the object and then clicking the style thumbnail. The object changes its appearance to match the style definition.

You can also modify the style definition. This changes all the objects that have had the style applied to them. To modify a style, make whatever changes you want to an object. Then hold the Alt key (Option key on the Mac) as you drag that object into the Styles palette and onto the original style square. The style definition updates within the Styles palette as well as in all objects that have had the style applied to them.

If you want, you can unlink an object from its style definition. This allows you to change the definition of that style without changing the appearance of that particular object. Select the object and then click the Break Link to Style button. The object no longer will change with the new definition of the style.

Importing Styles

Another way that styles are like swatches is that they are stored within the document. You can import styles from other documents. Choose Window » Style Libraries and then choose one of the listings. If you choose Other Library, you can import the styles from a separate Illustrator document. The styles appear in a separate Styles palette. Click the style in the imported palette and the style will automatically be added to the Styles palette for the current document.

Transferring Attributes

As useful as styles are, there are times when you'd like to quickly copy the effects and other attributes of one object and apply them to another. Transferring attributes means you don't have to scribble down notes about how different objects are styled when you want to create new objects that match exactly. Happily, Illustrator has a method to suit this means of styling an object as well. When you want to do this, you can suck up attributes with the eyedropper tool and pour them down with the paint bucket. Although the two objects won't have a link as they would with styles, the eyedropper and paint bucket do make it easy to make two objects look alike.

If you paid attention in Chapter 10, these are the same eyedropper and paint bucket tools that sampled and applied text attributes. However, there are a few more controls when working with objects.

Using the Eyedropper

The eyedropper lifts attributes from objects and stores them in the Appearance palette. To use the eyedropper, click inside a path. The eyedropper cursor becomes partially black to show that you're lifting attributes, as shown in **Figure 19.10**. You can then use the paint bucket tool to transfer the attributes to other objects.

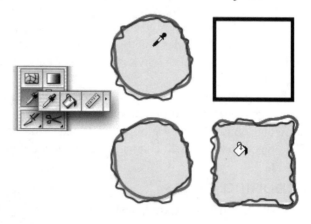

Figure 19.10: Use the eyedropper to sample the attributes of one object. Use the paint bucket to apply those attributes to other objects.

 If any objects are selected as you sample attributes with the eyedropper, those objects will automatically pick up the attributes of the sampled object.

If you Shift-click with the eyedropper, it transfers only the color directly under the eyedropper. This allows you, for example, to sample the color of the stroke of an object and transfer it to the fill of another. It also allows you to sample the colors of placed images, patterns, or gradients, as shown in **Figure 19.11**.

Figure 19.11: Hold the Shift key to sample only the color of an object. This allows you to sample colors from the rasterized images and use them elsewhere, such as in this circle.

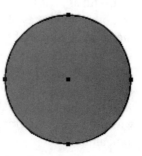

You can sample colors from background windows, including an image open in another application, or from the background color of your computer screen. Instead of releasing the mouse as you click, continue pressing the mouse button. Then move the mouse anywhere around the screen. As you drag, the color of the active icon changes to reflect the color under your cursor. When you sample the color you like, release the mouse.

Ordinarily, each time you sample an object with the eyedropper, you replace the attributes in the Appearance palette with the attributes of the sampled object. However, if you sample while holding Alt+Shift (Option-Shift on the Mac), a plus (+) sign appears next to the eyedropper cursor. This indicates that the eyedropper will *add* the attributes of the object to the Appearance palette. **Figure 19.12** shows how this allows you to combine the fills and strokes of different objects into multiple fills or strokes.

Figure 19.12: Hold Alt+Shift (Option-Shift on the Mac) to add the attributes to the sampled appearance. Then click with the paint bucket to apply the multiple fills or strokes.

Using the Paint Bucket

The paint bucket tool—the first alternate tool in the eyedropper tool slot— applies colors from the Color palette to objects in the illustration window. To use the tool, specify the desired fill and stroke attributes in the palettes, and then click the target object, as shown back in Figure 19.10.

 Although you can choose the paint bucket tool in the toolbox, I find it much easier to sample with the eyedropper and then hold the Alt key (Option key on the Mac) to switch to the paint bucket. As a pal of mine from Adobe likes to say, this method allows you to alternately "suck and dump" colors without changing tools. (Now if they'd only put that into the manual!)

If an object has no fill, you need to click with the paint bucket on the path outline.

Controlling the Sampled and Applied Attributes

Double-click either the paint bucket or the eyedropper in the toolbox to display the dialog box full of check boxes shown in **Figure 19.13**. When Appearance is checked, you will sample or apply all the attributes of the object, including multiple fills or strokes, transparency attributes, and effects. When Appearance is unchecked, only the focal fill or stroke and the transparency attributes are sampled. Effects and multiple fills or strokes are ignored. (The focal fill or stroke is the fill or stroke currently active in the toolbox.) Uncheck the Transparency option to not sample or apply the transparency attributes. Deselecting the Focal Fill or Focal Stroke check box turns off all corresponding options in that group.

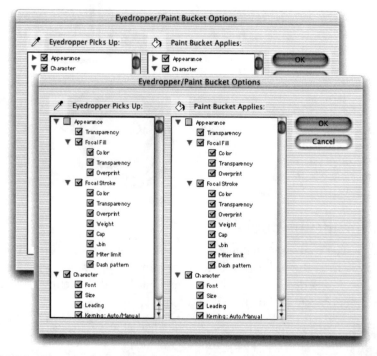

Figure 19.13: When Appearance is checked, all the attributes of an object will be sampled or applied. When Appearance is unchecked, you can choose which specific transparency, fill or stroke attributes will be sampled and applied.

The Scary Path Wigglers

Now that you're filled to the brim with how to use and manage effects, styles, and the Appearance palette, let's have some fun and look at some of the actual effects and the playful havoc they can wreak on your artwork. As Chapter 8 makes very clear, Illustrator has ways of making your objects quite perfect. Trouble is, many people don't want that kind of perfection in their illustrations. They want more organic, natural looks. Fortunately, commands in the Filter » Distort or Effect » Distort & Transform submenus let you apply imperfections to otherwise perfect paths. This can give your illustrations a much more spontaneous or traditional appearance. (I call these commands "path wigglers.") Depending on the filter, you can adjust the amount, direction, size, and details of the imperfection. You can also specify what becomes imperfect.

Figure 19.14 demonstrates how each of the path wigglers shakes up lines of boring old Helvetica Inserat. The word "ghosts" is the product of the Roughen filter, "zombies" comes from Zig Zag, "monsters" was scrambled by Scribble & Tweak, and "vampires" received the sharp-puckers of Pucker & Bloat. (I used the free transform tool and the twist filter to abuse "Halloween.") Also worth noting: the frayed outline was a standard rectangle before I subjected it to the roughen filter.

Figure 19.14: The path wiggler commands can turn common, dreary typefaces into something very frightening.

Two of the filters—Roughen and Scribble & Tweak—produce random results within a specified range. You can force Illustrator to generate new results without changing the range by turning the Preview check box off and back on.

Roughing Out Paths

Choose Filter » Distort » Roughen or Effect » Distort & Transform » Roughen. The roughen filter and effect creates roughness by adding nooks and crannies to paths. (For the sake of easy reading, when a feature exists as both a filter and an effect, I refer to it as a command.) The Roughen command adds points to selected objects and then moves the points in random directions, giving your paths a serrated, spiky look. The controls for the Roughen command are shown in **Figure 19.15**.

- **Size** indicates the distance that each point can move, expressed as a percentage of the longest segment in the path.

- The **Relative** and **Absolute** radio buttons set the Size value either relative to the size of the path or an absolute amount. Using the Relative setting means that the same setting applied to small objects creates a similar look to how it appears when the setting is applied to larger objects.

- **Detail** determines the number of points that Illustrator adds to each inch of segment.

- The **Smooth** radio button converts all points in the paths to smooth points; **Corner** makes them all corner points. As **Figure 19.16** demonstrates, corner points create a more jagged appearance, whereas smooth points are a little more curved. Think of corner points as the jagged edge created immediately after tearing a piece of paper; smooth points are more like the edge of burnt paper.

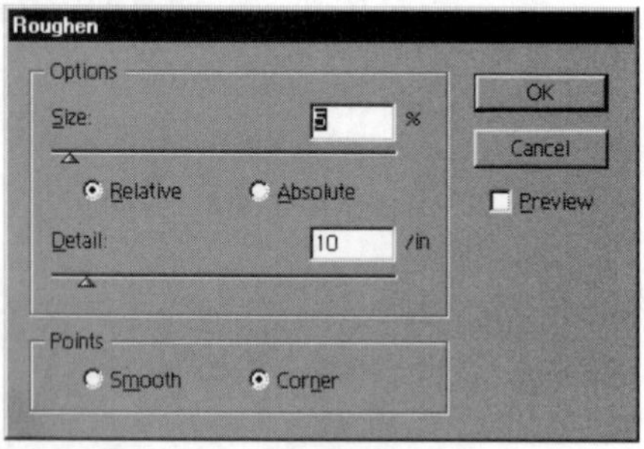

Figure 19.15: The Roughen dialog box creates a more natural look by adding points to paths.

Figure 19.16: Different settings of the Roughen command create more distorted paths. The letters of the illustration provide the size (S) and detail (D) settings for the text. Smooth points were applied to the left examples. Corner points were applied to the right.

Zigzagging Around Paths

Choose Filter » Distort » Zig Zag or Effect » Distort & Transform » Zig Zag to display the Zig Zag dialog box, as shown in **Figure 19.17**. The Zig Zag command is really a variation of the Roughen command. Instead of a random position of the new points and segments, the Zig Zag command gives your paths an electric jolt by arranging the points and segments evenly on either side of the path. The Amount value controls the distance that each point can move, which in turn determines the size of the wiggles. Use the Ridges per segment option box to specify how many zigzags Illustrator adds to each segment. As you can see in **Figure 19.18**, long segments—like the sides of the As—get long wobbly ridges, whereas the ridges along short segments—as on the bottoms of the characters—are more tightly packed.

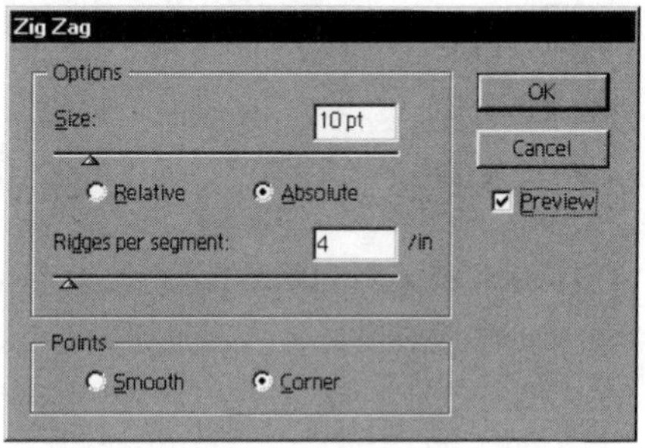

Figure 19.17: The Zig Zag dialog box is actually just a variation of the Roughen command.

Figure 19.18: Different settings of the Zig Zag command create orderly distorted paths. The letters of the illustration provide the amount (A) and Ridges per segment (R) settings for the text. Smooth points were applied to the left examples. Corner points were applied to the right.

Scribbling and Tweaking Paths

Unlike Roughen or Zig Zag, Scribble & Tweak (Filter » Distort » Scribble & Tweak or Effect » Distort & Transform » Scribble & Tweak) does not add points to selected objects. Rather, it moves existing points and control handles in random distances and directions. The name of this command is a leftover from the days when a pull-down menu offered the choice between a Scribble mode or a Tweak mode. Now, the differences are controlled by the Relative (percentage) or Absolute (actual amount) radio buttons as shown in **Figure 19.19**.

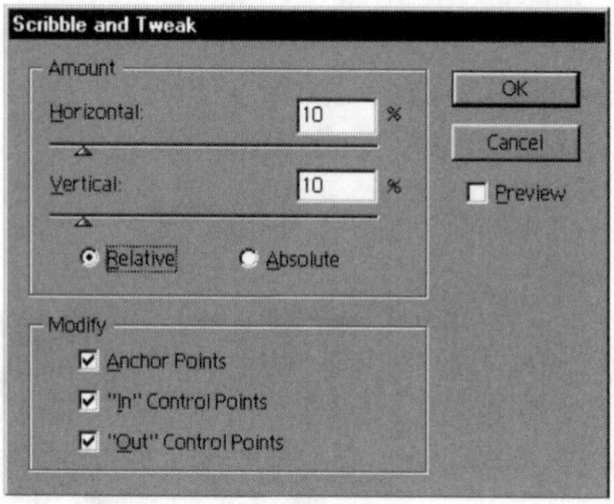

Figure 19.19: The differences between Scribble and Tweak are controlled by the radio buttons for Relative or Absolute.

Use the Horizontal and Vertical values to specify the maximum distance that points and control handles can move. Use the check boxes to decide which elements move. If you want to move the points but not the handles, turn off the two Control Points options. (The In option controls handles associated with segments entering points; the Out option controls handles for outgoing segments.) If you want to make the points stationary and move just the handles, turn off the

Anchor Points check box and turn on the other two. You can see the results in
Figure 19.20.

Figure 19.20: The Scribble &
Tweak command moved
anchor points (on the left)
and control handles (on the
right). The amounts are listed
in the percentage figures
shown in the text.

Puckering and Bloating Paths

Choose Filter » Distort » Pucker & Bloat or Effect » Distort & Transform » Pucker
& Bloat to open the Pucker & Bloat dialog box (shown in its complete simplicity
in **Figure 19.21**). This command features a single slider bar and related option
box. Negative values (which tend toward Pucker) move points outward from the
center of a path and twist segments inward. This creates an angular, almost
Gothic, look. Positive values (on the Bloat side) move segments inward and curve
segments outward, turning them into puffballs. The left column of **Figure 19.22**
demonstrates a few Pucker values, whereas the right column shows off Bloat.
Illustrator users will notice that this used to be called the Punk and Bloat command. I'm not sure why they changed it. Maybe Adobe decided the term "punk"
was too 1970s for the twenty-first century. We may never know.

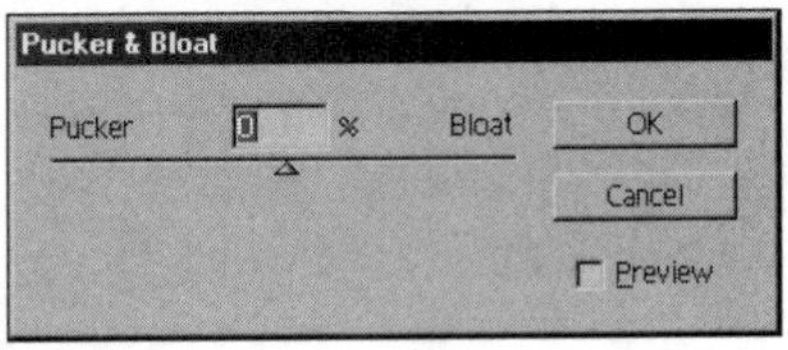

Figure 19.21: The deceptively
simple Pucker and Bloat
dialog box controls two
totally different effects.

Figure 19.22: A sampling of the values applied with the Pucker & Bloat command.

Orderly Distortions and Transformations

After all the chaos of the path wigglers, it's a relief to settle back with some controlled distortions and transformations in the Free Distort and Transform commands. The Free Distort command is a stripped-down version of the free transform tool, whereas the Transform command is an enhanced version of the Transform Each command.

Free Distortion

So why would you want a weakened version of the free transform tool? Because unlike the free transform tool, the Free Distort command allows you to apply a distortion through the Filter menu. The filter dialog box has an interactive preview area where you can experiment with your distortion before applying it. If you decide that it is better off left untouched, simply click the Cancel button. You can also create a distortion that is live and can be applied to editable text through the Effect menu. These features alone make Free Distort a worthy command.

Choose Filter » Distort » Free Distort or Effect » Distort & Transform » Free Distort to open the Free Distort dialog box as shown in **Figure 19.23**. This box couldn't be simpler. Just drag the four handles any which way you want to apply a distortion to the selected objects. Don't bother looking for special modifier keys to make one corner react to the motions of another. These handles don't have any of that sophistication. Just remember, the effect version of this feature can be modified or deleted at any time. It can also be made part of a style so that it can be applied automatically to objects. It works with paths and with editable type but not with bitmap images.

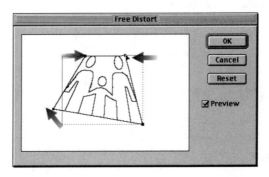

Figure 19.23: Drag the handles to change the appearance of the selected image in the Free Distort dialog box.

The one tricky thing about this feature is that the Preview option doesn't work like it does everywhere else. When you turn Preview on, you won't see the effect of your actions on the artboard, only in the dialog box. When you turn Preview off, the only difference is that you don't get to see the path outline in the dialog box.

Transform Effect

One of the problems with transformations is that they are so permanent. You make an object very wide, and there's no way to remember how much it was elongated—unless you write it down, which I don't know about you, but I rarely do. And if you want to restore the object back to its original size, you have to do all this involved math where the numerator is the original size and the denominator is the new size and X equals something else that you can't remember. And things get even worse when it comes to rotating objects, because you have to think in degrees.

Wouldn't it be cool if there were a way to apply live transformations to objects so you could change your mind later on without an advanced calculus degree? And as long as we're talking about transformations, wouldn't it be great if you could apply both a rotation and a scale to an object so it seems to get smaller and smaller as it rotates around? And, gee, now that you mention it, wouldn't it be terrific if you could make copies of the object as it rotates and scales, and flips, and does other transformations?

Yeah, it would. And that's what the mildly named transform effect does. Look at the options by choosing Effect » Distort & Transform » Transform. At first glance, the Transform Effect dialog box as seen (in triplicate) in **Figure 19.24** looks almost identical to the Transform Each dialog box covered in Chapter 9. But instead of a Copy button, the Transform dialog box has a Copies option box on the right. That is the secret to creating multiple copies of the selected object. When you enter a number in the Copies option box, you instruct Illustrator to make a copy of the selected object. That copy is in addition to the original. So 1 copy means two images, 2 copies means three images, and so on.

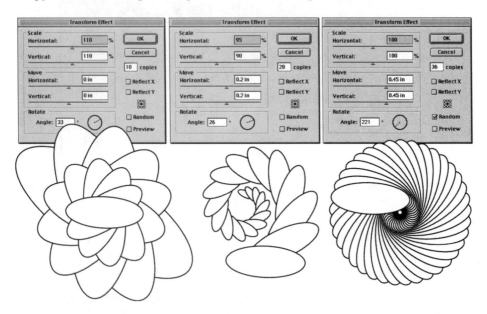

Figure 19.24: The same oval created three different images by changing the Transform dialog box settings shown above each image.

Look at the three images in Figure 19.24. Each one was created from the same single oval. The only differences are the scaling, moves, rotations, and number of copies applied in the Transform dialog box. In the example on the left, the oval is made to grow and rotate ten times around the original. In the middle example, the oval spirals and shrinks by combining scaling, movement, and rotation. Finally, on the right, the oval rotates without changing size.

Round Corners

I know—the round corners filter and effect are not to be found under the now-familiar Distort & Transform submenu, but under the category Stylize. Still, they are an orderly transformation, so I'm including them here, and that's that.

Stylize seems to be Adobe's word for "commands we can't think of a more descriptive name for." It's hard to find a theme for this useful hodgepodge of filters and effects. Some add a raster image such as a glow or drop shadow (which is why I cover them in Chapter 20, which deals with rasters). Another adds arrowheads, squares, and other markers to the ends of open paths (arrowheads are covered in Chapter 16, when I talk about Brushes and Strokes). Finally, Round Corners changes the shape of objects. Maybe someone at Adobe has a logic for grouping all these, but I can't see it.

As I mentioned in Chapter 5, the rounded rectangle tool is pretty lame. Once you've created a rounded rectangle, it's practically impossible to change the roundness of the corners. You're much better off just drawing a whole new object. Choose Filter » Stylize » Round Corners and you're in a similar situation. Once you've applied the round corner filter to objects, you have permanently rounded the corners with very little choices to fix what you've done later on. The sole advantage of the filter over the rounded rectangle tool is that the filter can round off all corner points, not just those in rectangles.

However, it's as a live effect that round corners really shakes up the world. Choose Effect » Stylize » Round Corners, and a dialog box appears where you can set the corner radius for how much roundness you want applied to corner points. As **Figure 19.25** shows, these objects maintain their original structures but display the round corner effect. The amount of rounding can be changed or deleted at any time.

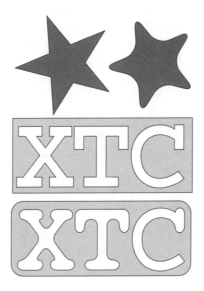

Figure 19.25: Round corners applied to a star, a rectangle, and some plain old Courier Bold text.

Pathfinder Effects

The Pathfinder effects were a lot more awe-inspiring before the dawn of the enlightened era in which we were given compound shapes. If you've read Chapter 7, you know that four of the major Pathfinder palette commands were awarded superpowers in this new version of Illustrator. The Add, Subtract, Intersect, and Exclude commands are now live. This means that, like effects, they are fully editable and can be expanded and released (undone), giving you tons of flexibility. Where effects still shine over the Pathfinder commands, however, is with the remaining commands that do not fall under compound shapes. The live effects versions of these commands don't permanently chop up your art, but provide you instead with the powers of editability and removal. By this time I probably don't have to tell you (OK, I can't resist) that one of the times this can really save you is when a client of yours loves the work you've done (that, of course, involves a layered-looking kind of image where one thing peeks through to another) but wants to move one of the pieces "just a tad bit" to convey just exactly the right message.

Because we've already covered the specifics of each individual Pathfinder command, we'll now take a look at how you can apply a few of the Pathfinder effects. One of the great things about using Pathfinder effects is that you can use them on combinations of complex paths, as you'll see in the first example.

 When you apply a Pathfinder effect, you may get an alert box telling you that Pathfinder effects work best on groups, layers, or type objects, and that the effect you are trying to apply may not work on the selected object. If this happens, give it up. Illustrator knows darn well that the type of object you've got selected isn't going to display the Pathfinder effect at all. And unless you know some technique that I've never heard of, applying the effect is going to be useless.

1.   Set up the basic illustration.

In **Figure 19.26**, I created a ten-step blend between two black bars, one wide and one thin. I then placed a compound path illustration of a chair on top of that blend.

2.   Target the layer.

In order for the effect to work, you must first target the layer. Click the circle next to the name of the layer inside the Layers palette.

Figure 19.26: A chair in front of venetian blinds is transformed into a striped settee by using the Minus Back effect.

3. **Apply the effect.**

Select Effect » Pathfinder » Minus Back. The chair clips out the bars anywhere they fall outside of the path of the chair. The wonderful thing is that everything is still live. I can edit the live blend. I can alter the anchor points of the compound path of the chair. Or I can remove the live effect altogether. None of this is possible with the run-of-the-mill Minus Back Pathfinder palette command.

Two effects you won't even find anymore on the Pathfinder palette are the Hard Mix and Soft Mix effects. These two commands give the illusion of transparency by mixing the colors of overlapping objects.

 Hard Mix mixes the colors in the objects at their highest percentages—that is, the highest amounts of cyan, magenta, yellow, and black from all overlapping objects.

 Soft Mix lets you specify what percentage of the inks you want to blend, thus resulting in lighter colors than the Hard Mix command.

Simply create your artwork and then choose Effect » Pathfinder » Soft Mix or Hard Mix. Both examples are shown in **Figure 19.27**. Unfortunately, the grayscale figure doesn't do the feature much justice.

Figure 19.27: These everyday grooming products take on a transparent appearance with the Soft Mix (left) and Hard Mix (right) effects. The original is at the top.

Warps

Up to now, the effects you've seen have been rather linear in nature. In other words, they've affected objects consistently from edge to edge. A twist is a uniform twist, and a free distortion still looks like a flat surface seen at an angle. But what do you do when you want an effect that seems to bend the plane of the object? That's when you want to try the warps that make up the rest of this chapter. If you're a Photoshop 6 user, some of these warps might look familiar. But where warps can be applied only to type in Photoshop, Illustrator 10 lets you apply them to anything, including images and editable type. And that's the way it should be, right?

The warp effects are somewhat predefined, although you can create many variations, as I did in **Figure 19.28**. If that isn't enough for you, you'll want to go back to Chapter 9 and try the mesh distortions.

Figure 19.28: A few of the wacky warps you can get away with in Illustrator 10.

You'll find all warp effects under the Effect » Warp menu. But it really doesn't matter which warp command you choose, because when the dialog box opens, you'll find out that they all share the same dialog box (**Figure 19.29**), and you can switch the warp effect at any time using the Style pop-up menu. That's because all warps use exactly this same set of options.

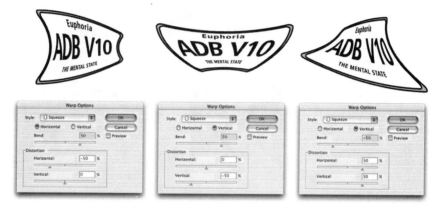

Figure 19.29: The same license plate distorted three different ways by changing the settings in the Warp Effect dialog box for the Squeeze warp. The perspective effects were added by changing the Horizontal and Vertical values.

- **Horizontal** and **Vertical** simply determine whether the effect runs along an object's horizontal or vertical axis.

- **Bend** controls the warp amount. A Bend value of 0 results in no warp at all. So the important thing to remember here is that you usually want this to be something other than 0, since at 0 all of the warps look pretty much the same. The bigger the positive or negative Bend value, the more extreme the warp factor, Mr. Scott!

- **Horizontal and Vertical Distortion** control the basic distortion of the object. If you want to see what this really means, set the Bend value to 0, then play with Horizontal and Vertical distortion. You'll find that Horizontal and Vertical are really about 3D rotation before the actual warp is applied, like the free transform or bounding box distortions we saw earlier. Like Bend, setting these values to 0 equals no change. Changing these away from 0 is like applying an additional illusion of perspective to a warp.

It can be hard to remember exactly what each warp name means. If you choose any warp and look at the Style pop-up menu inside the Warp Options dialog box, you see a little icon next to each warp name to jog your memory.

So you might actually want to apply any warp first and change it from inside the Warp Options dialog box.

Arc

Arc distorts the object around a center. This might be useful if you're designing graphics for package shapes such as bottles. The basic Arc distorts two sides and leaves the other two sides straight, which can be useful for some map projections. Arc Upper and Arc Lower distort one side but leave the other three straight, as you can see in **Figure 19.30**.

Figure 19.30: Using the square original at top left as a starting point, I applied, in clockwise order, the Arc, Arc Upper, and Arc Lower warps.

Arch

The Arch warp is like the Arc except it doesn't distort around a center. Instead, two sides are distorted in the same direction by the same amount, leaving the opposite two sides unaltered (whereas the standard Arc affects all sides).

Figure 19.31: Starting with the original on the left, I applied the Arch and Bulge warps to the center and right copies, respectively.

Bulge

The Bulge warp is like the Arch except that instead of distorting two sides in the same direction, two sides are distorted in opposite directions. **Figure 19.31** illustrates the difference.

Shell

The Shell warps distort three sides of an object. Use the Bend option in the Warp Options dialog box to customize the distortion.

- Negative values accentuate the shell shape.

- Positive values make two sides flare out like bell-bottom pants.

- Clicking the Vertical radio button points the warp to the left or right instead of up or down.

The only difference between the Lower and Upper warps is whether the undistorted side is at the top or bottom (or left or right if you've selected a Vertical orientation).

 If the orientation options seem counterintuitive to you, just remember that the terminology is all relative to the default orientation of the warp. For example, the default Shell Upper orientation is Horizontal and leaves the bottom side unaffected, so to leave the right side unaffected, you have to select Vertical. Is that too much to keep straight in your head? Well, it is for me! So instead of bothering to remember how it works, in this case it's better and more fun to play with the controls until you get what you want.

Figure 19.32 shows the basic forms of the Shell warps.

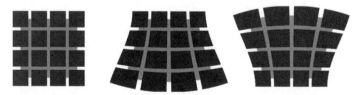

Figure 19.32: Starting with the original on the left, I applied the Shell Lower and Shell Upper warps, respectively.

Flag

The Flag warp does what it says. By distorting two opposite sides in the same way, it turns an object into a wavy shape as if it were imprinted on a flag in a stiff wind. It's kind of like the Arch except with two bends per side instead of one.

Figure 19.33: Here you see four closely related warps, starting with the original object at top left. Going clockwise from the middle-top object, I applied the Flag, Wave, Rise, and Fish warps.

Wave

The Wave warp is a lot like the Flag, except that it keeps the entire distortion within the object's bounding box. You can achieve a funhouse-mirror type of warp if you set this warp to Vertical. You can predict the difference when you look at the icons in the Style pop-up menu in the Warp Options dialog box, because the Flag icon looks like a flag, and the Wave icon looks like a flag in a box. It's the little things.

The next two warps, Fish and Rise, are similar to the Wave. Check out **Figure 19.33** to see the basic differences.

Fish

The Fish warp (not to be confused with fish wrap!) is a lot like Wave, except that the two opposing distorted sides are manipulated in opposite directions. You can flip the little fishy around by making the Bend value positive or negative.

Rise

The Rise warp is like the Flag warp except that one side is anchored to the bounding box. The side opposite the anchored side ends up higher or lower depending on (you should know this part by now) whether the Bend value is positive or negative. You enter a positive Bend value if you want to get a rise out of your object.

Fisheye

The Fisheye warp is a basic bulge type of warp. You can get a fisheye-lens look by entering a positive Bend value. The entire effect always stays within the object's bounding box. Again, you can know this in advance because the Style pop-up menu icon for Fisheye is in a little box. In **Figure 19.34**, you can compare the Fisheye warp to the Inflate warp, which is coming up next on the menu and very similar.

Figure 19.34: On the left is our original, in the middle is the Fisheye warp, and at the right is the Inflate warp. Notice how Fisheye mostly preserves the original outline, while Inflate extends well beyond it.

Inflate

The Inflate warp is really just the Fisheye warp with the object's edges turned loose from the object's bounding box. Extremely positive Bend values will push the object's edges way out into the layout, and negative values will suck it in.

Squeeze

The Squeeze warp distorts all four sides. Two opposing sides are curved out, and the other two are curved in, as shown in **Figure 19.35**. It's the perfect warp for making boxing-equipment logos. With this particular warp, you can trade the outward and inward distortions either by switching the Horizontal and Vertical options or by changing the Bend value from positive to negative or vice versa.

Figure 19.35: The Squeeze warp in action, pulling in the sides and pushing out the top and bottom. If you wanted the sides to push out and the top and bottom to pull in, you would simply change the warp axis from Horizontal to Vertical.

Twist

The Twist warp is essentially the same as the Twist distortion under the Effect »
Distort & Transform » Twist command covered earlier. See for yourself in **Figure
19.36**. Why does Illustrator provide a twist effect in two places? I really don't
know, but you should remember that there are still some important differences
between the two. If you use the Twist warp you also get to change horizontal and
vertical warp options, giving you more control and the ability to create more variations. Also, you can use the Twist warp on images! Because of these useful options,
the twist warp may be the twist distortion you'd want to use most of the time.

*Figure 19.36: The original
version is on the left, and the
version with the Twist warp
applied is on the right.*

CHAPTER 20

BECOMING MASTER OF THE RASTER

Used to be that pixel-based *raster* images were as useful in Illustrator as a can of Pepsi at a Coca-Cola sales conference. You could look at the raster image but couldn't touch it. Today, it's a different story. Not only does Illustrator allow you to import and manipulate raster images from programs such as Adobe Photoshop, but it also lets you create your own raster effects within Illustrator. You can apply transformations, filters, effects, or transparency techniques to images and even apply raster effects such as drop shadows, glows, and feathers that create raster images without actually losing your original path information.

Raster Effects on Vector Shapes

As I was going hog-wild in Chapter 19, I put off covering some of the filters and effects commands because they seemed more appropriate for this chapter. Some of Illustrator's effects do not simply manipulate path information; rather, they create displays of pixel images that conform to a path shape. These pixel images cannot be actually printed in anything except raster data.

For example, **Figure 20.1** shows a comparison between the type of drop shadow that was created by the drop shadow filter in older versions of Illustrator and the one created by today's drop shadow filter. The sharp edge of the old drop shadow was the best that Illustrator offered. The new drop shadow has a warm and fuzzy edge—an edge that could only come from pixels. Let's take a look at the various effects that can be applied to vector images.

Figure 20.1: The old drop shadow (left) doesn't hold a candle to today's drop shadow (right).

Drop Shadow Filters and Effects

Drop shadows can be applied as either filters or effects. While identical in their initial appearance, filters and effects are different in their characteristics. For more on those differences you'll want to stay tuned to this entire chapter and also check out Chapter 19. Choose Filter » Stylize » Drop Shadow or Effect » Stylize » Drop Shadow. The Drop Shadow dialog boxes appear as shown in **Figure 20.2**. Although most of the settings are identical, there are some differences between them. Here is the lowdown on each of the settings.

- **Mode:** This option controls how the drop shadow blends with any other objects behind it. The default setting, Multiply, creates the most realistic effect, which allows the colors of other objects to be added to the color of the shadow. I cover all the mode settings in painstaking detail in Chapter 19.

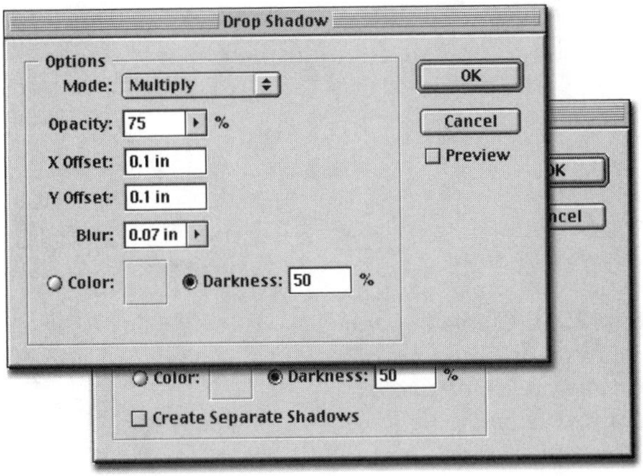

Figure 20.2: The Drop Shadow effect dialog box (top) provides a Preview checkbox. The Drop Shadow Filter dialog box (bottom) allows you to set separate shadows for multiple objects.

- **Opacity:** This controls how transparent the shadow appears. The higher the opacity, the less transparent the shadow will be. In real life, a low opacity setting would be similar to a low amount of light. However, there is no real-life equivalent to a 100 percent opacity setting.

- **X and Y Offsets:** This lets you choose the position of the shadow. The higher the numbers, the farther away from the object the shadow will be positioned. If you have not moved the zero point, positive X numbers move the shadow to the right; positive Y numbers move the shadow down.

- **Blur:** This controls how much blur is applied to the shadow. The higher the number, the more diffuse the shadow.

- **Darkness:** The Darkness setting starts with the basic color of the object and then adds black to make the shadow darker. Lowering the darkness setting makes the shadow closer to the color of the original object.

- **Color:** I don't know for sure, but there must be some planet where the shadows are green or red or pink. The Color setting lets you create shadows for those worlds. Or you can use it as a glow that can be positioned. After you click the Color radio button, click the small color box to open the color picker where you can choose your color.

- **Preview:** Use the Preview check box in the effect dialog box to preview the shadow as you change the settings.

- **Create Separate Shadows:** This setting is missing from the Drop Shadow effect dialog box. If you have selected multiple objects, you need to decide how they are creating the shadow. Turn this on to have each selected object cast its own shadow. Turn it off to create a single shadow from the selected objects as a group. **Figure 20.3** shows how the setting affects multiple objects.

Figure 20.3: Create Separate Shadows was turned on for the flame on the left and off for the flame on the right.

 Even though the dialog box for the drop shadow effect doesn't have the separate shadows setting, you can still create the same look. First group the objects and use the Layers palette to target the group. Then apply the effect to the group. The shadows will be applied to the group as a whole without creating individual shadows for each object.

Feathering

Feathering is the name of the technique in Photoshop that blurs selections into transparency. Those selections can then be filled with color, used to copy images, or deleted from layers. In Illustrator, the feather effect fades the edges of selected objects into transparency.

Choose Effect » Stylize » Feather. The amount of feathering is measured as a radius amount. This defines the size of the fade that is applied to the edge of the path. The higher the feather, the greater the blur that is applied to the image. Feathering in Illustrator is actually a live effect applied on a vector shape. That means that in Illustrator you can always resize the object, or better yet, change the feather value. You can't do either in Photoshop, because feathering there actually feathers the pixels in the selection. **Figure 20.4** shows the effect of feathering bubbles against a dark background.

Outer and Inner Glows

Glows are actually feathers that have colors rather than transparency. An outer glow extends out from an object. An inner glow extends from the edge of an object and moves inward or fills the entire object and moves toward the center. **Figure 20.5** shows the two dialog boxes for the outer and inner glow effects. I've created some sample glows shown in **Figure 20.6**.

Figure 20.4: Feathering allows you to create soft transitions between objects and the background.

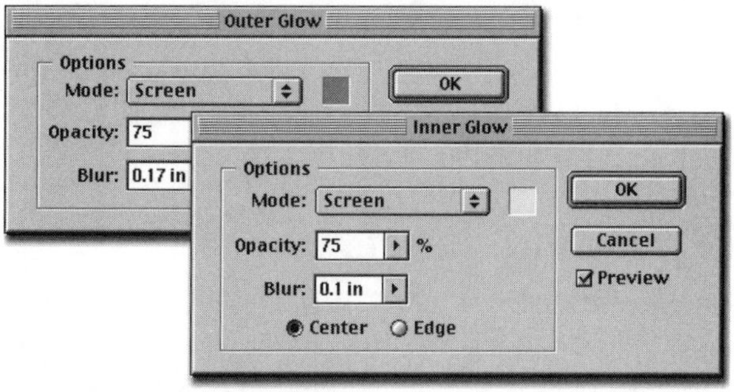

Figure 20.5: The dialog boxes for outer and inner glows. Notice the additional controls for the inner glows.

Figure 20.6: A lone snowflake takes on an outer glow (left) and an inner glow (right).

Here's how to control the glows.

- **Mode:** Like the drop shadows, this option controls how the glow blends with colors. For the inner glow, that is the color of the original object. For outer glows, it is the color of any objects behind the glow. The default setting of Screen causes the glows to lighten colors behind them.

 *The default setting of Screen makes it difficult to see an outer glow if it is on a white background. Move the object over a color to see the effect of the outer glow.*

- **Opacity:** This controls how transparent the glow appears. The higher the opacity, the less transparent the glow will be.

- **Blur:** This controls how much blur is applied to the glow. The higher the number, the more diffuse the glow.

- **Center:** The Center radio button for an inner glow creates a glow that starts from the center of the object. The lower the blur, the closer the glow will extend to the edge of the object, and the less you will see of the original fill of the object.

- **Edge:** The Edge radio button for an inner glow creates a glow that starts at the edge of the object and extends toward the center of the object, as demonstrated in Figure 20.6. The lower the blur, the closer the glow will be to the edge of the object, and the more you will see of the original fill of the object.

Expanding Effects

One way to discover what's happening behind the scenes when you apply the raster filters and effects is to look at what happens when you convert the live effect into dead objects—a procedure called *expanding*. (This is the equivalent of looking at the man behind the curtain.)

Select an object that has a raster effect such as the drop shadow applied to it. Choose Object » Expand Appearance. This separates the vector object from the effect, in this case the shadow. Then choose Object » Ungroup. As **Figure 20.7** shows, the drop shadow has been detached and you are left with the original vector object layered above the raster shadow.

 If you have used a filter, rather than an effect, you can separate the vector object from the raster shadow by simply choosing Object » Ungroup.

Figure 20.7: A sideways view of how the drop shadow effect actually layers vector objects over a raster image.

Filters and Effects for Raster Images

Illustrator also offers a large number of filters and effects that you can apply to both vector and raster images. Usually, however, these filters and effects provide a more dramatic result when applied to raster images, especially those with a wide range of color. If you've glanced at the Filter and Effect menus you've probably noticed that the there are several commands that appear under both menus. Your artwork will look the same whether you have applied a filter or an effect, but there are some differences between the two commands that aren't initially and readily visible to the eye. Briefly, when you apply a filter, you change the structure of an object, and that change is permanent. When you apply an effect, you change only the look, or appearance, of an object, not its underlying structure. Effects can be edited or deleted at any time. For more details, refer to Chapter 19. But before you do, here are few pointers to remember when working with filters and effects on raster images.

- As I mentioned in Chapter 19, once you apply a filter to an image, it cannot be modified or deleted (with the exception of the Edit » Undo command). Effects can be modified or deleted at any time.

- Effects require loads of RAM and a rather fast processor. You may find that complicated images can slow down screen redraw.

- The bottom set of filters can be applied only to raster images. The bottom set of effects can be used on either vector or raster images.

- You must first embed the raster image within the Illustrator file to apply the commands under the Filter menu. This adds to the size of the Illustrator file. (Embedding will be covered later in this chapter.) However, you do not have to embed the raster image if you apply the command from the Effect menu.

- Most of the filters and effects work only within the RGB colorspace. So you may have to switch from CMYK to RGB to apply a command.

Photoshop-Compatible Filters

When you install Illustrator, you can install 50-some plug-ins divided into ten different categories. As stated earlier, these plug-ins appear in both the Filter and Effect menus. These filters are the same ones that ship with Photoshop. As a general rule, they work best on tonal images rather than flat art. It would take hundreds of pages to show you the results of all the filters and all their variations using different settings. However, I put together a small sample of nine of the different categories of the plug-ins in **Figure 20.8**. (I skipped the Video category because it is primarily

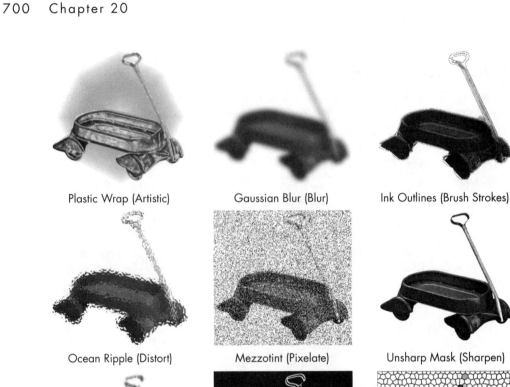

Plastic Wrap (Artistic)   Gaussian Blur (Blur)   Ink Outlines (Brush Strokes)

Ocean Ripple (Distort)   Mezzotint (Pixelate)   Unsharp Mask (Sharpen)

Waterpaper (Sketch)   Glowing Edges (Stylize)   Stained Glass (Texture)

Figure 20.8: Nine of the Photoshop plug-ins that are installed along with Illustrator. The categories are listed in parentheses next to the command name.

used for images from video cameras.) Looking through ten categories can be a little overwhelming. Here's a brief summary of what each category of filters does.

- **Artistic:** Tries to simulate traditional or natural media such as pastels or sponge painting. These are excellent for making your artwork appear less computer-generated and more hand-created.

-  **Blurs:** The Gaussian blur acts similarly to the Feather command. However, where Feather will fade only to the edge of a vector path, Gaussian Blur fades the image so that it lies on either side of the path. The Radial Blur causes the image to look as if it were spinning.

- **Brush Strokes:** Similar to the Artistic category, these create effects such as those created with pen and paintbrush strokes.

- **Distort:** These filters do not change the colors of the pixels in the image. Rather, they move them in various ways, causing distortions.

- **Pixelate:** Groups pixels of similar colors to simulate various effects, such as an impressionistic look.

- **Sharpen:** Allows you to apply the Unsharp Mask command, which helps improve the sharpness or focus of scanned images.

- **Sketch:** Adds texture to images, simulating traditional, hand-created effects.

- **Stylize:** Allows you to apply the Glowing Edges command for a neonlike glow.

- **Texture:** Adds an overlay texture, such as grain, glass or tiles, to images that simulate traditional media.

- **Video:** Contains two corrections for working with images from video sources.

Pointing to Filters

Choose Edit » Preferences » Plug-ins & Scratch Disk (Illustrator 10 » Preferences » Plug-ins & Scratch Disk in Mac OS 10.1) to change which folder or directory Illustrator looks at to find the filters and effects. In theory, you could point Illustrator to your Photoshop Plug-ins folder. Don't do it! The Illustrator Plug-ins folder contains your startup file along with tools and other important parts of the program. If you want, create an alias or shortcut of your Photoshop Plug-ins folder and put that inside the Illustrator Plug-ins folder.

You can also use this technique to bring in third-party (non-Adobe) Photoshop filters into Illustrator. These include filters from Alien Skin and the KPT filters.

 Don't trash all the Photoshop plug-ins inside the Illustrator Plug-ins folder. If the Photoshop filters and effects are not available, errors will appear when you create new documents that use the default startup files. If you don't wish these effects and filters to be present, you need to create startup files that don't use any of the Photoshop filters or effects such as Feather, Inner Glow, Outer Glow, and Drop Shadow. Or you can create an alias or shortcut of the Photoshop Plug-ins folder and place that in your Illustrator Plug-ins folder. This will avoid the error messages.

Converting Pixels into Vectors

Despite the lack of a sophisticated auto trace tool, Illustrator does have two commands that can convert pixel images into vector objects. The first is the Object Mosaic filter, which converts pixel information into small rectangles. The other is the Photo Crosshatch, which creates the effect of an old-fashioned custom halftone screen.

Finding the Mosaic in an Image

Imagine you had a large photograph that covered your bathroom floor. If you could apply it, the Object Mosaic filter would carve the photograph up into individual tiles (rectangles) that would create the look of the photograph on the floor. The smaller the rectangles, the more detail in the finished image.

Select an image and choose Filter » Create » Object Mosaic to convert the image into a series of colored rectangles. The rectangles imitate pixels—and each rectangle takes up the same amount of room on disk and in memory as a similarly sized pixel would—but you can edit the rectangles just as if you had drawn them with the rectangle tool.

When you choose Filter » Create » Object Mosaic, Illustrator displays the dialog box shown in **Figure 20.9**. It contains a lot of options, but they're fairly easy to use.

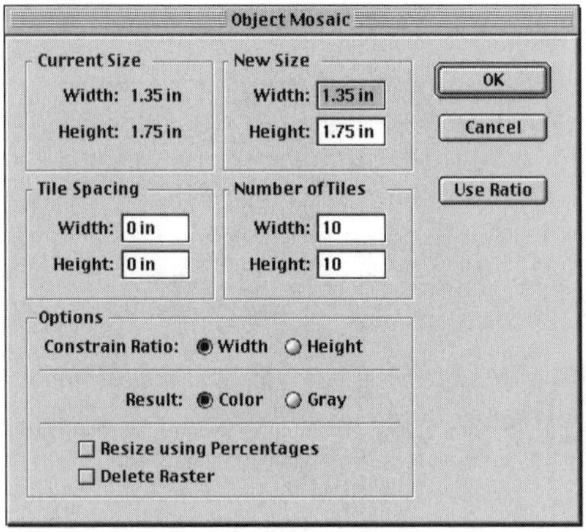

Figure 20.9: Use this dialog box to convert an embedded image into a series of object-oriented rectangles.

- **Current Size, New Size:** The Current Size area shows the dimensions of the image in points. You can adjust the size of the mosaic picture by entering new values in the New Size option boxes.

- **Tile Spacing:** Enter the amount of space (grout) you want Illustrator to insert between rectangles in the Tile Spacing option boxes. To make the rectangles fit snugly together, leave the values set to 0.

- **Number of Tiles:** Enter into the Number of Tiles option boxes the number of rectangles that Illustrator should draw horizontally and vertically. If you enter a Width value of 40, for example, Illustrator draws 40 rectangles across the width of the image. The greater the number, the more detail in the finished tiles.

- **Use Ratio:** If you want the New Size and the Number of Tiles values to conform to the ratio of the original image, you can enter the desired values into either the two Width or the two Height option boxes and then click the Use Ratio button. For example, let's say you want the mosaic to be 300 points wide with 30 tiles across. First, enter each value into the appropriate Width option box. Then select the Constrain Ratio Width radio button to tell Illustrator to change the Height values and leave the Width values intact. And finally, click the Use Ratio button to automatically adjust the Height values so that you'll get a proportional mosaic made up of perfect squares.

- **Color/Grayscale:** If you want Illustrator to fill the tiles with CMYK colors, select the Color radio button. Select the Gray option to fill the rectangles with shades of black.

- **Resize using Percentages:** If you want to use percentages to determine the change in width and height instead of specifying the exact dimensions in the New Size option boxes, select this option.

- **Delete Raster:** Select this option to delete the image after converting it to a mosaic. To retain the original image, turn off the check box.

After you apply the Object Mosaic command, Illustrator draws the rectangular tiles and groups them to facilitate editing.

 An interesting way to modify the tiles is to choose Object » Transform » Transform Each, where you can rotate, scale, or move the tiles ever so slightly with the Random setting turned on. This simulates the look of an old, broken-down bathroom floor.

If you want the mosaic rectangles to look like true mosaic tiles, you need to add highlights, such as those shown in **Figure 20.10**. I started out with the top photograph. I used Filter » Create » Object Mosaic to create a mosaic 40 tiles wide and 21 tiles tall. In the second example, I cloned the mosaic by choosing Edit » Copy and then Edit » Paste in Front. Then I used the Transform Each command to shrink the tiles to 80 percent horizontally and 20 percent vertically. (Random was turned off.) After nudging the tiles into position, I filled them with white and set their strokes to None.

To create the bottom example in **Figure 20.10**, I again cloned the mosaic. Then I used Object » Transform » Transform Each to reduce each tile to 60 percent horizontally and vertically. To lighten the tiles, I chose Filter » Colors » Saturate (a command I discuss in the next chapter) and entered a value of –30 percent. And I set the strokes to None. That's it; I didn't even have to move the tiles.

Figure 20.10:The top image was transformed using Object Mosaic and then highlights were added using Transform Each and changing the colors.

Mosaics can slow down Illustrator's redraw speed dramatically, and they can take a very long time to print. If you're not sure what kind of effect you want to apply, try it out on a small mosaic pattern with ten tiles or fewer. Then after you have the effect figured out, apply it to a larger mosaic. This will save you a considerable amount of time and help to prevent general exasperation.

Hatching a Sketch

With the Photo Crosshatch filter, Illustrator will transform an embedded graphic into a vector object by approximating the graphic with a number of little lines or hatches. Illustrator first converts the graphic to grayscale and then applies hatches to those gray values that fall within a certain range. **Figure 20.11** displays the same image converted with the Photo Crosshatch filter, with the dialog box showing the different settings.

Figure 20.11: By varying the hatch
settings I was able to change the look
from a perfect halftone screen to a more
sketched appearance.

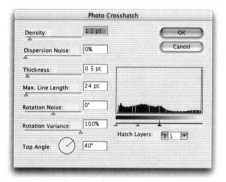

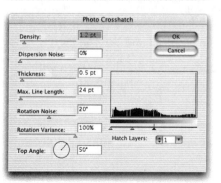

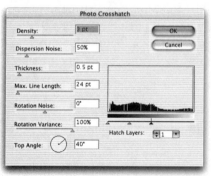

Unlike the Object Mosaic filter, the Photo Crosshatch does not give you the option of keeping the original image. So always work on a copy of your original. Also, the filter can easily create more objects than McDonald's has sold hamburgers. Your best bet is to put the image on its own layer so you can easily select or work with the tremendous number of objects.

Each and every time you choose the Filter » Pen & Ink » Photo Crosshatch command you're presented with the Photo Crosshatch dialog box, shown in Figure 20.11. The different settings let you take the static, uniform hatches that make up each layer and subtly adjust them as a whole to give the final effect a more realistic appearance.

The settings work as follows:

- **Density:** This setting dictates the distance between the lines that form the crosshatch. Use the slider bar to choose a value from 0.5 to 10 pixels. Unlike what you might expect, the higher the density, the fewer objects on the page.

- **Dispersion Noise:** This option affects the Density setting. For example, with the Dispersion Noise set to 50 percent and the Density at 3 points, the distance between the hatches can range from a maximum of 7.5 pixels all the way down to 0 points. Well, not quite zero. In fact, the minimum distance is dictated by the Thickness setting. A Thickness of 0.5 point means that the minimum distance will be 0.5 point. Enter a nonzero value in the Dispersion Noise option box to give the result a more realistic look.

- **Thickness:** Choose a stroke weight for all the hatches anywhere between 0.1 and 10 points.

- **Max. Line Length:** This value determines the longest length of any hatch.

- **Rotation Noise:** To vary the amount that each hatch is rotated from the default, enter a value into the Rotation Noise option box. For example, with a value of 20 degrees and a Top Angle of 50 degrees, the hatches on the top layer could vary anywhere between 30 and 70 degrees.

- **Rotation Variance:** If you have more than one hatch layer, then with this setting you can choose the amount of the angular difference between the different layers.

- **Top Angle:** No matter how many hatch layers you have, the hatches on the topmost layer will appear at this angle (plus or minus the value in the Rotation Noise option box).

Hatch Layers: You can choose to have from one to eight hatch layers. Each of these layers can cover a different range of grayscale values.

Linked or Embedded

Before I get into the discussion of whether to link or embed images, let's back up and review how you get images into Illustrator in the first place. There are three ways to import raster images into Illustrator.

 Choose File » Open to open your image as a new Illustrator file. This automatically embeds your image.

You can use the Clipboard and drag an image from an application, such as Photoshop, and drop it—kerplunk—onto an Illustrator window. This also automatically embeds your image.

You can use the File » Place command to either link or embed your image.

This brings us to our dilemma, one of those important issues like paper or plastic, and there are important advantages to both sides. When you bring a raster image into Illustrator, you have to decide how you want the information handled. If you choose Link, Illustrator creates a link to the image file on disk. All the information needed to actually print the file is stored outside the Illustrator file. What is inside the Illustrator file is actually only a preview image, which adds minimal file space, regardless of how much space the original image takes up on disk. What can you do to your linked image in Illustrator? You can use the transformation tools to scale, rotate, reflect, or shear the image. And you can apply those commands found under the Effect menu that I mentioned earlier in the chapter.

 If you link an image, don't throw away the original file. Illustrator needs that file to print the linked image.

 If you happen to place a file as a link and all you see is an outlined box with an X, don't panic. It means the file was saved without a preview in its original application. If you have access to the original application, go back and save the file with a preview.

If you deselect the Link option in the Place dialog box, Illustrator imports all the pixels into the illustration and converts the pixels into PostScript code, an operation known as *embedding* (or *parsing* in the olden days). Because Illustrator incorporates all the pixel information into the file, the image will add to the file size. However, if an image is embedded, you can apply the special features such as the Photoshop filters or effects to images.

So, should you embed or link images? Choose link if you never expect to manipulate the image within Illustrator. If you only link you can skip the rest of this chapter; however, you can't become a master of the raster if your pixels are all residing outside the Illustrator file.

You should embed if you want to take advantage of the filters within Illustrator. You also need embedded images to use the new and nifty liquify tools. And the new enveloping features won't work with linked images, with the exceptions of TIFFs, JPEGs and GIFs. If you have a linked image, you can easily embed it. Select the image and choose Embed from the Links palette menu.

If you are unsure as to whether or not an image is embedded or linked, look at the image in the document. Linked images have two diagonal lines that go from corner to corner. Embedded images do not. You can also check the Links palette as shown in **Figure 20.12**. The embed icon lets you know the image is incorporated into the Illustrator file. The Links palette is great for identifying, monitoring, and updating your links. For more details on the inner workings of links and the Links palette, see Chapter 4.

Figure 20.12: The embedded icon in the Links palette tells you that all the information necessary to print the file is embedded within the Illustrator document.

Illustrator doesn't completely ignore linked images. Whether an image is linked or embedded, Illustrator lets you move, scale, rotate, reflect, or shear it. You can view black-and-white versions of any image in the outline mode (if the Show Images In Outline check box is turned on in the Document Setup dialog box).

Hoist that Raster and Rake those Pixels

You know you've finally reached the enviable status of Hopeless Computer Dweeb when you know the meaning of the word "rasterize." In regular human terms, it means to convert objects to pixels. You probably aren't aware of it, but your computer is constantly rasterizing things. Every time you edit an object, Illustrator and your system software rasterize paths to display them as pixels onscreen. Illustrator rasterizes characters of type to screen pixels. And when you print your artwork, your printer rasterizes the mathematical path definitions as teeny printer pixels.

Legend has it that the word "rasterize" was coined during the early days of monitor development. Your monitor displays stuff on screen by projecting pixels in horizontal rows. It's almost as if the monitor were raking pixels across the screen, which is where the word raster—Latin for rake—comes in. Nowadays, rasterize is used for any kind of pixel creation, whether onscreen, inside a printer, or inside a program such as Illustrator.

You might think that the only way to create pixel images in Illustrator is to bring them in from a pixel program such as Photoshop. But you would be wrong. You can use the Object » Rasterize command to convert priceless vector objects into mundane pixels.

Illustrator 10's live effects feature has greatly reduced the importance of the Rasterize command. For example, rasterizing an image used to be the only way to apply Photoshop filters to Illustrator artwork. Now, however, you can apply the same commands under the Effect menu.

Still, there are a few good reasons to rasterize within Illustrator.

- Object » Rasterize is the only way to convert *all* Illustrator objects into grayscale. The Filter » Colors » Convert to Grayscale command works on most Illustrator paths but does not work on gradients, patterns, and linked images.

- Object » Rasterize lets you combine two raster images or raster and vector images into one raster image. You can use this technique to help clean up or enhance photographs.

- When you rasterize objects to a black-and-white image using the Bitmap option, you can then select a Fill color in the Color palette to specify the color of the black pixels. For this technique to work, make sure you check Transparent for your Background option. Add the fact that those black-and-white images take up relatively little room on disk, and you have a great means for creating quick texture patterns.

- You can rasterize raster images, too! That's a great way to convert CMYK files to grayscale.

The Rasterizing Options

When you choose Object » Rasterize, Illustrator greets you with the dialog box shown in **Figure 20.13**. This is where you control all the aspects of the final rasterized image.

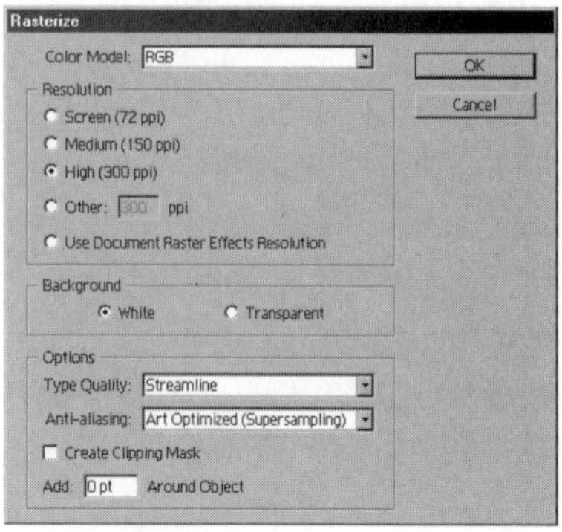

Figure 20.13: Use the Rasterize dialog box to convert vector objects into pixels. Or you can change the number of colors and pixels inside an image.

- **Color Model:** Use this pop-up menu to specify whether you want to create a color image, a grayscale image, or a black-and-white image. If you are working in the CMYK color space, your choice for color is CMYK; RGB documents let you choose RGB. For more information about the wonderful world of RGB and CMYK color spaces, read Chapter 14.

  To convert a selection to a grayscale image, select the Grayscale option. Select Bitmap if you want the image to contain only black-and-white pixels.

- **Resolution:** Select one of the first three radio buttons or enter a value into the Other option box to specify the number of pixels in the image. Select Screen for 72 ppi, Medium for 150 ppi, and High for 300 ppi. **Figure 20.14** demonstrates the effect of converting vector artwork using the three different settings.

The new Use Document Raster Effects Resolution allows you to use global resolution settings. Illustrator accesses these settings when you apply filters and effects to both raster and vector images. You can established those global settings by choosing Effects » Document Raster Effects Resolution.

As you can see in the figure, a high-resolution image looks smoother than a low-resolution one. However, the higher the resolution, the more space the image takes up on disk. As a general rule of thumb, an image with twice the resolution takes up four times as much space on disk.

Figure 20.14: Clockwise, the effects of converting an image at Screen, Medium, and High resolutions.

- **Background:** Choose between White and Transparent. White adds white pixels wherever there are any transparent areas in the image. Transparent leaves the transparent areas clear in the raster image. The transparency option creates an image similar to the transparent layers in Photoshop.

- **Type Quality:** Choose Streamline if you want your type rasterized in a fashionably sleek way. Choose Outline if you want your type rasterized on the bulkier side.

- **Anti-aliasing:** Anti-aliasing adds a very soft blur to the edges of an image and softens the transition between neighboring pixels. Version 10 now gives you more options to determine the type of anti-aliasing to apply to your image. Choosing None will apply no anti-aliasing. Use this option when rasterizing line art where you want to maintain hard, crisp, albeit somewhat jagged, edges. Choose Art Optimized to apply anti-aliasing to artwork where type isn't the focal point of the piece. Choose Type Optimized when your artwork contains primarily type. **Figure 20.15** compares an image created with and without anti-aliasing. The image on the left has a much more jagged appearance.

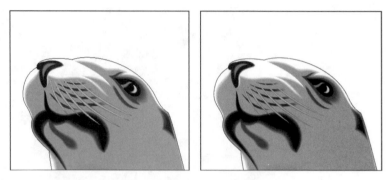

Figure 20.15: An image rasterized at 150 ppi with Art Optimized Anti-aliasing (right) and no Anti-aliasing (left).

 Create Clipping Mask: Choose this option to create a path that is used to mask transparent portions of the original vector objects to keep them transparent. For more information on working with masks, see Chapter 17.

Add Space Around Object: This option lets you automatically add extra space around an image. If you've chosen a white background, you add extra white around the image. If you've chosen a transparent background, you add extra transparency to the image.

 Because you can apply the transparency option to rasterized images, I find there are very few instances where you will need to create masks when you rasterize.

Lowering Resolutions

When you embed an image into Illustrator, all the pixels are contained in the file. If you use any of the scale tools to make the image smaller, you increase the resolution of the file. If your image was the correct resolution to begin with, you don't need the higher resolution.

You can use the Object » Rasterize command to lower the resolution of the image. Just make sure you won't want to scale the image up later on. Changing the number of pixels in this way is called *resampling*, because Illustrator has to generate new pixels by averaging the old ones. In technospeak, this averaging is called *interpolating*. Raising the resolution value is never a good idea; Illustrator isn't smart enough to generate detail out of thin air, so doing this just increases the number of pixels without providing any benefit.

If you're an experienced Photoshop user, you may be wondering what kind of interpolation Illustrator uses when resampling images. When Anti-alias is turned on, Illustrator uses bilinear interpolation, which means the program averages five pixels at a time. (Photoshop's more sophisticated bicubic interpolation factors in nine pixels.) When Anti-alias is off, Illustrator doesn't average pixels at all; it just throws away the pixels that it deems inappropriate. (This is the same as Photoshop's "nearest neighbor" interpolation.)

Fusing Objects and Images

You can fuse objects and imported images into a single image using Object » Rasterize. For example, I started with the image of the train on the left side of **Figure 20.16**. I wanted to add some perfect circles and lines to enhance the image.

Figure 20.16: Starting with an ordinary image (left), I added some circles and lines and then rasterized the paths into the image (right).

I then checked the resolution, in this case 300 ppi, using Window » Document Info palette. You need to choose either Linked Images or Embedded Images, depending on which you used, from the palette pop-up menu to view Resolution data. I selected the image and all the paths and chose Object » Rasterize. I selected the Grayscale Color Model option, used 300 as the resolution, selected Art Optimized Anti-Aliasing to soften the edges of the paths, and selected a Transparent background. Illustrator rasterized the paths into the image, as you can see on the right side of Figure 20.16.

Although Photoshop now offers its own object-oriented tools—including the pen and shape tools—Illustrator still provides a much wider range of drawing options. So if you find that you can't accomplish a certain effect in Photoshop, try turning the job over to Illustrator. You can use the File » Export » Photoshop (PSD) command to get the image back into Photoshop.

You can also use this technique to add a special colored background behind transparent images.

Outlining Objects

The Outline Object effect lets you create borders around images. Unlike some less-sophisticated programs, Illustrator recognizes transparency and even allows you to create outlines around shapes.

1. **Start with a placed Photoshop image. Be sure to embed the image. In the Photoshop Import dialog box, check Convert Photoshop layers to objects.**

Although you could use a flattened image such as a TIFF file, I prefer the native Photoshop file, especially if it is on a transparency layer. This lets you outline around the shape of the image, not just in a rectangle.

If you flatten the Photoshop layers, you can apply the rest of these steps to the image as a whole. However, by converting the Photoshop layers as individual Illustrator objects, you need to target the individual layers in the Layers palette to apply the outline.

 If your Photoshop file has a clipping path assigned to it, you need to change the path back to a regular path in Photoshop or release the path within Illustrator. I cover clipping paths and masks in Illustrator in Chapter 17.

2. **Target the image in the Layers palette.**

Click the circle next to the name of the image to target it. If you have multiple Illustrator objects, click the specific object.

3. **Add the stroke to the object.**

This is simple; just select the Add New Stroke command in the Appearance palette.

4. **Choose Effect » Path » Outline Object.**

Nothing much will happen except the command will appear listed under the Stroke in the Appearance palette. If your image suddenly disappears, though, it's because you forgot to target the Stroke in Step 3. Just drag the Outline Object listing under the Stroke listing so it appears as shown in **Figure 20.17**.

5. **Target the Stroke listing in the Appearance palette and choose a color.**

The reason nothing much happened in Step 4 is that you don't have any color chosen for your stroke. When you target the stroke listing, you can then choose a color from either the Color palette or the Swatches palette. As soon as you do, the outline appears around the image as shown in Figure 20.17.

Figure 20.17: To outline the area of a placed image, make sure the Outline Object command sits inside the Stroke listing of the Appearance palette as shown here. Notice the transparency indicated by the document grid.

 "Oh, good grief," I can hear you say. "Do I have to do all that every time I want to create a frame around an image? Isn't that a little time consuming?" Well, fret not. You actually have to do all that only once. After that you just need to save the settings as an image style that can be applied to other images with a single click.

"Cool," I can hear you say, "Now if only Illustrator provided a cropping tool." In fact, Illustrator provides arguably the best cropping capabilities of any program on earth. But it's a big topic that's equally applicable to objects and images, so I won't discuss it here. Turn to Chapter 17, and keep an eye out for the many appearances of the word "mask."

The Rasterize Effect

As useful as Object » Rasterize is, it is a permanent commitment to a specific resolution and color mode. If you don't feel comfortable making those decisions, you can use Effect » Rasterize » to apply the command as an effect. Effects allow you to change the *appearance* of an object without actually altering the original object. The other great thing about effects is that you can modify or delete the effect at a later date. For further details on effects, see Chapter 19.

In **Figure 20.18** I chose Effect » Rasterize and rasterized the logo at 72 ppi. I also added a white background and added 18 points of space around the object. You'll notice that the Rasterize effect displays in the Appearance palette. If you suddenly have a change of heart, simply drag the Rasterize effect to the palette's trash and your artwork will be "re-vectorized."

Figure 20.18: An object rasterized with an effect allows for modifications later.

Trading Artwork with Photoshop

Illustrator and Photoshop have been able to trade paths and pixels back and forth for a few years now. You can copy and paste, drag and drop, export, or just open. The results vary depending on which direction you drag—from Illustrator into Photoshop or vice versa—and what kind of objects you have selected. The following sections tell all.

Drag (or Copy/Paste) Objects into Photoshop

You can drag objects from Illustrator into Photoshop. Because Photoshop does not quite have the sophisticated drawing capabilities of Illustrator, you may find it easier to work in Illustrator and then drag objects into Photoshop. But you should keep the following in mind.

 You must have enough RAM to run Illustrator and Photoshop at the same time. These days that could mean easily 128 MB of RAM split between the two programs.

- Make sure that an image window is open in Photoshop so you have a place to drop the objects from Illustrator.

- You can drag any path or text object from Illustrator into Photoshop.

- By default, Illustrator objects are copied as raster images

- Although you can drag placed images from Illustrator into Photoshop, the resolution of the image will be resampled to the resolution of the Photoshop file.

- The placed objects appear in Photoshop as an independent layer. This permits you to move the objects into place before applying them to the underlying image.

- Hold the Shift key as you drag to position the objects in the center of the Photoshop window.

- Hold the Cmd/Ctrl key as you drag to place Illustrator paths as Photoshop paths. These paths can then be used for selections, strokes, or clipping paths.

- You can also copy and paste from Illustrator into Photoshop. In which case, a handy dialog box asks you if you would like to convert the paths to pixels, paths, or a shape layer. If you copy and paste from Illustrator into Photoshop and you don't get a dialog box asking your preference, don't panic. Go to Edit » Preferences »Files & Clipboard (Illustrator » Preferences » Files & Clipboard in Mac OS 10.1) and be sure to check AICB. Check either Preserve Paths or Preserve Appearance. Both will enable the Paste dialog box to appear.

Exporting from Illustrator

As handy as it is to drag from Illustrator into Photoshop, the best route uses File » Export—especially if you have any editable type in your Illustrator file. You don't have to lose the ability to edit type when you move from Illustrator to Photoshop.

Choose File » Export. In the Export dialog box, choose Photoshop (PSD) from the Format pop-up menu. You will then see the Photoshop Options dialog box shown in **Figure 20.19**. Most of the options have been either explained earlier or are self-explanatory, but here are a few points to note:

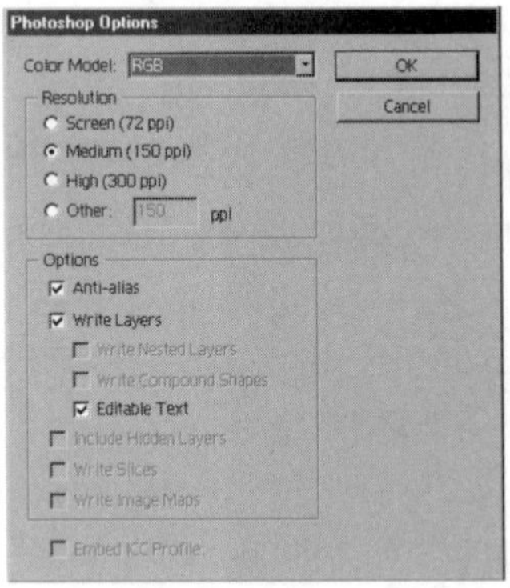

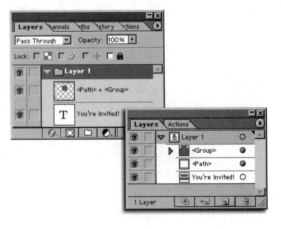

Figure 20.19: The Photoshop Options dialog box allows you to control how Illustrator layers and objects are translated into Photoshop.

Check the Write Layers option to enable your Illustrator layer to be translated into Photoshop layers. **Figure 20.20** shows how the layers from Illustrator are converted into Photoshop layers.

Figure 20.20: A comparison of the layers in an Illustrator file (bottom) next to how those layers are converted into Photoshop layers (top). Notice that the text in Illustrator is converted into Photoshop text.

Check the Editable Text option if your artwork contains text. The text will be translated into a Photoshop text layer.

 Illustrator can't export area type or path type as editable text in Photoshop.

Because there are no nested layers in Photoshop, the Write Nested Layers option writes each top-level sublayer from Illustrator to a separate Photoshop layer. For more on layers see Chapter 23.

The Write Compound Shapes option creates a Photoshop shape layer (a vector layer in Photoshop) for each Illustrator compound shape.

Of course, you can also export the Illustrator artwork as a TIFF file and then open it in Photoshop. But that simply creates a flat image without any layers or editable text. Layers and text are too valuable to lose.

From Photoshop into Illustrator

If you're an old-time Photoshop/Illustrator user, you are probably used to dragging images from Photoshop into Illustrator. You are also used to losing any transparency that was in the Photoshop layer. A much better solution is to save the Photoshop file with its layers and then use Illustrator's File » Place to import the image.

When you import Photoshop files, a dialog box appears that asks how you want to handle Photoshop's multiple layers (**Figure 20.21**).

Figure 20.21: Before you place Photoshop files, you need to choose how to handle multiple layers.

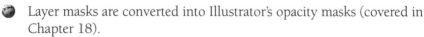

- Convert Photoshop layers to objects maintains all the individual layers with their transparencies.

- Flatten Photoshop layers to single image merges all the individual layers but does maintain the overall transparency of the merged layers.

If you have layer effects, type layers, and layer masks, they are converted as follows:

- Type layers and layer styles are rendered into pixels.

- Layer masks are converted into Illustrator's opacity masks (covered in Chapter 18).

PART FIVE
GOING PUBLIC

CREATING WEB GRAPHICS

As a longtime print person, I was skeptical when I first heard about the Web. "A fad," I thought. "It'll never catch on." Oh, all right, I was wrong, OK? Hey, I was in good company (move over, Mr. Gates). Now, of course, I've moved on, and I create Web sites, banner ads, and animations without the least trace of egg on my face. As it has for so many, the Web has become an important part of my life. It's the same with Illustrator—for years Illustrator had very primitive, almost negligible, Web features. Today, though, Illustrator's Web features are so robust it is possible to create exceptional Web graphics and animations without using any other software.

This chapter looks at all the options you have for creating Web graphics within Illustrator. This includes the traditional formats such as GIF and JPEG as well as newer formats such as PNG, SWF, and SVG. (I'll explain all these acronyms in just a bit.) I'll show you how to add special code within Illustrator so that your Web graphics contain links to other Web sites and how to take advantage of Illustrator's new SVG filters to create awe-inspiring graphic effects without creating awe-inspiringly large files.

The Ascent of Web Graphics

When Adobe Illustrator version 1.1 was released for the Macintosh way back in 1987, the computer graphics world was a very different place. Users produced graphics onscreen, but the final product was always printed on paper. Designs produced with Illustrator could be used in advertisements, newsletters, fliers, and a host of other print-based publications. During this time, the quality of the graphics' appearance onscreen was unimportant. What really mattered was how the illustrations looked when printed.

Almost 15 years later, Adobe Illustrator 10 is released into a much different environment. While print remains a very important medium, the Web has grown exponentially, and the demand for original images continuously increases. There are more similarities then differences between Web and print images, but these differences must be considered in the production of Web graphics. The essential difference between Web and print graphics is also the easiest to understand: unlike traditional print graphics, Web graphics must be optimized to look their best onscreen, because that is where they will be viewed.

Illustrator 9 took the first major steps into the Web graphics arena with the addition of features such as Web-safe swatch libraries, image maps, and the Save for Web application. With these new features, Web graphics could be created entirely in Illustrator and exported to a Web-friendly file format such as JPG or GIF. Illustrator 10 has several new features that allow the creation of more interactive, powerful, and polished Web graphics. With these new features, Illustrator 10 is no longer a primary tool just for the creation of print graphics, but for the creation of Web graphics as well.

Differences between Print and Web Graphics

Many users who have been creating traditional print images often ask why there is such a big difference between graphics for the screen and graphics for the Web. A picture is just a picture, right? Well, not quite. There are several issues to consider when producing Web graphics. I'll discuss Web graphics extensively in this chapter and the next two, so this is a good time to introduce the important differences between print graphics and Web graphics.

 In the past, most of the instruction I gave involved teaching legions of traditional, print-trained designers about the constraints of the Web. Nowadays, it's just as likely for a designer to have started out in Web design and need training to do good work for print.

The most important thing to remember is this: For print, everything serves print quality. The file has to have enough detail, and color must be absolutely correct. For the Web, everything serves file size. While detail and color accuracy are both important, they can be sacrificed to get the graphic down to a size that won't make impatient Web surfers give up on your Web page. Here is how those priorities play out in graphics production.

- **File size, great and small:** Illustrator files can get quite large—especially when the illustrations have raster objects in them. I have seen illustrations that used more than 100 MB of disk space when complete. When the image is printed, of course it doesn't really matter how much disk space the file takes up. Print images have to be huge because a printing press is a high-quality, high-resolution output device that mercilessly reveals lack of detail and other flaws. On the Web, however, disk space translates to download time, which is critical when your audience uses regular, slow dial-up modems. (I won't make any predictions about the future of dial-up so that I don't have to say I was wrong again later.) Studies have shown that the average user will wait less then 10 seconds for a page to download before getting bored and moving on to another page. Illustrator's tools not only support prepress quality, but they can also crunch a file down for the Web.

- **Resolution:** Print designers must usually supply 300-dpi images to get good quality on a printing press. This kind of resolution would be absolute overkill on the Web, where most monitors are set for 72 or 96 dpi. It's a good thing, too…imagine how hard it would be to make 300-dpi images download quickly over a 56K modem! So if you're a print designer moving to the Web, lower your resolution expectations. And if you're going the other way—from Web to print design—get used to much higher resolutions and much bigger files. Don't ignore this fact, because if you supply Web-resolution images that look embarrassingly bad on press, you're not going to look so good either.

- **Formats at odds:** Print and Web images have radically different requirements for file formats. Print veterans know that TIFF is the format of choice for bitmaps, and EPS for vector line art. Web designers think in terms of GIF for flat color art and JPEG for photographs and continuous tones, with Flash or SVG thrown in for vector art. Why such a large difference in formats across media? Again, it all goes back to the priorities of each medium. TIFF and EPS meet the print requirement for quality, while GIF and JPEG meet the Web requirement of maximum data compression.

- **Slicing things up:** Print graphics generally come in one piece. Web graphics are often sliced into sections and displayed as a reconstituted matrix of smaller graphics. While it's up for debate whether or not this is a more efficient method for displaying large graphics, slicing allows designers to accomplish several important tasks. Firstly, behaviors such as rollovers or pop-ups can be associated with the different slices. Secondly, each slice can be optimized differently for efficient rendering by the Web browser.

- **Can I touch it?:** Here's how print graphics work: you look at them. On the other hand, Web graphics can be designed to interact with the user. For example, Web images can be designed to execute hyperlinks, disappear, reappear, or animate when clicked. Sometimes these images support a necessary function on the Web page, such as allowing the user to receive more information or make a purchase. Illustrator 10 takes interactivity to a new level by letting you control the appearance of graphics from a database—a very important feature for e-commerce.

- **Getting a move on:** On the Web, animation is increasingly popular as more designers use animated sequences to set their pages apart. Whatever the purpose, there are several features in Illustrator to help make Web graphics both responsive and compelling.

- **The perception of color:** Because Web graphics are designed to be displayed on the screen rather than printed, they use (or, I should say, they *should* use) a different color system. Many who have designed for print have used the familiar CMYK color system, in which colors are produced from varying amounts of cyan, magenta, yellow, and black inks. However, computer monitors use the RGB color model to display color. I discuss RGB and CMYK extensively in Chapter 14. If you create Web graphics in CMYK, they may look fine, but you'll unnecessarily limit the range of colors available to you. If you create print graphics in RGB, they won't color-separate for the press (except under very specific workflows) and may cause delays in the job.

Another important difference is that printed color comes from a single source—a printing press—which makes it relatively easy to control the colors in a print run. On the other hand, the computer monitors all over the Web—which is to say, all over the world—can be calibrated in different ways. For example, Windows monitors are usually set to a gamma value of 2.2, and Mac monitors are usually set to 1.8. In reality, most of the monitors out there are simply out of adjustment, since most people wouldn't know how to calibrate their monitors even if they were told that it was possible. So, sadly, you can never be sure that, to the surfers out there, the colors in your Web graphics will look anything like you wanted them to. Web designers can get colors right only on their own monitors and hope for the best.

(Web) Graphically Speaking

Just in case you've been living in a cave for the past five years, here's a quick glossary of terms you should know when working with Web graphics.

- **Browser:** The software that people use to view Web pages. The two most popular browsers are Microsoft Internet Explorer and Netscape Navigator (part of Netscape Communicator), but there are many others as well.

- **Flash (SWF):** A file format for publishing vector artwork and sounds in interactive Web sites and animations. SWF stands for Shockwave Flash. (The proper name for these files is Macromedia Shockwave Flash, although many people call them Flash or SWF files.) Originally, you could create Flash (SWF) documents only using Macromedia software. However, the format has become so popular that other applications, such as Illustrator and Adobe LiveMotion, also let you export as Flash (SWF) files. You can export primitive Flash (SWF) animations— no sounds, no interactivity—from Illustrator. To create more sophisticated animations and Web sites, you need an application such as Adobe LiveMotion or Macromedia Flash.

- **GIF:** Short for Graphic Interchange Format. This is a format developed by CompuServe (now part of AOL Time Warner). It allows you to save graphics that are much smaller than the color images normally created by scanners and digital cameras and used in print, which use thousands to millions of colors. GIF images are limited to 256 colors, one of which can represent transparency. GIF can be pronounced *gif*—with a hard g—or *jif*—with a j.

- **HTML:** Stands for Hypertext Markup Language. This is the set of instructions that is used to format text. For instance, when you see text that is **written like this,** the source code for that text would actually be written like this,.

- **Internet:** The system of linked computers that makes Web sites accessible, sends email, downloads files, and contains newsgroups. Also called the *Net*. Note that the Web is only part of the Internet and is not synonymous with the whole thing.

- **JPEG or JPG:** Stands for Joint Photographic Experts Group. This is a format that compresses images differently than GIF. As a general rule, GIF images should be used for flat colors. JPEG is better used for photographs and images that need more than 256 colors. (JPEG is pronounced *jay-peg*.)

- **PNG:** Short for Portable Network Graphics. This file format was developed specifically to block the efforts of CompuServe to collect royalty payments on all GIF images used in Web pages. It lets you have millions of colors and soft-edged transparency. It has not been widely adopted, however, because only the newer browsers automatically let you see PNG files. (PNG is pronounced *ping*.)

- **SVG:** Stands for Scalable Vector Graphics. This is the new kid on the block as far as Web file formats are concerned. In fact, Illustrator is one of the first major applications to support SVG. Unlike SWF files, which rely on their own proprietary code, SVG files are based on an XML-based standard language approved by the World Wide Web Consortium (W3C). SVG files can be easily combined with HTML and JavaScript in Web pages. Because they are XML-based, they can be used in XML workflows and databases more easily than Flash files.

- **URL:** Acronym for Uniform Resource Locator. Most people think of this only as the address that lets you go to specific Web pages and the thing that's always frustrating to type. For instance, both www.dekemc.com and www.funpix.com take you to my site. A URL can also be the address that lets you download files or send email. For instance, an address that starts with http will send you to a Web page; an address that starts with ftp lets you download files; and an address that starts with mailto will take you to your email program. For humanitarian reasons, I won't bother telling you what things like http and ftp actually stand for.

- **Web:** Short for World Wide Web. Strictly speaking, the Web is only one part of the Internet—the part that displays pages linked together into Web sites. Each of these Web pages can contain text or graphics. However, the difference between Web and Internet is rapidly disappearing; most people use the terms Web, Net, Internet, and World Wide Web interchangeably.

I wonder just how long my copyeditor will still make me capitalize the W in Web. I suspect it won't be too long before I can create web graphics, not Web graphics.

Creating Web Graphics

There really isn't much difference in Illustrator between creating Web graphics and graphics for print. All the tools are the same, and you still work in the same document window. The major differences have to do with colors and some preview options. And there are a few special controls you can add to graphics so that they do special things when they are posted on the Web.

Web Safe RGB Palette

As I mentioned when we looked at color in Chapter 14, Illustrator lets you pick colors using a special Web Safe RGB palette, shown in **Figure 21.1**. To use the palette, choose Web Safe RGB from the Color palette menu. This palette makes it easier for you to use the set of 216 colors common to both the Macintosh and Windows operating systems. These colors are often referred to as the Web-safe colors.

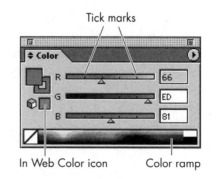

Figure 21.1: The Color palette set for the Web Safe RGB palette.

The Web Safe RGB palette defines colors using the hexadecimal color-naming system. Hexadecimal colors use RGB colors, but instead of numerals alone, they name the colors with a combination of the letters A through F and the numbers 0 through 9. So where a light turquoise color would be defined as R: 58, G: 230, B: 204, the same color would be defined in hexadecimal as R: 3A, G: E6, B: CC.

To pick the Web-safe colors, make sure the sliders are located on one of the short tick marks along the slider area. If you drag the slider, it will automatically jump to each tick mark. All hexadecimal colors are labeled with pairs of the numbers 00, 33, 66, or 99 and the letters CC or FF. So R: 33, G: CC, B: FF is a Web-safe color. (Many Web designers leave out the RGB letters and just label the color with a string such as #33CCFF.)

If you click the color ramp at the bottom of the Web Safe RGB palette, you automatically get the nearest Web-safe color. If you have selected a color that isn't Web-safe, you can convert it to the nearest Web-safe color by clicking the In Web Color icon in the Color palette. (This icon appears or disappears depending on whether your colors are all Web-safe.)

 Most Web graphics are colored using RGB colors. If you create Web graphics from scratch, you will want to set the color mode to RGB. However, if you have a CMYK document, you can convert it to RGB by choosing File » Document Color Mode » RGB. This allows you to select colors that are outside the CMYK color space.

Using Web-Safe Colors

There is much confusion regarding the need for Web-safe colors. What happens if you don't use Web-safe colors? Will your files be seen on the Web? Will the Web police come to arrest you? Will it be the end of civilization as we know it? Here's a little background that should help.

If someone has a computer monitor that displays only 256 colors, any other colors shown on that monitor will not be seen exactly as they were defined. They will be *dithered*. Dithering puts pixels of different colors next to each other so your eye will mix them. While dithering is good at its mission—to simulate colors outside the current palette—it also creates a splotchy effect that can make graphics look bad. It also makes text very hard to read. **Figure 21.2** shows dithering in all its glory.

If you use only Web-safe colors, you can be sure that anyone who views your Web site will see the color exactly as you defined it. This means that if the person has a monitor that displays only 256 colors, they will see the color without any shifting or dithering.

But Web-safe colors are important only for those people who have the oldest, cheapest computer monitors and video cards—the ones that display only 256 colors. Five years ago that was important, but today, most people have monitors that display millions of colors. This means that if you choose only Web-safe colors, you are limiting your color choices to satisfy the needs of a very small percentage of Web viewers.

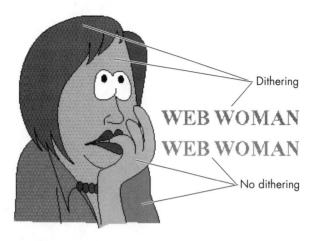

Dithering

WEB WOMAN

WEB WOMAN

No dithering

Figure 21.2: Dithering makes the artwork splotchy. This is how non-Web-safe colors appear on computers that can't display more than 256 colors. Using Web-safe colors avoids dithering.

How necessary is it to limit yourself to only Web-safe colors? If you are creating graphics for a weather Web site, you probably want to use colors that are Web-safe. You want to reach the largest possible audience without dithering. For the small percentage of viewers who have older monitors, dithering will make it difficult to read the graphics—especially the isobars and other weather indicators. However, if you're creating graphics for most companies, you really don't have to worry about using Web-safe colors. I prefer to be able to use a wider choice of colors, rather than cater to the needs of a very small percentage of viewers.

For accuracy's sake, you should know that in most cases, the number of colors a monitor can display isn't necessarily limited by the monitor itself, but by the video subsystem that drives the monitor. A lot of people who can see only 256 colors on their monitor could upgrade to millions of colors just by installing a better video card. Even stranger, many users have the right hardware but have never turned up the number of colors in their system software. (In Windows, right-click on the desktop, choose Properties, and then click Settings. On Mac OS 9 and before, open the Monitors control panel. On Mac OS X, open System Preferences and click Displays.)

Web-Safe Swatch Libraries

You can also choose Web-safe colors using one of two swatch libraries that ship with Illustrator. Choose Window » Swatch Libraries » Web to display the Web-safe swatch colors supplied by Adobe. This palette arranges the Web-safe colors based on the order of their hexadecimal names. Or you can choose Window » Swatch Libraries » VisiBone2. The VisiBone2 swatch library displays the Web-safe colors in a more logical order according to hue. (The VisiBone swatch palette was provided by Bob Stein at VisiBone.) To see the correct arrangement of the VisiBone2 palette, adjust the size of the palette so that you can see the white squares at all four corners, as shown in **Figure 21.3**.

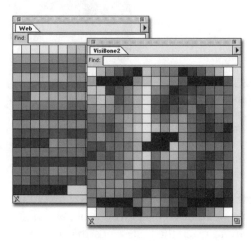

Figure 21.3: The Web-safe swatches palette (left) and the VisiBone2 swatches palette (right).

Creating Image Maps

Image maps are Web graphics with interactive areas that allow the viewer to click to start an action, such as switching to a new Web page or opening an email address. Although image maps are not as sophisticated as the JavaScript rollovers you can create by using the SVG Interactivity palette or other Web graphics programs, they are an option you can use to add interactivity to your graphics.

Image maps can be applied to individual objects or to groups of objects. Simply select the object, open the Attributes palette, and make sure all the options are visible. You can use the Image Map pop-up menu to apply an image map to the shape. Choose Rectangle to have the image map follow the bounding box of the selected object. Choose Polygon to create an image map that most closely follows the shape of the selected object. Use the URL options box to enter the address of the Web page you want to link to, or specify another action you want the image map to perform. For instance, **Figure 21.4** shows how I've created an image map for the sphere that the man is pointing to. I filled in the Attributes palette while the sphere was selected. If you were to click the sphere you would be transferred to my Web site.

If you want to preview the interaction of your image map area, you can use the Save for Web feature covered next.

Click the Browser button in the bottom-right corner of the Save for Web dialog box to automatically switch to your Web browser, which will take you to the Web address listed in the URL options box.

Figure 21.4: To set up an image map, select the object and then use the Image Map options in the Attributes palette.

Slicing Web Graphics

I'm sure you've seen many Web pages where the page is obviously chopped up into pieces and reassembled in an HTML table. Why not just make it one big image with image maps to the links? Well, here are a few reasons:

- If you want to add graphic links, you can't do dynamic rollovers with an image map. If you want just a piece of a page to change during a rollover, that piece has to be its own slice, so it can be swapped out with another piece that represents its change of appearance during a rollover.

- A sliced-up page can appear to display faster than waiting for one big image to download. Note that this doesn't mean it actually *does* appear faster. Technically, a big image is supposed to download faster than many small ones, because it takes more data to transmit many little images than one big one. (Think of it this way: Sending a ten-page letter in ten envelopes involves much more time and effort than sending all ten pages in one envelope.) However, sliced images feel faster because you see complete images faster.

- Some images benefit from having different optimization settings applied to different parts of the image. For example, if you have a home page image containing some lines and solid areas, and a photo in the middle, the image may retain more quality after compression if the photo was compressed as a JPEG and the rest as a GIF. By slicing up the image, you can apply the optimization that's most effective for each area. By the way, this example is the one way in which a sliced version might download faster. If a big graphic contains both solid areas and photos or soft-edged areas, customizing the optimization of each slice can take the most advantage of the compression potential for the image. But it will save time on the Web only if the time saved by the optimized slices more than makes up for the time lost to the additional overhead of transmitting multiple slices.

It wasn't too long ago that if you wanted to slice Web graphics you drew in Illustrator (so you could take advantage of vector drawing), you had to move over to Adobe Photoshop or ImageReady and cut 'em up over there. Thankfully, those days are gone. Now you can draw, slice, and dice straight from Illustrator to your Web page.

Once you create a slice, slices must also be created to account for the rest of the image to fill in the other cells in the HTML table that will contain the slice. Fortunately, Illustrator automatically creates slices for any areas you haven't manually defined as a slice. Illustrator calls these automatic slices subslices, as seen in **Figure 21.5**. *You can't change subslices directly— you can override them only by making an object or manual slice.*

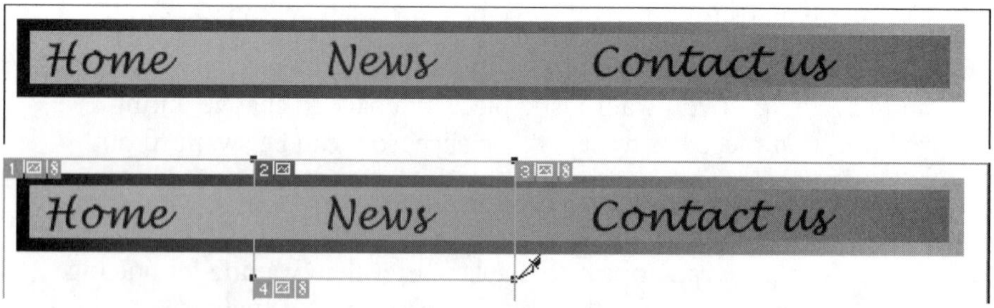

Figure 21.5: When you draw a slice and there aren't enough other slices to fill in empty areas, Illustrator creates whatever subslices are necessary.

The slice tool and the Slice submenu on the Object menu are new in Illustrator 10.

Creating Object-Based Slices

In the days when it was necessary to slice Illustrator graphics in Photoshop or ImageReady, updating an Illustrator Web graphic was a pain. You had to go through the entire exporting and slicing workflow again, adjusting slices manually to fit the changed graphic. In the new world of Illustrator 10, you can use object-based slices so that when objects change size you don't have to adjust the slices.

What exactly is an object-based slice? It's a slice that sizes itself automatically, based on the current size of an object. Say you designed a Web page in Illustrator. You've already sliced everything and are ready to go home, when your boss walks in and wants you to make a "slight change" to the layout. Without object-based slices, you have to remember to readjust the slice sizes after things shift around. With object-based slices, Illustrator takes care of this for you automatically, as you can see in **Figure 21.6**.

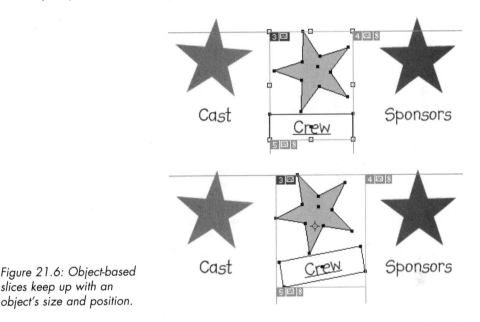

Figure 21.6: Object-based slices keep up with an object's size and position.

Creating object-based slices is a piece of cake.

1. Select one or more objects.

2. Choose Object » Slice » Make. You'll see the result in **Figure 21.7**.

 If you select more than one object and choose Object » Slice » Make, each object gets its own object slice. If you want a slice to automatically encompass multiple objects, group them first, then select the group before you make the slice.

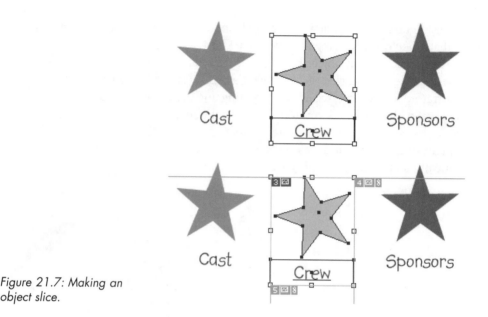

Figure 21.7: Making an
object slice.

Creating Manual Slices

If automatic object-based slices are so convenient, why would you want to use
manual slices? One good example is that you're already working with a design
that expects slices to be at certain sizes and positions, such as an HTML table
that's been set up by someone else. Fortunately, there are so many ways to slice
an image in Illustrator, it's like getting a full set of kitchen knives.

 *Illustrator thinks of slices as objects in the stacking order. They even show
up in the Layers palette, and you can use the Object » Arrange stacking
commands on slices when slices are selected. Why is stacking order
important? Because the top-down view of a stack of slices will determine
the final layout of the slices when you export them, as you can see in **Figure 21.8**.*

Using the Slice Tool

You can easily figure out the slice tool. Just drag to create a rectangular slice, as
shown in **Figure 21.9**. You can also use the slice tool to select slices (so that you can
set the slice options covered later in this section) or drag slices to a new location.

 *The slice tool works only on manual slices. Object slices are far more
transparent to manage: they change when you modify the object's size
or position.*

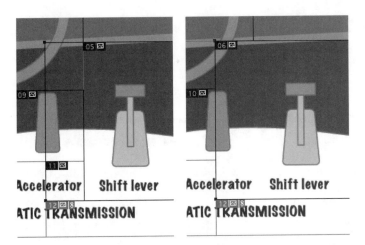

Figure 21.8: When slices overlap, the slice in front wins. Slice 5 starts out in back (left). It's brought to the front, overriding the slices that are now under it (right). Because the number of slices changed, Illustrator also renamed slices as needed.

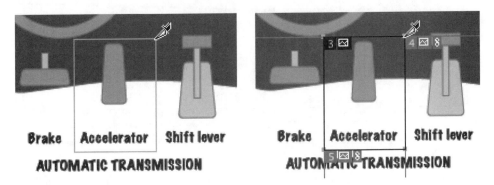

Figure 21.9: To make a slice with the slice tool, just drag the tool.

Creating Slices from a Selection

To create a slice from a selection, select one or more objects and choose Object » Slice » Create from Selection. **Figure 21.10** shows an example of the result.

Creating Slices from Guides

To create a slice from Illustrator's regular page guides, pull guides out of the rulers to mark slice borders, and then choose Object » Slice » Create from Guides, as shown in **Figure 21.11**. Of course, this will create an entire grid of new slices, as opposed to the single new slice you'd get by making object slices, or by creating slices with the slice tool or the Create from Selection command.

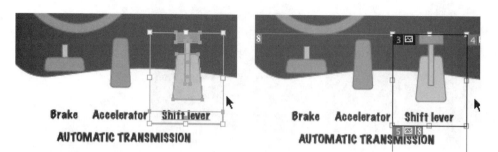

Figure 21.10: The Object » Slice » Create from Selection command makes a manual slice based on whatever's selected.

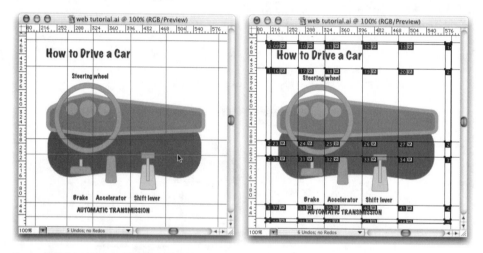

Figure 21.11: You can make slices by positioning ruler guides (left) and choosing Object » Slice » Create from Guides, which turns every rectangular guide area into a slice (right).

You can use the following techniques only on manual slices. Object slices always follow the size and position of the object you selected when you made the slice.

Moving Slices

When you want to move slices, position the slice select tool (the alternate tool in the slice tool slot in the toolbox) over the interior of a slice, and drag. As you can see in **Figure 21.12**, if you move a slice, Illustrator will automatically adjust any subslices around it.

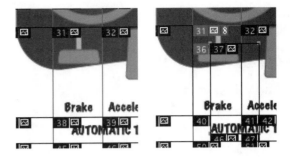

Figure 21.12: Moving a slice is just a matter of dragging it with the slice select tool. In this example, the slice was moved down, which makes it necessary for Illustrator to rearrange many of the surrounding subslices.

Resizing Slices

To resize a slice, position the slice select tool over the corner or edge of a slice, and drag. You'll know you're ready to resize when the pointer appears as a double arrow, as in **Figure 21.13**.

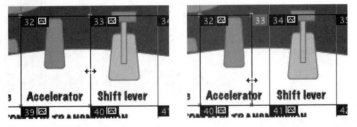

Figure 21.13: Drag a corner or edge of a slice to resize it. In this example, Illustrator needs to create a new subslice to fill the resulting gap.

Duplicating Slices

Say you want another slice that's exactly the same size as a slice you've already got. Just select the slice with the slice select tool and choose Object » Slice » Duplicate Slice. The new slice will be offset, as in **Figure 21.14**. Don't forget to move the new slice to the place where you really want it to be. If you don't move the duplicate slice, it will remain in its default position, which covers up the original at a slight offset. The difference between duplicating and moving a slice is that duplicating will leave a manual slice behind.

Figure 21.14: The Object » Slice » Duplicate Slice command makes an instant copy of a slice.

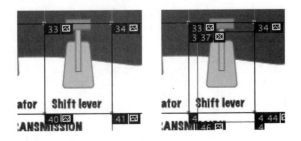

The shortcut for duplicating a slice is to use the slice select tool to Alt-drag (Option-drag on the Mac) a slice. The advantage of this shortcut is that you can position the duplicate slice as you create it.

Dividing Slices

You can divide an existing slice into smaller slices, as shown in **Figure 21.15**. Use the slice select tool to select the slice and choose Object » Slice » Divide Slices. Then change the options in the dialog box, shown in **Figure 21.16**, based on how you want to divide the slice horizontally and vertically.

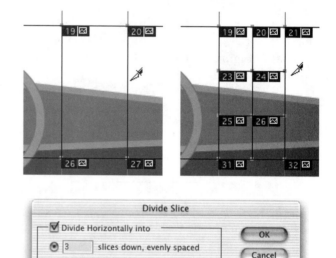

Figure 21.15: When you need to make smaller slices out of a big one, choose Object » Slice » Divide Slices.

Figure 21.16: The Divide Slice dialog box gives you great flexibility in cutting up a slice.

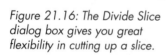 If you're dividing it into horizontal strips, select Divide Horizontally Into. The options in this section let you divide into a specific number of strips of the same height or strips of a specific pixel height. If you enter a pixel value that doesn't divide evenly into the pixel height of the original slice, the leftover amount (or "remainder" if you like long division) becomes a somewhat smaller bottom slice.

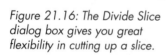 If you're dividing it into vertical strips, select Divide Vertically Into. The options in this section let you divide into a specific number of

strips of the same width or strips of a specific pixel width. Just as described above, if you enter a pixel value that doesn't divide evenly into the pixel height of the original slice, the leftover amount shows up in the last slice on the far right.

 Of course, you can select both Divide Horizontally Into and Divide Vertically Into. This will cut up the selected slice into rectangles according to the division options you enter here.

 Click OK when you're done, and the slice will suddenly become a number of smaller slices.

 Can't see your slice boundaries? You might want to change their color. Choose Edit » Preferences » Smart Guides & Slices (Windows and Mac OS 9) or Illustrator » Preferences » Smart Guides & Slices (Mac OS X). At the bottom of the dialog box, choose a color from the Line Color pop-up menu.

Combining Slices

Combining slices is pretty straightforward. Simply use the slice select tool to select the slices you want to combine, and choose Object » Slice » Combine Slices. **Figure 21.17** is an example of the result.

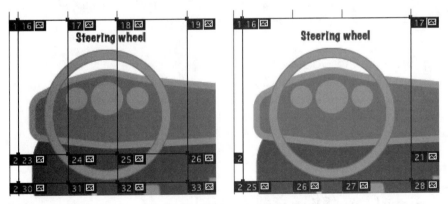

Figure 21.17: Combining slices is a good way to get rid of unnecessary slices.

The one slightly tricky thing to understand about combining slices is that the new slices will become the smallest rectangle that encloses the slices you selected. This has the effect of gobbling up any slices in between. If the slices are not very close in position, size, or shape, then combining the slices could affect a very wide area of your document.

Locking Slices

Manual slices are almost too easy to shift around by accident. (Object slices always stay with their object.) To prevent this, choose View » Lock Slices. You can also lock slices using their lock icons in the Layers palette.

Deleting and Releasing Slices

Before you delete any slices, be sure you know what you really want to do. If you delete a manual slice, you get what you expect—the slice goes away. But if you delete an object slice, you will also delete the actual object it was based on—deleting means deleting. So what do you do if you want to delete an object slice but not the object? Release the slice instead. This will remove the slice but leave the original object standing.

- To delete a manual slice, use the slice select tool to select it, and press the Delete key.

- To release an object slice, use the slice select tool to select it, and choose Object » Slice » Release.

- To delete all slices, choose Object » Slice » Delete All.

Good news—the Delete All command is an exception to the slice-deleting rule described above. Delete All deletes both manual and object slices, but it won't delete any objects.

Making Slices Fit the Document

Let's say you've drawn a few objects around the page and made slices for them, but the slices don't match the entire page size, which you set up as your Web page size. Do you have to laboriously draw slices that match the page size? Not at all. Just choose Object » Slice » Clip to Artboard. This will automagically fill in every gap between any existing slices and the page edges, as you can see in **Figure 21.18**.

Changing How Slices are Displayed

Slices are, of course, all about how your drawings display on the Web. And for the most part, you don't have to worry about them in Illustrator. There are a few things you can and can't change about slice display in Illustrator.

- You can't control how slices are numbered. Illustrator always numbers them from left to right and from top to bottom. Expect slices to be renumbered if you add or delete slices or change slice sizes and positions.

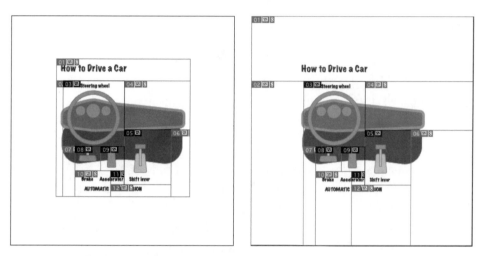

*Figure 21.18: If the artboard matches the size of your Web page, choosing Object » Slice »
Clip to Artboard can fill in empty areas with slices.*

- You can control whether slices are visible and what color they are.
  You'll see the slice color only in Illustrator; it doesn't affect the final
  output.

- To see slices or get them out of your way, choose View » Show Slices
  or View » Hide Slices.

- Open slice preferences by choosing Edit » Preferences » Smart Guides
  & Slices (Windows and Mac OS 9) or Illustrator » Preferences » Smart
  Guides & Slices (Mac OS X). The slice options are down at the bottom
  of the dialog box, in the Slices section. Two options are available.

  Show Slice Numbers controls whether or not you see the slice numbers generated by Illustrator.

  Line Color lets you change the color of the slice boundaries when
  slices are displayed.

*The Other option in the Line Color pop-up menu doesn't
work the way you might think. It appears to randomly
change color every time you open it. While it looks like a
bug, it's not. It automatically tries to set a color that has
high contrast against the colors in use on the artboard.*

Changing Slice Options

The Slice Options dialog box controls the behavior of the slice when it's converted to HTML. Illustrator uses these options during HTML export. Letting Illustrator do the work can save you from having to recode the HTML for these objects in your HTML application when you update the exported images.

To see the Slice Options dialog box, use the slice select tool to select any slice (object or manual), and then choose Object » Slice » Slice Options. Now, before you start pressing buttons and typing things, you need to know what kind of a slice you're making. The Slice Type menu at the top of the dialog box lets you change the very nature of a slice, and it changes the available options. You have three choices in the Slice Type pop-up menu:

- **Image** is the default, and the kind most people are used to. An Image slice consists of the exact image area you sliced out of the larger image.

- **No Image** slices don't include the image during export. If you export HTML, what you get in place of the slice is a blank cell in the resulting HTML table. (The cell can display text if you entered some in the Slice Options dialog box.) This might be OK if, for example, a slice represents empty space that would be transmitted faster as just a background color and plain text instead of an image.

- **HTML Text** slices are like No Image slices, except they contain text in HTML form. The distinguishing characteristics of this kind of slice are that it can contain only text, it's available only when an Illustrator text block is selected, and the text in the slice can only come from the Illustrator text block it's based on.

You can see examples of these in **Figure 21.19**. Once you choose the Slice Type, you can set the options for that type. I'll cover those now.

Image Slice Options

The Image slice options let you add the following information to the slice if you generate an HTML page with the sliced images:

- **Name:** This will become the filename for the image. If you don't change the name, Illustrator will number the image file automatically.

- **URL:** If you want the image to be an HTML link, enter the URL of the destination. Remember to check the pop-up menu just in case the URL you want is already entered, because if it is, you can just choose it from the menu instead of typing it.

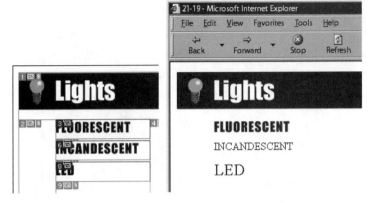

Figure 21.19: The three subheadings in Illustrator (left) exported into three types of slices (top to bottom on the right): Image, No Image, and HTML Text.

Target: This is handy when working with HTML framesets. You can specify exactly how the link opens into its destination. You can choose from four standard HTML targets in the pop-up menu: Blank opens a new blank window without closing the current one; Self replaces everything in the current frameset; Parent opens in the link's parent frameset; and Top replaces everything in the current window, escaping all framesets. Or, if you know the name of the frame in which you want the link to open, just enter the frame name.

Message: Whatever text you enter here will appear in the Web browser's status bar when someone moves the mouse over the slice. It may not work on older browsers or browsers where JavaScript is turned off.

Alt: Supplies text for the HTML Alt tag. It's a good practice to enter descriptive text here, because it appears in the slice when images are not visible (for example, when the user has turned off image display, or when a blind Web surfer uses screen-reading software).

You are free to leave blank any of the items in these boxes. **Figure 21.20** shows the dialog box for Image slice options.

No Image Slice Options
The No Image slice options let you add the following information to an HTML page you export:

Text Displayed in Cell: If you want to display text in place of the image, enter it here. You can adjust the appearance of the text using any HTML formatting codes.

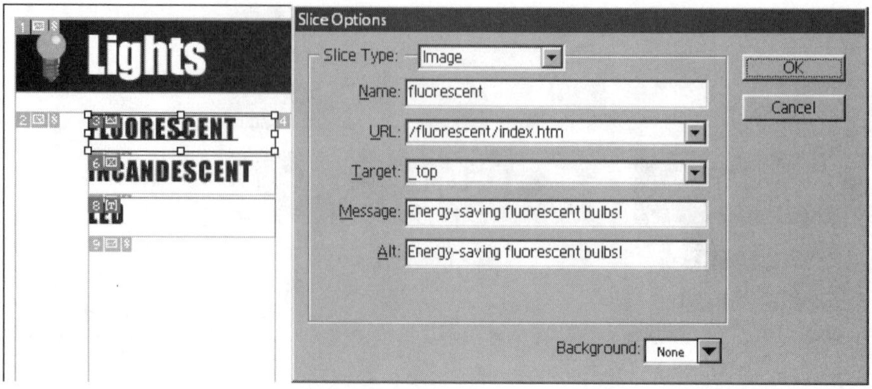

Figure 21.20: Options for an Image slice.

Be careful about the amount of text you enter in this cell. Keep in mind that sliced images are held together by an HTML table (which Illustrator can generate for you). If the text doesn't fit in its HTML table cell when displayed in a Web browser, the cell containing it will have to enlarge, and that will mess up the table layout. Since the display of text can vary among browsers, test this; since users can change their browser text size, leave plenty of room for possible expansion.

🌑 **Cell Alignment:** The horizontal (Horiz.) and vertical (Vert.) pop-up menus in this section control the alignment of the text in the cell.

🌑 **Background:** Since there's nothing in the slice's table cell (except text you may have entered in the Text Displayed in Cell option), you might want to make it match the background color of your Web site. None applies no color, so it will simply be transparent. Matte lets you specify the matte color by clicking on the word *Matte* after you choose the color.

You are free to leave blank any of the items in these boxes. **Figure 21.21** shows the dialog box for No Image slice options.

You won't be able to see the Background color in Illustrator. You have to export the page to your Web browser to see the effect.

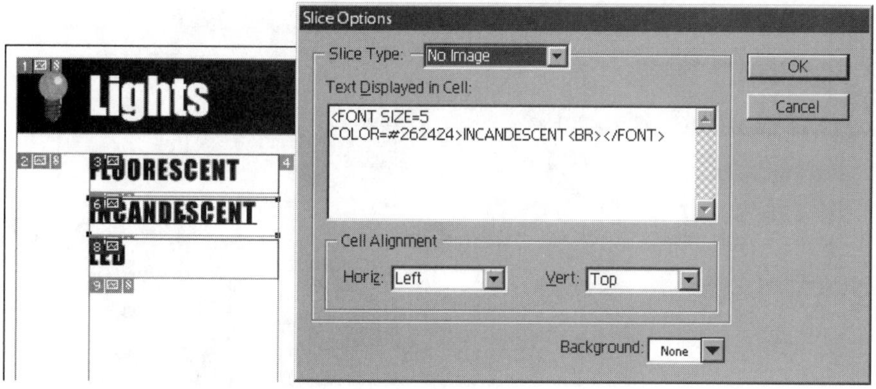

Figure 21.21: Options for a No Image slice.

HTML Text Slice Options

If the HTML Text option is dimmed in the pop-up menu, click Cancel and make sure you selected a text block with the selection or direct selection tool.

The difference between a No Image slice and an HTML Text slice is that the latter takes text from an Illustrator text block instead of a graphic. HTML Text slice options let you add the following information to an HTML page you export:

- **Text Displayed in Cell:** Don't be too surprised that you can't edit this text. It's because the text is inextricably linked to the text block you selected. If you want to change the text, change it in the text block. If you don't want the text to follow the text block, choose No Image from the Slice Type pop-up menu.

If you don't want the text in a No Image slice to use the HTML formatting code you see in the dialog box, go back out to the original text block and add the characters <unformatted> (including the brackets) to the very beginning of the text.

- The **Cell Alignment** and **Background** options work just as they do for No Image slices.

You are free to leave blank any of the items in these boxes. **Figure 21.22** shows the dialog box for HTML Text slice options.

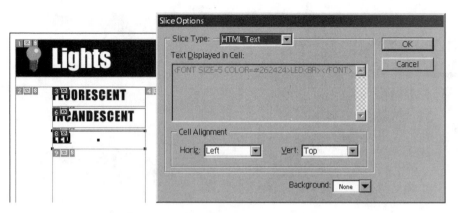

Figure 21.22: Options for an HTML Text slice.

SVG Filter Effects

Illustrator 10 contains an entirely new category of special effects that you can apply to your Illustrator artwork: SVG filter effects. What's so special about them? If you apply a regular effect like Gaussian Blur or Ocean Ripple, the artwork must be rasterized. With SVG filters, no rasterization is necessary. Now if you've been paying attention, you're probably asking: "So if it's vector artwork, and Illustrator's not rasterizing it, where does the SVG effect become rasterized?" Good question. The answer is a bit of a surprise: The Web browser rasterizes the effect (or more accurately, the SVG plug-in in a Web browser rasterizes the effect). SVG allows this by including the SVG filter effect as a set of XML instructions that Illustrator exports along with the file. A sample of this is shown in **Figure 21.23**. For you and your Web audience, the big win is that the filter instructions take up a lot less space than a rasterized version of the same effect, for the same reasons that vectors take up less space than a raster bitmap does.

Figure 21.23: SVG filters, such as the AI_shadow_2 effect applied in the example at the far right, are not rendered until they reach the Web browser.

Of course, for all of this to work, the viewer at the other end of the Web must have a Web browser or Web browser plug-in that supports SVG. If you're not sure if your audience meets these requirements, you can pretty much ignore this section and continue rasterizing your effects into GIF or JPEG as usual.

To apply an SVG filter, just select an object and choose the effect from the Effect » SVG Filters submenu. There aren't any options to adjust—at least, none that are obvious. I'll explain what I mean in a bit.

Alternatively, you can try out different SVG filter effects by choosing Effect » SVG Filters » Apply SVG Filter. In the ensuing dialog box (shown in **Figure 21.24**), turn on the Preview option and click different filter effects in the list. Click OK when you see what you want.

Figure 21.24: The Apply SVG Filter dialog box not only lets you apply SVG filters; it also lets you manage the filter list.

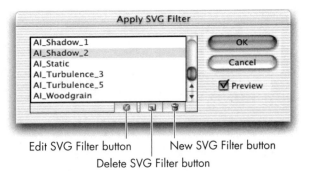

Edit SVG Filter button   New SVG Filter button
Delete SVG Filter button

 Be careful! If you apply an SVG filter effect and then apply a non-SVG effect, the SVG effect will have to be rasterized so that any subsequent non-SVG effect can be calculated, causing you to lose the benefit of SVG. For this reason, if you apply multiple effects to an object, make sure that any and all SVG effects are listed last for that object in the Appearance palette.

What I've talked about so far is the most basic way to work with SVG filters. It's also the only way most designers will be comfortable working with them. Not sure what I mean? Look again at the Apply SVG Filter dialog box, specifically at the buttons across the bottom. Click the Edit SVG Filter button...and don't faint. Yes, folks, what you see in **Figure 21.25** below are in fact the options in an SVG filter, in the form of the raw XML code that defines the filter effect. It would be nicer to have the sliders and buttons found in the other filters, but it's just not that way yet.

If you don't know XML, but you've worked with HTML, you can actually achieve a fair amount of customization in the Edit SVG Filter dialog box by locating and changing parameter values (usually a number in quotes) and clicking Update Preview. Since you have to save a filter to save your changes, I recommend you do this on copies of the built-in filters in case you make a mistake.

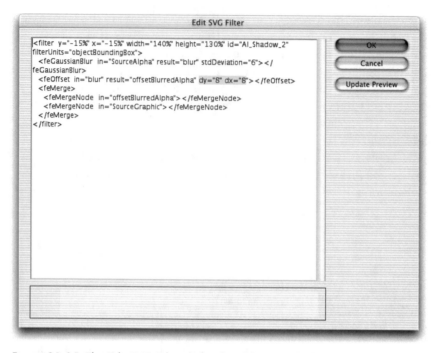

Figure 21.25: The Edit SVG Filter dialog box lets you edit the XML code that defines the filters—if you dare!

If you're comfortable editing this XML craziness, you can do whatever you want in here. SVG is still young, and I'm sure this will all become much friendlier in Illustrator 11, but at the moment, it's kind of like looking into a vat of slimy squid that hasn't yet been expertly cooked into a tasty calamari appetizer.

Of course, the New SVG Filter button brings up the same Edit SVG Filter dialog box, but this time it's nearly empty. If you click New SVG Filter, you *really* have to know your XML.

If you've been putting together your own SVG filters in XML, you can bring them in from wherever you've been storing them on your computer. Just choose Effect » SVG Filters » Import SVG Filter.

When you're not in the Edit SVG Filter dialog box, you can use the Apply SVG Filter dialog box to delete any SVG filters you don't ever want to use. Just select the filter and click the trash can icon. But don't use this to remove a filter from an object, because it deletes the filter from being available in Illustrator. Use the Appearance palette to remove filters from objects.

To edit or study the default SVG filters, use a text editor to open the file Adobe SVG Filters.svg. You'll find it in the Adobe Illustrator application folder, inside the Plug-Ins subfolder.

Save for Web Dialog Box

Hidden deep within the bowels of Illustrator is a whole 'nother application called Save for Web. This is the same feature that was introduced in Photoshop 5.5 and is quickly being added to the rest of Adobe's graphics line. Save for Web allows you to save images in GIF, JPEG, or PNG formats. For most designers, Save for Web is all that you will ever need to create simple Web graphics.

Save for Web Interface

When you choose File » Save for Web, the Save for Web dialog box opens, as seen in **Figure 21.26**. If you have a small monitor, this dialog box will pretty much take over your screen. Don't worry. Your document is still there, hiding in the background. For now, though, everything you need is contained within this window.

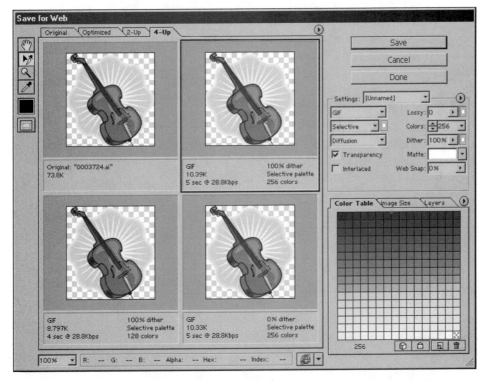

Figure 21.26: The Save for Web window is your one-stop shopping center for all the features you need to create Web graphics.

There are five major areas in the Save for Web dialog box: The tools; the preview area; the optimization settings; the (three) tabs controlling the color table, image size, and CSS layers; and the magnification, color and alpha information, and "jump to" controls along the bottom of the window.

Save for Web Tools

As shown in **Figure 21.27**, the Save for Web window has four tools that work somewhat similarly to their Illustrator equivalents, plus a couple of site-specific options as well:

- **Hand tool:** Lets you move around within the preview area. Press the spacebar to access the hand tool while in one of the other tools.

- **Slice select tool:** Lets you select slices so you can optimize them individually if necessary.

- **Zoom tool:** Lets you zoom in to the preview area. Hold the Alt key (Option key on the Mac) to switch to the zoom-out mode. Hold Ctrl+spacebar (Cmd-spacebar on the Mac) to access the zoom tool while in one of the other tools.

- **Eyedropper tool:** Lets you sample colors from the illustration area.

- **Eyedropper color square:** Displays the color sampled from the eyedropper tool. Click the square to open the Color Picker.

- **Toggle slices visibility tool:** Shows or hides slices when they exist in the artwork.

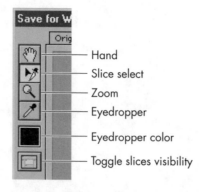

Figure 21.27: The tools area of the Save for Web window.

Preview Area

As shown in **Figure 21.28**, there are four tabs at the top of the preview area in the Save for Web window. They change the display of the preview area as follows:

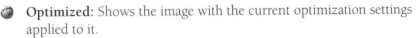

- **Original:** Shows the original image as seen in the Illustrator window.

- **Optimized:** Shows the image with the current optimization settings applied to it.

- **2-Up:** Splits the preview area into two separate sections. Each section can show either the original image or the display of different optimization settings.

- **4-Up:** Splits the preview area into four separate sections.

Figure 21.28: The four tabs at the top of the preview area let you see different views of the image to be saved.

The split preview windows are an excellent way to compare the differences between two different output formats (such as GIF vs. JPEG) or two different settings of the same format.

 The regular view and zoom shortcuts, such as pressing the spacebar for the hand tool, work in the Save for Web preview area.

Optimization Settings

There are six different displays for the optimization area, as shown in **Figure 21.29**. When you choose GIF, JPEG, PNG-8, PNG-24, SWF, or SVG, this area changes its controls. I'll cover each of these options in detail later in this chapter. (SWF and SVG options are described in Chapter 22.)

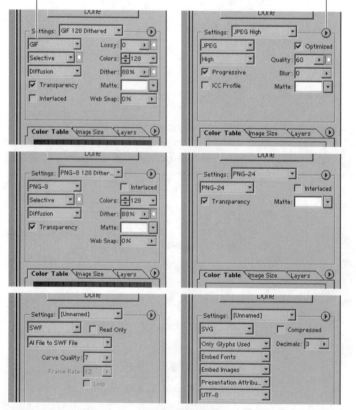

Figure 21.29: The optimization settings change depending on which export option is chosen from the optimization list.

Color Table

When you click the Color Table tab, shown in **Figure 21.30**, this area shows the colors that are included in GIF and PNG-8 images. Because JPEG, SWF, and SVG images don't use color tables, this area is left blank when one of those formats is chosen.

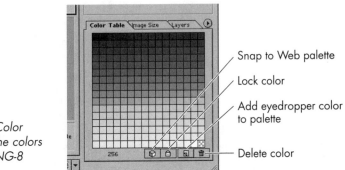

Figure 21.30: The Color Table tab displays the colors used for GIF and PNG-8 images.

Color tables are necessary only for files that use 8-bit color or below. Because 8 bit gives you no more than 256 colors, you have to take the best 256. Formats like JPEG or PNG-24, which support more than 8 bits, would create a color table so large you'd need a couple of monitors to see all of the swatches.

Image Size

When you click the Image Size tab, as shown in **Figure 21.31**, this area shows you the current dimensions of the image. You can also set new export sizes for the image. I'll show you each of these options in just a bit.

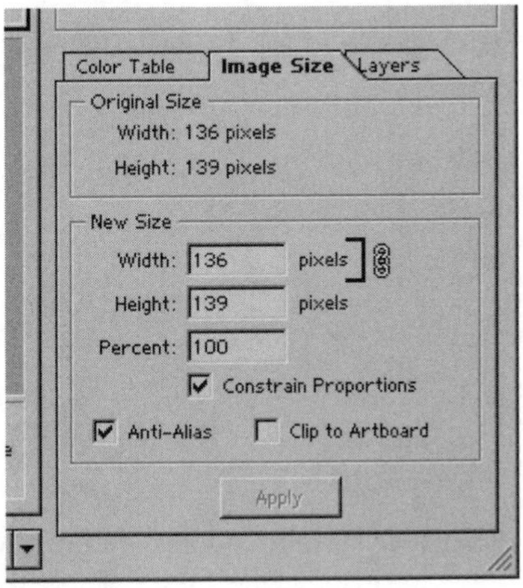

Figure 21.31: Click the Image Size tab to display the controls for changing the size of the exported image.

Layers

When you click the Layers tab, as shown in **Figure 21.32**, this area shows you options for exporting layers as CSS layers. These options will be covered later.

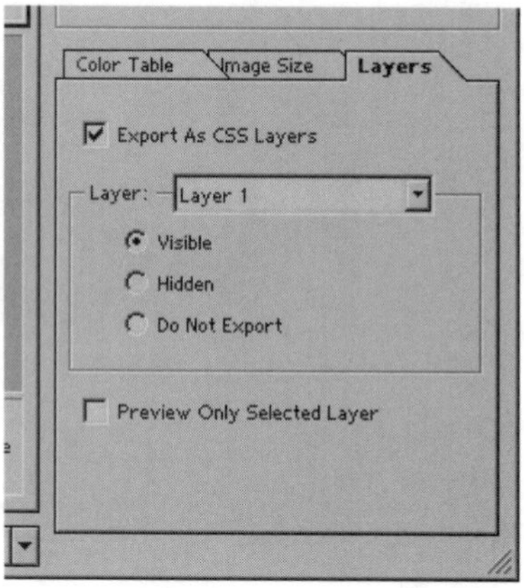

Figure 21.32: Click the Layers tab to display the controls for CSS layer export.

Magnification, Color and Alpha, and Jump to

The bottom of the Save for Web window contains the final three controls shown in **Figure 21.33**. The magnification option box and pop-up list lets you set numerical values for the size of the image shown in the preview area.

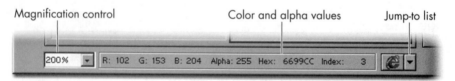

Figure 21.33: The bottom area of the Save for Web window lets you change the preview size of the image, check the color and alpha information, and switch to a browser to preview the image.

The color and alpha information shows you the color values of selected colors or the area underneath the eyedropper cursor.

The jump-to-browser control lets you automatically select and switch to a browser to see how an image will appear in that browser. This is also where you can see the interactivity of any image maps.

Choosing an Export Format

Before you can save your image as a Web graphic, you should understand the different optimization formats in the Save for Web application. Each of the formats has its own advantages and disadvantages.

GIF Images

GIF images are used primarily for images with flat areas of color. They can be used for blends and gradients if other formats are not acceptable. Because GIF images are limited to 256 colors, they are rarely used for photographic images that require many tonal changes. You can lower the size of GIF images by reducing the number of colors in the file. So if an image contains only a few colors, GIF images can become extremely small. GIF images are also used when the final image needs to have a transparent background (for instance, an image that will be placed over a multicolored background). **Figure 21.34** shows a sample of the kind of image that does best when exported as a GIF.

Figure 21.34: These are the types of graphics that do well when exported as GIF images. Even those images with blends and gradients are OK because they do not have many different color blends.

 The GIF format is also used to create simple animations. However, Illustrator does not let you create GIF animations. For that you need a program such as Adobe ImageReady or Macromedia Fireworks.

JPEG Images

JPEG images allow you to have millions of colors in your graphics and are used primarily for photographs. However, the JPEG format may also be best if you have used many blends, gradient fills, drop shadows, or glows in your Illustrator artwork. **Figure 21.35** shows the type of images that are best saved in the JPEG format. You reduce the size of JPEG images by applying a compression setting. The smaller you make the file, the more the quality of the file is degraded. When you apply a low quality setting to JPEG images, flat areas of color become distorted and gradations become blocky. Figure 21.35 also shows an example of this distortion.

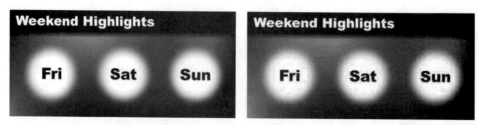

Figure 21.35: An image saved as JPEG because of its subtle gradations. The left example looks better because the compression quality was set for Maximum. The right example was with compression set to Low, causing distortion at edges and transitions.

PNG-8 and PNG-24 Images

PNG is the Web format that doesn't seem to get any respect. For a long time, you couldn't view PNG graphics unless you had special plug-ins in the browser. This kept most Web designers from using the PNG format. (They didn't expect visitors to their Web sites to go out and download a plug-in.) However, since Netscape 4.0 and Internet Explorer 4.0 were introduced, support for the PNG format has been built into the browsers. Even so, and despite the fact that the PNG format has many advantages over GIF and JPEG, many designers are still afraid to use PNG images.

Illustrator lets you save files in either the PNG-8 or the PNG-24 formats. The PNG-8 format saves files similarly to GIF images, supporting up to 256 colors. PNG-24 images can have millions of colors.

SWF (Shockwave Flash) Graphics

Flash has become a very popular way to show vector line art on the Web. Flash has had several years for its Web browser plug-in to reach nearly every corner of the Web—and it doesn't hurt that most browsers come with the plug-in. If a graphic has line art and flat color, your audience has recent browsers, and you'd like them to be able to resize it smoothly, exporting it as Flash might be a good idea. Just keep in mind that the same things that make an Illustrator file large will also make a Flash file large: a large quantity of individual paths and the use of rasterized objects (such as some effects). If you're not sure, try exporting a graphic in SWF and GIF, and see which one's bigger. You might also export as Flash if you want to use the graphic in a project you're assembling in Flash, since use of Flash animation has become so widespread that entire sites are built out of it.

SVG (Scalable Vector Graphics)

SVG is another Web-friendly vector format that allows animation and interactivity, but SVG hasn't yet become as pervasive as Flash. Like Flash, it creates high-quality resizable vector graphics but needs a plug-in to work in a browser. Adobe does its part by installing an SVG browser plug-in with all of its applications that handle it (yes, you got one with Illustrator). However, SVG has good prospects for the future. While Flash is a Macromedia proprietary format, SVG is an open standard officially sanctioned by the World Wide Web Consortium. It is also based on and completely compatible with XML, so it can be written or manipulated as a text file—for example, it is easy to search for text in an SVG file. For now, you'll want to choose SVG when the project really demands it, and that kind of project may look like a Web site driven by an XML-based database. SVG can be expected to ride the coattails of XML's rapidly increasing popularity with efficiency-minded organizations.

Like Flash, having lots of objects or using rasterized objects will make an SVG file larger and slower. However, SVG has one interesting advantage in this area. Illustrator includes SVG effects, which are specifically designed to work with SVG art. These filters are also XML files, and they're rendered at the browser, not on your computer. Because they don't have to be rasterized and stored as space-consuming bitmaps in the graphics file, they don't increase the size of the files you use them on.

Saving an Image for the Web

Even if you've never created Web graphics, it's really not as difficult as it may seem. In fact, there's actually only one important rule to remember: make the file as small as possible while still looking good. Everything else is just a nuance. Here are the overall steps for creating an image using the Save for Web command. I'll cover the specific details in just a bit.

1. Select slices if necessary.

If you want to export a few slices instead of the whole thing, grab the slice select tool and select the slices.

2. Choose File » Save for Web.

Make sure that only the artwork you want to export is visible. The Save for Web command will take all visible artwork, even outside the page. If there's too much artwork outside the page, Save for Web may take forever to open.

3. Use the preview area to view the artwork.

If you want to compare settings, click the 2-Up or 4-Up tabs. Otherwise, click the Optimized tab to see one version of the final image.

If you want to change the download time estimate or simulate browser dither, click the lonely little round menu button above the top-right corner of the preview area to get a list of options. If you right-click within the preview area (Control-click on the Mac), you'll also get to change the magnification.

4. Set the controls for GIF, JPEG, PNG-8, PNG-24, SWF, or SVG.

The optimization controls change depending on which format you have chosen. I'll cover how to set the controls for each of the formats separately.

5. Click the Image Size tab.

Use the Width and Height option boxes to change the size or enter a value in the percent field. Constrain Proportions keeps the image from being distorted when scaled. Checking Anti-Alias allows a soft blur to be added to the edges of objects. This keeps them from looking harsh or jagged. Check Clip to Artboard to use images only within the artboard area. Click the Apply button in the Image Size area to apply the changes.

If you choose the Anti-Alias blur, the anti-aliasing will result in more colors added to GIF images. Each additional color adds to the file size. You may have to delete colors that were automatically generated as a result of anti-aliasing.

If you use Clip to Artboard on a large document, Illustrator will take a long time to optimize the image. Change the image size first.

6. Preview in a browser (optional).

Choose a browser from the jump-to list. This lets you compare how the image will look for different viewers.

7. Click Save to name and save the file.

Or, if you want to save the changes and go back to the illustration, click Done.

If you clicked OK, name the file and save it to the location where you store your Web graphics. If you have applied an image map to the graphics, you need to save the HTML file along with the graphic.

The Done button is new in Illustrator 10. And I'm glad to see it...no more exporting just to apply the settings to the document.

Setting the GIF Options

The primary thing to remember about GIF images is that you are limited to 256 colors. Your mission is to use as few colors as possible while still making the image look good. When you choose the GIF format, the optimization settings appear as shown in **Figure 21.36**. Here's a complete rundown of what each of the controls does.

- **Color list:** This lets you choose the type of color palette that is applied to the image. *Perceptual* tries to maintain colors closest to the way the human eye perceives color. *Selective* creates images with the most color integrity, although it may shift some colors to the Web palette. *Adaptive* creates a set of colors that appear most in the image. This gives you the most fidelity to blends and gradients. *Web* limits the colors to the 216 colors in the Web-safe palette.

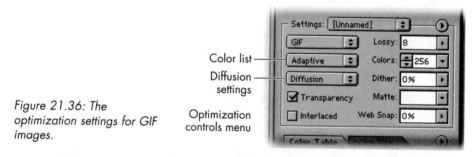

Figure 21.36: The optimization settings for GIF images.

- **Dither settings:** This lets you choose what type of dithering, if any, is applied to the image. *None* turns off dithering. *Diffusion* creates a random, but adjustable, pattern of dithering. *Pattern* creates a uniform grid of dithering. *Noise* creates a random pattern of dithering. **Figure 21.37** shows the difference in the three types of dithering.

- **Dither:** If you choose diffusion dithering, this setting lets you control how much diffusion dithering is applied. (The pattern and noise dithering do not let you adjust the amount of dithering.)

- **Colors:** Use this control to add or delete the number of colors in the image. This is how you can delete the colors that were added by anti-aliasing.

Figure 21.37: The three types of dithering that can be applied to images. From left to right: diffusion, pattern, and noise.

Lossy: This control reduces the size of GIF images by applying a compression scheme similar to that found in JPEG images. At low numbers, the lossy compression is not noticeable. However, as you increase the lossy compression, you will start to see distortion in your images.

 Sharp-minded readers may ask how lossy GIF can be possible when the GIF file format is lossless. The way it works is that Illustrator performs a neat little trick, applying lossy techniques before saving the file as lossless GIF.

Web Snap: As you increase this setting, Save for Web shifts colors to their nearest Web-safe equivalent. This allows you to have a mixture of some Web-safe colors while still keeping important colors that aren't Web-safe.

Transparency: Check this to create a transparent background to the GIF image. The transparency settings for GIF images are hard-edged. So although you may have applied a soft drop shadow to your artwork, the transparency for the GIF image will end abruptly, not fade out.

 And how do you control what becomes transparent? You don't have to—any empty areas will become transparent. The other side of this coin is that if you really want areas to be transparent, don't be leaving stray or white objects lying around, and definitely don't cover up things with white objects—delete or cut off any parts of objects you don't really want.

Matte: Once you apply transparency, you can use the Matte control to choose what color should be mixed into the edges of the transparent areas. For example, if you have a white matte and the image is placed over a black background, you will see small white pixels on the edge of the image. A better choice would be a black matte.

- **Interlaced:** Check this to have the image appear in stages as it is downloaded. **Figure 21.38** shows a representation of this effect.

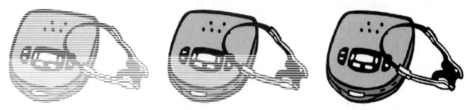

Figure 21.38: The different stages that interlaced GIF images appear as they download.

Here are a few hard-learned tips for making the best possible GIF images.

- **Lower the number of colors.** The Anti-Alias setting increases the number of colors. Use the Color Table tab to delete some of the colors that are added by anti-aliasing.

- **Apply dithering to reduce banding.** As you decrease the number of colors, you may see banding—abrupt changes in blends. Add a small amount of dithering to decrease the banding.

- **Lock important colors.** As you reduce the number of colors, you may lose important colors that do not appear very frequently in the image—for instance, a client's logo may have a distinctive color in a very small area. Use the color table to select that color and lock it so it is not deleted as you reduce colors.

- **Watch the preview size.** Use the information in the preview area to judge how small the final file will be.

Setting the JPEG Options

The options for creating JPEG images, as shown in **Figure 21.39**, are much simpler. Because JPEG images rely on image compression, you adjust a slider control to reduce the size of the image. Here's an explanation of what each of the settings does.

- **Quality (preset menu and options box):** There are four presets: Maximum, High, Medium, and Low. These simply move the slider in the Quality options box to the amount of 80, 60, 30, and 10, respectively. However, once you have applied a preset, you can then adjust the Quality options box to choose amounts in between the presets.

- **Optimized:** Check this setting to apply an automatic optimization that decreases the size of the JPEG image to as small as possible.

- **Blur:** As you decrease the quality to lower the file size, you may see small distortions in the image. Use the Blur control to soften the appearance of these distortions.

- **Progressive:** Turn on this option to have JPEG images appear gradually (similar to the interlaced setting for GIF images).

- **Matte:** Although there is no transparency for JPEG images, you can still set the color that the image fades into using the Matte control.

- **ICC Profile:** If you have assigned an ICC profile to help maintain the color of your image, you can use this setting to add the ICC profile to the JPEG image. ICC profiles are not yet supported by most browsers.

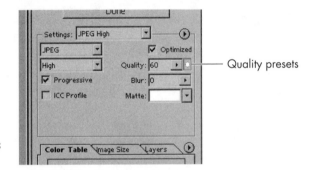

Figure 21.39: The optimization settings for JPEG images.

Setting the PNG Options

There are two types of PNG options, as shown in **Figure 21.40**. The PNG-8 settings are very similar to the GIF settings. You reduce the size of the image by lowering the number of colors. The PNG-24 settings let you set only transparency, matte, and the interlaced options.

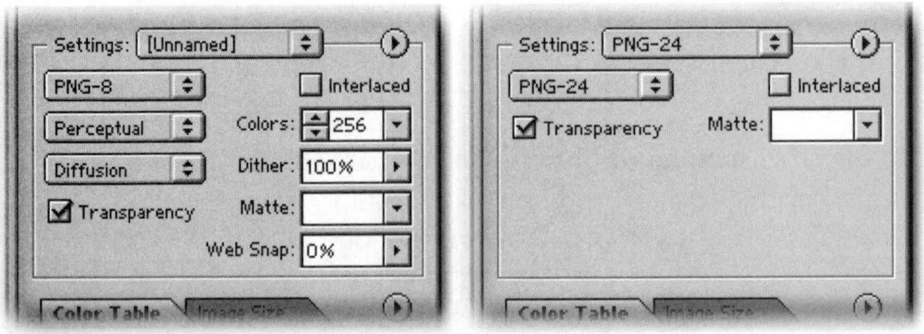

Figure 21.40: The optimization settings for PNG-8 and PNG-24 images.

Saving the Optimization Settings

Probably the items that have taken you the most time in this Save for Web dialog box are the optimization controls in the Settings area at the top right. But here's a piece of heartening news: once you've set those to your satisfaction for any or all of the kinds of files, you can save those settings for future images. With the optimization controls set the way you want them, choose Save Settings from the optimization controls menu (see that little round button right next to the Settings pop-up list?). You can then name and save the settings, which will then appear in the Settings pop-up list (where they will be available for all other documents as well).

You can apply any of the saved settings by simply choosing them from the Settings pop-up list. If you feel the list is too long, choose Delete Settings from the optimization controls menu.

Saving to a Specific Size

Don't you have anything better to do than sit and play with the settings to get your files under a certain size? I thought so. So you can just choose Optimize to File Size from the optimization controls menu. The dialog box shown in **Figure 21.41** appears. Simply enter the desired file size in the options box. Choose Start With: Current Settings to use the optimization settings that are currently in effect. Or choose Auto Select GIF/JPEG to have the Save for Web application automatically choose either a GIF or JPEG format. Either way, Save for Web will figure out the best possible settings that keep your file below the desired file size.

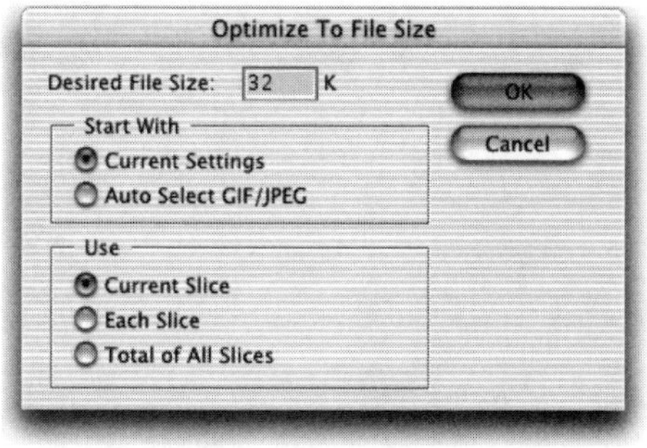

Figure 21.41: Use the Optimize To File Size dialog box to set a specific file size to which the Web graphic should be reduced.

 The Use section in the Optimize To File Size dialog box accounts for slices you create.

 Click Current Slice to have the desired file size represent the selected slice only.

- Click Each Slice to optimize individual slices to the desired size.
- Click Total of All Slices to have the desired file size represent the total of all slices in the graphic.

Optimizing Slices

The Save for Web dialog box makes it easy to optimize slices. Version 10 adds the slice select tool, the Toggle Slices Visibility button, and slice exporting options to Save for Web, which you can see in **Figure 21.42**. Any slice can have different optimization settings from any other slice; you simply select the slice you want and change the settings.

1. Choose File » Save for Web.

2. If you can't see the slices, click the Toggle Slices Visibility button.

3. With the slice select tool, select any slices to which you want to apply the same optimization settings. Use the same selection techniques you'd use with the slice select tool on the artboard; for example, Shift-click to select multiple slices.

4. Change the optimization settings for the selected slices.

5. Repeat for any other slices that need unique optimization settings, then click Save or Done. (The Done button lets you optimize slices without having to continue the export process.)

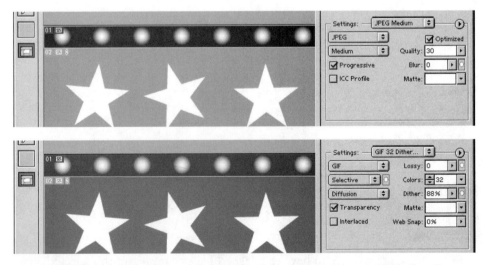

Figure 21.42: Slice 1 (top) has gradients, so it's being optimized as a JPEG. Slice 2 (bottom) has flat color areas, so it's being optimized as a GIF. The optimization options on the right change depending on the selected slice.

Sometimes a visible edge appears between adjacent GIF or PNG-8 slices if different color palettes were generated for each. To prevent this, select the slices and choose Link Slices from the optimize pop-up menu.

 If you forgot to set slice options before, or want to change them while in the Save for Web dialog box, double-click a slice. If you selected more than one slice, double-click the last slice you selected.

Setting CSS Layer Options

When you save an Illustrator document for the Web, you can export each Illustrator layer as a CSS (Cascading Style Sheet) layer. These are the layers supported in HTML 4.0 as part of the Dynamic HTML specification, and supported in version 4.0 or later of Microsoft Internet Explorer or Netscape Navigator. The advantage to doing this is that you can use CSS layers to add layout flexibility or animation to Web pages. For example, instead of trying to use tables for layout (a use for which they were not originally intended), you can use floating boxes, much like you might in a page-layout program for print. If you use this option, keep in mind that only named layers will be exported as individual units, not every object listed in the Layers palette.

The options for controlling CSS layer export are in the Layers tab in the Save for Web dialog box, as shown in **Figure 21.43**.

- **Export As CSS Layers:** Select this to enable the options in this tab panel.

- **Layer menu:** This pop-up menu lists all of the layers in the document. The way this works is that you select each layer in turn, and then you set the options for the current layer in the section below this menu.

- **Layer options:** Each layer can be set to any of these three options. *Visible* will export the layer so that it's visible by default, while *Hidden* exports the layer so that it isn't visible by default. You can change these attributes later in an HTML editor, but it's nice that Illustrator lets you set them from here. *Do Not Export* does what it says.

- **Preview Only Selected Layer:** This is just a way of hiding all layers other than the one you see in the Layer menu, so you can confirm which layer you're setting options for.

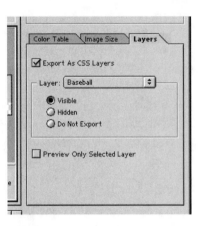

Figure 21.43: Options for exporting as CSS layers, which become available only if you select the Export As CSS Layers option.

Changing HTML Output Settings

Illustrator provides the Output Settings dialog box so that you can control the exact form of the HTML it generates. This makes it easier for Illustrator-generated HTML to work with other HTML workflows, editing applications, or browsers. Output settings don't change the function of the code, just things about the code you'd never see on a Web page, such as how the code is capitalized. If you've used Adobe ImageReady, you already know what's coming.

To see the Output Settings dialog box, choose the Edit Output Settings command from the optimize menu in the Save for Web dialog box. There, you'll find four settings groups in the pop-up menu at the top of the main settings group—HTML, Background, Saving Files, and Slices. (The pop-up menu at the very top can contain predefined settings you manage using the Load and Save buttons.)

HTML Settings

The settings shown in **Figure 21.44** control the HTML code in general.

- **Formatting:** Controls the appearance of the code when you edit the code itself. *Tags Case* and *Attribs Case* control the capitalization of HTML tags and attributes, respectively. Note that the tags listed in the pop-up menus are simply examples of capitalization. *Indent* controls how Illustrator formats indents, and *Line Endings* specifies the character to use to denote the end of a line in the HTML code. The Always Quote Attributes check box determines whether or not quotation marks are added around attributes. Even if you select this, some tags always have quotation marks around them.

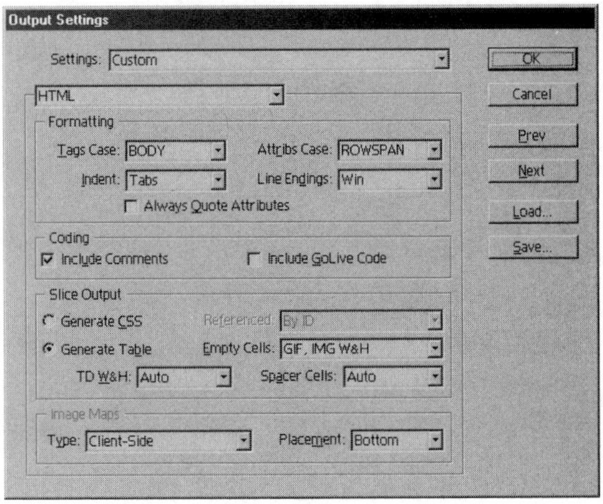

Figure 21.44: HTML Output Settings control the code of the HTML page that contains the page slices you export.

- **Coding:** Include Comments inserts comments that help identify certain sections of code, such as when tables start. While helpful for understanding the Illustrator-generated code, you might want to deselect this if you want the smallest possible file. Include GoLive Code sets up the code so that Adobe GoLive will understand it, allowing GoLive to reoptimize Illustrator images.

- **Slice Output:** The first thing to do here is understand whether you want to export slices using CSS (for recent browsers) or as a table (for older browsers). Once you select that, the appropriate options on the right become available.

  If you chose Generate CSS, you can then use the Reference By pop-up menu to select the method used to reference each slice. If you chose Generate Table, you can specify how to handle empty cells, table data (TD) cells, or spacer cells.

  In the Empty Cells pop-up, the two GIF options use a GIF to hold open empty cells. The difference is whether the dimensions of the empty cell are applied to the GIF or to the table cell. The NoWrap option uses a truly empty table cell (no GIF) and a nonstandard NoWrap tag.

  TD W&H specifies whether or not width and height are applied to table data cells. Auto lets Illustrator decide; Always and Never either include or exclude the dimensional values completely.

Spacer cells are an invisible outline of empty table cells around a table to make sure all table cells stay aligned, since not all browsers align table cells reliably. Auto means Illustrator decides when tables are always exported with a spacer border depending on the design. Always and Never either include spacer cells with or exclude them from all sliced tables it exports.

Image Maps: These options control exactly how Illustrator will write out the code for image maps.

The Type options let you specify that image maps are either client-side (run by the Web browser) or server-side (run by the server). They can also use the NCSA or CERN image map specification. To get this right you have to know how the Web server is set up, so if you have to, ask the server administrator before making a choice.

The Placement options have nothing to do with the placement of the image map on the Web page. It has to do with the placement of the image map code in the body of the HTML document. Top puts it just before the body, Body puts it just before the image map's IMGSRC tag, and Bottom puts it right after the body.

Background Settings

Use the settings shown in **Figure 21.45** to set up the following background attributes of the exported HTML code. The main choice is between Image and Background.

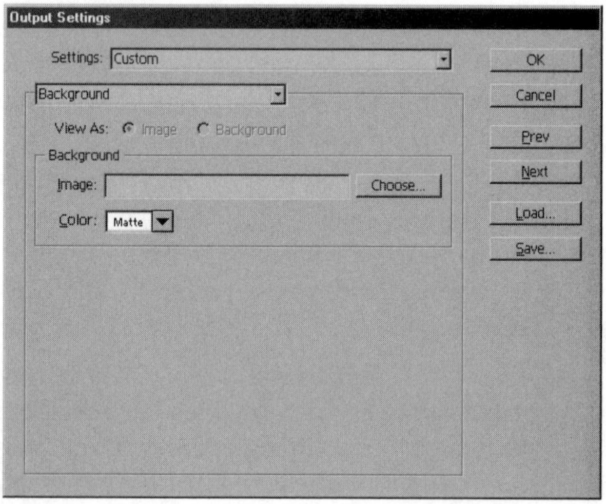

Figure 21.45: Background Output Settings control what's displayed behind the HTML page.

Image enables the additional Image option farther down, where you can specify a background image that will tile behind the page. You also get the Color option, which can use the Matte color if you already set one up in the Save for Web dialog box, or any other color you choose there.

 Background will specify a single solid background color in the HTML file. Accordingly, the only option available farther down is Color.

Saving Files Settings

The options shown in **Figure 21.46** control the way the filenames are written out.

 File Naming: If you're working on a Web project with specific requirements for the filename setup, you can probably get Illustrator to write out the filenames however you need them. Simply use the pop-up menus to set up the correct sequence of filename data. These options include data such as slice numbers, rollover states, and date and time. If you need filenames to include something that isn't on the list, just type it in the appropriate sequence box.

 Filename Compatibility: This lets you specify the platform naming convention with which your filenames will be compatible. Note that this is not just about your computer—it's about the platforms others might use to edit the files, and especially the platform on which the Web server runs (many Web servers run on Unix, for example). If one of them is dimmed, it's because Illustrator always makes sure the filename will work on the computer you're using.

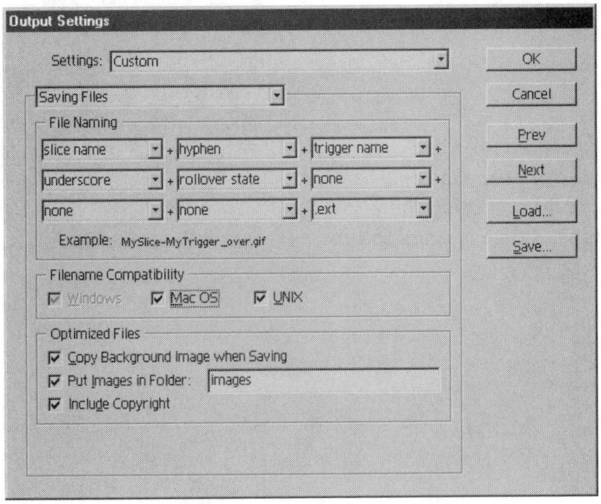

Figure 21.46: You can control HTML filenaming and file management of the exported slices from the Saving Files Output Settings dialog box.

🌐 **Optimized Files:** These options tell Illustrator what to do when saving optimized files (the ones exported by Save for Web, as opposed to the original Illustrator file).

Copy Background Image when Saving makes sure the background image (if you specified one) is copied into the folder where the rest of your images and slices are exported; otherwise, it will just leave it where it was.

Put Images in Folder lets you put slices and other images into a subfolder of the folder where you export the HTML, so that the files are a bit tidier. You can name the folder here, too.

Include Copyright inserts the copyright information, if you entered some using the File » File Info command.

Slices Settings

There's really just one section here, and it's about how slices are named. It works much like the File Naming option you saw in the Saving Files settings. Just pick and choose the order of name elements, as shown in **Figure 21.47**.

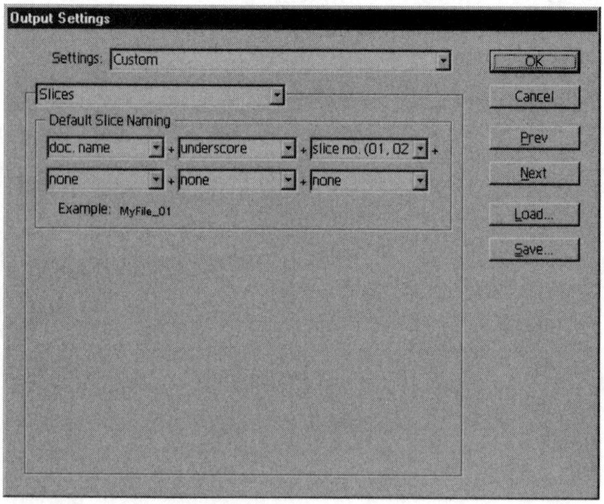

Figure 21.47: You can control how slices themselves are named using the Slices Output Settings dialog box.

Creating a Navigation Bar with Slices and CSS Layers

You can take the ideas you've learned so far and apply them to a real-world project: a navigation bar for a Web page. You can check out the final navigation bar in a Web browser in **Figure 21.48**, and its Illustrator source in **Figure 21.49**. It takes advantage of many of the Web features in Illustrator 10:

 Each link is a separate slice.

 All slices are created as object slices, giving you (or me) the freedom to reposition or resize them without worrying about slice alignment.

 Each slice was exported as a CSS layer. While it could have been implemented as a table, using tables for page layout is actually an old workaround. The World Wide Web Consortium says to let tables be tables and recommends doing page layout using CSS. Also, CSS layers can be moved around in an HTML editor such as Adobe GoLive instead of having to go all the way back to Illustrator.

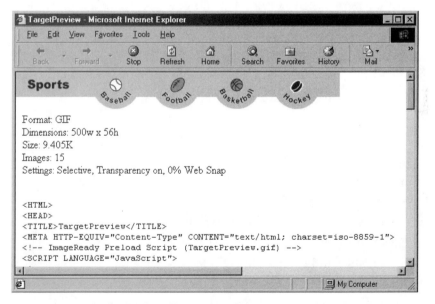

Figure 21.48: The finished toolbar in a Web browser, previewed using a browser jump-to button in the Save for Web dialog box. The file information below the toolbar is included by the Save for Web browser preview and won't be part of the final exported toolbar.

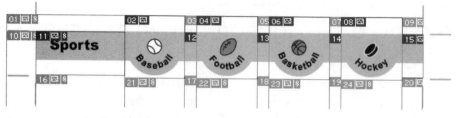

Figure 21.49: The finished, sliced navigation bar in Illustrator.

Before getting started, it's a good idea to set up the document so that it's Web-friendly. Here are two basic things I did to the document:

- Since the Web uses RGB colors, I chose File » Document Color Mode » RGB Color.

- Since the Web is a screen medium, I chose Edit » Preferences » Units & Undo, and changed the General units to pixels.

And here are the steps I used to build the toolbar.

1. Draw the toolbar.

Be sure that every design element that you want to become a slice can be somehow easily defined. In this case, the toolbar was organized around layers, because slices can be defined at the layer level. Each sport icon and text label is on its own layer, and the long rectangle with the word *Sports* is also on its own layer (Head).

2. Select an entire layer with Layers palette, and choose Object » Slice » Make.

Repeat for each layer.

3. To clip the design, set up crop marks by drawing a rectangle around the exact outside edge of the design, and then choose Object » Crop Marks » Make.

If you don't, when you go to Save for Web you may find that extraneous objects add unwanted area to the image.

4. Select each slice and choose Object » Slice » Slice Options to set up links and slice data, as shown in Figure 21.50.

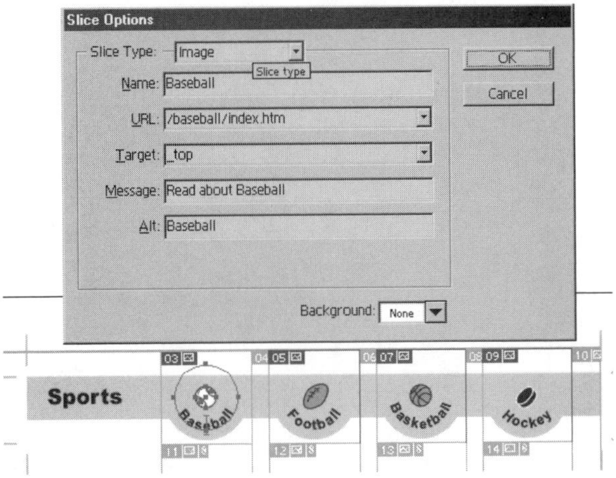

Figure 21.50: The Slice
Options dialog box when the
Baseball slice is selected.

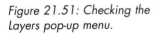

5. Choose File » Save for Web, and click the Layers tab.

6. Select Export As CSS Layers.

If you don't, it will be exported as a table. As you see in **Figure 21.51**, you can use the Layers pop-up menu to cycle through the layers and confirm the visibility and optimization settings for each layer.

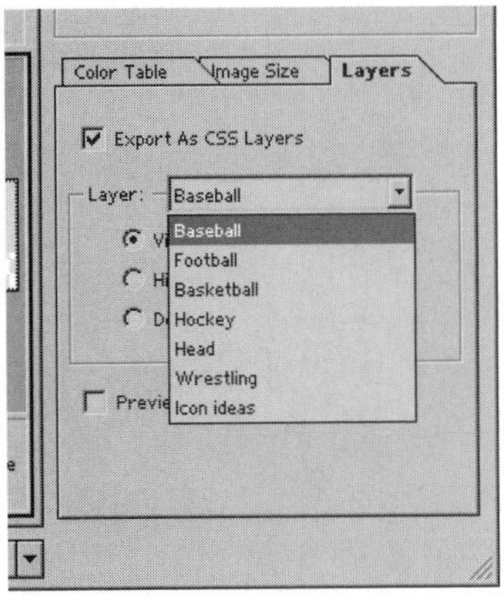

Figure 21.51: Checking the
Layers pop-up menu.

7. If necessary, choose Edit Output Settings from the optimize menu, and edit what you will.

8. Click the jump-to-browser button to test the page in the browsers you want to support.

9. Click Save when the Save for Web settings meet with your approval.

CHAPTER 22

ANIMATION AND DATA-DRIVEN GRAPHICS

The Macromedia Shockwave Flash (SWF) format is the Cinderella story of Web graphics. Before there were SWF animations, the only way to get motion on the Web was to create GIF animations, which required compiling multiple images into one big file.

Then Web designers discovered SWF. Instead of big, bulky pixels, SWF uses lean, mean vectors (like the paths found in Illustrator) to create images and animations. This allows SWF files that create Web graphics and animations to be much smaller than GIF files and animations. You can also add interactivity to SWF graphics or animations; SWF interactivity is built into the file instead of being added on in the Web page, as you would have to do if you were using GIF or JPEG files.

Originally, the only way to create SWF files was to use the Macromedia Flash application or Macromedia FreeHand. Today, Illustrator also lets you create SWF files. With it, you can use some special features to create simple SWF animations. However, if you want to add interactivity to SWF graphics, you'll have to finish them in a full-fledged animation program such as Macromedia Flash or Adobe LiveMotion.

In addition to SWF, Illustrator lets you create Scalable Vector Graphics (SVG) files, an up-and-coming open standard that exists as an XML-compatible alternative to SWF for vector Web graphics.

Designing SWF Files

There are three types of SWF files. A single-frame SWF file is a static image. Although not as exciting as an animation, static SWF files are extremely useful for displaying maps, technical illustrations, or other drawings that work better as vectors. Because these illustrations are vectors, they are much smaller than either GIF or JPEG graphics. And because you can zoom in on SWF files, your viewers can move in to examine details without losing sharpness. A single Illustrator document can easily be turned into an SWF file by using the Macromedia Flash Export option.

Multiframe SWF files create animations by playing all the frames one after another. This allows you to simulate motion, fades, transformations, and other effects. Because Illustrator doesn't have multiframes, you need to use multiple layers to simulate the multiframes. I'll cover how to do this very shortly in the section "Turning Blends into Animations."

Multiframe SWF files can also be used to create interactive Web sites. This is accomplished by displaying a frame and pausing the action of the movie. The viewer then clicks a button to move to the next frame. This sort of interactivity cannot be accomplished within Illustrator. For that you need to use Macromedia Flash or Adobe LiveMotion. These programs are also the only way to add sounds to your SWF files.

Viewing Shockwave Files

Once you have created SWF files, they can be inserted into HTML Web pages using a program such as Adobe GoLive. This allows you to use single-frame maps or illustrations as part of larger HTML Web pages. The benefit of this is that the SWF files are much smaller than GIF or JPEG images, and your viewers can zoom in or out to see details in the illustration. Or you can insert small multi-frame animations into an HTML page. This adds excitement to static Web pages. Or each SWF file can be posted individually as its own Web address.

 To see SWF files, you need to have the Shockwave Flash Player plug-in installed in your browser. The current versions of Netscape Navigator and Microsoft Internet Explorer install this plug-in automatically as part of their regular installation from a CD. However, if you install Internet Explorer from a Web download, you will not get the Shockwave Flash Player plug-in. In that case, you need to go to www.macromedia.com to download the Shockwave Flash Player plug-in.

Turning Blends into Animations

As mentioned in Chapter 17, the morphs you create using blends can be used as the basis for nifty Web animations. The steps to create these animations are rather simple. You first create the blend. The trick is to use Illustrator's Release to Layers command to separate the blend into steps that can be exported as SWF files. Here's your step-by-step guide to creating SWF animations.

1. **Create the blend.**

   Use the Blend command or blend tool to create the blend. Make whatever changes you want to the blend steps or spine.

2. **Target the blend in the Layers palette and choose Release to Layers (Sequence) or Release to Layers (Build) from the Layers palette menu.**

   To target the blend, make sure you see a double circle next to the name of the blend object in the Layers palette. If it isn't a double circle, click that circle to target it.

   The Release to Layers commands expand each blend step into its own individual object to create the incremental steps of the animation and send each newly expanded blend step to its own layer. Choose Release to Layers (Sequence) if you're making an animation where each frame appears only once, like movement across the graphic. Choose Release to Layers (Build) if you're making an animation where frames build up until the final frame, which will include everything in the preceding frames. If you have a blend between groups, each grouped step will be on its own layer after you apply the Release to Layers command. **Figure 22.1** shows the difference between before releasing to layers and after.

Expansion destroys the live blend, so make a copy of the blend if you think you may want to change the blend later. The blend appears as a group in the Layers palette.

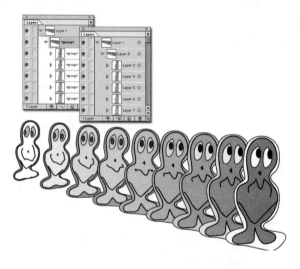

Figure 22.1: This blend of objects was expanded into individual group objects, as seen in the Layers palette on the left. After the Release to Layers command, each group appears on its own layer.

The Release to Layers command can be applied to more than just objects created by blends. Any objects or grouped objects on a layer can be released to their own layers.

3. **Set the SWF export options.**

First choose File » Export, which opens the Export dialog box. Name the file and choose Macromedia Flash (SWF) from the Save as type pop-up list. Then click the Save button to open the Macromedia Flash (SWF) Format Options as shown in **Figure 22.2**.

4. **Set the Export As menu to AI Layers to SWF Frames.**

This will convert each layer into an SWF frame.

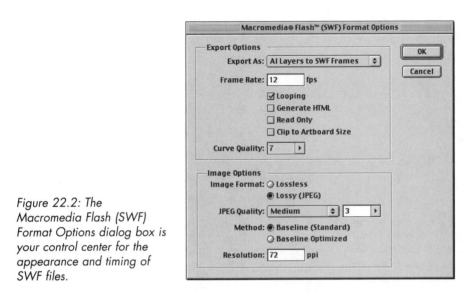

Figure 22.2: The
Macromedia Flash (SWF)
Format Options dialog box is
your control center for the
appearance and timing of
SWF files.

I'll cover the rest of the options in just a moment, but for now just click OK. This creates an SWF file that is ready to post on the Web as an SWF animation. If you want, at this point you can drag the finished file into a Web browser to see how it came out (if the browser has the Shockwave Flash Player plug-in installed).

 Apple QuickTime now supports SWF directly, so another way to preview an SWF file is to open it in QuickTime Player.

Setting the SWF Format Options

Once you have set up a file for SWF export, you can use the Macromedia Flash (SWF) Format Options dialog box to control how the final file is created. These controls not only change the appearance of your graphic, but also control the size of the file.

 *In most cases, you can generate Web formats such as SWF by choosing File » Export or by choosing File » Save for Web (which lets you preview the optimized version). The same options are usually available both ways, but in the Save for Web dialog box, they may be confusingly arranged, as shown in **Figure 22.3**, and in pop-up menus in the Save Optimized As dialog box you see after clicking Save in the Save for Web dialog box. If you can't find a certain option, it's probably there somewhere, though it might be labeled slightly differently. I just keep pushing buttons, clicking tabs, and popping up menus until I find what I want.*

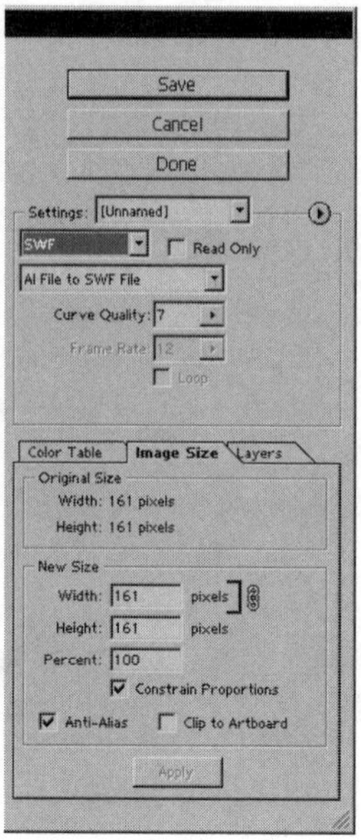

Figure 22.3: The Settings and Image Size panels from the Save for Web dialog box provide access to the same options you'll get after clicking Save in the Export dialog box.

Export Options

- **Export As AI File to SWF File** saves your Illustrator artwork out as a single-frame SWF file. Even if you have artwork on separate layers, choosing this option moves all the artwork to a single SWF frame. Use this option for maps and other single-frame illustrations.

- **Export As AI Layers to SWF Frames** converts each Illustrator layer into an SWF frame. Use this option to turn blends and other Illustrator objects into animations.

- **Export As AI Layers to SWF Files** converts each Illustrator layer into a separate SWF document. This option makes it easier to work with your Illustrator SWF file in the Macromedia Flash program itself.

- **Frame Rate** controls how fast multiframe animations play in frames per second (fps). The default value of 12 fps is the most commonly used rate to create smooth animations. Lower this value to slow down the animation.

- **Looping** (Loop in the Save for Web dialog box) does what it says, setting the exported SWF file to loop when it plays.

- **Generate HTML** exports a separate HTML file that refers to the SWF document. If you're not exactly sure how to write the HTML code for embedding an SWF document in your Web page, you may want to turn this on.

- **Read Only** sets a control so that your animations can't be copied from the Web and used by others. Turn this option on to protect your valuable artwork from showing up on other people's Web pages.

- **Clip to Artboard Size** (available in Export command only) uses the size of the artboard as the total size of the movie. If this option is turned on, the size of the movie is clipped to the size of the bounding box of the artwork in the illustration.

- **Curve Quality** controls how smooth curves in the Illustrator artwork are converted into SWF objects. The lower the curve quality, the smaller the final file size. However, very low curve quality can cause text to become hard-edged and distorted.

Image Options

The Image Options control how bitmapped images and effects in your file are converted into SWF objects. In other words, they don't apply to the vector portions of an SWF document.

- **Image Format Lossless** keeps the highest-quality display for bitmapped images. No compression is applied to the images. This option will create very large SWF files and should not be used for ordinary Web graphics. However, it can be practical and raise quality for projects where the files are stored locally, so that compression isn't as big an issue.

- **Image Format Lossy (JPEG)** allows you to adjust the amount of compression using the JPEG Quality pop-up list. The lower the quality you select, the more compression will be applied, and the smaller the final SWF image you'll get.

- **Method Baseline (Standard)** saves the JPEG with the standard type of compression. Use this setting if you have viewers who have difficulty reading the Baseline Optimized JPEG files.

- **Method Baseline Optimized** adds another level of optimization to the compression.

- **Resolution** lets you set a resolution amount for any bitmapped images. Set the resolution to 72 ppi for most purposes and to keep file size down. Use a higher resolution if you expect viewers to zoom in on the SWF files and you don't want your bitmapped images to look jagged.

Creating SVG Graphics

Wouldn't you have loved to be one of the first people to broadcast television? Or make one of the first telephone calls? Or send the first fax? Well, that's what it is like creating SVG graphics in Illustrator. Illustrator was the very first major application that could export Scalable Vector Graphics (SVG). And now, Illustrator 10 is the first major application to import SVG graphics.

Working with SVG is a little like being a pioneer in the old West. The SVG format is still relatively new, so most people need to download an SVG viewer. They can get it from the Adobe Web site. Many Adobe programs, including Illustrator, now install the SVG Viewer when you install the Adobe program.

Designing SVG Files

The simplest type of SVG file is a graphic with no animation or interactivity. These graphics can be easily created in Illustrator. However, SVG also allows you to create interactive animation graphics—for instance, you can click an object and it will change color or reveal information.

At the moment, the only way to create interactive or animated graphics in Illustrator is to use the SVG Interactivity palette where you enter code in the JavaScript language. Compared with SWF animations, which can be created by placing objects on their own layers, I find this method extremely difficult for most designers. (Entering code in a palette reminds me of the old days of DOS where you typed commands rather than used pull-down menus.) I would rather wait for a more visual approach to creating SVG graphics before I embrace the format for animations.

Setting the SVG or SVGZ Export Options

There are two types of SVG files you can export from Illustrator: SVG is the ordinary SVG format containing plain text code that describes the appearance of the artwork. SVGZ is a compressed version of the SVG format that makes smaller file sizes. If you are familiar with changing HTML code, you can easily modify the attributes within an SVG file. An SVGZ file can be uncompressed using any utility that understands the popular Zip compression standard. Once you have created your artwork, it is rather simple to export as either SVG or SVGZ formats.

1. Choose File » Save As or File » Save a Copy.

2. Select the folder where you want to save the file, and type in a name for the file in the File name text box.

3. In the Save as type box, choose SVG or SVG Compressed from the pop-up menu.

4. The SVG Options dialog box appears as shown in **Figure 22.4**. This is where you can set the export options for the SVG or SVGZ files, which I'll describe next.

> *You can also set these options by choosing File » Save for Web. They're the same options, but you'll find them in the Settings panel on the right side of the Save for Web dialog box.*

Export Options

You use the SVG Options dialog box, shown in Figure 22.4, to control what information is saved within the file. These options affect both the size and the appearance of the final SVG file.

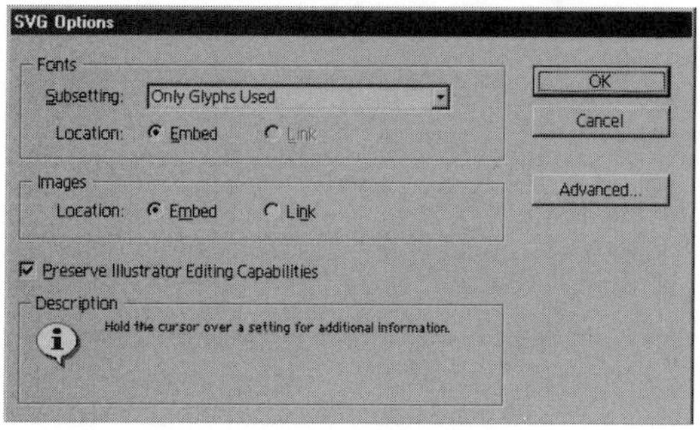

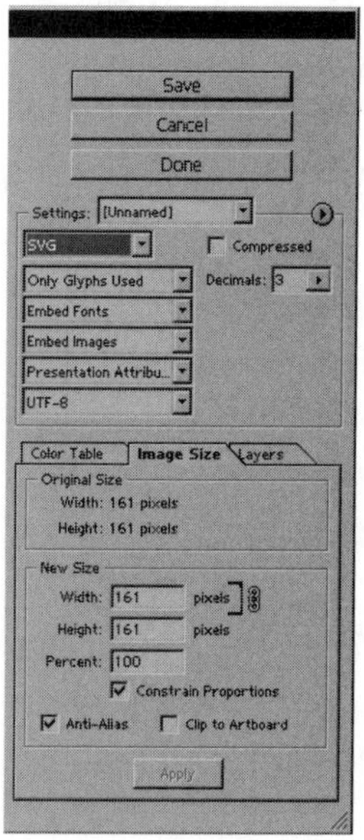

Figure 22.4: Main SVG Options dialog box and the similar panel in the Save for Web dialog box, in case you decided to export it that way. Note that some of the options in the Save for Web SVG panel appear in the Advanced dialog box if you chose the Export command.

The Compressed check box appears only in the Save for Web dialog box. This applies Zip file size compression to the SVG file, making it an SVGZ file. You won't see this option in the Save As dialog box because you make the SVG/SVGZ choice from the Save as type pop-up in the Save As dialog box.

Fonts Subsetting lets you control how the fonts are embedded or linked from the exported SVG file.

- **None (Use System Fonts)** embeds no fonts within the file. Use this option if you have no text in your file or you can rely on the necessary fonts being installed on the end user's system.

- **Only Glyphs Used** includes only the glyphs or characters for the text that exists in the current artwork. This adds to the file size, but only the smallest amount necessary to view the file. Do not use this option if you have a JavaScript action that allows the user to change the text in the file or if you want to edit the text directly in the SVG file without using Illustrator.

- **Common English** embeds all the text characters found in English-language documents.

- **Common English & Glyphs Used** adds the characters used in the artwork to the English-language characters.

- **Common Roman** embeds all the characters in Roman-language documents.

- **Common Roman & Glyphs Used** adds the characters used in the artwork to the Roman-language characters.

- **All Glyphs** embeds all the characters in the font. Use this to add non-Roman characters such as Japanese characters.

You choose Fonts Location to specify where the embedded fonts should be.

- **Embed** includes the fonts inside the document. This ensures that the fonts are present when the file is viewed.

- **Link** allows you to point the document to a different exported file where you've stored the fonts. This option is very helpful if you have multiple SVG files that all use the same fonts.

Like the embedded font location, the Images Location options allow you to specify where embedded raster images should be located.

- **Embed** keeps bitmapped images in the exported SVG file. This increases file size but makes sure that the image is included with the file. Raster images that have no alpha channel (transparency) are converted to JPEG images. Raster images with transparency are converted into the PNG format.

Link lets you point to a different exported file. Use this option if you have multiple SVG files that all use the same common bitmapped images.

The Preserve Illustrator Editing Capabilities option includes a copy of the Illustrator file with the SVG file, so you don't have to keep the Illustrator version of the file just to be able to update it later. Of course, turning this on makes the file bigger. This option doesn't appear in the Save for Web dialog box.

If you used Illustrator 9 to export SVG files, you might notice that a few options seem to be missing. They're not. Adobe simply moved them into a subdialog box to simplify things a bit. To get to them, click the Advanced button and you'll see the dialog box shown in **Figure 22.5**, where you'll find the options I'll describe next.

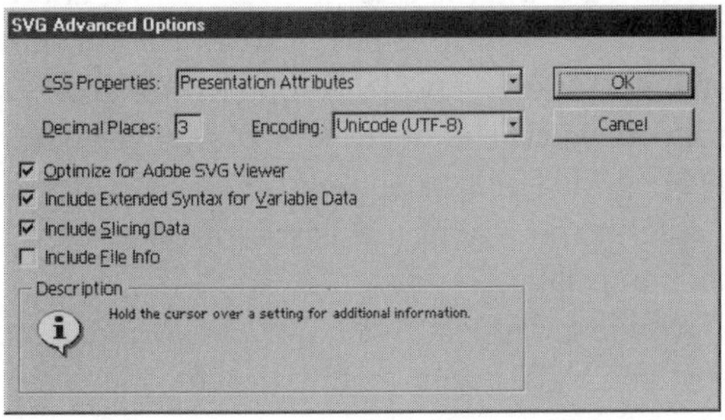

Figure 22.5: The SVG Advanced Options dialog box controls the finer nuances of exporting an SVG file.

The CSS Properties option determines how the file's appearance will be represented in the SVG file. Remember, SVG is based on XML, and XML uses CSS to describe appearance. You have to know your way around CSS to take advantage of these options, so if you either don't know CSS or don't want to know, just leave it set to the default option, Presentation Attributes. (If you're sending these graphics to a Web team that's setting up an XML-based project, they may be able to tell you which one to use.)

 Presentation Attributes is the default because it works well in most cases.

 Style Attributes is a good choice if you plan to use the SVG file with CSS transformations. It can also be useful if you plan to edit the file by hand, because the code it generates is more readable to human eyes.

 Style Attributes (Entity References) is a lot like Style Attributes but is faster and more compact. Choose this if you want to use Style Attributes but you're not so concerned about reading the file in a text editor.

- **Style Elements** is likely to be used with HTML (non-XML) pages. It makes the SVG style elements CSS styles that are also compatible with HTML pages that you also want to reference the style sheet, but it's not the fastest option for rendering.

The Decimal Places option (called Decimals in the Save As dialog box) lets you specify the precision of the vectors in the exported artwork. You can set a value of 1 to 7 decimal places. A high value results in a larger file size but maintains the highest image quality.

The Encoding options let you choose between ASCII characters or characters encoded using the Unicode Transformation Format (UTF). Although ASCII is fine for many European languages, UTF-8 and UTF-16 are preferred for non-Roman languages like Japanese, Chinese, or Hebrew. If you want to include information entered using the File Info command, choose UTF-8.

The Optimize for Adobe SVG Viewer option should be on if you went beyond just drawing and used special Adobe SVG features such as Illustrator's SVG filters, and you expect the file to be viewed through the Adobe SVG Viewer browser plug-in. This option will preserve the special Adobe info so that the Adobe plug-in can render it as fast as it can, and it makes it easier to edit the file with Illustrator later.

The Include Extended Syntax for Variable Data option is intended for when you're passing SVG graphics on to graphics servers (such as Adobe AlterCast) that need the variable information from Illustrator to fill in Web page templates properly. If you're not doing this kind of thing, you don't need to select this option.

The Include Slicing Data option exports the information an SVG viewer needs to reconstruct an SVG graphic you sliced up. If you didn't slice your graphic, you don't need to select this option.

The Include File Info option exports the data entered into the File Info command. This option is available only when you've selected UTF-8 as the Encoding option further up in the dialog box.

Data-Driven SVG Graphics

Data-driven graphics are Illustrator 10's way of decreasing drudgery for sites that have their foundation in a database. You can find examples of such a site in anything from an e-commerce shopping site to a site that documents the statistics for your fantasy baseball league. Before Illustrator 10, Illustrator really had no part in this process. Sure, you could have used Illustrator 9 to create Web graphics for a database-driven site, but your graphics would have to be perfectly and manually aligned to the Web pages someone else was coding up. In addition, the feedback loop—the time between designing a site and actually testing it with the live database—was so long that design problems might not be discovered until late in the process. Or if the site wasn't automated, you might have had to spend long hours generating endless variations on a page, so that a site could show products with different colors and options.

Illustrator 10 makes this whole thing much easier by letting you use Illustrator to design a page around the variables in the Web site's database. These variables can display different photos, text, or graphics that are stored in a database, as you can see in **Figure 22.6**. They can even (like a certain British tyke with a special cape) disappear entirely if need be. What will ultimately appear in the Web browser depends on the choices that a user makes when viewing that page on the Web.

The page design, complete with these variables, is known as a *template*, because the real content gets filled in somewhere else (by a database). You can test the template using actual data that you can set up or import from the database (either way, that's called a *data set*), so that you can troubleshoot the interaction of the template with the data before you hand off the design. When it works the way you want it to, you export the Illustrator page as an SVG template. Illustrator will mark the variable objects as variables and leave them empty, to be filled in using data from the site's database, pulled into the layout by a script (usually written by the programmers that maintain the Web site). Because SVG is based on XML, it can be seamlessly integrated with standard XML databases and scripts. When it's all working, the user's Web browser sends data about user choices to the Web server, which uses a script to change parts of the page based on those choices. The script can be encoded in the Web page (as JavaScript, for example) or be stored on the Web server.

Figure 22.6: All three graphics come from the same file. Changeable areas were linked to variables and arranged into data sets. The only difference among the three graphics is that each of them uses a different data set.

So what is XML then? XML stands for eXtensible Markup Language. If you're familiar with HTML, it's similar to that, but it's intended to be more flexible. For example, you can make up your own tags, which makes it easier to create tags that fit the types of data you have, instead of figuring out which of the available tags you should use. This tag customizability also makes XML more readable by humans. Another key idea behind XML is that form is separate from content. While HTML lets you store both the data and its appearance in the same file, this means an HTML document made for a Web browser would look terrible on a cell phone, or you'd need redundant data documents for each device. With XML, you need only one XML data document for both the Web browser and the cell phone, plus a lay-out template (no data) for a Web browser and a layout template for a cell phone. While the layout templates can be HTML (and often are these days), Illustrator tem-plates are SVG, to preserve vector graphics and type information, to provide the additional flexibility of SVG, and to work better with XML (on which SVG is based).

When Illustrator 10's new features were announced, more than a few print professionals thought that SVG and XML were examples of Illustrator forsaking their print world for the Web. But they are quite mistaken. XML is becoming a major force in database-driven print production, and there's nothing stopping you from using the concepts in this chapter—everything from data templates to scripting—to automate the creation of printed business cards, product datasheets, ads customized for different regions or languages, or package designs for a product family. You don't even have to use XML—you can use Visual Basic or AppleScript (already widely used in the Mac prepress world) to automate Illustrator production tasks.

 All of the data-driven graphics features in this section are new in Illustrator 10.

Creating a Web Site Template

The first thing you need to do is figure out which parts of a Web page are going to change (based on the database) and which parts aren't going to change. So, for example, on an online store page, the company logo and header at the top won't change, but the section displaying the product, options, and colors would need to change.

Next, figure out what the variables are going to be. Generally, you're going to need one variable for each item on the page that can change. Some variables will control objects on the page, but other variables will be controlled by a variable that is in turn controlled by user input.

For example, if a Web shopper chooses Cell Phone Model 3000, the model number variable (which is now set by the user to "Cell Phone Model 3000") will determine the state of other variables, such as the phone's picture, feature list, and price. If you're working on a team with Web programmers, they might have already worked out what the site's variables are and how they will change. That makes it easier for you. Just go get the list from them and make sure you know where the variables go. While you're at it, you might also ask for some sample data sets, which you can use to test your Web template in Illustrator.

The Variables Palette

The new Variables palette is where you set up the variables for a data-driven Web page. Open it by choosing Window » Variables, and you'll see the variable list and controls shown in **Figure 22.7**.

You can sort the Variables palette list by clicking the Variables or Objects headers.

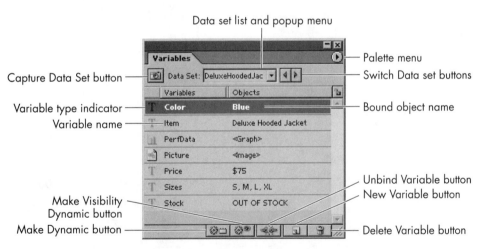

Figure 22.7: The Variables palette.

The Four Kinds of Variables

Illustrator knows about four kinds of variables that can be controlled by the interaction between the Web site's scripts and the database that the script works with.

- **Graph Data:** This variable type represents tabular spreadsheet data as the variable data here, the kind you'd enter into the Graph Data window you saw in Chapter 13.

- **Linked File:** This represents a separate, externally stored image that will be switched in and out of the Web page. It's a great way to dynamically insert the right product photo from a database.

- **Text String:** This lets the text in a text object be replaced with different text data. Use this for any text or numbers that will change.

- **Visibility:** This simply lets the script control whether an object is visible or hidden. In Illustrator, you set this by using the eye icon in the Layers palette to hide or show the object.

Figure 22.8 gives you a few examples of how variables can be used in a Web page you design in Illustrator.

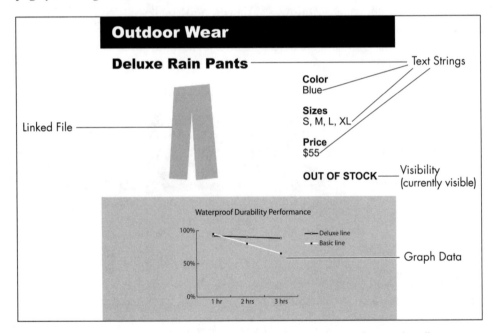

Figure 22.8: Four variable types on the same Web page being designed in Illustrator.

Setting Up Variables

If you know that an XML variable library already exists for your project, skip to the next topic, "Importing and Exporting Variable Libraries." Otherwise, you need to create a list of variables.

If you've set up your variables, you're done. Right? Wrong. Normally, each variable must be bound to an object on the page. We know that a variable represents data that will change. But Illustrator (and later, the Web site's script) won't know *what* to change on the page until you *bind* a variable to an object. Binding basically says "When variable X changes, change object Y." Now Illustrator and the Web site will know what to do. That's what you'll be setting up in the following procedures.

There's more than one way to do this. Here's one quick and dirty way.

1. Click the New Variable button in the Variables palette as many times as the number of variables you need. You now have a list of variables with default names.

2. Bind variables to objects. Double-click a variable, set its options in the Variable Options dialog box seen in **Figure 22.9**. The four types are explained in the previous section, "The Four Kinds of Variables." Click OK, and continue down the variable list until they're all set up.

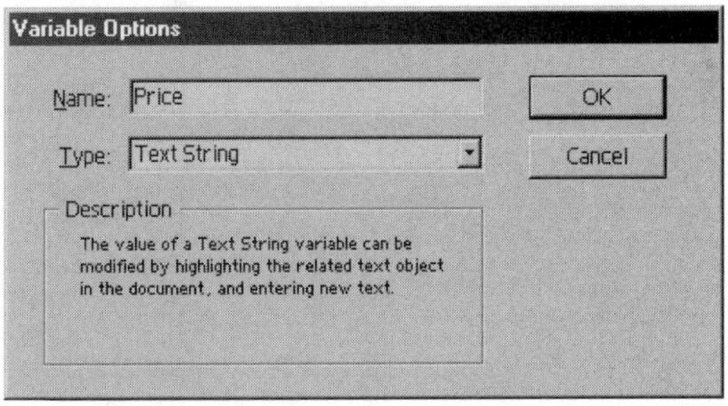

Figure 22.9: The Variable Options dialog box.

If you're a more systematic type, you can Alt-click (Option-click on the Mac) the New Variable button so you can set up each variable as you go.

If the variable will be used in an XML workflow, make sure the name is valid in XML (no spaces, and starting only with a letter, underscore, or colon). If you want to work with variables as XML IDs, choose Edit » Preferences » Units & Undo (Illustrator » Preferences » Units & Undo on Mac OS X), and in the Names section, select XML ID. The other choice is Object Name, which is the name of the object as it appears in the Layers palette.

Now, if you would rather design first and deal with variables later, do it this way.

1. Draw the Web page layout, making sure that you make separate objects for each thing that will be controlled by a variable.

2. Select an object.

3. Bind variables to objects using the Make Dynamic or Make Visibility Dynamic button. (The actual tool tip name for the Make Dynamic button will change depending on what you selected, and for some objects only Make Visibility Dynamic is available). Illustrator makes a new variable, guessing at the variable type based on what was selected.

4. Edit the new list of variables by double-clicking each of them to set their name in the Variable Options dialog box seen in Figure 22.9, and if necessary, change their type as well.

If you ever come across objects that need to be bound to variables, just select the object, then select a variable, click the Make Dynamic button, and then if necessary, double-click the variable to edit it.

Once you set this up, when you export the template and use a script to hook it up to a database, the objects will be controlled by the script that changes the variable data. **Figure 22.10** shows you what the Variables palette will look like before and after variables are bound.

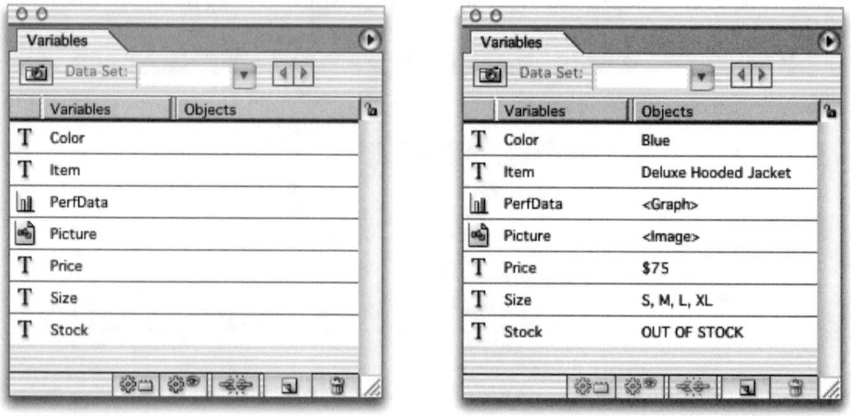

Figure 22.10: A variable list before binding (left) and after all have been bound to objects (right).

You can lock the entire variable list by clicking the Lock icon at the top-right corner of the list in the Variables palette. When it's locked, you can't change the list or edit any variables. As with locking elsewhere in the program, you'd lock the variable list to prevent accidental changes to it.

Importing and Exporting Variable Libraries

If you're working with Web database programmers who already have a list of variables stored in an XML file, you can import those variables right into Illustrator and save some setup time. Just choose Load Variable Library from the Variables palette menu, and voilà, the variable library will show up in the Variables palette. When you can see them in the Variables palette, don't forget to bind them to something on the layout (by selecting an object and using one of the Make Dynamic buttons at the bottom of the Variables palette, as covered in the previous section).

If you worked out a list of variables in Illustrator and want to hand it to your Web developers, you can export a variable library by choosing Save Variable Library from the same menu.

Selecting Bound Objects

Alt-click (Option-click on the Mac) a variable name to select the object bound to it. This is the same as choosing Select Bound Object from the Variables palette menu.

If you have a need to select all bound objects at once, choose Select All Bound Objects from the Variables palette menu.

Working with Data Sets

To avoid embarrassment at the hands of the nerds over in the Web programming department, test your template using data sets. A data set is a particular combination of variables and data. For example, a single data set for a sales force might include a salesperson's name, photo, region, and sales performance spreadsheet. Switching to another salesperson's name would change all of that data to a different data set representing the other salesperson.

Before you make a data set, at least one bound variable must exist so that the data has some meaning in the layout.

Creating a Data Set

Making data sets is pretty straightforward.

1. Make everything the way it should be for the new data set.

For each variable, edit its bound object with the correct data for the set. In **Figure 22.11**, the catalog layout is fully designed, and each variable is in the proper state for the Deluxe Rain Pants data set.

The way you edit has to match the variable type.

- Edit a graph data variable by editing the Graph Data window for the graph.

- Edit a linked file variable by using the Links palette to relink to a different file.

- Edit a text string variable by editing the text in a text block.

- Edit visibility by changing the object's visibility in the Layers palette.

2. Capture the data set.

Either click the camera icon next to the data set name, or choose Capture Data Set from the Variables palette menu.

Outdoor Wear

Deluxe Hooded Jacket

Color
Blue

Sizes
S, M, L, XL

Price
$75

Waterproof Durability Performance

Outdoor Wear

Deluxe Rain Pants

Color
Blue

Sizes
S, M, L, XL

Price
$55

OUT OF STOCK

Waterproof Durability Performance

Variables		Objects	
T	Color	Blue	
T	Item	Deluxe Hooded Jacket	
ⅠⅡⅠ	PerfData	<Graph>	
🖼	Picture	<Image>	
T	Price	$75	
T	Size	S, M, L, XL	
T	Stock	OUT OF STOCK	

Data Set: DeluxeHooded

Variables		Objects	
T	Color	Blue	
T	Item	Deluxe Rain Pants	
ⅠⅡⅠ	PerfData	<Graph>	
🖼	Picture	<Image>	
T	Price	$55	
T	Size	S, M, L, XL	
T	Stock	OUT OF STOCK	

Data Set: DeluxeRainPa

Figure 22.11: The same Illustrator Web page showing different data sets. Note that on the right, there is a text string ("Out of Stock") that is not visible on the left. Using a script, the site's Web programmers will tie the Out of Stock text string variable's visibility to an inventory value from the Web shopping site's database.

3. Rename the data set.

If you want a friendlier name than the one Illustrator provides by default, just edit the data set name in the box, or choose Rename Data Set from the Variables palette menu.

You can use scripts to create data sets or import them from other programs, which will make your template testing more accurate. Check out the information on the Illustrator product CD, inside the Illustrator Extras \ Scripting \ Datasets folder.

Using Data Sets
Data sets are easy to work with.

- While testing, you can try out different data sets by clicking the arrows to the right of the data set name or by choosing one from the pop-up menu next to the data set name.

- If you need to edit the object states in a data set, make sure the right data set is active, make your changes, and then choose Update Data Set from the Variables palette menu.

- To delete a data set, make sure you've selected the data set you want to remove, then choose Delete Data Set from the Variables palette menu.

- If the data set name is in italics, that means the data on the artboard doesn't match any data sets. If the data is correct, you can make a new data set for it, update the current data set to match (by choosing Update Data Set from the Variables palette menu), or reselect the data set without saving data set changes.

Saving the Template

When everything's tested and ready, export the file as SVG. Follow the steps in the section "Setting the SVG or SVGZ Export Options," but be sure to turn on one required setting: In the SVG Options dialog box, click the Advanced button, and make sure Include Extended Syntax for Variable Data is selected. That will export information necessary for the template to interact successfully with the downstream workflow. What's the downstream workflow? It could be the site scripts and an Open Database Connectivity (ODBC)-compatible database, or Adobe GoLive 6 (which can work with the dynamic links generated in Illustrator 10), or Adobe's AlterCast image server, which can substitute all template variables with the right data.

Scripting for Data-Driven Graphics

Scripting relates to Illustrator in two ways. There are the scripts that can run inside Illustrator and the Web-based scripts that will fill the variables in templates you create with Illustrator.

In version 10, Illustrator can now be scripted using JavaScript, Visual Basic in Windows, and AppleScript on the Mac. Many designers shy away from scripting, and there's nothing wrong with that if you really want to concentrate on being a designer. But if you have an interest in automating graphics production (also known as an interest in saving time, repetitive labor, and money), and you're not intimidated by a little coding, you can script Illustrator's data-driven templates, variables, and data sets to generate graphics while you sit back and sip a drink on the porch.

"Now wait a minute," I hear some of you saying. "Why do I need scripts if Illustrator already has actions?" Well, that's a good question. While power users automate Illustrator with actions, power-user programmers quickly realize that there are useful things actions can't do, such as conditional statements (*if* the linked graphic is Logo1998.eps, *then* relink it to Logo2002.eps). Scripting opens up a much wider range of automation possibilities, including making it easier to integrate Illustrator automation with other programs that support standard scripting languages but don't support Adobe-style actions (for example, so that you can make multiple programs exchange data to assemble and produce artwork).

Here's a script you can run yourself. It exports all open documents in SWF format. With some documents open, choose File » Scripts » ExportDocsAsFlash (File » Scripts » Export Open Documents as Flash on the Mac). Notice the other scripts listed in the Scripts submenu. Just think of all the keystrokes and time this would save if you had to do an entire site's worth of these conversions! Here's what the JavaScript version of the script (installed with the Windows version) looks like:

```
// save all open documents as flash documents
//$.bp();      //      Uncomment this line to cause the script to be
run in the JavaScript debugger window.


numDocuments = documents.length;


for ( i = 0 ; i < numDocuments; i++)
{
        aDocument = documents[i];
        theDocumentName = aDocument.name;

        flashOptions = new ExportOptionsFlash();

        flashOptions.jpegQuality = 10;
        flashOptions.curveQuality = 10;
        flashOptions.replacing = SaveOptions.SAVECHANGES;

        docPath = aDocument.path;
        docPathStr = docPath.toString();

        if (docPathStr.length > 1)
        {
                documentPath = docPath + "/" + aDocument.name;
```

```
        }
        else
        {
                // This is a brand new file and doesn't have a path
yet,
                // so put it in the illustrator application folder.
                documentPath = path + "/" + aDocument.name;
        }

        theFile = new File(documentPath);
        aDocument.exportFile(theFile, ExportType.FLASH,
flashOptions);
}
```

The Mac version is written in AppleScript. If you are conversant in scripting languages, you can see that you can preset the Shockwave Flash options (as seen in the flashOptions lines). You can always examine a script by opening its file in a text editor. AppleScript scripts can be opened in Script Editor on the Mac. Built-in scripts are stored in the Presets \ Scripts subfolder. If you want more examples and documentation, grab your Illustrator 10 CD and check out the scripting resources in the Illustrator Extras \ Scripting folder.

Outside of Illustrator, a Web server can run scripts that mediate between the SVG/XML templates created by Illustrator and the database that populates the templates. Illustrator itself is not involved with these scripts other than providing the XML templates for the scripts to work with. If you're a Web designer but not a programmer, you may not need to worry too much about Web scripting. If you are involved in helping design the database scripts and the templates, simply work with the Web programmers to make sure you all agree on what the variable names and purposes will be. The scripts written by the Web programmers will be referring to the variable names to change the content of the layout, and they may be working in common Web database scripting languages such as JavaScript.

ILLUSTRATOR AND OTHER PROGRAMS

Way back when Illustrator was born in the mid-1980s, its creators expected it to be used in exactly two ways. Either you could print drawings out directly from Illustrator (in glorious black-and-white, no less), or you could take them into a layout application such as PageMaker and print them as part of a layout. That was it.

Things have changed. Having once driven typesetting machines and then imagesetters, all in the service of the printing press, computers have moved beyond paper to serve Web sites and edit digital camera footage. In addition, the blurring of lines between the raster and vector worlds has let Illustrator gain access to areas where it used to be irrelevant. Today you find Illustrator users not just at newspapers and magazines, but at Web design companies, TV stations, and film studios. The downside to Illustrator's multimedia expansion is the bewildering range of options and choices to be made when trying to make Illustrator files for a medium in which you're not familiar. In this chapter I'll try to smooth out the bumps you may encounter in getting Illustrator to play nice with, well, everybody.

 A general tip for using Illustrator in other programs: If you can't get an Illustrator file to import into another program, first try saving and then importing an EPS version of it. You can also try saving the document into an older version of the Illustrator format.

Working with Adobe Photoshop

Adobe Photoshop and Illustrator are naturals at working together, since Photoshop is the raster specialist and Illustrator is the vector specialist. You *could* say that Photoshop is a generic bitmap image editor, and treat it as such. If you take this approach, you would simply make TIFFs out of your Photoshop files and place them in Illustrator, or you would make TIFFs out of your Illustrator files and place them in Photoshop. But to do so would be to miss the point—big time—because Adobe has worked especially hard to get these two programs to work well together. Given their opposite approaches to graphics creation, the current versions are surprisingly compatible.

Opening an Illustrator File in Photoshop

If you open an Illustrator file in Photoshop, Photoshop will simply rasterize it using the options you set in the dialog box shown in **Figure 23.1**. This is fine, but you can do better.

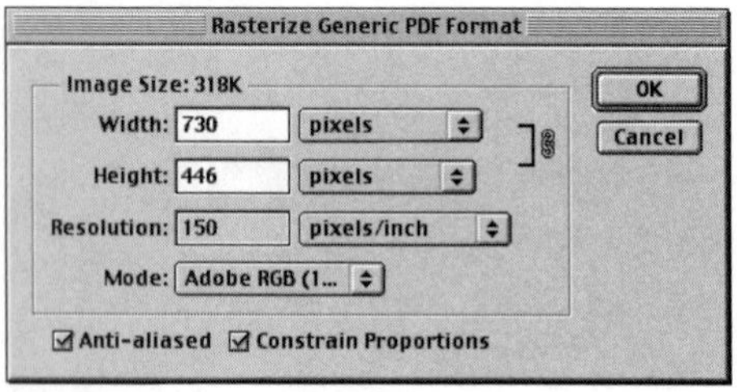

Figure 23.1: Photoshop's dialog box for converting an Illustrator file into Photoshop pixels. Note that the dialog box title is Rasterize Generic PDF Format. That's because the Illustrator 10 file format is a form of PDF.

Rasterize Generic PDF Format

Image Size: 318K

Width: 730   pixels

Height: 446   pixels

Resolution: 150   pixels/inch

Mode: Adobe RGB (1...

☑ Anti-aliased ☑ Constrain Proportions

OK

Cancel

If you really want Photoshop to get the most flexibility out of an Illustrator file, add another step: export the Illustrator file as a Photoshop file. While this step is neither obvious nor easy to remember, it's much more powerful than simply letting Photoshop make a flat image out of your carefully layered Illustrator file. The Photoshop Options dialog box, seen in **Figure 23.2**, is essentially a long list of the bonus features you get by performing this step before going to Photoshop.

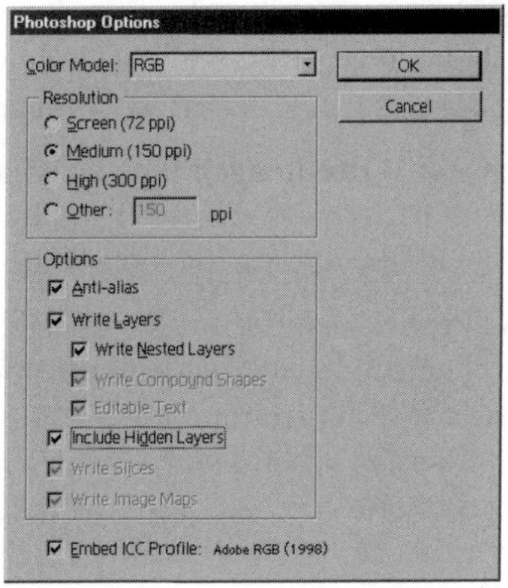

Figure 23.2: The Photoshop Options dialog box provides all sorts of enticements to use this method of transferring files between Illustrator and Photoshop.

- **Color Model** exports the file in one of the color models covered in Chapter 14. The choice is important for some uses: CMYK is best for printing, RGB for Web and video projects, and Grayscale for black-and-white projects. If you don't need CMYK, it's good to choose one of the others because where CMYK requires four color channels, RGB requires only three, and Grayscale only one, which translates into smaller file sizes.

- **Resolution** sets the pixels per inch at the current physical size of the artwork. Obviously, you need low resolution for the Web and high resolution for print, with the usual effect on file size.

- **Anti-Alias** helps smooth lines as they make the export transition from Illustrator vectors to Photoshop bitmaps. It also helps when exporting to a low resolution.

- **Write Layers** preserves Illustrator layers in the form of Photoshop layers. Note that it preserves only the highest layer level from the Layers palette—it doesn't preserve layers nested at a lower level.

- **Write Nested Layers** needs to be on if you want to preserve Illustrator layers that are not at the highest layer level in the Layers palette. Note that Illustrator may not let you choose this if doing so won't preserve the look of the original artwork.

- **Write Compound Shapes** preserves compound paths if they're at the first layer level in the Layers palette. Again, if Illustrator needs to flatten a compound shape into a layer to preserve how the original artwork looks, it will override this choice and do that.

- **Editable Text** preserves text so that it can continue to be edited in Photoshop. Again, this works on text only in a first-level Illustrator layer. Another limitation is that it doesn't work on area text or text on a path.

- **Write Slices** and **Write Image Maps** do what they say—they preserve these Web options if you've created them in Illustrator and if they can be preserved without altering the look of the original artwork.

- **Embed ICC Profile** includes a color-management profile in the document so that Photoshop can maintain the appearance of colors as created in Illustrator (if Illustrator color settings are set up correctly). Turn this on if you've synchronized color-management settings across Illustrator and Photoshop, as covered in the section "Making Color Appear Consistent across Programs" later in this chapter.

Here are the steps for exporting Illustrator files in Photoshop format.

1. Choose File » Export in Illustrator.

2. Adjust the settings in the Photoshop Options dialog box, shown in Figure 23.2. In particular, you might want to turn on the Write Layers option to preserve your Illustrator layers.

Sometimes options are dimmed and unavailable. Usually this is because Illustrator can't export with that option without changing the appearance of the artwork, as may happen with certain kinds of layered effects. Illustrator's priority is to make the exported file look like the original artwork as much as possible, sometimes at the expense of flexibility.

3. Click OK.

Opening a Photoshop File in Illustrator

To open a Photoshop file in Illustrator, simply use Illustrator's File » Open command. When you do this, Illustrator asks you how you want to open the Photoshop file, using the dialog box you see in **Figure 23.3**.

Figure 23.3: The Photoshop Import dialog box lets you determine how to import a Photoshop file.

Convert Photoshop layers to objects will turn each Photoshop layer into an image on its own Illustrator layer. Illustrator can make nested layers out of Photoshop layer sets.

Flatten Photoshop layers to a single image will convert the entire Photoshop file to a single bitmapped image, no matter how many interesting layers were in the original Photoshop file. If you don't need to work with the original Photoshop layers in Illustrator, choosing this will certainly save disk space and let you edit faster than making Illustrator track all of the layers.

Either way, Photoshop will keep a clipping path if it finds one in the Photoshop document, but if multiple paths exist, it will take only one clipping path.

Two more options exist in the dialog box: Import Image Maps and Import Slices. If you set up these Web features in Photoshop, Illustrator can read them and apply them to the Illustrator version.

If you chose Convert Photoshop layers to objects, Illustrator preserves the following features of a Photoshop file:

- Layers
- Opacity masks
- Transparency
- Blending modes
- Vector shapes (converted to Illustrator paths)

Most everything else is converted to images on Illustrator layers that mirror the Photoshop layers.

Moving Vector Objects between Photoshop and Illustrator

If you haven't really plumbed the depths of the latest versions of Photoshop, you may be surprised to find out just how much you can do with vector graphics in Photoshop. For a while now, Photoshop has had an Illustrator-like pen tool, added for its usefulness in creating clipping paths. More recently, Photoshop added shape layers, which are special layers containing vector paths. They are most often used as clipping paths (vector masks), but because they really are paths, you can move these paths back and forth between Illustrator and Photoshop with a minimum of fuss.

You'll find Photoshop paths either on a shape layer or in the Paths palette, so when you're moving paths between the two programs, it's a good idea to have the Paths and Layers palettes open in Photoshop.

To move Photoshop paths to Illustrator:

1. Select paths as vectors in Photoshop.

You can do this with Photoshop's direct selection tool, which looks exactly like Illustrator's. If it's a shape, select the shape layer in the Layers palette, then Alt-click (Option-click on the Mac) the Shape Clipping Path in the Paths palette to select the shape as a vector. Make sure all handles on the paths are solid; otherwise, you haven't selected entire paths. A completely selected path will look like the crescent on the right side of **Figure 23.4**.

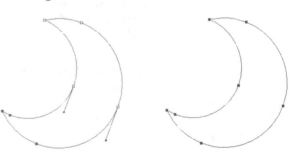

Figure 23.4: The Photoshop path on the left isn't completely selected; some of the upper points are hollow (unselected). The one on the right is, so the entire path will copy over to Illustrator.

Another way to select an entire Photoshop path is to Alt-Click (Option-click on the Mac) the path with the direct selection tool.

2. Move the paths to Illustrator.

Either use the direct selection tool to drag the selected paths to an Illustrator document window, or use the Edit » Copy command in Photoshop and then the Edit » Paste command in Illustrator.

Moving Illustrator paths to Photoshop can be trickier. Illustrator can transfer its objects to the Clipboard in several ways. You have to set a preference first, to make sure Illustrator really puts paths on the Clipboard. Here's the whole story.

1. Get Illustrator ready.

Choose Edit » Preferences » Files & Clipboard (Illustrator »
Preferences » Files & Clipboard in Mac OS X). In the dialog box,
shown in **Figure 23.5**, make sure that in the Clipboard section, the
AICB and Preserve Paths options are switched on and the PDF option
is switched off. Click OK to close the dialog box. You should have to
do this only once, or at least until you reset your preferences.

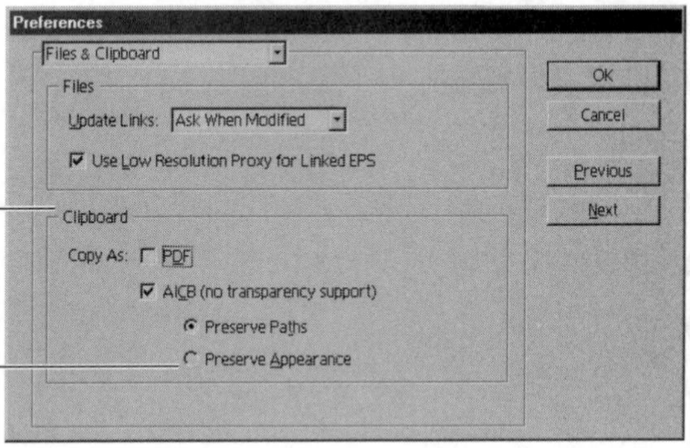

Clipboard export options ——

*Figure 23.5: You have to set
Illustrator's Files & Clipboard
Preferences to properly move
Illustrator paths to Photoshop.*

2. Copy and paste.

Use the solid arrow tool to select the path, choose Edit » Copy, switch
to Photoshop, and choose Edit » Paste.

3. Choose to paste as vectors.

A Paste dialog box, shown in **Figure 23.6**, appears in Photoshop
when you paste (unless you forgot to change the Illustrator Files &
Clipboard Preferences). To preserve the vector path, you can choose
either Path or Shape Layer, depending on how you want to work with
it. Now you can use Photoshop's arrow or pen tool to edit the path.

*Figure 23.6: You must select
either Path or Shape Layer in
Photoshop's Paste dialog box
to preserve your Illustrator
paths when pasting into
Photoshop.*

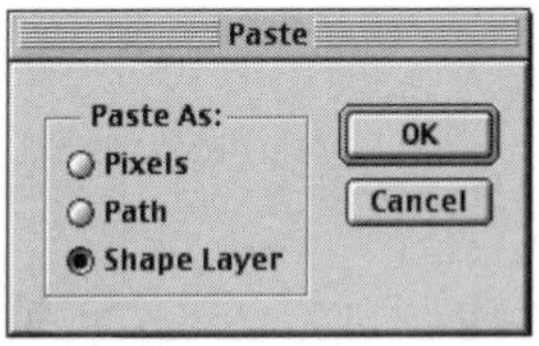

 *If you don't need to see the pasting choices, just use this shortcut.
Ctrl-drag (Cmd-drag on the Mac) the Illustrator path to Photoshop,
and when you drop it in Photoshop, it will import as a path.*

Working with Other Image Editors

While Illustrator works easiest with Photoshop, Illustrator can import and export a number of other bitmap file formats.

Thanks to the inclusion of Photoshop-format import plug-in filters, you can use Illustrator's File » Place or Open command to import:

- Amiga IFF
- BMP (Windows bitmap)
- FLM (Filmstrip)
- GIF
- Kodak Photo CD
- JPEG
- PCX
- Pixar
- PNG
- TIFF
- TGA

Illustrator can export:

- BMP
- FLM
- JPEG
- PCX
- PICT
- Pixar
- Targa
- TIFF
- WMF

You can use either the File » Open or File » Place command to import graphics. The behavior of the two commands is very similar, but there are important differences.

File » Open creates a new file with the imported graphic in it, included as a linked file. The new file takes on the filename of the imported file.

 File » Place inserts the graphic as a new object in the currently open Illustrator document. This means Place works only when you already have an Illustrator document open. When you choose File » Place, a Link check box appears at the bottom of the Place dialog box. If you select it, the graphic imports as a linked graphic; otherwise, it will be embedded.

Either way, the graphic you import can be managed using the Links palette, which was covered in Chapter 4.

Working with Page-Layout Programs

Illustrator has traditionally gotten along well with the software friends it made early on—page-layout applications such as QuarkXPress, Adobe PageMaker, and Adobe InDesign. The time-honored method is to save an EPS version of the Illustrator file, then import the EPS version into the page-layout program. The fact that you're creating printed materials dictates some basic ideas to keep in mind when you prepare Illustrator files for them.

 Use CMYK color mode for a press. If your artwork's final destination is a printing press, set up your Illustrator document in CMYK (choose File » Document Color Mode » CMYK Color). If it will be printed only on an inkjet printer, leaving it in RGB is fine, since inkjet printer drivers expect RGB data even though they use CMYK inks. (Really, it's true.)

 Save as EPS or export as TIFF. The natural choice for Illustrator files is Illustrator EPS, which preserves vectors. Sometimes, EPS issues with missing fonts, transparency, or other effects can challenge your deadline. When that happens, you might decide to export the Illustrator file as a 300-dpi TIFF instead, since bitmapped images are pretty reliable (but can take up a lot more disk space). Also, EPS and TIFF directly support the CMYK color model of a printing press. EPS and TIFF are about it as far as print-friendly file formats go. Don't even bother using computer-screen formats such as GIFs, WMFs, or BMPs in print documents; most of these aren't capable of CMYK color, and some don't even support high resolutions.

Avoid using JPEG images for work going to a printing press. Unlike TIFF, JPEG uses lossy compression, which degrades image quality. You may not notice this on the Web, but you will on a high-resolution image-setter and press. It's not impossible to use JPEGs for print work, but if you insist on doing so, you must ask your printer what settings are going to make it work properly.

 Save as the right version. If you want to preserve spot colors, transparency, and fonts as characters, select version 9.0 or later when saving the file.

 Use high resolutions. This not only applies to the images you place, but also to the resolution you set in Effect » Document Raster Effects Settings and the Transparency panel in the File » Document Setup dialog box.

 Consider embedding fonts. When you Save As or Save a Copy, you may want to select Include Document Fonts. You don't have to do this if you're diligent about sending all relevant project files to the printer; turning it on can make files a lot bigger.

 Consider embedding links. Your printer may prefer that you turn on the Include Linked Files option in the EPS Format Options dialog box, so that any files you placed in Illustrator are taken along to wherever else the Illustrator EPS file goes.

 Be careful with spot colors. Each spot color you use adds a plate to the print job. Just be aware of how many spot colors you use and talk to your printer about it so that they know it's coming.

Following these suggestions can help keep your printer from rolling his eyes every time you walk in the door. They work well with QuarkXPress and most page-layout applications. (But as you'll see in the next section, Adobe InDesign offers a simpler and more enhanced workflow with Illustrator.) When in doubt about an option, always ask your printer for advice since they're the ones that will have to make it print.

 Adobe PageMaker 7.0 has one advantage over most page-layout programs: You can import Illustrator files without saving them as EPS first.

InDesign and Illustrator

If you work with Illustrator and InDesign, you might reflexively do the old save-as-EPS-then-import routine. Remember earlier in this chapter when I talked about the special relationship between Illustrator and Photoshop? You'll find the same thing going on between Illustrator and InDesign. Adobe has set it up so that using Illustrator 10 and InDesign 2.0 together is easier and more flexible than any other combination of illustration and layout software.

The most amazing thing about using these two programs together is that InDesign can import Illustrator files directly. You don't need to save Illustrator files as EPS before importing them, saving a step. If you do this all day long, you'll save lots of steps! Equally amazing is that InDesign also preserves Illustrator transparency and effects, again without any special intervention on your part.

In InDesign 2.0, choose File » Place to import the Illustrator file. This method preserves as much of the Illustrator appearance as possible, but it comes in as one big chunk you can't edit. However, you can use the Edit Original command to open the file straight from the layout back into Illustrator. To use Edit Original in InDesign, right-click the graphic (Control-click on the Mac) and choose Graphics » Edit Original from the context menu that pops up.

If you want to edit Illustrator objects in InDesign, you can also move objects from Illustrator to InDesign using the Clipboard or by dragging and dropping, but realize that some effects may not transfer over this way. By changing a couple of preferences, you can preserve more of the appearance, but it may be less editable:

- In Illustrator, choose Edit » Preferences » Files & Clipboard (Illustrator » Preferences » Files & Clipboard on Mac OS X). In the Clipboard section, selecting PDF will preserve appearance and selecting AICB will preserve editability. You may need to turn PDF off if you can't edit what you paste. These are the same options that were covered in Figure 23.5.

- In InDesign, choose Edit » Preferences » General. In the Clipboard section, as shown in **Figure 23.7**, selecting Prefer PDF When Pasting will preserve appearance but not editability, and Copy PDF to Clipboard will let you edit InDesign paths in Illustrator after copying and pasting.

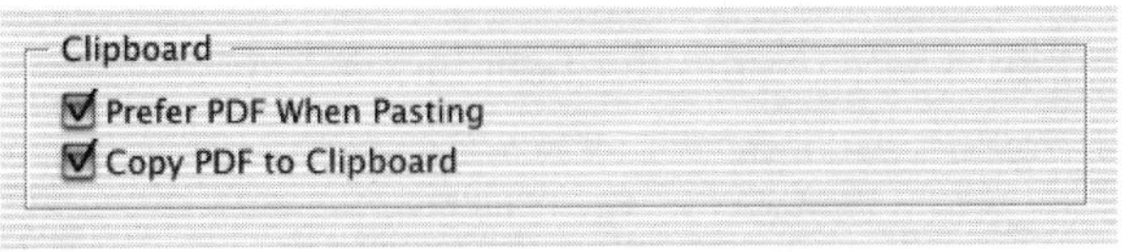

Figure 23.7: InDesign's Clipboard preferences let you choose whether to preserve appearance or maximize editability.

Clipboard
- ☑ Prefer PDF When Pasting
- ☑ Copy PDF to Clipboard

All told, if you want to preserve appearance, you're better off just placing the Illustrator file. Use the Clipboard when you want to edit some Illustrator paths in InDesign.

If you want to move InDesign elements to Illustrator, you can export InDesign pages as PDF, which Illustrator can open. Just choose File » Export in InDesign, and choose Adobe PDF from the Formats menu.

 Illustrator can import and export text files. This means you can prepare text in a word processor and then place it in Illustrator or reuse text in Illustrator in another program.

Acrobat and Illustrator

Acrobat isn't exactly a layout program, but it's so often used to interchange layout files that it bears mentioning here for one important reason: With version 10, Illustrator's file format is now a variation of the PDF file format. That's right, there isn't much of a practical difference between the PDF and Illustrator 10 formats. Illustrator has been able to edit PDF files for a couple of versions now, but surprisingly, Acrobat can now open and print Illustrator 10 files, and that's with no alterations to Acrobat! So if you run into others who need to print an Illustrator 10 file but don't have Illustrator 10, tell them they can print it from Acrobat. Other programs that import PDF may identify Illustrator 10 files as PDF files, so don't be surprised if that happens.

Working with Other Drawing Programs

Illustrator works well with other drawing programs. Its arch rival, Macromedia FreeHand, can open Illustrator files. In addition, Illustrator can open and export in many common formats, so you can interchange files even with non-PostScript-based drawing programs. However, copying and pasting will usually work best with PostScript-based drawing programs.

Illustrator imports:

- Older Illustrator files
- AutoCad DXF/DWG
- CGM (Computer Graphics Metafile)
- CorelDraw
- EPS (Encapsulated PostScript)
- FreeHand

- PDF
- Photoshop
- SVG/SVGZ
- PICT
- PostScript Level 1
- WMF/EMF

Illustrator exports:

- CGM
- DXF/DWG (AutoCad)
- EPS
- EMF
- FLM
- PDF
- PICT
- PostScript
- SVG
- SWF (Shockwave Flash)
- WMF

 *Some formats are listed here and in the bitmap formats list. That's because some formats can include bitmap or vector data.*

Working with Web Authoring Programs

Chapters 21 and 22 go into great detail about converting Illustrator artwork into Web file formats. Here I'll talk a little more about the other end—using Illustrator files in Web authoring. The lists of file formats earlier in this chapter include standard Web formats, including GIF and SWF (Shockwave Flash).

For basic site design, it's simple. Just export to one of the Web file formats as discussed in Chapters 21 and 22, trying to keep quality up and file size down, and use them in Web authoring programs such as Macromedia Dreamweaver or Microsoft FrontPage. But if you're working with Adobe GoLive, the story changes—for the better. Have you guessed by now that Adobe Illustrator and Adobe GoLive are friendlier to each other than to non-Adobe products? If you did, you guessed right. Read on...

GoLive and Illustrator

Here comes one of the coolest product integration tricks you'll see. Well, some of you may think the layer preservation between Illustrator and Photoshop is pretty cool, but the GoLive/Illustrator collaboration is right up there with it. GoLive has a concept called Smart Objects, which turns the timeworn import/export paradigm on its head. Instead of starting from Illustrator and importing to GoLive, you start in GoLive.

There's two ways to use Smart Objects. You can lay down a Smart Object for an Illustrator graphic you've already created, and GoLive will open Illustrator and bring the file through the Save for Web optimization process, while you sit back and wait for GoLive to receive the optimized version and lay it out in the place where you put the Smart Object. Or, you can just drag an Illustrator file directly into GoLive's layout window, where GoLive will sense that it's an Illustrator file and automatically make it into a Smart Object for you. Here's the manual way to do it:

1.   Create the Illustrator file.

Even though the Smart Objects method is not supposed to require any special preparation for the Web, this will work best if the Illustrator file is close to the size it will be on the Web page.

2.   Make a Smart Object in GoLive.

Open the Objects palette in GoLive (Window » Objects), and run your mouse over the icons until you see the Smart Illustrator label at the bottom of the Objects palette. Drag that icon to the layout and use the handles to size it. **Figure 23.8** shows you what it should look like when you're done.

3.   Link to the file.

With the icon selected on the GoLive page, click the folder icon next to the Source option in the Inspector Basic palette (Window » Inspector) in GoLive. Locate the file.

GoLive automatically opens Illustrator (if it isn't open already), runs Save for Web (you may have to set some Save for Web options here, which were covered in Chapters 21 and 22), and imports the file into the position and size you marked with the Smart Object. You are done.

To edit the Illustrator file from GoLive, just double-click the Smart Object.

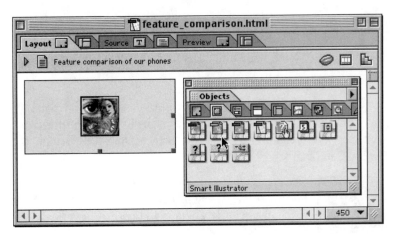

Figure 23.8: An Illustrator Smart Object in GoLive, ready to be linked. On the right is the arrow over the Smart Illustrator object, which you would drag from the Objects palette to the page.

After you import the Illustrator file, you can resize the Smart Object and GoLive will make Illustrator reoptimize the graphic at the new size if it's a bitmap Web graphic. If it's a vector Web graphic such as SVG, GoLive won't waste your time reoptimizing it because it's a resolution-independent vector, after all.

Slicing, Dicing, and Going Live

If you're using GoLive 6, you can even slice an Illustrator file, save it as a single Illustrator file, and when it comes into GoLive, it will come in sliced back up. You can also take the variables that you've created in Illustrator (see Chapter 22 if you've forgotten what those are), import the file into GoLive, and have GoLive hook up with a database to replace those variables for you. Also, in the Save for Web dialog box in Illustrator, when you choose to save as HTML, you can choose Include GoLive Code, which will save an HTML file with an Images folder containing all the slices you made, plus, in another folder called Source, a bunch of SVG files that GoLive can use to reoptimize those slices without your having to go back into Illustrator and resave them (as you would if they were just Smart Objects).

Working with Macromedia Flash

As the current champion of vector graphics on the Web, it would make sense to pair up Macromedia Flash graphics with the vector capabilities of Illustrator, especially if you prefer Illustrator's drawing tools. In Chapters 21 and 22, I talked a lot about Flash from Illustrator's point of view. This section gives you an idea of how to handle the Illustrator/Flash relationship from the Flash side.

Moving SWF graphics from Illustrator to Flash 5

Illustrator 10 can directly export vector graphics into the Macromedia Flash SWF format, making it easy to use your Illustrator art in Flash. There are just a few steps.

1.   Export SWF from Illustrator.

Use File » Save for Web to export the graphic to SWF. If necessary, you can use the procedures described in the "Saving an Image for the Web" section in Chapter 21 and the "Setting the SWF Format Options" in Chapter 22.

Don't forget that you can set up animation in advance using Illustrator layers, and then select AI Layers to SWF Frames in the Export As box in the Macromedia Flash (SWF) Format Options dialog box.

2.   Import into Flash.

Switch to Flash 5, and make sure you have the Flash document open. Choose File » Import, locate the file, click Add, then click Import. It will appear as a group on whatever Flash layer is active.

Don't use the File » Open command, because that will simply open the Flash graphic as a movie to play back, and your editing tools will disappear.

3.   Edit as necessary to complete your animation.

If you need to edit the graphic after it appears in Flash, use the Flash drawing tools and commands. However, you might find that you can't get at some of the objects. All you have to do is select the object and use Flash's Modify » Group or Modify » Break Apart commands until it breaks down the way you want it to (**Figure 23.9**).

Remember that many of Illustrator's advanced features will automatically be flattened or expanded to work in Flash, but some items, such as symbols, will be preserved in Flash.

Another way to transfer the artwork is to save the Illustrator file as Illustrator 88, 3.0, 5.0, or 6.0 format, and then import that into Flash. You usually don't want to do this because this trick won't support features like exporting layers to SWF frames or preserving symbols. But this knowledge can be handy if you own a lot of the clip art that's been saved in older Illustrator format, since there's no need to re-export them to use them in Flash.

Figure 23.9. An Illustrator 10 graphic in Flash. One of the raindrops from Illustrator is about to be ungrouped for further Flash-specific editing and animation.

Moving Flash 5 Graphics and Animations to Illustrator

To edit a Flash frame in Illustrator, in Flash simply choose File » Export Image, and choose Adobe Illustrator as the format. The dialog box doesn't say so, but the export format is Adobe Illustrator 6.0. Because it's such an old format, the artwork will be expanded and flat, without support for features such as symbols or transparency created in Flash. Unfortunately, you can do this only one frame at a time.

If you want to export the multiple frames of a Flash animation, in Flash choose File » Export Movie, and choose Adobe Illustrator Sequence from the Format menu. Because Illustrator handles only a single page, you'll get a sequence of separate Illustrator files.

Because of the way Flash handles shapes, you may find that shapes are cut up in unexpected ways. For examples, fills and strokes are likely to import as two separate paths.

LiveMotion and Illustrator

LiveMotion is Adobe's answer to Macromedia Flash. With LiveMotion, you have a large degree of control over animated Web graphics. And if you don't like the Flash timeline, you might prefer the LiveMotion timeline, which was modeled after the timeline in Adobe After Effects (which I talk about in the next section).

LiveMotion has a few vector drawing tools of its own, but, obviously, Illustrator's are much more powerful. Fortunately, LiveMotion takes advantage of the vector data in Illustrator files, so you can scale an Illustrator file up in LiveMotion without worrying about the jaggies you'd get from scaling up bitmaps. This means you can do all of your drawing using Illustrator's drawing tools and take full advantage of them in LiveMotion.

To move an Illustrator file into LiveMotion 1.0, you have to save an EPS version of the Illustrator file first. Then go into LiveMotion, choose File » Place, locate the file, and you're ready to go. LiveMotion 2.0, though, reads Illustrator files directly. Either way, you can happily enjoy the benefits of Illustrator vectors in LiveMotion, as seen in **Figure 23.10**.

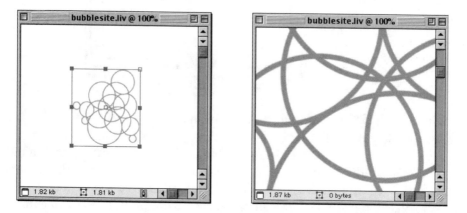

Figure 23.10: Vector objects in an imported Illustrator file can be scaled in LiveMotion with no loss of quality.

If you're using LiveMotion 2.0, you can simply drag an Illustrator file into LiveMotion 2 and animate it. Because LiveMotion understands Illustrator's layers, if you organize your art well, animating it becomes quite easy. You can use the Release to Layers feature to easily animate blends. And you can use LiveMotion's Edit Original command to edit the file in Illustrator and it will be updated automatically in LiveMotion when you close the file—even if you've already broken it apart and animated it.

Working with Video

Ah, television. Swooping logos, text zooming in and out. With all of this motion, you'd think a fixed-resolution bitmap would be clunky to work with, and you'd be right. Illustrator is ideal for today's constantly moving video graphics because vectors are more flexible than bitmaps.

Adobe also happens to make Premiere and After Effects, two of the dominant video-editing programs for personal computers. By now you might guess that there's more to Illustrator's relationship with these programs than would be obvious at first glance.

Premiere and Illustrator

Premiere, the editing program, can import Illustrator files directly. There's no need to save Illustrator files in another format, as you might have to with a non-Adobe video editor. Given Illustrator's control over type, Illustrator's a natural for video titles and other graphics that can't easily be drawn in Premiere's anemic titler.

In Premiere, simply choose File » Import » File, and locate the Illustrator file. Premiere rasterizes the Illustrator vector into an anti-aliased bitmapped version. Unfilled areas become transparent areas so you can easily superimpose the Illustrator graphic. **Figure 23.11** shows an Illustrator file being used as a title in Premiere.

Figure 23.11: An Illustrator file in Premiere's Monitor window, where it is serving as a title.

As Adobe product releases leapfrog each other, file format compatibility between programs can get out of sync. If you have trouble importing an Illustrator file, try saving the file to an older Illustrator version or to an EPS version.

While it's nice that you don't have to pre-rasterize an Illustrator file, Premiere will rasterize it only at its original Illustrator size. If you plan to make it bigger in Premiere, it's better to enlarge it in Illustrator first. Otherwise, Premiere will scale it up after the rasterization, and that could put you face to face with the jaggies.

 To see through transparent areas when an Illustrator file is on a Premiere superimposition track, in Premiere choose Clip » Video Options » Transparency for a selected clip and set the Key Type to White Alpha Matte.

 If the Illustrator file doesn't have exactly the same proportions as the Premiere project frame size, it may be stretched or squeezed to fit. To stop this distortion, select the clip in the Premiere timeline and choose Clip » Video Options » Maintain Aspect Ratio.

After Effects and Illustrator

After Effects is widely used for compositing—the act of layering video or film elements such as characters, space ships, and backgrounds into a complete version. After Effects actually works a lot more closely with Illustrator than Premiere does.

As you might expect, After Effects can import Illustrator files without making you save them in a different format. Here's how it works.

1.   In After Effects, choose File » Import » File, and locate the file.

But don't click the Import button just yet, because you still have a choice to make.

2.   From the Import As menu in the Import File dialog box, choose either Footage or Composition.

After Effects can import an Illustrator file as a single graphic or as an After Effects composition. If you choose Footage, you get a single graphic (all layers merged). But if you choose Composition for a multi-tilayered Illustrator file, you get an automatically created After Effects composition that holds all the layers in the Illustrator file in their original positions on the page, and you also get a new folder in the Project window to store all of the layers from the Illustrator file. This means you can arrange complicated graphics in Illustrator, and when you get them into After Effects, they are already ready to animate. See **Figure 23.12** for an example of this.

3. Now click Import.

Whatever you selected is now in the After Effects Project window, ready to use.

Illustrator layers in Project window folder

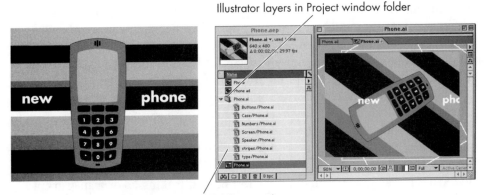

Composition containing Illustrator layers

Figure 23.12: An Illustrator file (left) imported as a composition (right) and animated in After Effects.

After Effects has one more surprise for unsuspecting Illustrator users. I've already mentioned how Premiere can rasterize only at the original size of the Illustrator file. After Effects doesn't have this limitation. If you turn on the Continuous Rasterization switch in the After Effects timeline, the Illustrator vectors will always be rasterized at whatever size you've scaled it to, as you saw in LiveMotion. (After Effects makes it switchable because video resolutions are much higher than Web resolutions, which can slow you down).

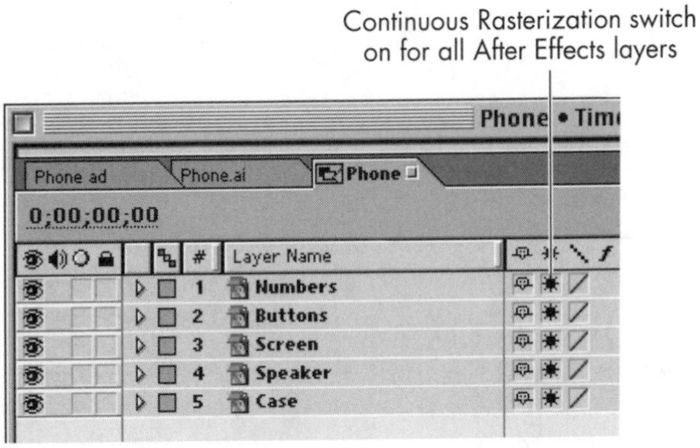

Continuous Rasterization switch
on for all After Effects layers

Figure 23.13: The Continuous Rasterization switch in the After Effects Timeline window ensures that Illustrator vectors are rasterized at full quality at any size. You may want to turn it off for a faster draft display mode when editing.

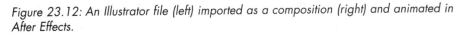

Making Color Appear Consistent across Programs

Who among us has not been unpleasantly surprised when a graphic that looks perfect in one program turns out with completely different colors after being imported into another program? Mismatched color is, in fact, one of the most annoying problems in the graphic arts. Chapter 14 introduced you to color management, the industrywide effort under way to rectify this problem. That chapter talks about color management within Illustrator, but color management is most valuable when it solves the question of color across programs.

But if you think color management is a challenge to understand within just one program, it can be a real bear to deal with when you try to make different programs handle color the same way. Compared with the rest of the industry, Adobe has put an unusual amount of effort behind making color management useful to regular people like you and me, and Illustrator is now more integrated into Adobe's big color-management picture. As seen in **Figure 23.14**, Illustrator 10 uses the Color Settings dialog box that Adobe is adding to its professional graphics applications.

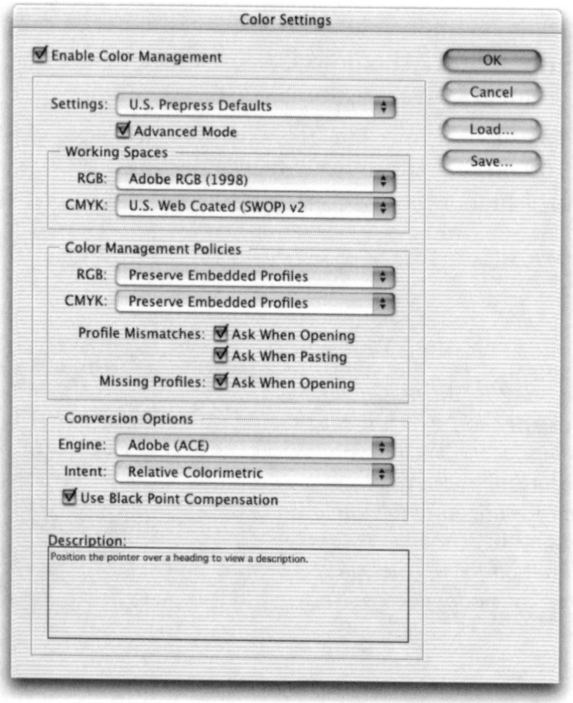

Figure 23.14: Illustrator's Adobe-standard Color Settings dialog box is the place to synchronize your settings between Illustrator and other programs.

When you change color settings in some recent Adobe programs (by choosing Edit » Color Settings), the program may ask you if you want to synchronize color settings with other Adobe programs. As long as you set up color settings that you want all of your Adobe programs to use, it's usually a good idea to go ahead and synchronize. Now, not all Adobe programs do this yet, so you may want to double-check the color settings yourself. If they don't match, and the Color Settings dialog box looks like the one in Illustrator, you can use the Load and Save buttons to make them match. Here's how to synchronize your color settings:

1. **Switch to the program where color settings are already set up the way you want them.**

Let's say, for example, that you've already set the color settings the right way in InDesign 2.0.

2. **Choose Edit » Color Settings, and click Save.**

Name the settings and save them in the folder it automatically goes to. If you're lucky, it will already be pointed to the Settings folder where Adobe stores color-management settings files; if not, here is where you should save them:

Windows: My Computer/Program Files/Common Files/Adobe/Color/Settings/

Mac OS X: Computer/Library/Application Support/Adobe/Color/Settings/

Mac OS 9: Hard Disk/System Folder/Application Support/Adobe/Color/Settings/

3. **Switch to the program that doesn't match your preferred settings.**

In this case, we'll pretend it's Illustrator 10.

4. **Choose Edit » Color Settings.**

5. **From the Settings menu, select the color settings you saved, and click OK.**

If you're trying to load settings from another location, such as a server, you may need to click Load instead and locate the file yourself.

Unfortunately, if you're using an Adobe program that doesn't have the same Color Settings dialog box as the latest versions of Illustrator, Photoshop, and InDesign, you may need to try to match up the settings option by option (such as Working Space).

If you're interchanging files with a program that isn't using color management, the Color Management Off setting may be a reasonable choice, although the level of color consistency may not be as good as with color-managed programs.

PRINTING YOUR ILLUSTRATIONS

Sure, Illustrator images and effects look fantastic on the computer monitor. But the real proof of a program is in the printing. (If you're using Illustrator only to create Web graphics or screen illustrations, please feel free to skip this chapter.) Illustrator has a great track record when it comes to printing objects exactly as you see them on the screen, with the lowest likelihood of error. However, printing problems don't just happen randomly. Those people who manage to avoid problems usually have a good understanding of how to create their files and set their options with the output in mind.

This chapter explains how to print your illustrations to a PostScript-compatible printer (also called an *output device*). Although Illustrator is capable of printing to non-PostScript printers, such as inkjet devices, this is not its forte. I don't mean to be a PostScript elitist—heck, I love my color inkjets—but every high-resolution, professional-quality device includes a PostScript interpreter. And even those who proof their artwork on inkjet devices will eventually have their files separated using high-resolution PostScript printers.

Printing Composite Pages

A composite is a single-page representation of an illustration. A black-and-white composite, printed from a standard laser printer or professional imagesetter (which I'll describe in a few pages), translates all colors of an illustration to gray values. A color composite, printed from a color printer or film recorder, prints the illustration in full color. Composites are useful when you want to reproduce the illustration in black and white, proof an illustration, or fire off a few color photocopies. But you can't use composites for professional-quality full-color reproduction. For that, you need to print *separations,* which I'll discuss later in the section "Printing Color Separations."

Printing a composite illustration is a five-step process (Windows users can skip to Step 2).

1. If your computer is hooked up to a network, use the AppleTalk control panel to select the network to which the printer is connected. On Mac OS X, use the Network control panel.

2. Choose the appropriate composite printer. Windows users can choose from the list of available printers in the Print Setup dialog box. Mac OS 9.1 or 9.2 users can use the Chooser desk accessory to activate the AdobePS driver and select the network printer. Mac OS 10.1 automatically selects your printer if you are connected to a USB printer. If you are using network printers, use Print Center to select your printer from the Printer list.

 AdobePS is the PostScript printer driver direct from Adobe, the inventor and custodian of PostScript. It helps Illustrator and the system software translate the contents of an illustration to the output device.

3. Choose File » Print Setup (File » Page Setup on the Mac) to determine the size and orientation of the printed page. Close the dialog box when you're finished. Mac OS 10.1 users can also choose the printer from the Format for pop-up menu.

4. If needed, position the page-size boundary in the drawing area with the page tool.

5. Choose File » Print to print the illustration to the desired output device.

I'll explain each of these steps in detail in the following sections.

Selecting a Network on a Mac

The newer Macintosh computers include two kinds of printing ports: a Universal Serial Bus (USB) port and an Ethernet port. The USB port connects directly to a printer. The Ethernet port connects to an Ethernet printer or a large-scale network. If you work in a larger office, you're probably connected to other computers and printers via Ethernet, which is the standard networking protocol used throughout the world. If you work in a small office or at home, you may print by way of your USB port. Older Macintosh computers also include two kinds of printing ports: the serial LocalTalk port (printer port) and the Ethernet port. The LocalTalk port connects directly to a printer or to an AppleTalk network. And like the newer Macs, the Ethernet port connects to an Ethernet printer or a large-scale Ethernet network.

In Mac OS 9.1/9.2, if you have access to multiple networks, you can switch from one network to another using the AppleTalk control panel. Choose Apple » Control Panels » AppleTalk to bring up the appropriate window. The AppleTalk control panel is shown in **Figure 24.1**. Depending on your model of computer, you'll probably find at least two options—Printer Port and Ethernet. You may see a third option, Remote Only, which allows you to print through your modem to a remote network. (This is a function of Apple Remote Access, a handy tool for telecommuters.) Select the kind of network that contains the printer you want to use, and then click the close box in the upper-left corner of the window.

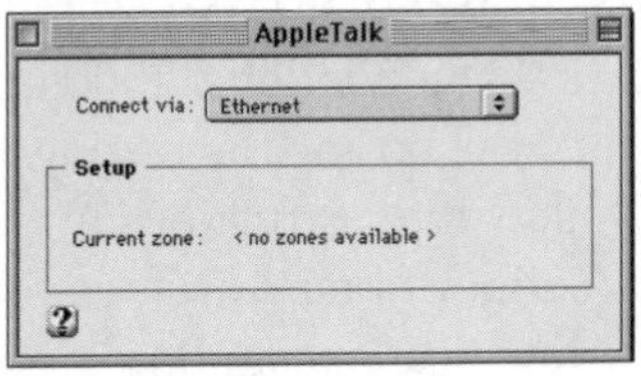

Figure 24.1: If your computer is hooked up to multiple networks, use the AppleTalk control panel to select the network that includes the printer you want to use.

Mac OS 10.1 has the ability to work with multiple networks. You choose all of your available networks and then the operating system continually senses which are available and uses them in the order you specify. For example, let's say you utilize three networks— Ethernet, Airport, and a Dialup modem. You prioritize your three networks in the order listed. If you send a document to print, Mac OS 10.1 first checks your Ethernet connection. If it doesn't find anything there, it looks at the Airport network. If it can't find what it is looking for on that network, it goes to the internal dialup modem. Once your network is set up you should never have to go back and change the settings. But if for some reason you need to, you can do so by using the Network Preferences. Choose Apple » System Preferences and click on the Network icon to bring up the Network window shown in **Figure 24.2**. Mac OS 10.1 supports both TCP/IP and AppleTalk protocols. You'll find Built-In Ethernet in the Show pop-up menu. If you want AppleTalk, click on the AppleTalk tab and then check the Make AppleTalk active box. Click the close box in the upper-left corner of the window.

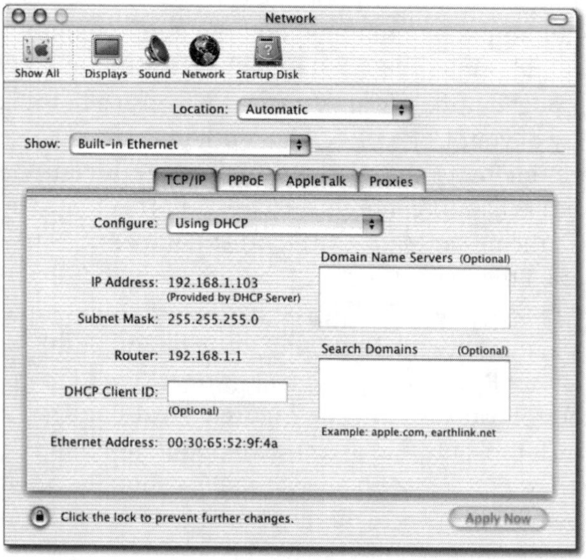

Figure 24.2: Control your connection preferences in Mac OS 10.1's Network window.

Choosing a PostScript Printer in Windows

If you're using the Windows 98 or Windows 2000 operating system, you select a printer from the Start menu by choosing the Settings » Printers command. Click the Add Printer icon and follow the instructions in the Install Wizard. If you don't have the most current PostScript printer driver, go to the Adobe product Web page (www.adobe.com/support/downloads/main.html). Scroll down to Printer Drivers, select Windows and download the Adobe Universal PostScript Windows Driver Installer 1.0.5, which consists of AdobePS 4.5.2 for Windows 98 and PScript 5 for Windows 2000. After you've downloaded it to your hard drive, double-click on the ".exe" file to access the file's contents. You'll be asked to select the Printer Port and a default PPD during the installation. The Illustrator CD comes with a number of PPDs, and you can also find some additional ones at the Adobe Web site.

After you have installed the printer drivers you want, choose File » Print Setup. You can then choose the printer you want to use from the pop-up menu inside the Print Setup dialog box. If you want to change to another printer, one for which you've already installed a driver, choose it from the Name pop-up menu whenever the mood strikes you while using Illustrator.

Choosing a PostScript Printer on a Mac

To select a printer on a Macintosh using System 9.1/9.2, locate the Chooser desk accessory in the list of items under the Apple menu. The Chooser dialog box comes up, as shown in **Figure 24.3**. The dialog box is split into two halves, with the left half devoted to a scrolling list of printer driver icons and network zones and the right half devoted to specific printer options.

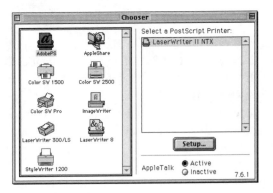

Figure 24.3: Select the AdobePS icon in the Chooser window to select and initialize a PostScript printer.

Select the AdobePS icon, highlighted in Figure 24.3. As mentioned earlier, AdobePS is the PostScript printer driver direct from Adobe.

If AdobePS is not available in the list of printer driver icons, or if you haven't yet installed the newest version, AdobePS 8.7.2, insert the CD-ROM that came with your copy of Illustrator and open the Adobe PostScript Drivers 8.7.3 folder. Open it and double-click the Installer program. This installs the AdobePS driver as well as lots of PostScript printer description files, which I'll describe in a moment. Together, they make Illustrator print in top form. You should also visit Adobe's product Web page at www.adobe.com/prodindex/printerdrivers/main.html. Here you can get the most recent printer drivers and PostScript printer description (PPD) files.

The AdobePS driver supports the all-important PPD files. The printer driver itself, which promises to serve pretty much all PostScript printers, can't account for the tiny differences among different models of PostScript printers, so each PPD serves as a little guidance file, customizing the driver to accommodate a specific printer model. After selecting a printer, you can associate the proper PPD with it by clicking the Setup button. (Or just double-click the printer name in the list.) A new dialog box appears, as shown in **Figure 24.4**. Click the Auto Setup button to instruct the system software to talk to your printer and automatically determine the proper PPD. If the system fails, or if it selects the dreaded Generic option, click the Select PPD button and try to locate the proper PPD file inside the Printer Descriptions folder in the Extensions folder in your System folder. When you finish, click OK or press Return.

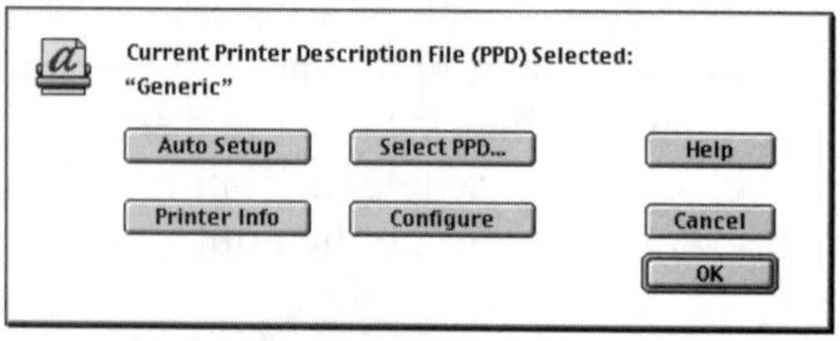

Figure 24.4: Use this dialog box to select the proper printer description file for your particular brand of PostScript printer.

Selecting a printer in Mac OS 10.1 is quite a bit different. If your computer is connected directly to a USB printer, it is automatically selected for you—no fuss, no muss. If you want to select a network printer, you must use the new Print Center, shown in **Figure 24.5**. The Print Center application is located in the Utilities folder in the Applications folder. If your printer does not show up in the Printer list, click the Add Printer button. First choose the type of connection and then either select a printer from the Printer Model or enter the necessary information (IP address or Name) to connect to the printer. You can establish a default printer by selecting a printer in the list and choosing Make Default from the Printers menu.

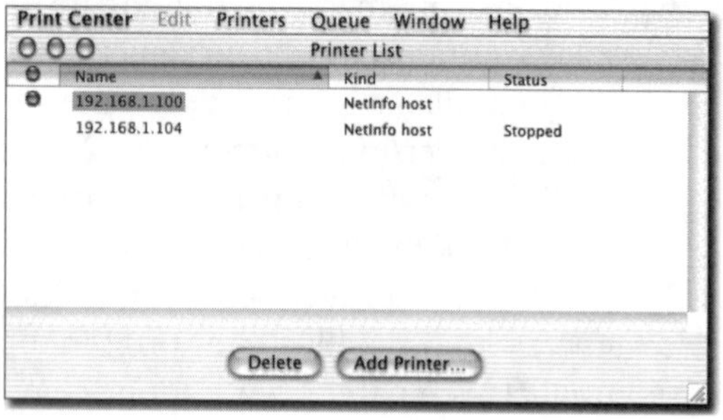

Figure 24.5: To select a network printer in Mac OS 10.1, you must select it from those listed in the Print Center's Printer List.

Setting Up the Page

Many of the printing-related options appear in completely different locations within the two different platforms. So wherever possible, I'll present both the Windows and Mac dialog boxes together to help you.

Your next step is to define the size of the page on which you intend to print your illustration. Choose File » Print Setup (File » Page Setup on the Mac) to display the Page Setup dialog box shown in **Figure 24.6**, which contains the following options:

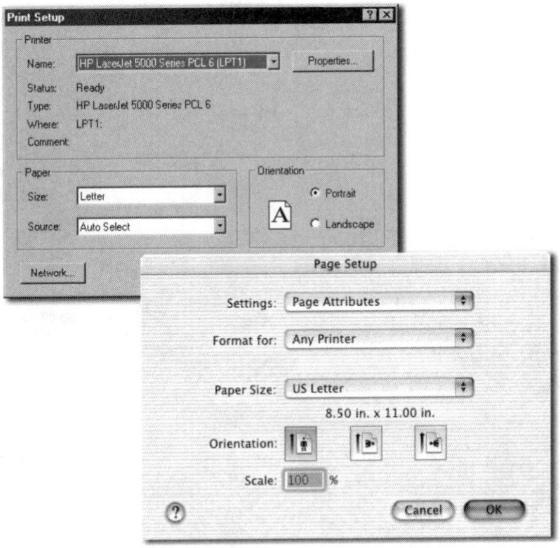

Figure 24.6: The Print Setup or Page Setup dialog boxes for Windows or Mac.

- 🌐 **Paper:** Select the size of the paper on which you want to print. The specific options available from this pop-up menu depend on which PPD file you have selected.

- 🌐 **Scale:** Generally, you'd use this option to reduce large artwork when proofing it on a laser printer or on another device that's limited to letter-sized pages. But it can scale artwork (as it prints) anywhere from 25 to 400 percent. This option is not immediately apparent in Windows, but you can get to it by clicking on the Properties button, selecting the Effects tab, and using the slider bar or entering a value in the % of Normal Size box.

- 🌐 **Orientation:** There are two orientation options (Mac OS 10.1 users are blessed with three; the third is a flipped landscape option). By default, the page is positioned upright, in the Portrait position. But if you want to print a wide illustration, you can select the Landscape option.

PostScript Options

Mac OS 9.1/9.2 users can use the pop-up list at the top of the Page Setup dialog box to open the PostScript Options panel shown in **Figure 24.7**. (Windows users will find some of these options dispersed throughout the Properties panel of the

Print Setup dialog box and the Print dialog box.) Select the options in this dialog box to perform a few printing effects that may come in handy. The sample page in the dialog box demonstrates the effect of the selected options. On the Mac the little dog represents the illustration on the page, and the dotted line represents the margin size. In Windows you will see a letter H with lines representing text and a picture of a graph representing a graphic. You won't find any PostScript options in Mac OS 10.1.

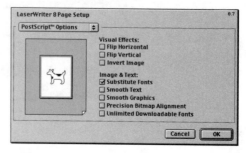

Figure 24.7: The PostScript Options dialog box lets you perform certain printing effects, which range from moderately useful to nonfunctioning.

The options in the PostScript Options dialog box are most useful when you're printing an illustration to a midrange output device, such as a laser printer. If you're printing to more sophisticated devices such as an imagesetter, some of the options—particularly Flip Horizontal, Flip Vertical, and Invert Image—may duplicate or nullify settings in the more important Separation Setup dialog box.

The check boxes in the PostScript Options dialog box work as follows:

- **Flip Horizontal:** Select this option (called Print as a Mirror Image in the Graphics panel for Windows users) to flip the objects in an illustration horizontally on the printed page. Although this option was originally created to help print film negatives, you should use Illustrator's Separation Setup to properly control the horizontal orientation. I explain film negatives more thoroughly in the "Printing Color Separations" section later in this chapter.

- **Flip Vertical:** Same as Flip Horizontal, this option will change the orientation of the image. And again, this option is better controlled in Separation Setup.

- **Invert Image:** This option will turn the artwork into a negative of itself. (This is called Print as a Negative Image in the Graphics panel for Windows users.) And like the flips, this setting is better controlled in Separation Setup.

- **Substitute Fonts:** This check box supposedly substitutes the fonts Geneva, Monaco, and New York with their respective PostScript equivalents of Helvetica, Courier, and Times. But if you try to use the option with Illustrator, the program automatically turns off the check box and prints the TrueType versions of Geneva, Monaco, and New York. In other words, you can ignore this option.

Smooth Text: Back in the old days when people used dot-matrix and first-generation inkjet printers, the Smooth Text option would adjust the text so that it looked smoother. The great high-resolution printers we use now make this option obsolete.

Smooth Graphics: Again turning back the clock, when MacPaint was a hot program, folks were bound and determined to get their jagged black-and-white images to print with smooth edges. Smooth Graphics did just that, averaging pixels to give them smooth, though gummy, edges. Well, it doesn't matter how you have this option set in Illustrator (or the similar option in the Windows Print dialog box). Imported black-and-white images always have jagged edges, just as Mother Nature meant them to have.

Precision Bitmap Alignment: This option reduces a typical 72-ppi image dragged over from Photoshop to 96 percent of its original size, making it compatible with a 300-dpi laser printer. This increases the resolution of a 72-ppi image to 75 ppi, which is evenly divisible into 300. Unless the laser printer is your final output device, I recommend that you leave this option unchecked.

Unlimited Downloadable Fonts: This check box is designed to help moron applications that don't know how to properly download fonts. This check box tells the program to wise up. Illustrator manages its fonts just fine without this silly option.

In Windows you can stamp your pages with watermarks. In the Print Setup dialog box, click the Properties button and then select the Effects tab. Choose Draft, Confidential, or Sample from the Watermarks pop-up menu. A light gray watermark will print diagonally across the page. This is a handy feature for the production workflow.

Adjusting the Page Size

You can modify the page boundaries in the artboard by selecting one of the View radio buttons inside the Document Setup dialog box (introduced back in Chapter 3). To display the dialog box, choose File » Document Setup, and then select the desired radio button.

● **Single Full Page:** Select this radio button to display a single page size inside the artboard. This ensures that you will print just one page for the entire illustration.

● **Tile Full Pages:** Select this radio button to display as many whole pages as will fit inside the artboard. Use this check box to print a multipage document such as a flier or a two-page ad.

● **Tile Imageable Areas:** Select this radio button to subdivide the artboard into multiple partial pages, called tiles. I'll talk more about tiling large artwork in the "Tiling Oversized Illustrations" section later in this chapter.

After you select one of these options and press Enter (Return on the Mac), you can use the page tool to position the page size relative to the objects in your illustration. If the dotted page boundaries are not visible, choose View » Show Page Tiling. If you selected the Tile Imageable Areas option in the Document Setup dialog box, the page number of each tile is listed in the lower-left corner of the tile. This way, you can specify the particular pages that you want to print when outputting the illustration.

Printing Pages

To initiate the printing process, choose File » Print. The Print dialog box appears, as shown in **Figure 24.8**. The default options and names will vary somewhat between operating systems, but unless you've never printed a document from a computer, you should be familiar with these options.

● **Copies:** Enter the number of copies you want to print. You can choose up to 999, but if you want to print more than 10, you're better off having them commercially reproduced. Commercial reproduction provides better quality for less money, and it means less wear and tear on your printer.

● **Print Range (Pages on the Mac):** Specify a range of pages for output. By default, the All radio button is selected. If the drawing area displays a single page size, Illustrator will print just that page. If the drawing area contains multiple pages or tiles, Illustrator prints all pages that contain objects. To define a specific range of pages or tiles to be printed, enter the page numbers in the From and To option boxes. These numbers should correspond to the page numbers displayed in the lower-left corners of pages in the drawing area.

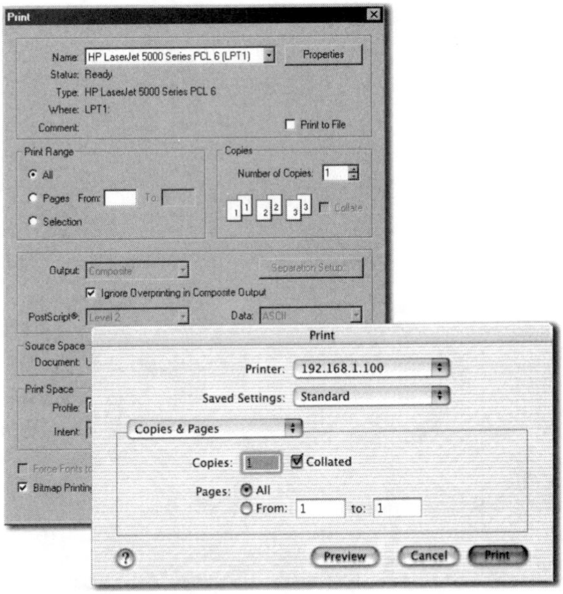

Figure 24.8: You can print
the pages in your illustration
to a PostScript-compatible
printer from the Print dialog
box. Pictured here are the
Windows and Mac OS 10.1
interfaces.

- **Paper Source (Mac OS 9.X only):** If you want to print your illustration on a letterhead or other special piece of paper that you manually feed into the printer, select the specific paper source. Mac OS 10.1 users select the Paper Feed option from the pop-up menu. Windows users will find the paper source option by clicking the Properties button and clicking the Paper tab.

- **Print to File (Destination in Mac OS 9.X):** This option allows you to generate a PostScript-language definition of the file on disk rather than printing it directly to your printer. Windows users simply check the Print to File check box, then enter a filename and click OK. Mac users select the File destination, enter a name, and click Save. You can then submit the saved file to a service bureau for output. To print regular pages to your printer as usual, just don't select any of these options.

Most of the time, printing is going to be a pretty straightforward affair. But when you want to specify particular items to print, print separations, or further customize your printer options, you may need to delve into your output options. In Windows, the Output options are in the main Printer dialog box. On the Mac, these options are available by choosing Adobe Illustrator 10 from the pop-up list as shown in **Figure 24.9**. Here's how these options work.

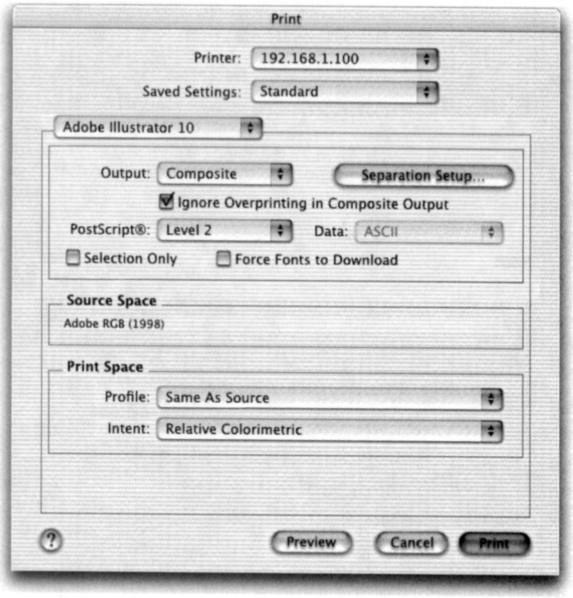

Figure 24.9: The Adobe Illustrator 10 options for a specific output device.

- **Output:** Select the Composite option from the Output pop-up menu to print a black-and-white or color composite of your illustration. Select the Separate option to print color separations. I'll explain the latter option in more detail in the next section.

- **PostScript:** Select Level 1, Level 2, or Level 3, depending on the kind of PostScript that's built into your output device. PostScript printers made in the past two years are very likely to be Level 3—the most sophisticated. Older PostScript printers are Level 2. Extremely ancient machines are Level 1. If your machine is brand new, set this option to Level 3. If it doesn't work, move down to Level 2.

- **Data:** If your network doesn't support binary encoding, select the ASCII option to transfer data in the text-only format. The printing process takes much longer to complete, but at least it's possible. When in doubt, however, leave this option set to Binary.

- **Selection (Selection Only on the Mac):** If you just want to print the selected objects in the illustration, select this check box. When the option is turned off—as it is by default—Illustrator prints all objects, selected or not.

- **Separation Setup:** This button opens the all-powerful Separation Setup dialog box that allows you to specify settings for printing color separations. I'll explain this dialog box from A to Z in the next section.

The last two options concern using color management. If you skipped Chapter 14, you may want to check it out to get a better handle on these two options.

- **Source Space:** This option tells you what color profile is currently embedded in your document. Nothing to choose here; it's purely informational.

- **Print Space:** The Profile option allows you to choose a color profile for your document. Same As Source will print your file using the current color profile (mine says Adobe RGB 1998). No color conversions are made with this option. You can choose a different profile to print to by choosing it from the Profile pop-up menu. If you choose PostScript Color Management, Illustrator will send the color data and color profile in your file to a PostScript printer. The document then gets converted to the printer's color space. The Intent option allows you to choose a translation method if your colors have to be adjusted from one color space to another. Leave the rendering Intent at the default setting unless you are a total color guru.

All of these color profile conversions can vary from one printer to another, so be sure to run multiple tests. It's your best assurance to achieve good output results.

 If your Source Space says Untagged RGB or Untagged CMYK and your Print Space options are grayed out, it means that you haven't established your Color Settings. Go to Edit » Color Settings. If this dialog box is scary, get help in Chapter 14.

Once you've made all your settings, just click the Print button and sit back and watch as your beautiful creation works its way out of the printer. Or, depending on your beautiful creation and your printer, step outside for a breath of well-deserved fresh air.

Printing Color Separations

Professional color reproduction requires that you print an illustration using color separations. This means you print a separate sheet of paper or film for each of the process-color primaries—cyan, magenta, yellow, and black—or for each spot color used in the illustration. You can even add spot colors to the four process primaries to enhance the range of colors in the final document, or target the colors in a logo or another color-sensitive element. But keep in mind that every additional separation you print incurs additional costs—additional ink has to be applied to the pages, and someone has to make and run the plates.

The only category of printer up to the job of creating the originals for color separations is an *imagesetter,* which is a high-resolution device. Imagesetters print onto special photosensitive paper or film, which is then turned into printing plates. (Some imagesetters print directly to the printing plates.)

 Although your laser printer is too primitive to use for final color separations, you can certainly use it to make paper separations. It is always wise to run separations through a laser printer to count how many pieces of paper come out. If the job is supposed to be two-color, and four pieces of paper come out, you know you need to adjust the colors in the document.

You can print color separations of an illustration in one of the following ways:

- Take the Illustrator file to a service bureau or commercial printer and let a qualified technician deal with it.

- Import the illustration as an EPS file into InDesign, PageMaker, or QuarkXPress. Then take that file to a service bureau and let those folks do their jobs.

- Print the separations directly from Illustrator to an in-house imagesetter or to a PostScript file that you can later deliver to a service bureau. (Or you could import the illustrations into InDesign, PageMaker, or Quark-XPress as mentioned above, and print the separations from there.)

The last option—printing the color separations directly from Illustrator on your own—is perhaps the most unlikely scenario of them all. But it is the reason that Illustrator integrates color-separation capabilities, which is why I explain it in great detail in the next few pages.

To print color separations from Illustrator, do the following:

1. Prepare the illustration just as you did when printing the composite, as discussed way back in the early pages of this chapter.

2. Choose File » Separation Setup.

3. Modify the settings as desired.

4. Choose File » Print. Choose the settings there.

5. Click the Print button.

Only Step 3 requires much effort, but it requires quite a bit. **Figure 24.10** shows the Separation Setup dialog box in full regalia. The dialog box is divided into two parts—the separation preview in the upper-left corner and a series of options below and to the right of it.

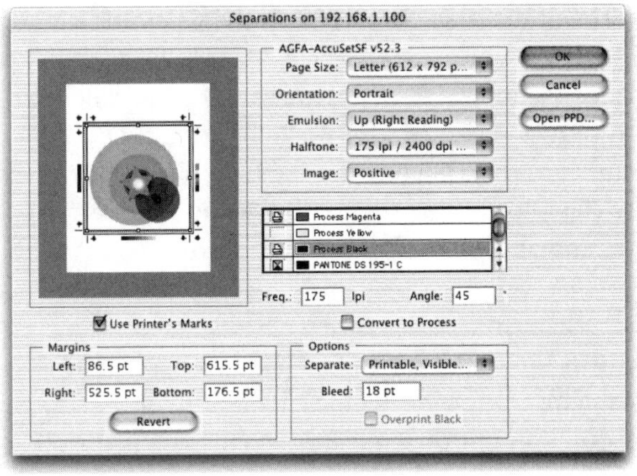

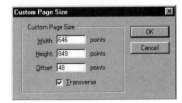

Figure 24.10: You can access this dialog box either by clicking the Separation Setup button inside the Printer dialog box or by choosing File » Separation Setup.

If this is the first time you've opened this dialog box, you'll need to select a PPD file. Click the Open PPD button, and then locate the desired PPD file. The PPD file you select will determine which options are available in the pop-up menus throughout the Separation Setup dialog box.

Page Size

This pop-up menu lists the page sizes available for your output device based on the active PPD. Next to the common name of each page size is the imageable area of the page, measured in points. Keep an eye on the preview to make sure the illustration and all of the printer marks around the illustration fit on the page.

If you've selected the PPD file for an imagesetter, you can define your own page size by selecting the Custom option from the Page Size pop-up menu. This displays the dialog box shown in **Figure 24.11**. The default values for the Width and Height options are the dimensions of the smallest page that will hold all the objects in your illustration. The Offset option allows you to add space between your illustration and the right edge of the paper or film. If the Offset value is left at 0, the output device will automatically center the illustration on the page.

Figure 24.11: This dialog box allows you to specify a custom page size as well as a distance between pages.

The Transverse check box in the Custom Page Size dialog box controls the orientation of your custom page relative to the paper or film. By default, the printer places the long side of portrait artwork parallel to the long edge of the film. You can reduce paper or film waste by rotating the illustration so that its short side is parallel to the long edge of the film. This is known as *transverse orientation*. Then use the Offset value to specify the amount of space that lies between your illustration and any printed image that follows it.

Orientation

Set this option to Portrait or Landscape, just as you have in the Page Setup dialog box. This option works independently of the Transverse check box; if the Orientation option is set incorrectly, you'll cut off part of your illustration.

Emulsion

The Emulsion options control how the illustration prints relative to the emulsion side of photosensitive film. The names given to the options, Up and Down, refer to the sides of the film on which the emulsion is located. When printing film negatives, you probably want to select Down from the pop-up menu; when printing on paper, Up is usually the correct setting. (Be sure neither Flip Horizontal nor Flip Vertical is selected in the PostScript Options dialog box—shown back in Figure 24.7—because either option will nullify the Emulsion setting.) Consult your commercial printer to confirm which option you should select.

Halftone

Weird as it may sound, traditional printing presses aren't capable of applying shades of color to paper. They can apply solid ink or no ink at all. That's it. So to represent different light and dark values, imagesetters generate thousands of little *halftone dots*, as illustrated in **Figure 24.12**. The halftone dots grow and shrink to represent darker and lighter shades, respectively, of a color.

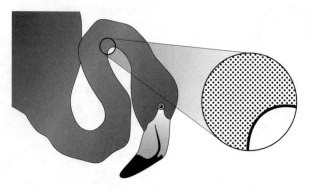

Figure 24.12: A gray value is printed as thousands of little halftone dots. The dots can grow and shrink to imitate different shades.

You can specify the density of the halftone dots by selecting an option from the Halftone pop-up menu in the Separation Setup dialog box. The first value before the slash represents the screen frequency, which is the number of halftone dots per linear inch. The second value represents the printer resolution, which is the number of tiny printer pixels that print in a linear inch. You can figure out the number of printer pixels that fit inside the largest possible halftone dot by dividing the second number by the first. For example, in this book, all illustrations are printed at a resolution of 2,540 dpi and a screen frequency of 133 lpi. If you divide 2,540 by 133, you get a little more than 19, which means that a halftone dot inside a very dark shade of gray is 19 printer pixels tall and 19 pixels wide.

Fascinating as this may be, the real question is, as always, which option should you use? Unless you have a specific reason for doing otherwise, set the printer resolution (the second value) as high as it will go. If you're printing to paper, you probably don't want to set the screen frequency (the first value) any higher than 120 lpi, because the dots may grow and clog up as the illustration is transferred to film and then to plates. When printing to film, screen frequencies of 133 lpi and higher are acceptable. Consult your service bureau or commercial printer if you are at all unsure.

Image

The Image option controls whether the illustration prints as a positive or a negative image. If you're printing to paper, the default Positive is usually the correct setting. However, when printing to film, you'll probably want to select Negative. (The Invert Image check box in the PostScript Options dialog box should be turned off; otherwise, it will interfere with the Image setting.)

Color list

The scrolling list of colors that appears below the Image pop-up menu allows you to specify exactly which colors you want to print to independent separations. The process colors are listed first, followed by any spot colors. A couple of different icons may appear in front of the colors, as shown in **Figure 24.13**. These icons specify whether a color gets its own separation or whether a spot color is converted to its process ingredients. If there is no icon, the color does not get printed at all.

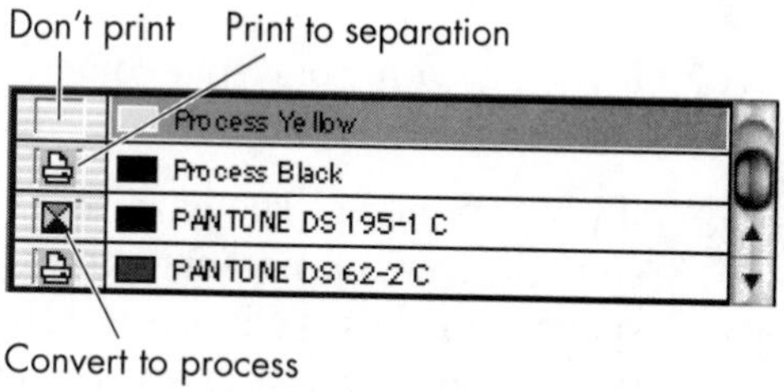

Figure 24.13: To decide which spot colors you want to separate and which you want to convert to their CMYK ingredients, turn off the Convert to Process check box (shown here in its default on position).

Don't print   Print to separation

Convert to process

By default, Illustrator is ready to convert all spot colors to their process ingredients. If you want to print at least one spot color to its own separation, turn off the Convert to Process check box. The spot colors in the list should immediately change from dimmed to black. The printer icon in front of each spot color indicates that the color will print to its own separation. If you want a specific spot color to be converted to process, click the printer icon so that it changes to a process color icon. For example, in Figure 24.13, the color Pantone DS195-1C is set to convert to CMYK colors. But Pantone DS62-2C is set to print onto its own plate.

Frequency and Angle

In addition to changing the overall screen frequency of the illustration, you can modify the frequency of a single separation. You can also change the angle of the halftone dots. Back in Figure 24.12, for example, you can see that the halftone angle is 45 degrees—that is, each dot is angled 45 degrees from its closest neighbor. To change either the frequency or angle, select a color from the list and enter a new value in either the Frequency or Angle option box.

Why would you want to change either of these values? To avoid creating weird patterns (called moirés) between the halftone dots from different separations. By default, all process colors are set to the same frequency. Black is angled at 45 degrees, cyan is set to 15 degrees, magenta is 75 degrees, and yellow is 0 degrees. Rotations of 90 degrees or more are repetitive, because the halftone dots extend in all different directions. This means that cyan, magenta, and black are each rotated 30 degrees from each other; only yellow is closer—measuring only 15 degrees from cyan and magenta—but yellow is so light, its halftone dots don't create a patterning effect.

So far, so good. There's no reason to change the process colors. The problem is, how do you prevent a spot color from clashing? Unless you know exactly what you're doing, you shouldn't mess around with the Frequency value. And there aren't really any good angles left. This leaves you with the following frequency and angle options:

- If you're printing an illustration that contains one or two spot colors and black—but not cyan, magenta, or yellow—leave black set to 45 degrees and set the spot colors to 15 and 75 degrees. It doesn't matter which color you set to which value.

- If you have only one spot color, pick an angle—15 or 75—and go with it.

- If you're printing a spot color in addition to CMYK, pick a process color —black, cyan, or magenta—that the spot color never overlaps. If the spot color overlaps all three, return to your illustration and modify it so the overlap no longer exists. Then mimic the angle of that color. For example, if the spot color and cyan never mix—you don't blend between the two colors, mix them together in a gradation, or overprint one on top of the other—then you would set the angle of the spot color to 15 degrees.

Use Printer's Masks

This option lets you print a predefined collection of printer's marks. Turn on this check box to print the marks; turn it off to hide them.

The printer's marks include star targets and registration marks to aid in registration. To register plates is to get them into exact alignment, so one color doesn't appear out of sync with another. Illustrator also prints crop marks around the entire illustration and different types of progressive color bars along the edges. Most important, Illustrator labels each separation according to the ink it goes with. There is no good reason to turn off this option. But I sure do wish Illustrator still let you customize the marks.

Separate

Use this pop-up menu to specify which layers you want to print inside your illustration. (If the file contains just one layer, skip this option and move on.) Choose the Printable, Visible Layers option to print just those layers that you have set to print; if you turn off the Print check box for a layer in the Layer Options dialog box (as discussed in the "Working with Drawing Layers" section of Chapter 8), the layer won't print. Select the Visible Layers option to print all layers that are visible onscreen, even if the Print check box is off. And select the All Layers option to print all layers, whether hidden or turned off. The preview shows the results of the option you select.

Overprint Black

Select this check box to overprint all black ink inside the illustration. Overprinting black is a common way of anticipating registration problems. Also, it permits you to create so-called saturated blacks. Although black is theoretically as dark as dark can be, you can create colors that are visibly darker by adding cyan, magenta, or yellow to solid black. The result is a rich, glossy black.

But overprinting every black in your illustration has its drawbacks. If a black rectangle is positioned on top of a dark CMY object, for example, you can end up applying more ink than the page can absorb. Most paper stocks max out at about 300 percent saturation. If you go over that—for example, 90%C 80%M 70%Y 100%K, which adds up to 340 percent saturation—the ink can actually puddle or run, creating some messy results. Unless you're sure your illustration is safe from oversaturation, avoid the Overprint Black check box and use the more selective Filter » Colors » Overprint Black command, as I explain near the end of this chapter.

Margins

The Margin options—Left, Right, Top, and Bottom—allow you to adjust the size of the area Illustrator allots to the illustration. The default values represent the smallest bounding box that can be drawn around the illustration. Printer's marks appear in the margins around the bounding box in the preview; the bounding box itself appears as a rectangle.

You can modify the bounding box either by dragging the corner handles in the preview or by changing the values in the Left, Right, Bottom, and Top Margin option boxes. These values represent the distance from the edge of the page (specified with the Page Size pop-up menu) and the edge of the bounding box. Therefore, entering smaller values increases the size of the bounding box; entering larger values shrinks the bounding box. Illustrator automatically moves the printer's marks so they stay outside the bounding box inside the preview.

 If you have totally mucked up the margins, and you want to hand the reins over to Illustrator, click the Revert button. Illustrator will reset the margins back to their defaults.

Bleed

Although this last option may sound like a practice that died along with leeching, it actually controls the distance from the edge of the bounding box to the beginning of the crop marks. In printing, a bleed is the distance that an image extends off the printed page. For example, a bleed of 18 points ensures that even if the page shifts 1/4 inch on the press or the trim is 1/4 inch off, the illustration still fills the entire page and extends off the sides. How you set the bounding box affects the amount of illustration that is permitted to bleed off the edge. The Bleed value (which can vary from 0 to 72 points) determines how much of this bleed gets printed and offsets the crop marks and other printer's marks so they don't overlap too much of the printed artwork. Unless you're running out of room on the film, you're better off leaving the Bleed value set to its default, 18 points.

Unusual Printing Considerations

So much for the huge array of printing options that are crammed into the major printing dialog boxes. Although these options are very important—some clearly more important than others—you'll spend most of your time pressing Ctrl+P (Cmd-P on a Mac), hitting the Enter key (Return on a Mac), and going off to get some coffee.

Unfortunately, things don't always go according to plan. Sometimes you have to spend a few minutes massaging your illustration to get it ready to deliver the most ideal results in less-than-ideal conditions. Most problems can be overcome using the options that I've already described, but others can't. Those that can't are the subject of the remaining pages in this chapter.

The following sections explain all the preparatory alternatives that Illustrator permits prior to printing your artwork. Though none of these measures is obligatory—or even customary—they are the sorts of options with which you'll want to be at least vaguely familiar. For example, you can slice and dice large illustrations, insert your own crop marks or trim marks, overcome printing errors, and anticipate registration problems using tools and commands that are spread out from one end of the illustration window to the other. These are the fringe printing features, out of touch with the common illustration, and miles away from the automated worlds of the Print and Page Setup commands. But when things turn slightly uncommon, you may be very glad to have these features around.

Tiling Oversized Illustrations

By virtue of the Print Setup (Page Setup on a Mac) dialog box, Illustrator provides access to various common page sizes. But many artists require custom page sizes that midrange printers can't accommodate. So how do you proof oversized artwork using a typical laser printer?

To proof your artwork to letter-sized pages, choose File » Document Setup and select the Tile Imageable Areas radio button. Illustrator automatically sections your illustration into separate tiles as indicated by the dotted lines in the drawing area. If these breaks will not permit you to easily reassemble your artwork, use the page tool (the alternate tool in the hand tool slot) to manually reposition the dotted lines.

Even after you meticulously set up and print the tiles, your pages may not fit together properly. Most notably, the tiles may fade toward the outside of the paper, so that the pasted artwork appears to have gutters running through it. The only solution is to adjust the tiles with the page tool, print a page, adjust the tiles again, print another page, and so on until you get it right. Illustrator doesn't provide any automated means for creating an overlap from one tile to the next.

Creating Crop Marks and Trim Marks

Crop marks indicate the boundaries of an illustration. Most imagesetters print pages between 12 and 44 inches wide, regardless of the actual size of the illustration. When you have the illustration commercially reproduced, the printer will want to know the dimensions of the final page size and how the illustration should be positioned on the page. Crop marks specify the boundaries of the reproduced page, and properly positioned crop marks help to avoid miscommunication and additional expense.

Illustrator automatically creates crop marks around an entire illustration when you print color separations (as discussed in the "Printing Color Separations" section). But what if you want to print a color or grayscale composite to your desktop printer? Or perhaps you want to more precisely control the placement of the crop marks in the illustration window. In either case, you can take advantage of Object » Crop Marks » Make, which lets you manually position crop marks inside the illustration window.

To create crop marks, draw a rectangle that represents the size of the final reproduced sheet of paper. Then, with the rectangle selected, choose Object » Crop Marks » Make. Illustrator converts the rectangle into crop marks. For example, in **Figure 24.14**, I drew a business card, and then a rectangle around the card (in the first example) and converted the rectangle to crop marks (in the second example). Notice that the marks are positioned well outside the rectangular boundary, preventing them from appearing on the final card. The checkered borders and lines of music that extend outside the crop marks will bleed off the edge of the business cards.

 If no object is selected and a single page is displayed in the drawing area (i.e., the Single Full Page radio button is active in the Document Setup dialog box), choose Object » Crop Marks » Make to create crop marks around the page.

Unfortunately, only one set of crop marks can exist in an illustration. When you choose Object » Crop Marks » Make, you delete any previous crop marks as you create new ones. Also, you can't move crop marks after you create them. You have to convert the crop marks back to a rectangle by choosing Object » Crop Marks » Release, edit the rectangle as desired, and then choose Object » Crop Marks » Make again to move the crop marks.

When you display the Separation Setup dialog box, Illustrator automatically sizes the bounding box in the preview to the exact size of the area surrounded by the crop marks. This is a handy method for sizing the boundary, typically more accurate and easier to manipulate than the bounding box controls inside the Separation Setup dialog box.

Illustrator also offers the Trim Marks filter that adds printable guides to your illustration. Trim marks are similar to crop marks in appearance. They differ from crop marks in that they will print inside the printable area, they don't affect printing boundaries (or any other printing considerations), you can use as many sets of them as you wish in a single illustration, and they can encompass any shape.

Trim marks are intended to help you or your printer cut your final print into its components. Say you wanted to print a number of the business cards shown in the bottom portion of Figure 24.14. Instead of using crop marks, you would select the rectangle that surrounds the card and choose Filter » Create » Trim Marks to have Illustrator add eight little lines that look just like crop marks.

These trim marks will surround the rectangle. Because the trim marks filter does not modify the rectangle (like the Crop Marks command does), you will need to delete the rectangle around the card. If you don't like the placement of the marks, you can move them—something that's not possible to do with crop marks unless you first release them. To move trim marks, simply select the marks and then move them to their new locale.

Figure 24.14: After drawing a rectangle to specify the size of the trimmed illustration (top), choose Object » Crop Marks » Make to convert the rectangle to crop marks (bottom).

Select all the card elements and the trim marks and cut and paste them so that you fit as many as you can into the printable area. After you print your drawing, you can cut along the trim marks to form several individual cards.

Flatness and Path Splitting

You can encounter a fair number of errors when printing an illustration, but one of the most common is the limitcheck error, which results from a limitation in your printer's PostScript interpreter. If the number of points in the mathematical representation of a path exceeds this limitation, the illustration will not print successfully.

If you have a sufficient amount of memory in your printer and have a newer PostScript Level 3 printer, most likely you will never be burdened with limitcheck errors.

Unfortunately, the "points" used in this mathematical representation are not the anchor points you used to define the object. Instead, they're calculated by the PostScript interpreter during the printing process. When presented with a curve, the interpreter has to plot hundreds of tiny straight lines to create the most accurate possible rendering. So rather than draw a perfect curve, your printer creates an approximation with hundreds of flat edges. The exact number of edges is determined by a variable known as flatness, which is the maximum distance a flat edge can vary from the mathematical curve, as illustrated in **Figure 24.15**.

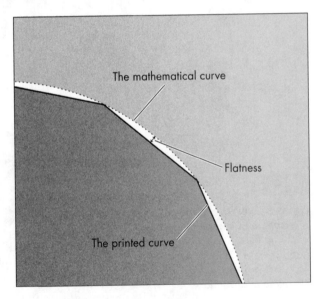

Figure 24.15: The flatness value determines the greatest distance between the center of a flat edge and the closest point along the true mathematical curve.

The default flatness value for a typical laser printer is 1 pixel, or 1/300 inch. This means the center of any flat edge of the printed curve can be at most 1/300 inch from the closest point along the perfect mathematical curve. If you were to raise the flatness value, the printer could draw fewer flat edges, which quickens the print time but results in more blocky curves. Each tiny line in the polygon rendering is joined at a point. If the number of points exceeds your printer's built-in path limit, you'll see the telltale words "limitcheck error" in the progress area on your screen, and the illustration will fail to print. The path limit for the original LaserWriter was 1,500, seemingly enough flat edges to imitate any curve. But when you factor in such path variations as compound paths and masks, both of which merge shapes with hundreds or thousands of flat edges together, things can get extremely complicated.

You can overcome limitcheck errors several ways:

 Increase the flatness. This is usually just a matter of lowering the Output Resolution in the Printing & Export section of the Document Setup dialog box. (The Output Resolution in the Document Setup will be applied to all objects in the illustration.)

The default value for the output resolution is 800. For an imagesetter with a resolution of 2,400, this translates to a flatness of 3. This is because Illustrator uses the equation Flatness = Printing Device Resolution/Output Resolution (2,400/800 = 3). A flatness of 3 is usually high enough to avoid limitcheck errors. If the Output Resolution is the same as the resolution for the final output device, you have set the flatness to 1. This is a low flatness and could cause problems.

As mentioned above, the default output resolution for every illustration you create is 800 dpi. This means that curves printed to a 2,540-dpi imagesetter will be treated to a flatness of approximately 3, whereas lower-resolution printers will use lower flatness values. You can print a test version of an illustration by lowering the Output Resolution in the Document Setup dialog box to, say 300, and leaving the Split Long Paths check box turned off. This will significantly speed the print time at the expense of the curves.

 *All Output Resolution values are saved with an EPS file and included with the illustration even if you import it into another application. So don't expect an illustration to print better from PageMaker or QuarkXPress than it does directly from Illustrator.*

 Select the Split Long Paths check box in the Printing & Export section of the Document Setup dialog box. The next time you save or print the current illustration, Illustrator will automatically break up every path that it considers to be at risk into several smaller paths. In most cases, this won't affect the printed appearance of your illustration.

 Unfortunately, there's no way to automatically reassemble paths after Illustrator splits them apart. If you ever need to join them back together, you have to do so manually, which complicates the editing process. So be sure to save your illustration before selecting the Split Long Paths check box, and then use File » Save As to save a copy of the split illustration under a different name.

- Use masks and patterns wisely. This is the best solution. If a complex mask isn't printing, for example, select the mask group and click the Pathfinder palette's Crop button to permanently crop the content elements. Though this may necessitate some manual edits on your part, it will almost always solve the printing problem, and it allows you to print smooth curves without worrying about strange printing issues such as flatness.

- *Some of the Pathfinder commands have a habit of producing alert boxes when they complete, warning you that they may have generated paths that are too complicated to print. Ignore these messages! They are almost always inaccurate. Wait until you encounter a limitcheck error before you worry about an overly long path.*

Printing Patterns

Patterns can also cause limitcheck errors, but more commonly they can cause out-of-memory errors by overwhelming the amount of RAM available to your printer. (Yes, like computers, PostScript printers have RAM.) It works like this: Illustrator downloads the tile pattern (called tiles because they are based on repeating rectangular artwork) as if it were a font to your printer's memory. In this way, the printer accesses tile definitions repeatedly throughout the creation of an illustration. So if the illustration contains too many tile patterns or if a single tile is too complex, the printer's memory may fill up, in which case the print job is canceled and you see an out-of-memory error onscreen. (If your printer just stops working on a job, even though Illustrator seems to have sent the illustration successfully, this is likewise an indication of an out-of-memory error.)

Out-of-memory errors are not as common when you're printing to modern, high-resolution imagesetters, because these machines tend to include updated PostScript interpreters and have increased memory capacity. And actually PostScript Level 3 printers in general have also remedied a lot of the printing problems experienced in the past. Therefore, you will most often encounter an out-of-memory error when proofing an illustration to a midrange laser printer or to another low-memory device. Try one of the following techniques to remedy the problem:

- Change all typefaces in the illustration to Times, Helvetica, or some other printer-resident font. Better yet, convert all characters to paths using Type » Create Outlines. This way, Illustrator won't have to download both tile and font definitions.

- Rasterize the vector art. This will convert the pattern tiles into pixels, thereby simplifying the data the printer has to interpret. Be warned that the printed art will lose a little quality from the rasterization process.

- Save the Illustrator file as a PDF. Converting to PDF resolves a lot of the complex instructions in things such as patterns, masks, and compound paths.

- Print objects filled with different tile patterns in separate pages. Then use traditional paste-up techniques to combine the patterns into a composite proof.

When you print the illustration to an imagesetter, it will probably print successfully because of the imagesetter's increased memory capacity. But if the illustration still encounters an out-of-memory error, you'll have to delete some patterns or resort to traditional paste-up techniques, as suggested in the last item above.

Printing Transparency Objects

Transparency is a revolutionary advancement. However, there are some drawbacks to working with transparency files. As I mentioned back in Chapter 18, some of the transparency options may create raster images during a process called flattening. Flattening is where Illustrator analyzes the transparency in your artwork and divides the overlapping transparent objects into individual pieces. Depending on the complexity, Illustrator decides whether those pieces will be retained as vector art or rasterized. This can cause your files to print a bit differently than you might expect, especially if you artwork contains complex, overlapping transparent objects. If you want some input into how Illustrator makes the vector versus raster determination, you can change the settings in the Transparency section of the File » Document Setup dialog box. Here is a very brief description of the options.

- **Raster/Vector Balance:** The higher the value, the less your art will be rasterized, and the more your vector data will be retained. The default is 100%, and that is also the recommended setting. This setting creates the highest-quality artwork that can be scaled up without losing image details.

- **Rasterization Resolution:** This option allows you to input a resolution for any artwork that will be rasterized during the flattening process. You can use the formula of doubling the linescreen of the final output. For example, if you are going to have your artwork printed on an offset press, the linescreen is usually 150 lines per inch (lpi). Double that and you get the typical 300 pixels-per-inch (ppi) resolution amount. However, if you are going to have your artwork printed by a newspaper, for example, the lpi is usually 85 to 110 lpi, so you can lower the resolution to 170 to 220 ppi. If you don't know how your artwork will be printed, a value of 300 is usually fine, unless you have very small type or a lot of intricate detail in your artwork. In this case, you may want to shoot up to 600.

- **Convert Text to Outlines:** Does just what it says—converts text into paths, complete with anchor points and segments. Checking this option ensures that the width of all your text stays consistent. The downside is that some smaller type may appear thicker and less legible. It is recommended that if you want to convert any text to outline, you do so by selecting your text and choosing Type » Create Outlines. For more details on type, see Chapters 10 and 11.

- **NEW 10** You have another option when it comes to opaque text, however. Rather than convert your text to outlines, you can rearrange the stacking order of your text, if possible. The Flattener in Illustrator takes the stacking order of artwork into account. And it is so intelligent that it also knows to "ignore" opaque text when it flattens to best avoid getting text that's partially vector and partially rasterized. Once you've created all of your artwork, select all of your opaque text and either bring it to the front, or put it on a new layer at the top of the layer stack. This will ensure that your text remains in vector form and you don't get the ugly thick and thin type.

- **Convert All Strokes to Outlines:** This option takes the strokes in your artwork and converts them to filled objects. This will ensure that the stroke widths remain constant. And, as with the text outlines, thin strokes will look thicker. Again, you are better off converting your strokes to objects by selecting them and choosing Object » Path » Outline Stroke.

- **Clip Complex Regions:** This option allows Illustrator to apply a clipping mask to the rasterized objects. For more on masks, check out Chapter 17. The upside is that it allows for a better transition between the vector and raster objects and reduces some of the funky artifacts that can occur during the flattening process. The downside is that it can occasionally produce complex clipping paths and cause potential printing problems. It's probably worth taking a chance and leaving this option checked.

● **Preserve Overprints When Possible:** Select this option when you are printing color separations and have objects set to overprint. This will allow those objects that are not involved with transparency to overprint properly. You will find more details on overprinting later in this chapter.

An optional plug-in called the Flattening Preview Palette can help you identify flattening problems by allowing you to preview the results of your various flattening settings. See Chapter 18 for more on this great palette.

There are some instances where transparency effects will print with less-than-desired results. For instance, if you have extremely fine strokes in your document, they may be rasterized where transparency effects are positioned over them. This may cause a change in the stroke weight. Converting text and strokes can help by ensuring that your width remains constant, but it can also cause small type and thin strokes to appear thicker, as mentioned above. Also, some colors may print differently if they are in elements that are divided into both vector and raster images. This is called *stitching*. One way to avoid these problems is to set the slider all the way to Rasters. This causes the entire document to be rasterized, which avoids inconsistencies between vector and raster images. You can export your entire file as a high-resolution TIFF image, which you can then output.

For a very detailed explanation on printing transparency issues, see the document named Flattening Guide.pdf in the White Papers folder in the Adobe Technical Info folder on the Illustrator program CD. There is also a paper copy of the Flattening Guide in your Illustrator 10 product box.

Trapping Selected Paths

Registration problems can sometimes occur when printing full-color documents. *Trapping* is the term used to describe a number of techniques used to help cover up these problems. If your commercial printer's plates are slightly out of register—as they frequently are—gaps may form between high-contrast edges. It's always a good idea to employ a professional printing company that has lots of experience in color printing and guarantees its work. But even the most conscientious printers may be off by as little as a half point, enough to cast a shadow of shoddiness across your artwork.

Full-service (read mega-expensive) printers will trap your work for you using dedicated systems from Scitex or Crosfield. Other printers may charge you a little extra to trap your illustration with software such as TrapWise or Trapeze. If your printer does not provide trapping services, however, you may want to create your own traps in Illustrator.

Illustrator's Trap command works by creating a new path of a specified thickness that overprints the neighboring paths below it. The result is a slight darkening of colors where two paths meet, an imperfect solution that is nevertheless vastly preferable to a white gap.

You can't trap an entire illustration. Instead, you trap two or more neighboring paths at a time. Also, the filter works only on paths with flat fills. It can't handle gradations, tile patterns, strokes, text, or imported images.

If you want to trap a stroke, first convert it to a filled path by choosing Object » Path » Outline Stroke. To trap text, convert the characters to paths with Type » Create Outlines. You'll want to trap only large text, such as headlines or logos. Traps around small letters can make the text blurry and illegible.

The trick when using the Trap filter is to recognize which paths need trapping and which do not. Here are a few elements or combinations where trapping may be helpful:

- Two paths filled with different spot colors

- A path filled with a spot color next to a path filled with a process color

- Two paths filled with process colors that don't share any primary color in common. For example, you'd want to trap an 80-percent cyan path next to a 50-percent yellow, 40-percent magenta path.

If two neighboring paths are both filled with process colors, and they have one or more primary colors in common, trapping is not necessary. For example, if a 50-percent cyan, 20-percent magenta path overlaps a 70-percent cyan, 30-percent yellow path, a continuous screen of cyan will occur between the two paths even if the magenta and yellow plates are incorrectly registered. Likewise, you don't have to trap between two paths filled with different tints of a spot color. Registration problems have no affect on paths printed from the same plate.

The Trap filter is pretty smart about telling you when you need and don't need to trap. If the filter refuses to work, it means that the paths are too similar to require trapping. This assumes that the paths are filled with flat colors. The Trap filter won't create traps for gradations, strokes, or other sophisticated fills. That's not to say those objects don't need trapping—it's just that the Trap filter can't work on those types of objects.

To trap two or more selected paths, choose Window » Pathfinder and then select Trap from the palette's pop-up menu, which displays the Pathfinder Trap dialog box shown in **Figure 24.16**. The options in this dialog box work as follows:

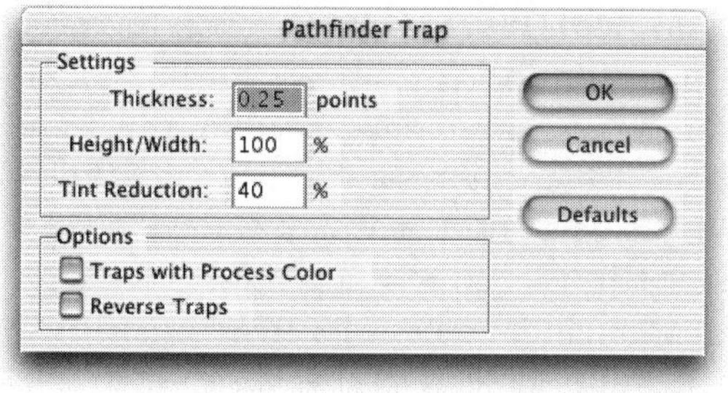

Figure 24.16: From this dialog box, you can create a sliver of a path that traces the border between a pair of selected paths.

Pathfinder Trap

Settings
Thickness: 0.25 points
Height/Width: 100 %
Tint Reduction: 40 %

OK
Cancel
Defaults

Options
☐ Traps with Process Color
☐ Reverse Traps

- **Thickness:** This is the key option in the dialog box. Here you specify the width of the overprinting path created by the filter. The default value, 0.25 point, is awfully small, only sufficient to remedy extremely slight registration problems. If your commercial printer is a top-of-the-line operation, this is sufficient. If your printer is more the workaday, get-the-job-out variety, a value of 0.5 or 1 might be more appropriate.

- **Height/Width:** This value represents the ratio between the vertical and horizontal thickness of the trapping path. A value of 100 percent means that the trap will be the same thickness—as specified in the previous option—throughout its length. Raise the value to increase the vertical thickness of the trap; lower the value to decrease the vertical thickness. The horizontal thickness is always the exact width entered into the Thickness option box. The purpose of this option—in case you're wondering—is to account for differences in vertical and horizontal misregistration. Check with your printer to find out if any compensation is needed.

- **Tint Reduction:** When trapping paths are filled with spot colors, Illustrator fills the trap with a tint of the lightest color. So if a selected yellow path neighbors a selected brown path, the trap is filled with a tint of yellow. The light yellow trap looks lighter than either of the neighboring paths on the screen, but because it overprints, the trap leaves the yellow path unaffected and slightly darkens the brown path.

  When trapping process-color paths (or if you convert the trap applied to spot colors to a process color using the Convert Custom Colors to Process check box), Illustrator mixes a 100-percent tint of the darker color with a lighter tint of the lighter color.

  Whether you're trapping spot or process colors, the Tint Reduction value determines the tint of the lighter color. A light tint appears less intrusive than a dark one, so the default 40 percent is a good value for most jobs.

⚫ **Traps with Process Color:** Select this check box to fill the trap with a process color regardless of whether the trapped paths are filled with spot or process colors. Generally, you'll want to leave this option off. If the lighter color is a spot color, it stands to reason that the trap should be a tint of that spot color. Only if the darker of two neighboring paths is filled with a process color and the screen angle of the spot color might interfere with those of the process colors should you select this option. Never select it when trapping two neighboring paths filled with spot colors.

⚫ **Reverse Traps:** Select this option to change the fill of the trap to favor the darker color instead of the lighter one (maybe you disagree with Illustrator over which of two neighboring colors is lighter). For example, when trapping a red path and a blue path, Illustrator will most likely see the blue path as lighter, whereas you may see it as darker. If you don't like the way Illustrator fills the trap, undo the operation and reapply it with Reverse Traps selected.

After you press Enter (Return on the Mac), Illustrator creates a trapping path along the border between each pair of neighboring selected shapes. **Figure 24.17** shows two trapping scenarios (converted to grayscale for purposes of this book). In each case, just the outlined paths were selected. As you can see, Illustrator creates traps around the neighboring borders of the selected paths only; portions of selected paths that do not neighbor other selected paths are ignored.

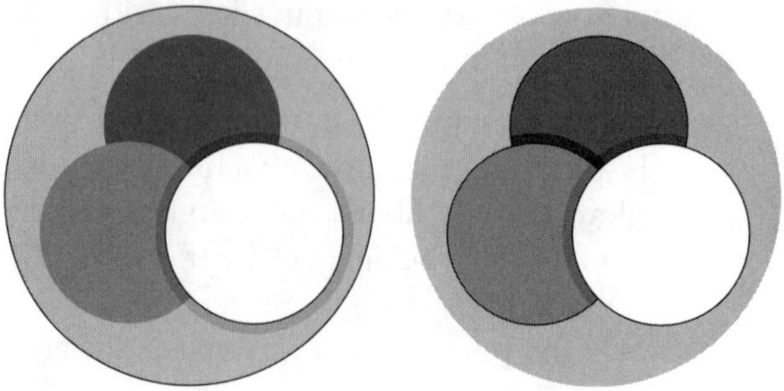

Figure 24.17: The results of two trapping operations. In each case, the outlined paths were selected; paths without outlines were not. The dark strips are the traps.

This system works great when trapping spot colors, but it gets a little weird when trapping process colors. For example, suppose in the left example in Figure 24.17 that the small selected circle is yellow and the large selected circle is deep purple. The overprinting trap will have hints of both yellow and purple, even when it overlaps the deselected circles, which may be green, orange, or any other color. The fact is, the purple of the background circle has no business being there.

To avoid the problem of unwanted colors in a trap, remove the tint of the background path from the trap. In the case of our purple objects in the above example, you would simply remove the purple from the trap and leave the yellow intact. A yellow trap surrounding a yellow path is always acceptable, regardless of the paths it overprints.

Overprinting Black Paths

Another way to trap two objects is to overprint one on top of the other. If a text block is full of small black type, you'll probably want to select the Overprint Fill check box in the Attributes palette. This way, Illustrator prints the text on top of any background colors to ensure that no gaps appear between character outlines and neighboring colors.

Overprinting black is such a common practice that Illustrator provides a filter to automate the process. This filter allows you to overprint a specific percentage of black through the fills and strokes of all selected objects. Select all the objects you might want to overprint, and then choose Filter » Colors » Overprint Black. Illustrator displays the Overprint Black dialog box shown in **Figure 24.18**.

Figure 24.18: Use the Overprint Black filter to overprint all selected objects that contain a specific percentage of black.

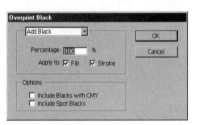

The options in this dialog box work as follows:

- **Add Black and Remove Black:** If you want to overprint colors, select the Add Black command in the pop-up menu. If you want to remove overprinting from selected objects—so that they knock out the colors behind them—select Remove Black.

- **Percentage:** Enter the intensity of black ink that you want to overprint. All objects with that exact percentage of black will overprint.

- **Apply to Fill and Stroke:** Use these check boxes to overprint—or to remove the overprinting from—fills, strokes, or both fills and strokes. By default, both check boxes are selected.

- **Include Blacks with CMY:** To overprint CMYK objects that contain a specific percentage of black, select this check box. For example, if you set the Percentage Black value to 40, and a selected object is filled with 30%C 20%M 10%Y 40%K, this check box must be turned on for the filter to affect the object.

- **Include Spot Blacks:** When this check box is on, any spot blacks in your document will also overprint. If you intend for your objects to print as spot colors, you should check this option. (Because the CMYK values are for screen display purposes only, the Black value in a spot color has nothing to do with the printed ink.) But if you plan to convert all spot colors to CMYK, you don't have to worry about this option.

This filter would be better if it would allow you to change a range of blacks all at a time (an oversight that I'm still hoping Adobe might fix in the future). And it would be nice if the filter could automatically detect oversaturations and make sure that overprinted blacks don't smudge on the printed page. Still, it's safer than simply selecting the Overprint Black check box in the Separation Setup dialog box.

Remember that you can choose View » Overprint Preview to—you guessed it—preview your overprints and see how they'll look when you finally get to the printing stage.

Creating PDF Files

One of the more exciting developments in computer graphics in the past few years has been the acceptance and widespread use of Adobe's Portable Document Format (PDF). PDF files can be created from almost any application and then read using Acrobat Reader (which is available free from the Adobe Web site).

Originally the folks at Adobe created PDF as a way to transfer and read documents without printing them—part of their grand plan for a paperless office. And although PDF has been accepted for that, its real glory has been its role in the prepress process. PDF documents allow you to package a file for a service bureau and include all the fonts and graphics necessary to print the file. Unlike a self-contained PostScript file, which can only be sent to a printer, PDF files can be opened, examined, modified slightly, and even added to other documents. This makes them ideal for advertising and illustrations that need to be incorporated into magazines, newspapers, books, and other publications.

Saving a PDF File

It's very easy to save your Illustrator documents as PDF files. All you have to do is choose File » Save As and then choose the Adobe PDF format from the pop-up list. Name the file and then click Save. This opens the Adobe PDF Format Options dialog box. This box will display its Default options, with the General controls visible as shown in **Figure 24.19**. You use the pop-up list to change the General options to the Compression options as seen in **Figure 24.20**.

 Illustrator provides two option sets. The Default set is more appropriate for PDF files that will be output by a service bureau on an imagesetter. The Screen Optimized set creates a smaller file that is more appropriate for onscreen or Web viewing. The Screen Optimized set also changes the color space of the file to RGB. When you select your own combination of options, the name of the set will change to Custom.

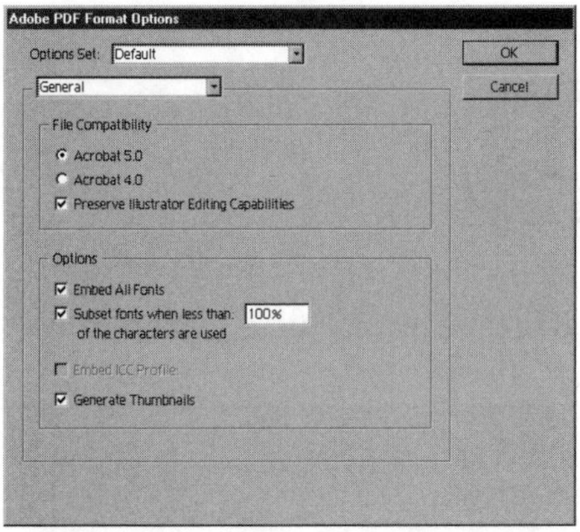

Figure 24.19: The General options for saving files as PDF files.

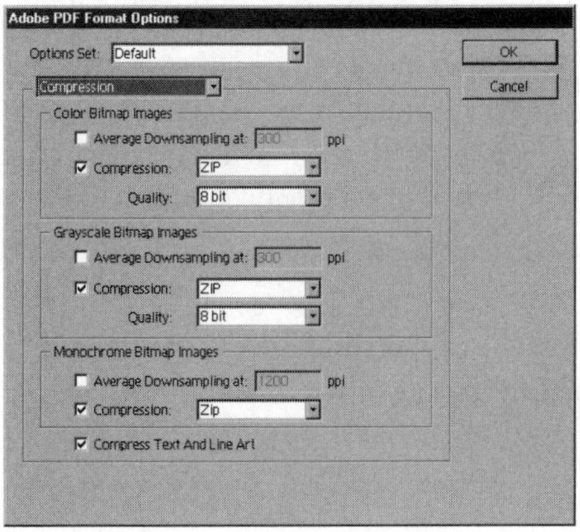

Figure 24.20: The Compression options for saving files as PDF files.

Setting the General PDF Options

Select either Acrobat 5.0 or 4.0 in the File Compatibility panel. This determines which version of Adobe Acrobat will be able to read your PDF file. The Acrobat 5 format supports the widest range of Illustrator features, but if you are concerned that not everyone who you want to read your files has version 5 yet, choose version 4.

- Select Preserve Illustrator Editing Capabilities to export the file in a PDF format that allows you to reopen and edit the file in Adobe Illustrator. Turning this option off will create a slightly smaller file, which may be desirable if you are going to post your Acrobat file on the Web.

- Select the Embed All Fonts option to save the fonts used in the file with the saved file. This option embeds all the characters in each font. This can create larger files than necessary if you've used only a few characters in the file. For instance, do you really need to embed all the characters in a font if the only text in the file is one small trademark symbol?

If you find that a font has not been included in the file, it may be that it has been set to be protected by its manufacturer and cannot be embedded in PDF files.

- Choose the Subset fonts when less than __% of the characters are used option to minimize the file size. This embeds only those characters of the font that are used in the document. (The technical term for this is a subset.) Enter the percentage of the characters that determines when a font subset is created. For instance, if you have used just a few of the characters, you can lower the percentage to 25 percent. If the percentage of characters used in the document exceeds this setting, then the entire font set is embedded in the file rather than the subset.

Do not embed subsets if you think that you might need to edit the Illustrator file in Acrobat—for instance, if you are sending the PDF to a service bureau for output. You cannot edit the text if only the subset of the font is included with the file.

- Select the Embed ICC profile option to embed a color profile into the saved file. The color profile is determined in the Color Settings dialog box located under the Edit menu. This embedded color profile is then applied to the file when it's reopened in Adobe Illustrator.

- Select the Generate Thumbnails option to save a thumbnail image of the artwork with the saved file. This adds a small amount to the file size and should not be used for files that are to be posted to the Web.

Setting the Compression PDF Options

- Select the Average Downsampling at __ppi option in any of the compression panels if you want to set downsampling for the PDF file. *Downsampling* is the term used for lowering the resolution—and therefore the detail—in raster images. You should not downsample PDF files that will be printed using high-resolution output devices. However, there should not be any problem downsampling images that will be viewed only onscreen.

- Select the Automatic compression option to have Illustrator automatically apply the best compression. For most files, this option produces satisfactory results.

- Select ZIP compression for images with large areas of single colors or repeating patterns, and for black-and-white images that contain repeating patterns. Use the 8-bit compression for the most flexibility if your images have many colors. Use the 4-bit compression only for images with limited colors.

- Select JPEG compression for grayscale or color images. JPEG is lossy, which means that it removes image data and may reduce image quality. Choose from five quality settings. Minimum will result in the smallest file size but the lowest quality. Maximum will give you the best quality but the largest file size. Because JPEG eliminates data, it creates smaller files sizes than ZIP.

- Use the Consultative Committee on International Telegraphy and Telephony (CCITT) compression method when compressing as monochrome bitmap images. No information is lost with CCITT compression. Group 4 is a general-purpose method that produces good compression for most monochromatic images. Group 3, used by most fax machines, compresses monochromatic bitmaps one row at a time.

- Use the Run Length option for images that contain large areas of solid black or white. This compression method does not lose any data.

- Select the Compress Text and Line Art option to apply the ZIP compression method to text and line.

ILLUSTRATOR ACTIONS

As you probably know by this stage in its evolution, the Action palette, rightly enough, stores actions that are groups of steps designed to complete a specific procedure. And it's another one of the handful of miraculously timesaving and sanity-saving devices that a lot of people don't take the time to use despite how it can change their life, or at least their workday.

The Actions palette, shown in **Figure 25.1**, allows you to display its actions in either the Default mode or the Button mode. Default mode allows you to see every detail of every entry, should you so desire, and make some further refinements to those entries as well. Button mode shows only the action names, as shown on the right of Figure 25.1. Although it provides no details, Button mode can show you more actions at once.

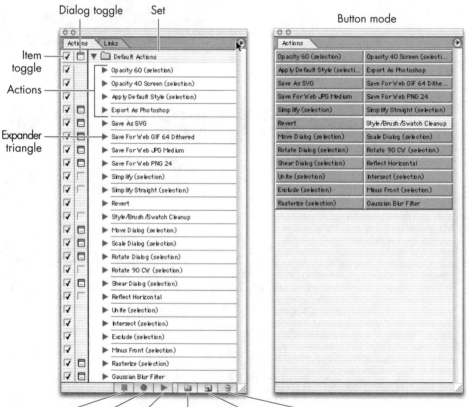

Figure 25.1: Within the Actions palette, you can choose to display the actions and set hierarchies or just display the action buttons.

It's human nature, or maybe the semi-Pavlovian response that passes for it in this technical age, to want to double-click on something to make it work. Double-clicking on the name of an action to run it will only, frustratingly, bring up its puny Options dialog box, so you will quickly be cured of the temptation to do this.

Creating a New Action

Before you construct an action anew, you should give some thought to what kind of action you want to make. Illustrator lets you create two types of actions: the *construction action* and the *modifying action*.

The construction action is a self-contained action that creates objects from scratch and requires nothing of you except your desire to use the action. Construction actions are useful when you want to create the exact same object over and over (for example, if you always need a rounded rectangle at a certain size). But construction actions limit you to *exactly* the same object each time.

The modifying action is designed to make changes to an existing path. Before you execute a modifying action, you must first create the path that you want the action to modify, and select that path before you play the action. I like the modifying actions more because they are more flexible and allow me to consistently transform whatever path I choose to use as a starting point. In the example below, I've designed an action that's intended to give selected text a spiky effect.

Getting Organized

The Actions palette is your headquarters for action design, but it also lets you organize your actions into folders or directories called *sets*. Illustrator's preset actions are all stored in the set called Default Actions. When you create a new action, you can choose to add it to the Default Action set, or you can create a new set that better reflects the nature of your new action. To create a new set, either click the New Set button located at the bottom of the Actions palette or choose the New Set command from the palette's pop-up menu. Either way, you see the New Set dialog box. You have but one decision to make with this dialog box: what to name the set. Since the action that I'm going to create is one that modifies text, I'll call the new set "Text Modifiers."

 Actions are available to all new documents, not only to the document that was open when they were created.

Recording an Action

In recording an action, you show Illustrator all the steps you want it to follow. For my example, I first created a line of point text and then selected it with the arrow tool. **Figure 25.2** shows the text I'm using as my starting object. The content and font of the text are completely open-ended, since they have no bearing on the action. But since the action I'm going to make will be designed for 72-point type, I'll set its size to 72 points in the Character palette.

Figure 25.2: This 72-point text is the starting point for the action that I'm about to record. I'll modify this text to show Illustrator the steps involved in the action.

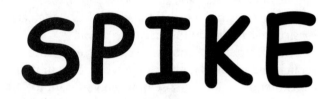

Now that my "raw material" is ready, it's time to start designing and recording.

1. **Click the New Action button, or choose the New Action command from the palette menu.**

The New Action dialog box will display, as shown in **Figure 25.3**. Here you name the action and choose the set in which it should reside. I named this action "Spike Effect 72pt" and directed it to the Text Modifiers set that I created above. If you think you're going use the action often and want it to have its own keyboard shortcut, you can assign it a function key. If you display your Action palette in the Button mode, you can choose a color for the action's button.

Bear in mind that Illustrator already has shortcuts for all the function keys, so if you choose a shortcut for your action, be sure to also check either or both the Shift and Command check boxes. Otherwise, you could lose a preset shortcut.

Figure 25.3: In the New Action dialog box, you can name your action and choose the set to which it belongs.

2. **Click the Record button, or press Enter (Return on the Mac).**

Illustrator will add your new action to the set you specified and start recording, as shown in **Figure 25.4**. When Illustrator is recording, the Record button changes from black to red. Now any changes I make will become part of the Spike Effect 72pt action.

3. **Set the fill to None and give it an 8-point black stroke.**

The number of steps that Illustrator assigns to this task and the nature of the individual steps depend entirely on how you go about changing the fill and stroke. Don't worry about it, since you can streamline the action after you're done recording it. I discuss this in an upcoming section, "Changing an Action."

Figure 25.4: The Actions palette ready and rearing to record the new Spike Effect 72pt action.

4. Convert the text to paths by choosing the Type » Create Outlines command.

Or press Ctrl+Shift+O (Cmd-Shift-O on the Mac).

> *I could have also started my action with this step. After I'm done recording the action, if I decide that this should be the starting point, I can move this step, as discussed in the "Changing an Action" section.*

5. Choose Object » Transform » Move.

I entered –0.5 into the Horizontal and 1 into the Vertical option boxes. This nudges the paths up 1 point and to the left 0.5 point.

6. Click the Copy button.

A slightly displaced clone appears in front of the original.

7. Change the stroke attributes.

I changed the stroke to a dash pattern with a 0-point dash and a 10-point gap and selected round caps and joins.

8. Change the color to 90 percent black.

Now I have my 90 percent black clones covering the original 8-point black paths.

9. **Choose Object » Transform » Transform Again.**

Or simply press Ctrl+D (Cmd-D on the Mac) to repeat the move and copy transformation.

10. **Reduce the stroke to 7, and change the stroke's color to 80 percent black.**

This second copy is slightly lighter and smaller than the first.

11. **Repeat the last two steps six more times.**

This means that each time I pressed Ctrl+D (Cmd-D on the Mac) I reduced the stroke by 1 point and lightened its color by 10 percent.

12. **Click on the Stop button located at the bottom of the Actions palette.**

The action is complete.

 *The top line of **Figure 25.5** shows the modifications that I made to my original path. To repeat all these steps by hand to a new bit of point text would take me almost as long as it took to create the Spike Effect 72pt action. But now that it's recorded, the actions will re-create the effect in just a few seconds. In the bottom portion of Figure 25.5, I created a new line of text and applied the Spike Effect 72pt action. It took Illustrator about 6 seconds to spike up this new line.*

Figure 25.5: The top line is the end result of all the changes I made to the original line of text. The bottom line is the result of Illustrator applying the action that I just created.

Inserting Menu Items

You can also use the Insert Menu Item command from the Actions palette menu. This opens the Insert Menu Item dialog box, as shown in **Figure 25.6**. Although the instructions say you can type the first few characters of a menu command in the field or use the Find button, I find it much easier to just move to a menu and choose the item you want to insert. This inserts the full path name in the field.

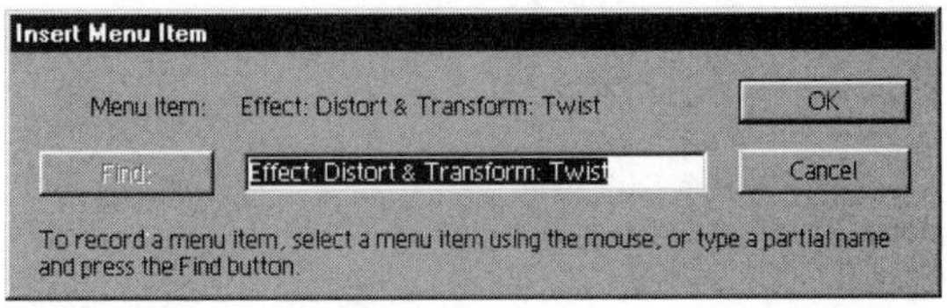

Insert Menu Item

Figure 25.6: The Insert Menu Item dialog box allows you to add menu items that cannot be recorded while creating the action.

| Menu Item: | Effect: Distort & Transform: Twist | OK |
| Find: | Effect: Distort & Transform: Twist | Cancel |

To record a menu item, select a menu item using the mouse, or type a partial name and press the Find button.

The Insert Menu Item command is extremely helpful for including in an action any items from the Effect menu that can't be captured as part of the recording. For instance, the Twist effect must be inserted using the Insert Menu Item. Sadly, all menu items inserted from the Insert Menu Item must be stopped with a dialog box. So there is no way to run the action without getting the dialog box.

Inserting Paths

As you create actions, you may notice that although rectangles and ellipses can be made part of an action, paths created with the pen, brush, or pencil tool cannot be recorded. These paths rely on recording the mouse movements, which unfortunately cannot be made part of an action. Fortunately, you can insert simple paths as part of an action using the Insert Select Path command.

As you are recording the action, draw the path. With the path still selected, choose Insert Select Path from the Actions palette menu. In the Actions palette you will see the phrase *Set Work Path* appear. This indicates that the path will be created at that point. Once you have made the path part of the action, you can then modify it using any of the recordable action commands such as transformations, opacity settings, and so on.

Selecting Paths

You may also notice that selections made with any of the selection tools cannot be recorded. Fortunately, the generous engineers at Adobe added the Select Object command. This command allows you to use the little-known Note options box in the Attributes palette to select objects.

The best way to understand how the Select Object command works is to use it to create an action. Here, I'll create one to perform a cleanup task that I always think is a good idea and never want to take the time to do. When you use the Offset Path command, Illustrator creates a copy of the selected path, but it doesn't delete the original—a perfect opportunity for an action! (Thanks to Dave Burkett, group product manager, who posted this action way back when actions were first introduced into Illustrator.)

1. **Select a path and start a new action.**

Click the New Action icon to open the New Action dialog box. I named the path Delete Offset Path, and then clicked Record to start recording the action.

2. **Add a note to the selected path.**

Use the Note options box of the Attributes palette to add a note that tags the object with a word, as shown in **Figure 25.7**. It doesn't matter what the note says; I just happen to like to use the word *original*.

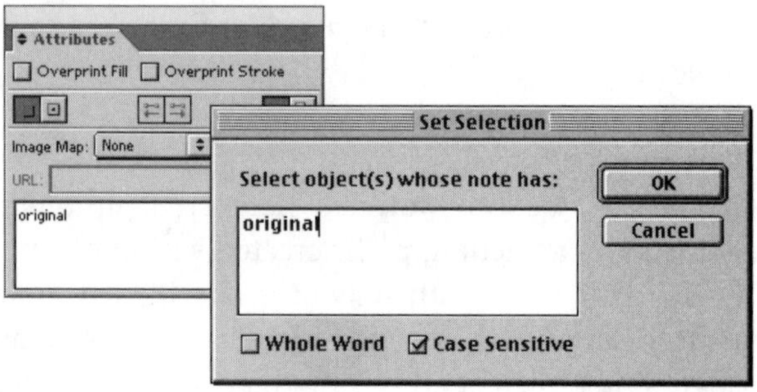

Figure 25.7: By typing a note in the Attributes palette (left), you make it possible to choose Select Object in the Actions palette to open the Set Selection dialog box (right) to delete that object later.

3. **Press Enter (Return on the Mac) to apply the note.**

The note is not made part of the action until you press the Enter key. You'll see the note added with the label "Attribute Setting" in the Actions list.

4. **Choose Object » Path » Offset Path.**

Make whatever settings you want in the dialog box and click OK. The new path appears offset from the original.

5. **Delete the note word from the Attributes palette and press Enter (Return on the Mac).**

When you offset the path, the same note is applied to the new path. With that path still selected, you need to delete the second note so that only the original object has the note applied to it. (There can be only one original, right?) Select the note in the options box and delete it. Don't forget to press the Enter key to set the step in the Actions palette.

6. **Choose Select Object from the Actions palette.**

This opens the Set Selection dialog box, as shown in Figure 25.7. Type the same word you used to label the original object. (See why I like the word *original*?) Click OK. This selects the original object.

7. **Press the Backspace key (Delete key on the Mac) on the keyboard.**

This deletes the original object, leaving only the path that was offset from the original.

8. **Click the Record button to stop recording.**

Congratulations—you've just selected and deleted a path within an action. And they said it couldn't be done! Your steps should be listed in the Actions palette, as shown in **Figure 25.8**.

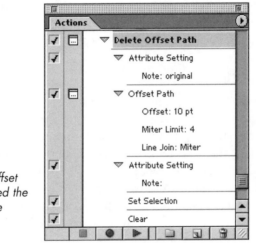

Figure 25.8: The steps created by the Delete Offset Path exercise. I've opened the triangles to show you the details for each of these steps.

I admit, it may seem like a lot of work; but trust me—once you've created the action, it's so much easier to just run it than executing the individual steps by hand. And with a function key applied to the action, it is just as easy to execute the action as it is to run the Offset Path command.

Changing an Action

After you create an action, you'll probably find that it contains more steps than necessary or that you want to add a step or two. Fortunately, Illustrator allows you to make changes to an action with relative ease.

Deleting Steps

When logic, aesthetics, or your boss whispers to you that you have too many steps, or the wrong steps, you can just select those steps in the palette and click the Delete Selection icon (aka the trash can). To select a series of steps, click the first and then

Shift-click the last of the ones in the series. To select discontiguous steps, click one, and then Ctrl-click (Cmd-click on the Mac) any others you'd like to delete.

 You can also choose Delete from the palette menu. Illustrator is always very polite and asks if you're sure you want to delete the selection. If you get tired of this solicitous behavior, just drag the selections directly to the trash, or Alt-click (Option-click on the Mac) the trash can.

Of course, you can use the Delete command to get rid of an entire action as well, in exactly the same manner as that I've described for steps.

 If you're deleting steps in hopes of streamlining an action, it would probably be best to duplicate the action before you commence surgery. Then you have the original to refer back to if things go wrong.

Adding Steps

Just as you can easily delete steps from an action, so can you easily add them. To add steps, select the action in the Actions palette and click the Record button. Define the desired steps, and then click the Stop button when you're done. Illustrator will tack the new steps onto the end of the action; and you can then move them to their proper position.

For example, say I want to add two steps to my Spike Effect 72pt action: a Roughen command that should follow the Create Outlines step and a Deselect command at the end. First I would create a new bit of point text and convert it to paths by pressing Ctrl+Shift+O (Cmd-Shift-O on the Mac). If you're wondering why, it's because I have to convert before I can apply the Roughen filter. With this path selected, I select the action and click the Record button. Then I choose the Filter » Distort » Roughen command, set the options to my liking, click OK, and then choose the Select » Deselect command. After applying these two new commands, I press the Stop button. Illustrator records two new steps at the end of my action. Since I want the Deselect command at the end of the action to inform me that the action is complete, I leave it where it is. The Roughen step needs to follow the Create Outlines step, so I drag the new step into place.

Reordering Steps

Here are a couple of things you might want to know about moving parts of your actions around once you've got them recorded.

- You can switch the order of an action's steps by dragging a step to a new position within the stack.

  You can even move multiple steps at once. Select the first step and then Ctrl-click (Cmd-click on the Mac) on each additional step you want to move. When you've selected all the steps you want, drag them to their new location. Illustrator will drop them as a contiguous block in which the original order of the steps is preserved.

One of my favorite techniques is to drag steps from one action to another within the palette. This allows you to create small action sequences and then combine them in longer action commands. Regular dragging will move the steps; if you don't want to lose the steps from one action, just hold the Alt key (Option key on the Mac) to copy the steps from one action to another.

Controlling User Input During Actions

For the most part, Illustrator needs your input only at the beginning of an action and doesn't bother you while it completes all the steps. But you can allow for user input in two ways. The first relies on commands that have a dialog box associated with them. The second actually pauses the action for some kind of input.

Toggles

If a step involves the use of a dialog box, Illustrator inserts a Dialog Toggle box to the left of the command in the palette. For example, every time I used the Move command in my Spike Effect 72pt action, a Dialog Toggle box appeared with the step. By default, Illustrator turns all of these boxes off when you record your action. When the Dialog Toggle box is off, or empty, Illustrator will apply your original settings without asking you for new input. If you want Illustrator to pause at a step that uses a dialog box and display the box for your use or perusal, click the empty Dialog Toggle box in the palette to activate the interactivity. A small icon will then show up in the box. You can see these icons, or lack thereof, in **Figure 25.9**.

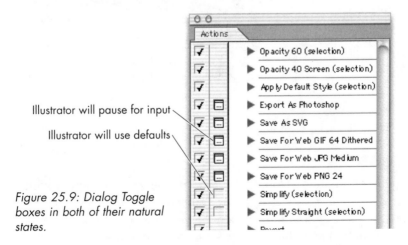

Illustrator will pause for input

Illustrator will use defaults

Figure 25.9: Dialog Toggle boxes in both of their natural states.

When the Dialog Toggle is active, Illustrator will display the appropriate dialog box when it comes to that step. You can then make changes to the box's settings or choose to go with the original settings. Before Illustrator moves to the next step, you will have to close the dialog box.

Stops

Another way to allow for user input in the execution of an action is to add a stop to the action. A stop forces Illustrator to halt the execution of an action, and it won't resume the action until you tell it to do so.

- To add a stop to an action while you're creating it, choose Insert Stop from the Action palette's pop-up menu.

- To add a stop to an existing action, select the step that you want the stop to precede, and choose Insert Stop from the pop-up menu.

In either case, you will see the Record Stop dialog box, as shown in **Figure 25.10**. In the Message field, you can explain to the user why Illustrator is pausing here. (This could be a simple explanation of what the following step is about to do, or it could be instructions to the user about what the user needs to do.)

For example, I could insert a stop at the beginning of my Spike Effect 72pt action to explain to a user that the action works best for 72-point text or to explain that the action adds eight new paths.

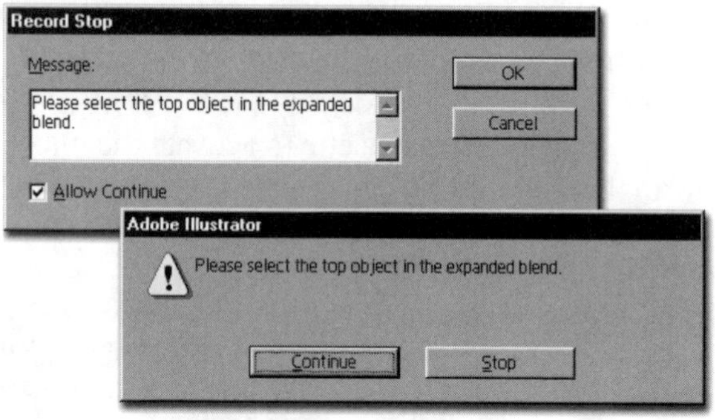

Figure 25.10: When you insert a stop, Illustrator will prompt you for a message in the Record Stop dialog box (top). When Illustrator comes across a stop while playing an action, it will display a warning box with your message (bottom).

You can change the dialog box settings for a step by double-clicking the step in the Actions palette. This opens the dialog box as it was set during the recording of the action. You can then make whatever changes you want to the settings in the dialog box.

When Illustrator encounters a stop, it displays a warning box, complete with your instructions, also shown in Figure 25.10. Depending on whether you activated the Allow Continue option in the Record Stop dialog box, the warning may include a Continue button in addition to the standard Stop button. In cases in which you only want to provide information and you want the user to be able to quickly move on, be sure to check the Allow Continue check box. This will allow the user to simply click the Continue button, and Illustrator will resume the next step in the action. If the user clicks the Stop button, Illustrator terminates the action at that point, but it remembers where it is in the action. At this point, for example, the user could apply some changes to the artwork and, when finished, have Illustrator complete the rest of the action by clicking the Play button.

 If you like an action as is, but you can see how it may be more useful in some cases with a couple of the steps removed, you can temporarily turn off steps. To do so, click on the Item Toggle box located to the far left of the step. The checkmark will disappear from the box, indicating that Illustrator will bypass the step when it next carries out the action. To turn the step back on, click on the Item Toggle box again and the checkmark will return.

Setting the Playback Options

Actions play back fast—really fast. So fast, in fact, that you certainly wouldn't have time to select an item during the playback. Fortunately, those clever Adobe engineers (aren't they clever?) have anticipated the need to slow down actions. Simply choose Playback Options from the Actions menu. The dialog box shown in **Figure 25.11** appears.

- 🌐 Accelerated plays the actions lickety-split (and is the default).

- 🌐 Step by Step allows all the objects to be created and the screen to redraw before the next step plays. This is somewhat slower than Accelerated, but not if you have a very fast computer.

- 🌐 Pause For __ seconds allows you to specify a time interval between each step of the action.

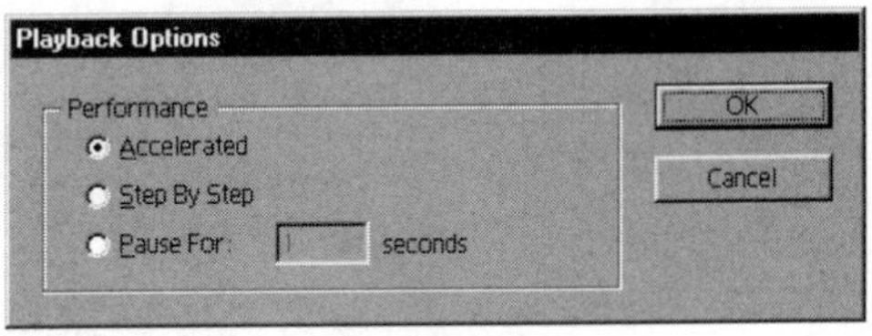

Figure 25.11: Use the Playback Options dialog box to control the speed of how actions are played.

Batch Processing Actions

Batch processing is the term used to describe doing something to a large number of files at the same time. The batch command for actions allows you to apply an action to a large number of files. Let's say you have a folder of Illustrator art. You can use the batch processing command to apply the Save for Web command to convert all the files to a GIF or JPEG. In less time than it takes to feed the cat, you've converted all your files into Web graphics.

To apply the batch processing command, choose Batch from the Actions palette menu. The Batch dialog box opens, as shown in **Figure 25.12**. Set each of the options as follows:

- Use the Set and Action pop-up lists to choose the action you want to play.

- Use the Source controls to choose which files should be converted. If you have specified an "Open" command in the action, you can override that setting by checking Override Action "Open" Commands. Check Include All Subdirectories if you want to open subfolders.

- Use the Destination controls to choose where the finished files should be saved. If you have specified a "Save In" command in the action, you can override that setting by checking the Override Action "Save In" Commands checkbox. If you are using the Export command in the action, you can use the controls to choose where the exported files should be saved. You can also override any existing directories for exported files by checking Override Action "Export" Commands.

- Use the Errors controls to choose whether the action should be stopped if there are errors in how the action is created. Or use the pop-up list to choose Log Errors to File, which creates a text file that lists any errors that were created in the batch processing.

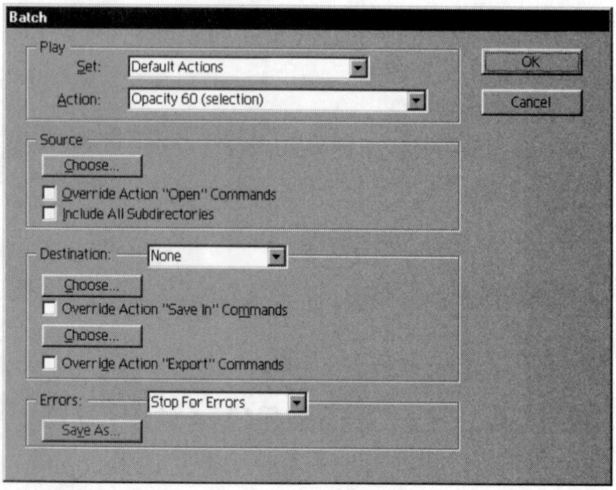

Figure 25.12: The Batch Processing dialog box allows you to apply an action to many files at once.

The Log Errors to File setting is very helpful when you want batch processing to run while you are away from your computer—perhaps going off to lunch. This allows all the files to be processed without getting stuck on one particular file.

Saving and Loading Actions

Hey, boys and girls, once you create actions, you can save and trade 'em with your friends! Use the Save Actions command in the Actions palette menu to save your Actions to a separate file, which you can copy onto a separate computer. Then use the Load Actions command in the palette menu to add the actions, or use the Replace Actions command to replace the current actions with the new set. You can also use the Reset Actions command to delete new actions and reset the palette to its default settings. Or you can choose Clear Actions to completely wipe out all the actions from the palette.

INDEX

Q